Steve Emanuel's First Year Questions & Answers

Second Edition

This edition revised by
ALEX RUSKELL
Associate Director of Academic Support
Roger Williams University School of Law

Prior edition by
STEVEN L. EMANUEL
Founder and Editor-in-Chief, *Emanuel Law Outlines and Emanuel Bar Review*
Harvard Law School, J.D. 1976
Member, NY, CT, MD, and VA bars

Wolters Kluwer
Law & Business

About Wolters Kluwer Law & Business

Wolters Kluwer Law & Business is a leading global provider of intelligent information and digital solutions for legal and business professionals in key specialty areas, and respected educational resources for professors and law students. Wolters Kluwer Law & Business connects legal and business professionals as well as those in the education market with timely, specialized authoritative content and information-enabled solutions to support success through productivity, accuracy and mobility.

Serving customers worldwide, Wolters Kluwer Law & Business products include those under the Aspen Publishers, CCH, Kluwer Law International, Loislaw, Best Case, ftwilliam.com and MediRegs family of products.

CCH products have been a trusted resource since 1913, and are highly regarded resources for legal, securities, antitrust and trade regulation, government contracting, banking, pension, payroll, employment and labor, and healthcare reimbursement and compliance professionals.

Aspen Publishers products provide essential information to attorneys, business professionals and law students. Written by preeminent authorities, the product line offers analytical and practical information in a range of specialty practice areas from securities law and intellectual property to mergers and acquisitions and pension/benefits. Aspen's trusted legal education resources provide professors and students with high-quality, up-to-date and effective resources for successful instruction and study in all areas of the law.

Kluwer Law International products provide the global business community with reliable international legal information in English. Legal practitioners, corporate counsel and business executives around the world rely on Kluwer Law journals, looseleafs, books, and electronic products for comprehensive information in many areas of international legal practice.

Loislaw is a comprehensive online legal research product providing legal content to law firm practitioners of various specializations. Loislaw provides attorneys with the ability to quickly and efficiently find the necessary legal information they need, when and where they need it, by facilitating access to primary law as well as state-specific law, records, forms and treatises.

Best Case Solutions is the leading bankruptcy software product to the bankruptcy industry. It provides software and workflow tools to flawlessly streamline petition preparation and the electronic filing process, while timely incorporating ever-changing court requirements.

ftwilliam.com offers employee benefits professionals the highest quality plan documents (retirement, welfare and non-qualified) and government forms (5500/PBGC, 1099 and IRS) software at highly competitive prices.

MediRegs products provide integrated health care compliance content and software solutions for professionals in healthcare, higher education and life sciences, including professionals in accounting, law and consulting.

Wolters Kluwer Law & Business, a division of Wolters Kluwer, is headquartered in New York. Wolters Kluwer is a market-leading global information services company focused on professionals.

Preface

Every year, I ask law professors, "What is the biggest problem you see in your students' exams?" And year after year, they answer, "My students don't base their answers on correct statements of the black letter law." "Black letter law" is an informal term that refers to the basic principles of law recognized by the courts. (The term stems from the former practice of printing compilations or statements of law in bold type.) This book is designed to help you recall, memorize, recognize, and focus on the black letter law (also referred to as the "rule of law") during your first-year exams. Consequently, for every short-answer and essay question, the relevant black letter law has been written in bold to remind you that this **must** be the basis for any of your answers.

If you don't understand and memorize the black letter law for your classes, you won't be able to spot issues on the exam, and you won't be able to write analysis for your answers that is well thought out and structured. For example, black letter law "burglary" is the "breaking and entering into the dwelling of another at night with the intent to commit a felony within." "Burglary" is not anything less than that. You can't write a good essay by stating that "burglary" is "going in someone's building and taking stuff," because that is not what "burglary" is. Keep in mind that the absolute worst essays on any exam are essays that either only reference random cases brought up in class or speak in general terms of fairness. To succeed in your first year of law school, you need to take all the individual cases or "trees" you study in class and synthesize them into a "forest" of torts, contracts, criminal law, property, or civil procedure. When you get a hypothetical situation on an exam, you need to figure out where this new "tree" fits.

Working through the short-answer questions in this book will help you recall and master the black letter law and help you build the "forest" of the subject area. In working through the essay questions, you will apply your knowledge of the black letter law and practice expressing it in a clear, concise manner in a well-structured argument. "Guidelines for Writing Successful Essay Exam Answers," which begins on page 1, walks you step-by-step through the essay writing process using the "IRAC" (**I**ssue, **R**ule [or black letter law], **A**nalysis, **C**onclusion) method.

The essays in this book are designed to be written in 30 minutes. As you do them, time yourself. You will be under extreme time pressure on your exams, so get used to working with the clock ticking. The essays are also likely shorter than those on your first-year exams, and the issues are slightly more apparent than in the essay questions on your first-year exams. There is a reason for this: to get you practicing spotting issues and referencing the appropriate law for those issues. On your first-year exams, you will likely have longer essays and more time to do them, so your professors will probably expect more of you (e.g., statements of policy, more counterarguments, references to a Restatement or a case, etc.). For examples of longer essay questions and sample answers, check your law school library or with your professor, or check your law school bookstore or online for commercially available resources. This book is meant to give you practice in the particular skill of recognizing and stating the black letter law, a skill that is absolutely vital for your success in law school (and, in fact, your later career as a lawyer).

As Associate Director of Academic Support, I advise students to start practicing issue spotting and essay writing early in the semester, rather than just during their exam prep time. As an aid in doing this, each section of this book begins with a basic table of contents of the major topics in the subject area. After each topic, the short-answer and essay questions that cover the topic are indicated. While your professor may not address the topics in the same order as the table of contents, with minimal effort, you should be able to find questions on topics you are currently studying.

Use this book to practice focusing on the black letter law—you can't write a good essay answer without it. Stay positive, have courage, keep healthy, and good luck on your first-year exams!

Alex Ruskell
Associate Director of Academic Support
Roger Williams University School of Law

Summary of Contents

Abbreviations Used in Text

CIVIL PROCEDURE

F,K&M—Friedenthal, Kane & Miller, Civil Procedure (2d ed., 1993)

Wr.—Charles A. Wright, Law of Federal Courts (5th ed., 1994)

CONTRACTS

Rest. 2d—American Legal Institute, Restatement of the Law Second, Contracts (1981)

UCC—Uniform Commercial Code (2001 and 2003)

CRIMINAL LAW

M.P.C.—Model Penal Code, Proposed Official Draft (1962) and Tentative Drafts 1-13 (1953-1962) (American Law Institute) [Note: The Model Penal Code has not changed since 1962. However, the Official Commentaries to Parts I and II were revised in 1985 and 1980, respectively.]

CRIMINAL PROCEDURE

L&I—LaFave & Israel, Criminal Procedure, 3 vol. unabridged vers. (West, 1984 w/1991 supp.)

PROPERTY

Rest. 2d—American Law Institute, Restatement of the Law Second, Property (Landlord & Tenant; Donative Transfers) (1977-1979, 1983, 1986)

TORTS

Rest. 2d—American Law Institute, Restatement Second of Torts (Student edition)

Rest. 3d—American Law Institute, Restatement Third of Torts: Liability for Physical Harm (Pop. Final Draft No. 1, 2005); Products Liability (1998) and Apportionment (2000)

Guidelines for Writing Successful Essay Exam Answers

The best way to write a good law school essay exam answer is to imagine speaking to a client: The client comes into your office, sits down, and tells you the story of what happened. Your job is to cut everything down into discernible parts and link those discernible parts to clear statements of the law in a way that the client can understand. A common student mistake is to think, "I am writing to my professor, who knows the law." You will likely fail if you do this—your professor is not a mind reader, and if you write an essay in which the professor has to guess what you think the black letter law is or has to guess how you think the particular facts in the question connect to that black letter law, you have not demonstrated your knowledge and therefore have not written a sucessful essay. You need to clearly spot the relevant issues, lay out the law that applies, and connect the facts of the question to that rule.

HOW TO ORGANIZE YOUR ANSWER

The IRAC method is a standard form for addressing a legal issue. You will likely cover IRAC (or one of the variant forms—CRAC, TRRAC, ARAC) in your legal writing class in your first year. IRAC stands for Issue, Rule, Analysis, and Conclusion.

- "Issue" is the legal issue—for example, "The issue is whether one dollar is sufficient consideration to support a contract for the sale of a boat."
- "Rule" is the black letter law—for example, "Consideration is any bargained-for benefit or legal detriment. In general, courts do not question the sufficiency of consideration."
- "Analysis" is where you connect the black letter law to the question, explaining how the law and the facts interact—for example, "Here, a dollar is a benefit, however slight. On the other hand, Skip could argue there was no way a reasonable person could have believed a boat could be conveyed for so little money. However, courts will not question the sufficiency of the consideration."
- "Conclusion" is how you believe a court will rule on the issue—for example, "Consequently, a dollar is likely sufficient consideration to support the contract for sale of the boat."

For every issue you spot, you should write a single IRAC (a common mistake is to try and make one giant IRAC answering the entire question). On a law school exam, *you must use* IRAC (or a variant)! You will miss points if you do not. However, there is a very slight caveat to this: while you can use the IRAC method as an unchanging formula if you find it easier to do so ("The first issue is whether Skip committed burglary. The rule for burglary is . . . . Here, Skip did . . . . On the other hand, Skip could argue . . . . Consequently, ..."), you don't have to twist your writing into a pretzel to do so. The goal is clarity. To reflect this, some of the suggested answers in this book may not have a clearly stated issue for every paragraph (but only when it was unnecessary to do so for the reader's understanding). In fact, some professors will tell you not to use the IRAC method or not to worry about it; however, they don't actually mean "don't use IRAC"—they only mean that they don't want you to spend all your time on potential convoluted IRAC formatting and not answer the question. But keep in mind that no professor will ever take off points just because you used the IRAC method when you wrote your exam answer.

HOW TO APPROACH AN ESSAY QUESTION

On an exam, you will be under extreme time pressure, so you need to practice answering questions so you can learn to do the steps of writing a good essay answer as quickly as possible. The following sections explain the steps you should use in writing your essay and include a simple hypothetical question.

Step 1: Read the Question Once, Just to Get Your Bearings

First, quickly read through the question to get an idea of where it is trying to lead you. Keep in mind that when a professor writes a question, she is inserting different specific facts to prompt you to reference a discrete piece of law (e.g., a character is 12 years old, a contract is not in writing, a child is driving a car, a lawyer is requesting the other side's will and banking statements, etc.). That is why it is important to memorize the black letter law—otherwise, you won't know what specific facts make a difference. (This applies to open-book exams as much as closed-book exams—on an open-book exam, it will use up too much time if you have to look in your books for everything.)

Simple Example Question

Mary owns and operates Mary's Bovine Boutique, a store featuring shirts with images of cows, in the Uptown Mall. She rents her space from Uptown Mall as her landlord. Jimmy is carrying a large box (which he can't really see around) through the mall's common hallway when he trips over a three-inch crack in the floor in front of Mary's shop. Jimmy falls and breaks his leg. He then sues Mary for his injuries. Discuss Mary's potential liability.

Step 2: Circle, Highlight, or Underline the Important Characters and Facts

Read the question a second time, slowly. Every character in an exam question likely represents something (and needs to be discussed). Also, the details of how the characters get into the situation they are in are important. Mark these characters and details, so you can be sure not to drop them when you write your answer. (Try to mark only words or short phrases—otherwise, you'll end up marking up the entire essay question, which won't help you.)

Example Question Markup

Mary owns and operates Mary's Bovine Boutique, a store featuring shirts with images of cows, in the Uptown Mall. She rents her space from Uptown Mall as her landlord. Jimmy is carrying a large box (which he can't really see around) through the mall's common hallway when he trips over a three-inch crack in the floor in front of Mary's shop. Jimmy falls and breaks his leg. He then sues Mary for his injuries. Discuss Mary's potential liability.

Step 3: Outline Your Answer

A good answer needs to be well organized. Most professors will tell you that you need to spend at least one-third of your time outlining your answer before writing it. Although you won't get points for things that don't make it from your outline to your complete answer, you will lose points if your answer is not written in a logical fashion. Outline the relevant facts you are going to use, and pin them to the correct statement of the rule of law (which you don't need to write in full in your outline; you'll write it in full in your answer, and it wastes time to do it twice).

Sample Outline

| Common area | Jimmy falls in front of Mary's store common area, three-inch crack, Uptown Mall landlord's responsibility, not Mary's |
| Contributory negligence | Carrying large box—can't see, three-inch crack could reduce |

Step 4: Write Your Answer in IRAC Form

While this is a simple example, with a simple suggested answer, this suggested answer should alert you to two important points. First, there is such a thing as meaningful ambiguity. In an exam question, if the question doesn't tell you an important fact, you have to write the answer to cover possible variations for the missing fact. In this example, we don't know that there is any relationship between Jimmy and Mary, so we need to address that missing fact, and we also need to address issues that would come up if there were some type of relationship between them that creates liability. The same applies for the law—if the question does not tell you what law applies, you have to list the relevant variations. Here, for example, we don't know what contributory negligence scheme the jurisdiction uses.

Importantly, a meaningful ambiguity is not a signal for a brain dump. Remember, the most important thing is that you *answer the specific question asked*. Here, the question does not ask about the mall's liability, so only write about the mall's liability in relation to Mary's liability (which the question is asking about). Also, don't write absolutely everything you know about tort law (the "brain dump"). For example, there's no indication that Jimmy is a minor, that Jimmy is drunk, that Jimmy is a government agent, or that Jimmy is an agent for Uptown Mall, so don't address liability as it would apply to those scenarios. However, the stated rule for "common area" does contain the point that if there is some kind of relationship, Mary might have had a duty to warn. Also, all you know about Jimmy is that he is carrying a large box and that he can't see around it. You need to ask yourself: *Why is that fact in the question? Why is this the one thing I am told about Jimmy?* Here, based on what you've probably covered in torts, the question is clearly trying to get you to write something about contributory negligence. Think of it from the standpoint of speaking to a real client. Imagine your elderly client asks you to help her get out of a contract. You wouldn't say, "Actually, you know, if you were a minor, and this wasn't a contract for necessaries, you could . . . ." Your client wouldn't care, because she clearly isn't a minor.

The second important point is that a good exam answer shouldn't be too conclusory. Always think about "the other hand." On a real exam, you always need to think about the potential counterarguments or defenses that exist. A really good exam question has a hypothetical that lies right in the middle of the situation and has arguments that could go both ways.

The following is a simple suggested answer (again, not necessarily the "A" answer, depending on how much time you have). The black letter law appears in bold type (don't highlight it in any way on your exam; this is just in the book to point out the placement of the black letter law in the IRAC form). Also, when you write your answer on the exam, divide each IRAC with an underlined heading. The underlined headings make it easier for your professor to grade. This makes your professor happier. And a happier professor is likely to award more points.

Sample Answer

Jimmy/Common Area

The issue is whether Mary could be held liable for Jimmy's fall in the common area. **A tenant is only liable for those areas as to which he or she is in actual possession. Thus, common areas, such as stairways, elevators, and corridors, are usually deemed to remain in control of the** landlord, at least where the building is a structure with multiple tenants. The tenants therefore can have no liability for defects in these areas (except perhaps for a non-possession-related liability for failing to warn of the defect to a person to whom they had a general duty of due care, such as a social guest). Here, Uptown Mall, as a mall, likely has multiple tenants, and tenants are likely not responsible for the common areas in front of their stores. Jimmy tripped and fell over a defect in the common area. Mary, as a tenant of the mall, would not be liable for defects in the common areas, unless there was some relationship between Jimmy and Mary giving rise to a general duty to warn.

Jimmy's Contributory Negligence

Assuming Mary could be found liable based on some relationship between Jimmy and Mary and Mary's failure to warn, Jimmy's recovery would likely be reduced or barred because of his negligence. **At common law, the doctrine of contributory negligence applies. The doctrine provides that a plaintiff who is negligent, and whose negligence contributes proximately to his or her injuries, is totally barred from recovery. A comparative negligence system reduces the amount the plaintiff can recover based on the amount of his or her negligence. In a pure comparative system, the recovery is simply reduced by a proportion equal to the ratio between his or her own negligence and the total negligence contributing to the accident. In a "50 percent" system, a plaintiff is completely barred from recovery if his or her negligence is as great or greater (depending on the state) as that of the defendant.** Here, Jimmy was carrying a large box that he couldn't see around when he tripped over a three-inch defect. A three-inch defect is likely a fairly noticeable defect (as opposed to a three-millimeter defect), so a court would likely find that Jimmy's own negligence in carrying the large box contributed to his injury. In a traditional contributory negligence system, Jimmy would likely be barred from recovery. In a comparative system, his recovery would likely be reduced by the proportional amount of his negligence, or even barred if a court finds his negligence outweighs Mary's.

Ultimately, taking a law school exam is a skill, and as with any skill (whether it's playing the piano, shooting a basket, or catching a fish), the best way to improve is with practice. Many students make the mistake of simply reading cases and making an outline. But think about whether you would feel comfortable getting into a boxing ring if you had only read about boxing and organized some notes, and not practiced throwing punches, jumping rope, and sparring. When you are preparing for exams, it is important to set aside time to do as many practice questions as you can. By using the questions in this book and the essay writing guidelines above, you will reinforce your knowledge of the black letter law and become proficient at issue spotting and essay writing.

CIVIL PROCEDURE

Civil Procedure Table of Contents

JURISDICTION OVER THE PARTIES

SUBJECT MATTER JURISDICTION

PLEADING

TRIAL PROCEDURE

MULTIPARTY AND MULTICLAIM LITIGATION

Civil Procedure Short-Answer Questions

1. In New York, D made oral statements to X concerning P, including the statement that P was a thief. P learned of these statements while he was in New York on business. P then returned to his home in Colorado. P happened to learn that D would be motoring through Colorado as part of a New York to San Francisco cross-country drive. As D pulled into a gas station in Boulder, Colorado (his only stop in Colorado), he was served with a summons in a Colorado state court defamation action brought by P. May the Colorado courts constitutionally take jurisdiction over this action?

Not sure ☐

2. D resided in Connecticut until five years ago. His company then transferred him to California to take over a troubled operation. Even though D expected to return to Connecticut eventually, he sold his Connecticut house, figuring that when he returned there he would buy a different house. D did not know for sure how long he would be residing in California, but he did not expect to remain there for more than two or three years. After D took up residence in California, he was sued in the Connecticut state courts concerning a transaction that he had carried out in New York some years before. Can the Connecticut state courts constitutionally take jurisdiction over this suit?

Not sure ☐

3. D, a wealthy heir, owns homes in New York, Florida, and California. He spends about six months of the year in the New York home and about three months per year in each of the other two homes. D has been sued in the Florida courts in a suit that relates to transactions that took place entirely outside of Florida. Service was made on him in New York pursuant to a Florida long-arm statute that allows jurisdiction over any "resident of Florida." May the Florida courts constitutionally take jurisdiction over this action?

Not sure ☐

4. P, a resident of Michigan, has virtually no contacts with California. P was injured in Michigan in an auto accident in which he drove one car, and D, a resident of California, drove the other car. P sued D in California, alleging negligence as to this accident. In the same action, D then counterclaimed against P, alleging that it was P, not D, whose negligence caused the accident. Evidence developed during discovery made it apparent that D had the better case. P therefore discontinued his action. D continues to assert his counterclaim against P, who now moves to dismiss on the grounds that the California courts do not have jurisdiction over him. Will P's motion be granted?

Not sure ☐

5. D owns and runs a small bakery in Portland, Maine. P is a truck driver who lives in South Carolina. One day, P visited D's bakery just before embarking on the long truck ride from Maine to South Carolina. He bought a dozen cream-filled doughnuts from D and remarked, "I'm going to eat one of these every two hours, so I'll still have a couple left by the time I get home to South Carolina." P followed this plan and ate the last two doughnuts while inside the South Carolina state limits. P then fell violently ill of food poisoning, causing him to lose control of his truck, which went off the road and flipped over, seriously injuring P. Later, medical evidence showed that it was one of the last two doughnuts, eaten in South Carolina, that caused the food poisoning. P sued D in the South Carolina courts. Not only was P a resident of South Carolina, but at the time of the suit he was also hospitalized there, and all witnesses to the accident, as well as all witnesses to the medical findings concerning the food poisoning, resided in South Carolina. Assuming that the South Carolina long-arm statute can fairly be interpreted to give jurisdiction over D on these facts, may the courts of South Carolina constitutionally hear the suit?

Not sure ☐

6. D operates a women's leather-goods store in Tulsa, Oklahoma. Until five years ago, D bought all of his goods from an Oklahoma-based jobber. But five years ago, D decided to travel to New York City's leather district to see what goods he could buy there. He purchased $10,000 of merchandise in New York and then flew back to Tulsa. Two months later, while vacationing in Pennsylvania, D collided with a car driven by P, a New York resident. P sued D in New York state court. Except for the buying trip, D has never been in New York or had any other activities connected with New York. May the New York courts constitutionally take jurisdiction over D for purposes of this negligence suit?

Not sure ☐

7. Corporation is a manufacturer of ladies' dresses. In the state of Arkansas, Corporation does not maintain any official office. Corporation conducts no advertising directed at Arkansas residents and derives only a small portion of its total revenues from that state. Corporation's sole activities in the state consist of the activities of Jones, a commission salesman for Corporation, who works out of his house soliciting orders from Arkansas-based department stores. When an Arkansas department store places an order, the order is not accepted by Jones, but instead is sent to the home office in New York for approval. All orders are shipped from New York directly to the department store that placed the order. P, an Arkansas department store that placed one order with Corporation via Jones, received what it believed to be defective merchandise and sued Corporation in the Arkansas courts. May the Arkansas courts constitutionally take jurisdiction over Corporation?

Not sure ☐

8. D is an insurance company with its principal (and in fact only) office in Connecticut. D writes life insurance policies in ten carefully selected states, including Oklahoma but not Kansas. D offered P a policy by sending him a direct-mail solicitation to his Oklahoma home; P accepted the policy and paid the first premium from Oklahoma. Two months thereafter, P moved to Kansas. The month after that, P died without ever having made a premium payment other than the first one from Oklahoma. Only when P's widow, the beneficiary under the policy, filed a notice of claim from Kansas did D realize that Kansas was where P last resided. D, suspecting that P's death was due to suicide (which would not be covered by the policy), has refused to pay. P's widow has sued D in the Kansas state courts. All witnesses to the manner of P's death are in Kansas. May the Kansas courts constitutionally take jurisdiction over D in this action?

Not sure ☐

9. Husband and Wife both lived in Texas during their marriage. They then were divorced, and Wife moved to Oregon. After the divorce, their only child, Son, lived with Husband in Texas for one year. Son then asked Husband for permission

to go live with Wife in Oregon. Husband agreed. While Son was living with Wife in Oregon, Husband fell behind in the child support payments that he and Wife had agreed upon in a contract that they signed in Texas just before the divorce. Wife has sued Husband in Oregon for the unpaid child support. May the Oregon courts constitutionally take jurisdiction over this action?

Not sure ☐

10. D was in the business of manufacturing car batteries. D had only one customer, Car Co., a large car manufacturer. D and Car Co. were both based in Michigan, and any battery sold by D to Car Co. was delivered to Car Co.'s various plants in Michigan. Car Co. sold the cars it produced in Michigan to buyers located all over the nation and world. About 20 percent of Car Co.'s cars were sold to California consumers. One of these California consumers, P, bought in California a Car Co. car with a battery made by D. P was injured in California when the battery exploded while P was trying to change it. All witnesses to the accident reside in California. Because Car Co. has since gone bankrupt, P has sued D rather than Car Co., and has brought that suit in California. May the California courts constitutionally take jurisdiction over D in this action?

Not sure ☐

11. D is an individual who sells personal computers at retail. She resides in Illinois and conducts her business there. P is a large computer manufacturer, all of whose operations are in Texas. P and D signed a "dealership agreement," by which the parties agreed that (1) D was to place mail and phone orders from Illinois to P's Texas headquarters, (2) P was to ship the computers from Texas to D's Illinois place of business, (3) D was to pay for the goods by sending checks to Texas, and (4) Texas law would apply to the contract. The agreement did not state where suits on the contract may be brought.

The only representatives of P that D ever actually met personally were P's two Illinois-based salespeople. After D had ordered and paid for a number of computers as contemplated by the agreement, D ordered a computer that she then did not pay for, claiming it was defective. P has sued D in Texas state court for payment. Since P is a large corporation that does business nationwide, P would probably find it easier to sue in Illinois than D would find it to defend in Texas. The Texas long-arm statute provides that the Texas courts shall have jurisdiction over any contract "in which either of the parties is a Texas resident or, in the case of a corporation, has its principal place of business in Texas." D concedes that the long-arm applies to this situation, but contends that the exercise of jurisdiction by Texas on these facts would violate her constitutional rights. May the Texas courts exercise jurisdiction?

Not sure ☐

12. D is a somewhat raunchy men's magazine, with a 1 million-copy circulation. P is a prominent evangelist. D published a satirical cartoon asserting (humorously) that P has sex with barnyard animals. After seething for a considerable time, P finally decided to sue D for intentional infliction of emotional distress. By this time, the statute of limitations on an intentional infliction of emotional distress claim had passed in every state except Rhode Island. Therefore, P sued D in Rhode Island, even though the only contact either P or D had with Rhode Island was the sale by D in Rhode Island of 10,000 copies of the magazine containing the offending cartoon. May the Rhode Island courts exercise jurisdiction over D for purposes of

awarding damages for all of the injuries suffered by P due to the nationwide publication of the cartoon?

Not sure ☐

13. Same facts as in the previous question. Now, however, assume that of the 1 million total copies of the offending cartoon published, only 15 were sold in Rhode Island. Does this change the answer?

Not sure ☐

14. D is a toy manufacturer whose sole office is located in New York. P is a young Florida citizen who claims to have been seriously injured in Florida by a toy made by D in New York and shipped to a store in Florida, from which P's mother bought it. P has brought a diversity action against D, based on strict product liability, in the U.S. District Court, Southern District of Florida. Assume that if the action had been brought in the Florida state courts, no Florida statute would have permitted P to serve process on D outside the boundaries of Florida. In the federal action, P caused a licensed process server to travel to New York, where the process server visited D's headquarters and personally handed the summons and complaint to D's president. Does the federal court for the Southern District of Florida now have personal jurisdiction over D?

Not sure ☐

15. Same facts as in the previous question. Now, however, assume that Florida has a long-arm statute providing that service may be made on a corporation located outside of the state, by first-class mail sent to any officer of that corporation, in any suit in which the claim arises out of a tort allegedly committed by the defendant outside of the state but causing injury in the state. P caused a summons in his Florida federal court action to be sent by first-class mail to the president of D in New York. May the U.S. District Court for the Southern District of Florida take jurisdiction over D?

Not sure ☐

16. Coca Cola Corp., a Georgia Corporation (Coke GA), owns the federal trademark for "Coke" when applied to beverages. The Coke Den is a restaurant in Reno, Nevada, that serves illegal drugs, including cocaine, to its guests along with meals. Only people who are known to the owners of the Coke Den as being Reno residents (and non-law-enforcement members) are permitted to dine at the Den. The Den also operates a website, *thecokeden.com*, accessible to anyone anywhere with an Internet connection. The website prominently displays the name "The Coke Den" and the slogan "We sell the freshest Coke in the world." The website invites Reno residents to dine at the Coke Den and allows anyone to send an electronic message to people who operate the restaurant, but it does not facilitate any other form of transaction (for instance, no food or merchandise can be ordered on the site). About 2,000 people a year from outside Nevada browse the website each year, of whom about 100 are from Georgia. Coke GA sues the Coke Den in federal district court for the Northern District of Georgia, alleging that the Coke Den website, by repeatedly using the word "Coke," is infringing Coke GA's federal trademark. The Georgia long-arm statute allows the state courts of Georgia to assert personal jurisdiction over any person or entity "having constitutionally sufficient contacts with the state of Georgia." The Coke Den moves to have the case dismissed for lack of personal jurisdiction. Should the court dismiss the suit?

Not sure ☐

17. P, a resident of New York, wished to bring a diversity action in the U.S. District Court for the Southern District of New York against D, a resident of California. The

suit involved an automobile accident to which D was a party, and which occurred in New York. The New York long-arm statute allows the New York courts to take jurisdiction over any suit arising out of a motor vehicle accident within the state. P caused there to be sent to D by first-class mail a notice that the action was being commenced, a request that the defendant waive service of the summons, a copy of the complaint, and a stamped self-addressed return envelope. D received the mailing, but made no response. May the New York federal district court exercise personal jurisdiction over D?

Not sure ☐

18. Software Co. is a Washington-based publisher of computer software, particularly a program called "3-2-1." Clone Co., which is also a software publisher, has come out with a competing program called "4-3-2." Clone Co. has sold more than 1,000 copies of 4-3-2 in the state of Washington. Software Co. has sued Clone Co. for federal copyright infringement in U.S. District Court for the Western District of Washington. The complaint alleges that 4-3-2 is so similar to 3-2-1 that it has the same "look and feel" and is therefore a violation of Software Co.'s copyrights. Assume that Clone Co., by selling more than 1,000 copies in Washington, has the constitutionally required minimum contacts with Washington to make it not violative of due process for Clone Co. to have to defend a suit there. Assume further, however, that due to the Washington state legislature's desire to cut down on the "litigation explosion," Washington's long-arm is quite restrictive and would not permit the Washington courts to take jurisdiction of any suit against a company that, like Clone Co., has no contacts with the state except for selling 1,000 copies of a product in the state. May the federal court for the Western District of Washington take personal jurisdiction over Clone Co. for purposes of the Software Co. copyright suit? (Assume that the method by which service is made on Clone Co. is satisfactory.)

Not sure ☐

19. Driver borrowed a car owned by Owner (a New Mexico resident) with Owner's permission. While Driver was driving the car in Arizona, he hit and injured Pedestrian, an Arizona resident. Pedestrian, realizing that Driver is so poor as to be judgment-proof, has brought a diversity action against Owner in Arizona Federal District Court. Applicable Supreme Court decisions indicate that Owner, by permitting his car to be driven into Arizona, has such minimum contacts with Arizona that it is not a violation of due process for him to be required to defend a suit brought in the Arizona state courts arising out of the accident. However, Arizona's nonresident motorist statute is relatively restrictive; it allows suit against one who is the driver in an Arizona-based accident, but not against one who owns a car (which he is not driving) that is involved in an Arizona accident. Therefore, Pedestrian would not have been permitted to sue Owner in the Arizona courts unless Owner was served while in Arizona. Pedestrian instituted his federal court suit by making personal service on Owner in New Mexico. May the Arizona district court hear the suit against Owner?

Not sure ☐

20. Computer Co. is a New York–based manufacturer of personal computers, many aspects of which are protected by U.S. patent laws. Knockoff Co. is a Taiwan-based manufacturer and exporter of personal computers. To make a splash for its new Model 543 personal computer, Knockoff Co. brought a machine from Taiwan to California and conducted a press conference there, at which it issued

news releases about the computer. It sent three of these news releases to news organizations located in New York. Computer Co. sued Knockoff Co. in New York Federal District Court, claiming that the Model 543 violates Computer Co.'s patents, asserting that the sample machine brought to California violates the U.S. statute barring importation of patent-infringing goods and seeking an injunction against any further importing into the United States. Assume that under applicable Supreme Court decisions, Knockoff Co. does not have minimum contacts with New York, but does have minimum contacts with California. May the New York Federal District Court constitutionally exercise jurisdiction over Knockoff Co.?

Not sure ☐

21. D is a resident of Pennsylvania. While driving one day in Pennsylvania, D collided with P, a pedestrian, an Ohio resident who happened to be visiting his sister in Pennsylvania. D has no contacts with Ohio except for the fact that D works in Pennsylvania for a corporation whose state of incorporation and principal place of business are Ohio. P commenced an action for negligence against D in the Ohio state courts. P obtained from the Ohio state courts an order of prejudgment garnishment (authorized by Ohio statutes) whereby D's employer was required to deposit with the court each week 20 percent of D's take-home pay until the action is resolved. Under the terms of the garnishment order, if P prevails, P will be given the garnished amount (up to the amount of his judgment), but D will have no other liability, assuming that he does not make a general appearance. May the Ohio courts constitutionally proceed with P's action on this basis?

Not sure ☐

22. P is a resident of Kansas. D is a resident of Missouri. D lent his car to a friend, who injured P with the car in Kansas. Kansas has a very restrictive long-arm statute, which does not permit the Kansas courts to take jurisdiction over actions against nonresident owners of cars even where an accident involving the car takes place in Kansas, unless the owner was also the driver. Therefore, P cannot bring an ordinary suit against D in the Kansas courts.

Not sure ☐

However, P has discovered that D is owed money as the beneficiary under an insurance policy, and the insurer happens to be based in Kansas. Kansas attachment statutes permit P to attach this debt of the insurer to D, and would permit P to show that under the relevant law of both Kansas and Missouri, D is responsible for P's injuries from the accident. P obtained such an attachment (issued by the Kansas state courts) against the debt owed by the insurer to D. P then instituted a diversity action against D in Federal District Court for the District of Kansas. P would like to have the court hear the suit and, if P prevails, award P the attached insurance proceeds up to the amount the court finds to have been P's damages from the accident. May the federal court properly do this?

Not sure ☐

23. P wished to bring a federal court suit against D, a large multinational corporation with its headquarters in a suburb of New York City. P's process server arrived at D's headquarters building at 5:15 P.M. on Monday, after the offices were officially closed. Near the reception desk, he encountered Edward, who identified himself as secretary to the director of D's personnel department. The process server stated that he had "important papers" for the corporation, and Edward agreed to take them and get them to the proper person. Edward meant well, but forgot to give the

papers to D's in-house legal department (the proper action). Assuming that there is no relevant New York State statute, has P properly served D?

Not sure ☐

24. P wished to bring a federal trademark infringement action against D, an individual. The statute of limitations would run against P's claim on July 1. On June 1, D's process server rang the doorbell of D's residence. A maid who appeared to speak very little English answered the door. The process server asked for D, and the maid merely shook her head and said, "No here." The process server gave the papers to the maid. The maid in fact gave the papers to D, who did not answer them. The maid then went home for the night (since she was a day worker, not a live-in). Four months after this encounter, P moved for a default judgment. At that point, D not only opposed the entry of the default judgment but also argued that the complaint should be dismissed (with the result that it would now be time-barred). Assuming that the issue boils down to whether service on the maid was suitable, and assuming that there is no state statute on point, does D have a respectable chance of prevailing on his dismissal motion?

Not sure ☐

25. A statute of the state of Ames provides that in any action for personal injuries arising out of an automobile accident, the plaintiff may obtain a prejudgment attachment of the defendant's bank account simultaneously with the filing of the plaintiff's suit. However, the plaintiff may obtain the attachment only by filing an affidavit stating that, to the best of P's knowledge, D was involved in and was the cause of the accident; the judge must then find that P appears to be acting in good faith. The statute also provides that the court must grant D a hearing within one month after issuance of the attachment, at which D may show that he will probably not be found liable in the suit; if D makes such a showing, the attachment must be rescinded. D now attacks the statute as a violation of his right to due process. Should D prevail?

Not sure ☐

26. P resides in Indiana; D resides in Illinois. While D was driving his car in Indiana on vacation, he hit and injured P. P started a suit against D in the Indiana state courts and made service upon D in Illinois pursuant to the Indiana long-arm statute. (Assume that application of the long-arm to allow service on and jurisdiction over D in these facts is constitutional.) D has no assets in Indiana, but P has learned that D performed some home remodeling work for a couple who live in Indiana, and that the couple has not yet paid D's bill for this work, which is for $4,000. Acting pursuant to Indiana's prejudgment garnishment statutes, P has obtained a court order garnishing this debt owed to D; that is, the debtor (the couple who had the work done) has been ordered to pay the $4,000 into an account held by the court, with the proceeds to be turned over to P or D at the end of P's lawsuit, depending on who wins. Indiana law provides that as long as P shows some "reasonable probability" that he will prevail at trial on the merits, the garnishment will stand until the trial is finished (which is likely to take one to two years). D argues that this attachment procedure has deprived him of his property (the $4,000) without the right to be heard and is therefore a violation of his constitutional due process rights. Will D's argument succeed?

Not sure ☐

27. P is a resident of New Mexico. D is a resident of Arizona. P sued D in diversity in federal court for New Mexico and made service on D in Arizona in a manner that he believed to be authorized by the New Mexico long-arm statute. D filed a motion under Federal Rule 12(b)(6) for failure to state a claim upon which relief can be granted; this motion asserted that P's claim was barred by the applicable statute of limitations. The court considered and rejected D's motion. D then made a motion claiming that the federal court lacked personal jurisdiction over D. D does not in fact have minimum contacts with New Mexico. Should the court grant D's second motion?

Not sure ☐

28. Same facts as in the previous question. Now, however, assume that D has not made a 12(b)(6) motion or a motion to dismiss for lack of jurisdiction. This is because he has placed his lawyer on a tight budget and has told her not to make any motions at all. What should D's lawyer do to assert D's claim of lack of personal jurisdiction, without subjecting D to the court's general jurisdiction by the very act of raising the lack-of-jurisdiction objection?

Not sure ☐

29. Same facts as in the previous question. Now, however, assume that D has not made either motion, but has served an answer raising several defenses, including the defense of statute of limitations, the defense of statute of frauds, and the defense of lack of personal jurisdiction. Assume that D's jurisdictional objection is a valid one on the merits. P argues that when D submitted an answer containing the other nonjurisdictional defenses, he thereby waived his right to make the simultaneous jurisdictional objection. Is P's argument correct?

Not sure ☐

30. P is a resident of New York. D is a resident of New Jersey. While P was driving through New Jersey, D (who operates a fast food restaurant) served P a hamburger. P ate the hamburger in New Jersey, but became violently ill upon his return to New York. P sued D in New York state court for negligence and product liability. Service on D was carried out by means authorized by the New York long-arm statute. D made a special appearance in the New York court (as is permitted by New York procedural law) for the sole purpose of contesting personal jurisdiction over him. The New York court found that it had personal jurisdiction over D.

D then failed to answer the complaint, and the New York court issued a default judgment against him. Since all of D's assets were in New Jersey, P brought a suit in New Jersey to enforce the New York judgment. In the New Jersey suit on the judgment, D convinced the New Jersey court that under applicable U.S. Supreme Court decisions, the New York court had erred in deciding that it could constitutionally exercise personal jurisdiction over D, because D did not knowingly and voluntarily take action that would bring his products into New York. Must the New Jersey court enforce the New York judgment against D, thus allowing P to seize D's property to satisfy that judgment?

Not sure ☐

31. Same facts as in the previous question. Now, however, assume that D never appeared in the New York courts at all, whether to contest jurisdiction or anything else. The New York court issued a default judgment against D. When the suit was brought for enforcement in New Jersey, the New Jersey court agreed with D's argument that D lacked minimum contacts with New York and that therefore the New York courts could not constitutionally take personal jurisdiction over him. Must the New Jersey courts permit P to enforce his judgment against D's New Jersey assets?

Not sure ☐

32. P is a resident of Connecticut. D is a resident of New York. P wished to sue D on a cause of action unrelated to Connecticut. P realized that D was very unlikely to come to Connecticut voluntarily. Therefore, P printed up some stationery bearing the name "Litchfield Farms" and a Connecticut address, and sent D a "mailgram" printed on the stationery, stating, "By a random drawing, you have won a one-acre luxury vacation home site at fabulous Litchfield Farms, located in prestigious Litchfield, Connecticut, favorite second-home spot for movie stars and other celebrities. To collect your prize, you must come to the above address no later than April 1." D, believing that the letter was real, showed up at the Connecticut address on March 31. When he arrived, P immediately served him with the summons and complaint in a Connecticut state court action. D now moves in the Connecticut court for a dismissal for lack of personal jurisdiction. Will the Connecticut court grant D's motion?

Not sure ☐

33. Same basic fact pattern as in the previous question. Now, however, assume that although D has a residence of record in Connecticut, he is rarely to be found there. Also assume that Connecticut has very limited methods of substituted service, so that P's lawyer concluded that only personal service upon D within the state of Connecticut would suffice. P sent the letter (described in the previous question) to D's Connecticut address. The mail was forwarded to D's out-of-state address, where he read it, and traveled to Connecticut to claim his prize. If D moves to dismiss the Connecticut action for lack of personal jurisdiction over him, will the court grant his motion?

Not sure ☐

34. Davis was a member of the New York–based law firm of Dewey, Cheatham & Howe. However, Davis practiced only in the firm's Miami office. The firm became insolvent due to poor financial planning. Peters, a New Jersey resident whose financial printing firm (also based in New Jersey) had done work for the firm and had not been paid, instituted suit against all partners individually (since any debt of a partnership is binding on all the individual partners) in the New Jersey state courts. During discovery in this suit, Peters served Davis in Florida with a notice of deposition, the deposition to take place in Peters's lawyer's office in New Jersey.

Although the notice of deposition was not binding outside of New Jersey, Davis voluntarily complied, traveling to New Jersey. While Davis was at Newark Airport on his way to the lawyer's office, he was served with a summons and complaint by Parker, a former client of his; this suit was in the New Jersey state courts, and was for malpractice allegedly committed by Davis on Parker (now a New Jersey resident) when Parker was a Florida resident. The work leading to the alleged negligence was all performed in Florida. Will the New Jersey state courts hear Parker's suit against Davis?

Not sure ☐

35. P and D are both individuals. P is a resident of the Eastern District of Michigan; D resides in the Northern District of Ohio. P and D are both designers of children's clothing, and both have their offices in Detroit, in the Eastern District of Michigan. P wishes to bring a federal court action asserting that certain clothing designs created by him have been taken and used by D, and that this use constitutes a violation of Michigan's unfair competition laws. Since P and D are both fairly small-time operators, each sells his designs and clothing only in the Detroit area. Assuming that there is no problem of personal jurisdiction, in what judicial district(s) may P bring his action?

    Not sure ☐

36. Same facts as in the previous question. Now, however, assume that (1) the designs by D that P claims to be unfairly competitive with P's own designs are sold primarily in the Northern District of Indiana; and (2) P wants to join to his suit D's main customer, Jones, who is a resident of the Northern District of Indiana. Where may P's suit be brought?

    Not sure ☐

37. Same facts as in the previous question. Now, however, assume that P adds to his action a claim that D's conduct violates federal copyright laws. Assume that there is no statute setting a special rule for venue in copyright actions. Where may P's suit be brought?

    Not sure ☐

38. D is a small electronics company, with its headquarters in the Southern District of Texas. P is an individual who resides in the Northern District of Texas. P wishes to sue D for violation of the federal patent laws; P asserts that D has sold a product that infringes on a patent held by P. All of the sales by D that P cites as infringing took place in the Southern District of Texas. D is a Delaware corporation. D has no contacts with the Northern District of Texas (or any other part of Texas except for the Southern District, where it is based and where it makes its sales). May P bring her suit in the Northern District of Texas?

    Not sure ☐

39. P, a resident of Los Angeles (in the Central District of California), sued D, a resident of Las Vegas (in the District of Nevada), for trademark infringement, a federal cause of action. The cause of action arose in Nevada. This suit was initially brought by P in the California state court system, in a court located in Los Angeles. (Actions claiming violation of the federal trademark laws, even though based on a federal statute, are not exclusively federal actions—P may sue in either federal or state court.) D now attempts to remove the case to federal court.

  (a) Assuming that removal is proper on these facts, in what federal court will the action be heard?

    Not sure ☐

  (b) What is strange about the answer to (a)?

    Not sure ☐

40. P is a resident of the Southern District of New York. D1 is a resident of the District of New Jersey. D2 is a resident of the Eastern District of Pennsylvania. P sued D1 and D2 in federal court for federal copyright infringement; P's cause of action arose in the Northern District of Ohio, where P has brought his suit. Both Ds have collaborated on a petition stating that Ohio is an inconvenient place to try the case and asking that the case be transferred to the Southern District of New York. It is clear that although the cause of action arose in Ohio, most of the witnesses are in New York or New Jersey, and the convenience of all parties (even P) is best served by having the action proceed in New York. May the Ohio federal judge grant the Ds' motion to transfer the case to New York?

    Not sure ☐

41. Same basic fact pattern as above question. Now, however, assume that P brought suit in the Southern District of New York. The Ds submitted their answers, and then noticed that venue was improper. Both Ds moved to have the case transferred to federal district court for the Northern District of Ohio (where the claim arose).

The federal judge hearing the motion (the federal judge for the Southern District of New York) has decided that while the case could and should have been brought in Ohio federal district court originally, convenience of the parties dictates that she hear the case herself in New York. Is the New York federal judge entitled to hear the case?

Not sure ☐

42. P is a resident of the Southern District of New York. D is a resident of the Southern District of Florida. P brought, in the Southern District of New York, an action alleging that D violated a patent belonging to P. The cause of action arose in the Southern District of Florida. The action was filed shortly before the statute of limitations ran on P's claim. D has moved in a timely manner under Rule 12(b)(2) to dismiss the case on the grounds that the federal court lacks jurisdiction over D's person, because D does not have minimum contacts with New York. Also, D has pointed out that venue does not properly lie in the Southern District of New York. The New York federal judge agrees with both of D's assertions. However, the judge realizes that if he dismisses the case, P will lose his remedy because the statute of limitations will now have run and any service on D in a new action brought in an appropriate forum (e.g., federal court for the Southern District of Florida) will be time-barred. What, if anything, may the federal court do to avoid this unfair result?

Not sure ☐

43. P is a resident and citizen of Canada. P reasonably believed that D was a permanent resident alien of the United States and that D resided in Michigan. D is in fact an illegal immigrant who remains a citizen of Mexico. P sued D in federal court for the Eastern District of Michigan for breach of contract; the suit presented no federal question. D made no jurisdictional objection, and the case proceeded through trial. After the jury rendered a verdict in favor of P, D disclosed to the court that he was an illegal immigrant. What, if anything, should be the effect of this disclosure on the status of the case?

Not sure ☐

44. D's sole residence is in Connecticut. Under a contract with P, D performed some construction work on P's weekend home in Connecticut. P also has a principal residence, located in New York (where P resides during the week). When D failed to do the work in the contracted-for manner, P sued D in federal court for the District of Connecticut for $100,000 (a reasonable assessment of the damages suffered by P). No federal questions are presented by P's suit. May the federal court for Connecticut hear the case?

Not sure ☐

45. P is an American citizen who resided in New York until the age of 30. P has since moved to France; he has not applied for French citizenship (so he remains American), but he has no plans ever to return to the United States. D is an American domiciled in Illinois. P has sued D on a contract action in the Northern District of Illinois; no federal question is present. The amount at stake is $90,000. May the Illinois federal court hear the case?

Not sure ☐

46. P1 is a citizen of New York. P2 is a citizen of New Jersey. D1 is a citizen of California. D2 is a citizen of New Jersey. P1 and P2 have brought a federal court action in the Southern District of New York against D1 and D2, alleging that D1 and D2 have breached a contract. No federal question is present. The Southern

District of New York is the district where the claim arose. The amount at stake is $100,000. May the Southern District of New York hear the case?

Not sure ☐

47. Insurance Co., whose principal place of business and state of incorporation are both Connecticut, issued a life insurance policy on the life of Father. Father originally designated Son as his beneficiary. Later, Insurance Co. received what purported to be a change of beneficiary notification from Father, designating Daughter instead of Son as the beneficiary. Shortly thereafter, Father died. Both Daughter and Son have claimed the $100,000 proceeds, with Son arguing that the change of beneficiary form was a forgery perpetrated by Daughter. Son is a citizen of New York; Daughter is a citizen of Connecticut. No federal question is presented. What, if anything, may Insurance Co. do to obtain a federal court forum for determining whether Son or Daughter is entitled to the policy proceeds?

Not sure ☐

48. Paul Tulip is a player for the major-league Cleveland Blues baseball team. Tulip is a citizen of Ohio, which is also the principal place of business and state of incorporation of the Blues. Tulip learned that the commissioner of Major League Baseball was about to bar him from the game for life for gambling. Tulip instituted a state court action in the Ohio courts against Major League Baseball and the Blues, seeking to block them from removing him from the game, on a state-law theory. Major League Baseball is a corporation with its principal place of business and state of incorporation in New York. The Blues actually hope desperately that Tulip will win his suit to prevent the commissioner from barring him, since Tulip is the Blues' best player. Nonetheless, the Blues have reluctantly joined (after lots of threats and browbeating by the commissioner) in Major League Baseball's petition to remove the case to federal court for the Northern District of Ohio (the district in which the Blues are located). Tulip opposes removal, arguing that there is not complete diversity.

    (a) What can Major League Baseball (represented by the commissioner) do to counter Tulip's argument?

Not sure ☐

    (b) Will the step taken by the commissioner pursuant to (a) succeed?

Not sure ☐

49. Pete, while crossing the street in his hometown of Oxford, Mississippi, was struck by a car driven by Dave, an Alabama resident. Pete's injuries were serious, and while he did not die immediately, he and his family tort lawyer realized that he might soon die of the injuries. The lawyer also realized that if Pete (or, in case of his death, his executor) were to bring a tort action against Dave, he would be likely to fare better in the Mississippi state courts than in federal court. Accordingly, the lawyer prepared a new will for Pete in which he appointed as his executor Edward, a resident of Alabama. Pete then died. Edward, as his executor, sued Dave in the Mississippi state courts; the case was captioned *Edward v. Dave*. Dave has attempted to remove the case to the federal court for the Southern District of Mississippi. No federal question is present, and the amount at stake is more than $75,000. Should the federal judge in Mississippi allow removal?

Not sure ☐

50. P, a citizen and resident of Mexico, sued D, a citizen of Texas. The suit, for breach of contract, was brought in federal court for the Southern District of Texas, the district in which D resides. The amount at stake is $85,000. Does the Texas federal court have subject matter jurisdiction over the dispute? Not sure ☐

51. P, a citizen and resident of France, has sued D, a citizen and resident of England. The suit has been brought in the federal court for the Southern District of New York and arose out of an automobile accident that took place in the Southern District. The amount at stake is $100,000. No federal question is present. May the federal court for the Southern District of New York hear the case? Not sure ☐

52. P1, a citizen of France, and P2, a citizen of New York, have sued D1, a citizen of England, and D2, a citizen of Texas. The suit has been brought in the Southern District of New York. Assuming that there is no federal question present, and that any amount in controversy requirement is satisfied, does the New York federal court have subject matter jurisdiction over the case? Not sure ☐

53. P1 is a citizen of Delaware; P2 is a citizen of New Jersey. They have brought a federal court action against D, a corporation with its principal place of business in New York and incorporated in Delaware. No federal question is present. $80,000 is at stake. Putting aside questions of venue, does the federal court have subject matter jurisdiction over the dispute? Not sure ☐

54. P1 is a citizen of Pennsylvania; P2 is a citizen of New Jersey. They have brought a federal court suit against D, a corporation that is incorporated in New York, has its headquarters in New York, makes 53 percent of its sales in New York and 47 percent in New Jersey, and whose board of directors meets in New Jersey. No federal question is present in this suit. Do the federal courts have subject matter jurisdiction over the dispute, assuming that the amount in controversy requirement is satisfied? Not sure ☐

55. Peter is a citizen of South Carolina. A car he was driving was involved in an accident with a car driven by Dennis, also a citizen of South Carolina. Peter wished to sue Dennis for negligence. He was aware that procedural rules would be more favorable for him in the federal court for South Carolina than in the South Carolina state courts. However, he realized that he would not be able to obtain diversity of citizenship in an action against Dennis. Therefore, he assigned his claim to his sister Paula, a citizen of North Carolina, for $1. Such an assignment is fully enforceable under the laws of both South Carolina and North Carolina. Peter and Paula had an implicit understanding that if Paula recovered, she would return the vast bulk of the award to Peter. Paula then sued Dennis on the claim in South Carolina federal court. The amount in controversy requirement is satisfied. Does the South Carolina federal district court have subject matter jurisdiction over the case? Not sure ☐

56. Pedro is a citizen of Wisconsin. Doris is a citizen of Michigan. Pedro wished to sue Doris for breach of contract. The amount at stake was $200,000. Pedro wanted to be sure that the suit remained in state court (where procedural rules were favorable to him), and was afraid that Doris would remove the suit to Wisconsin federal court. Therefore, solely for the purpose of defeating removal, Pedro assigned one-twentieth of his claim to Peggy, a friend who lived in Michigan, in return for a nominal payment. Pedro and Peggy then sued Doris as co-plaintiffs in Wisconsin state court. May Doris remove the case to Wisconsin federal district court? Not sure ☐

57. P1, an individual, is a citizen of Ohio. P2, also an individual, is a citizen of Michigan. D is a corporation, with its principal place of business in Ohio and incorporated in Delaware. P1 and P2 have sued D in federal court for the Northern District of Ohio. The Ps' complaint alleges that D has violated a patent jointly held by the two Ps. $100,000 is at stake. Does the Ohio federal court have subject matter jurisdiction over the action?

Not sure ☐

58. P is a franchiser of fast food restaurants. D holds a franchise issued by P for a particular restaurant location. P is incorporated in Delaware and has its principal place of business in New York. D is incorporated in Delaware and has its principal place of business in Florida. P wishes to terminate D's franchise. Therefore, P has brought an action in Florida federal district court for a declaratory judgment that by the terms of the franchise contract, P is entitled to terminate D's franchise. P's complaint raises no substantive issues other than issues of state contract law. D has submitted an answer asserting that P wishes to terminate D's franchise so that P can operate D's store itself; D asserts that this cancellation would be a violation of federal antitrust laws. Both P and D wish the action to proceed in federal court, to avoid the congestion of the Florida state courts. The federal judge is convinced that D's antitrust defense is not frivolous. Any applicable amount in controversy requirement is satisfied. Does the federal court for Florida have subject matter jurisdiction over the case?

Not sure ☐

59. P is an individual who is a citizen of Missouri. D, also an individual, is a citizen of Indiana. P asserts that he sold goods to D under a contract whereby D was to pay him $40,000 and that D has not paid for the goods. If suit is brought in federal court for the Southern District of Indiana (the district in which D resides), may that court hear the suit?

Not sure ☐

60. P is an individual who is a citizen of California. D is an individual who is a citizen of New York. P brought suit against D in federal court for the Western District of New York (the district including D's home), alleging that D injured P by hitting P with D's car. The damages asked for in the complaint by P, including damages for pain and suffering, totaled $85,000. This total was arrived at in good faith by P and P's lawyer, based on an analysis of what juries had awarded in similar cases, and on P's lawyer's belief that there was a significant chance that P would recover this amount of money if he showed that D was negligent. The case was tried before a jury. The jury found D liable but awarded damages of only $30,000.

(a) Should the trial judge enter a judgment in P's favor for this $30,000 amount?

Not sure ☐

(b) Apart from entering or not entering judgment for P, what action should the trial judge consider taking on these facts?

Not sure ☐

61. P is a citizen of New York. D is a citizen of New Jersey. P claimed that D, P's doctor, performed plastic surgery on P and did so in a negligent manner. P brought suit in the Eastern District of New York (where the operation took place). P sought $25,000 of compensatory damages and $60,000 of punitive damages. The case was tried before a jury, which awarded P $25,000 of compensatory damages and $60,000 of punitive damages. After the verdict and before judgment, D called to the court's attention a decision by the highest court in New York state (whose law applies to this action, due to *Erie* principles), holding that as a matter of public policy, the New York courts will not permit punitive damage awards in medical malpractice actions. What, if any, action should the federal judge take?

Not sure ☐

62. P, whose domicile is in New Haven, Connecticut, also owns an undeveloped one-half acre in rural Litchfield, Connecticut. D, a corporation incorporated in Massachusetts and with its principal place of business there, proposes to build a steel mill on property in Litchfield adjacent to P's property. P has brought a suit against D in federal court for the District of Connecticut, seeking an injunction on the state-law grounds that D's plant will, if built, constitute a private nuisance that will diminish the value of P's property. Since P's property has a market value of only $40,000, it appears virtually certain that the injury to P's ownership interest can be no more than $40,000. However, the cost to D, if its right to build the mill is enjoined, will be over $1 million (due to land acquisition costs, planning costs, etc.). No federal question is present. May the federal district court for Connecticut hear the case?

Not sure ☐

63. P, an individual, is a citizen of Vermont. D, a corporation, is incorporated in and has its principal place of business in Washington State. In 2010, P signed a contract with D giving D marketing rights to a software program developed by P, 4-3-2. In 2011, D issued a press release (unrelated to the P-D contract), stating that P "is a good programmer, but he's not a very good or honest guy, as evidenced by his 2005 conviction for armed robbery." P has brought suit against D in federal district court for Vermont alleging (1) in count one, breach of the contractual royalty provisions, for which P claims damages of $40,000; and (2) in count two, libel, for which P claims damages of $40,000. Assume the court has personal jurisdiction over D. May the court hear the case?

Not sure ☐

64. P1 and P2 are individuals who are citizens of Kentucky. D is a corporation that is a citizen of North Carolina. The Ps both signed identically worded contracts with D, whereby the Ps were each to raise broiler chickens, which they would sell to D for a stated price per pound. D unilaterally canceled both contracts at the same time. The Ps wish to sue jointly in North Carolina federal court for breach of contract and plan to join together as plaintiffs against D under Federal Rule 20. The damages asserted by P1 are $80,000, and the damages asserted by P2 equal $40,000. May the claims by P1 and P2 be heard together in a single federal action?

Not sure ☐

65. Same facts as in the previous question. Now, however, assume that P1 and P2 each have a claim for $45,000. May they join their claims against D together pursuant to Rule 20, so that they can be adjudicated in a single federal court suit?

Not sure ☐

66. P1 and P2 formed a partnership to grow broiler chickens. Each owns 50 percent of the partnership, and each is to bear 50 percent of any losses. The partnership signed a contract with D, whereby D agreed to buy at a stated price per pound all broilers grown by the partnership. D then refused to buy the contracted-for chickens, and the partnership suffered $80,000 of losses. There is diversity of citizenship between the Ps on one hand and D on the other hand. May P1 and P2 bring suit in the name of their partnership against D in federal court for this breach of contract?

Not sure ☐

67. P is a citizen of Tennessee. D is a citizen of Louisiana. P sued D in Louisiana state court on a breach of contract claim, seeking $30,000 in damages. D counterclaimed

for $80,000 damages for his injuries in an auto accident in which he was struck by a car driven by P. Assume that Louisiana law regarding when a counterclaim is compulsory and when it is permissive is the same as under the Federal Rules of Civil Procedure. May D remove the entire case to Louisiana federal court?   Not sure ☐

68. P and D are competing furniture stores. Each is operated in the form of a corporation headquartered in Georgia (and incorporated in Georgia); both stores serve the same small town. P has sued D in federal district court for the Middle District of Georgia. P makes two claims: (1) that certain advertising and marketing practices engaged in by D are a violation of the federal antitrust statutes; and (2) that those same practices are a violation of a Georgia statute prohibiting "unfair competition." Each claim involves more than $100,000. D moves to dismiss claim (2) on the grounds that federal subject matter jurisdiction is lacking over it.

    (a) What doctrine determines the validity of D's motion?   Not sure ☐

    (b) Should D's motion be granted?   Not sure ☐

69. Same fact pattern as in the previous question. Now, however, assume that the federal court, in response to a motion by D, has dismissed the antitrust claim before discovery, on the grounds that it failed to state a claim upon which relief may be granted (Rule 12(b)(6)), in that it is barred by the statute of limitations. The court concludes, however, that the state-law unfair competition claim is not time-barred. Should the federal court try the state-law claim?   Not sure ☐

70. Paula, a pedestrian, was seriously injured when a mail truck owned by the United States and driven by Dexter (a post office employee), hit her while she was crossing the street. Paula reasonably believed that both the United States and Dexter may be liable to her. Applicable statutes and court decisions interpreting those statutes indicate that a suit against the United States under the Federal Tort Claims Act may only be brought in federal court. Therefore, Paula sued both the United States and Dexter in federal district court for Nevada. Both Paula and Dexter are citizens of Nevada. Paula's claim is for more than $200,000 against each of the defendants. Paula's claim against the United States is based on the Federal Tort Claims Act; her claim against Dexter is based on a state-law theory of negligence. Dexter has moved to have the claim against him dismissed for lack of subject matter jurisdiction. Should Dexter's motion be granted?   Not sure ☐

71. P and D were both injured (P more seriously than D) when a car driven by P collided with a car driven by D. P is a citizen of Oklahoma; D is a citizen of Kansas. P has sued D in federal district court for the District of Kansas, asserting a claim whose amount in controversy is $100,000. D, who sustained only a few scratches and some damage to his car, has counterclaimed against P for $12,000. P moves to dismiss D's claim for lack of subject matter jurisdiction.

    (a) What doctrine determines whether D's claim should be dismissed?   Not sure ☐

    (b) Should P's motion be granted?   Not sure ☐

72. Same facts as in the previous question. Now, however, assume that there was a third car involved in the collision, driven by Xavier, a citizen of Kansas. P has not filed suit against Xavier, only against D. But D has concluded that both P and

Xavier were at fault and were responsible for his injuries. Therefore, he has joined Xavier as an additional party (defendant) to the counterclaim that he is making against P; he seeks $12,000 against each of P and Xavier. If Xavier moves to dismiss the claim against him for lack of federal subject matter jurisdiction, should the court grant his motion?

Not sure ☐

73. P is a citizen of Washington. D is a citizen of Oregon. P has sued D for negligence, arising out of an auto accident in which a car driven by D collided with a car driven by P. The amount at stake for P is $100,000. This suit has been brought in federal court for the District of Oregon. D has taken advantage of the pending suit to file a counterclaim against P for breach of a contract that the two had signed several years ago (before the auto accident). D has added Wanda as a defendant to this counterclaim, on the grounds that Wanda induced P to breach the contract with D. Wanda is a citizen of Oregon. D's counterclaim plausibly seeks $200,000 in damages from each of P and Wanda. Wanda moves to dismiss D's claim against her on the grounds that the court lacks subject matter jurisdiction over it. Should the court grant Wanda's motion?

Not sure ☐

74. Pedro, a pedestrian, was hit and injured in New Jersey by a car owned by Denise, and driven by her employee, Ted. Pedro (a citizen of New York) has sued Denise (a citizen of New Jersey) in federal district court for the Southern District of New York; his claim is for $100,000. Ted is a Pennsylvania resident, but Pedro has not bothered joining him (because he believes Ted is judgment-proof.) Pedro began the action by serving Denise pursuant to the New York long-arm. Denise (knowing, as Pedro does not, that Ted has a small nest egg) has brought a third-party claim against Ted, in which she asserts that if she is forced to pay anything to Pedro, Ted owes that amount to her. Denise has served Ted, claiming authority of the New York long-arm. Ted has no connection with New York, but Denise has substantial connections with New York. Ted now moves to dismiss, on the grounds that the New York federal court has no personal jurisdiction over him. Should Ted's motion be granted?

Not sure ☐

75. Same fact pattern as in the previous question. Now, however, assume that the accident occurred in New York, and suit has been brought by Pedro in New Jersey. Ted now moves to dismiss the action for improper venue; he argues that he and Denise are both defendants, and that suit must be brought in a district where any defendant resides if all reside in the same state, where a significant part of the events leading to the claim took place, or where the defendants are subject to personal jurisdiction at the time the action is commenced. Should the court grant Ted's motion?

Not sure ☐

76. Same basic fact pattern as in the previous two questions. Assume that Pedro (citizen of New York) has sued Denise (citizen of New Jersey) out of an accident caused by the driving of Ted (Pennsylvania resident) in New Jersey. Pedro has brought his action in the Southern District of New York after serving Denise pursuant to the New York long-arm. Denise has served Ted for her third-party claim, again pursuant to the New York long-arm. Ted has no connection with New York, but Denise has substantial connections with New York. Ted now moves to dismiss, on the grounds that the New York federal court has no personal jurisdiction over him. Should Ted's motion be granted?

Not sure ☐

77. Patricia, a citizen of New York, ate dinner one night at a restaurant operated in New York by David, a citizen of Connecticut. For dessert, Patricia had an apple pie bought by David from Terry, a New York citizen who is in the business of baking and selling pies to restaurants. Patricia became violently ill shortly thereafter, and tests indicated that the pie contained botulism. After months of hospitalization, Patricia commenced a product liability action in New York federal district court against David. Her claim is for $100,000.

David then impleaded Terry as a third-party defendant pursuant to Federal Rule 14, asserting that if he is liable to Patricia, Terry is liable to him. (This represents a correct statement by David of the applicable substantive rule in a product liability action brought against a restaurateur who makes a claim over against his supplier.) Patricia then made a product liability claim against Terry for $100,000, as allowed by Federal Rule 14. Terry now moves to dismiss Patricia's claim against her for lack of subject matter jurisdiction. Should Terry's motion be granted?   Not sure ☐

78. Same basic fact pattern as in the previous question. Now, however, assume that after David impleaded Terry, Patricia did not make any claim against Terry. Assume also, however, that after the accident, Patricia called a news conference in which she stated, "My terrible illness is the result of contaminated ingredients knowingly placed by Terry in pies she sold to David and other restaurateurs in the area." In the basic litigation, Terry now, as third-party defendant, has made a claim against Patricia for slander, seeking $200,000 in damages. Patricia seeks to dismiss Terry's claim against her for lack of subject matter jurisdiction. Should Patricia's motion be granted?   Not sure ☐

79. Paul, a pedestrian, was injured when a car driven by Dennis and owned by Dexter ran him down in Connecticut. Paul is a citizen of Connecticut, Dennis a citizen of Massachusetts and Dexter a citizen of Connecticut. Paul has sued Dennis and Dexter in federal court for the District of Connecticut on a negligence theory; he seeks $200,000 in damages from each. The joinder of Dennis and Dexter together as defendants was done pursuant to Federal Rule 20(a). Dexter now moves to dismiss the action against him on the grounds of lack of subject matter jurisdiction. Should Dexter's motion be granted?   Not sure ☐

80. Peter, a pedestrian, was injured when a car driven by Dale collided with a car driven by Dolores, and Peter was thrown to the sidewalk while walking nearby. Peter is a citizen of New Hampshire; Dale and Dolores are both citizens of Vermont. Peter, believing that both Dale and Dolores were negligent, has brought a negligence suit against them in federal court for New Hampshire. His claim is for $200,000. Dale suffered only property damage of $10,000 in the collision; she has made a Rule 13(g) cross-claim against Dolores for this amount, asserting that Dolores was negligent, and she, Dale, was not. Dolores now moves to dismiss Dale's claim against her for lack of federal subject matter jurisdiction. Should Dolores's motion be granted?   Not sure ☐

81. Homeowner owns a home next to a restaurant owned and operated by Restaurateur. Homeowner is a citizen of New Jersey, and Restaurateur is a citizen of Pennsylvania. A fire that started in Restaurateur's restaurant spread to Homeowner's home, damaging it. Homeowner commenced an action against Restaurateur in federal court for the District of New Jersey, alleging that Restaurateur behaved negligently. The suit seeks $400,000 in damages.

Shortly after the suit was commenced, Insurer, which insured Homeowner against some but not all of the damage to his house from the fire, sought permission from the court to intervene as a co-plaintiff, pursuant to Federal Rule 24. (Insurer's claim is that if Restaurateur was negligent, some of the damages will be owed to Insurer for money it has already paid over to Homeowner, rather than owed directly to Homeowner.) The federal judge agreed with Insurer that Insurer's claim has a "question of law or fact in common" with Homeowner's claim against Restaurateur. Therefore, the court granted Insurer's motion. Restaurateur now correctly points out that Insurer is incorporated in Pennsylvania. Restaurateur therefore moves to have Insurer's claim against him dismissed for lack of subject matter jurisdiction. Should the court grant Restaurateur's motion?

Not sure ☐

82. Same facts as in the previous question. Now, however, assume that Insurer has sought to intervene in the action (for purposes of making a claim against Restaurateur similar to Homeowner's claim) of right, under Federal Rule 24. Assume further that the court has concluded that Insurer claims "an interest relating to the property or transaction which is the subject of the action and the applicant is so situated that the disposition of the action may as a practical matter impair or impede the applicant's ability to protect that interest." Therefore, the court has granted Insurer's motion to intervene of right. Restaurateur now notes that Insurer has the same citizenship as himself and moves to dismiss Insurer's claim for lack of subject matter jurisdiction. Should the court grant Restaurateur's motion?

Not sure ☐

83. Same facts as in the previous question. Now, however, assume that the court has become convinced that Insurer's interest is so closely allied to that of Homeowner that Insurer is an indispensable party as that term is used in Federal Rule 19. (The court has concluded that it would not be fair to Restaurateur to have Homeowner's suit proceed without Insurer, because Insurer would not be bound by the judgment and could relitigate with Restaurateur even if Restaurateur won as against Homeowner.) What, if anything, should the court do as a consequence of having made this determination of indispensability?

Not sure ☐

84. P is a citizen of New York. D is a citizen of New Jersey. P has sued D in the New York state court system, alleging that D drove his car negligently, and thus injured P. P seeks damages of $90,000. D has heard that New York state juries tend to give unreasonably large awards in negligence cases. As a tactical matter, what should D consider doing shortly after being served in P's action?

Not sure ☐

85. P is a citizen of Ohio. D is a citizen of Kentucky. P has brought suit in the Ohio state courts, asserting that D drove his car negligently, thereby injuring P. P has incurred $65,000 in medical bills, plus significant pain and suffering. If P prevails at all, the likely award will be at least $120,000. Nonetheless, in the state court action P seeks only $65,000. (P is aware that under Ohio law, the jury is not limited to the sum demanded in the complaint.) D has filed a timely notice of removal with the federal district court for Ohio. P has made a timely motion to have the case remanded to the Ohio state courts due to the federal court's lack of removal jurisdiction. Should P's motion for remand be granted?

Not sure ☐

86. P is an individual who is a citizen of Pennsylvania. D is a corporation with its principal place of business in New Jersey, but incorporated in Delaware. P has sued D in the New Jersey state courts for breach of contract. P's claim seeks $100,000. D has filed a prompt notice of removal with the federal district court for New Jersey. P has moved to have the case remanded to the New Jersey state courts, on the grounds that removal was improper. Should P's motion be granted?   Not sure ☐

87. P is a citizen of Arizona. D is a citizen of New Mexico. P has sued D in the New Mexico state courts for violation of a federally registered trademark held by P. Suits alleging violation of the federal trademark laws may be brought in either state or federal court. D has filed a timely petition removing the case to federal court for the District of New Mexico. P moves to have the case dismissed for lack of subject matter jurisdiction. Should P's motion be granted?   Not sure ☐

88. P is a citizen of New York. D1 is a citizen of New Jersey. D2 is a citizen of Pennsylvania. P has sued D1 and D2 in the New Jersey state courts, on a cause of action alleging negligence. The claim arose in New York and is for $80,000. D1 and D2 have filed a joint petition to remove the case to the federal court for the District of New Jersey. P now moves to have the case remanded to state court for lack of subject matter jurisdiction. Should P's motion be granted?   Not sure ☐

89. P, a citizen of New Jersey, has brought an action in the New Jersey state courts against D1 (a citizen of New Jersey) and D2 (a citizen of Pennsylvania). The suit alleges that D1 and D2 have jointly violated a federally registered trademark held by P. (Both federal and state courts have jurisdiction over trademark-infringement claims.) The alleged violations occurred in New York.

   (a) If D1 and D2 join to file a notice of removal, and P opposes removal, will the removal stand?   Not sure ☐

   (b) What anomaly is produced by this fact pattern and your answer to part (a)?   Not sure ☐

90. P is a citizen of Pennsylvania. D is a citizen of Ohio. P has brought a negligence action against D in the state courts of Kentucky. The amount in controversy is $80,000. D has made a counterclaim against P for $200,000; the counterclaim arises out of an unrelated transaction (making it permissive under Kentucky law), and is based on state law. P has filed a notice of removal with the Kentucky federal district court. D now moves to have the case remanded to the state courts. Should D's motion be granted?   Not sure ☐

91. P, a citizen of Pennsylvania, has sued D, also a citizen of Pennsylvania, in the Pennsylvania state courts. P's suit seeks a declaratory judgment that a contract previously signed between P and D may be terminated at will by P. D has asserted, as a defense, that P's right of termination would, if exercised, violate federal anti-trust laws. The amount at stake is more than $100,000. D has filed a notice of removal with the Pennsylvania federal district court. P now moves to have the case remanded to state court for lack of jurisdiction. Should P's motion be granted?   Not sure ☐

92. P, a citizen of North Carolina, has brought a state-law products liability suit against D1, D2, and D3, all citizens of South Carolina. P's suit has been brought in the North Carolina state courts. One million dollars is at stake. D1 and D2 have signed and filed a notice of removal with the Eastern District of North Carolina (embracing the area where the state courthouse handling P's suit is located). D3 does not care whether the suit is removed or not, and has not signed the notice of removal. P moves to have the case remanded for lack of subject matter jurisdiction. Should P's motion be granted?

Not sure ☐

93. P is a citizen of Maryland; D is a citizen of Virginia. On July 1, P filed a complaint against D for negligence in the Maryland courts; service was properly made on D in this action on July 5. The amount in controversy is $100,000. On August 15, D filed a notice of removal with the Maryland federal district court. On September 1, P moved to have the case remanded to the Maryland courts for lack of jurisdiction. Should P's motion be granted?

Not sure ☐

94. On July 1, P (a citizen of Virginia) brought a negligence action against D1 (a citizen of Maryland) and D2 (a citizen of Virginia). The action was brought in the Virginia state courts. The amount at stake is $100,000 with respect to each defendant. On November 1, the Virginia court granted D2's motion to have P's claim against her dismissed. On November 20, D1 filed a notice of removal with the Virginia federal district court. Shortly thereafter, P moved to have the case remanded to the Virginia state court due to lack of federal subject matter jurisdiction. Should P's motion be granted?

Not sure ☐

95. One day, Paul called Larry, a lawyer whom Paul had never met. Paul said to Larry, "Larry, I've been in a terrible car accident. I was a passenger in a car driven by Dave. Dave ran a stop sign, plowed into another car, and I was badly injured. I've been in the hospital for two months, I've got severe lower-back damage, and the doctors say I'll never be able to work again. I'd like to sue Dave." Larry accepted the truth of Paul's statements, asked only a few questions about how the accident occurred, and then prepared a complaint stating that Paul had been permanently injured, had lost the ability ever to work again, and was entitled to $1 million in damages. Who, if anyone, must sign this complaint before it is served on Dave in a federal court action based on diversity?

Not sure ☐

96. Same facts as in the previous question. Assume that Larry honestly and in good faith believed everything that Paul told him. Larry did not ask for a copy of the police report. The actual police report showed that the driver was Dennis, not Dave. The case then went to trial. At trial, it turned out that Dennis, not Dave, was the driver, and that the suit was just Paul's attempt to find a "deeper pocket" to sue, since Dennis was judgment-proof. It also turned out at trial that Paul had only minor injuries and had already been back at work at the time he made the telephone call to Larry. Dave has now finally won the case, but only after spending $10,000 in attorney's fees to defend the case. What, if any, action should Dave's lawyer take now that Dave has prevailed at trial?

Not sure ☐

97. A lawyer for P has caused an action to be brought against D in federal district court. P is an individual; D is a corporation that operates a television station. The first claim in P's complaint (denominated as "Count 1") recites a certain statement made about P by a third person on D's television station and asserts that this statement constitutes libel. A second count repeats by reference the factual allegations

of the first count and alleges that the statement constitutes slander. It is not clear from applicable law whether defamatory statements made on a television station are libel or slander. D has brought a motion under Federal Rule 12(b)(6) to have one or the other of the claims dismissed. D's argument is, in substance, that "the same statement cannot be both libel and slander; P must pick one of these two inconsistent theories of the case and proceed solely on that theory." Should the judge grant D's motion?

Not sure ☐

98. P was injured in an automobile accident when his car was hit by a car driven by D. P has brought a negligence suit in federal court for the district in which P resides. The complaint states that P is a citizen of New York and that D is a citizen of New Jersey. The complaint also recites the facts of the collision, asserts that D was negligent, and asserts that P has suffered serious injuries (in an amount not specified). Nothing else in the complaint refers to any dollar amount. Is P's complaint a sufficient one?

Not sure ☐

99. P brought a diversity action against D in federal district court. P asserted that D was guilty of negligence in the way D drove her car, thereby injuring P. The complaint closed with a "demand for judgment" in the amount of $200,000. The case was tried to a jury, which awarded P $300,000 of compensatory damages and $200,000 of punitive damages. (The jury was apparently motivated by evidence that D knew she was drunk before she took the drive that injured P.) After the verdict, D's lawyer moved to have judgment limited to $200,000, the amount P asked for in his complaint. Should D's motion be granted?

Not sure ☐

100. Same basic fact pattern as in the previous question. Now, however, assume that D never responded to the complaint or appeared in the action in any way. The federal judge before whom the action is pending now conducts a hearing pursuant to Federal Rule 55(b)(2) to compute the damages suffered by P (since his damages are not "liquidated" ones and cannot be determined except by an evidentiary hearing). At this hearing, the judge is convinced that P has suffered $300,000 of actual damages, including medical expenses and lost wages. May the trial judge enter a judgment for P in this amount?

Not sure ☐

101. P and D entered into a contract. The contract turned out to be very unfavorable to P. P has uncovered evidence suggesting that D misrepresented certain major facts about the proposed contractual arrangement in order to induce P to enter into the contract. Therefore, P has brought a federal court action, based on diversity, against D. P's complaint recites the date and general subject matter of the contract, and then states, "D fraudulently induced P to enter into this contract." On account of this fraud, P asks the court to grant the equitable relief of rescinding the contract.

(a) Putting aside the correctness of the complaint's jurisdictional allegations and the adequacy of its demand for judgment, does the complaint satisfy the pleading requirements of the Federal Rules?

Not sure ☐

(b) In light of your answer to (a), what procedural steps should D take?

Not sure ☐

102. P, an individual, brought a federal diversity action for libel against D, a television station. Before filing an answer, D made a timely motion under Federal Rule 12(b)(6) for dismissal for failure to state a claim upon which relief can be granted. The

essence of D's motion was that under applicable substantive law, a statement made over the airwaves by a television station cannot be libel, and is at most slander. The federal judge agreed with D, and ordered P's claim dismissed. P now wishes to amend his pleading to allege slander rather than libel. Must P get the court's permission to amend his pleading in this manner?   Not sure ☐

103. P agreed to have D (a plastic surgeon) perform a certain operation on P in which D used "dissolving thread" to suture the wound. The thread failed to dissolve as it should have, leaving P with scars. P brought a strict product liability action in federal court against D, based on diversity. D made a motion under Rule 12(b)(6) for failure to state a claim; this motion asserted that D was a supplier of a service rather than a seller of a good, and that strict product liability was therefore inappropriate. The federal district court judge agreed with D and ordered that P's claim be dismissed. P then amended his pleading to drop the strict product liability count and instead to assert that D behaved negligently and was liable for malpractice. This claim went to trial, and P lost on the merits. May P now appeal the court's earlier dismissal of the product liability claim, if P can show that the federal court misapplied applicable (state) law on the issue of whether a medical device used by a doctor on a patient constitutes a "sale" from doctor to patient?   Not sure ☐

104. P brought a federal diversity action against D, alleging that D breached an oral agreement to employ P for a five-year period. D, in his answer, denied each and every allegation of P, as permitted by Federal Rule 8. In what respect, if any, could D's answer have been improved?   Not sure ☐

105. Same facts as in the previous question. Now, assume that the case has come to trial one year after service of the complaint. D realizes that his best defense is to argue that the contract is unenforceable due to the Statute of Frauds, and to present evidence that the contract by its terms was one that could not possibly be fulfilled within one year (thus bringing it within the Statute). P objects to this proffered evidence as being not within the scope of the pleadings. What should D do?   Not sure ☐

106. P began a diversity suit against D by filing a complaint with the court on July 1. Service was made upon D on July 5. (D was served within the state in which the action is pending.) Assuming that D has not made any motion against the complaint, what is the last day upon which D may serve his answer?   Not sure ☐

107. On July 1, P filed with the federal court for the District of New Jersey a diversity complaint against D. Since D is not a citizen or resident of New Jersey, D had to be served in his home state of New York. P arranged for personal service on D on July 5 in New York, carried out pursuant to the New Jersey long-arm statute. That long-arm statute allows personal service out of state with respect to suits arising out of in-New Jersey activities; the long-arm allows the defendant 30 days in which to answer. On July 29, D submitted an answer. Is D's answer timely?   Not sure ☐

108. On July 1, P commenced a federal-question suit against D by filing a complaint with the district court. On July 15, D made a motion under Rule 12(b)(6) to dismiss the complaint for failure to state a cause of action. On September 1, the court denied D's motion; D received notice of the denial that same day. What is the last day for D to serve his answer?   Not sure ☐

109. On July 1, P Co. filed with the federal court a complaint alleging that D violated a particular patent belonging to P; the complaint alleged that D imported a certain machine into the United States on a particular day, thereby committing the patent violation. According to federal trademark statutes, P's time for commencing the action expired on July 5. On July 10, P made personal service of the complaint upon D. On July 25, P, after realizing that it had cited the wrong patent number in its complaint, served upon D an amended complaint listing the correct patent number. All other aspects of the complaint are the same. Is P's amended complaint time-barred?

Not sure ☐

110. Pedestrian was severely injured when a car driven by Driver and owned by Owner struck him. Pedestrian brought a diversity action alleging negligence; the complaint was filed on July 1 and listed Driver as the sole defendant. According to applicable state law, the statute of limitations would be satisfied only if Pedestrian commenced the action no later than July 5; under state law, the filing of a complaint with the court is deemed to commence the action (as it is under Federal Rule 3). On July 10, Pedestrian made personal service upon Driver. That same day, Driver gave a copy of the suit to Owner, saying, "I'm surprised they didn't bring you into the suit as well." On July 11, Pedestrian filed an amended complaint listing Owner as a co-defendant. On July 12, this complaint was served on both Driver and Owner. Owner now moves to dismiss the amended complaint as being time-barred, at least as against him. Should Owner's motion be granted?

Not sure ☐

111. P, while standing on the sidewalk, was injured when a car driven by Driver and manufactured by Carco suddenly swerved in the street and struck her. P brought a federal court diversity action against Carco. Her complaint asserted that Carco had produced a dangerously defective product and that Carco is strictly liable for P's injuries. At trial, P offered evidence that Carco was negligent in not ascertaining that the design of the car produced a significant likelihood of a sudden swerve to the right. Carco's lawyer did not object to this proof of negligence. The judge (the case was tried to a judge rather than to a jury) found that strict product liability does not apply to injuries caused to a bystander such as P, but also found that Carco is liable to P because of Carco's negligence in designing the car. Carco now moves to have the trial judge's verdict set aside, on the grounds that it is based upon a claim (negligence) that was not contained in P's complaint. How should the trial judge respond to this motion?

Not sure ☐

112. Same facts as in the previous question. Now, however, assume that when P presented her evidence of negligence, Carco objected on the grounds that the complaint did not allege negligence. How should the court respond to this objection?

Not sure ☐

113. P was injured in an auto accident involving a car driven by D. P's lawyer deposed D. During this deposition, the fact emerged that D stood by the car after the accident and watched while W, an eyewitness to the accident, gave a statement to the police. P's lawyer asked D during the deposition, "What was the substance of W's statement to the police about what occurred?" D's lawyer objected on the grounds that any answer would be hearsay, and instructed D not to answer. (Assume that it would indeed be hearsay for D to testify at trial regarding W's statement.) P now moves for an order compelling D to answer this question. Should the court grant the order sought by P?

Not sure ☐

114. P brought a federal court diversity action against D. P's claim was that D willfully breached a contract with P. D raised the defense that the contract is unenforceable due to the Statute of Frauds. During a deposition of D conducted by P's lawyer, L, L ascertained that D had consulted with his own lawyer, X, before signing the contract. L then asked D, "Did you discuss with X the enforceability of the contract before you signed it?" D objected to the question on the grounds of attorney-client privilege. (This matter would indeed be privileged under the law of the state where the district court sits if the question were asked of D at trial.) P now moves to compel D to answer the question. Should the court grant P's motion and issue an order compelling an answer?

Not sure ☐

115. P was injured in an automobile accident involving a car driven by D. P brought a federal diversity suit against D on a negligence theory. After commencement of the suit, D's lawyer, L, conducted an interview with an eyewitness to the accident, W. L wrote down those aspects of W's account of the accident that seemed most interesting to L. P's lawyer, after learning about this interview, submitted to D a Rule 34 Request for Production of Documents, requesting "any notes taken by L of any interviews with W." D and L refused to comply, so P made a motion to compel discovery. Should the court grant P's motion to compel production of the notes?

Not sure ☐

116. P brought a negligence action against D in federal court, based on diversity. To prepare for trial, D's lawyer hired an investigator, I. I interviewed a number of potential witnesses, including W. When I interviewed W, he tape recorded the interview. In the interview, W recited certain facts known only to W, and these facts have a close bearing on the action. I then had a transcript made of W's statement.

(a) Assuming that W is now available to be interviewed directly by P's lawyer, may P obtain discovery of the transcript prepared by I of W's statement given to I?

Not sure ☐

(b) Suppose that shortly after giving the statement to I, W died. Is P entitled to a copy of the transcript of W's statement to I?

Not sure ☐

117. In a diversity action, P sued D for what P's complaint calls "product liability." P alleges that a can opener manufactured by D severely cut P's hand. D's lawyer has submitted a Rule 33 interrogatory to P, which states, "State whether your claim asserts strict product liability, negligence, or both." P objects on the grounds that this request violates the work-product immunity rule of Rule 26, including particularly the ban on disclosure of the "mental impressions, conclusions, opinions, or legal theories of an attorney . . . concerning the litigation." Should P be required to comply with this interrogatory?

Not sure ☐

118. P and D were involved in an automobile accident. P sued D in federal court based on diversity; the suit alleges that D behaved negligently. Shortly after the accident and before P filed his lawsuit, P furnished a statement to D's insurance company, at the insurer's request. At the time of the interview, P was not given a copy of the statement (which was in the form of a tape recording that was later transcribed). P's lawyer now submits, pursuant to Federal Rule 34, a request that D give P a copy of the transcript of P's statement. Is D obligated to give P a copy of this statement, assuming that P makes no showing of special need for this statement?

Not sure ☐

119. P (the U.S. government) has brought a federal court antitrust action against D (Macrosoft, a large software company), contending that D has illegally monopolized certain software markets. One of P's key allegations is that D incorporated a free browser into the latest version of D's operating system, Macrosoft Doors, so as to illegally extend D's operating system monopoly into the browser market. D is in possession of two documents that bear directly on P's claim: (1) a market research report prepared for D before the government filed suit, which recites that D's share of the operating system market is 48 percent; and (2) a confidential email written by D's vice president to its chairman, saying, "Let's put the browser into the operating system at no extra charge to customers to make sure no competitors can get a foothold in the browser market." D expects to present item (1) as part of its case if the suit goes to trial but does not expect to use item (2) as part of its case. No discovery request has been served by P. The parties have had a pretrial meeting as required by Rule 26(f). What, if anything, must D now disclose to P concerning documents (1) and (2)?   Not sure ☐

120. Pedestrian was hit by a car driven by Driver. The accident occurred on a busy city street, and there were a number of eyewitnesses. Pedestrian brought a federal court diversity action based on negligence against Driver. Driver learned that an investigator hired by Pedestrian's lawyer had conducted extensive inquiries (including the placement of newspaper advertisements) to get the names of as many people as possible who personally witnessed the accident. Driver therefore submitted the following interrogatory question to Pedestrian: "State the names and addresses of all known eyewitnesses to the accident." Must Pedestrian and/or Pedestrian's lawyer answer this interrogatory?   Not sure ☐

121. P, driving one car, was injured by a collision with a car driven by D. (P believes that the accident occurred because D went through a stop sign.) P sued D for negligence in federal court based on diversity. P's lawyer hired an expert accident reconstructionist, Rufus T. Firefly, to (1) examine the skid marks, the damage to the two automobiles, and any other physical evidence of how fast each car was going at the time of the accident; and (2) determine whether this speed proves that D definitely did not stop at the stop sign. As a result of his investigation, Firefly has formed an opinion that D definitely did not stop at the stop sign. P plans to call Firefly to testify at trial to this effect.

    (a) How, if at all, can D learn that P will be calling Firefly at trial?   Not sure ☐

    (b) How, if at all, can D get details of what Firefly will say at trial?   Not sure ☐

    (c) Assume that D has learned of Firefly's identity and the fact that he will be called to testify at trial about the results of his investigation. If D wishes to take the deposition of Firefly to hear in detail Firefly's conclusions about what caused the accident, is D entitled to do so? If so, when?   Not sure ☐

122. In a federal court action for antitrust, P, a corporation, claimed that D's predatory conduct had caused X to terminate a contract with P that was valuable to P. In a set of interrogatories, D asked P to state when and how the alleged interference by D with the P-X contract had occurred. P, in a set of answers signed by Prexy, P's president, responded that the interference had been in the form of a phone call by D's chairman, Charm, to X, on September 15, in which Charm told X that P was preparing to breach the contract. Subsequent to the filing of this interrogatory answer, Prexy has learned that the conversation between Charm and X was a face-to-face one, and that it took place on September 18. What obligation, if any, does P have to amend its interrogatory answer?

Not sure ☐

123. D, a plastic surgeon, performed cosmetic surgery on P's face to reduce the size of her chin. P was mildly displeased with the results and found a lawyer, L, willing to bring a malpractice action (in federal court based on diversity) against D. L has commenced the action and now would like to know whether D is covered by malpractice insurance for any verdict that P might recover here. L would also like to know the limits of the policy, if one exists. How may L get this information?

Not sure ☐

124. P brought a federal court action against D in connection with an automobile accident. P learned that the accident was personally observed by W. P served upon W a set of interrogatories asking W to describe the accident as he saw it. Must W answer the interrogatories?

Not sure ☐

125. P brought a diversity-based negligence action against D in federal district court for the Southern District of New York. One of the witnesses to the accident in question was W (who is not a party). W is an individual who was visiting in New York at the time of the accident, but who resides in the Southern District of Florida. P's lawyer wished to take W's deposition, but P's lawyer did not wish to travel to Florida to do so. Consequently, P served upon W at W's residence in Miami a notice of deposition, together with a notice stating that W's reasonable travel and lodging expenses for a trip to New York (where the deposition was to be held) would be paid by P. W has indicated that she will not submit to any deposition unless subpoenaed to do so. If P is ready to bear W's travel and lodging expenses to New York, may W be subpoenaed to appear in New York for her deposition?

Not sure ☐

126. P sued D in federal court, on a diversity theory, for breach of contract. P's claim was that D signed a contract whereby D was to employ P for two years. P then served upon D a copy of what P claimed was the written contract signed by both parties and requested that D admit that the enclosed document was signed by D. D's lawyer, trained in the "hardball" school of litigation, knew that his client had signed the document, but served upon P an answer stating, "D does not recall signing the document in question." At trial, P called, at considerable expense, a handwriting expert who presented detailed testimony tending to prove that the signature on the contract belonged to D. The jury found that the contract was signed by D, but was not breached by him. Therefore, the trial judge entered a verdict in D's favor. What tactical move should P's lawyer now make in the trial court?

Not sure ☐

127. P and D were involved in an automobile accident. P sued D for negligence in federal court, based on diversity. P discovered the existence of a police report, issued by the police department of the City of Langdell (where the accident occurred). P served upon that police department a Rule 34 Request to Produce Documents, listing the police report as the document to be produced. Assuming that the City of Langdell is within the district where the action is pending, must the police department comply with the request?

Not sure ☐

128. P was hit by an automobile driven by D. P brought a federal diversity action against D alleging negligence. P claimed that he suffered serious whiplash in the accident and that he has been physically disabled from working. D's lawyer had doubts

about whether P was as severely disabled as he claims. Therefore, D's lawyer served upon P a notice to undergo physical examination, which stated, "Please present yourself at any time within the next two weeks at the office of Dr. John Smith, who will conduct a physical examination of you to determine the degree of your disability." Must P comply with this request?

Not sure ☐

129. P has brought a diversity action against D for negligence. The essence of P's claim is that D is an epileptic, knew that he was an epileptic, nonetheless drove a vehicle and had a seizure, which caused him to lose control of the car, thus injuring P. P obtained a court order directing D to submit to a physical examination regarding his alleged epileptic condition. The examination took place, conducted by Dr. Brown, who prepared a report.

(a) Is D entitled to a copy of this report if P does not wish to give it to D?

Not sure ☐

(b) Assume that D asks for a copy of Dr. Brown's report, and P gives it to him. P now asks for copies of any reports prepared by physicians who have examined D at D's request. D refuses on the grounds that any such reports are protected by the patient-physician privilege. Must D turn over the reports?

Not sure ☐

130. P and D are each corporations engaged in the pharmaceutical business; they compete with each other. P has brought a federal patent infringement suit against D, and has added to it a pendent state claim alleging that D, by hiring a former employee of P, effectively stole certain trade secrets belonging to P. During the discovery phase, P has served upon D a Rule 34 document production request seeking documents containing details of certain secret manufacturing processes used by D, so that P can determine whether these are derived from P's own trade secrets. D is afraid that if it complies, two bad results may occur: (1) P may use the information, including the trade secrets, to compete with D; and (2) P may disclose those trade secrets to the world, thus stripping D's competitive advantage. What should D do to deal with these problems?

Not sure ☐

131. P was injured when the steering wheel of the car he was driving suddenly came loose and P was unable to steer the car. P has brought a federal diversity suit for strict product liability against D, the manufacturer of the car. P suspects that employees of D who designed the car probably knew that the design they chose for the steering wheel raised a significant probability of such accidents. However, P has no idea which employees within D may have had the relevant design and safety information. Therefore, P cannot designate any particular person within D whose deposition is to be taken. What should P do?

Not sure ☐

132. In a federal action, P took D's deposition. During the deposition, D's lawyer objected to a particular question asked by P's lawyer, on the grounds that the answer would involve the disclosure of privileged information. D then refused to answer the question. P's lawyer continued with the deposition, asking and getting answers to other questions. After the session was over, P moved for an order compelling D to answer the objected-to question, on the grounds that the material is not in fact privileged.

(a) Did P, by continuing with the deposition after D objected, waive his right to seek a court order compelling D to answer the question?

Not sure ☐

    (b) What risk, if any, is there to D in declining to answer the objected-to question and requiring P to seek an order compelling discovery?

Not sure ☐

133. P brought a product liability suit (based on diversity) against D. D is a corporation. P served D with a notice of deposition, which stated that D or its representative would be asked questions concerning how the product in question was designed. D designated Smith to be deposed on its behalf. Smith was D's director of product safety at the time the product in question was designed but had since left D's employ. Now, at trial, P seeks to introduce in evidence answers given by Smith in the deposition. The answers are offered for substantive purposes and are offered even though Smith is available to testify at trial. Are the deposition answers admissible under these circumstances?

Not sure ☐

134. P and D were involved in an auto accident while each was driving a car. P brought a diversity action against D for negligence. D took the deposition of W, a bystander who observed the accident. W is available (indeed eager) to testify at trial, but neither party has called her. D now offers a portion of W's deposition testimony as evidence. Will this testimony be admitted if objected to by P?

Not sure ☐

135. Same facts as in the previous question. Now, however, assume that W was called to the stand by P and gave live testimony. D now seeks to offer into evidence portions of W's deposition testimony that would cast doubt upon the accuracy of W's statements made at trial. Is this deposition material admissible?

Not sure ☐

136. A car driven by P, in which W was a passenger, collided with a car driven by D. P brought a diversity-based negligence action against D. P took W's deposition testimony regarding the accident. The trial is now taking place in the Southern District of New York. By the time of the trial, W had returned to her home in Los Angeles (she was visiting P in New York at the time of the accident). P now seeks to introduce into evidence a portion of W's deposition testimony, in which W stated that she saw D run a stop sign. This testimony is offered as part of P's prima facie case. Is the deposition testimony admissible?

Not sure ☐

137. Cars driven by P and D were in an accident. P sued D in federal court for negligence. During the discovery process, P served upon D an interrogatory containing the following question: "State what, if anything, you told the police officer investigating the accident regarding whether you stopped at the stop sign located at the corner of Main and 21st Street just before the accident." D submitted the following response to this question: "I told the police officer that I did not stop at the stop sign."

    (a) Suppose that at trial, D does not take the stand. May P introduce D's interrogatory statement for the purpose of proving that D did not in fact stop at the stop sign?

Not sure ☐

    (b) Assume that at trial, (i) D testifies that he did stop at the stop sign, and (ii) P is permitted to introduce the interrogatory answer to impeach D's testimony. Will a properly instructed jury be permitted to conclude that D stopped at the stop sign?

Not sure ☐

138. Perry brought a diversity action against Donna, alleging that Donna had breached a contract that the two of them had signed. In this action Perry served upon Donna a Rule 36 request for admission; the request attached a copy of a document and asked Donna to admit that Donna signed the document (which was the contract upon which suit had been brought). Donna, a businessperson with many complex affairs, was not certain whether she had signed the contract, but served an admission to avoid litigating the issue. The case was then settled, with the payment by Donna of a small amount to Perry. Subsequently, Donna discovered that Perry had forged Donna's signature on the contract in question. Donna brought a diversity action against Perry for the tort of fraud, on account of this forgery. Perry now asserts that Donna is barred from contesting the authorship of the contract because of Donna's response to the request to admit. Putting aside any issues of merger, bar or collateral estoppel, is Perry's assertion correct?

Not sure ☐

139. P has brought a negligence action against D (based on diversity) in federal district court for the District of Iowa. P's complaint alleges that P was a social guest in D's house, that P fell when a wooden step on a stairway inside the house broke, and that had D used ordinary reasonable care in keeping his house safe, he would have discovered the danger and avoided it. (The complaint does not claim that D knew of the defect, merely that a reasonable person in D's position would have learned of the defect and fixed it.) A five-year-old decision of the Iowa Supreme Court holds that a social guest is only a "licensee," not an "invitee," and that a property owner owes a licensee no duty of inspection. A number of courts in other states have in the last few years abolished the licensee/invitee distinction, and have held that a property owner owes a duty of reasonable inspection to a licensee as well as an invitee. The federal district judge in whose court P's action is pending believes that these newer decisions represent the much better view. However, there is no evidence that the Iowa Supreme Court would change its attitude on this issue, since the court has on more recent occasions rejected other chances to expand tort liability. Should the federal judge impose upon D the duty of making reasonable inspection of his premises?

Not sure ☐

140. Same basic fact pattern as the in the previous question. Now, however, assume that the Iowa Supreme Court has never ruled on the issue of whether a property owner owes a duty of inspection to a licensee. Assume further that the only Iowa court to ever rule on the matter is the Iowa Appeals Court (the sole intermediate-level court in the state), which has recently held that no such duty is owed to a licensee. The federal court believes, however, that due to the somewhat "liberal" tendencies of the Iowa Supreme Court at the present time, that court would probably impose such a duty of inspection on behalf of a licensee if the issue were before that court today. Should the federal court impose a duty of inspection upon D?

Not sure ☐

141. Same basic fact pattern as in the previous two questions. Now, however, assume that the only ruling on point is a 50-year-old decision by the Iowa Supreme Court, in which the court refused to impose any duty of inspection on behalf of a licensee. Since the courts of most states that have considered the matter within the past five years have rejected the traditional rule and imposed a duty of inspection on behalf of a licensee, the federal judge believes that the Iowa Supreme Court would probably follow this modern trend if it heard the case today. Should the federal court impose a duty of inspection on D?

Not sure ☐

142. Same facts as in the previous question. Now, assume that the federal trial court imposed the duty of inspection on D, reasoning that this is what the Iowa court would do. The jury rendered a verdict in favor of P. D appealed. While the case was on appeal in the federal courts, the Iowa Supreme Court heard and decided a case presenting the same issue of whether a property owner owes a duty of inspection to a licensee. To the surprise of most commentators, the Iowa Supreme Court reaffirmed its 50-year-old view, holding that no duty is owed to the licensee. Should the federal appeals court affirm the federal district court's judgment?   Not sure ☐

143. P has sued D in federal district court for the Central District of California. The suit is based on diversity (since P is a citizen of California and D is a citizen of Arizona). P claims that D negligently drove an automobile, thus injuring P in an accident. The accident took place in Arizona. Under California state court decisions, any suit brought in the California state courts arising out of an auto accident is to be decided under California law if the plaintiff is a California resident, even if the accident took place in another state. This California approach is a minority and old-fashioned one; nearly every other state applies the rule of "lex locus delicti," whereby in auto accident cases the law of the state where the accident took place is the law that is used. The federal judge hearing the P-D suit believes that the majority "lex locus delicti" approach is the sounder one. In the P-D suit the issue arises whether California state substantive law (under which contributory negligence is not a defense) or Arizona law (under which contributory negligence is still a defense) should be applied. The federal judge hearing the case believes that the California (no contributory negligence defense) is the better approach. Which state's substantive law of negligence, California's or Arizona's, should be applied by the federal judge?   Not sure ☐

144. P has sued D in diversity in federal court for the District of Nevada. The suit claims that P was struck by a foul ball while attending a baseball game put on by D, and that D was negligent in not covering the seating area. D claims that P assumed the risk by disregarding the warning on the back of his ticket stub and by sitting in the unscreened seats. P claims that this does not constitute assumption of risk. Under Nevada law, the burden of proof on the issue of assumption of risk belongs on the plaintiff (who must affirmatively produce evidence that he did not assume the risk once this issue is raised by the defendant). Under the policy suggested by Federal Rule 8(c) (requiring assumption of risk to be affirmatively pleaded by the defendant), the burden of proof on assumption of risk would normally be on the defendant. In this suit between P and D, who bears the burden of proof on assumption of risk?   Not sure ☐

145. P has sued D in diversity in federal court for the Northern District of Georgia. P seeks to assert against D a tort claim relating to an accident, as well as a breach of contract claim arising from a prior business relationship between P and D, having nothing to do with the accident. Under a Georgia statute, a tort claim may not be joined with a contract claim against the same defendant in state court if the two claims relate to different transactions. However, joinder of unrelated contract and tort claims against a single defendant is expressly allowed by FRCP 18. In the federal action, may P join his contract and tort claims against D in a single action?   Not sure ☐

146. P and D signed a contract whereby P was to perform personal services for D. Almost immediately, it became clear to P that D was not living up to his part of the bargain with respect to the duties that P was to be given. However, P tried to work things out with D for a long time (reasonable conduct by P in the circumstances), and therefore took no legal action for more than two years. He then brought a diversity action against D in federal district court for the District of Kansas, the state in which the contract was signed and was being performed. Under Kansas law, any action (whether legal or equitable) related to performance of a contract must be brought within two years of the performance or nonperformance complained of. P does not seek damages in his federal suit; instead, he seeks to have the contract declared rescinded on account of D's nonperformance.

The federal courts have traditionally regarded actions to rescind a contract as being primarily equitable, and they apply the equitable doctrine of laches rather than any strict statute of limitations doctrine when the action is primarily equitable. Thus, under general federal principles, P's suit will not be time-barred so long as P has acted within a "reasonable" period of time considering the circumstances. Should the federal court for the District of Kansas regard P's action as time-barred?

Not sure ☐

147. On July 1, P filed with the clerk of the federal district court in New Jersey a complaint against D alleging breach of contract; the suit was based on diversity. According to the New Jersey law of contracts (which would apply to this controversy if the case were brought in the New Jersey courts), the statute of limitations on P's action ran on July 10. On July 15, a process server for P made service of the summons and complaint on D at his residence in New Jersey. Under New Jersey law, a civil action is deemed to have been "commenced" (for statute of limitations purposes) by service on the defendant. Under Federal Rule 3, a civil action is deemed commenced by filing a complaint with the court. Assuming that the New Jersey statute of limitations applies to this action, has P's suit been commenced in a timely manner?

Not sure ☐

148. P has brought a diversity-based medical malpractice action against D in federal court for the Northern District of Ohio. The Ohio statute of limitations for medical malpractice actions provides that suit must be brought within one year of the time P "knew or should have known" of the existence of the malpractice. In P's suit, there is a disputed factual issue as to when P should have known that D, a surgeon, had left a sponge in P's body after performing an operation on P. Under a decision of the Ohio Supreme Court, the issue of when a plaintiff discovered or should have discovered medical malpractice is to be made by the judge. Under a broader federal policy (inspired by, but not strictly required by, the Seventh Amendment), all issues that are essentially factual should in a case tried to a jury be decided by the jury; the issue of when P discovered or should have discovered the malpractice would be such a "primarily factual" case under this federal principle. The federal principle is not embodied in any particular Federal Rule of Civil Procedure (or any other federal statute). In P's federal court suit, should the issue of when P discovered or should have discovered the malpractice (and thus the issue of whether P's claim is time-barred) be decided by the judge or by the jury?

Not sure ☐

149. P has brought a diversity suit in Illinois federal district court against D1 and D2. P is a citizen and resident of California. D1 is an individual who is a citizen and resident of Illinois. D2 is a Delaware corporation, with its principal place of business in Indiana. D2 has minimum contacts with Illinois. The cause of action arose in England. Before bringing the suit, P considered suing in state court, but could not find any state other than Illinois that would have jurisdiction over both D1 and D2 (since D1 did not have minimum contacts with any state other than Illinois, thus preventing a suit in Indiana). An Illinois statute provides that no suit may be brought in the Illinois state courts against a corporation not residing in Illinois, unless it is the case that either the plaintiff is an Illinois resident or the cause of action arose in Illinois. Legislative history indicates that the sole purpose of this statute is to reduce congestion in the Illinois state courts. May the Illinois federal district court hear the case?

Not sure ☐

150. P has brought a diversity suit against D in federal district court for Montana; the suit alleges negligence. In both the Montana state trial courts and the federal district court of Montana, the applicable rules provide for a six-person jury. By Montana statute, the verdict in a civil case needs to be by only a five-sixths majority. The state rule allowing a five-sixths majority was adopted to reduce the number of hung juries and retrials, thus reducing court congestion. By a long-standing federal policy, a federal civil jury must reach a unanimous verdict. (There is no federal statute or Rule of Civil Procedure that directly requires unanimity.) Should the federal district judge recognize a verdict on which five out of the six jurors agree?

Not sure ☐

151. P has sued D in diversity in federal court for the District of Kansas. P's suit was filed with the court on July 1 and served on D on July 2. The complaint alleges that a product sold by D to P was negligently manufactured and injured P; this is a cause of action sounding primarily in tort. On August 1, P amended his complaint to add a claim that the product sold by D breached the implied warranty of merchantability, and that D is therefore liable regardless of fault. Under Kansas law, a breach of warranty claim is deemed to be a contract claim. Also under state law, P's time to sue expired on July 15. Under Kansas law, a claim added by an amendment to a previously filed action dates from the date of the amendment, for statute of limitations purposes. But according to Federal Rule 15, a claim added by amendment against the original defendant and arising out of the same transaction as the original claim "relates back," so that it is deemed to date from the filing of the original action. Should the federal court treat P as being time-barred?

Not sure ☐

152. On July 1, P filed a diversity suit against D1 in Wyoming federal district court and served the complaint that same day. P's suit alleged that the sidewalk in front of a residence at 523 Main Street, owned by D1, was negligently maintained, thus causing P to trip and injure herself. P's suit against D1 stemmed from the fact that D1 was shown in local public records as being the owner of 523 Main Street. On July 30, P learned through independent sources that before the accident, 523 Main was sold to D2. Therefore, on July 30, P amended his complaint to add D2 as a defendant and drop D1; this complaint was served on D2 that same day. Under Wyoming state law, P's claim for negligence became time-barred on July 15. However, Wyoming law also provides that where a new party is added to a pleading by amendment, the new claim "relates back" to the original filing date, even if the newly added party did not know of the action until he was actually served by it. By contrast, Federal Rule 15(c) allows relation back in the case of a newly added defendant only if the new defendant received notice of the suit before the running of the statute of limitations (so that under Rule 15(c) the claim against D2 does not relate back to the original July 1 filing date). Is P's claim against D2 time-barred?

Not sure ☐

153. Steve was a soldier in the U.S. Army. While off duty (but dressed in uniform), he jaywalked across a crowded street in the town of Ames, Ohio. While doing so, he was struck by a van owned by Express Delivery Corp. and driven by its employee. Steve was seriously injured, and had to be hospitalized and cared for at U.S. government expense for six months. The United States has brought suit in federal district court for Ohio against Express Delivery, asserting that Express's negligence led to the United States' expenses. Express has raised the defense of contributory negligence. Under Ohio law, even a slight degree of contributory negligence is an absolute defense to a negligence claim. Under the law of most other states, and under general federal principles, a small degree of contributory negligence is not an absolute bar, but merely reduces the plaintiff's recovery. In deciding whether Steve's slight contributory negligence bars the United States from recovering against Express, must the federal district court apply Ohio law?

Not sure ☐

154. D, driving her car, struck and injured P, a pedestrian. P sued D in the courts of the state of Ames, which follows the Federal Rules of Civil Procedure and the Federal Rules of Evidence. P's suit charged that D drove negligently. The substantive law of the state of Ames imposes on P both the burden of production as to negligence and the burden of persuasion (by a preponderance of the evidence) on this issue. The case was tried to a jury. As part of P's case, P showed that shortly after the accident, D was stopped by the police and asked to take a Breathalyzer exam but refused to do so. According to the substantive law of Ames, refusal to take a Breathalyzer upon request by the police gives rise to a presumption of intoxication (which under state law is a form of negligence when the person is the driver). During his case, P came up with no evidence of D's negligence other than the refusal to take a Breathalyzer exam. At the close of P's case, D made a motion for a directed verdict based on P's failure to prove negligence. Should the trial judge grant D's motion?

Not sure ☐

155. Same facts as in the previous question. Now, however, assume that the trial judge allowed the case to go forward, and D came up with some evidence indicating that she was not in fact intoxicated despite her refusal to take the Breathalyzer exam. At the close of D's case, the judge instructed the jury as follows: "Under our law, the defendant's refusal to take a Breathalyzer exam when asked to do so by the police gives rise to a presumption of intoxication. If you find that D refused to take the Breathalyzer, then you must find that D was intoxicated unless D persuades you by a preponderance of the evidence that she was not intoxicated." Are the judge's instructions appropriate?

Not sure ☐

156. P, a black male, has brought an employment discrimination suit against D, a corporation that declined to offer him a job. The suit is pending in federal district court and is being tried to a judge. During P's case, P proved that he was not offered a job but did not come forward with any proof regarding D's motives in not giving him a job. Applicable substantive law provides that a plaintiff can only win an employment discrimination suit if he shows by a preponderance of the evidence that the defendant denied him a job because of his race, rather than for some other reason. At the end of P's case, what tactical move should D's lawyer make?

Not sure ☐

157. P has brought a medical malpractice suit against D in federal court based on diversity. P's complaint asserts that D performed an operation upon P to reduce the size of P's nose, and that the results were disastrous. The complaint asserts that the operation took place on October 13, 2010. D has moved for summary judgment pursuant to Rule 56 and has submitted in support of that motion an affidavit stating that he was not in the United States on October 13, 2010 (and has attached to the affidavit an exhibit purporting to be his calendar for that date, showing an entry that reads, "Continued to tour in South of France"). P, in opposition to D's motion, has submitted an affidavit stating merely, "On October 13, D performed an operation on my nose, with disastrous results." P has not submitted any other information in opposition to D's motion. Should the court grant D's summary judgment motion?

Not sure ☐

158. Same facts as in the previous question. Now, however, assume that in opposition to D's motion for summary judgment, P has submitted an affidavit that furnishes a couple of details about the alleged operation (e.g., "On October 13, 2010, I went to D's offices at 456 Main Street. D was a brown-haired man of about 50 years of age who wore glasses, and he performed the surgery on me"). D's moving papers, by contrast, give much more information, all of which tends to indicate that D could not have performed the operation on the date P said D performed it (e.g., an affidavit from D's travel agent stating that D was in the South of France that day, as well as charges on D's phone bill showing calls made from the South of France to D's office on that date). In reviewing these moving papers, the federal judge concludes that there is about a 90 percent chance that P is either honestly mistaken or is lying when she asserts that D performed the operation on her on that date. Should the federal judge grant D's motion for summary judgment?

Not sure ☐

159. P sued D in federal district court for employment discrimination. The case was tried to a judge. Both sides put on their case. The judge announced from the bench that she would decide the case within several weeks. After four weeks, the judge issued a written opinion, which read in its entirety as follows: "The judge finds for D, on the grounds that while P has proven that D did not hire P, P has not proven that this refusal was on account of D's race, as required by the federal civil rights statute under which P brought suit." The judge has not issued any other statements or documents in connection with the case. Has the judge complied with applicable procedural requirements?

Not sure ☐

160. P brought a federal court suit against D for employment discrimination. P alleged that D failed to give P a promotion because P was a woman. The case was tried without a jury. At the close of P's case, D made a motion pursuant to Federal Rule 50 for a directed verdict in D's favor. The judge immediately denied the motion and ordered D to present his case. The judge did not give any reasons or findings

relating to her denial of D's motion. From a procedural point of view, did the judge act correctly?

161. P brought a federal suit against D for negligence relating to an automobile accident in which P was injured. The suit was based on diversity. The essence of P's claim was that D went through an intersection while the light was red, striking P's car. The case was tried without a jury. At trial, P presented a witness, W, who testified to having seen D go through the intersection when the light was red against D. P himself also testified that the light was green for him (and thus red for D) when D entered the intersection. The only witness or other evidence on behalf of D was D's own testimony, in which D asserted that the light was yellow when D passed through the intersection. The trial judge found in favor of D. The judge's findings of fact, after summarizing the testimony given by each of the witnesses, stated, "Although the only apparently objective witness supports P's account, I find that D's testimony was more credible, and I therefore conclude that the light was yellow at the time D entered the intersection. Accordingly, I find that D did not act negligently and is therefore not liable."

P appealed the case to the Court of Appeals. The three-judge panel hearing the appeal has concluded, after reading the entire trial transcript, that there is a 70 percent or so chance that the light was red against D at the time D entered the intersection. The only issue on the appeal is whether the trial judge's finding of fact as to the color of light was a correct one. Should the appeals court affirm the lower court judgment?

162. P brought a diversity suit against D, alleging that D drove negligently and thereby injured P. The case essentially boiled down to whether D was traveling materially in excess of the 35 mph speed limit. P testified that in his opinion, D was travelling at least 45 mph; D testified that he adhered strictly to the speed limit. The only other evidence on this point was (1) a photograph of the skid mark left by D as D tried to stop just before the impact and (2) a police report analyzing this skid mark and concluding from the skid mark that D was traveling at approximately 44 mph just before slamming on the brakes. The trial judge, sitting without a jury, concluded that D was traveling at the speed limit and therefore found D not liable. P appealed the case. The three appeals judges, after reviewing the oral and written evidence, have concluded that there is a 65 percent chance that D was traveling materially faster than the speed limit (probably at about the rate of 44 mph found by the police report). Assuming that there are no other issues of fact or law in the case, should the appellate court affirm the trial court's judgment in favor of D?

163. P sued D for negligence in federal court, based on diversity. P alleged that D drove a car at well beyond the speed limit, thus making it impossible for D to stop her car in time to avoid striking P, a pedestrian. P sought to introduce into evidence a police report, in which a police detective summarized his analysis of the skid mark left by D, and concluded that based on the skid mark D was traveling at least 45 mph (10 mph over the speed limit). The trial judge refused to allow this report into evidence, stating, "It's hearsay, but the officer who wrote the report is available to give live testimony, so that's the testimony you must use." P failed to put on that live testimony (due to his lawyer's negligence in not subpoenaing the officer in a timely manner), and the trial judge (sitting without a jury) found in favor of D. On appeal, the appeals court has concluded that the trial judge's decision not to admit the police report was erroneous, on the grounds that the report came within the "public records and reports" exception to the hearsay rule given by Federal Rule of Evidence 803(8)(C). Assuming that there are no other factual or legal issues raised on P's appeal, what should the appeals court do?

Not sure ☐

164. P has sued D in a diversity action brought in the federal court for the District of Iowa. According to properly adopted local court rules for the Iowa District Court, a civil jury shall consist of six members. P's claim against D was tried before a six-person jury, and the jury split 5-1 in favor of P. No aspects of the jury trial procedure have been agreed upon between the parties. May a verdict be entered in favor of P?

Not sure ☐

165. Same facts as in the previous question. Now, however, assume that before the trial, P and D signed a stipulation providing that any verdict reached by four or more of the six jurors shall be taken as the verdict of the entire jury. The jury split 4-2 in P's favor. Should the judge enter a verdict in favor of P?

Not sure ☐

166. P sued D in federal court for the District of Colorado. The suit, which was based on diversity, alleged that D negligently injured P in an automobile accident. At the close of D's case, the judge instructed the jury that under Colorado law of comparative negligence (applicable here because of *Erie* doctrine) any contributory negligence by P would not bar P from recovery. However, the judge omitted to point out, as requested by D, that under Colorado law if P's fault was greater than D's, P may not recover at all. D's lawyer made no comment on the judge's jury instructions. The jury found in favor of P. On appeal, D now asserts that the trial judge's failure to give the requested "P more negligent than D" instruction constitutes reversible error. Assuming that the appellate court agrees that the judge's instruction was erroneous, should the appellate court affirm the verdict?

Not sure ☐

167. P brought a breach-of-contract suit, based on diversity, against D in federal court. The case was tried before a jury. During the voir dire, each juror was asked whether she or any member of her family knew or had had dealings with either party or with any member of either party's immediate family. Juror number two answered no to this question and was seated. The jury returned a unanimous verdict in favor of D. (The parties did not stipulate that a less-than-unanimous verdict would suffice.) One month after the trial, P's lawyer discovered that (1) juror number two's brother works for D's son; and (2) juror number two was aware of this fact at the time of the voir dire, believed that the fact would be considered material by P's lawyer, and chose not to disclose the fact because she wanted to be on the jury to have a chance to help D, her brother's employer's father. P's lawyer now makes a motion for a new trial based on this evidence. Does the trial court have discretion to grant the new trial, assuming that the judge believes the new evidence shown by P?

Not sure ☐

168. P has brought a diversity-based contract action against D in federal court. The sole issue in the case is whether D in fact signed the document that P has proffered as "the contract." At trial, the only witnesses were P and D. P testified that D signed the contract. D testified that he did not sign the contract. No documentary evidence

was produced (except for the alleged contract document itself). After both sides rested, the judge instructed the jury, and the jury found in favor of P. D has now moved for judgment as a matter of law (after having complied with any procedural prerequisites for this motion). In considering the JML motion, the trial judge has a fairly strong belief that D told the truth and that P lied; however, the judge also recognizes that if P's testimony is believed rather than D's, P should win the case. The judge has also concluded that a person would not be completely irrational in concluding that it was D, rather than P, who had lied. Should the judge grant the JML motion?

Not sure ☐

169. P brought a negligence action against D in federal court, based on diversity. At the close of P's case, D immediately presented his first and only witness, and at no time made any motions. The jury found in favor of P. D then made a motion for JML. Assuming that the trial judge agrees with D's contention that a reasonable jury could not possibly have found in favor of P, should the trial judge grant D's JML motion?

Not sure ☐

170. P has brought a diversity-based product liability action against D in federal court. The jury has awarded damages (compensatory only) of $3 million, a sum that the trial judge believes to be at least twice what a reasonable damage award would be. However, the judge agrees with the jury's finding that D should be liable. The judge does not want to waste the litigants' and court's time by ordering a new trial. What should the judge do?

Not sure ☐

171. P brought a negligence action against D in federal court, based on diversity. At the close of P's case, D immediately presented his first and only witness. The jury found in favor of P. D then made a motion for JML. Assuming that the trial judge agrees with D's contention that a reasonable jury could not possibly have found in favor of P, should the trial judge grant D's JML motion?

Not sure ☐

172. P has sued D for negligence in Colorado state court. A recently enacted Colorado statute provides, "In any civil suit in which the amount in controversy is less than $10,000, the case shall be tried before a judge sitting without a jury." P's claim is for $9,000. P asserts that the statute, insofar as it deprives him of the right to have his claim tried before a jury, violates the Seventh Amendment. Is P's contention correct?

Not sure ☐

173. On July 1, P served on D a summons and complaint for a federal district court action alleging breach of contract. On July 15, D served an answer on P. There were no pleadings after the answer. At no time did P make a demand for a jury trial. On September 1, shortly before the case was to be tried, D served upon P a demand that the case be tried before a jury. Is D entitled to a jury trial?

Not sure ☐

174. P has brought a federal trademark infringement action against D. P seeks two types of relief: (1) an injunction prohibiting D from further violating P's trademark and (2) money damages for the past violations. D seeks a jury trial on any issues for which he has a jury trial right.

(a) On which, if either, of the two claims does D have a jury trial right?

Not sure ☐

(b) What rule should the court follow with respect to the order in which the issues should be tried?

Not sure ☐

175. Insurer wrote a $100,000 policy on the life of X. X, who owned the policy, notified Insurer that the beneficiary should be W, X's wife. Two years later, just before X died, he wrote to Insurer, "I wish to change the beneficiary from W to S, my son." After X's death, both W and S made a claim to the policy proceeds (W's claim was on the basis that X was not mentally competent at the time he purported to change the beneficiary). Insurer instituted a Rule 22 interpleader action in federal court, with W and S as the defendants. Insurer and S were content to have the case heard by a judge, but W demanded a jury trial. Is W entitled to a jury trial on the issue of whether she is the proper beneficiary?

_____
Not sure ☐

176. P and D were each seriously injured when a car driven by P collided with a car driven by D. P sued D in federal district court on a negligence theory; the case was based on diversity. D submitted a general denial as his answer. The jury found in favor of D. D has now brought a separate federal diversity-based action against P relating to the same accident; D's suit asserts that P's negligence caused the accident. Will D's suit be permitted to go to trial?

_____
Not sure ☐

177. P and D were both involved in a car accident in Iowa. P commenced a diversity-based negligence action against D in Iowa. P is a citizen and resident of Iowa; D resides in North Dakota. D has minimum contacts with Iowa, at least for the purpose of this suit (since the accident occurred there). However, to save money, P declined to cause personal service to be made on D in North Dakota even though the Iowa long-arm statute would allow this. Instead, P discovered that D maintained a bank account in Iowa and caused a notice of attachment to be served on D's Iowa bank, covering the $80,000 in the account. The federal court permitted D to make a limited appearance in the suit (as permitted by Iowa law). The jury found in favor of D. D has now brought suit against P in a second Iowa federal suit, alleging that it was P's negligence that caused the accident. May D's suit proceed?

_____
Not sure ☐

178. P and D, each driving his own car, collided in an accident. P brought a negligence action, based on diversity, against D in federal district court. P's claim was for $80,000. D, in his answer, counterclaimed for $100,000. No further pleadings were served by either party. P lost interest in his suit, and it was dismissed for want of prosecution. What should D do now?

_____
Not sure ☐

179. Pedestrian was injured when she was struck by a delivery van driven by Worker. The van was owned by Boss and was being driven by Worker as part of the job that Worker did for Boss. Pedestrian brought a federal court diversity-based action against Boss alleging that Worker drove negligently and that Boss was liable for that negligence under the doctrine of respondeat superior. Boss impleaded Worker as a third-party defendant under Federal Rule 14(a), on the theory that if Boss was liable to Pedestrian based on respondeat superior, Worker must indemnify Boss. The jury found against Pedestrian and thus in favor of Boss. Worker has now commenced a new federal action, alleging that Boss knowingly gave Worker a defective van to drive, thus preventing Worker from stopping and contributing to injuries suffered by Worker in the same accident in which Pedestrian was injured. Should Worker's suit against Boss be allowed to go forward?

_____
Not sure ☐

180. In Connecticut, a car driven by Alan collided with a car owned by Bob but driven by Carol. Bob has sued Alan for negligence in Connecticut federal district court; the case is based on diversity. Bob's claim is for $100,000. Alan and Carol are citizens of Massachusetts; Bob is a citizen of Connecticut. The Connecticut long-arm allows out-of-state mail service on anyone who is involved in an accident that takes place inside the state. Now, Alan wishes to make a counterclaim (relating to the same accident) against Bob; Alan's claim is such that Carol must be made a codefendant if it is feasible to do so (see FRCP 19(a)). Alan's claim is for $20,000 against Bob, and would be for another $20,000 against Carol if she is joined.

(a) May Alan bring a counterclaim against Bob and Carol together?

Not sure ☐

(b) If Alan does not bring his counterclaim against Bob or Carol, may he bring a later state court suit against them both? (Ignore jurisdictional problems with this second suit.)

Not sure ☐

181. Same basic fact pattern as in the previous question. Now, assume that the Connecticut long-arm statute is a very narrow one, and that it would not permit service out-of-state on Carol, even though she was involved in an in-Connecticut accident. If Alan doesn't bring his counterclaim in federal court, may he bring a later state court suit against Bob and Carol?

Not sure ☐

182. P has brought a tort action against D, arising out of an automobile accident. The case is pending in federal district court. The case is based on diversity, and P's claim is for $100,000. D now seeks to assert a counterclaim against P; the counterclaim is for $30,000, and alleges that P breached a contract with D entered into before (and unconnected with) the automobile accident.

(a) Is D's counterclaim compulsory?

Not sure ☐

(b) May D bring that counterclaim?

Not sure ☐

183. P and D were injured when cars driven by each in the state of Ames collided on July 1, 2009. Under the state law applicable to suits brought concerning the accident, there is a one-year statute of limitations. On June 25, 2010, P filed with the federal court for the District of Ames a diversity-based negligence action; that same day, he caused D to be served with the summons and complaint in the action. On July 5, 2010, D filed an answer containing a counterclaim for negligence relating to the same accident; P was served that same day. State law is silent concerning when an action brought by counterclaim is deemed commenced for statute of limitations purposes. Is D's counterclaim timely?

Not sure ☐

184. P brought, in federal court, an action against D for violation of P's federally registered copyrights. (The suit alleged that D plagiarized language in a novel written by P.) Before D's time to answer ran, P amended his suit to add a second claim that D libeled P by calling P a "dishonest writer." The alleged libel has nothing to do with the alleged copyright violation. Putting aside questions of personal and subject matter jurisdiction, is P entitled, procedurally, to add this second claim to his action?

Not sure ☐

185. Same basic fact pattern as in the previous question. Now, however, assume that P and D are citizens of the same state. Assume also that both the copyright claim and the libel claim are for more than $75,000. May the federal court hear the libel claim?

186. P and D were both injured in a car accident when the cars driven by each collided. P brought a federal court diversity action against D for negligence, seeking $100,000 in damages. D brought a counterclaim against P for negligence (relating to the same accident) in that same action; D joined to that counterclaim a second person, X (the owner of the car driven by P). D claimed that P and X each owed $30,000 on D's counterclaim. D then joined a second claim against X, for breach of contract, in an unrelated transaction; this claim was for $15,000. P is a citizen of Alabama, D is a citizen of Georgia, and X is a citizen of Florida.

(a) May the court hear D's claim against X for damages from the car accident?

(b) May the court hear D's claim against X for breach of contract?

187. P, a motion picture company, is the owner of the "Richie Rat" cartoon character. Because of Richie Rat's enormous popularity, a number of small entrepreneurs produce T-shirts, sweatshirts, dolls, and other objects with the Richie Rat character on them, but without authorization from P. P has brought a federal district court action against D1 and D2, alleging federal copyright violation. D1 and D2 have no connection with each other or with P, except that P claims that D1 has put Richie Rat on a series of T-shirts, and that D2 has put the character on a series of dolls, both without authorization. Is P justified in joining D1 and D2 in a single action?

188. P1 and P2 were both passengers in a twin-engine aircraft owned and operated by D1 (a commuter airline) and manufactured by D2. Both P1 and P2 were seriously injured when the plane caught fire while landing. P1 and P2 are both citizens of New York; D1 is a citizen of Wisconsin (i.e., it is incorporated there and has its principal place of business there) and D2 is a citizen of Kansas. P1 and P2 have brought a single federal court diversity action in which D1 is charged with negligent inspection and operation, and D2 is charged with strict products liability. P1 and P2 each meet the amount in controversy requirement. Is the joinder of both defendants and both plaintiffs proper?

189. Same basic fact pattern as in the previous two questions. Now, however, assume that D1 has its principal place of business in New York. May the action be heard as pleaded?

190. X, shortly before dying, signed a contract in which he promised to leave P $100,000 in his will in consideration for services performed for him by P. X then died, and his will did not mention P. P has brought a federal court diversity action against D1 (X's estate), seeking to enforce this contract to make a will. P's suit does not list as defendants D2 and D3 (X's children, who are his beneficiaries under the will). Neither P nor D1 seems troubled by the absence from the suit of D2 and D3. Assuming that D2 and D3 can be subjected to the personal jurisdiction of the federal court, and that they are not citizens of the same state as P, what if any action should the federal judge hearing the suit take?

191. In 2000, X, a wealthy citizen of New York, gave possession of a valuable Van Gogh painting to P, a museum located in Florida. X assured P that she wanted P to have the painting forever, and that this would be confirmed in X's will. In 2010, X died. X's will left all of X's property (including, specifically, the Van Gogh) to Y, X's daughter, who is a citizen of Florida. (Y has no contacts with New York.) P has brought a diversity suit against D (X's estate) in New York federal district court, seeking a judgment that the 2000 transfer of possession of the Van Gogh to P was a completed gift, and that the painting now belongs to P. (X's estate is deemed a citizen of New York.) P has not joined Y as a codefendant because Y's presence would destroy diversity of citizenship and because the court could not get personal jurisdiction over Y. Y is afraid that if the action proceeds without her and P wins, P may sell the painting, lend it to a museum outside the United States, or otherwise put the painting beyond Y's reach. Assuming that there is no way for Y to become part of the pending action, should the New York federal district court dismiss the action on account of Y's absence?

Not sure ☐

192. Same facts as in the previous question. Now, however, assume that Y, because of regular business dealings with New York, has such minimum contacts with the state of New York as to make it constitutional for Y to be subjected to the personal jurisdiction of the New York courts (and, by extension, to the personal jurisdiction of the New York federal district court sitting in diversity). Also, the New York long-arm would reach Y in a New York state court action. Should the New York federal court order Y to be joined, order the action to go on without Y, or dismiss the action because Y cannot be joined?

Not sure ☐

193. A cooperative located in the City of Langdell has 16 apartments and, thus, 16 shareholders. The members of the co-op wish to bring a federal court securities action against the previous owner of the building; the suit would allege that the prior landlord created a false prospectus (concealing defects in the building's structure known to him) and then sold shares in the corporation holding title to the building, in violation of a federal securities law provision. Each of the 16 members has a claim worth in excess of $100,000. The co-op members would like to bring their suit as a class action. Are they likely to be able to do so?

Not sure ☐

194. Peter owned one share of stock (worth $20) in Huge Motors, a large publicly traded automobile manufacturer. Acting at the urging of his friend Larry, a young, inexperienced would-be securities litigator, Larry brought a federal securities law action against Huge, claiming that Huge, by failing to disclose certain facts in its prospectus accompanying its initial public offering (IPO) in 2007, defrauded everyone who bought Huge stock in that offering (approximately 30,000 individuals and entities). The action was certified as a class action under Federal Rule 23(b)(3). Notice by mail was given to the 7,000 people shown on Huge's stock transfer books as being ones who bought Huge stock at the IPO. (Personal notice given to the remainder was found by the court not to be feasible, because these were people whose stock was held in "street name," and their names and addresses were thus not directly available to Huge. Publication notice was used instead.)

At trial, Larry, due to his inexperience, presented a weaker case than could have been made, and the judge found in Huge's favor on all claims. Shortly thereafter, Phil, who had bought $2 million worth of Huge stock at the IPO, brought a similar securities act suit against Huge. Phil demonstrated that he had not received actual notice of the suit brought by Peter, because he, Phil, held his stock in street name. Will Phil's suit be permitted to go forward as an individual action, given that the claim is substantially the same as that asserted by Peter on behalf of the class in the earlier action?

Not sure ☐

195. P1 and P2 are individuals whose applications to live in a particular federally subsidized housing project were rejected by D, the state agency that administers the project. P1 and P2 brought a federal action alleging that D's refusal to furnish them with a statement of reasons for their rejection constituted a deprivation of their right to due process, in violation of a federal civil rights statute. P1 and P2 now seek to certify as a plaintiff class all individuals whose applications for this project were rejected where the rejection was not accompanied by a statement of reasons. They seek a declaratory judgment that D violated the civil rights of each class member, and an injunction against further violations. (They don't seek damages.) The identities of the would-be class members can be compiled quite readily from the records of D; there are approximately 700 such individuals. Assuming that the trial judge believes that the lawyers for P1 and P2, and P1 and P2 themselves, can adequately represent the interests of the 700 absent members, should the judge permit the action to go forward as a class action? If so, under what subdivision of Rule 23?

Not sure ☐

196. Same basic fact pattern as in the previous question. Assuming that the federal judge certifies the plaintiff class as requested by P1 and P2, must P1 and P2 pay for notice to all 700 absent class members?

Not sure ☐

197. D operates a chemical plant in the Town of Pound. Late one night, an explosion occurred in the plant, and a cloud of toxic gas was released. The cloud drifted for several miles before dispersing, and hundreds of people appeared to be injured by it in various ways. One year after the explosion, P1, a resident of Pound who claimed to have been seriously injured by his exposure to the toxic cloud, filed suit against D for violation of federal environmental protection statutes. P seeks certification of a class consisting of all individuals residing within five miles of the plant who were or may have been injured by the toxic substance released. The suit seeks compensatory damages on behalf of each class member. Assuming that P can adequately represent the absent class members, should class certification be granted? If so, under what subdivision of Rule 23?

Not sure ☐

198. Same basic fact pattern as in the previous question. Now, assume that the federal judge certified a class action, under Rule 23. Notice was given to each resident of Pound, including X. All residents were notified that they may "opt out" of the action, and X elected to so opt out. The judge found that D violated the federal environmental statutes by allowing the toxic cloud to be released, and that D was therefore liable to any resident who could prove that the cloud proximately caused injuries to her. After the class action was complete, X started a separate federal action against D. In the suit, he seeks to collaterally estop D from denying that it released a cloud in violation of federal statutes. Should X be granted the benefit of collateral estoppel on this issue?

Not sure ☐

199. P1 instituted a federal class action against D. D is a large investment banking firm, and P1's suit alleged that D broke federal securities laws when it sold stock on behalf of Z Corporation. D and Z are both Delaware corporations with their

principal place of business in New York. The suit took place in New York federal district court. The court certified as a class all persons who purchased Z Corp. stock during a certain time period. One of these individuals was X, a California resident with no significant contacts with either Delaware or New York. X ignored the notice telling him he had the right to opt out. The class action was decided in favor of D. X then instituted his own individual suit against D in California federal district court. D now argues that X should be bound by the prior class action results. X points out in rebuttal that he, X, had no minimum contacts with New York, and argues that he should not be bound by the results in the New York class action suit given this lack of minimum contacts. Is X's contention correct?

Not sure ☐

200. P1 and P2 have instituted a federal suit against D, a large bank that issues many credit cards. The suit contends that credit cards issued by D were misleadingly advertised, in violation of the law of New York (the state where the federal action is pending). P1's claim is for $80,000, and P2's claim is for $90,000. P1 and P2 are both citizens of New Jersey. D is a citizen of New York. No federal question is present. P1 and P2 seek certification of a class consisting of all those who ordered credit cards from D in reliance on the misleading advertising, regardless of the amount of damage suffered by that person. (All these others have damages of at most $20,000 each.) Assuming that the requirements of Federal Rule 23 are satisfied, should the court grant certification of the proposed class?

Not sure ☐

201. Biff is the publisher of Biff's Notes, a series of study aids sold to college and high school students. Each year, Biff's acquires about 1 million new customers for its study aids, which cost an average of $3 each. P, a college student who is a customer of Biff's Notes, brought a federal antitrust suit against Biff, accusing him of price fixing, predatory tactics, and other congressionally forbidden tactics to maintain a dominant share of the study aid market. P has asked the court to certify a class consisting of all customers who have bought any study aids from Biff during the past four years. (Of the approximately 4 million Biff's customers during this period, the names and addresses of about 800,000 are identifiable by Biff's from its records, because they have sent in a card requesting free updates.) The court has certified this class under Rule 23.

(a) Which, if any, of these customers must receive individualized notice of the pendency of the class action?

Not sure ☐

(b) Assuming that at least some customers must receive such notice, who must pay for it?

Not sure ☐

(c) What if anything can the person who must pay for notice pursuant to (b) do to reduce the cost?

Not sure ☐

202. Same facts as in the previous question. Now, assume that prior to certifying the class, the district court determines that P's probability of success on the merits at trial is small (less than 10 percent). Should this diminish the court's willingness to certify a class?

Not sure ☐

203. Same basic fact pattern as in the previous two questions. Assume that after the court has certified the action as a class action, P's lawyer and the lawyers for Biff work out a proposed settlement, by which a $1 discount coupon will be sent to each identifiable class member, and Biff's will reduce its prices by 10 percent for the next two years. What procedural steps, if any, must be taken?

Not sure ☐

204. Same basic fact pattern as in the three previous questions. Assume that P obtains class certification, proceeds to trial, and wins on the merits. The court orders that the class be paid damages of $2 million. P's lawyer applies for attorney's fees. The antitrust statute under which P sued makes no mention of court-awarded attorney's fees for suits brought under that statute. May the court award P's lawyer a reasonable fee?

Not sure ☐

205. P and X were passengers aboard an airplane owned and operated by D. The plane caught fire while landing, and P and X were both seriously injured. P filed a diversity suit against D in federal district for the Southern District of Michigan, arguing that D flew the plane in a negligent manner. X now plans a separate suit against D. Before filing that suit, X has learned that P and he are both planning to use the same expert witness at trial, Edward, who will testify that D's pilot did not land the plane in accordance with the manufacturer's instructions. X's lawyer fears that if P tries his suit first and does not properly prepare Edward for testimony, Edward will be seriously attacked in cross-examination and will be a less useful witness in X's own later action against D. In this situation, what tactical step should X consider?

Not sure ☐

206. Same facts as in the previous question. Assume that P is a citizen of Michigan, D is a citizen of Ohio, and X is a citizen of Ohio. Will the tactic you suggested in your answer to the previous question still work?

Not sure ☐

207. Same facts as in the previous question. Now, however, assume that the federal district court rules that X is entitled to intervene as of right in the action. Does X's presence in the action satisfy the requirements of federal subject matter jurisdiction?

Not sure ☐

208. Same basic fact pattern as 206. Assume that X has moved the court for leave to permissively intervene in the action as a co-plaintiff. Assume also that there are no jurisdictional problems. The district court has denied X's application. X has now appealed this denial. Will the appeals court reverse the district court's denial of leave to intervene?

Not sure ☐

209. The U.S. government (represented by the Justice Department) has brought a federal court suit against the Ames Board of Education, charging that Ames is administering its public schools in a racially discriminatory manner. The essence of the complaint is that intradistrict boundaries are being intentionally drawn on racial lines, and that predominantly black schools within Ames are receiving fewer resources than predominantly white schools. P, the parent of a black Ames public school student, wishes to intervene as of right in the action as a co-plaintiff. Should such intervention be granted?

Not sure ☐

210. Same facts as in the previous question. Assume that the district court denies P's motion to intervene, holding that P is not entitled to intervene as of right under Rule 24, and that permissive intervention under Rule 24 is unwise because it would "clutter up this lawsuit." If P appeals this determination, will the appeals court reverse?

Not sure ☐

211. A car driven by Xavier hit and injured two pedestrians, Al and Betty. The only insurance policy on Xavier's car was issued by Insurer and has a $30,000 policy limit. Al is a citizen of the Southern District of New York; Betty is a citizen of the Western District of Oklahoma; Insurer is a citizen of the Western District of New York. Insurer is worried that it will have to defend Xavier in two distinct actions (one brought by Al and the other brought by Betty) and that defense costs plus judgments may total more than $30,000. Also, Insurer is worried that Al, Betty, or both may sue in states allowing a direct action against the defendant's insurer. Insurer wants to be sure that it doesn't have to pay out more than $30,000 as the result of this accident. No suit has been commenced yet by either Al or Betty. Tactically, what should Insurer do?   Not sure ☐

212. If an action is brought, as you recommend in your answer to the previous question, where would venue lie?   Not sure ☐

213. Same fact pattern as in the previous question. Suppose that Insurer believes that Xavier fraudulently procured the policy and that Insurer is therefore not liable to either Al or Betty (even if Xavier were found to be liable to one or both of these claimants). May Insurer deny its liability while still using the tactical device you referred to in your answer to the previous two questions?   Not sure ☐

214. Same fact pattern as in the previous three questions. Can Insurer bring an action pursuant to Federal Rule 22 on these facts?   Not sure ☐

215. H and W, a married couple, jointly applied for a homeowner's insurance policy from Insurer. They then got entangled in a nasty divorce proceeding. While this proceeding was pending (and when the status of the marital home was still in doubt), a tornado destroyed the home. H now asserts that he is entitled to the entire proceeds by virtue of a prenuptial agreement signed between H and W; W asserts that she is entitled to the sole proceeds because she is the sole occupant of the house at the moment. W is a citizen of Indiana, where the home is located; H has now moved to Ohio, of which he is currently a citizen. Insurer is a citizen of Kentucky. Insurer's assets are heavily invested in junk bonds, which are relatively illiquid at the moment. Therefore, Insurer would like to delay as long as possible having to pay out the claim or even deposit the $500,000 policy proceeds in court during an interpleader proceeding. Assuming that none of the three states involved (Ohio, Kentucky, and Indiana) has helpful interpleader laws, what tactical step should Insurer take?   Not sure ☐

216. A commercial aircraft owned and operated by Airline Inc. crashed into the tip of a peak in the Himalayas while en route from San Francisco to Nepal. Investigation of the black box and other instruments found in the wreckage indicated that the pilot believed that he was flying at 20,000 feet above sea level when he was in fact flying at only 9,000 feet above (less than the height of the mountain). The estate of P, one of the passengers killed in the accident, has sued Airline and Doeing (the plane's manufacturer) in a single federal court diversity action. The suit alleges that Airline was negligent in not discovering the altimeter problem, and that Doeing breached the implied warranty of merchantability by delivering a plane containing an altimeter that would fail.

Doeing's lawyer realizes that if the altimeter was defective, Doeing will be liable even if it behaved without negligence. The lawyer also realizes that if Doeing has breached the implied warranty of merchantability with respect to the altimeter, then the warranty has also been breached by Altimeters R Us, the manufacturer of the altimeter (which is not a defendant thus far). What tactical step should Doeing take to ensure that Doeing does not get unfairly saddled with liability for an act (manufacture and delivery of a defective altimeter) that is really the fault of Altimeters R Us?   Not sure ☐

217. Same facts as in the previous question. Suppose that Doeing's lawyer concludes that it would be more desirable not to bring Altimeters into the action but to bring a later separate federal or state action against Altimeters if in fact Doeing is held liable on breach of warranty. Will Doeing be able to bring such a later action if it does not bring Altimeters into the current action?   Not sure ☐

218. P, suffering from a heart attack, was taken to Ames General Hospital. While there, P was subjected to unreasonable delays in treatment, with the result that he suffered permanent brain damage. P's lawyer, believing that Ames General Hospital was run by the City of Ames, brought a federal diversity action against the City of Ames, charging negligence. In fact, the Ames Hospital Foundation, a charitable foundation, runs Ames General Hospital, and the hospital's operation has nothing to do with the city. Given this fact, what tactical step should the lawyer for the city take?   Not sure ☐

219. Paula, a citizen of Ohio, wished to have a house constructed for her on land she owned in Ohio. She contracted with Dave, a builder who is a citizen of Kentucky; the contract stated that Dave would build a house according to Paula's specifications on Paula's land for a total construction price of $200,000. Because the capital and risk associated with this project were too much for Dave to deal with alone, he entered into a side contract with Ted, a financier, whereby Ted agreed to put up half the capital needed for the project in return for half the profits from the job. This side contract also provided that the two would share equally in any losses or liabilities that might result from the project. Ted did not contract directly with Paula in any way. Dave lives in the town of Covington; Ted, a citizen of Ohio, lives in Cincinnati (about 50 miles from Covington).

Dave constructed the house; Paula paid for it and moved in. Paula then discovered certain latent defects that rendered the house substantially less valuable. Paula has brought a suit against Dave in federal court for the Eastern District of Kentucky (where Covington is located); the suit is based in diversity and seeks $80,000 in damages for breach of contract. Paula has not joined Ted in the suit. Dave would now like to bring Ted into the suit somehow, so that if Dave is required to pay up to $80,000 damages, Ted, in the same action, will be required to pay half of this amount over to Dave (so that they will end up having to pay equal shares of any damage award). Although Ted has minimum contacts with Kentucky, the Kentucky long-arm statute is a very limited one that would not allow service on Ted in an action by Paula or Dave concerning either the Paula-Dave or the Dave-Ted contract.

(a) What can Dave do to bring Ted into this action?   Not sure ☐

(b) Describe any procedural intricacies associated with your answer to (a).   Not sure ☐

(c) What special FRCP provision will help you solve a problem relating to jurisdiction?

Not sure ☐

220. Same basic fact pattern as in the previous question. Assume that Ted now wishes to file a claim against Paula, alleging that Paula libeled him by writing a letter to the local newspaper, which stated, "Ted secretly and crookedly induced Dave to save them both a few bucks by building my house in a sloppy and dangerous way." Ted's claim is for $100,000. Will the court hear Ted's claim against Paula?

Not sure ☐

221. Same basic fact pattern as in the previous two questions. Now, assume that after Paula has sued Dave, Dave has impleaded Ted, and Ted has made a claim against Paula for libel, Paula wishes to make a claim against Ted for deceit—she alleges that Ted conspired with Dave to induce her to pay for an improperly constructed house. The claim does not involve a federal question and is for $80,000. Will the court hear Paula's claim against Ted?

Not sure ☐

222. Same basic fact pattern as in questions 219-221. Assume that Paula's claim against Dave, Dave's claim against Ted, and Ted's claim against Paula go forward. Ted's lawyer determines that much of the damage cited by Paula is due to improper plumbing on the house. This plumbing was performed by Steve, who entered into a subcontract with Dave and Ted, whereby Steve was to do all plumbing needed for the house, and to do so in a merchantable fashion. Dave does not want to bring Steve into the case because Steve is Dave's brother-in-law. Ted, however, would like to bring Steve into the action. May Ted do so, and if so, how?

Not sure ☐

223. Deborah and Dell, each driving a separate car, decided to drag race one day. While doing so, one or both of them (this is not clear) collided with a car driven by Pete, injuring him. Pete has brought a federal diversity action against both Deborah and Dell, alleging that each, because of negligence, is jointly and severally responsible for his injuries. Pete is a citizen of Michigan; Deborah and Dell are both citizens of Wisconsin. Deborah would like to be able to make a claim against Dell for damage to her car suffered in the same accident. However, Deborah does not want to make the claim in the current action, because she thinks that the federal judge assigned to this case is hostile to women drag racers. If Deborah does not assert her claim against Dell in the present action, will she be able to bring a separate suit against Dell in Wisconsin state court after Pete's case is completed?

Not sure ☐

224. Same facts as in the previous question. Suppose that Deborah does bring a claim against Dell as part of Pete's original action. Assume that Deborah's claim is for $30,000. Will the federal court take jurisdiction over Deborah's claim against Dell?

Not sure ☐

225. Same basic fact pattern as in the previous two questions. Now, assume that Deborah does not want to make any claim against Dell for injuries arising from the accident. Instead, Deborah wishes to assert against Dell a claim for breach of contract. This claim asserts that Dell agreed to sell Deborah his house but refused to do so when Deborah tendered the purchase price. The claim is for $85,000. Putting aside any problems relating to lack of diversity, may Deborah assert this claim against Dell as part of the action brought by Pete?

Not sure ☐

226. P and D, each driving a car, collided. P suffered serious personal injuries, and her car was totally demolished. P brought an action in Ames state court for damages for her personal injuries but not for any loss of property. P won the suit. P then commenced a second action against D, for the damage to her car, in Ames state court. Will the court hear this second action?

227. Peg, a cartoonist, created the enormously popular Tiny Tom animated character. Peg has licensed this character to various entrepreneurs, including some who put the character on T-shirts. Dennis did not purchase a license from Peg but put Tiny Tom on T-shirts for resale anyway. Peg brought a federal court action for a preliminary injunction against Dennis, alleging federal trademark infringement and seeking to stop Dennis from putting the Tiny Tom character on any additional T-shirts. The district judge granted the injunction sought by Peg. Peg then instituted a second suit against Dennis, again in federal court, seeking to recover from Dennis, on a federal trademark infringement theory, the profits that Dennis made from those shirts he sold before issuance of the injunction. Will the federal court hear Peg's money-damages claim?

228. Pauline and Doug collided while each was driving. Pauline suffered personal injuries and damage to her car. Pauline brought a federal court diversity action against Doug for her personal injuries but not for her property damage. Suit was brought in Iowa federal district court, where Pauline resides. Service was made by mail upon Doug, who resides in New York. Doug successfully moved under Federal Rule 12 to have the action dismissed for lack of personal jurisdiction over him, since he has no contacts with Iowa. Pauline then filed a new action in federal court for the Southern District of New York and properly served Doug. This suit seeks only damages for Pauline's personal injuries from the accident. Doug now seeks dismissal on the grounds that the earlier Iowa suit bars Pauline from bringing the present New York suit. Will the court grant Doug's motion to dismiss?

229. Same fact pattern as in the previous question. Now, however, assume that in the first action (in the federal court for Iowa), Doug did not make any jurisdictional objection. Instead, he made a motion under Rule 12(b)(6) for failure to state a cause of action; he asserted that Pauline's claim was barred by the statute of limitations. The federal judge agreed with this assertion and dismissed the case. The order of dismissal did not say whether the dismissal was with prejudice. Pauline has then brought another action, again in federal court for Iowa, seeking to recover for the property damage she sustained in the accident (in contrast to the personal injury damages she sought in the first action). Should the federal judge hear Pauline's second claim on the merits?

230. Same facts as in the previous two questions. Now, however, assume that Pauline's personal injury claim against Doug was litigated through to a jury verdict, which was in favor of Doug. Doug made no claims of his own against Pauline in this suit. After final judgment in Doug's favor was entered, Doug instituted a claim in Iowa state court against Pauline for property damage that he sustained in the accident with Pauline. Under Iowa laws of procedure, all counterclaims are permissive, not compulsory. Will the Iowa court hear Doug's claim against Pauline?

231. Same basic fact pattern as in the previous three questions. Now, assume that Pauline's claim in Iowa federal court proceeded to a decision on the merits. The judge applied Iowa state law, which is that contributory negligence by the plaintiff, no matter how small in degree, completely blocks plaintiff from recovering. The judge found in favor of Doug on the grounds that Pauline was slightly negligent. The judge entered a final judgment in favor of Doug. One month later, the Iowa Supreme Court reversed its prior decisions and held that comparative negligence, rather than contributory negligence, will henceforth be the official doctrine of Iowa. Pauline has now brought a second suit against Doug in federal court for Iowa for property damage from the original accident. Should the federal judge allow Pauline's action to go forward?

Not sure ☐

232. Phillip was injured when a car he was driving collided with a car driven by Doreen. Phillip sued Doreen for negligence in Ames state court. The case was tried before a jury, and the jury found for Phillip, awarding him substantial damages. Judgment was entered. Then, Doreen brought a negligence suit against Phillip for property damage arising from the same transaction. This suit, too, was brought in Ames state court. Ames follows traditional negligence law, by which even a small amount of contributory negligence on the part of the plaintiff prevents the plaintiff from recovering. Ames has no statute or judicial policy making any cause of action a compulsory counterclaim. In Doreen's suit, may she assert, and prove, that Phillip's negligence caused the accident?

Not sure ☐

233. Same basic fact pattern as in the previous question. Now, assume that after Phillip sued Doreen in Ames state court for negligence, Doreen declined to answer. A default judgment was entered against her for $100,000 in damages. Doreen then instituted an action, in Ames, against Phillip for negligence. Will the court allow Doreen to assert and prove that Phillip was negligent?

Not sure ☐

234. Same basic fact pattern as in the previous two questions. Now, assume that Phillip's suit against Doreen was actively litigated, with Phillip claiming that Doreen was negligent, and Doreen claiming that Phillip was contributorily negligent.

The jury found in favor of Doreen. In response to two special interrogatories, the jury stated that Phillip was contributorily negligent and that Doreen was also negligent. (Remember that according to Ames law, even a small amount of contributory negligence bars recovery, even if the defendant was also negligent.) In a second Ames action, Doreen then sued Phillip for negligence. Will Doreen be collaterally estopped from denying her own contributory negligence in this second action?

Not sure ☐

235. Penny and Dan, each driving a car, were involved in what at first appeared to be a minor fender bender. Penny sued Dan for negligence in municipal court for the town of Langdell, a small claims court whose jurisdiction is limited to cases involving less than $5,000. This court has quite informal procedures; for instance, there is no right to jury trial, and there are no formal rules for the admissibility of evidence. The jurisdiction applies common law contributory negligence. Penny sought $2,000 for property damage suffered by her. The judge found that Dan drove negligently and that Penny did not; he awarded the full $2,000 to Penny.

Dan shortly thereafter developed back trouble, which, in the opinion of his doctor, stemmed from the collision with Penny. Dan sued in a court of general jurisdiction (in the state where Langdell is located) for $100,000 of compensatory damages for medical expense, and pain and suffering. Penny now asserts that Dan is collaterally estopped from either (1) showing that Penny was negligent or (2) denying that Dan himself was negligent. Which, if either, of these assertions is correct?

Not sure ☐

236. Perry sued Denise for negligence, arising out of an auto accident. Since Perry was seeking only a modest sum for actual medical expenses, Denise agreed to settle the case for a $2,000 payment to Perry. The settlement document recited these facts and made no statement about what effect the settlement would have on any other litigation. A judgment was entered in accordance with this settlement. Shortly thereafter, Xavier, who was injured in the same accident, sued Denise. Putting aside the issue of whether the mutuality doctrine or Xavier's status as a stranger to the first action prevents him from using collateral estoppel, is Denise entitled to deny her negligence as part of her defense of the action brought by Xavier?

Not sure ☐

237. Jones, who had not been ordained by any recognized religious institution, asserted that he was a minister, that his house was therefore a parsonage, and that he need not pay real estate taxes to the town of Ames, where the house was located. In an attempt to collect real estate taxes for the 2009 tax year, Ames took Jones to court and litigated the issue of whether Jones was a bona fide minister as required by the state's property tax exemption laws. In this proceeding, the court concluded that Jones met the requirements for the exemption. Jones then refused to pay the 2010 property taxes, and Ames again took him to court. Ames argues that the issue of Jones's entitlement to the exemption is an issue of law, which therefore does not qualify for collateral estoppel in the second proceeding. In this second proceeding, may Jones's entitlement to the exemption be disputed by the town?

Not sure ☐

238. The Agriculture Department of the state of Ames bars any milk wholesaler from selling milk within Ames at a wholesale price of less than $1 per quart. Potter, an out-of-state wholesaler who wanted to sell milk at less than the $1 price, sued the Department of Agriculture in Ames state court. Potter's claim was that the price law discriminated against out-of-state commerce, in violation of the dormant Commerce Clause of the U.S. Constitution. The trial judge who heard the suit agreed with Potter's assertion. Potter, immediately after his victory, began selling milk at 90 cents per gallon. The Agriculture Department did not appeal. Instead, it actively defended a similar suit brought by Xavier and lost that one at the trial level as well. Subsequently, the Department appealed the loss to Xavier to the Ames Supreme Court (the highest court in the state), which found that the price floor was valid as a constitutional matter. Potter continued to sell milk for 90 cents per gallon after the decision in Xavier's suit. The Agriculture Department then brought a suit to obtain an injunction against Potter's continuing to sell milk at less than $1 per gallon. Potter asserts that his victory in the earlier suit against him collaterally estops Ames from relitigating that issue with him now. Will Potter get the benefit of collateral estoppel on these facts?

Not sure ☐

239. Worker served as a full-time chauffeur for Boss, a wealthy tycoon. One day, while Worker was driving on an errand for Boss (Boss was not in the car), Worker ran over Pedestrian. Pedestrian sued Boss in state court on a respondeat superior theory (alleging that Worker drove negligently and that Boss was automatically responsible for that negligence). Boss gave Worker notice of this action, but Worker

declined to hire his own lawyer or to get involved in the suit. The jury found in favor of Pedestrian, but awarded only $50,000 in damages (much less than the $250,000 sought by Pedestrian). Pedestrian has now brought a second action, this time against Worker, again in state court. This action similarly claims that Worker drove negligently and seeks the same $250,000 of damages (though Pedestrian is happy to give a credit for the $50,000 already paid by Boss).

(a) May Worker claim, and prove, that he was not negligent in the accident?　Not sure ☐

(b) Assuming that Worker is liable, may Pedestrian recover anything beyond the $50,000 awarded against and already paid by Boss?　Not sure ☐

240. Peter and Paul were neighbors who agreed to share a cab ride to the airport one night. David drove the cab. On a poorly lit city street, the cab smashed into an abandoned car (whose owner was never traced), and Peter and Paul were both seriously injured. Peter brought a suit against David in Ames state court. Peter's lawyer aggressively and expertly litigated the case, but the jury found in favor of David. Special interrogatories given to the jury made it clear that the jury simply believed that David used all due care and could not have prevented the accident by ordinary precautions. After this verdict, Paul brought a suit against David in Ames state court, also alleging negligence relating to the same accident. Assuming that Paul has no evidence of David's negligence to put forth except evidence used by Peter in the first suit, may Paul nonetheless assert and prove that David drove negligently and caused the accident?　Not sure ☐

241. Parker was a lifelong smoker. The only two brands he ever smoked were Acme and Baker. On average, he smoked two packs of Acme per day and one pack of Baker. He contracted lung cancer and then brought a products liability suit against Acme in Ames state court, asserting that Acme was responsible for his lung cancer. Acme presented evidence that Parker's lung cancer was of a type not usually associated with cigarette smoking, that it was of a type usually associated with asbestos exposure, and that Parker had worked around asbestos for many years. The case was tried to a judge, who concluded that Parker had failed to prove by a preponderance of the evidence that cigarette smoking (regardless of brand) contributed substantially to his getting lung cancer. Parker then brought a suit against Baker, again in Ames state court, making the same type of allegations he had made against Acme. Baker now argues that Parker should be collaterally estopped from asserting that his lung cancer was caused by any brand of cigarette. Granting Baker's request will result in Parker's claim being dismissed before trial. Should Baker be permitted to use collateral estoppel to bar Parker from claiming that cigarettes caused his lung cancer?　Not sure ☐

242. The Attorney General for the state of Ames had evidence that Natural Foods, a cereal company, was making inflated health claims about its new Oat Bits cereal. Natural Foods claimed that Oat Bits "cuts by 90 percent your chances of getting colon cancer." The Attorney General brought a civil suit against Natural Foods, seeking a declaratory judgment that this claim was false, and also seeking a civil fine. Natural Foods defended the case vigorously, but lost, with the court finding that the health claim was false and awarding a $10,000 civil fine against Natural Foods.

Subsequently, Paul, a consumer, filed a $1 million strict product liability and negligence action against Natural Foods. This suit alleges that Paul ate Oat Bits constantly, relied on the message, ignored pains in his stomach, and thus did not consult a doctor for the pains. When he finally consulted a doctor, Paul alleges, he found out that he had advanced colon cancer, which might have been caught and treated earlier while it was still curable had he not been lulled into a false feeling of security by Natural Foods' health claims about Oat Bits. Paul seeks to prevent Natural Foods from relitigating the issue of whether Oat Bits really cuts down one's risk of colon cancer by 90 percent. Should Natural Foods be so estopped?

Not sure ☐

243. Fred and Greg went one day to a diner operated by Dave. Fred ordered a bowl of clam chowder. The meal went uneventfully, and Fred and Greg left. One week later, Fred sued Dave for strict product liability, alleging that the chowder was dangerously defective and gave Fred food poisoning. The suit was tried in a court of general jurisdiction of the state of Ames, and Fred sought $500 in damages. Dave defended by trying to show that Fred's illness was in fact the flu, but the judge found in Fred's favor and awarded $500 in damages. Nowhere during the trial was Greg mentioned.

Shortly after Fred's verdict against Dave, Greg instituted a suit against Dave in Ames state court. His suit alleges that he ate some of Fred's order of clam chowder and that he too was food poisoned. Greg's suit seeks $100,000 in damages, stating that while the hospital was treating him for food poisoning, it gave him a drug that caused him to go into convulsions, and that Dave must be liable for all of the resulting injury to Greg. At the trial, Greg seeks to collaterally estop Dave from denying that the clam chowder was dangerously defective (though he is willing to let Dave attempt to prove that the defectiveness was not the proximate cause of Greg's own injuries). Should Greg be allowed to use collateral estoppel in this manner?

Not sure ☐

244. A group of plaintiff lawyers decided that the time was ripe for bringing a serious strict product liability action against one or more of the leading cigarette companies. They singled out the Deadly Tobacco Co. as their primary defendant. They then advertised in consumer magazines for possible plaintiffs who had suffered cigarette-related illnesses. After interviewing dozens of potential plaintiffs, they finally settled upon Angie as their first plaintiff. They picked Angie because her case was especially appealing for several reasons: (1) she began smoking while she was still a minor and did so in response to repeated television advertising by Deadly and other cigarette companies (this was before the ban on televised cigarette advertising); (2) she repeatedly tried to stop smoking through methods such as hypnosis but appears to be simply addicted; and (3) she would make a very appealing witness, in part because she has the most serious of all cigarette-related illnesses, lung cancer. Angie's case was tried to a jury in Ames state court. After a long trial, the jury found that cigarettes produced by Deadly were dangerously defective, that Deadly did not issue adequate warnings, and that Deadly should be liable to Angie for $200,000 (a higher figure was rejected since the jury believed that some of the fault was Angie's).

After this victory, the same group of lawyers selected Betty as the next plaintiff. Her case also seems to be strong, though not as strong as Angie's for several reasons (e.g., she did not start smoking until she was an adult and never saw televised cigarette advertising). Betty's lawyers now propose that Deadly be collaterally estopped from denying that its cigarettes are a dangerously defective product, and from denying that its warning labels (at least during the years that were at issue in Angie's suit) were inadequate. Should this use of collateral estoppel be allowed?

Not sure ☐

245. The governor of the state of Ames issued an executive order requiring any educational testing company conducting operations within the state to release to the public the text of any test question asked within the state. The state was immediately sued by the College Testing Service (CTS), which asserted that the order was a violation of CTS's First Amendment rights. An Ames state court judge agreed and issued a declaratory judgment that CTS could continue to keep its questions secret. Shortly thereafter, another testing service, Midwest Testing Service, filed a similar suit against the state, again in Ames state court. This suit is being heard by a different judge from the one who decided the CTS case. Midwest seeks to collaterally estop the state from denying that its executive order is a violation of the First Amendment rights of any testing company doing business in the state. Should Midwest be given the benefit of collateral estoppel in this situation?

Not sure ☐

246. Dick, while driving his car, failed to stop at a stop sign and ran over Patricia, badly injuring her. A police officer who arrived at the scene arrested Dick for drunk driving. Dick was tried on the drunk driving charge (a felony under state law) and was convicted of that crime. Patricia then filed a civil tort suit against Dick for her injuries. Patricia now asserts that Dick should be estopped from denying that he was drunk at the time of the accident (which, if true, under state law makes him automatically liable for negligence). Should Patricia be given the benefit of collateral estoppel here?

Not sure ☐

247. In the courts of the state of Ames, Abel sued Baker for negligence arising out of an automobile accident. The judge concluded that Baker was negligent and entered judgment in favor of Abel. Shortly thereafter, Conroy sued Baker for negligence arising out of the same auto accident; this suit is taking place in the courts of the state of Bates. The Ames Supreme Court allows broad offensive use of collateral estoppel, and would allow Conroy to make use of collateral estoppel against Baker on the issue of Baker's negligence in the accident, if Conroy's suit had been filed in Ames. The Supreme Court of Bates, by contrast, is a more old-fashioned jurisdiction that almost never allows offensive use of collateral estoppel by a stranger to the first action. Conroy seeks to collaterally estop Baker from denying Baker's negligence in the accident.

(a) Should Conroy be given the benefits of collateral estoppel here?

Not sure ☐

(b) Is the answer left to the court's discretion, or is it imposed by some nondiscretionary requirement?

Not sure ☐

248. Same basic fact pattern as in the previous question. Now, however, assume that the second action (by Conroy) was filed not in the state courts of Bates, but rather in federal district court for the District of Bates. Should/must the federal judge give Conroy the benefit of collateral estoppel against Baker?

Not sure ☐

249. Same basic fact pattern as in the previous two questions. Now, however, assume that the first suit is in federal court for the District of Ames (sitting in diversity) and the second suit is in the state court of Bates. Assuming that the federal judge sitting in Ames would grant offensive use of collateral estoppel against Baker in this situation, must the state court of Bates do the same?

Not sure ☐

Civil Procedure Answers to Short-Answer Questions

1. Yes, probably. **The defendant's presence in the forum state at the moment of service of process, no matter how transitory that presence, will almost always suffice to allow the forum state to constitutionally take jurisdiction over the defendant.** The Supreme Court's 1990 decision in *Burnham v. Superior Court*, 495 U.S. 604 (1990), seems to confirm that transitory presence in the forum state at the moment of service will automatically constitute the required "minimum contacts."

2. Yes. **A court may constitutionally exercise jurisdiction over anyone who is *domiciled* in that state. A person's domicile is the last place where he or she resided with the indefinite intent to remain there.** Even though D has temporarily changed his residence to California, his domicile remains Connecticut. This is because one's domicile is the last place of which it was true both that one resided there and that one had the indefinite intent to remain there. Since D does not intend to remain in California, California cannot be his domicile, so courts look at the next prior place he resided, Connecticut. (In fact, Connecticut would still be D's domicile even if he intended to move to New York after he finished his California job.)

3. Yes. **A number of states, like Florida in this question, purport to exercise personal jurisdiction based on residence, even where the resident is not a "domiciliary" of the state. Courts have generally accepted the constitutionality of such residence-based jurisdiction. However, the Supreme Court has not recently addressed the issue of jurisdiction over nondomiciliaries based solely on residence, and it is possible that in light of *Shaffer v. Heitner*, 433 U.S. 186 (1977), jurisdiction over someone who happened to own a house in the forum state but rarely visited it and was domiciled elsewhere might be found to violate constitutional due process.** Under this approach, D would be a resident of New York, California, and Florida simultaneously and could be sued in all three. The odds are, however, that maintaining a residence in the state, without more, would be enough for jurisdiction; certainly on the facts here, where D actually lives in the state three months a year, D can be subjected to suit based on his Florida residence.

4. No. **Once a person institutes suit in the forum state, he or she is deemed to have consented to the court's jurisdiction over any counterclaim that may be asserted against him or her. See *Adam v. Saenger*, 303 U.S. 59 (1938).**

5. No, probably. **According to *Worldwide Volkswagen v. Woodson*, 444 U.S. 286 (1980), the mere fact that a product finds its way into a state and causes injury there is not enough to subject the out-of-state manufacturer or vendor to personal jurisdiction there. Instead, the defendant must have made some effort to *market* in the forum state.** Here, D was not attempting to market in South Carolina, even though he knew that the doughnuts in question would find their way to South Carolina. Therefore, even though P resides in and is presently located in South Carolina, and all the witnesses are there, it would probably be a violation of due process for the South Carolina courts to subject D to personal jurisdiction there.

6. No. **If D were being sued on a claim *arising out of D's New York–based activities* (e.g., an auto accident that occurred while he was in New York on the leather-buying trip), jurisdiction would probably be constitutional. According to *Perkins v. Benguet Consolidated Mining Co.*, 342 U.S. 437 (1952), and *Helicopteros Nacionales de Columbia v. Hall*, 466 U.S. 408 (1984), claims that do not arise from in-forum-state activities may only be litigated in the forum state if the defendant**

has had *"systematic and continuous"* contacts with the forum state. Here, the claim does not relate to D's in-forum-state activities. Since a onetime three-day buying trip to New York does not constitute "systematic and continuous" activities, D cannot constitutionally be subjected to the jurisdiction of the New York courts.

7. Yes. **These facts are quite similar to those of *International Shoe v. Washington*, 326 U.S. 310 (1945), in which the Supreme Court held that the out-of-state company had the requisite *"minimum contacts"* with the forum state.** Since Corporation sought business from within Arkansas and had a salesman based there, the fact that it had no office, conducted no advertising directed at the state, and derived only a small portion of its total revenues from the state are all irrelevant. The basic idea is that Corporation purposefully availed itself of the opportunity to sell goods within Arkansas, so it is therefore not unfair for Corporation to be required to defend suits there relating to those sales.

8. No, probably. **This case is distinguishable from *McGee v. International Life Insurance Co.*, 355 U.S. 22 (1957), where the insured mailed premiums to the defendant from California until his death, and lived in California at the time the policy was most recently renewed (leading the Supreme Court to allow jurisdiction in California). The facts here are actually more similar to those of *Hanson v. Denckla*, 357 U.S. 235 (1958), where the settlor of a trust lived in Pennsylvania at the time she created the trust and then moved to Florida; since the only contacts with Florida were not voluntarily made by the defendant trustee, the trustee was not subjected to jurisdiction in Florida. The Court held in *Hanson* that there must be "some act by which the defendant *purposefully avails itself of the privilege of conducting activities within the forum state. . . ."* D** has not purposefully availed itself of the opportunity to do business in Kansas. D offered P the insurance policy at a time he lived in Oklahoma, not Kansas. D did not receive any premiums sent from Kansas or have any other way of even knowing that there was a Kansas connection with the policy. Consequently, D has not purposefully availed itself of the privilege of conducting activities within Kansas, so it cannot constitutionally be subject to jurisdiction there.

9. No. **On virtually identical facts, the Supreme Court held in *Kulko v. Superior Court*, 436 U.S. 84 (1978), that a father does not acquire minimum contacts with a forum state merely by permitting his minor child to go there to live with her mother.** (But the Oregon courts would be constitutionally entitled to award Wife a divorce if she didn't already have one; in that case, the Oregon court would merely be adjudicating status, rather than exercising *in personam* jurisdiction, and it may do this in whatever state *either* spouse is domiciled.)

10. Yes, probably. **The Supreme Court has never decided a case such as this, involving jurisdiction over a component manufacturer who made no sales directly into the forum state, but who knew that his components would be incorporated in products, some of which would be sold in the forum state. The closest fact pattern to this was in *Asahi Metal Industry Co. v. Superior Court*, 480 U.S. 102 (1987), but the case was different enough that it is not dispositive of our fact pattern here. Five members of the Court in *Asahi*, however, believed that if a defendant puts his or her goods into a stream of commerce under circumstances making it clear that a substantial minority will end up in the forum state, the defendant has minimum contacts with the forum state.** Therefore, D here probably has minimum contacts with California even though it never sold directly to any California buyers—D certainly knew that many of the cars incorporating its product would be sold in California, and D clearly benefitted from the existence of the California market.

Apart from the requirement of "minimum contacts" with California, P will also have to show that it would be "reasonable and fair" for the California courts to exercise jurisdiction over D. Since Car

Co. is no longer in business, P is based in California, and the witnesses to the accident are California-based, it does not seem unfair or unreasonable for California to exercise jurisdiction over the one plausible solvent defendant, so the court would probably find it not violative of due process for the suit to proceed.

11. Yes, probably. **The facts of this question are sufficiently similar to those of *Burger King Corp. v. Rudzewicz*, 471 U.S. 462 (1985), that the Supreme Court would probably find jurisdiction to exist, as it found in *Burger King*.** Three main factors are likely to lead the court to conclude that jurisdiction over D by the Texas courts would not violate her due process rights: (1) D signed a contract with a party based in the forum state (even though D did not come into the forum state to sign the contract), (2) D agreed to let Texas law govern any disputes, and (3) D agreed to send her payments into the forum state. None of these three factors by itself would probably be sufficient for due process, but taken together they probably will be. All in all, it probably cannot be said that D was unfairly surprised by being required to defend in Texas. The fact that it might be easier for P to sue in Illinois than for D to defend in Texas is irrelevant, since D should reasonably have anticipated out-of-state litigation.

12. Yes, probably. **The facts are similar to those of *Keeton v. Hustler Magazine*, 465 U.S. 770 (1984), where the Supreme Court found that jurisdiction could constitutionally be exercised in the forum state over the defendant publisher based on the sale of 10,000 copies there, even though neither plaintiff nor defendant had any other contact with the forum state.** The idea seems to be that although P may not have resided in (or even been present in) Rhode Island, the damage to P—inflicting emotional distress on him due to the satirical attack—resulted in part from reading that took place in Rhode Island (as in every state).

However, the suit in *Keeton* was a libel suit, and it could be said that Ms. Keeton's reputation was actually blackened in the forum state—people in the forum state had a lower opinion of her after reading the article. Here, by contrast, any emotional distress suffered by P was suffered outside the forum state. But probably this distinction would not make a difference—since P's suffering was due in part to reading that took place in Rhode Island, the Court would probably find that the Rhode Island courts could constitutionally take jurisdiction.

13. Yes, probably. **Now, since such a very tiny fraction of the total injury suffered by P occurred in the forum state, a court would probably conclude that it offends notions of fair play for D to have to litigate in Rhode Island.** Also, if jurisdiction can be predicated on such a small number of copies, publishers might decide not to sell at all in small states like Rhode Island, for fear that the cost of possible libel defenses in the state would be greater than the financial benefit from the small circulation there—this is a factor a court could probably reasonably consider in deciding whether it is fair to make a defendant defend in the forum state.

14. No. **Normally, service in a federal court action (whether based on diversity or federal question) must either take place within the confines of the state where the federal court sits, or must be made out of state in a way that is expressly permitted by that state's own long-arm statute. (There is an exception for situations where Congress has allowed for nationwide service of process, and for the 100-mile bulge provision of Federal Rule 4(f), neither of which is applicable here.)** Since the facts tell us that Florida would not allow service on the New York corporation to be made in New York on these facts, and since D is not found within Florida (as it would be if, say, it had its principal place of business there), the federal court may not take jurisdiction either.

15. Yes. **According to Federal Rule 4(e), if the long-arm statute of the state in which the District Court is located would permit a particular type of out-of-state service on a particular defendant,**

that same form of out-of-state service will suffice to confer jurisdiction on the federal district court (whether the case is based on diversity or federal question).

16. Yes. **By merely making information available to people in other states, the operator of a passive website is unlikely to be found to have subjected himself or herself to personal jurisdiction in every state where the site can be viewed.** No activities by the Coke Den other than the operation of the website even arguably involve significant contacts with Georgia, so the issue is whether the operation of the Coke Den website gives rise to minimum contacts with Georgia. The website is a relatively passive site that merely posts information and does not attempt to consummate business transactions with Georgia residents. There's no indication that the operators are attempting to lure Georgia residents to the restaurant (and, indeed, company policy is that out-of-staters will not be accepted as customers.) So it can't be said that the Den has "purposely availed" itself of the opportunity to do business in Georgia. This case is similar to the situation in *Cybersell, Inc. v. Cybersell, Inc.*, 130 F.3d 414 (9th Cir. 1997). Therefore, the fact that about 100 Georgians a year find their way to the site won't suffice.

   Furthermore, a court might well say that Coke GA's suite does not even really "arise out of" the Coke Den's forum-state activities since there's very little if any trademark infringing happening in Georgia. (The only "consumers," in the sense of customers, who might become confused about whether the Den has something to do with Coca-Cola are Nevada residents, not Georgia residents.) If the courts take the view that the suit arises solely out of non-Georgia activities, then the fact that the Coke Den's contacts with Georgia are not "systematic and continuous" will result in a finding of no jurisdiction, even if the Den did have "minimum contacts" with Georgia.

17. No. **It is true that Federal Rule 4(d)(g) allows a request for waiver of service to be made by first-class mail, but that service takes effect only if the recipient returns the waiver within 30 days of the date of mailing (60 days for a foreign defendant). If the defendant does not so waive, service must be made personally, as set out in Rule 4(e).** This is what happened here, so there is not yet jurisdiction over D.

18. Yes. **In federal question suits, the federal court will hear the case if the defendant has minimum contacts with the forum state, even though the courts of the state might not (for reasons of fairness or judicial economy) have heard a suit against that defendant.** Software Co.'s suit is a "federal question" suit. That is, Software Co.'s claim "arises under the constitution, laws, or treaties of the United States," since the source of the claim is the federal copyright statute. So the fact that the Washington long-arm would not permit the courts of Washington to hear any suit against Clone Co. is irrelevant—since Clone Co. has the constitutionally required minimum contacts with Washington, the federal court will hear the suit. (But this is not the rule for suits based on diversity.)

19. No. **In diversity cases, the federal courts only exercise the personal jurisdiction that is allowed by the statutory law of the state in which they sit, even if the state statutory law does not go to the limits of what the state could do commensurate with due process. See, e.g., *Arrowsmith v. United Press International*, 320 F.2d 219 (2d Cir. 1963).** So the rule for diversity actions is quite different from that for federal question actions—this fact pattern is virtually identical to the fact pattern of the prior question, except for the fact that we are dealing with diversity rather than federal question, yet the result is that here there is no federal court jurisdiction and in the prior question there is.

20. No, probably. **A defendant may not have to defend itself in a particular jurisdiction if to do so would be so burdensome as to violate its due process rights.** A court would probably conclude that even though the case involves federal question jurisdiction, rather than diversity jurisdiction, and even

though Knockoff Co. has minimum contacts with the United States as a whole, it would be unfair to make it defend in New York. That is, the court might conclude that it is so burdensome to require Knockoff to defend on the East Coast, where it has virtually no contacts, that to do so would violate Knockoff's due process rights.

21. No. **The landmark case of *Shaffer v. Heitner* states that *quasi in rem* jurisdiction over a defendant may not be exercised unless the defendant has such minimum contacts with the forum state that *in personam* jurisdiction could be exercised over him or her.** Since D has no contacts at all with Ohio (except for the very fortuitous fact that D's Pennsylvania-based job is with an Ohio-headquartered company), the Ohio courts could not exercise personal jurisdiction over D. Consequently, under *Shaffer v. Heitner*, Ohio may not achieve the same result by seizing part of D's wages to serve as the means for satisfying a possible judgment. The fact that P happens to be an Ohio resident is irrelevant—what counts is D's contacts with the forum state. The type of garnishment-based action described in this fact pattern is similar to that of *Harris v. Balk*, a pre-*Shaffer* case in which *quasi in rem* jurisdiction over a debt located in the forum state was permitted—but *Harris v. Balk* is almost certainly now invalid in light of *Shaffer* (though the Supreme Court has not expressly so held).

22. Yes. **The Federal Rules allow original *quasi in rem* jurisdiction in the federal courts if the law of the state in which the federal court sits permits such *quasi in rem* jurisdiction.** Here, the Kansas state courts would permit P to bring a *quasi in rem* action against D based on attachment of the insurance policy, even though Kansas would not (due to its refusal to enact a long-arm that goes to the outer limits of due process) allow full *in personam* jurisdiction over D. Consequently, the federal courts may follow Kansas's principle and allow a *quasi in rem* suit against D, to be satisfied only out of the insurance proceeds.

   Also, realize that *quasi in rem* jurisdiction is allowable here only because D has minimum contacts with Kansas, stemming from his having let his car be used in the state, where it caused an accident—*Shaffer* holds that *quasi in rem* cannot be a substitute for minimum contacts, but it can still be a substitute for a state long-arm.

23. No, probably. **Federal Rule 4(h)(1) states that service upon a domestic or foreign corporation shall be made "by delivering a copy of the summons and of the complaint to an officer, a managing or general agent, or to any other agent authorized by appointment or by law to receive service of process. . . ."**
   By this standard, Edward seems clearly improper, since he is not a member of management, has not been appointed by the corporation to receive service, and has not received any special training instructing him as to what to do with legal papers. This, coupled with the fact that Edward in fact did not give the papers to the proper person within D, would probably lead a court to conclude that there had not been proper service on D. (Observe that the fact that the recipient did not give the papers to the appropriate person is *not by itself dispositive*—if the recipient was a person contemplated by the statute as being proper to receive service, the fact that he or she did not discharge his or her duty and give the papers to, say, the corporation's legal department is irrelevant.)

24. Yes, D has a respectable chance of prevailing. **According to Federal Rule 4(e)(2), service shall be made upon an individual "by delivering a copy of the summons and of the complaint to the individual personally or by leaving copies thereof at the individual's dwelling house or usual place of abode with some *person of suitable age and discretion then residing therein*. . . ."** Given the maid's apparent inability to speak English, D can make a strong argument that the maid was not a person of suitable "discretion." Also, since the maid was a day worker, D could make a plausible argument that she did not "reside" at D's house. A court might well conclude that service had not been made as

required by 4(e)(2), in which case the court could dismiss the action under Rule 4(m) (which allows dismissal if service does not occur within 120 days after filing of the complaint and P cannot show good cause why service was not made within that period).

The fact that D actually received the papers would not automatically make his argument fail, since service-of-process statutes are usually strictly construed and are not necessarily satisfied merely because the defendant actually eventually receives the papers. On the other hand, the fact that D did in fact receive the papers would probably be considered by the court as bearing on whether the maid was a person of suitable "discretion." If the court did dismiss the complaint under Rule 4(m), it is possible (though not likely) that the claim would be treated as time-barred so that it could not be reserved.

25. **Yes. Under *Connecticut v. Doehr*, 501 U.S. 1 (1991), the court is to apply a three-part balancing test in determining whether a statute allowing for prejudgment attachment satisfies the due process rights of the person whose property is being attached: The court weighs the harm to D's property right, the risk of an erroneous deprivation, and the strength of the other party's interest in obtaining the prejudgment attachment.** Here, the impact on D is significant, since D can't spend the money in the account (and even a temporary, up-to-one-month deprivation would probably be found to be material). The risk of erroneous deprivation is substantial because P's one-sided conclusory allegations (with no rebuttal by D or opportunity to cross-examine P or to present witnesses) leave the judge no real ability to assess the likelihood that P will prevail on the merits. The strength of P's interest in the attachment is weak, because the statute does not require P to show that D is about to transfer funds or do anything else that would make it hard for P to collect any judgment he might obtain. All in all, the statute here is marginally better than the one struck down in *Doehr*, but similar enough to it that it, too, would almost certainly be found to violate due process.

26. **No, probably. D is entitled to notice and an opportunity to be heard before his property is "taken." But as long as the property (here, the $4,000) is kept safely by the court, and as long as D is given the opportunity to show that there is no reasonable likelihood that P will prevail, the court will probably conclude that D got enough of a hearing to pass constitutional muster.** However, it is not absolutely clear how this would come out if the Supreme Court were to decide the issue. Observe that if the procedure here will not suffice, then presumably no prejudgment garnishment statute would be likely to survive, since the "hearing" that would have to be given to D would have to amount to a virtual trial of P's case.

27. **No. A person has *waived* his or her meritorious claim of lack of personal jurisdiction by failing to make it as part of the initial motion under Rule 12(b). Under Rule 12(h)(1), a defense of lack of jurisdiction over the person is waived if it is omitted "from a motion in the circumstances described in subdivision Rule 12(g)(2)," which is a subsection that allows a party only one 12(b) motion per case.** (If D had not made his 12(b)(6) motion, he could have asserted his claim of lack of personal jurisdiction as part of his answer.)

28. Assert the defense as part of D's answer. **Any defense, including the defense of lack of jurisdiction, may in the federal system be asserted as part of the defendant's answer. The defendant's right to do this is implied by Federal Rule 12(b) and 12(h)(1)(B).**

29. **No. A defendant may not only raise his or her jurisdictional argument in his or her answer (assuming that he or she has not already waived that objection by making a motion under Rule 12(b) from which the jurisdictional objection is omitted), but he or she may even combine this jurisdictional objection with other more substantive defenses.**

30. Yes. **The Full Faith and Credit Clause of the Constitution (Article IV, Section 1) provides that where a judgment from State 1 is sued upon in State 2, the courts of State 2 must give that judgment the same effect as it would have in State 1. There is an exception if the State 1 judgment was by default, but there is an exception to this exception if the defendant *actually litigated the jurisdictional question* in State 1 and lost.** Since here, D litigated the jurisdictional issue in the New York courts and lost, he may not "collaterally attack" the New York judgment when it is sued upon for enforcement in New Jersey, even if the New Jersey court is absolutely convinced that the New York courts misunderstood federal due process principles. (D should have appealed the New York decision to the Supreme Court, rather than trying to make a collateral attack in New Jersey.) See *Baldwin v. Iowa State Travelling Men's Association*, 283 U.S. 522 (1931).

31. No. **These facts illustrate the one situation in which the defendant will be permitted in the State 2 proceedings to collaterally attack the judgment issued against him in State 1: It must be the case that State 1 issued a default judgment against the defendant *and* the defendant did not appear for *any reason* in the State 1 proceeding (even to unsuccessfully contest jurisdiction there).** Observe, however, that D took a big chance by letting a default judgment be issued against him in the New York proceedings: If the New Jersey court had disagreed with D's jurisdictional argument, D would have lost his right to defend on the merits in the New Jersey courts, since under the Full Faith and Credit Clause the New Jersey courts would have had no choice but to enforce New York's judgment against D once the court concluded that the New York court had personal jurisdiction over D.

32. Yes, probably. **Most courts will not hear a case where jurisdiction stems solely from the fact that the defendant has been fraudulently induced to enter the jurisdiction so that he can be served there.** When a court declines to hear such a case, it is doing so as a matter of its own discretion, not because this result is required by constitutional due process principles. Rest. Conflicts 2d, §82.

33. No, probably. **In this situation, the Connecticut court is not gaining any power that it would not otherwise have had, so the court will probably conclude that it should hear the case despite the trickery. See, e.g., *Gumperz v. Hofmann*, 245 App. Div. 622 (N.Y., 1st Dept. 1935).** Here, D could constitutionally have been subjected to suit in Connecticut even if he never entered the state—the problem was simply that Connecticut did not allow substituted service (e.g., a mailing to or posting on D's Connecticut property) even though it constitutionally could have established jurisdiction over D by this means. But again, this would be a matter for the Connecticut court's discretion.

34. No, probably. **Most jurisdictions give to nonresidents of the forum state *immunity* from service of process while they are in the state to attend a trial or deposition, either as witnesses, parties, or attorneys.** Especially here, where Davis did not have to come to New Jersey and did so as an accommodation to Peters's counsel, the court will almost certainly conclude that Davis should be given immunity from service in an unrelated suit.

35. In either the Northern District of Ohio or the Eastern District of Michigan. **Where a suit is based solely on diversity of citizenship, it may be heard in a judicial district where any defendant resides, if they all reside in the same state (the Northern District of Ohio in this case) or in the district where a substantial part of the events giving rise to the claim occurred (the Eastern District of Michigan here). See 28 U.S.C. §1391.** It is also possible for the case to be heard in another district where D is subject to personal jurisdiction, as §1391(a)(3) provides, although based on the facts D is likely to be subject to personal jurisdiction in Ohio or Michigan only.

36. In the Northern District of Indiana. **Since there is no state where all the defendants reside, the suit can be heard only in the Northern District of Indiana, where a substantial part of the events**

giving rise to the claim occurred (unless there is another district in which D and Jones are subject to personal jurisdiction and that would satisfy the "catch-all" provision in 28 U.S.C. §1391(a)(3)).

37. Only in the Northern District of Indiana. **According to 28 U.S.C. §1391(b), in federal question cases, proper venue will lie either in a district in which any defendant resides (if all defendants reside in the same state), in a district in which a substantial part of the events leading to the claim occurred or a judicial district in which any defendant may be found, if there is no district in which the action may otherwise be brought.** Since the defendants reside in different states, §1391(b)(1) is not applicable. This leaves the Northern District of Indiana, where the events took place (§1391(b)(2)). Since a district has been found, §1391(b)(3)'s "catch-all" provision does not apply, so the Northern District of Indiana is P's only choice.

38. No. **Again, the relevant statute is 28 U.S.C. §1391(b): Since the suit is not founded solely on diversity, it may be brought in the district where any defendant resides (if all defendants reside in the same state) or where a substantial part of the events leading to the claim arose.** P's only chance to get venue in the Northern District would have been by showing that D "resides" in the Northern District. However, 28 U.S.C. §1391(c) clearly ruins this argument for P: "In a state which has more than one judicial district and in which a defendant that is a corporation is subject to personal jurisdiction at the time an action is commenced, such corporation shall be deemed to reside in any district in that State within which its contacts would be sufficient to subject it to personal jurisdiction if that district were a separate State. . . ."

By this test, D resides only in the Southern, not the Northern, District, since it is only with the Southern District that D has the "minimum contacts" needed to subject it to jurisdiction if the Southern District were a separate state. Therefore, there is nothing that would make venue in the Northern District proper, even though D is headquartered, and does all of its business, in the state of which that Northern District is a part.

39. **(a)** Central District of California. **28 U.S.C. §1441(a) says that a case removed from state to federal court passes to "the district court of the United States for the district and division embracing the place where such action is pending."** Since the action was pending in the California state court in Los Angeles, it passes to the federal court serving Los Angeles, namely the Central District of California.

(b) This is a court in which P could not have originally brought the action. **In cases presenting a federal question, there is venue in the district in which a defendant resides (if all defendants reside in the same state), or where a substantial part of the events leading to the claim occurred, or in the alternative, in a district in which any defendant may be found. See 28 U.S.C. §1391(b).** There is no "plaintiff's residence" venue. So if P had originally filed in federal court, the District of Nevada would have been the only suitable district, according to the federal venue statute.

40. No. **28 U.S.C. §1404(a) states that "for the convenience of parties and witnesses . . . a district court may transfer any civil action to any other district or division where *it might have been brought*."** In *Hoffman v. Blaski*, 363 U.S. 335 (1960), the Supreme Court held that this language means that the case may be transferred only to those districts where the plaintiff would have had the right, *independent of the wishes of the defendant*, to bring the action. This in turn means that the action may not be transferred to a place where venue would have been improper had the suit originally been filed there.

On our facts, since there is a federal question, venue could lie in a district where any defendant resides (if all reside in the same state), or in a district where a substantial part of the events leading to the cause of action occurred (here, N.D. Ohio). Since the two defendants reside in different states, the action could have only been brought originally in Ohio federal district court (as it was indeed brought). Since the action could not have been brought in New York federal court originally, the Ohio federal judge is powerless to order transfer to New York despite the fact that this would be clearly for the convenience of all parties. (This is why many commentators feel that *Hoffman v. Blaski* was a bad decision.)

41. Yes. **Federal Rule 12(h)(1) provides that a defense of improper venue (like the defense of lack of personal jurisdiction) is *waived* if it is not made either as a pre-answer motion under Rule 12 or as part of the defendant's answer.** Therefore, when the Ds submitted their answers without asserting the venue defense, they waived that defense. 28 U.S.C. §1406(b) states that "nothing . . . shall impair the jurisdiction of a district court of any matter involving a party who does not interpose timely and sufficient objection to the venue." So the federal judge for New York gets to hear the case even though venue was, strictly speaking, improper.

42. Order the action transferred rather than dismissed. **28 U.S.C. §1406(a) states that if a case is filed in a district where venue does not properly lie, the court, "if it be in the interests of justice, [may] transfer such case to any district or division in which it could have been brought."** Here, since the case could have been brought in the Southern District of Florida, the New York court may order it transferred there, even though the New York court itself has neither venue nor personal jurisdiction.

43. The case must be dismissed. **Since there was no federal question, jurisdiction could only be based on diversity (or its close cousin, alienage jurisdiction; see 28 U.S.C. §1332(a)(2)).** But D's belated disclosure that he was an illegal immigrant deprives the court of alienage jurisdiction, because although a properly admitted resident alien is deemed a citizen of the United States (and of the state where he is domiciled; see 28 U.S.C. §1332(a)), an illegal immigrant is simply a foreigner. Therefore, P and D are both foreigners, and there is no alienage jurisdiction. Consequently, the court completely lacked subject matter jurisdiction. Federal Rule 12(h)(3) provides that when the court lacks jurisdiction of the subject matter, the court shall dismiss the action. Thus the court was required to dismiss the action for lack of federal subject matter jurisdiction even though the trial had already been concluded. See *Louisville & Nashville R.R. v. Mottley*, 211 U.S. 149 (1908) (case is tried and reaches Supreme Court, which dismisses it for lack of subject matter jurisdiction).

44. Yes. **For there to be subject matter jurisdiction, there must of course be diversity of citizenship. That is, P and D must be "citizens" of different states. "Citizenship" for this purpose is not synonymous with "residence." Instead, a person is a "citizen" only of the state where he is *domiciled*—that is, has his or her principal residence.** On these facts, P's principal residence is clearly New York, and Connecticut is merely his secondary residence. Therefore, P is a "citizen" of New York, and he has diversity of citizenship with D. Consequently, the court may hear the case.

45. No. **There is no diversity jurisdiction, because P is not a citizen of *any particular state* even though he is a citizen of the United States.** Therefore, there is not a suit between "citizens of different states." Furthermore, alienage jurisdiction is not present, because P is not a citizen of a foreign country, merely a resident of a foreign country. Since no federal question is present, there is no basis for federal subject matter jurisdiction. See *Hammerstein v. Lyne*, 200 F. 165 (W.D. Mo. 1912).

46. No. **Since there is no federal question present, the federal subject matter jurisdiction must be supplied by diversity if at all. But by a judge-made construction of the federal diversity statute, there must be "*complete*" diversity. That is, it must be the case that no plaintiff is a citizen of the same state as any defendant.** Since P2 and D2 are both citizens of New Jersey, diversity is deemed not to exist even though there is also a pair of opponents (P1 and D1) who are citizens of different states from each other. See *Strawbridge v. Curtiss*, 3 Cranch 267 (1806).

47. Institute a statutory interpleader proceeding. 28 U.S.C. §1335(a) allows **federal court jurisdiction over any interpleader proceeding (based on certain procedural rules, such as deposit by the stakeholder of the stake into the federal court) if there are "two or more adverse claimants, of diverse citizenship. . . ."** Since Son is a citizen of New York and Daughter a citizen of Connecticut, this requirement is satisfied. The fact that Insurance Co. is deemed to be a citizen of Connecticut (because of its principal place of business and state of incorporation), which is the same state as Daughter's state of citizenship, is irrelevant in a statutory interpleader proceeding. (But if Insurance Co. tried to proceed under Rule 22 interpleader, or by bringing a declaratory judgment action in which both Son and Daughter were defendants, there would be no subject matter jurisdiction—in that situation, the fact that Insurance Co. as plaintiff was a citizen of the same state as Daughter, a defendant, would violate the ordinary rule requiring complete diversity. Statutory interpleader is practically the only exception to the general rule requiring complete diversity.)

48. **(a)** Move to realign the parties according to their real interests. **The federal court will recognize the necessity of aligning the parties to their real interests.** The commissioner can make the strong argument that Tulip and the Blues are really on the same side of the controversy (both want the court to order the commissioner not to bar Tulip from the game). Therefore, the commissioner should argue, the real alignment of the parties is Tulip and the Blues as plaintiff against Major League Baseball as defendant. On that realignment, there is complete diversity of citizenship, and the case may therefore be heard by the federal court under its removal jurisdiction.

(b) Probably, but not certainly. **The federal court will indeed try to align the parties according to their real interests.** If the court concludes that the Blues really do have substantially the same interest in the litigation as Tulip does, it will order the realignment. But if it finds significant differences of interest between Tulip and the Blues (e.g., the Blues are subject to discipline by the commissioner, and will therefore during the litigation probably take actions urged by the commissioner even if these are against Tulip's interest), the court may decline to disturb the original alignment chosen by Tulip, in which event there will be no removal. See *Rose v. Giamatti*, 721 F. Supp. 906 (E.D. Oh. 1989), holding on similar facts that Pete Rose and the Cincinnati Reds were not really adverse parties, so diversity existed in Rose's suit against the commissioner and the Reds, and removal was proper.

Thus, a wise litigant in Tulip's position can, with some planning, concoct an alignment that will make the case harder to remove to federal court, but the defendant always has the opportunity to try to undo this cleverness by seeking a realignment.

49. Yes. **A special statutory provision provides that the executor's citizenship is irrelevant: "[T]he legal representative of the estate of a decedent shall be deemed to be a citizen only of the same state as the decedent. . . ." 28 U.S.C. §1332(c)(2).** Even though the case is captioned *Edward v. Dave*, and Edward and Dave are both citizens of Alabama, the case is treated as being one between a citizen of Mississippi and a citizen of Alabama; as such, it is removable at the urging of the defendant. So Pete's lawyer's clever strategy doesn't work.

50. Yes. **This case falls within the so-called *alienage* jurisdiction of 28 U.S.C. §1332(a)(2), covering suits between "citizens of a state, and citizens or subjects of a foreign state."**

51. No. **There is no federal statutory provision giving subject matter jurisdiction to a U.S. federal court over this suit. The closest statute is 28 U.S.C. §1332(a)(2)'s alienage jurisdiction, but that requires that there be a citizen of some American state (or a permanent resident alien living in**

some American state) on at least one side of the controversy. So a suit between two foreign citizens, even if it involves a cause of action that arose in the United States, may not be tried in federal court unless a federal question is presented.

52. **Yes. According to 28 U.S.C. §1332(a)(3), the federal courts have subject matter jurisdiction over suits between "citizens of different States and in which citizens or subjects of a foreign state are additional parties."** But for this provision to apply, there must be American citizens (from different states) on opposite sides of the controversy. Thus, if D2 were not a party, the suit could not proceed because there is nothing conferring nonfederal question jurisdiction over a case between a citizen of a state and a foreign citizen on one hand and a foreign citizen alone on the other hand.

53. **No. A corporation (whether plaintiff or defendant) is deemed to be a citizen *both* of the state where it has its principal place of business *and* the state where it is incorporated. 28 U.S.C. §1332(c)(1).** Putting this rule together with the rule requiring complete diversity, it becomes the case that D can be sued only if none of the Ps are citizens of *either* Delaware or New York. Since P1 is a citizen of Delaware, complete diversity is lacking and there is no diversity jurisdiction.

54. **Yes, probably. A corporation is deemed to be a citizen both of the state where it has its principal place of business and the state where it is incorporated.** There is no hard-and-fast test for determining where a corporation's principal place of business is. However, here, where the day-to-day headquarters are New York, and most business derives from New York, the court would almost certainly conclude that New York was the principal place of business even though a substantial minority of the business is done in New Jersey and the board of directors meets there.

55. **No. 28 U.S.C. §1359 provides that "a district court shall not have jurisdiction of a civil action in which any party, by assignment or otherwise, has been improperly or collusively . . . joined to invoke the jurisdiction of such court."** Since the sole reason for which Peter made the assignment to Paula was to create diversity, and since this assignment was collusive in the sense that it was not the product of an arm's-length economic bargain between Peter and Paula, the court will invoke §1359 and refuse to take jurisdiction. The fact that the assignment may have been valid and enforceable under South Carolina law is irrelevant for purposes of §1359.

56. **Yes, probably. There is no federal statute that directly bars the use of improper or collusive joinder for the purpose of defeating diversity (as there is a statutory provision, 28 U.S.C. §1359, barring improper or collusive joinder to *create* diversity).** However, federal courts have tended to disregard collusive or fraudulent joinders that are undertaken solely for the purpose of blocking diversity, and have therefore tended to allow the removal to take place as if the joinder had not occurred. See, e.g., *Rose v. Giamatti*. But it is not certain, merely likely, that a given federal court would so rule on these facts.

57. **Yes. There *is*, of course, *federal question jurisdiction*: A suit brought for damages based on the patent laws is based on a federal statute and thus presents a federal question.** There would not be diversity jurisdiction over this case, since D is deemed to be a citizen of both Ohio and Delaware, and there is a plaintiff who is nondiverse with D (P1, who is a citizen of Ohio). (The Constitution gives the federal government exclusive control over patents, so that states may not award patents; furthermore, a congressional statute gives the federal courts exclusive jurisdiction over actions to enforce patent rights.)

58. **No. The subject matter jurisdiction must be of the federal question sort. But it is well established that the federal question must be part of a "well-pleaded complaint." In other words, the federal question must be an integral part of the plaintiff's cause of action (as revealed by the plaintiff's complaint); it is not enough that the plaintiff anticipates a defense based on federal law or even

that the defendant's answer explicitly states a federal defense. Clearly there is no diversity of jurisdiction (since both parties are incorporated in Delaware and are thus deemed to be citizens of Delaware as well as of the state where they have their principal place of business). Since P's claim is founded solely upon state law (contract law), it is irrelevant that D has asserted a defense that derives entirely from a federal statute. See *Louisville & Nashville R.R. v. Mottley*, 211 U.S. 149 (1908).

59. No. **For diversity actions, the *amount in controversy* must exceed $75,000. See 28 U.S.C. §1332(a).** Since P is claiming only the amount of money due under the contract, and that amount comes to less than $75,000, this requirement is not satisfied. (Nor can costs, interest, or attorney's fees generally be included to meet the amount.)

60. (a) Yes. **Only if the court concluded that there was no possible way that P could recover more than $75,000 should the court have dismissed the action for the failure to meet the amount in controversy requirement.** The trial judge should not dismiss the action for lack of diversity jurisdiction merely because the amount finally recovered was less than the jurisdictional amount of $75,000. At the outset of the case, it appeared possible that P might recover more than $75,000. That being so, the court is not ousted of jurisdiction merely because the amount finally recovered is less.

   (b) The court should consider *denying costs* to P and in fact *imposing* costs on him. **According to 28 U.S.C. §1332(b), if a diversity plaintiff is finally found to be entitled to less than $75,000, the court may effectively penalize him or her for bringing a small case by denying him or her costs (even though he or she technically prevailed) and imposing the defendant's costs on him or her.** However, this is very rarely done, as long as the judge believes that the plaintiff acted in good faith in asserting his claim for more than $75,000. On the facts of the question, the trial court would probably not deny P costs or award costs to D.

61. Dismiss P's complaint for lack of subject matter jurisdiction. **For subject matter jurisdiction to be proper, there must at least be a chance that P would properly be entitled to recover more than $75,000.** Despite the jury verdict, the federal judge now knows that there was no chance that P would properly be entitled to recover more than $75,000, due to the unavailability of punitive damages. Therefore, the court now knows that it never had subject matter jurisdiction at all, so it should (and indeed must) dismiss the case even though the expense of a trial has already been incurred.

62. Unclear. **Courts are split as to whether what counts, for amount-in-controversy purposes, is the value "to the plaintiff" or the value "to the defendant."** One authority says that "the majority rule is that the jurisdictional amount is to be tested by the value to the plaintiff of the object that is sought to be gained." See F,K&M, p. 46. If so, the court will not hear the case since the value to P is less than the required $75,000.

63. Yes. **A plaintiff may "*aggregate*"—that is, add together—all of his claims against a single defendant for purposes of meeting the $75,000 diversity amount in controversy requirement.** This is true even if no single claim meets the jurisdictional amount by itself.

64. Yes. **In *Exxon Mobil Corp. v. Allapattah Services, Inc.*, 125 S. Ct. 2611 (2005), the Supreme Court held that when multiple plaintiffs join under Rule 20, as long as one satisfies the amount in controversy requirement, the doctrine of supplemental jurisdiction permits the other(s) to join in with claims that don't meet the requirement.** So here, because P1's claim is for more than $75,000, P2 can join the action under Rule 20(b) even though P2's claim is for less than $75,000.

65. No. **Supplemental jurisdiction can't be triggered unless at least one plaintiff independently satisfies the amount in controversy requirement.** Unlike the fact pattern where one claimant does meet

the jurisdictional amount and others do not, here neither plaintiff independently satisfies the amount in controversy requirement. Therefore, in this situation, supplemental jurisdiction does not apply. Given that supplemental jurisdiction does not apply, the question is whether aggregation among multiple plaintiffs is permitted. The answer is that aggregation is not permitted so long as the claims are "separate and distinct." See *Snyder v. Harris*, 394 U.S. 332 (1969). Here, even though the Ps both signed similarly worded contracts, and even though D carried out the alleged breach in a similar manner and at a similar time toward both Ps, a court would almost certainly regard the claims as "separate and distinct." Consequently, aggregation will not be allowed, and the case cannot go forward.

66. Yes. **Aggregation of claims is permitted as long as the claims are not "separate and distinct."** It is true that in a sense, P1 and P2 each have only $40,000 at stake, since each owns half the partnership. But here, the court would regard P1 and P2 as having a single "common and undivided interest" relative to D. Therefore, this fact pattern would fall within the narrow class of exceptions to the general rule that claims not individually meeting the amount in controversy requirement may not be aggregated—if the claims were "separate and distinct," aggregation would not be allowed (as in the prior question).

67. No. **It is well settled that the existence of a permissive counterclaim meeting the jurisdictional amount does not allow the defendant to remove the case to the federal courts.** P's claim and D's claim do not arise out of the same transaction or occurrence. Therefore, under federal law (and, therefore, by hypothesis, under Louisiana law), D's counterclaim is a permissive one and the case cannot be removed to federal court.

68. (a) **Supplemental jurisdiction.**

    (b) No, probably. **This fact pattern is a classic illustration of what was formerly known as pendent jurisdiction, and is now covered under the doctrine of supplemental jurisdiction. Supplemental jurisdiction, codified in 28 U.S.C. §1367, provides that in cases where "the district courts have original jurisdiction [over a federal question], the district court shall have supplemental jurisdiction over all other claims that are so related to claims in the action within such original jurisdiction that they form part of the same case or controversy under Article III." Supplemental jurisdiction applies to additional claims between the same two parties, as well as to "pendent parties" (third parties brought into the suit who are under the federal court's jurisdiction), provided that both claims derive from a common nucleus of operative fact (a requirement implied by the statute's reference to "Article III case or controversy").**

    Here, the federal court would not ordinarily have jurisdiction over the state unfair competition claim, because that claim apparently does not present a federal question, and there is no diversity between the parties (since both are citizens of Georgia). But since the antitrust claim presents a federal question, and since the practices that are being relied on by D to support that federal claim are the same as the practices that are alleged to violate the state statute, both claims derive from a "common nucleus of operative fact," and P would ordinarily be expected to try them all in one suit. The federal court would still be free to use its *discretion* to decline to hear the state-law claim, but on these facts it probably would hear the claim (since considerations of judicial economy and convenience militate in favor of hearing both claims).

69. No. **As a matter of federal subject matter jurisdiction, the federal court probably has the power to try the state-law claim on the grounds that that claim is within the court's supplemental jurisdiction, under 28 U.S.C. §1367. However, §1367 also provides (in subsection (c)(3)) that the court**

may "decline to exercise supplemental jurisdiction" if the federal claim is dismissed before trial. As a result, a court would most likely exercise its discretion and decline to hear the supplemental state claims.

70. No. **If a claim involves a "common nucleus of operative fact," it falls within the supplemental jurisdiction of the court. See 28 U.S.C. §1367.** Paula's second claim falls within the supplemental jurisdiction of the court, and Paula would normally try them both in the same proceeding. Before December 1990 (and the enactment of §1367), the Supreme Court's decision in *Finley v. U.S.*, 490 U.S. 545 (1989), meant that the doctrine of pendent jurisdiction did not offer Paula the right to bring in "pendent parties" unless Congress had expressly stated in the applicable statute (here the FTCA) that it would allow pendent parties.

However, when Congress in 1990 codified the doctrines of pendent and ancillary jurisdiction, one of the most important changes made was to specifically overrule *Finley* and allow "pendent parties" in federal question cases, as indicated by the last sentence of §1367(a): "Such supplemental jurisdiction shall include claims that involve the joinder or intervention of additional parties."

71. (a) Supplemental jurisdiction. **Where the plaintiff has a valid diversity claim against the defendant, the doctrine of supplemental jurisdiction often allows additional claims or parties to be brought into the litigation, even though the additional claim or party does not satisfy the requirement of diversity or the amount in controversy requirement ($75,000) applied in diversity actions.**

(b) No. **Supplemental jurisdiction (formerly known as ancillary jurisdiction in this context) will always encompass a defendant's compulsory counterclaim. According to Federal Rule 13(a), a counterclaim is compulsory "if the claim (A) arises out of the transaction or occurrence that is the subject matter of the opposing party's claim; and (B) does not require adding another party over whom the court cannot acquire jurisdiction."** By this test, D's counterclaim against P was a compulsory one, since both claims arose out of the same auto accident. Accordingly, the court will hear the counterclaim as part of its supplemental jurisdiction, even though that counterclaim does not independently meet the amount in controversy requirement for diversity suits.

72. No. **Just as the federal courts virtually always allow supplemental jurisdiction over a compulsory counterclaim, so they also allow supplemental jurisdiction over an additional party to a compulsory counterclaim.** Consequently, the fact that Xavier is a citizen of the same state as D (thus technically preventing complete diversity from existing) will be disregarded by the court. Although 28 U.S.C. §1367(b) does restrict certain types of joinder when the original claim is based on diversity, these restrictions do not apply to claims by defendants, nor do they apply to Rule 13 counterclaims.

73. Yes. **D's claim against P is a *permissive* counterclaim (Rule 13(b)), since it does not arise out of the transaction or occurrence that is the subject matter of the plaintiff's claim. Because this permissive counterclaim and the original claim do not derive from a common nucleus of operative fact, the counterclaim does not satisfy the standard of 28 U.S.C. §1367, and it will *not* fall under a court's supplemental jurisdiction.** For the same reason, D's claim against Wanda does not fall under supplemental jurisdiction. Therefore, D's claim must independently meet the federal subject matter jurisdictional requirements—that is, there must be either diversity or a federal question, and any applicable amount in controversy requirement must be satisfied. Since there is no federal question, and since D and Wanda are citizens of the same state (Oregon), the federal subject matter jurisdictional requirements are not satisfied, and Wanda is entitled to dismissal.

74. Yes. **A Rule 14 third-party claim brought by a third-party plaintiff (the defendant in the main action) against a third-party defendant is always considered to be within the supplemental jurisdiction of the court.** 28 U.S.C. §1367. However, the fact that supplemental jurisdiction will encompass the third-party claim against Ted under §1367 does not mean that the requirements of *personal* jurisdiction don't have to be satisfied as to Ted. For the third-party claim against Ted to be heard by the New York federal court, it must still be the case that Ted has minimum contacts with New York, which the facts say he does not.

75. No. **Where supplemental jurisdiction applies, courts generally hold that the supplemental claim need not independently satisfy the requirements of *venue*.** Thus, even if Denise and Ted are correctly regarded as both being defendants, the fact that all defendants do not reside in the same state or that the action was not brought where a substantial part of the cause of action arose will not make venue improper; the court will evaluate venue based on the original action (Pedro against Denise), and if it is proper there, the court will disregard the venue considerations as to the ancillary claim. Since the only defendant to the original claim (Denise) lives in New Jersey, venue is proper in that state.

76. Yes. **The fact that supplemental jurisdiction will encompass the third-party claim under §1367 does not mean that the requirements of *personal* jurisdiction don't have to be satisfied.** For the third-party claim against Ted to be heard by the New York federal court, it must still be the case that Ted has minimum contacts with New York, which the facts say he does not.

77. Yes. **A claim by the original plaintiff against the third-party defendant does not fall within the court's supplemental jurisdiction, so it must have independent jurisdictional grounds. §1367(b) excludes certain claims made *by plaintiffs* when the original claim is based on diversity. By specifically precluding claims by plaintiffs against persons made parties under Rule 14, §1367(b) preserves the result of *Owen Equipment & Erection Co. v. Kroger*, 437 U.S. 365 (1978).** Terry is a third-party defendant. In the absence of a federal question and in the absence of supplemental jurisdiction, Patricia and Terry must be citizens of different states, which they are not. Consequently, the court has no jurisdiction over Patricia's claim against Terry, and it must be dismissed.

Observe that there is a good rationale for denying supplemental treatment to Patricia's claim against Terry: Patricia would not have been able to institute an initial suit against both David and Terry, because of the lack of diversity between Patricia and Terry; it seems improper to allow Patricia to do indirectly (by dropping Terry from the initial suit, waiting for David to implead Terry as he will surely do, then making a third-party claim against Terry) what she may not do directly.

78. No, probably. **A claim by a third-party defendant against the original plaintiff is allowed by Federal Rule 14(a) if that claim arises out of "the transaction or occurrence that is the subject matter of the plaintiff's claim against the third-party plaintiff."** Since Terry's claim against Patricia arises out of the same tainted food episode as Patricia's claim against David, this "same transaction or occurrence" test seems to be satisfied. Since the two claims are so related, they will satisfy the "common nucleus of operative fact" requirement implied by 28 U.S.C. §1367 and will fall under the court's supplemental jurisdiction. Once supplemental jurisdiction applies, the fact that Terry is not of diverse citizenship is irrelevant, as long as the statute does not specifically preclude her claim.

Note that §1367(b), which restricts certain claims (including Rule 14) by *plaintiffs* in diversity cases, does not apply to the same claims by *defendants*. The theory in allowing the third-party defendant (here, Terry) to assert her claim while precluding the original plaintiff is that she has been hauled into federal court against her wishes. In allowing her to make a claim against the original plaintiff, we are not running the risk that she will thwart federal subject matter requirements by choosing to drop a party (as we risk in the case of a claim by Patricia against Terry).

79. Yes. **For diversity jurisdiction, there must be complete diversity between the parties.** Paul and Dexter are both citizens of Connecticut. Therefore, the requirement of complete diversity is not satisfied. Only if supplemental jurisdiction applies to Paul's claim against Dexter will there be federal subject matter jurisdiction (since there is no federal question). However, 28 U.S.C. §1367(b), the supplemental jurisdiction statute, clearly excludes claims by plaintiffs "against persons made parties under Rule 14, 19, 20, or 24." Therefore, Paul's claim against Dexter must independently meet federal subject matter jurisdiction requirements, which it cannot.

80. No. **Since §1367(b), which excludes certain types of claims in diversity actions, does not mention Rule 13 claims, Dale's claim can go forward.** Dale and Dolores are citizens of the same state, so Dale's claim against Dolores will have to be dismissed for lack of diversity (as well as failure to meet the amount in controversy requirement) unless the doctrine of supplemental jurisdiction applies. Because a cross-claim under Rule 13(g) must arise out of the same transaction or occurrence that is the subject matter of the original action, Dale's claim will satisfy the "common nucleus of operative fact" test that the supplemental jurisdiction statute requires. See 29 U.S.C. §1367(a). By not excluding claims like Dale's in diversity actions, §1367 preserves the general tendency of courts to allow what used to be called "ancillary" jurisdiction in defensive situations—i.e., claims by someone other than the original plaintiff.

81. Yes. **28 U.S.C. §1367(b), which excludes certain types of claims in diversity actions, specifically *bars* supplemental jurisdiction "over claims by persons . . . seeking to intervene as plaintiffs under Rule 24."** Since there is no diversity between Insurer and Restaurateur, and no federal question is present, Insurer's claim must be dismissed unless it comes within the court's supplemental jurisdiction.

82. Yes. **§1367(b) clearly bars claims by persons seeking to intervene under Rule 24 from falling under the court's supplemental jurisdiction.** Since Insurer's intervention would destroy diversity, and since there is no federal question posed, the court must grant Restaurateur's motion.

83. Probably dismiss the entire action! **Just as the supplemental jurisdiction statute disallows claims by persons seeking to intervene under Rule 24, it also will not permit claims by "persons proposed to be joined as plaintiffs under Rule 19." 28 U.S.C. §1367(b).** Because of the statute's general bias *against* plaintiffs who add parties, the net result here would be that Homeowner and Insurer have to co-sue Restaurateur in state court.

84. D should consider removing the case to New York federal district court. **Since the case could have been brought as a federal court action, D may cause it to be tried in the federal court system just as if P had filed it there. The suit will then take place in the district (and division, if there is more than one division in the district) encompassing the state courthouse where the suit was originally filed. See 28 U.S.C. §1441(a).**

85. Yes. **The federal courts only have removal jurisdiction of a case that could have been brought as an original action in the federal courts. For this purpose, "could have been brought" includes all requirements of federal subject matter jurisdiction, including any applicable amount in controversy requirement.** Since P's claim could only have been brought as a diversity action (no federal question is present), that claim must be for more than $75,000 to satisfy the amount in controversy requirement. P is deemed to be *master of her complaint*, and if she seeks less than $75,000, that is dispositive even though her claim could quite properly have been for more than the jurisdictional amount. So the federal judge, as in any situation where removal is not proper, should remand the case to state court.

86. Yes. Where a case is based solely on diversity, the defendant *may not remove if he or she is a citizen of the state where the action is pending*. (This restricts removal and diversity cases to situations in which the defendant would suffer from having to litigate "away" rather than "at home" if removal were not allowed.) Since a corporation is deemed to be a citizen of the state where it has its principal place of business as well as the state where it is incorporated, D is deemed a citizen of both New Jersey and Delaware, and may therefore not remove an action pending in the New Jersey courts.

87. No. **Where the plaintiff's claim raises a federal question, the defendant may remove even though the state court suit is pending in the state of which the defendant is a citizen.** This is the principal difference between removal jurisdiction in federal-question actions and removal in diversity suits (where a defendant may not remove if the suit is pending in his home state, as shown by the prior question).

88. Yes. **The rule that in a case founded solely on diversity, the defendant may not remove if he is a citizen of the state where the action is pending, applies quite strictly to multidefendant actions—it must be the case that *none* of the defendants properly served and joined is a citizen of the state where the action is pending. 28 U.S.C. §1441(b).** Since D1 is a citizen of New Jersey, where the suit is pending, D2's chance to remove is spoiled.

89. (a) Yes. **As long as a federal question is present, it does not matter that one (or indeed all) of the defendants is a citizen of the state where the action is pending.** The removal is proper, and it will stand.

    (b) **In suits involving a federal question, venue based on the residence of one of the defendants is available only if *all* defendants reside in the same state.** Since D1 and D2 are from different states, this provision does not apply. See 28 U.S.C. §1391(b)(1). Since venue would lie in New York if based on the district where a substantial part of the cause of action arose, there is nothing that would have allowed P to bring suit in New Jersey federal court. Since a district for venue is available (New York), the "catch all" provision of §1391(b)(3) (allowing venue where any defendant may be found) does not apply. Because of the peculiar operation of the removal statute, the case ends up in a district in which it could never have been brought. The anomaly is that the suit ends up in the New Jersey federal district court even though venue restrictions would have prevented P from bringing it there in the first place.

90. Yes. **A plaintiff may *never* remove.** This is true even if the plaintiff is a defendant to an unrelated (and unexpected) counterclaim, and even if the case is such that the defendant would have the right to remove (as D does here). So P must carefully consider the desirability of a federal forum before bringing any case in state court—by the act of suing first, he loses all right to remove, even if there should develop a counterclaim against him.

91. Yes. **Since there is no diversity of citizenship between P and D, the case could only be removed if it raises a federal question. The standard for determining whether a case presents a federal question is the same for removal cases as for cases originally filed in state court. That is, the federal question must be raised by the *plaintiff's* claim, not merely by the defendant's defense.** Here, P's claim is a purely state-law claim, so the fact that D's antitrust defense raises a federal question is irrelevant—no federal question is presented, and there is therefore no removal jurisdiction.

92. Yes. **Where there are multiple defendants, *all* defendants, not just a majority, must sign the notice of removal.** See Wr., p. 242.

93. Yes. **28 U.S.C. §1446(b) provides that the notice of removal must be filed within 30 days after the defendant received service of the complaint.** Since D filed the notice later than August 5, his right to remove was time-barred.

94. No. **Normally, a notice of removal must be filed within 30 days of the time when the defendant receives the complaint. But if the complaint as originally served is or seems to be ineligible for removal, and later events make the case removable, the defendant may file a notice of removal so long as he or she acts within 30 days of the time when the case became removable.** When the Virginia court dropped D2 from the suit on November 1 (thus creating the required complete diversity and also making it the case that no defendant was a citizen of the state where the action was pending), the case became removable. Therefore, D1 had until November 30 to file his notice of removal. See 28 U.S.C. §1446(b). (But in a diversity case, removal may not occur more than one year after commencement of the action even if the case has just recently become removable. *Id.*)

95. Larry. **Federal Rule 11 provides that "every pleading . . . must be signed by at least one attorney of record in the attorney's name."**

96. Move for Rule 11 sanctions against Paul and/or Larry. **Rule 11 states that "by presenting [a pleading] to the court . . . an attorney or unrepresented party is certifying that to the best of the person's knowledge, information, and belief, formed after an *inquiry reasonable under the circumstances* . . . (3) the factual contentions have evidentiary support." The rule goes on to say that if there is a violation, "the court may impose an appropriate sanction." Possible sanctions include "an order to pay a penalty to the court."**

    Although Larry acted in good faith in signing the pleading, he almost certainly did not act "after reasonable inquiry." For instance, reasonable inquiry would almost certainly have included getting a copy of the police report, which would have led Larry to realize that Dennis, not Dave, should be the defendant. Assuming that the court agrees that Larry acted without making reasonable inquiries, the court could award sanctions against either Larry or Paul. Since Paul is the guiltier of the two (his wrongdoing was deliberate), the court will almost certainly award sanctions against Paul, and possibly against Larry as well. The court should probably order Paul and/or Larry to pay Dave the $10,000 that Dave has spent in attorney's fees defending the suit.

97. No. **Federal Rule 8(d)(2) provides that "a party may set out two or more statements of a claim or defense alternately or hypothetically."** It will be up to the judge and/or jury at trial to decide which, if either, of P's claims has merit.

98. No. **Since the case is brought in diversity, the $75,000 amount in controversy requirement must be met. A federal court complaint is required to include "a short and plain statement of the grounds for the court's jurisdiction." Federal Rule 8(a)(1). This is interpreted to require, in the case of a diversity suit, a statement that more than $75,000 is at stake.** Consequently, P must amend her complaint to state something like, "As the result of D's negligence, P has suffered injuries aggregating more than $75,000."

99. No. **According to Federal Rule 54(c), "Except as to a party against whom a judgment is entered by default, every final judgment shall grant the relief to which the party in whose favor it is rendered is entitled, *even if the party has not demanded such relief in the party's pleadings*."** Therefore, the fact that P only asked for $200,000, and even the fact that P did not specifically request punitive damages, are irrelevant: If the jury (and the federal judge reviewing the jury's verdict) concludes that P is entitled to this relief, the fact that the complaint did not ask for it will make no difference.

100. No. **Federal Rule 54(c) provides that "a default judgment must not differ in kind from, or exceed in amount, what is demanded in the pleadings."** In other words, P may not recover more than the $200,000 he asked for in his complaint, given the fact that the judgment is by default. The rationale for this rule is that the defendant is entitled to know how much is at stake, and is entitled to rely on that amount in deciding whether it is worthwhile to contest liability.

101. (a) No. **Federal Rule 9 sets out certain matters that must be pleaded in extra detail, called "special matters." One of these is fraud, as detailed in Rule 9(b): "In alleging fraud or mistake, a party must state with particularity the circumstances constituting fraud or mistake."** P's conclusory statement that D fraudulently induced him to enter into the contract (without a statement of what the fraudulent misrepresentations were, or how D knew that these representations were false) seems not to satisfy this requirement of particularity.

(b) Make a Rule 12(e) motion for more definite statement. **Under Rule 12(e), a defendant can move for a more definite statement if the complaint is "so vague or ambiguous that [the defendant] cannot reasonably prepare a response."** If this motions fails, then at the least, D would be entitled in discovery to probe the details of how P thinks D behaved fraudulently.

102. No. **Rule 15(a) provides that "a party may amend its pleading once as a matter of course within . . . 21 days after service of a responsive pleading."** Since D has not yet served his responsive pleading (i.e., his answer), P has the right to make one amendment even without permission of the court or of his adversary. (D's filing of a motion against the complaint is not deemed to be a "responsive pleading" for this purpose.)

103. Yes, probably. **If a plaintiff's initial claim is dismissed by the court on a Rule 12(b)(6) motion and the plaintiff repleads, he or she will generally be able to argue (after the trial on the amended claim) that the original dismissal was improper, if the amendment was a substantively significant one.** Here, where P was forced to change the entire legal theory behind his action, the appeals court would probably hear and decide P's argument that he should have been allowed to sue on a product liability theory.

104. By asserting the affirmative defense of Statute of Frauds. **Rule 8(c) states that a party shall "set forth affirmatively" a number of defenses, including Statute of Frauds.** A defendant who does not specifically plead an affirmative defense may be held at trial to have waived the right to present evidence on that defense.

105. Move for leave to amend his answer. **According to Rule 15(a), the time on leave to amend as of right runs out after 21 days following service of the complaint.** Thus, it is too late for D to amend as of right so as to raise the affirmative defense of Statute of Frauds. So D must procure leave from the court. However, the rule states that "the court should freely give leave when justice so requires." On these facts, the prejudice to P from allowing the Statute of Frauds defense to be raised is small—P would not be in a materially worse position if the defense is allowed now than if it had been properly raised in the first instance. Therefore, the court will probably grant D's motion for leave to replead. In the amended answer, D should specifically assert the affirmative defense that the contract is unenforceable due to the Statute of Frauds.

106. July 26. **Even though the case is deemed commenced by filing the complaint with the court (see Federal Rule 3), D's time to answer does not start to run until he receives service. Under Rule 12(a) D generally has 21 days from receipt of summons and complaint within which to answer.**

107. Yes. **Normally, Rule 12(a) requires a defendant to serve his or her answer within 21 days after he received service of the summons and complaint. But that rule contains an exception: If service is made outside the forum state pursuant to Federal Rule 4(k) (allowing the use of the forum state's long-arm statute), the time that long-arm statute allows for service of the answer controls.** Since the New Jersey long-arm gives 30 days, D's time to answer has not yet expired on July 29.

108. September 14. **Rule 12(a)(4)(A) states that where the court denies a motion brought under Rule 12, the responsive pleading shall be served within 14 days after notice of the court's action.**

109. No. **In cases in which the Plaintiff's claim arises under the federal Constitution or a federal statute (i.e., federal-question cases), the action is deemed commenced, for statute of limitations purposes, by the filing of a complaint with the court. (Rule 3.)** Therefore, at least as to P's original complaint, P satisfied the statute of limitations by filing before July 5, even though service was not made on D until after this date.

    Second, when P served the amended complaint on July 25, P got the benefit of Rule 15(c)(1)(B), which provides that "[a]n amendment to a pleading relates back to the date of the original pleading when . . . the amendment asserts a claim or defense that arose out of the conduct, transaction, or occurrence set out—or attempted to set out—in the original pleading." The same transaction (importation of a particular machine violating P's patents) is charged in both complaints, despite the fact that the patent number changed. Therefore, the amended complaint relates back to the original July 1 complaint filing, and is timely.

110. No. **If there is a change of party, relation back may still help the plaintiff. But for the amended complaint to relate back in this changed-party situation, the plaintiff must pass three obstacles: (1) the claim must arise out of the same conduct, transaction or occurrence as the original complaint; (2) before the time for service of the summons and complaint has expired, the new defendant must have "received such notice of the action that it will not be prejudiced in defending on the merits"; and (3) before the time for serving the complaint and summons has expired, it must be the case that the new defendant "knew or should have known that would have been brought against it, but for a mistake concerning the proper party's identity." Federal Rule 15(c)(1)(C)(ii).** Since requirement (1) appears satisfied, the issue is whether (2) and (3) are.

    According to Rule 4(m), the time limit for service of the summons and complaint is 120 days after the complaint is filed. Since Owner was indeed served before this time expired (on July 12), and since Owner should have known that the action would be brought against him (from the conversation on July 10), the action is not time-barred and Owner's motion should not be granted.

111. Deny it. **Rule 15(b) provides that "when an issue not raised by the pleadings is tried by the parties' express or implied consent, it must be treated in all respects as if raised in the pleadings."** When Carco remained silent in the face of P's presentation of evidence on negligence, Carco was implicitly consenting to the trial of this issue, so the court will treat the case as if the complaint alleged negligence by Carco.

112. Allow P to amend the complaint to allege negligence. **Rule 15(b) states that "[t]he court should freely permit an amendment when doing so will aid in presenting the merits and the objecting party fails to satisfy the court that the evidence would prejudice that party's action or defense on the merits. The court may grant a continuance to enable the objecting party to meet the evidence."** Here, it is very unlikely that Carco will show that its ability to maintain its defense on the merits would be prejudiced by allowing P to bring a negligence claim: Negligence is so closely allied to strict product liability that Carco should have foreseen the possibility that the carefulness of

its conduct might be called into question. In any event, any possible prejudice to Carco can be cured by giving Carco a continuance, during which it can come up with evidence to rebut the negligence charge.

113. **Yes. Even though it is true that the answer would consist solely of hearsay material, which would be inadmissible at trial, Rule 26(b)(1) states that the information sought in discovery "need not be admissible at the trial if the discovery appears reasonably calculated to lead to the discovery of admissible evidence."** Here, D's answer to the question will at least tell P whether it is worthwhile to conduct discovery of W (which may in turn produce admissible evidence), and may lead to admissible evidence in other not easily foreseen ways. Therefore, the court will almost certainly hold that the defendant must answer the question.

114. **No. According to Federal Rule 26(b)(1), parties may obtain discovery "regarding any nonprivileged matter that is relevant to any party's claim or defense." In diversity actions, the rules of privilege are those of the state whose substantive law controls the action.** The facts tell us that according to state law here, the question asked by L would require D to divulge information protected by the attorney-client privilege. Therefore, the court will not order D to answer the question.

115. **No. The notes clearly fall within the *work-product immunity* of Federal Rule 26(b)(3). In fact, the notes probably come within the "absolute" protection given by 26(b)(3)(B), under which, if the court orders discovery of materials prepared in anticipation of litigation or for trial, the court "must protect against disclosure of the mental impressions, conclusions, opinions, or legal theories of a party's attorney or other representative concerning the litigation."** Since L has written down only what he thinks is important, his notes of necessity contain his "mental impressions" and probably his "opinions." Therefore, the court is almost certain to reject discovery of those notes even if P needs them very badly (e.g., because W has died).

116. (a) **No. Since the statement was prepared by a party "in anticipation of litigation," it falls within the work-product immunity of Rule 26(b)(3). Since the statement consists mostly of the words of W, and probably has no mental impressions, conclusions, etc., by I or anyone else working for D, it probably is covered only by the "qualified" rather than "absolute" immunity. Therefore, P can get the statement if he can show that he has "substantial need for the materials . . . and [he] cannot, without undue hardship, obtain their substantial equivalent by other means."** But since W is available to be interviewed directly by P, P probably cannot make this showing of hardship. Therefore, he probably cannot get discovery of the transcript.

(b) **Yes. Since W has now died, presumably P can show that he "cannot, without undue hardship, obtain their substantial equivalent by other means." Therefore, he should be able to override the qualified immunity given to this transcript by Rule 26(b)(3).**

As to both (a) and (b), observe that the work-product immunity provision of Rule 26(b)(3) applies not only to work product prepared by a lawyer but also to anything prepared by a party's "representative (including the other party's attorney, consultant, surety, indemnitor, insurer, or agent)." So the fact that I, who helped prepare the materials, is not a lawyer is irrelevant as long as he was acting as D's representative.

117. **Yes, probably. Despite Rule 26(b)(3), most courts have held that in an interrogatory, a plaintiff may be required to state his or her legal theories about the case, and his or her interpretation of how the law applies to the particular facts.** A court might reach this result by concluding that the question is only asking what the plaintiff is asserting as a public theory in this action and is not asking for P's (or her lawyer's) "secret" theories. A court also might rely on Rule 33(a), stating that "an

interrogatory is not objectionable merely because it asks for an opinion or contention that relates to fact or the application of law to fact." The questions here relate to the application of law to fact, rather than to pure legal theory; they are the equivalent of the question "State whether you are asserting that the defendant's particular conduct in this case constituted the tort of negligence, the tort of strict product liability, or both."

118. Yes. **Rule 26(b)(3)(C), provides that even though a party's statement made to the other party is technically work product, it is still discoverable: "Any party or other person may, on request and without the required showing [of special need], obtain the person's own previous statement about the action or its subject matter."** So P is entitled to the transcript even without any showing of special need.

119. D must furnish a copy or description of item (1) but need not disclose the existence of item (2). **Under Rule 26(a)(1)(A), "a party must, without awaiting a discovery request, provide to the other parties . . . (ii) a copy—or description by category and location—of all documents, electronically stored information, and tangible things that the disclosing party has in its possession, custody, or control and may use to support its claims or defenses, unless the use would be solely for impeachment."** So D must automatically furnish P with a copy or description of item (1) (the market research report), since D plans to introduce that as part of its substantive case at trial. (If D doesn't do this, the court must exclude the document from evidence, under Rule 37(c).) But D does not have to automatically furnish a copy or description of item (2) (the email), since D does not plan to use that document in its case. If P submits a valid discovery request that would call for disclosure of the email's existence (e.g., a Rule 34 document production request calling for "all documents or files in D's possession referring to D's decision to incorporate a free browser in D's operating system"), then D would have to produce the email—but D has no obligation to disclose the email automatically, as it does with the items it plans to use in its case.

120. Yes, probably. **Rule 26(a), allows discovery of "the name and, if known, the address and telephone number of each individual likely to have discoverable information."** Even though the names and addresses of eyewitnesses here were assembled only through work done by Pedestrian's representative in anticipation of litigation, a court will probably hold that this sentence overrides the work-product immunity. A court might well reason that it is more important for each side to be able to present at trial the testimony of any witness who has firsthand information than it is to protect a party's incentive to do substantial trial preparation without the disincentive of having to share that preparation with the other side. But this result is not certain.

121. **(a)** D need not do anything; P has an obligation to automatically disclose this information. **Under Rule 26(a)(2)(A), "A party must disclose to other parties the identity of any witness it may use at trial to present [expert] evidence."** This disclosure is "automatic," in the sense that the adversary does not have to ask for it. The disclosure must be made at least 90 days before trial. Rule 26(a)(2)(D).

     (b) Again, D need not do anything; P has an obligation to provide a report prepared by Firefly. **Under 26(a)(2)(B), the party preparing to call a retained expert must automatically provide to the other party "a written report—prepared and signed by the [expert] witness." The report must contain "a complete statement of all opinions the witness will express and the basis and reasons for them," as well as the data relied on, any exhibits to be used, the witness's qualifications and publications, the compensation to be paid the witness for testifying, and even a list of all cases in which the witness has testified as an expert in the previous four years.** *Id.*

(c) Yes, after the report is provided. **FRCP 26(b)(4)(A) says that a party may "depose any person who has been identified as an expert whose opinions may be presented at trial." The rule goes on to specify that where a report is to be provided by the expert, as Firefly would have to do here (see (b) above), the deposition may not be conducted until after the report has been provided.**

122. P must amend its response unless the error has already been called to D's attention. **Under Rule 26(e)(1), "[a] party who has made a disclosure under Rule 26(a)—or who has responded to an interrogatory, request for production, or request for admission—must supplement or correct its disclosure or response: (A) in a timely manner if the party learns that in some material respect the disclosure or response is incomplete or incorrect, and if the additional or corrective information has not otherwise been made know to the other parties during the discovery process or in writing."** Since P has now learned that its answer was materially incorrect (the place and date of this key conversation would surely be material), P must file an amended response, as long as D has not learned of the error in some other way.

123. L does not need to do anything; D's lawyer must disclose this information automatically. **Under Rule 26(a)(1)(A), "a party must, without awaiting a discovery request, provide to the other parties: . . . (iv) for inspection and copying as under Rule 34, any insurance agreement under which an insurance business may be liable to satisfy all or part of a possible judgment."** This mandatory disclosure must occur early on in the case.

124. No. **Only *parties* may be served with, and are required to respond to, interrogatories. See Federal Rule 33(a).** If a party wishes to get discovery from a nonparty witness, this must usually be done by taking the witness's deposition.

125. No. **Federal Rule 45(c)(3)(A)(ii), which protects persons subject to subpoenas, states that a court shall quash a subpoena if it "requires a person who is [not] a party . . . to travel more than 100 miles from where the person resides, is employed, or regularly transacts business in person."** Since a 1,300-mile trip from Miami to New York goes far beyond the 100 miles ordinarily contemplated for a subpoena, it is highly unlikely that a court would uphold the necessary subpoena. (But if P's lawyer is willing to travel to Miami to conduct the deposition, the lawyer can serve the subpoena for deposition on W at W's residence. And that's true even if P's lawyer is not admitted to practice in Florida. See Rule 45(a)(3)(B), authorizing an attorney as an officer of the court to issue a subpoena for a deposition in another district, "if the attorney is authorized to practice in the court where the action is pending.")

126. Move pursuant to Rule 37(c) for expenses for failure to admit. **Rule 37(c) provides: "If a party fails to admit what is requested under Rule 36 and if the requesting party later proves a document to be genuine or the matter true, the requesting party may move that the party who failed to admit pay the reasonable expenses, including attorney's fees, incurred in making that proof."** The court must grant the order unless it finds good reason for the failure to admit (including that the party failing to admit had reasonable grounds to believe that she might prevail on the matter). On these facts, however, there was no good reason for D's failure to admit the genuineness of the contract (the desire to play "hardball" is not a good reason), so the court will order D to pay to P the costs of retaining the handwriting expert and the attorney's fees associated with the proof of genuineness, even though D prevailed on the overall merits of the action.

127. No. **A Rule 34 request to produce documents may be served *only on a party*. To compel the police department to deliver the report, P must cause the clerk of the court to issue a subpoena *duces tecum* on the department, pursuant to Rule 45.**

128. No. **Unlike nearly all the other discovery tools, the right to require another party to undergo a physical examination may be accomplished only by *obtaining a court order*.** According to Rule 35(a), if the mental or physical condition of a party is "in controversy," the court where the action is pending may order that party to submit to a physical or mental examination. The order may only be made upon a showing of "good cause." Here, if D makes a motion to have P subjected to a physical examination, the court will almost certainly grant D's motion, since P's physical condition is clearly in controversy and there is no other good way to ascertain the truth of P's claim of disability.

129. (a) Yes. **Rule 35(b)(1) provides: "The party who moved for the examination must, on request, deliver to the requester a copy of the examiner's report, together with like reports of all earlier examinations of the same condition. The request may be made by the party against whom the examination order was issued or by the person examined."**

(b) Yes. **By making the request for a copy, D will be held to have *waived his physician-patient privilege* as to any prior or subsequent examinations made as to the same condition. Rule 35(b)(4).**

130. Seek a protective order limiting how the information can be used. **Federal Rule 26(c) allows the federal court to issue, on motion by a party from whom discovery is sought, a protective order protecting the requesting party from annoyance, embarrassment, oppression, etc.** One of the steps the court can order is "that a trade secret or other confidential research, development, or commercial information not be revealed or be revealed only in a specified way." D should seek an order that the information sought be used by P only for purposes of the litigation, that it not be used in P's business operations, and that it not be disclosed to any third parties. The Supreme Court has held that such an antidisclosure protective order will generally not violate the First Amendment free speech rights of the other party (here, P). See *Seattle Times Co. v. Rhinehart*, 467 U.S. 20 (1984).

131. Issue a notice of deposition to the corporation itself. **Federal Rule 30(b)(6) states, "It its notice or subpoena, a party may name as the deponent a public or private corporation, a partnership, an association, a governmental agency, or other entity and must describe with reasonable particularity the matters for examination. The named organization must then designate one or more officers, directors, or managing agents, or designate other persons who consent to testify on its behalf; and it may set out the matters on which each person designated will testify. A subpoena must advise a nonparty organization of its duty to make this designation. The persons designated must testify about information known or reasonably available to the organization."** P should therefore in its notice of deposition state that the examination will concern the procedure by which the steering wheel was designed and any facts known to the corporation regarding the safety of that design. It will then be up to D to designate one of its present or former employees to give the testimony; this employee, to the extent he or she does not have firsthand information, will be required to get it from others within D's organization.

132. (a) No. **Federal Rule 37(a)(3)(C) provides, "When taking an oral deposition, the party asking a question may complete or adjourn the examination before moving for an order [compelling discovery]."** Thus, P's lawyer had the choice between adjourning the deposition immediately, when D refused to answer, or continuing with the session while asking for an order later.

(b) D may have to pay P's expenses in obtaining the order compelling discovery. **According to Federal Rule 37(a)(5)(A), "if the motion is granted . . . the court must, after giving an opportunity to be heard, require the party or deponent whose conduct necessitated the motion, the party or attorney advising that conduct, or both to pay the movant's reasonable expenses incurred in making the motion, including attorney's fees. But the court must not order this payment** if: (i) the movant filed the motion before attempting in good faith to obtain the disclosure or discovery without court action; (ii) the opposing party's nondisclosure, response, or objection was substantially justified; or (iii) other circumstances make an award of expenses unjust." So, if the court finds that D's claim of privilege was not only incorrect but frivolous, the court will probably order D to pay P's expenses, including attorney's fees incurred in obtaining the order compelling discovery. So, it's not necessarily risk-free for D to play "hardball" during the discovery stage.

133. **Yes. Federal Rule 32(a)(3) states, "An adverse party may use for any purpose the deposition of a party or anyone who, when deposed, was the party's officer, director, managing agent, or designee under Rule 30(b)(6) or 31(a)(4)."** Here, at the time of deposition, Smith was a person designated under Rule 30(b)(6) (by which the deposing party serves a notice of deposition on the corporation without naming an individual, and the corporation designates the person to answer the questions). Therefore, Smith's answers can be used against D even though Smith was no longer in D's employ at the time of the deposition. This is true even if Smith is available to testify at trial.

134. **No. A nonparty deponent's deposition testimony may be admitted for substantive purposes only under narrowly defined circumstances, relating to the witness's unavailability to give live testimony. See Federal Rule 32(a)(4).**

135. **Yes. "Any party may use a deposition to contradict or impeach the testimony given by the deponent as a witness, or for any other purpose allowed by the Federal Rules of Evidence." Federal Rule 32(a)(2).** The use here is for impeachment, so it is covered by Rule 32(a)(2).

136. **Yes. The deposition of any witness (whether party or nonparty) may be introduced for substantive purposes if any of a number of special circumstances exist. One of these circumstances is "that the witness is more than 100 miles from the place of hearing or trial or is outside the United States, unless it appears that the witness's absence was procured by the party offering the deposition." Rule 32(a)(4)(B).** Since W is 3,000 miles away from the place of trial, and since she is at her home (making it unlikely that her absence was procured by P), P is entitled to offer the deposition as substantive evidence. This is true even though W has every reason to be friendly to P (since they were friends before the action), and it is true even though admission deprives D of the ability to cross-examine W.

137. (a) **Yes. Federal Rule 33(c) states that "an answer to an interrogatory may be used to the extent allowed by the Federal Rules of Evidence." Since an interrogatory may only be addressed to a party, and since by Federal Rule of Evidence 801(d)(2)(A), a party's statement is not classified as hearsay and is admissible against him of her for any purpose, an interrogatory answer will always be admissible against the party who made it.** Therefore, D's interrogatory answer may be used substantively against him.

(b) **Yes. Although a party's interrogatory answer is always admissible against him or her (whether for substantive or impeachment purposes), that answer is not "binding" on him or her.** That is, the party who has given the interrogatory answer is always free at trial to state that his or her answer was wrong, and it is up to the jury to decide whether to believe what the defendant says at trial or what he or she said in the interrogatory. (Contrast this with the response to a Rule 36 request to admit, which *is* binding on the party making the admission.)

138. **No. By the explicit terms of Rule 36(a), a request for admission is made "for purposes of the pending action only."** Therefore, Donna's admission is not even admissible in the second action, let alone binding on her.

139. **No. There is neither a state nor a federal statute on the matter. State common law creates the right being sued upon. Therefore, the federal court in diversity *must apply the common law (judge-made law) of the state where the federal court sits* and may not apply the federal judge's own opinion of what a desirable rule would be. See *Erie RR v. Tompkins*, 304 U.S. 64 (1938).** Since all of the evidence is that the Iowa Supreme Court would not impose any duty of inspection on D here, the federal court may not impose any such duty either.

140. **Yes. In an *Erie* situation, the issue is always "What would the highest court of the state where the federal court sits do today?" Existing precedents from intermediate-level courts (even precedents from the highest state court) are only clues to help the federal court answer this question; they are not dispositive.** So if the federal court's best judgment is that the Iowa Supreme Court would overrule the intermediate-level decision, then the federal court must behave the same way, by applying the duty of inspection to D.

141. **Yes. Again, the only issue is what the highest court of the state where the federal court sits would do if it heard the issue *today*.** Since the facts indicate that the Iowa Supreme Court would probably overturn its 50-year-old ruling today, the federal court is not bound by that old ruling, and is instead required to behave as it thinks the Iowa court would behave today, by imposing the duty on D.

142. **No. If an issue falls within the *Erie* principle, it is *never too late* to change the federal decision to conform to a new pronouncement of state law, until the final appeal has been disposed of.** Thus a federal appellate court must rely on a new decision of the state's highest court even if that decision is handed down after the federal district court action was completed.

143. California's. **In deciding an *Erie* case, the federal judge must apply the law of the state where the federal court sits. This principle includes the forum state's *conflict-of-laws principles* as well as its substantive principles.** Therefore, the federal judge must apply California's conflicts rules. Since California's conflicts rules would make California rather than Arizona law applicable, the court must follow California's substantive rules as well. One way to remember this is to apply the general principle that the federal court must *reach the same underlying decision* as the court of the state where the federal judge sits. (Observe that if California would apply Arizona law, then the task for the federal judge is not to apply what it thinks Arizona's state courts would decide but, rather, to apply what it thinks California's courts would think that Arizona's laws are!) See *Klaxon Co. v. Stentor Electric Mfg. Co.*, 313 U.S. 487 (1941).

144. P. **The federal court must follow the rules governing the allocation of the burden of proof in force in the state where the federal court is sitting.** In this sense, allocation of burden of proof is treated as being essentially "substantive" rather than "procedural." Consequently, even though there seems to be a weak federal policy in favor of putting the burden of proof on this issue on D (since he bears the burden of pleading it), the state policy will control. One way of rationalizing this approach is to note that the burden of proof on assumption of risk in a case like this is heavily *outcome determinative*; a plaintiff who knew that this would be an important issue on which there would be no clear evidence might well "forum shop" as between state and federal court based on the two forums' approaches, so the federal court should discourage this forum shopping by following state law. See *Palmer v. Hoffman*, 318 U.S. 109 (1943).

145. **Yes. This is an instance in which the federal policy is embodied in a Federal Rule of Civil Procedure that is exactly on point, and that is in direct conflict with the relevant state rule. In situations involving such a direct conflict, *Erie* doctrine (and the avoidance of forum shopping) does not apply at all. Instead, the sole question is *whether the federal rule is a valid one*.** See

Hanna v. Plumer, 380 U.S. 460 (1965). Since no Federal Rule of Civil Procedure has ever been found invalid under the Rules Enabling Act (i.e., no rule has ever been found to violate the Enabling Act's ban on the abridgement or enlargement of a litigant's substantive rights), Rule 18(a)'s rule of permissive joinder is certainly valid. Therefore, the federal court must follow Rule 18(a) and must disregard the policy behind the conflicting state rule. See *Har-Pen Truck Lines, Inc. v. Mills*, 378 F.2d 705 (5th Cir. 1967).

146. **Yes. In diversity suits, the federal court must *apply the state-law statute of limitations*.** Even though a statute of limitations has a "procedural" aspect, the choice of statute of limitations is heavily outcome determinative. For example, here P will be allowed to maintain his suit if the federal laches approach is used, but will not be allowed to maintain suit at all if the state statute of limitations is used—the choice of law, therefore, is *completely* outcome determinative. The doctrine that state statutes of limitations control in diversity actions is the central holding of one of the most important *Erie* cases of all, *Guaranty Trust Co. v. York*, 326 U.S. 99 (1945).

147. **No. In a suit based on diversity, state law controls on the issue of when the action is deemed "commenced" for statute of limitations purposes.** This is an instance in which a federal rule and state law seem to conflict, but really do not. That is, the U.S. Supreme Court has determined that Federal Rule 3 merely sets a commencement date for purposes of measuring other dates under the Federal Rules (e.g., the last date on which P may make service on D without seeking leave of court; see Rule 4(m)); Rule 3 was not intended by Congress to define "commencement" for statute of limitations purposes. Since there is no real conflict between the Federal Rule and the state law, state law must control. Therefore, New Jersey law holding that the action is not commenced for statute of limitations purposes until service is made on D controls, and P's action is time-barred. See *Walker v. Armco Steel Corp.*, 446 U.S. 740 (1980).

148. **The jury. Here, no valid federal rule applies on its face to the controversy; therefore, courts do not use a *Hanna v. Plumer* analysis. Instead, courts conduct a rough kind of balancing between the strength of the competing federal and state interests.** Here, the federal policy of having disputed factual issues determined by the jury is a strong one, as is the federal interest in having its procedural preferences control in federal trials. Conversely, the state interest in having the judge decide the issue appears to be a relatively weak one. Also, the likelihood that the choice of law on this issue will be outcome determinative is relatively small: It is hard to say that P has a significantly better or worse chance of prevailing on the issue based on whether state or federal law is used. Since the federal policy outweighs the state policy, the court should probably apply federal law and have the issue decided by the jury. See *Byrd v. Blue Ridge Rural Electric Co-op, Inc.*, 356 U.S. 525 (1958) (holding that the issue of whether plaintiff was a "statutory employee" should be determined by the jury rather than the judge, even though under state law the issue would be decided by the judge).

149. **Yes, probably. Here we have a situation in which there is no federal rule directly on point, and in which we must therefore balance the federal and state interests.** The state's interest (avoiding congestion in its courts) is a relatively weak one, and is in any event not ill served by having the federal court hear the case (since if the federal court hears it, congestion in the state courts is not worsened). There are at least two reasonably strong federal interests: (1) the interest in allowing joinder of multiple defendants, especially where the defendants reside in different states and could not both be served in any single state other than Illinois; and (2) the interest in preventing discrimination against nonresidents—Illinois' statute discriminates against out-of-state plaintiffs in favor of in-state plaintiffs, since the in-state plaintiff may sue a foreign corporation in Illinois, while the out-of-state plaintiff may not. On the other hand, the issue is very strongly outcome determinative—P simply cannot bring the suit

in the Illinois state courts, but can bring it in federal court if federal policies are followed, so there is a complete divergence of outcome based on the choice.

However, remember that outcome determinativeness is not dispositive: if strong federal policies are matched against much weaker state policies, the federal court may apply federal law even if this has a somewhat outcome-determinative effect. Consequently, it is probable (but by no means certain) that the federal court would apply federal policies, and would therefore allow the suit to proceed even though it could not proceed in state court.

150. No. **Here, there is a conflict between a federal policy not embodied specifically in a Federal Rule or statute and a state policy or statute. Therefore, the court must balance the two.** The state interest here is relatively weak, and is in any event not thwarted by following the federal policy (since the number of hung juries and thus retrials in state court will probably not be increased if the federal court has a hung jury). Conversely, the federal policy is a long-standing and apparently strong one—it is related to the Seventh Amendment's policy of giving maximum weight to the jury system, for instance. Similarly, there is a strong federal interest in having a treatment of the unanimity issue that is the same from one federal court to another. Also, the choice of law is quite unlikely to be out-come determinative—it is hard to say, for instance, whether having a less-than-unanimous jury verdict would help P or D, since it is unclear who would get five but not six votes. And the choice of law is unlikely to promote forum shopping—it is hard to imagine that P will sue in state rather than federal court, because jurors in the former don't have to be unanimous. All in all, the federal interests seem so much stronger than the state interests, and the risk of forum shopping so small, the court will probably decide to follow the federal policy requiring unanimity. See, e.g., *Masino v. Outboard Marine Corp.*, 652 F.2d 330 (3d Cir. 1981).

151. No, probably. **Here, there seems to have a flat-out conflict between an applicable Federal Rule (15(c)) and a state rule or policy. So as long as the Federal Rule is valid under the Rules Enabling Act (i.e., it does not enlarge or reduce a party's "substantive right"), it will prevail over the competing state policy.** The highly technical nature of Rule 15(c)'s relation back approach means that it is almost certainly valid. Therefore, a federal court will apply the Rule and allow P to add his breach of warranty claim, even though he could not do so in state court. This is true even though there is something of an outcome-determinative effect here: P gets to pursue his warranty claim even though he would not get to pursue it if the case were in state court. The important thing to remember is that we do not use the *Byrd v. Blue Ridge* "balancing" approach when a Federal Rule is directly on point; instead we apply the Federal Rule so long as it is valid (which every Federal Rule has been found to be so far). See, e.g., *Welch v. Louisiana Power & Light Co.*, 466 F.2d 1344 (5th Cir. 1972). See also *Hanna v. Plumer*, 380 U.S. 460 (1965), setting out the method of analyzing the conflict between an on-point Federal Rule and a state rule or policy.

152. No. **Under Rule 15(c), if the applicable state law would allow relation-back, relation-back should be allowed in the federal diversity action as well.** So there isn't any conflict between federal and state policies, and the state policy is expressly to be followed, making P's claim not time-barred.

153. Probably not. **This seems to be one of those relatively unusual cases where "federal common law" applies, notwithstanding Erie. Erie establishes that there is no "general federal common law." But where the case arises out of a federal statute, or relates to peculiarly federal interests, the federal court is still free to apply federal common law principles instead of following state law.** Here, where it is the rights of the U.S. government that are at stake, the court is probably free to apply what it perceives as general federal common law principles. See *U.S. v. Standard Oil Co.*, 332 U.S. 301 (1947), applying federal common law to a tort suit brought by the United States on roughly

comparable facts. (The federal court is always free to conclude that Ohio state law in this instance provides the soundest solution, but the point is that the federal judge is not *required* to apply state law if he disagrees with that law.)

154. **No. The trial judge should grant D's motion for judgment as a matter of law only if the judge believes that P has not carried his burden of production—that is, his burden of producing some credible evidence (evidence that might be believed by a reasonable jury) that D behaved negligently.** The presumption (failure to take a Breathalyzer equals intoxication and thus negligence) is enough to get P past this burden of production—by proving that D did not take the Breathalyzer (the basic fact), P will be deemed to have met the burden of producing evidence that D was negligent (the presumed fact). Unless D comes up with credible evidence of her nonnegligence, the court will in fact have to instruct the jury at the end of D's case that it should find for P on this issue.

155. **No. Under the "bursting bubble" approach to presumptions imposed by Federal Rule of Evidence 301, "a presumption imposes on the party against whom it is directed the burden of going forward with evidence to rebut or meet the presumption, but does not shift to such party the burden of proof in the sense of the risk of non-persuasion, which remains throughout the trial upon the party on whom it was originally cast."** Thus, although the presumption "refusal to take Breathalyzer equals intoxication" meant that once P showed such refusal, the burden of *production* as to intoxication shifted to D (see answer to prior question), this presumption did not help P get rid of the burden of *persuasion*. At the end of the trial, just as at the beginning, the burden remained on P to show by a preponderance of the evidence that D was in fact intoxicated. Thus if the jury believed that there was exactly a 50 percent chance that D was intoxicated, P loses, just as if there had been no presumption at all. To the extent that the judge's instructions indicate that D loses where the jury is completely undecided, those instructions are wrong.

156. Move for judgment on partial findings. Rule 52(c) states, **"If a party has been fully heard on an issue during a nonjury trial and the court finds against the party on that issue, the court may enter judgment against the party."** If the court agrees that P has not shown that D's motives were based on race, the court will enter judgment as a matter of law (a final judgment on the merits, preventing P from bringing the suit again), complete with findings of fact and conclusions of law as Rule 52(a) requires. If the court denies D's motion, D can then put on its own case.

157. Yes. **Federal Rule 56(c) provides, "[A] party asserting that a fact cannot be or is genuinely disputed must support the assertion."** P's opposing papers fail to satisfy this rule: P has merely repeated the conclusory allegation of her complaint that D performed the operation. In the face of D's quite specific demonstration that he was out of the country on that date, P was required to come up with something specific (e.g., an affidavit reciting in detail her trip to D's office, a copy of the bill rendered by D, or something else more detailed than the statement, "D performed this operation on me on October 13"). If P's opposing papers sufficed, it would be virtually impossible for a party ever to win a motion for summary judgment so long as his or her adversary came up with a facially adequate pleading.

158. **No. Federal Rule 56(a) states that the motion for summary judgment may be rendered only if all the materials submitted by both parties "show that there is no genuine dispute as to any material fact." It is not enough that the judge concludes that the moving party is very likely to win at trial—the judge must conclude that *as a matter of law* all issues must be decided in favor of the movant before the judge may grant summary judgment.** Here, there is some chance (although admittedly not a very good chance) that P will be able to come up with more evidence that D really did perform the operation on the day stated or will be able to show that D's evidence was fraudulent.

Alternatively, P may be able to show that D performed the operation on a different day. Since the issue of whether D performed the operation is very fact bound, and there seems to be an honest dispute, the court should deny D's motion even though it appears very probable that D will prevail at trial.

159. No. **Federal Rule 52(a) provides, "In an action tried on the facts without a jury . . . the court must find the facts specially and state its conclusions of law separately."** The judge has almost certainly failed to find the facts "specially"—this word indicates that the judge must state the facts with some particularity, so that a reviewing court will know whether the judge has conducted the trial in an adequate way and has reached a verdict in accord with the weight of the evidence. At a minimum, the judge should have summarized the evidence of intentional discrimination produced by P (if any) and should have described why she did not find this evidence sufficient. If P were to appeal this case, the appellate court would probably remand it to the district court for an opinion that recites the facts and conclusions of law much more specifically.

160. Yes. **Rule 52(a) requires that the judge make detailed findings of fact and conclusions of law when the case is decided on the merits.** But it also states that "the court is not required to state findings or conclusions when ruling on a motion under Rule 12 or 56 or, unless these rules provide otherwise, on any other motion." A Rule 50(a) motion is such an "any other motion."

161. Yes. **One of the most important sentences in the entire Federal Rules of Civil Procedure is in Rule 52(a): "Findings of fact, whether based on oral or other evidence, must not be set aside unless clearly erroneous, and the reviewing court must give due regard to the trial court's opportunity to judge the witnesses' credibility."** Here, each witness's testimony is internally consistent, and there are no documents that contradict any witness's story. Therefore, the case boils down completely to whether one believes P and W on the one hand, or D on the other. This is the very sort of credibility determination that the Federal Rules leave to the trial court. Thus, even though the appellate court believes that there is a 70 percent chance that the trial judge made an error, the appellate court should not reverse or even order a new trial. (The main rationale for this deference to the trial judge's findings, especially on matters of credibility, is that the trial judge can *see* things in court that are not apparent from the trial transcript. For instance, both P and W may have appeared to be evasive, pausing a long time before answering questions, failing to look the questioner in the eye, and so on; by contrast, D might have appeared to be a straight shooter whose demeanor strongly suggested honesty.)

162. Yes, probably. **The same rule as cited in the previous answer applies here; under Rule 52(a), "findings of fact, whether based on oral or documentary evidence, shall not be set aside unless clearly erroneous. . . ."** Note the phrase "whether based on oral or documentary evidence"—although it could be argued that the appellate court is just as competent as the trial court to review a document and determine whether it is believable (in contrast to the trial court's superior ability to judge the credibility of live witnesses), the quoted phrase makes it clear that even as to documentary evidence the findings must be disturbed only if they are clearly erroneous. It is doubtful that the evidence here, although it favors D, is so strong that it makes the finding in favor of P clearly erroneous. See *Anderson v. Bessemer City*, 470 U.S. 564 (1985) (applying the "clearly erroneous" rule to documentary evidence).

163. Remand for further factual findings. **The appeals court may *not* analyze the police report (even if it is part of the record on appeal) and conclude that had that evidence been admitted, the trial judge's finding in favor of D would have been clearly erroneous. Instead, the appeals court must remand so that the trial court (the finder of fact) can analyze this new evidence and decide whether it justifies a different conclusion.** If the trial judge on remand decides that no change in the judgment is warranted, then P can re-appeal and hope to persuade the appellate court that the findings are clearly erroneous. The key point to remember is that even when the federal trial judge makes a

mistake of law (here, excluding admissible evidence), the judge does not lose his or her primary role as finder of fact.

164. **No. The six-person jury is allowable; see *Colgrove v. Battin*, 413 U.S. 149 (1973) (holding that a six-person jury does not violate the Seventh Amendment right to jury trial in civil cases, and allowing such a jury where provided by local court rules). But it is required in federal civil trials that the verdict be unanimous. Rule 48 states, "[U]nless the parties stipulate otherwise, the verdict must be unanimous."** Since P and D did not stipulate that a less-than-unanimous verdict would suffice, the trial must be treated as a "hung jury" and the case retried.

165. **Yes. Federal Rule 48 expressly allows the parties to decide what majority shall control, stating that the verdict shall be unanimous *"unless the parties stipulate otherwise."***

166. Yes, probably. **Federal Rule 51 provides that "[a] party may assign as error: (A) an error in an instruction actually given, if that party properly objected; or (B) a failure to give an instruction, if that party properly requested it and—unless the court rejected the request in a definite ruling on the record—also properly objected."** A request for a particular instruction, made before the judge gives his or her instructions, is not a substitute for an after-the-instruction objection. Therefore, by the strict language of Rule 51, D waived his right to an instruction on this point by failing to object before the jury retired. There is some chance that the appellate court might conclude that this error was "plain error" that should be reversed despite the lack of an objection; however, most appellate courts in the federal system are reluctant to reverse even for plain error in instructions, on the theory that this wastes judicial resources (since a new trial is necessary, whereas with a timely objection the judge might have corrected his mistake and obtained a properly instructed jury verdict the first time around).

167. **Yes. Generally, judges frown on attempts to impeach the jury's verdict. But in federal courts, there is an exception where evidence is presented that a juror failed to disclose information during voir dire; a new trial may be granted, at the discretion of the trial judge, if there is evidence that (1) the juror failed to answer honestly a material question, and (2) a correct response would have provided a valid basis for a challenge for cause.** Since the relationship between the juror and D was material, and since a truthful response by that juror would have entitled P to challenge her for cause (bias), the trial judge has the discretion to order a new trial based on this information. (But the trial judge does not *have* to grant the new trial; if she refuses to grant a new trial, this finding will probably not be disturbed on appeal.) See *McDonough Power Equipment, Inc. v. Greenwood*, 464 U.S. 548 (1984).

168. **No. When a judge decides a JML motion (as when he or she decides a motion for directed verdict), the judge's job is not to substitute himself or herself for the jury. Instead, his or her task is to decide whether a reasonable juror could possibly find in favor of the nonmovant; if the answer to this is yes, the JML or directed verdict must be denied.** Where the nonmovant (here, P) presents testimony that, if believed, is adequate to make out a claim, the judge will rarely grant the motion even though the judge believes the contradicting testimony supporting the movant. On the other hand, if the trial judge believed that P's testimony was so implausible, so internally self-contradictory, or so completely contradicted by other evidence that no rational juror could believe it, then it would be proper for the judge to grant the motion.

169. No. **Rule 50(a)(2) says that a JML motion may be made "at any time before the case is submitted to the jury." Rule 50(b) then says that any JML motion made after trial must be a "renewed motion"—i.e., a repeat of a motion made before the case was submitted to the jury.** Since here

D never moved for JML before the case went to the jury, he has waived his right to seek a JML now (post-trial). This means that the most D can get, either from the trial judge or on appeal, is a new trial, not an entry of judgment in his favor.

170. Grant a remittitur. **The judge should conditionally order a new trial—the new trial will occur unless P agrees to a reduction of the damages to an amount set by the court, probably $1.5 million.** It will then be up to P whether to accept this "deal" or not. If P accepts, he may not appeal the remittitur thereafter and must be content with the $1.5 million. If P declines the remittitur, he must go through a new trial, which he may lose entirely.

171. No. **According to Federal Rule 50, the party seeking judgment as a matter of law must make a motion for that judgment before the case is submitted to the jury.** Since here D never moved for a JML, he has waived his right to seek a JML after the verdict was reached. This means that the most D can get, either from the trial judge or on appeal, is a new trial, not an entry of judgment in his favor.

172. No. **The Seventh Amendment is one of the few Bill of Rights provisions that has never been "incorporated" into the Fourteenth Amendment's due process guarantees.** Therefore, the Seventh Amendment applies only to federal, not state, civil trials. A state is free to deny juries entirely in civil trials if it wishes.

173. No. **According to Federal Rule 38(b), "[o]n any issue triable of right by a jury, a party may demand a jury trial by: (1) serving the other parties with a written demand—which may be included in a pleading—no later than 14 days after the last pleading directed to the issue is served; and (2) filing the demand [with the court]."** This means that the last time D could demand a jury trial was 14 days after he served his answer, or July 29. After that, he waived his right, and only in very exceptional cases will the court relieve him from this waiver.

174. (a) Only the damages claim. **Federal Rule 38(a) gives the right of jury trial "as declared by the Seventh Amendment to the Constitution."** That Amendment applies only to suits "at common law." Therefore, there is only a right to a jury trial (unless Congress specifically otherwise provides) where the suit is one that is "legal" rather than "equitable." An injunction suit is always regarded as "equitable," so there is no right to a jury trial on an injunction claim. A claim for damages, by contrast, is virtually always "legal," so it does carry with it a right to a jury trial.

    (b) The court should try the damages claim first. **If the court tries the injunction claim (without a jury) first, this will probably bind the jury when the jury hears the damages claim later, because of the doctrine of "law of the case."** Yet if the jury is not given comparatively free rein in deciding the damages claim, D's right to a jury trial is violated. Therefore, even though it may be somewhat inefficient, the federal judge should try the damages claim first, then the injunction claim, if there are significant issues in common between the two. (There are almost certainly such common issues here—e.g., the issue of whether P's trademark is valid and whether D has in fact infringed it.) See *Beacon Theatres v. Westover*, 359 U.S. 500 (1959).

175. Yes. **The issue is whether the action is legal or equitable. It may well be that prior to the enactment of the Federal Rules of Civil Procedure in 1938, interpleader was regarded as an equitable action. But today, the court determines whether a claim is equitable or legal not by reference to the procedural device by which the parties come before the court (here, interpleader) but, rather, by reference to the *underlying claim*.** Here, the underlying issue is basically an issue of contract law (was X competent to change the policy beneficiary?), and such a contract-law issue will almost always be legal rather than equitable. Since the underlying issue is legal, each party has the right to demand a jury trial as to that issue (and if one party so demands, there will be a jury trial even though the other

parties do not want one). See *Ross v. Bernhard*, 396 U.S. 531 (1970) (for determining whether the claim is legal or equitable, "nothing now turns upon . . . the procedural devices by which the parties happen to come before the court").

176. No. **Since D's present claim arises out of the same transaction or occurrence that was the subject of P's claim in the first suit, D's claim was a *compulsory* counterclaim in the first action. That is, D was required to assert that claim as a Rule 13(a) compulsory counterclaim in the first action, or face losing it.** Since D did not do so, he will be barred from bringing the claim as a separate suit now (even though the result in the first trial indicates that D is probably correct in asserting that the accident was caused by P's negligence).

177. Yes. **Federal Rule 13(a)(2) makes a counterclaim permissive rather than compulsory if "the opposing party sued on its claim by attachment or other process that did not establish personal jurisdiction over the pleader on that claim, and the pleader does not assert any counterclaim under this rule."** Since P's claim against D was based on *quasi in rem* rather than *in personam* jurisdiction, any counterclaim that D might have had in the first suit was automatically rendered permissive. (Otherwise, D would not really get the benefit of a limited appearance—he could limit his liability to the amount of the bank account, but only by forsaking his own claim. This results from the fact that most courts hold that a defendant who makes a counterclaim thereby subjects himself or herself to unlimited personal liability.)

178. Apply for a default judgment against P. **A counterclaim, just like an initial claim, must be responded to by an *answer*.** Since P served no further pleading after D's counterclaim, P failed to answer.

179. No. **The rule that compulsory counterclaims must be asserted in the initial action or waived applies not only to defendants but also to any other parties. Thus Federal Rule 13(a) does not refer to defendants specifically but instead to any "pleading" by any "pleader"—the pleader is required to raise any claim against "any opposing party" if that claim arises out of the same transaction or occurrence that is the subject matter of the opposing party's claim.** Since Worker's claim against Boss for injuries results from the same transaction or occurrence (the accident with Pedestrian) as Boss's third-party claim against Worker, Worker must assert his claim as a counterclaim against Boss, or lose it. Since he did not so assert it, he will be found to have waived it.

180. (a) Yes. **Compulsory counterclaims fall within the *supplemental jurisdiction* of the court under 28 U.S.C. §1367.** Since Alan's counterclaim arises out of the same transaction or occurrence as Bob's claim, Alan's counterclaim is compulsory and will satisfy the "same case or controversy" requirement of §1367. Since §1367(b), which excludes certain types of claims in diversity actions, does not mention counterclaims, Alan's claim will fall within supplemental jurisdiction, and it will not matter that Carol and Alan, opposing parties, are citizens of the same state. Nor does it matter that Alan's claim totals less than $75,000. (The supplemental jurisdiction statute, where it applies, obviates the need to meet the usual requirements of subject matter jurisdiction, such as complete diversity and amount in controversy.)

(b) No. **Alan's federal court counterclaim was compulsory, so by not asserting it, he lost it. If Alan had not been able to get *personal* jurisdiction over Carol, his counterclaim against Bob would not have been compulsory, because Rule 13(a) says the counterclaim is compulsory only if it "does not require adding another party over whom the court cannot acquire jurisdiction."** But since Carol had minimum contacts with Connecticut, and Connecticut had a long-arm statute authorizing service out of state on Carol, jurisdiction was not a problem. The supplemental jurisdiction statute would have taken care of any subject matter jurisdictional problem. Therefore, Alan's claim was an ordinary compulsory counterclaim, even though it needs for just adjudication the presence of a third person not previously a party to the action. Since a state court will normally bar a claim that would have been a compulsory counterclaim in an earlier federal action, Alan will be barred.

181. Yes. **As Rule 13(a) indicates, a counterclaim is compulsory only if it "does not require adding another party over whom the court cannot acquire jurisdiction."** Since the fact pattern assumes that Carol is required for a just adjudication of any claim by Alan, this language makes Alan's counterclaim against Bob (in the absence of Carol) permissive only. If Alan does not want to bring his counterclaim against Bob alone, he can decline to bring the counterclaim entirely, since it is permissive.

182. (a) No. **Since the two claims arise out of different transactions or occurrences, the counterclaim is permissive.**

    (b) No. **Permissive counterclaims do not fall within the court's supplemental jurisdiction, because by definition they do not derive from a "common nucleus of operative fact."** They must therefore satisfy the requirements of federal subject matter jurisdiction independently of the main claim. Consequently, most courts hold that a permissive counterclaim must independently exceed the amount-in-controversy requirement (i.e., the counterclaim cannot be aggregated with the main claim), which in diversity cases is $75,000.

183. Yes, probably. **Under *Erie* principles (especially *Guaranty Trust Co. v. York*), the state statute of limitations is binding on the federal court in this diversity action.** Probably the federal court should apply the same rule regarding whether D's time to sue is tolled as the state of Ames would apply. Assuming that we don't know what that state law is, probably the federal court should allow D to sue. Mostly, this is a question of simple fairness: Since P's claim is the same age as D's, and since P clearly had notice of the possibility of litigation within the one-year period (since P brought suit himself), it seems unfair to bar D. See *Azada v. Carson*, 252 F. Supp. 988 (D. Haw. 1966), reaching this conclusion. (But if D's counterclaim were a permissive one (i.e., one arising out of a different transaction or occurrence), then probably P's filing would not cause a tolling of the statute of limitations on D's counterclaim against P—the "same age" and "P is already on notice" arguments would not apply here.)

184. Yes. **Federal Rule 18(a) provides, "A party asserting a claim . . . may join, either as independent or as alternate claims, as many claims as it has against an opposing party."** Since P and D are opposing parties based on P's initial copyright claim, P has the right to add whatever claims against D he wishes, even if these other claims have nothing to do with the original copyright claim.

185. Probably not. **Since P and D are citizens of the same state, there is no diversity jurisdiction. This is not a problem for the copyright claim, since that is founded upon federal law. But the libel claim is based upon state law.** If the libel claim were closely related to the copyright claim (e.g., both related to the same transaction or occurrence), the libel claim could be heard together with the copyright claim under the doctrine of supplemental (formerly pendent) jurisdiction. The supplemental jurisdiction statute, 28 U.S.C. §1367, allows parties to join claims that are so related as to form part of the same case or controversy in the same suit. But since the two claims have nothing to do with each other, supplemental jurisdiction does not apply here. Therefore, there is no federal subject matter jurisdiction over the libel claim, and it cannot be heard by the federal court.

186. (a) Yes. **D's claim against X for the car accident is a compulsory counterclaim. (That is, D's claim against P is a garden-variety compulsory counterclaim, and X is an additional party to that counterclaim joined pursuant to Rule 13(h)). Compulsory counterclaims, and the joinder of additional parties to compulsory counterclaims, fall within the court's supplemental**

jurisdiction under 28 U.S.C. §1367 because they concern "part of the same case or controversy." Consequently, it does not matter that D's claim against X fails by itself to meet the amount in controversy requirement; supplemental jurisdiction obviates the need for the usual diversity jurisdiction in this case. (In fact, it wouldn't even matter that D and X were citizens of the same state.)

(b) No. **This second claim by D against X is allowed procedurally only because of Rule 18(a)'s joinder of claims provision (which allows any party, not just the plaintiff, to join additional claims against an opposing party who is already in the action). But Rule 18(a) joinder of claims does not fall within the court's supplemental jurisdiction unless the claims are so related as to form part of the same case or controversy (the "common nucleus of operative fact" standard).** Here, the breach of contract claim is based on an unrelated transaction. Since it does not fall under supplemental jurisdiction, the unrelated claim must independently meet federal subject matter jurisdictional requirements. Because D's second claim against X is not for more than $75,000, that second claim cannot be heard.

187. No, probably. **The circumstances under which a plaintiff may join two or more defendants are governed by Federal Rule 20(a)'s "permissive joinder" provision: "Persons . . . may be joined in one action as defendant if: (A) any right to relief is asserted against them jointly, severally, or in the alternative with respect to or arising out of the same transaction, occurrence, or series of transactions or occurrences; and (B) any question of law or fact common to all defendants will arise in the action."**

Here, there is a good chance that P could meet the second of these tests (common question of law or fact), since identical questions as to what constitutes federal copyright infringement, or whether Richie Rat is copyrightable, are likely to be involved in the case against D1 and D2. But the first test—that all claims involve the "same transaction, occurrence, or series of transactions or occurrences . . ."— probably is not satisfied. It is true that the transactions are roughly similar, but they are not the *same*. Just as a plaintiff probably cannot join in one federal action all defendants who owe him money where each defendant is liable under a separate contract, so it is probably the case that P cannot join independent copyright violators.

188. Yes. **Rule 20(a) makes joinder of D1 and D2 proper, since there is a single transaction and a common question of law or fact (who caused the accident?) involved in the claims against D1 and D2.** Similarly, Rule 20(a) allows multiple plaintiffs to join together if they meet both the "same transaction" and "question of law or fact common to all plaintiffs" requirements. Here, P1 and P2 meet these requirements since there is obviously a single transaction (the crash) and at least one major question of law or fact (who caused the accident?) common to their claims. The fact that there may also be questions of law or fact that are *not* in common between the two plaintiffs or two defendants is not a problem—for instance, the fact that P1 may have suffered dramatically different injuries from P2 is irrelevant.

189. No. **Since D1 has its principal place of business in New York, it is deemed to be a citizen of New York (as well as of whatever state it is incorporated in).** This means that there is no longer complete diversity of citizenship. Since the action involves no federal question, and there is no diversity, the action could go forward as pleaded only if supplemental jurisdiction somehow eliminated the requirement of complete diversity. But the supplemental jurisdiction statute, 28 U.S.C. §1367, states in subsection (b) that in diversity actions the district courts shall *not* have supplemental jurisdiction over claims by plaintiffs (like P1 and P2) against persons made parties under Rule 20 (such as D1) if the result would be inconsistent with the requirements of diversity. Because §1367 does not apply

in this case, each claim and each party must independently meet federal subject matter jurisdictional requirements. Consequently, D1 will have to be dropped from the action (though the action may proceed as a suit by P1 and P2 against D2.)

190. Order that D2 and D3 be joined as defendants. **Federal Rule 19(a) provides that if any of the three criteria stated there are satisfied by a person who is not currently a party to the action, that person must be joined if feasible.** One of these criteria is that the person "claims an interest relating to the subject of the action and is so situated that the disposition of the action in the person's absence may . . . as a practical matter impair or impede the person's ability to protect that interest." If D2 is not made a party to the action, and P prevails against the estate, then the estate will pay out the $100,000 to P immediately. In a strictly legal sense, D2's legal rights cannot be affected by a suit to which D2 is not a party—D2 is free to sue P and/or D1, and to relitigate the issue of whether the contract to make a will was enforceable. But as a *practical* matter, D2's interest will be impaired—D1 will already have laid out the money to P, and it will be harder for D2 to get this money back (since the estate will no longer have the money and P may spend it immediately) than if D2 were a party to the original P-D1 suit. The same analysis is true of D3. Therefore, even though neither P nor D1 moves to have D2 and D3 joined to the action, the court should on its own order that they be joined since joinder is (by the hypothesized facts) available.

191. Yes, probably. **Y is clearly a person who should be joined if feasible (Federal Rule 19(a)), but the facts make it clear that it is not "feasible" to join Y. Therefore, courts look at Rule 19(b) to determine whether Y's presence is so indispensable that it is better to dismiss the action entirely than to proceed in Y's absence. Rule 19(b) lists four factors to be considered by the court on this issue of indispensability. One of these factors is "the extent to which a judgment rendered in the person's absence might prejudice the person or the existing parties."** On this factor, Y's claim to have the action dismissed is very strong—a judgment entered in P's favor (especially since P already has possession) might make it very difficult indeed for Y to ever get her own day in court, since P might sell the property, lend it abroad, or otherwise effectively put it outside the court's jurisdiction.

Another factor also cuts in Y's favor—"whether the plaintiff would have an adequate remedy if the action were dismissed for non-joinder." Since P and Y are both Florida residents, and D (the estate) owns property currently located in Florida, it is almost certain that the Florida courts would have jurisdiction over an action by P against D and Y jointly; therefore, P would have an adequate remedy if the federal judge dismissed for nonjoinder.

Cutting the other way is still another factor listed in Rule 19(b): "the extent to which any prejudice could be lessened or avoided by: (A) protective provisions in the judgment." That is, the federal court could find in favor of P, but could simultaneously instruct P to hold the painting without disposing of it for, say, one year to permit Y to bring a separate action. However, this method only avoids prejudice by allowing a complete relitigation of the merits, a very wasteful approach.

So, putting it all together, the court will probably conclude that it is better to dismiss the action (and let P bring a Florida state court action or D bring a federal statutory interpleader action joining both P and Y) than to let the action proceed in Y's absence. See *Haas v. Jefferson National Bank of Miami Beach*, 442 F.2d 394 (5th Cir. 1971), finding the absentee to be an indispensable party, on analogous facts.

192. Dismiss the action because Y cannot be joined. **Y's minimum contacts with New York take care of the problem of personal jurisdiction over her.** But the problem of lack of diversity persists. Before 1991, there was some chance that the federal court might have applied ancillary jurisdiction to this situation (which would have the effect that complete diversity as between Y and P would not be needed).

But the supplemental jurisdiction statute enacted that year, 28 U.S.C. §1367, would *definitely not* allow jurisdiction in this case, thus preserving the policy established in *Owen Equipment v. Kroger*, 437 U.S. 365 (1978). *Kroger* only granted supplemental-type jurisdiction to parties in a *defensive* posture. Similarly, §1367(b) specifically excludes claims by plaintiffs against persons joined under Rule 19 if the result would destroy diversity. All Rule 19 parties, whether indispensable or not, must therefore each meet the usual subject matter jurisdiction requirements.

193. No. **One of the requirements for a federal class action, according to Rule 23(a)(1), is that the class be "so *numerous* that joinder of all members is impracticable."** Sixteen is such a small number that it is hard to see why the individual co-op members cannot simply join together as co-plaintiffs under Rule 20(a).

194. Yes, probably. **One of the requirements for a federal class action is that "the representative parties will fairly and adequately protect the interests of the class." Rule 23(a)(4).** Even if the judge in Peter's suit believed that Peter and Larry together could adequately represent the class (as the judge must have believed to certify a class action in the first place), a second judge in a later suit by a member of the class can reach a different conclusion. Therefore, the judge in Phil's suit would probably conclude, in retrospect, that Peter and Larry did not adequately represent the class, and that Phil should therefore not be bound by the results of the class action.

195. Yes, under Rule 23(b)(2). **A proposed class action must meet the four requirements of Rule 23(a): numerosity, common questions of law or fact, typicality of claims or defenses, and adequate representation.** Seven hundred members seem sufficiently numerous. There are certainly questions of law or fact common to the class—for instance, each class member's claim presents the issue of whether due process is owed to a rejected housing applicant. The claims of P1 and P2 seem quite typical of the claims of other class members, since all are rejected applicants claiming a due process right. Finally, the facts tell us to assume that there is adequate representation.

Now that Rule 23(a) is satisfied, the court must still find some subdivision of Rule 23(b) that is satisfied. The most likely candidate is (b)(2): "The party opposing the class has acted or refused to act on grounds that apply generally to the class, so that final injunctive relief or corresponding declaratory relief is appropriate respecting the class as a whole." Here, the plaintiffs are seeking a declaratory judgment that due process is owed to a housing applicant and an injunction against denying due process to future applicants. Since D is apparently treating all rejected applicants the same way (by not giving them a statement of reasons for the rejection, or other trappings of due process), the "generally applicable to the class" requirement seems satisfied.

196. No. **In a (b)(1) or (b)(2) class action, notice is not required by Rule 23 (in contrast to (b)(3) actions). Instead, Rule 23(c)(2)(A) leaves it up to the discretion of the judge whether to order notice to some or all members of a (b)(2) class action.** The reason for this is that if the suit is successful, it will result in an injunction or declaratory judgment applicable to *all* members of the class, whether notified or not, and class members will not be able to opt out, so that no good would probably come of class-wide notice. On these facts, it is unlikely that the judge will order notice given to each individual (though the judge might order publication notice, or notice sent to a small sample).

197. Unclear, but probably not. **Even assuming that the four requirements of 23(a) can be satisfied, P's only chance of certification would be as a (b)(3) action.** (A Rule 23(b)(1) action is out, because there is no risk of inconsistent or varying adjudications, or prejudice to the absentees—even if D was ordered to pay damages to P and not to some absentee, or vice versa, there would be no inconsistency or prejudice. Similarly, (b)(2) is out, because the suit does not seek declaratory or injunctive relief.)

For a (b)(3) action to be certified, the court must find that "questions of law or fact common to the members of the class predominate over any questions affecting only individual members." This requirement seems not to be met here: While there is a common question of liability, the more interesting and time-consuming questions will probably relate to causation (given that a particular class member was sick or injured, was this because of the toxic cloud?) and damages, issues that are not common. Similarly, it is unclear that the court should conclude that "a class action is superior to other available methods for fairly and efficiently adjudicating the controversy," as required by Rule 23(b)(3). Individual suits by each injured resident may be a superior way to proceed, because of the causation and damage issues. However, such suits may be less efficient and more costly in terms of legal fees. (The court might certify a class action only as to D's general liability, rather than as to causation and damages. But see *In the Matter of Rhone-Poulenc Rorer, Inc.*, 51 F.3d 1293 (7th Cir. 1995), refusing to allow even a liability-only class certification in a mass tort suit.)

198. Probably not. **Clearly a class member who opts out is not bound by any unfavorable judgment that may result. The converse should also be true: One who opts out should not be able to claim the benefit of a favorable decision.** Otherwise, it will be in each class member's interest to opt out and wait to see whether the class action turns out favorably. This would be unfair to the defendant (giving each potential plaintiff two bites at the apple), and would lead to wasteful multiple suits. Therefore, in all probability, the judge will conclude that X must relitigate from scratch the issue of whether D released the gas, and did so in violation of federal statutes. This is true even though nonmutual collateral estoppel might be given to X if the first suit were not a class action.

199. No. In ***Phillips Petroleum Co. v. Shutts***, **472 U.S. 797 (1985), the Supreme Court held that an "absent" member of the plaintiff class (i.e., one who does not participate in the suit, but who also does not opt out) will nonetheless be bound by the results of the case, even if the absent member does not have minimum contacts with the state where the class action is pending.** Thus, even though X had absolutely no contacts with New York, where the class action took place, he is bound by the results since he did not opt out.

200. Yes. **According to *Exxon Mobil Corp. v. Allapattah Services Inc.*, 125 S. Ct. 2611 (2005), as long as the named members of the class each have claims that satisfy the amount in controversy requirement, the supplemental jurisdiction statute is to be read so as to permit non-named persons with claims for less than that amount to be part of the plaintiff class.** So, the action will be certified even though the unnamed members don't independently have claims exceeding $75,000.

201. (a) All 800,000 identifiable members. **Individual notice must be given (usually by mail) to any class member who can be "identified through reasonable effort." *Eisen v. Carlisle & Jacquelin*, 417 U.S. 156 (1974).** Thus, the 800,000 customers whose names and addresses are on file at Biff's offices must each be sent notice by mail. This is true even though the average Biff's Notes costs $3, and thus even though the cost of notice is large, if not prohibitive, compared with the possible recovery. Additionally, the court may order publication notice to reach the approximately 3,200,000 customers whose names are not on file.

(b) P must pay the entire cost. **This is true even if the court concludes that P would probably prevail at trial, and even if the court concludes that the cost of notice is so great relative to P's possible recovery that imposing the cost of notice on P will effectively kill the action.**

(c) P could define a subclass and give notice only to that class. **P could restrict his suit only to those who bought during the most recent year, or only to those who bought more than a certain quantity of books, or to those who bought only certain titles.** The advantage would be that

P's costs of notice diminish. The disadvantage, of course, would be that any recovery would be reduced, and the fees awarded by the court to P's lawyer in the event of victory would be correspondingly reduced.

202. No. **As long as the requirements of Rule 23 are met (which do not include any requirement that P be likely to prevail on the merits), the court should certify the class even though P will probably lose at trial.** In fact, the Supreme Court in the *Eisen* case (see the answer to question 201(a) for cite) expressly forbade district courts from conducting any kind of preliminary hearing to determine the plaintiff's likelihood of prevailing on the merits.

203. Notice of the proposed settlement to absent class members, and judicial approval of the settlement. **Rule 23(e) provides, "The claims, issues, or defenses of a certified class may be settled . . . only with the court's approval. The following procedures apply to a proposed settlement . . . : (1) The court must direct notice in a reasonable manner to all class members who would be bound by the proposal."** In the case of a large class, each member of which has very small claims, the court will probably not order notice by mail to anyone, but will instead probably permit publication notice. In deciding whether to approve the settlement, the court will consider principally whether it is fair to the absent class members (since there is a danger that P's lawyer and Biff will collude, by agreeing to pay P's lawyer a large amount and paying smaller damages to class members than would be appropriate based on the strength of P's case).

204. No. **In suits brought under federal statutes, even class action suits, attorney's fees may be awarded only if the federal statute so provides. See *Alyeska Pipeline Service Co. v. Wilderness Society*, 421 U.S. 240 (1975).**

205. Seek the court's permission to intervene under Federal Rule 24(b). **Since X's proposed claim and P's existing action have a "common question of law or fact," X can move the Michigan federal court for leave to intervene as a co-plaintiff in P's suit.** Clearly there is one major question of law/fact that the two claims have in common: whether D flew the plane in a negligent manner. The fact that there is also at least one noncommon question of fact (each plaintiff's damages) should be irrelevant. It will be up to the district court's discretion whether to allow the intervention. (The requirements for intervention of right under Rule 24(a) do not seem to be satisfied—X is not really "so situated that disposing of the action may as a practical matter impair or impede the movant's ability to protect its interest," since X ought to be able to find a different expert witness, or to improve Edward's testimony even if he gives poor testimony in P's action.)

206. No. **The action is in diversity, which means that there must be complete diversity (no plaintiff from the same state as any defendant).** If X's motion for permissive intervention is allowed, X will be treated as a plaintiff. Since he will then be a citizen of the same state (Ohio) as D, diversity will be ruined. Supplemental jurisdiction would not apply for permissive intervention—28 U.S.C. §1367(b) provides that intervenors under Rule 24 must meet jurisdictional requirements for diversity actions and cannot rely on the court's supplemental jurisdiction. The statute thus treats permissive intervenors in the same way as the judge-made "ancillary" doctrine did.

207. No. **The supplemental jurisdiction statute makes no distinction between intervention as of right and permissive intervention. 28 U.S.C. §1367(b) clearly states that persons seeking to intervene under Rule 24 will not be allowed if their presence would destroy diversity (as it would here).**

208. No. **A motion to permissively intervene is within the discretion of the trial judge, and is very rarely reversed on appeal.**

209. Yes, probably. **For a person to be entitled to intervention as of right, Rule 24(a) requires that the applicant claim "an interest relating to the property or transaction that is the subject of the action, and [be] so situated that the disposing of the action may as a practical matter impair or impede the [applicant's] ability to protect its interest, unless existing parties adequately represent that interest."** P certainly has an interest relating to the same transaction as the main action: the procedure by which Ames draws district boundaries and administers its schools. There is also a danger to P that his ability to bring a successful action in the future might be compromised by a poor result in the United States' action—if the Justice Department does a lackluster job and loses the case (e.g., the court finds that there was no racially discriminatory intent on Ames's part), a subsequent court is unlikely to permit the issue of intentional discrimination to be completely relitigated (even though the rules of collateral estoppel do not formally bind P, since P was an absentee to the U.S.-Ames original action).

The toughest question is whether "existing parties adequately represent [the applicant's] interest"—either the United States or Ames can make a plausible argument that the Justice Department is adequate to represent P's interests. But P can argue in turn that the U.S. government may be pursuing other interests (e.g., a desire to settle such suits in return for partial relief, rather than litigating them to the fullest extent to get complete compliance with the law) and that P's interests are therefore not completely congruent with those of the United States.

On balance, the court will probably rule that P is entitled to intervene as of right (and will almost certainly at least allow P to intervene permissively). See *Smuck v. Hobson*, 408 F.2d 175 (D.C. Cir. 1969), allowing parents to intervene as of right in a similar litigation.

210. Yes, probably. **If the conclusion given in the prior answer is correct (that P is entitled to intervene as of right), the appeals court will overturn the trial court's determination here.** Indeed, the principal difference between intervention as of right and permissive intervention is that a district court's decision denying intervention of right will be overturned by the appeals court if the appeals court thinks the decision was wrong, whereas a district court's denial of permissive intervention will rarely be reversed on appeal, on the theory that this decision is within the trial court's discretion.

211. Bring a federal statutory interpleader proceeding, under 28 U.S.C. §1335. **That section allows a person holding property claimed by two or more adverse claimants to interplead those claimants.** Thus, Insurer can commence a federal proceeding "against" both Al and Betty, and say in effect to the court, "Here's the $30,000; you decide how this should be split among Al and Betty. Return any excess to us." Even though this is a suit brought, in essence, in diversity, the amount in controversy requirement is only $500 (not $75,000). Also, the requirement of complete diversity is canceled, and all that is required is that some two claimants be citizens of different states (satisfied here since Al is a citizen of New York and Betty is a citizen of Oklahoma).

212. Southern District of New York, or Western District of Oklahoma. **Venue in a statutory interpleader action lies in the judicial district in which one or more of the claimants reside.** So suit can be brought where either Al or Betty resides (in contrast to noninterpleader diversity actions, where suit must be in the district where all defendants or all plaintiffs reside, or in the district where the cause of action arose).

213. Yes. **The stakeholder in a federal statutory interpleader action may deny its liability entirely.** This liability issue will simply be one issue that is litigated in the proceeding (together with the issue of how the claimants should divide the fund if there is liability to both).

214. No. **Federal Rule 22 does allow an interpleader action to be brought by a stakeholder (whether the stakeholder acts as plaintiff, or is already a defendant in an existing proceeding brought**

by one or more claimants). **But Rule 22 interpleader, unlike statutory interpleader, does not give any relief from the normal requirements of personal jurisdiction, subject matter jurisdiction, and venue. In a Rule 22 interpleader action, there must be complete diversity between the stakeholder on the one hand and all of the claimants on the other hand.** Since Insurer and Al are both citizens of New York, the required complete diversity is not present. Also, a Rule 22 interpleader action must satisfy the ordinary $75,000 amount in controversy requirement for diversity actions, which the controversy here does not. (What counts for a Rule 22 action is the size of the stake, not the aggregated sizes of the various claims against the fund.)

215. Use Federal Rule 22 interpleader. **The most promising place for Insurer to start such a proceeding is in federal court for the District of Indiana where the home is located; H, as a former resident of Indiana and one who still asserts a property interest in Indiana real estate, certainly has minimum contacts with Indiana and is therefore subject to personal jurisdiction (assuming that the Indiana long-arm allows him to be served, which is quite likely).** Although Rule 22 suits require complete diversity (in the sense that the stakeholder not be a citizen of the same state as any of the claimants), this requirement is satisfied here, since neither H nor W is a citizen of Insurer's home state of Kentucky. The amount-in-controversy requirement is satisfied, since more than $75,000 is at stake. The district where the home is located also suffices for venue, since that is the district where a "substantial part of property that is the subject of the action is situated." 28 U.S.C. §1391(a)(2).

The big advantage for Insurer of Rule 22 interpleader versus statutory interpleader is that under Rule 22 interpleader, Insurer does not have to deposit the "stake" (the $500,000 policy proceeds) with the court at the outset of the proceeding, or post a bond in that amount, as it would for statutory interpleader. Therefore, Insurer gets the use of the money while the suit is pending.

216. Doeing should implead Altimeters pursuant to Federal Rule 14(a). **A defendant may, as a third-party plaintiff, cause a summons and complaint to be served "on a nonparty who is or may be liable to it for all or part of the claim against it." Rule 14(a)(1).** By impleading Altimeters, Doeing is stating that if it is liable for breach of warranty, Altimeters must be derivatively liable to it. (This is a correct statement of warranty law.)

217. Yes. **An impleader claim, even though it always relates to the same transaction or occurrence as the main claim, is always *optional*, not compulsory.** Thus, a defendant does not waive his or her impleader claim by failing to raise it in the first action, as he or she would waive a compulsory counterclaim that he or she failed to make.

218. Deny liability and move for a dismissal under Rule 12(b)(6), not implead the Foundation. **Impleader liability is always *derivative*—the third-party plaintiff is saying that if he is liable, then the third-party defendant is liable over to him.** Impleader cannot be used where the essence of the principal defendant's claim is, "I'm not liable at all, so-and-so is liable instead." Since the City would in effect be saying here, "We're not liable at all, only the Foundation is liable," the situation is not a proper one for impleader. Therefore, the City should simply raise its nonliability as a defense in its answer and seek a dismissal for failure to state a claim. It would then be up to P to join the Foundation in the action, or to dismiss and bring a new suit against just the Foundation.

219. (a) Dave can implead Ted pursuant to Federal Rule 14(a). **Since Ted will be liable over to Dave for half of anything that Dave is required to pay Paula, Ted's liability is derivative.** Therefore, it is appropriate for Dave to bring a third-party action against Ted, even though Paula has not made any claims against Ted directly.

(b) Dave has to solve three problems: **(1) diversity, (2) amount in controversy, and (3) personal jurisdiction.** As to (1), a claim by a third-party plaintiff against a third-party defendant will come within the court's *supplemental* (formerly ancillary) jurisdiction, provided that it and the main claim concern a "common nucleus of operative fact." The supplemental jurisdiction statute, 28 U.S.C. §1367, does not specifically exclude claims by third-party plaintiffs under Rule 14, as it excludes some claims made by plaintiffs. Thus, the fact that Paula and Ted are both citizens of Ohio, and are in a very general sense opposing parties (theoretically nullifying the complete diversity usually required), doesn't matter—as long as Paula and Dave, the original parties, are diverse, the citizenship of the third-party defendant is ignored. As to (2), similarly, the fact that Dave's third-party claim against Ted gets supplemental treatment means that amount in controversy is ignored as to the third-party claim. Therefore, the fact that Dave's claim against Ted is for only $40,000 (half of the up-to-$80,000 claim by Paula) is irrelevant—since Paula's claim against Dave, the original claim, is for more than $75,000, that's all that matters. As to (3), see the answer to (c).

(c) **FRCP 4(k)(1)(B)'s "100-mile bulge" provision.** Under ordinary principles, Dave would not be able to get personal jurisdiction over Ted, because he would not be able to make service on him—the federal court sitting in diversity only allows service on out-of-staters to the extent that the long-arm of the state in which the federal court sits would so allow. Here, since Kentucky would not allow service over Ted, the federal court would not normally be permitted to allow such service either (even though Ted has minimum contacts with Kentucky). But the special "100-mile bulge" provision of Federal Rule 4(k)(1)(B) comes to Dave's rescue: According to that Rule, anyone who is brought in as a third-party defendant pursuant to Rule 14 may be served in a place that is "not more than 100 miles from the place where the summons was issued." Since Cincinnati is within 100 miles of Covington (where the action is pending), Ted may be served at his residence.

220. Yes. **Rule 14(a)(2)(D) provides that the third-party defendant "may also assert against the plaintiff any claim arising out of the transaction or occurrence that is the subject matter of the plaintiff's claim against the third-party plaintiff."** Since Paula's claim against Dave and Ted's claim against Paula both relate to construction of Paula's house, Ted's claim against Paula will presumably be found to meet this "same transaction or occurrence" test. The bigger potential problem is that Ted and Paula are both citizens of Ohio, and all claims are based solely on diversity. There would thus not seem to be the complete diversity required. However, a claim by a third-party defendant against the original plaintiff falls within the court's supplemental jurisdiction, under 28 U.S.C. §1367, since the claim is closely related to the original claim. Since §1367(b) does not exclude claims by third-party defendants against original plaintiffs, the lack of diversity doesn't matter.

221. No. **A claim by the original plaintiff against the third-party defendant does *not* fall within the court's supplemental jurisdiction. The supplemental jurisdiction statute, in 28 U.S.C. §1367(b), specifically bars claims made by the original plaintiff against "persons made parties under Rule 14, 19, 20, or 24."** This provision codifies the result of *Owen Equipment Co. v. Kroger*, 437 U.S. 365 (1978). Paula's claim against Ted would have to be brought under Rule 14(b). Therefore, that claim must independently meet the requirements of federal subject matter jurisdiction. Since Paula and Ted are both citizens of Ohio, the requisite diversity is not present, so the claim cannot be heard. (Similarly, Paula's claim against Ted must independently meet the amount in controversy requirement of $75,000, which it does.)

222. Ted may implead Steve under Rule 14. **Rule 14's allowance of third-party claims does not benefit only the original defendant—*any* party to the action may implead someone who is not presently**

a party, if the nonparty is or may be liable to the other person for all or part of an existing claim against that other person.** Since Steve, under his contract with Dave and Ted, will be liable to Ted for some part of any amount that Ted is required to contribute to Dave, it is proper for Ted to implead Steve. This claim, like the original third-party claim by Dave against Ted, should fall within the court's supplemental jurisdiction and thus need not meet independent federal subject matter jurisdictional requirements (e.g., diversity of citizenship). As in the above questions, supplemental jurisdiction will encompass Ted's impleader of Steve because, by definition, Ted's claim is sufficiently related to Paula's original claim. In 28 U.S.C. §1367(b)'s exclusion from supplemental jurisdiction provisions, there is no exclusion for claims by defendants (including third-party defendants).

223. Yes. **If Deborah were to make a claim against Dell as part of Pete's existing action, Deborah's claim would be a *cross-claim* under Rule 13(g).** However, Deborah is *not required* to make this cross-claim against Dell—cross-claims under the Federal Rules are always optional, never compulsory (in contrast to counterclaims, which are compulsory if they arise out of the same transaction or occurrence as the original claim). Thus, Deborah will not be barred from bringing a separate state court action against Dell later on (though the doctrine of collateral estoppel will probably prevent her from relitigating issues that were actually litigated by her in the original action).

224. Yes. **Deborah's claim against Dell would be a cross-claim, asserted pursuant to Rule 13(g). Cross-claims fall within the court's supplemental jurisdiction, under 28 U.S.C. §1367, since they are by definition closely related to the original action and since they are not excluded by subsection (b).** Therefore, the ordinary requirements of federal subject matter jurisdiction are ignored. It does not matter that Deborah and Dell are both citizens of the same state, or that Deborah's claim is for less than the $75,000 amount in controversy ordinarily required for diversity suits.

225. No. **Since Deborah and Dell are codefendants, Deborah's claim against Dell must be a cross-claim, asserted pursuant to Rule 13(g). However, Rule 13(g) allows a cross-claim only if it "arises out of the transaction or occurrence that is the subject matter of the original action or of a counterclaim, or if the claim relates to any property that is the subject matter of the original action."** Since the Deborah-Dell contract has nothing whatsoever to do with the drag racing, it does not satisfy this requirement of relatedness, so it cannot be asserted by Deborah even if Dell is willing to have it heard in the basic action.

226. No, probably. **The twin doctrines of *merger* and *bar* (collectively known as "*claim preclusion*") prevent a plaintiff from splitting his or her cause of action between two suits.** If a plaintiff splits a cause of action and wins the first suit, his or her second claim is said to be "merged" into the favorable first judgment; if he or she loses the first suit, his or her second claim is held to be "barred" by the unfavorable first result.

Most courts today follow the "transaction" test for determining what constitutes a cause of action. By this test, both P's personal injury claim and her property damage claim formed a single cause of action, since they stemmed from a single transaction (the auto accident). Therefore, most courts would treat P as losing her property damage claim because it was merged into her previously asserted personal injury claim.

227. No. **The rule against splitting a cause of action applies even where the cause of action has both legal and equitable aspects.** Therefore, even though Peg's injunction claim is equitable and her damage claim is legal, the court will almost certainly treat them as being a single cause of action, since they arise out of a single transaction or series of transactions. Thus, the court will hold that Peg should have asked for damages in the same suit where she sought the injunction, and will hold that her damages claim was merged into her successful injunction claim.

228. No. Claim preclusion only applies where the first suit was resolved *"on the merits."* Federal Rule 41(b), last sentence, expressly provides that a dismissal for lack of jurisdiction does not operate as an adjudication on the merits. Therefore, Pauline is completely free to bring her new action (for the same damages) wherever she wants.

229. No. **Claim preclusion only applies where the first suit was resolved *"on the merits,"* so the question becomes whether the dismissal here was on the merits. Under Federal Rule 41(b), an order of dismissal is treated as being on the merits unless either the dismissal order specifies that it is without prejudice, or the dismissal is for lack of jurisdiction, improper venue, or failure to join an indispensable party.** Since none of these exceptions applies here, the dismissal is treated as being on the merits. As such, the result is the same as if Pauline had tried her case through to, say, a jury verdict. Her property damage claim is part of the same cause of action as her personal injury claim, so she is barred by the earlier dismissal from asserting the property damage claim here.

230. No, probably. **Most state courts will respect the policy behind the federal compulsory counterclaim rule and will bar an action on a claim that should have been raised as a compulsory counterclaim in a prior federal action.** This is true even if state law does not make any counterclaims compulsory. Since Doug's claim for property damage arose out of the same transaction or occurrence as Pauline's personal injury claim, Doug was required under Rule 13(a) to assert that property damage claim as part of Pauline's federal suit. Since he did not do so, he will be barred from making the claim in Iowa state court, just as he would be barred from making it in any federal court.

231. No. **Once a final judgment has been rendered, not even a change in the applicable law will prevent res judicata from operating.** The fact that Pauline would have won her original lawsuit if it were brought today is irrelevant. Since the property damage claim being asserted now and the personal injury claim asserted then are part of the same cause of action, Pauline's property damage claim will be barred just as if there had been no intervening change of law.

232. No. **Doreen is *collaterally estopped* from relitigating the issue of Phillip's negligence in the accident.** This is because (1) the issue of Phillip's negligence was *fully and fairly litigated* in the first action; (2) that issue was *actually decided* (since the finding in favor of Phillip, under the substantive law of Ames, was inconsistent with any negligence on Phillip's part); and (3) the finding was *necessary* to the verdict (since if Phillip had been negligent, he could not have recovered under Ames's law on contributory negligence).

233. Yes. **Collateral estoppel does not apply here.** For collateral estoppel to apply to an issue, that issue must have been actually litigated at the first trial. When a default judgment is entered, no issue is deemed to have been litigated.

234. No. **For collateral estoppel to apply to an issue, the disposition of that issue must have been *necessary* to the first verdict.** Here, once the first jury found that Phillip was contributorily negligent, it didn't matter whether Doreen was negligent (since Phillip couldn't recover even if Doreen were negligent). Since Doreen's negligence was not a necessary component of the first verdict, she will be permitted to relitigate the issue of whether she was (contributorily) negligent during the second suit. See *Cambria v. Jeffery*, 29 N.E.2d 555 (Mass. 1940).

235. Neither. **Where the first trial takes place in a court that has not only very limited jurisdiction but also very informal procedures, the findings of that court will generally *not* be given collateral estoppel effect.** The reason is that the findings of such a court are viewed as insufficiently trustworthy to determine the outcome of a much larger later controversy. (The mere fact that a jury trial was not available would not by itself be enough to deprive the first court's findings of collateral estoppel effect, but the absence of rules of evidence probably would be.) See F,K&M, p. 681-82.

236. **Yes. A *settlement* normally has *no collateral estoppel effect* on other suits.** Therefore, Xavier will not be able to treat the settlement as establishing Denise's negligence, even though a judgment against Denise was entered pursuant to that settlement. (Also, the rule against giving collateral estoppel effect to settlements can be viewed as a specific application of the general rule that collateral estoppel effect will only be given to issues that were litigated in the first action.)

237. **No. Although collateral estoppel does not usually apply to "pure" issues of law, it generally applies to "mixed" issues of law and fact (i.e., the application of a given legal principle to a particular fact situation), at least where the transactions in the two suits are similar or identical. See *U.S. v. Moser*, 266 U.S. 236 (1924).**

238. **No, probably. Collateral estoppel does not usually apply to "pure" issues of law, but does usually apply to "mixed" issues of law and fact—i.e., the application of a given legal principle to a particular fact situation. However, even if the first decision involves (as it does here) a mixed question of law and fact rather than a pure question of law, most courts believe that they have discretion to decline to apply collateral estoppel where there has been a significant change in legal principles between the first and second suits.** Courts are especially likely to exercise that discretion where use of collateral estoppel would "impose on one of the parties a significant disadvantage, or confer on him a significant benefit, with respect to his competitors." Rest. 2d Judgments, Section 28, Comment c. Here, use of collateral estoppel would give Potter a perpetual advantage over his competitors (he can undercut the price slightly, and they can never match him). The court is very unlikely to grant Potter, just because of the fortuity of his earlier victory, such a permanent advantage. This is especially true where, as here, the intervening decision was by a higher court than decided the original case in favor of the party now seeking collateral estoppel.

239. (a) **No. An indemnitor and indemnitee are usually held to be in *privity* with each other.** As such, a finding of fact adverse to one will normally be binding on the other. This is generally true of the employer/employee relationship: Since Worker was bound to indemnify Boss for any damages suffered by Boss as a result of Worker's negligence, Boss and Worker should be treated as privies. Especially where Worker had notice of the suit and could have intervened, there is no unfairness in binding him via collateral estoppel from relitigating the issue of whether he drove negligently.

(b) **No. If Boss and Worker are privies, then this should be viewed as a situation in which collateral estoppel is not being asserted by a "stranger" to the first action.** Instead, estoppel is being asserted by one who was in effect present in the first litigation. Therefore, Pedestrian should be collaterally estopped from claiming higher damages, even in a jurisdiction that looks unfavorably upon the offensive use of collateral estoppel by a stranger to the first action.

240. **Yes. *A stranger to the first action will never be bound*, either for claim preclusion or collateral estoppel purposes, by the results of that first suit.** Peter and Paul were not privies, since their cab-sharing relationship does not fall within any of the traditional relationships recognized as constituting privity by the common law (e.g., master/servant, insurer/insured, etc.). Thus, Paul is entitled to get his "day in court," even if that amounts to merely trotting out the same evidence as already used by Peter against David.

241. **Yes. Until the past 20 or 30 years, many courts might have automatically denied Baker's attempt to use collateral estoppel, on the now-discredited doctrine of mutuality (by which since Baker was a stranger to the first action, it could not claim the benefits of collateral estoppel in the second**

action). **Today, virtually all jurisdictions reject the automatic principle of mutuality.** Instead, most courts decide on a case-by-case basis whether to allow collateral estoppel use by a stranger. When it is the defendant in the second action who seeks to use collateral estoppel, and seeks to use it against a party who was a plaintiff in the first action, the case for allowing collateral estoppel is at its strongest. Thus here, Parker had the opportunity to fully and fairly litigate the causation issue during his first trial, and Baker is merely trying to use collateral estoppel as a shield rather than a sword in the second action. Nearly all courts would allow Baker to use collateral estoppel here. (This "use by the plaintiff in first action who is also plaintiff in second action" scenario matches the situation in *Bernhard v. Bank of America*, 122 P.2d 892 (Cal. 1942), the major case rejecting mutuality and allowing a stranger to use collateral estoppel.)

242. **Yes, probably. Here, Paul is not only a stranger to the first action but also an "*offensive*" user of collateral estoppel, so his case for getting the benefit of the doctrine is weaker than the case of Parker, the defensive would-be user of collateral estoppel in the prior question.** Nonetheless, the court will probably find that Paul is entitled to use collateral estoppel. First of all, Paul might not have been allowed to intervene in the first suit even if he had wanted to, since individuals are not always permitted to intervene in suits brought by government bodies. Second, there is every reason to believe that Natural Foods had an incentive to vigorously defend the first suit. Nor is there any evidence that Natural Foods would have procedural opportunities in the second suit that were not present in the first suit. All together, there seems to be very little risk of unfairness to Natural Foods in collaterally estopping it from relitigating the issue of whether Oat Bits reduces colon cancer risk. This fact pattern is somewhat similar to that of *Parklane Hosiery Co. v. Shore*, 439 U.S. 322 (1979), where the Supreme Court held that offensive collateral estoppel should be allowed on those facts.

243. **No. Greg is not only a stranger to the first action but also is attempting an offensive use of collateral estoppel. (That is, he is a plaintiff in the second action.) Therefore, the court will do a case-by-case balancing (similar to that performed by the Supreme Court in *Parklane Hosiery*) to decide whether to allow estoppel here.** Two factors strongly militate against allowing estoppel here: (1) the first suit was for relatively little money ($500), so Dave did not have an incentive to litigate it to the hilt; and (2) the possibility of a later action by Greg (or anyone else relating to that particular serving of chowder) was quite unlikely from Dave's perspective, so Dave was not at all on notice that issues might be decided as to which collateral estoppel would later be possibly applicable. Together, these factors make it most unlikely that the court would estop Dave from attempting to disprove Greg's allegation of dangerously defective chowder.

244. **No. Here there is a situation where a stranger to the first action is proposing to make offensive use of collateral estoppel.** Here, we have a stark case of the "*multiple plaintiff anomaly*"—if Deadly wins any given suit, it still has to completely relitigate the merits with the next plaintiff in line, yet under collateral estoppel one defeat by Deadly would cause it to lose against everyone later in line. The unfairness to Deadly from allowing collateral estoppel here is further exaggerated by (1) the fact that the plaintiffs' lawyers have intentionally chosen the most appealing plaintiff to go first, and (2) the fact that the lawyers intentionally declined to join the additional victims as plaintiffs in the first suit, preferring to have them "wait in the wings." Therefore, it is unlikely that Deadly will be deprived of its chance to relitigate the issue of whether its cigarettes are dangerously defective or its warnings inadequate.

245. **No. Nonparties to the first action will almost never be allowed to use offensive collateral estoppel against a *government body*.** A government will frequently have to defend multiple suits, and it is undesirable from a public policy viewpoint to require the government to fully appeal each adverse

decision or else lose the ability to litigate that issue when it arises in subsequent suits brought by other parties. (For instance, Ames would have had virtually no choice but to appeal, theoretically all the way to the U.S. Supreme Court, the adverse decision in the CTS suit.) See, e.g., *U.S. v. Mendoza*, 464 U.S. 154 (1984), holding that nonmutual offensive use of collateral estoppel will never be allowed against the federal government.

246. Unclear. **Most states at least allow the conviction to be used as evidence.** Some, but by no means all, take the further step of collaterally estopping the defendant from denying any fact that was an element of the crime of which he was convicted. (If Dick had been *acquitted*, it is absolutely clear that Patricia won't be estopped from showing that Dick was in fact drunk—first, as a stranger to first action, she cannot be bound, and second, the burden of proof was more favorable to Dick in the first action than it would be here, so collateral estoppel would not be allowed on that ground either.)

247. (a) Yes.

   (b) The answer is required by the Full Faith and Credit Clause of the U.S. Constitution. **The Full Faith and Credit Clause of the U.S. Constitution (Article IV, Section 1) requires each state to give to the judgment of any other state the same effect that that judgment would have in the state which rendered it. This requirement extends to the *res judicata effect* of the first state court's judgment.** Here, therefore, Bates must give to the judgment of the Ames court the same effect that the Ames court system would give to that prior judgment. Since Ames would grant preclusive effect to the judgment against Baker (i.e., Ames would let Conroy collaterally estop Baker), Bates must do the same. This is true even though the Bates courts, if left to their own devices, would prefer not to give collateral estoppel effect to the judgment against Baker.

248. Yes, the federal judge must do so. **A federal statute, 28 U.S.C. §1738, requires federal courts to give state court judgments the same effect (including res judicata effect) as the state itself would give them.** Except in a very few instances where later, more specific, congressional statutes indicate that Congress does not want the federal courts to have to honor the preclusive effect of a state court judgment, the federal court is bound by §1738 to give the state court judgment the same effect the state itself would give it. Therefore, since no special congressional statute is at issue here, the federal judge must grant collateral estoppel against Baker solely on the grounds that the Ames court would do so.

249. Yes. **No congressional statute, and no specific constitutional provision, requires the state court to follow the prior federal judgment's preclusive effect.** However, *Semtek v. Lockheed Martin*, 531 U.S. 497 (2001), requires the Bates state court to apply the same rule of preclusion as would be applied by the Ames courts (which are the courts of the state where the federal diversity court that rendered the first judgment sits). Since the Ames courts would allow Conroy to make offensive use of collateral estoppel against Baker on this issue if the first judgment had been rendered by an Ames state court, the courts of Bates must allow that same use.

Civil Procedure Essay Questions

QUESTION 1:   Tony is a sea captain based in New Bedford, Massachusetts, although he spends nine months out of the year at sea harpooning unicorn seals. One December, when he sails home for the Christmas holidays, he buys a bottle of Super Mustache from Otto's Drug Store in New Bedford. The maker of Super Mustache is Drugimi Drugs, Inc., a large drug company incorporated in Delaware. The company's headquarters are in Connecticut, and all of its factories are in Arizona. Tony uses Super Mustache and ends up liking it so much that he films himself using the product and posts it on YouTube, with a video of him singing a song called "Even Pirates Like Super Mustache!" The video goes viral and is soon being watched by more than 10 million people. Drugimi finds out about the video and incorporates it into its new advertising slogans. Tony is fine with this until one day he wakes up and finds that Super Mustache has turned his once luxurious black mustache bright purple. He files suit against Drugimi in Massachusetts state court, claiming damages of $100,000 for his destroyed mustache (he claims it is now impossible to captain a ship because no one takes him seriously), and also claiming copyright infringement in the amount of $50,000 for Drugimi using his video. Drugimi files a motion for both actions to be moved to federal court. Please advise the judge.

QUESTION 2:   Bruce and Andy are in a car accident. Bruce hires Herbert "The Harasser" Caulfield as his attorney. Caulfield files suit in federal court based on diversity (assume there is no issue regarding the case being heard in federal court). Caulfield sets up ten depositions, in which he asks Andy the same questions over and over again. Caulfield calls Andy and says he's set up five more. At the same time, Caulfield sends an interrogatory seeking "all papers, pictures, and anything else that Andy has ever touched." Andy calls Caulfield and says, "I'm not giving you anything, and I'm not doing anymore depositions! You're acting like Attila the Hun!" Caulfield says, "I'll get you for that one!" Caulfield then requests that the court subject Andy to a mental examination since he claims that Andy thinks Caulfield is in fact Attila the Hun. Judge Chan, the judge in the case, orders Caulfield and Andy to attend a pretrial conference. During the conference, Caulfield claims that his client should not be required to attend the pretrial conference, and then demands that Judge Chan issue discovery sanctions against Andy. Judge Chan refuses and tells Caulfield and Andy that the only issues in the trial are going to be whether Andy or Bruce were negligent in their driving. Caulfield storms out of the conference. Andy, realizing this whole thing is getting a bit out of hand, comes to you for advice.

QUESTION 3:   Mark, who has had what he considers to be a "rough life," decides to sue "Satan and his staff" for his injuries. He files a class action suit in federal court on behalf of anyone who has ever been tormented by Satan. Judge Ogala gets the case, and comes to you, her clerk. She says, "Look, this guy is bananas, but I want to give him some real reasons why he can't sue Satan in federal court. Assume there really is a Satan, and if there really is a Satan down in Hell tormenting people with fire and pitchforks and whatnot, why couldn't Mark sue him?" Please write the memo.

QUESTION 4:   Bear Insurance Agency is based in Massachusetts. It also conducts business in Connecticut through salespeople who live in the state and work out of their own homes. The salespeople send all insurance orders to the home office, which then handles the remainder of the paperwork. Each year, Bear salespeople in Connecticut make roughly $100,000 in commissions. As Bear grows, it decides to try to expand its business. To do so, it takes over some life insurance policies written by Bubbler Insurance, an insurance agency in Rhode Island. Bear sends out new life insurance policies, and the policyholders (Rhode Island residents) send their premiums to the home office in Massachusetts. Additionally, Urbe, a Maine resident, comes in and asks if Bear can set up a trust for her with it as the trustee. Thinking getting into the trust business might be a good idea, Bear agrees. Several years later, Urbe moves to Texas. Several years after that, a Rhode Island life insurance policyholder named Small dies in a freak hot-air balloon crash with Urbe. Small's family in Rhode Island sues Bear for payment under the policy in Rhode Island court. Urbe's family in Texas sues Bear in Texas court for payment of the trust funds. At the same time, a policyholder in Connecticut sues Bear in Connecticut court. Bear's CEO comes to you and asks, "Can we really be sued in these different states? I thought we could only be sued in Massachusetts!" Please draft your answer.

QUESTION 5: In preparation for her move from New York to Oklahoma, Marly buys a new Zoolet automobile from Big Dan's Auto Sales in Massapequa, New York. Zoolets are distributed by Miles Car Service, and are only distributed on the East Coast. A week after moving to Oklahoma, Marly is injured in an accident. An investigator discovers that the accident was caused by a defect in the car. Marly files suit against Big Dan and Miles in Oklahoma court for her product liability claim. Big Dan and Miles come down to Oklahoma to argue that they should not be sued in an Oklahoma court. The judge responds, "If something breaks in Oklahoma, we sue in Oklahoma! Anyway, all y'all are here now—we might as well do this thing!" The judge then allows the suit to proceed. Big Dan calls you up and asks if the judge is right about any of this.

Sample Answers to Civil Procedure Essay Questions

ANSWER TO QUESTION 1:

Claim for the Mustache

The issue is whether Tony's claim for his mustache meets the diversity requirements for removal to federal court. **Generally, any action brought in state court over which the federal courts would have original jurisdiction may be removed by the defendant to federal district court. In diversity cases, the action may generally be removed only if no defendant is a citizen of the state in which the action is pending. Under the rule of diversity jurisdiction, federal courts have jurisdiction over controversies between citizens of different states as long as the amount in controversy is more than $75,000. People are citizens of where they are domiciled. A person's domicile is where he or she has his or her true, fixed, and permanent home. A corporation is deemed a citizen of any state where it is incorporated and of the state where it has its principal place of business. The most commonly used test for principal place of business is the place in which the corporation carries on its main production or service activities, while a minority of courts base principal place of business on where the corporate headquarters are. The party seeking to invoke federal diversity jurisdiction does not have to prove that the amount in controversy exceeds $75,000. All he or she has to show is that there is some possibility that that much is in question.** Here, although Tony is away at sea most of the year, he is domiciled in Massachusetts, since that appears to be his permanent and fixed address. Drugimi, the defendant, is incorporated in Delaware, has its headquarters in Connecticut, and has all of its factories in Arizona. Although Tony bought Super Mustache in Massachusetts, from the facts it appears Drugimi is a citizen of Delaware, where it is incorporated; Arizona, where all its factories are; or Connecticut, where it has its corporate headquarters. Importantly, it does not appear to be a citizen of Massachusetts, so there is likely a complete diversity of citizenship. Tony is claiming $100,000 for his mustache, but considering he claims the damage to his mustache is defeating his ability to be a captain, damages of $100,000 do not appear to be completely out of the realm of possibility. Consequently, Drugimi may remove this claim to federal court.

Claim for the Copyright Violation

The issue is whether the copyright claim can be heard in federal court. **Federal courts have jurisdiction over all civil actions arising under the Constitution, laws, or treaties of the United States. Importantly, a claim of violation of copyright is a federal claim.** Consequently, since Tony is suing on a federal claim, it does not matter that the amount in controversy for this particular claim is less than that required for diversity jurisdiction (even if that were not the case, since the claims are closely related, the amount in controversy requirement could likely be met by aggregating the amounts together since both claims arise from the same transaction or occurrence). Thus, this claim can also be removed to federal court.

ANSWER TO QUESTION 2:

Interrogatories and Depositions

The issue is whether Andy can protect himself against Caulfield's discovery abuses. **A party may object to a discovery request the same way a question at trial may be objected to. Typical grounds are that the matter sought is not within the scope of discovery (i.e., not relevant to the subject matter) or that it is privileged. An objection to an interrogatory question is written down as part of the answers. Where** more than a few questions are at stake, the party opposing discovery may seek a protective order. **FRCP 26(c)(1) allows a judge to make "an order to protect a party or person from annoyance, embarrassment, oppression, or undue burden or expense.** This case is dealing with a simple car accident. The request for documents is much too large and is seeking evidence that is not relevant to the subject matter of the car accident. As for the depositions, Andy should request a protective order in which the judge orders that no further depositions of Andy may take place at all. The court will probably grant this request since Caulfield keeps asking the same questions (and there is likely no just reason to depose Andy 15 times for a car accident).

Request for Mental Examination

The issue is whether Caulfield can have Andy subjected to a mental examination. **When the mental or physical condition of a party is in controversy, the court may order the party to submit to a physical or mental examination by a suitably licensed or certified examiner under FRCP 35. Unlike all other forms of discovery, FRCP 35 operates only by court order. The discovering party must make a motion upon notice to the party to be examined, and must show good cause why the examination is needed.** Here, Andy's mental state is unlikely to have anything to do with the car accident. Also, the fact that he called Caulfield "Attila the Hun" does not imply that he actually believes Caulfield is Attila the Hun. Consequently, a court will be unlikely to order the mental exam.

Pretrial Conference

The issue is whether Bruce should be required to attend the pretrial conference with Judge Chan. **In the federal system, the judge has the authority to conduct a pretrial conference. The judge may use such a conference to simplify or formulate the issues for trial, and to facilitate a settlement. See FRCP 16(a) and 16(c). If the judge does hold a pretrial conference, he or she must then enter a pretrial order reciting the actions taken in the conference.** Here, Judge Chan had the authority to require the parties to attend the pretrial conference, and he could lawfully use that conference to narrow the issues at trial to the parties' negligence. However, he now has to enter a pretrial order stating the fact that negligence will be the sole issue at trial.

Sanctions

The issue is whether Caulfield can receive sanctions against Andy for failing to meet his discovery requests. **The court may order a number of sanctions against parties who behave unreasonably during discovery. Principally, these sanctions are used against a party who fails to cooperate in the other party's discovery efforts.** Andy appears to be reasonable in his refusal to submit to Caulfield's irrelevant interrogatory and harassing depositions. Consequently, the court is very unlikely to order sanctions against Andy.

ANSWER TO QUESTION 3:

Service of Process and Personal Jurisdiction

The issue is whether someone could serve process on Satan. **To determine whether a federal court has personal jurisdiction over the defendant, courts look at whether the defendant is served notice of the lawsuit in the appropriate territory, in the correct manner, and whether the defendant is amenable to federal suit. FRCP 4(k)(2) allows a federal question suit to be brought against any person or organization who cannot be sued in any state court (almost always because they are a foreigner).** Here, since Satan lives in Hell, which seems to be impossible to get to without dying, there is likely no way anyone could serve process on him. Also, while the location of Hell is a mystery, if it is thought of as a foreign country, Mark is not apparently suing on any federal question (he is only suing for his "rough life"). Consequently, since there is likely no way to properly serve Satan in Hell, a federal court would have no personal jurisdiction over him.

Class Action

The issue is whether Mark can file a class action on behalf of all those tormented by Satan. **Four pre-requisites must be met before any federal class action is allowed: (1) the class size must be so large that joinder of all members is impractical, (2) there must be questions of law or fact common to the class, (3) the claims or defenses of the representatives must be "typical" of the class, and (4) the representative has to show that he or she can "fairly and adequately protect the interest of the class." FRCP 23.** While the class of people tormented by Satan is likely numerous, this is likely one of the rare situations where the claims of the class members do not share common facts or questions of law (since everyone is likely tormented by Satan in unique ways). Consequently, a court is unlikely to certify this class despite its large size.

ANSWER TO QUESTION 4:

Connecticut

The issue is whether Bear can be sued in Connecticut based on its insurance policies. **A forum state may exercise personal jurisdiction over a corporation only if the corporation has "minimum contacts" with the forum state "such that the maintenance of the suit does not offend 'traditional notions of fair play and substantial justice.'" Usually, a corporation will be found to have the requisite "minimum contacts" with the forum state only if the corporation has somehow voluntarily sought to do business in, or with the residents of, the forum state.** Although Bear is based in Massachusetts, and its Connecticut salespeople were based in their own homes, it seems pretty clear that Bear has minimum contacts with Connecticut based on the large amount of business it does in the state. Consequently, Bear may be sued in Connecticut.

Rhode Island

The rule for personal jurisdiction over corporations is stated above. Here, Bear took over the policies from a Rhode Island company, and it again has voluntarily sought to do business in Rhode Island. Importantly, Bear offered a policy to someone it knew was a resident of the forum state. Consequently, Bear has minimum contacts in Rhode Island and can be sued there.

Texas

However, Bear will not have to face a lawsuit in Texas. **The rule for personal jurisdiction is stated above.** The important difference here is that Bear never voluntarily initiated business transactions with a resident of the forum state—it was only Urbe's unilateral decision to move to the forum state that established any kind of connection with that state, so minimum contacts did not exist (although this could change if Urbe's family can show that Bear has in fact purposely availed itself of the chance to do business in Texas).

ANSWER TO QUESTION 5:

Product Liability in Oklahoma

The issue is whether Oklahoma has jurisdiction over Big Dan and Miles since the Zoolet injured Marly in Oklahoma. **The mere fact that a product manufactured or sold by the defendant outside of the forum state finds its way into the forum state and causes injury there is not enough to subject the defendant to personal jurisdiction there. Instead, the defendant can be sued in the forum state only if it made**

some effort to market in the forum state, either directly or indirectly. Here, there is no fact stating that either Big Dan or Miles made any effort to market their products in Oklahoma. Consequently, they cannot now be sued in Oklahoma for the defective product, even though the product injured Marly in Oklahoma.

Big Dan's and Miles's Presence in Oklahoma

The issue is whether Big Dan and Miles can be sued in Oklahoma simply because they made an appearance there. **In a special appearance, the defendant appears with the express purpose of making a jurisdictional objection; his or her doing so is not a consent to the exercise of jurisdiction.** Here, Big Dan and Miles can enter Oklahoma to argue that Oklahoma jurisdiction shouldn't apply. Importantly, by doing so, they do not consent to the court having any personal jurisdiction over them. Consequently, the judge is wrong in saying he has jurisdiction over them now simply because they are physically in Oklahoma.

CONTRACTS

Contracts Table of Contents

OFFER AND ACCEPTANCE

CONSIDERATION

PROMISES BINDING WITHOUT CONSIDERATION

MISTAKE

PAROL EVIDENCE AND INTERPRETATION

CONDITIONS

ANTICIPATORY REPUDIATION AND OTHER ASPECTS OF BREACH

STATUTE OF FRAUDS

CONTRACTS INVOLVING MORE THAN TWO PARTIES

IMPOSSIBILITY, IMPRACTICABILITY, AND FRUSTRATION

MISCELLANEOUS DEFENSES: ILLEGALITY, DURESS, MISREPRESENTATION, UNCONSCIONABILITY, AND LACK OF CAPACITY

WARRANTIES

DISCHARGE OF CONTRACTS

Contracts Short-Answer Questions

1. Alex prepared a written offer to buy Barry's house; he put the offer in a stamped and addressed envelope. He then put it in a stack of other letters that he intended to mail. Shortly thereafter, Alex decided that he didn't really want to buy the house. However, he gathered up the whole stack of letters and mailed them, forgetting that the offer to Barry was in the stack. Barry received the offer and sent an immediate written statement: "I accept your offer." Barry did not know that Alex's offer letter was dispatched in error. Do Alex and Barry have a contract?

    Not sure ☐

2. Adam orally offered to buy Basil's Rolex watch for $400. Basil orally accepted. Both parties incorrectly believed that such an agreement was not enforceable because it was not in writing, and neither intended to be bound. However, neither party stated this intention not to be bound to the other (so that Adam thought that Basil intended to be bound, and Basil thought that Adam intended to be bound). Adam and Basil are neither relatives nor friends, but have done business together before. Do Adam and Basil have a contract?

    Not sure ☐

3. Same facts as in the previous question. Now, however, assume that Adam said to Basil, "You know, of course, that such contracts are not enforceable unless they are in writing, so I am not intending this as a binding contract." Basil said nothing out loud, but secretly reasoned to himself, "This is one of those agreements that is enforceable even though it's oral, so I'm going to treat it as binding." Is there a contract?

    Not sure ☐

4. Alfred and Bertha were classmates at Ames High School. Alfred asked Bertha to the junior prom, and Bertha said, "Sure." Alfred then changed his mind and attended the prom with someone else. Can Bertha recover from Alfred for breach of contract?

    Not sure ☐

5. Ava wished to sell her chain of ten radio stations; Bridget wished to buy the stations. They orally agreed on a price of $20 million but did not discuss other details. Ava then said, "It's a deal," and she and Bridget shook hands. Bridget said, "My lawyers will prepare the formal written agreement," and Ava said, "Fine." Later, Ava changed her mind and now claims that there was no binding agreement, merely an understanding that the parties would try to arrive at a formal binding written agreement. Bridget, by contrast, claims that although the parties intended to embody their agreement in a later written document, their oral agreement was itself intended as binding. On the issue of whether there was a contract, who will win, Ava or Bridget?

    Not sure ☐

6. Adlai, a distributor of home heating oil, sent a letter to Bellamy, a dealer in such oil. The letter said, "We quote you standard home heating oil at 98 cents per gallon, for immediate delivery. 1,000 gallon minimum." The letter itself did not have Bellamy's name on it and was clearly a form letter. Bellamy sent back a letter saying, "I accept your offer to sell 2,000 gallons at 98 cents. Please deliver to my depot next Wednesday." Do Adlai and Bellamy have a contract?

    Not sure ☐

7. Same basic fact pattern as in the previous question. Now, however, assume that Adlai sent Bellamy a follow-up letter. This one was personally addressed to Bellamy and stated, "We will sell you 5,000 gallons of heating oil at a special price of 96 cents per gallon, delivery to take place next week at your depot. Your order will not be shipped until approved by our office." Bellamy wrote back, "I accept." Do Adlai and Bellamy have a contract?

Not sure ☐

8. The Piano Store, a retail piano dealer, took out the following newspaper advertisement: "New Steinway Living Room Grand Pianos, $14,500 each. On sale through Friday, Feb. 24." Charles Consumer, who arrived at the store on February 23, tendered a check for $14,500 and said, "I'll take one of the Steinway living room grands in any color." The Piano Store's manager replied, "I'm sorry, sir; we're sold out." Can Consumer recover against the Piano Store for breach of contract?

Not sure ☐

9. Same basic fact pattern as in the previous question. This time, however, the Piano Store's ad read, "We will sell one Steinway Living Room Grand, black, at a special $13,900 promotional price to the first purchaser who arrives when we open next Thursday at 9:00 A.M." Consumer was the first customer in the store on Thursday at 9:00 A.M. and tendered his check for $13,900. The manager of the store replied, "I'm sorry; the owner decided to take that particular piano home for his wife, so it's not available. May I interest you in a white Steinway at our regular price of $15,900?" May Consumer recover against the Piano Store for breach of contract?

Not sure ☐

10. Spot, a beagle belonging to Arnold, had disappeared. Arnold placed an ad in the local newspaper saying, "Reward, $500, for return of my gray beagle Spot, last seen in the vicinity of my house at 481 Main Street. No questions asked." Bernice, who lived several blocks away from Arnold, read the ad and then noticed a dog resembling Spot pawing through her trash can. She brought Spot to Arnold. Arnold said, "Oh, thank you so much," but refused to pay the $500. Can Bernice recover from Arnold for breach of contract?

Not sure ☐

11. Same facts as in the previous question. Now, however, assume that Bernice never saw the reward ad. She picked up Spot from her front yard, read his name collar, and returned him to Arnold just because it was the neighborly thing to do. Shortly thereafter, she learned that a reward had been offered. May she recover the reward from Arnold?

Not sure ☐

12. Homeowner wrote to Buyer, "I hereby offer to sell you my house for $250,000. You must indicate your acceptance by signing this letter and returning it to me no later than August 15." On August 14, Buyer telephoned Homeowner and left a message on his answering machine stating, "I accept your offer." Homeowner listened to the message but disregarded it. On August 16, not having gotten the signed letter back, Homeowner sold the house to someone else. Putting aside the Statute of Frauds, is there a contract between Buyer and Homeowner?

Not sure ☐

13. Same basic facts as in the previous question. This time, however, Homeowner's offer said, "You may accept this offer by signing this letter and returning it to me no later than August 15." Buyer purported to accept on August 14 by leaving a

message on Homeowner's answering machine, as in the previous question. Is there a contract?

14. Seller wanted to sell and Buyer wanted to buy a computer system manufactured by Seller. Seller's salesman prepared a form called a "purchase order," which listed the equipment to be sold. Buyer signed that form. The purchase order form stated, "This order does not become a contract until signed by an officer of Seller." Seller's salesman brought the order back to Seller's office, where Seller's president immediately signed it. A copy of the signed order was sent to Buyer on March 1. On March 2, Buyer purported to cancel the deal. On March 3, Buyer received the copy of the order with Seller's president's signature on it. Can Seller enforce the agreement?

15. Same facts as above question. Now, however, assume that Seller never sent Buyer a copy of the purchase order signed by Seller's president, even though the form had in fact been signed. After 30 days went by, Buyer purported to revoke his offer. May Seller enforce the agreement against Buyer?

16. Seller advertised an IBM-compatible Pentium computer at a specified price in a newspaper ad. Buyer wrote to Seller, "Here's my order for the IBM-compatible Pentium computer. Ship by next Tuesday, August 13." Seller then sent a document that said, "Thanks for your order. We'll ship next Tuesday, the 13th." On the 11th, Buyer received the letter, changed his mind, and telephoned Seller with the message, "Since you haven't shipped the computer yet, cancel my order." Do Seller and Buyer have a contract?

17. Grandfather wrote to Grandson, "If you can gain acceptance to and complete a degree at an ABA-accredited law school, I will pay you $10,000." Grandson immediately wrote back to Grandfather, "I accept." Before Grandson actually made an application to any ABA law school, Grandfather wrote back, "I've changed my mind, and I revoke my offer. Sorry. I love you anyway." Grandson then applied to, got accepted by, attended, and graduated from an ABA-accredited law school. Assuming that contracts to make gifts are generally enforceable in the jurisdiction, does Grandfather owe Grandson $10,000?

18. Insurer had insured Owner's house against fire for many years. At the start of each year, Insurer mailed Owner a renewal notice and a bill, which Owner paid. On January 1, 2010 (the sixth year of the arrangement), Insurer mailed Owner a renewal policy and a bill. Owner retained the policy but did not pay the bill. On March 1, Owner told Insurer that he would not be paying the bill, and that he regarded the insurance as not having been in force at any time during 2010 because he, Owner, never accepted the policy. Assuming that there is no statute on point, is Owner liable to pay the premiums attributable to January and February?

19. Seller was in the business of selling widgets. Buyer, a large business, sent Seller a purchase order for one widget manufactured by Seller. The order stated the price and delivery terms for the widgets and also contained an extensive warranty. Seller sent back an "acknowledgment" form, which in its boilerplate (1) disclaimed all warranties, including the warranty of merchantability; and (2) stated, "Our acceptance of your order is hereby expressly made conditional on your assent to any

terms in this acknowledgement that are different from or additional to terms in your order form. If you do not so assent, you must notify us to that effect immediately." Buyer received this form, failed to read the boilerplate, and waited for the shipment. Seller, hearing nothing from Buyer, sent the widget. Buyer kept the widget and used it. The widget turned out to be unmerchantable.

(a) Is there a contract, and if so, when was it formed?   Not sure ☐

(b) Assume, for this part only, that the answer to part (a) is that there is a contract. What does the contract provide regarding the warranty of merchantability?   Not sure ☐

20. Seller was in the business of selling widgets. Buyer, a large business, sent Seller a "purchase order" form ordering 100 widgets at a stated price and time for delivery. The order form said nothing about warranties. Seller responded with an "acknowledgement form," which matched Buyer's purchase order form completely, except that it included a provision allowing Seller to ship any number of widgets between 90 and 110. After Seller sent this acknowledgement form (and before Seller shipped the goods), Buyer purported to revoke its order.

(a) Do the parties have a contract?   Not sure ☐

(b) Assume, for this part only, that the answer to (a) is yes. Does the contract allow Seller to ship (and be paid for) 110 widgets?   Not sure ☐

21. Buyer placed a purchase order with Seller for 100 widgets, stating price and delivery terms. Buyer's purchase order also provided that Seller warranted that the goods were merchantable. Seller responded with an "acknowledgement form" that agreed with Buyer's form as to description of the goods, quantity, price, and delivery. However, Seller's form stated that the warranty of merchantability (as well as all other warranties) was expressly disclaimed. Seller then shipped the widgets, and Buyer accepted them and used them. Buyer and Seller are both merchants.

(a) Do the parties have a contract, and if so, when was it formed?   Not sure ☐

(b) Assume, for this part only, that a contract exists. Does that contract contain the warranty of merchantability?   Not sure ☐

22. Same facts as in the previous question. Now, however, assume that Buyer's purchase order was silent on the issue of warranties, and Seller's acknowledgement expressly disclaimed the warranty of merchantability. All other facts remain the same. Assuming that the exchange of forms created a contract, does that contract contain the warranty of merchantability?   Not sure ☐

23. The market price of standard-grade 50-pound offset paper was 45 cents per pound. Printer sent to Paper Co. a purchase order for one carload of such paper, at a price of 40 cents per pound. Paper Co. sent back an "acknowledgement," stating that it would ship a carload of such paper to Printer, but at 50 cents per pound. Printer made no further response. Paper Co. failed to ship the paper on the delivery date (a date as to which both forms agreed). Is Paper Co. in breach?   Not sure ☐

24. Same facts as in the previous question. Now, however, assume that Paper Co. went ahead and shipped the carload of paper at the appointed date and sent Printer a bill

at 50 cents per pound. Printer used the paper, but refused to pay any more than 40 cents per pound.

   (a) Is there a contract, and if so, why?

   (b) Assume that there is a contract. What is the price?

25. In a telephone conversation, Buyer and Seller agreed that Seller would sell Buyer 100 widgets at a stated price and time. In this conversation, the parties did not say anything about Buyer's remedies in case Seller breached. Seller then sent a "confirmation" form, which repeated the essential terms of the oral agreement, but which added the following clause: "In case of breach by Seller, Buyer's remedy shall be limited to the right to return the goods and receive a refund of the purchase price." Buyer did not respond to this confirmation. Seller shipped the widgets at the agreed-upon time and for the agreed-upon price. Buyer used the widgets, but they were defective. These defects caused Buyer to in turn breach a larger contract to manufacture goods of which the widgets were one component. Seller offered to take back the unused widgets and to refund Buyer's purchase price, but Buyer seeks consequential damages. May Buyer receive such damages?

26. Owner offered to sell his house to Buyer for $200,000, the offer to be kept open for one week. A day after the offer was made, Buyer wrote to Seller, "I'll give you $180,000." Owner did not respond. Before the end of the original one-week deadline, Buyer wrote to Owner, "I've changed my mind, and I hereby accept your offer at $200,000." Do Owner and Buyer have a contract?

27. Same facts as in the previous question. Now, however, assume that the day after Owner's original offer, Buyer wrote to him, "Would you take $180,000?" Owner responded, "No." A day later (still before the original deadline), Buyer wrote to Seller, "I accept at $200,000." Is there a contract?

28. Owner offered, in a letter sent to Buyer, to sell his house to Buyer for $200,000. The letter stated that Owner must receive Buyer's acceptance by January 15. On January 15, Buyer purported to accept, by mailing a letter of acceptance that Owner received on January 16. Owner remained silent when he got this letter. On January 18, Buyer telegraphed, "I don't want to buy after all." May Owner successfully sue Buyer for breach of contract?

29. Buyer offered to buy Seller's house for $200,000. This offer said, "You may accept this offer until March 1." Seller received this offer on January 30. On February 1, Buyer dispatched another letter to Seller, this one saying, "I revoke my offer." On February 2, when Seller had not yet received Buyer's February 1 letter, Seller dispatched a letter to Buyer saying, "I accept." On February 3, Seller received Buyer's February 1 revocation letter. On February 4, Buyer received Seller's February 2 acceptance letter. On February 5, is there a contract?

30. On February 1, Seller wrote a letter to Buyer, in which Seller offered to sell his home for $200,000. On February 2, Seller unexpectedly died. On February 3, Buyer (who did not yet know of Seller's death) mailed a letter saying, "I accept."

On February 4, Buyer learned that Seller had died. On February 5, Buyer's acceptance letter arrived at Seller's house (the place to which, according to Seller's offer, the acceptance should be directed). May Buyer force Seller's estate to sell him the property for $200,000?

Not sure ☐

31. Seller and Buyer were negotiating for Buyer to buy Seller's house. Seller gave Buyer a letter that said, "I will sell you my house for $200,000. In return for your payment to me of $1, receipt of which is hereby acknowledged, I agree to keep this offer open for two years. [signed, Seller]." This $1 was not in fact paid. $200,000 was a fair price for the house based on the market as it then stood. After 30 days, Seller got an offer for $250,000 from someone else and purported to revoke the offer. Buyer now shows that he would have been willing and able to buy the house at some point during the two-year period. May Buyer recover for breach of contract?

Not sure ☐

32. Printer asked Paper Co. to quote him a price for one carload of 50-pound white offset paper. Paper Co. responded by means of a letter signed by its president, which recited the price at which Paper Co. was willing to supply such paper and further stated, "This offer will be held open for two weeks." Printer did not pay anything for this promise of irrevocability; nor did the document state otherwise.

Before Printer relied in any way on this offer, paper mills announced a general price increase of 10 percent, and Paper Co. realized that it had been imprudent. Therefore, one week after the initial offer, Paper Co. sent Printer a letter stating, "Due to the unexpected price rise, we must withdraw our offer. We would be happy to sell you the paper at a price 10 percent higher than the originally quoted price." Printer sent back a letter saying, "I accept your original offer." Paper Co. refused to perform. May Printer recover against Paper Co. for breach?

Not sure ☐

33. Fred Frozen was in the business of selling freezers door to door. Consumer agreed to buy one of Frozen's freezers on credit, and was given an order form prepared in the name of Frozen's employer (the Frozen Foods Corporation or FFC), which stated, "All orders are subject to acceptance by the home office, following a check of Buyer's credit." The order form also said, "This order form, when signed by Buyer, shall remain irrevocable for a period of three days." Consumer signed the order form, initialed the irrevocability clause as requested by Frozen, and understood that the order form would become effective as a contract when (and if) signed by an officer of FFC. The day after Consumer signed the form, while FFC was still checking Consumer's credit, Consumer telephoned Frozen and said, "I'm canceling my order." Frozen said, "You can't do that. You signed a firm offer." That same day, FFC approved Consumer's credit, and FFC's president signed the order form. Do Consumer and FFC have a contract?

Not sure ☐

34. Arthur, who lived in San Francisco, wanted to have his automobile brought back from his former residence in New York. He therefore wrote to his friend Brian, "If you'll drive my car from New York to San Francisco, I'll pay you $500 when you arrive. You can find the keys under the doormat of my house. No need to respond, just show up with the car." Brian, without contacting Arthur, went to Arthur's house, got the key, hopped in the car, and started to drive. After 100 miles,

he telephoned Arthur to say, "I'm on my way." Arthur said, "I've been trying to reach you. I've gotten an unexpected good offer for the car from someone back in New York, so I'm calling off my offer. Drive the car back to New York, and I'll pay you $50 for your trouble." Brian, who needed the $500 desperately and had nothing else to do with his time, replied, "No, we've got a deal." He got back in the car and kept driving west, arriving in San Francisco six exhausting days later. Does Arthur owe Brian $500?

Not sure ☐

35. Same facts as in the previous question. Now, however, assume that to take the trip in the time frame demanded by Arthur, Brian knew that he would have to give up a free ticket (worth $50) to the Super Bowl, offered to him by his employer. Brian explained to Arthur that he didn't know whether he could do the drive, that he would have to give up the ticket to do the drive, and that if he (Brian) decided to do the drive he would just start driving without further contact with Arthur. Brian then decided to do the trip, told his boss he wouldn't be using the ticket, and the boss gave it to someone else. Brian went to Arthur's house to get the keys, but instead of finding the keys, found a letter under the doormat addressed to him, saying, "Sorry old man. I've had a change of plans. I don't want the car in San Francisco after all. Just leave it where it is. Hope you haven't been inconvenienced. [Signed, Arthur]." Brian never did the drive. Does Brian have a claim for breach against Arthur? If so, for how much?

Not sure ☐

36. Owner wanted to sell his house. He said to Broker, a real estate broker, "If you find me someone who is willing to pay $200,000 for the house, I'll pay you a 6 percent commission." Broker responded, "I'll find you someone." Owner replied, "Talk is cheap. I don't want your promises—just let me know if and when you come up with a buyer. For the next month, while you're working on the deal, I won't use any other brokers." Broker, after considerable effort and canvassing, learned of a possible buyer, Bertrand, with whom he began discussing the merits of Owner's house. Before Bertrand could make up his mind, Owner telephoned Broker and said, "Forget our deal, I've found another buyer." Assuming that Broker can show that Bertrand would indeed have bought Owner's house for $200,000, is Broker entitled to a commission?

Not sure ☐

37. Contractor Co. was one of several bidders competing for a contract to construct a new jail for the City of Pound. Contractor solicited bids for the plumbing portion of this work from several potential subcontractors, including Plumbing Co., which submitted a bid of $100,000. This was the lowest of the plumbing bids that Contractor received, and it was lower than the next lowest by $20,000. Contractor incorporated this bid into its own master bid to construct the jail. The terms of the bidding arrangement required Contractor to list all of its subcontractors, and it listed Plumbing Co. as one. The terms also provided that when a contractor submitted a bid to the city, that bid would be irrevocable for 60 days. Thirty days after Contractor submitted its bid, Plumbing Co. sent a letter to Contractor stating, "Due to a major new contract we've gotten, we no longer wish to do the plumbing work on the Pound jail project. Consider this letter a termination of our offer to you." Contractor was then awarded the master contract from Pound. Contractor sent a letter to Plumbing saying, "We accept your bid." Plumbing refused to perform.

Contractor was forced to hire a different plumber, who charged $120,000. May Contractor recover $20,000 from Plumbing on a breach of contract theory?   Not sure ☐

38. Seller and Buyer were both jewelers. Seller wrote to Buyer, "I have a grade-A flawless white diamond, two carats, which I offer to you at $8,000. You may reply by mail or telephone." On February 1, Buyer put a properly addressed letter of acceptance into the mail. Seller ordinarily would have received such a letter on February 4, but it was unaccountably delayed in the post office. When Seller had not received any response on February 5, he telephoned Buyer to say, "Someone has offered me a better deal. I am therefore canceling my offer." Buyer responded, "No, I was just about to call to confirm that you got my letter of acceptance; I'm holding you to the deal." Do Seller and Buyer have a contract?   Not sure ☐

39. Same facts as in the previous question. Now, however, assume that Buyer carelessly put the wrong zip code on his February 1 acceptance letter. When Seller had not received the letter on February 5, he called Buyer and purported to revoke. A properly addressed letter would have arrived by the 4th. Buyer disregarded Seller's revocation and said, "I stand on my acceptance." Buyer's acceptance letter arrived at Seller's office on February 6. Do Buyer and Seller have a contract?   Not sure ☐

40. In response to Seller's written offer to sell Buyer a particular rare postage stamp for $1,000, Buyer sent a letter on February 1 offering Seller $500 instead. Then, Buyer thought things over a while longer, realized Seller's offer was a good one, and telegraphed Seller on February 3 (the telegram was delivered that same day), "I accept your original offer. Disregard the written counteroffer you will be receiving." On February 4, Seller received Buyer's February 1 letter. Do the parties have a contract on the terms of Seller's original offer?   Not sure ☐

41. Same facts as in the previous question. Now, however, assume that when Buyer decided to accept after all, he sent a letter instead of a telegram. He dispatched this letter of acceptance on February 3, but it did not arrive until February 6. Buyer's original February 1 letter containing the $500 counteroffer arrived on February 5. On February 7, do the parties have a contract on the terms of Seller's original offer?   Not sure ☐

42. Seller sent Buyer an offer to sell Buyer a postage stamp for $1,000. On February 1, Buyer dispatched a letter accepting this offer. On February 2, Buyer sent a telegram (delivered the same day) saying, "Disregard my February 1 letter. I'm not willing to pay $1,000, but I'll give you $500 for the stamp." On February 3, Buyer's original letter of acceptance arrived. Do the parties have a contract at $1,000?   Not sure ☐

43. Produce Co. was a wholesaler of produce. Ron Rest owned a restaurant. One day, Rest telephoned Produce and said, "I want to buy 50 pounds of spinach, 20 pounds of iceberg lettuce, and three pounds of asparagus. Send the order today to my restaurant at 481 Main Street in Ames." The clerk at Produce Co. said, "Okay." Neither party mentioned price or a time for payment. The order never arrived that day, and Rest had to turn away a party of ten who loved vegetables and who would have paid him $200 for dinner. Rest sued Produce for breach of contract. Produce responded that the contract was void for indefiniteness. Can Rest recover for breach of contract?   Not sure ☐

44. Ron Rest, the restaurateur in the previous question, opened a large salad bar. He stocked two kinds of lettuce, carrots, and green peppers, as well as some other items not relevant to this question. He agreed with Produce Co. that with respect to the four types of vegetables mentioned here, he would buy some of his needs for the next year from Produce Co. The parties agreed that the price would be the price charged by Produce Co. to its largest restaurant customer. The parties further agreed that during the year, Rest would buy at least 2,000 pounds of vegetables from Produce Co. One month after the contract was put into effect (and after Rest had bought only 100 pounds of vegetables from Produce), Rest was offered a better deal by a different wholesaler and stopped ordering any vegetables from Produce Co. Produce Co. then sued for breach. Rest now defends on the grounds that the contract is too vague to furnish a basis for awarding a remedy and is thus unenforceable. Will Rest prevail with this defense?

Not sure ☐

45. Owner was a collector of vintage automobiles. He owned two 1936 Rolls-Royce Silver Shadows, one white and one black. Buyer knew about the white Rolls (because his friend was the one who had sold it to Owner), but he did not know about the black one. Owner put an ad in the local *Pennysaver* saying, "I offer to sell my 1936 Rolls-Royce for $60,000." Owner subjectively intended to sell the black Rolls. $60,000 would have been a fair price for either Rolls. Buyer telephoned Owner and said, "I'd like to buy your Rolls for $60,000." Owner said, "Fine." Assume for this question that Owner had no reason to know that Buyer was talking about the white Rolls, and Buyer had no reason to know that Owner was talking about (or even owned) the black Rolls. Do the parties have a contract? If so, for which color Rolls?

Not sure ☐

46. Same facts as in the previous question. Now, however, assume that Owner drove his white Rolls around town every weekend and kept the black Rolls hidden in the garage all the time. Owner advertised, "1936 Rolls for sale; $60,0000." Buyer phoned him and said, "I'll take you up on your offer. I've seen the car around town, and I've always admired it." Owner intended to sell the black Rolls. Owner was not really paying attention and failed to deduce that Buyer must be talking about the white car, since he could not have seen the black car around town. Again, assume that $60,000 is a fair price for either car. Do the parties have a contract? If so, for which car?

Not sure ☐

47. Same facts as in the previous question. Now, however, assume that the white Rolls was in vastly better condition than the black one, so that the white Rolls had a value of $300,000 compared with the black Rolls' value of $60,000. Assume further that Buyer should have known (although he did not in fact know) that for a 1936 Rolls in the obvious mint condition of the white car, $60,000 would be much too low a price. If Buyer sues to enforce what he asserts is a contract to sell the white car, will he win?

Not sure ☐

48. Tycoon, a wealthy entrepreneur who grew up in poverty, resolved that his children should lead lives of comfort. Therefore, Tycoon wrote to his 17-year-old son, Stewart, "When you become 21, I will give you $10,000." Tycoon died when Stewart was 19, and Tycoon's will left Stewart nothing. When Stewart turned 21, he demanded that his father's executors pay him $10,000. The executors refused.

Assuming that the estate must honor any binding contract entered into by Tycoon before his death, may Stewart recover the $10,000 from his father's estate?

Not sure ☐

49. Same basic facts as in the previous question. Now, however, assume that Tycoon wrote to Stewart, "On your 21st birthday, I will give you $10,000. However, I will give you this money only if you need it, so you must present me with a personal financial statement on that date, showing me a net worth of less than $50,000, or else I will not give you the money." Stewart turned 21, and diligently prepared a detailed personal financial statement, showing a net worth of $20,000. He presented the statement to his father, who said, "I've changed my mind." May Stewart recover the $10,000 from Tycoon?

Not sure ☐

50. Same basic fact pattern as in the previous two questions. Now, assume that Tycoon wrote to Stewart when Stewart was 17, "I deplore the tendency of modern youth to delay childbearing until their 30s or later—among other things, it is very unfair to their parents. Therefore, if you marry and have a child by your wife before you reach the age of 30 (thus making me a grandfather before I'm 60), I will give you $10,000 upon the birth of that child." Stewart married at 28 and had a child by his wife the next year. Tycoon refused to pay the $10,000. If Stewart sues Tycoon for breach of contract, will he recover $10,000?

Not sure ☐

51. Tycoon wanted to make a $500 gift to his son Stewart. Tycoon knew that promises to make gifts are generally not enforceable. Therefore, he had Stewart transfer, from Stewart to Tycoon, title to Stewart's 1972 Ford Mustang, which had a market value of $500. Simultaneously, Stewart and Tycoon signed a document in which Tycoon promised to pay $1,000 for the car, payment to be made two months later. When the two months were up, Tycoon refused to pay. May Stewart recover the $1,000?

Not sure ☐

52. Tycoon desired to help his son Stewart financially. Tycoon knew that promises to make a gift are ordinarily not enforceable. Tycoon and Stewart signed a document that said, "In return for transfer by Stewart of title to his 1972 Mustang to Tycoon, which transfer was made this same day, Tycoon hereby agrees to pay Stewart $1,000 in two months." This recital was a false one, in that Stewart did not in fact transfer title to the Mustang. After two months, Stewart demanded payment, Tycoon refused, and Stewart sued. Will he win?

Not sure ☐

53. Same facts as in the previous question. Now, however, assume that the two months went by and Tycoon paid the $1,000. The next day, he thought better of it and sought to get the payment back from Stewart, on the grounds that a gratuitous payment is not binding. Can Tycoon succeed in recovering the payment?

Not sure ☐

54. Peggy, who had worked for Employer for 30 years, decided to retire of her own volition. Her last day of work was January 30. On February 1, Employer wrote to Peggy, "In consideration of your many years of devoted service, I hereby agree to pay you a retirement benefit of $300 per month for the rest of your life." After making just two such monthly payments, Employer then wrote to Peggy, "Sorry, but I'm not going to be able to pay you anymore." Does Peggy have a claim for breach of contract against Employer?

Not sure ☐

55. Peggy had worked for Employer for 20 years, and she was now 50. Employer wrote to Peggy, "In view of your long service to me, if you will promise to work for me for just one more year, I will then pay you a retirement benefit of $500 per month for the rest of your life." Peggy promised to work another year. After she had worked one month of this year, Employer said, "I'm sorry, I've changed my mind about the pension." Assuming that Peggy works the remainder of the year, can she then sue to enforce Employer's promise?

Not sure ☐

56. Patrick, who was 23 years old, hitchhiked around Europe. In France, Farmer, a wealthy farmer, picked Patrick up, invited him home, and let him eat and sleep rent free with the family for one week (though Patrick never expressly asked for such treatment). When Patrick returned home, he told Fred, his father, about this great generosity. Fred wrote to Farmer, "If you are ever in New York, where we live, I'd be happy to reciprocate by offering you and your family rent-free accommodations for up to a month." Farmer happened to come to New York on business (which he would have done even had Fred not made his invitation), and demanded that Fred keep his promise. Fred said, "I'm sorry, but I acted imprudently—I don't have enough room." Can Farmer sue Fred for enforcement of this promise?

Not sure ☐

57. Parker borrowed $100 from Loanshark with the promise to repay it in a week. The interest rate was 10 percent per week. With one day left to go, Parker did not have the money. Loanshark threatened that if Parker did not repay on time, Loanshark would put a bullet through both of Parker's knees. Parker (who was a hopelessly compulsive gambler) had no more relatives or friends left from whom he could borrow, but he did have a diamond-studded watch worth $1,000. However, it was already seven o'clock in the evening (with payment due the next day), and all the local pawnshops had closed. Parker told his story of woe to his neighbor, Denise, who said, "I'm willing to trade you $100 in return for your watch." Parker said, "I don't have the watch here; it's in my safe deposit box at the bank. As soon as I pay off Loanshark in the morning, I can get it for you." Parker and Denise therefore signed a document in which Denise agreed to give Parker, immediately, $100, and Parker agreed to give Denise the watch early the next morning. Parker took the money, paid off Loanshark, and then refused to hand over the watch (though he offered to return Denise's $100). Denise sued Parker for the value of the watch ($1,000). Parker defends on the grounds that the contract lacked consideration, because of the extreme inequity of the bargain. May Denise recover the $1,000?

Not sure ☐

58. Archie, an architect, agreed with Owen, the owner of a vacant lot, to draw plans for an office building that Owen wanted to construct on the lot and to supervise the construction. Archie agreed to handle the project for a total flat fee of $10,000 (a fair fee for the work that would be involved). Two months later, after Archie had already drawn the plans and construction had commenced, Archie received a much larger and more lucrative commission from someone else. Archie refused to continue supervising Owen's job. Owen became desperate, because he knew that it was foolhardy to have an architect supervise the job who had not drawn the plans. He therefore said to Archie, "I'll double your fee to $20,000 if you resume working." Archie agreed to come back to work and finished supervising the job. At the conclusion of the job, Owen refused to pay Archie more than the originally agreed-upon $10,000 fee. If Archie sues for the second $10,000 on a contract theory, will he recover?

Not sure ☐

59. Same facts as in the previous question. Now, however, assume that Archie refused to continue the supervision without a raise because construction was proceeding twice as slowly as expected because of a work slowdown by unionized employees of the construction contractor. Neither Archie nor Owen foresaw the possibility of such a slowdown when they made their agreement. Owen agreed to double Archie's fee, Archie came back on the job, Owen refused to pay the increased fee at the end of the job, and Archie sued. Will Archie be able to recover the full $20,000 on a contract theory?

Not sure ☐

60. Same basic facts as question 58. That is, Archie refused to continue with the contract because he found more lucrative work elsewhere. Owen begged him to reconsider and offered to double his fee. In return for this doubling, Archie agreed that in addition to coming back to work, he would make best efforts to find an alternative contractor who would speed up the work. Archie tried to do so but failed, so he and Owen used the original slow contractor. After the job was finished, Owen refused to pay anything more than the original $10,000. Archie now sues for the balance. Will he recover?

Not sure ☐

61. Debtor owed Creditor $100, to be repaid on July 1. On June 30, Debtor realized that he would not have enough money to repay the debt on July 1. He went to Creditor and said, "I've got enough money to pay you $80 on July 1, but I will only pay it to you if you will give me a release from your full claim. I'm not going to part with my hard-earned $80 and still have a $20 debt hanging over my head." Creditor, to save the expense and bother of suing Debtor for the other $20, agreed to take $80, payable on July 1, in full satisfaction of the original $100 debt. Debtor paid the $80 on July 1. Creditor then changed his mind and sued Debtor for the remaining $20. May Creditor recover this $20?

Not sure ☐

62. Same facts as in the previous example. Now, however, assume that on June 30, Debtor said to Creditor, "I can't pay you the full $100, but I can pay you $80. If you don't accept my offer of partial payment in release of your claim, I will file a bankruptcy petition tomorrow, and after the costs of administration you will get nothing." Creditor agreed that if Debtor promised to refrain from filing a bankruptcy petition until the $80 was paid to Debtor, Creditor would take the $80 in full settlement. Debtor paid the $80 on July 1 (without filing for bankruptcy), and Creditor turned around and sued for the balance. Can Creditor recover the $20?

Not sure ☐

63. E.T. signs up for a long-distance calling service with MCI. The calling plan says that calls made "between 7 and 11" will be 10 cents a minute, and calls made at all other times will be 15 cents a minute. E.T. gets a bill for $187 for one month's calls, properly computed based on MCI's assumption that "between 7 and 11" means between 7 and 11 P.M. E.T. thinks "between 7 and 11" should also apply to the A.M. period (assume that a court would probably find for MCI on this issue, but that E.T.'s reasoning is not crazy and is done in good faith). E.T. decides to pay only what he thinks he owes, and sends in a check for this lesser amount ($125). At the bottom of the check, he writes in neon green ink, "Paid in full." He sends the check, along with a note explaining why he believes this is all he owes. MCI cashes the check, but writes next to its endorsement, "Under protest, and with reservation of rights." MCI then sues E.T. for the $62 difference. Can MCI recover? Not sure ☐

64. While Pamela was crossing the street, Derrick, driving his car at an unreasonably high speed, nearly hit her. Pamela, to escape the impact, threw herself out of the way and fell hard on the pavement. Pamela threatened to sue Derrick unless Derrick paid for Pamela's chiropractic bills for having the back pain treated. Derrick agreed to pay these bills. Unbeknownst to Derrick, Pamela had been having these same back pains for many years, and they were in no way worsened by the near-accident (nor did Pamela in fact suffer any other injury from the episode). Derrick reneged on his promise to make the chiropractic payments, and Pamela sued him for breach of contract. Assuming that all of the above facts become clear in the litigation, will Derrick's promise to make the payments be enforced? Not sure ☐

65. Same basic fact pattern as in the previous question. Now, however, assume that Pamela had never suffered back pains before the accident, and indeed, she did not get back pains until six months after the accident. As Pamela was aware, there is a one-year statute of limitations on tort actions. Thirteen months after the accident, she told Derrick that she was about to sue him for her medical bills unless he agreed to pay them. Derrick so agreed. At the time of Derrick's promise, Pamela honestly but unreasonably believed that in her state, the tort statute of limitations does not start to run until the injury is or should have been discovered. (A simple question to any tort lawyer in the state would have given Pamela the correct reading—that the statute starts to run at the time of the wrong.) If Derrick fails to make the promised payments, and Pamela sues for enforcement of his promise, may Pamela recover? Not sure ☐

66. Arthur Agent was attempting to build a reputation as a successful agent for movie stars. He therefore said to Steve Star, an internationally famous film star, "I will be your nonexclusive agent for one year. I will spend full time trying to get you parts. If I succeed in getting you parts, you will only have to pay me what you think my services are worth. You may terminate the arrangement at any time without notice." Star agreed. After one month, Agent took a salaried job with an established talent agency and stopped trying to get Star parts. Star sued Agent for breaching the promise of full-time efforts to get Star parts. May Star recover for breach of contract? Not sure ☐

67. Same facts as in the previous question. Now, however, assume that the parties agreed that Star would pay Agent a commission equal to what Screen Actors Guild guidelines determined to be a "reasonable" commission, and that although Star could cancel at any time, the cancellation would not take effect for 30 days. Agent got a better job offer from an established talent agency and stopped working on Star's behalf after only one month, without notice. Star has sued. May Star recover for breach of contract? Not sure ☐

68. Merchant, a supplier of widgets, wrote to Customer as follows: "We offer to sell you as many widgets as you want to purchase, up to 10,000 in any month, for each of the next six months, at a price of $6 per widget." Customer responded, "Fine. I agree that for any widgets I order from you in the next six months, the price will

be $6. I expect to place an order sometime in the next few months." Four months later, Customer placed an order for 1,000 widgets at $6. Merchant responded, "I'm sorry, we've had much higher orders from other customers than expected. I'm sorry we can't fill your order." Customer (who did not refrain from making other widget arrangements because of the deal, and who did not rely in any other way on the arrangement) now sues Merchant for breach of contract. May Customer recover?

Not sure ☐

69. Same basic facts as in the previous question. Now, however, assume that in response to Merchant's offer to sell widgets at $6, Customer responded, "Fine, I agree that for any widgets I need in the next six months, I'll buy them from you at $6 per widget." After four months, Customer placed an order, which Merchant refused to fill. May Customer recover for breach?

Not sure ☐

70. Seller was the owner of a house that Buyer wanted to buy. Seller and Buyer signed a contract under which Buyer agreed to buy the house 60 days later for $200,000. The contract was expressly made conditional upon Buyer's being able to obtain a mortgage for 80 percent of the purchase price. Buyer got the mortgage and was ready to close, but Seller refused to go through with the sale. Buyer sued Seller for breach. Seller now defends on the grounds that since Buyer's obligation to buy was contingent upon his getting the necessary financing, and since Buyer could have chosen not to get the necessary financing, Buyer was never really bound, and therefore his promise was not consideration for Seller's promise to sell. Can Buyer recover for breach?

Not sure ☐

71. Debtor owed Creditor $1,000. Debtor got into a financial predicament, filed a petition in bankruptcy, and obtained a bankruptcy discharge of all his debts (including the one to Creditor). Debtor then, simply because he liked Creditor, wrote to Creditor, "Despite the fact that my debt to you was recently discharged in bankruptcy, I will pay it as soon as I am able." Debtor then won the California state lottery. Creditor now sues for the $1,000. Debtor defends on the grounds that there was no consideration for his promise to Creditor to pay the debt. May Creditor recover?

Not sure ☐

72. Grandfather, a wealthy landowner, was aware that the price of land near New York City had grown exorbitant. Although Grandfather now lived in California, he owned a half-acre parcel in the New York suburbs. He said to his daughter's son, "Grandson, if you build a house on my land and live in it for two years, I will deed the land to you." Grandson spent $100,000 to construct a house on the parcel. The land itself was worth $200,000. Grandson then lived on the property for the required two years. At the end of that period, Grandfather refused to convey the property to Grandson. Grandson sued to enforce the promise of a deed.

(a) May Grandson recover from Grandfather on the promise? If so, upon what doctrine would the recovery most likely be based?

Not sure ☐

(b) If the promise is enforced, what recovery should Grandson obtain?

Not sure ☐

73. On September 1, Deborah, a wealthy tycoon, promised Peacock University that next January 1, she would make the school an unrestricted gift of $1 million. The university responded immediately by a letter, thanking Deborah for her generosity.

The university planned to use the money as a down payment on a new science center. Before the university could begin with plans for the science center, however, Deborah sent it a letter in October saying, "I'm sorry, but due to the recent stock market decline, I will be unable to keep my promise." The university sued Deborah to enforce the gift. Will the university prevail?

Not sure ☐

74. Driver and Passenger were riding in Driver's car when Driver went through a stop sign and slammed into an oncoming car. Passenger's new sable coat, worth $5,000, was ripped and thereby ruined in the collision. Passenger herself, however, seemed fine; a medical examination that day showed no injuries. One week after the accident, Driver and Passenger both signed an agreement in which Passenger released Driver from "all liability with respect both to property damage and personal injury arising out of [the accident]," in return for Driver's payment to Passenger of $5,000. One week after that, Passenger developed a severe case of whiplash, which both doctors who examined Passenger agree was almost certainly caused by the accident. May Passenger rescind the release so that she may sue Driver for her whiplash? What legal doctrine furnishes the basis for your answer?

Not sure ☐

75. Same basic facts as above question. Now, however, assume that Driver urged Passenger to see a doctor after the accident, but Passenger declined because she felt fine. Had Passenger seen a doctor, the doctor would have told her that there was no way to know whether she had suffered whiplash, since such soft-tissue injuries usually do not manifest themselves for some time after an accident. As in the previous question, at the time they signed the release in return for $5,000, both Driver and Passenger honestly believed that Passenger had suffered only property damage. May Passenger obtain rescission of the release so that she can sue Driver for her personal injuries?

Not sure ☐

76. Builder, who was in the business of constructing deluxe homes, agreed to construct such a home for Owner on a parcel owned by Owner. Both parties understood that Builder would have to excavate at least ten feet down into the soil to construct a foundation for the house. Both believed that this excavation would require only excavation of soil, and would not cost Builder more than $10,000. The parties agreed on a fixed price for the construction of the house. After Builder started to work, he discovered that the area where the excavation was to take place consisted of bedrock underneath a small coating of soil, so that excavation would cost $60,000 rather than $10,000. (The overall price for the house was $300,000, and if Builder were forced to complete the contract, he would suffer a loss of $10,000 rather than the expected profit of $40,000.) May Builder obtain rescission of the contract on grounds of mutual mistake?

Not sure ☐

77. Owner owned a 20-acre farm in Oklahoma. She contracted to sell the farm to Buyer, who intended to continue farming there. Neither party realized, or had any reason to realize, that there were valuable oil deposits underneath the land. Shortly after the contract was signed, and before the scheduled closing date, Owner's neighbor brought in, most unexpectedly, a huge oil gusher. Owner immediately conducted a test bore and discovered that there was oil underneath her land as well. Instead of being worth $500,000, the farm is now worth $5,000,000. Owner refused to close, and Buyer sued for breach. May Owner have the contract rescinded because of mutual mistake?

Not sure ☐

78. Same facts as in the previous question. Now, however, assume that before the contract was signed, Buyer learned (but Owner did not) that the owner of the neighboring parcel had brought in a substantial well. Before closing, Owner learned of this and refused to close. May Owner avoid the contract for mistake?

Not sure ☐

79. Contractor bid $1 million on a contract to build a new jail for the Town of Langdell. Due to the complexity of the ingredients of the job, Contractor made an arithmetic error in adding up the various components, so that it turned in a bid of $1 million instead of the $1.2 million that it would have bid had it done the addition correctly. After the deadline for withdrawing bids had passed, Contractor discovered its mistake and tried to withdraw its bid. The town refused, and Contractor refused to honor its bid. The town awarded the contract to the next lowest bidder (who bid $1.1 million) and sued Contractor for the $100,000 difference. Contractor shows that if it had been forced to perform for the $1 million mistaken figure, it would have lost $100,000 instead of making $100,000. May Contractor avoid the contract on grounds of mistake?

Not sure ☐

80. Same facts as in the previous question. Now, however, assume that the source of Contractor's mistake was not a clerical error but, rather, a judgment by Contractor's president that erecting the building's superstructure would take a total of 2,000 man-hours, rather than the 4,000 hours it will in fact take. After Contractor was awarded the job, but before it began construction, it discovered the true time needed to complete the job by discussing this issue with a more experienced contractor. May Contractor avoid the contract on grounds of mistake?

Not sure ☐

81. Contractor was bidding for a contract to build a new headquarters building for Mega Corporation. Due to a computational error, Contractor submitted a bid of $1 million, when without the error it would have submitted a bid of $1.3 million. The next lowest bid was for $1.4 million, and all bids other than Contractor's fell in the range of $1.4 to $1.6 million. If Contractor is forced to perform, it will have to do the job at a loss of $5,000. May Contractor avoid the contract on grounds of mistake?

Not sure ☐

82. Borrower wished to borrow $100,000 from Bank. Veep, the vice president of Bank, conducted extensive oral negotiations with Borrower, during which the terms of the possible loan were discussed. During the course of these discussions, Veep said to Borrower, "We try to be an understanding bank. When a borrower fails to make a payment on time, we will give him or her a 90-day grace period before instituting suit." Eventually, the parties completed their negotiations, and the loan was consummated by the parties' taking several simultaneous steps: (1) Borrower supplied collateral to Bank; (2) Borrower supplied a financial statement on which, at Bank's request, he wrote, "I warrant and represent that this is my complete financial condition as of the date hereof"; and (3) Borrower signed a note prepared by Bank. This note recited the amount borrowed and the due date (July 1); it also recited that if Borrower did not pay, Bank could "institute suit or otherwise employ any rights given to it by law." But the note did not state whether Bank must give Borrower a grace period, nor did it refer to the collateral or to the financial statement.

Borrower failed to make the repayment on July 1, and Bank instituted suit on July 10—i.e., without giving Borrower any grace period. Borrower now defends on the ground that Veep's oral representation that there would be a 90-day grace period was part of the contract and that Bank's collection suit is therefore premature. Will Borrower prevail with this assertion?

Not sure ☐

83. Same facts as above question. Now, however, assume that the note signed by Borrower recites, "Upon Borrower's failure to make the required repayment on July 1, Bank may, with no further delay or grace period, institute an immediate suit." Assume that this provision appears in legible type, and that Borrower was represented by counsel when he signed the note. If Borrower argues that the oral agreement regarding the grace period should be enforced, will he prevail?

Not sure ☐

84. Same facts as in the previous question. This time, however, assume that Borrower was clever enough to get a preliminary "deal letter" from Veep while they were still carrying out their negotiations. In this deal letter (which spelled out the anticipated terms of the agreement) Veep stated that "there will be a 90-day grace period." Later, however, Borrower and Bank signed the note, which expressly provided that there would be no grace period. Will Borrower prevail in his argument that the prior grace period provision is part of the agreement?

Not sure ☐

85. Same basic fact pattern as in the previous three questions. This time, however, assume that at the end of their negotiations, Bank and Borrower signed a single formal "Loan Document," which covered not only the amount, due date, and borrower but also collateral, financial statements, and every other topic that the parties intended to cover in their deal. Veep had previously orally promised Borrower that there would be a 90-day grace period. The Loan Agreement says nothing one way or the other about whether there will be a grace provision. If Borrower fails to make the required prepayment on July 1, and Bank sues on July 2, may Borrower successfully argue that the grace period is part of the contract?

Not sure ☐

86. Same basic fact pattern as in the previous four questions. This time, however, assume that during their discussion on the proposed loan, Borrower promised to keep 10 percent of the loan proceeds in a checking account at Bank throughout the life of the loan (known in the industry as a "Corresponding Balance" provision). The parties then signed a comprehensive Loan Agreement that covered amount borrowed, due date, interest rate, collateral, financial statement, and virtually everything else the parties had discussed; however, the Loan Agreement did not mention the Corresponding Balance provision. Assume that a Corresponding Balance provision is so customary in the banking industry that it would be natural for the parties to omit putting the provision into their complete written agreement even though they intended the provision to be in force. Assume further that the Loan Agreement contains a provision that reads as follows: "This document contains the entire agreement between the parties relating to the loan contemplated herein, and there are no oral or written representations, promises, or agreements between the parties except those recited in this document." Borrower has complied with the terms of the loan, except that he has not kept 10 percent of the loan proceeds in a checking account at Bank. If Bank tries to enforce the Corresponding Balance provision, will it succeed?

Not sure ☐

87. Seller and Buyer agreed in writing that Seller would manufacture and deliver to Buyer by July 1 a customized semiconductor-manufacturing machine for a stated

price. On June 15, Seller told Buyer, "I'm having a lot of trouble making the machine. May I have until August 1 to complete it?" Buyer responded, "Okay." On July 15, Buyer canceled the contract for nondelivery and sued Seller for breach. Seller now defends on the grounds that Buyer's oral postponement of the delivery date is enforceable. Buyer counters that if he made such an oral agreement, it is unenforceable because of the parol evidence rule. Is Buyer's assertion correct?   Not sure ☐

88. Same basic fact pattern as in the previous question. Now, however, assume that the written agreement between Seller and Buyer stated, "No subsequent modification of this agreement shall be effective unless in a writing signed by both parties." This time, on June 15, Seller called Buyer and said, "I'm having trouble finishing the machine on schedule. If I put my workers on double overtime, I can finish it by July 1 [a true statement]. But I'd much prefer it if you would give me an extension until August 1. Will you?" Buyer responded, "Okay." When Seller had not delivered by July 15, Buyer canceled the contract and sued for breach. Seller asserts that the oral modification is binding. Buyer points to the "no oral modifications" clause. Is Buyer's oral agreement to postpone the delivery date binding upon him?   Not sure ☐

89. Seller and Buyer negotiated for Buyer to buy a business, the ABC Bar Review Course, operated by Seller. Seller showed Buyer financial statements that purported to demonstrate that the business operated at a profit. Seller and Buyer then signed a written agreement that appeared to cover all aspects of the sale. This final agreement did not mention the financial statements; it did contain a clause that read as follows: "This document represents the entire agreement between the parties relating to the sale by Seller to Buyer of the ABC Bar Review Co., and any prior discussions, agreements, or promises between the parties shall be of no effect." After the closing, Buyer discovered that (1) the financial statements shown to him by Seller were false (the business in fact lost lots of money); and (2) Seller knew that these statements were false (he told a third person, "I've dummied up some financial statements to make the business look more appealing").

Buyer refused to pay a balance due on the sale contract. Seller has sued to collect this amount. Buyer wishes to present evidence concerning the false financial statements to support a defense of fraud. Seller argues that the evidence should not be admitted because the contract contains a merger clause indicating that it is a complete integration, and thus may not be varied even by consistent additional terms. If the case is tried to a jury, should the judge permit evidence to be submitted to the jury concerning Seller's knowing use of false financial statements?   Not sure ☐

90. Same facts as in the previous question. Now, however, assume that the contract contains a provision stating, "Buyer expressly agrees that although Seller has shown Buyer prior financial statements for the business, Buyer has not in any way relied upon these statements and has made his own independent investigation into the financial condition of the business." Should the judge allow the jury to hear Buyer's evidence that Seller knowingly submitted false financial statements to Buyer?   Not sure ☐

91. Owner and Contractor signed an agreement whereby Contractor was to install aluminum siding on Owner's house. Before they signed the agreement, the parties agreed orally that the agreement would only be effective if and when Owner was

able to cancel a contract he had made with somebody else for the same kind of siding. The signed agreement did not refer to this special provision, and contained a clause stating, "This document represents the entire agreement between the parties, and no oral agreements or promises that may have been made with respect to the subject hereof shall be enforceable." Owner was unable to cancel the other contract and notified Contractor that he regarded their deal as never having become effective. Contractor has sued Owner for breach of contract. Owner wishes to produce evidence of the prior oral agreement regarding cancellation of the other contract. If the case is tried to a jury, should the judge allow this evidence?

Not sure ☐

92. Computer Co., a manufacturer of computers, contracted to supply 1,000 IBM-compatible computers to the Department of Justice (DOJ). The machines were to be delivered at the rate of 200 per year for five years. The contract document (which was intended as a final and complete expression of the parties' intent) stated that the price would be $1,000 per computer, but that "the price will be reduced to the price listed by Computer Co. for comparable equipment under the price schedules filed by Computer Co. with the U.S. General Services Administration (GSA)." At the time the contract with DOJ was signed, the applicable price schedule filed by Computer Co. with GSA listed a price of $1,100 per unit. But two years into the Computer Co.-DOJ contract, Computer Co. filed a revised price schedule with GSA, showing a price of $900. DOJ now demands that the price to be reduced (both prospectively and retrospectively) to $900. Computer Co. asserts that the intent of the parties was that a lesser GSA price should control only if that lesser price was on file at the time of the Computer Co.-DOJ contract. May Computer Co. present evidence that this more limited meaning of "GSA price" should control?

Not sure ☐

93. Seller, a used farm equipment dealer, sold a used hay baler to Buyer. The parties signed a written agreement covering the purchase, and that agreement said nothing about the warranty of merchantability. The baler broke down as soon as Buyer ran it, and Buyer sued Seller for breach of the implied warranty of merchantability under UCC §2-314. Seller has presented evidence that buyers and sellers of used farm equipment virtually always understand that the equipment is being sold "as is" (i.e., without any kind of warranty), and that Buyer, as one who on previous occasions has bought used farm equipment (though never from Seller), should have known this. What is the technical term for what the Seller is trying to establish with this evidence?

Not sure ☐

94. Diskette Drive Co. was a manufacturer of floppy disc drives for personal computers. Computer Co. was a manufacturer/assembler of personal computers. The two signed an agreement whereby, for a period of five years, Computer agreed to buy all of its requirements for 360K 5.25-inch floppy drives from Diskette at a fixed price per drive. Computer's records showed that, as of the time of the contract, Computer had needed an average of one million such drives per year during the previous three years. As Diskette knew, approximately half of these each year had gone to Mega Store, a large computer retailer who was far and away Computer's biggest customer. Only six months into the contract (after Computer had ordered 500,000 drives), Mega Store stopped buying computers from Computer. Computer therefore slashed its orders from Diskette in half. May Diskette recover for breach of contract?

Not sure ☐

95. Same basic facts as the previous fact pattern. Now, however, assume that the computer industry has developed in such a way that smaller diskette drives (3.5-inch drives) have become substantially cheaper than the 5.25-inch drives called for in the contract. Assume further that the smaller drives are no "better" in any meaningful sense. Computer Co. has shifted its machine designs from the 5.25-inch drives to the 3.5-inch drives solely to escape from the contract with Diskette Co., and to therefore be able to buy drives more cheaply. Now, Computer Co. has informed Diskette that it has no more requirements for 5.25-inch drives. May Diskette recover for breach?   Not sure ☐

96. Same basic fact pattern as in the previous question. This time, however, assume that the 3.5-inch diskette drive represents a major new technological development, one that customers of Computer Co. are anxious to have. Computer has decided (rationally) that it is too expensive to offer both sizes of diskette drives, so it has standardized on the 3.5-inch type, which, at the same wholesale price as the 5.25-inch drive, represents a better economic and technological buy for Computer and its customers. This decision has had the effect of reducing to zero Computer's requirements for drives covered under the Diskette-Computer contract. May Diskette recover for breach?   Not sure ☐

97. The Peoria Mud Hens were a major league baseball team. The Mud Hens were worried that their star slugger, John "Bigbelly" Johnson, was getting so fat that his speed on the base paths would diminish. The Mud Hens and Johnson therefore made a contract covering the 2010 season, in which Johnson was given a base salary of $200,000, and was also to be paid an additional $100,000 "on condition that he report to training camp on March 1 at a weight of no more than 210 pounds." (Nothing in the contract imposed an affirmative duty on Johnson to report at less than 210 pounds.) Johnson traveled the "rubber chicken" banquet circuit extensively during the off-season before the 2010 season and made no attempt to watch his weight. He reported to training camp at 240 pounds, and as a result performed materially less well during the season. (For instance, he was thrown out 17 times while sliding into second on what should have been routine stand-up doubles.) The Mud Hens have not only not paid Johnson the $100,000 bonus, but they have also withheld $25,000 of his base $200,000 salary (based on their reasonable estimate that Johnson's excess weight over 210 pounds cost the team $25,000 of "value" from his play). Have the Mud Hens breached Johnson's contract?   Not sure ☐

98. Owner wished to have Architect draw plans for a new house to be built for and lived in by Owner. As Architect was aware, Owner was somewhat idiosyncratic with respect to houses. The two agreed that Architect would draft plans for an ultracontemporary 20-room house; they further agreed, "If Owner is satisfied, Owner shall pay Architect $10,000 for the plans; otherwise, Owner shall owe Architect nothing." Architect worked diligently on the plans and came up with a design that architectural experts acclaimed as masterful; most homeowners who like contemporary homes would have been happy to use these plans. However, Owner honestly concluded that he was not satisfied with the plans and refused to pay Architect anything. May Architect recover $10,000 under the contract?   Not sure ☐

99. Same basic fact pattern as the in the previous question. This time, however, assume that Owner lost $3 million in the stock market between the time he signed the contract and the time Architect delivered the plans. Owner was so short of funds that he did not even look at the plans; he simply told Architect that he was not satisfied and refused to pay anything. May Architect recover the $10,000?

Not sure ☐

100. Farmer owned a 20-acre tract of land that he wished to sell for $200,000. Developer paid Farmer $10,000 for an option to purchase the property for $200,000 any time during the next year (i.e., before July 1, 2010). Developer's right to purchase under the option was made "expressly conditional on Developer's delivery to Farmer of a cashier's check for $200,000 no later than July 1, 2010." For unknown reasons, Developer did not deliver a $200,000 certified check to Farmer until July 3, 2010. Farmer (who had in the interim received an offer of $300,000 for the property) responded, "Your check is too late. The option has expired," and refused to take the check. Is Farmer contractually obligated to sell the property for $200,000 in return for the July 3 check?

Not sure ☐

101. Insurer wrote a fire insurance policy on Homeowner's home. The policy provided: "Insurer's obligation to pay any loss insured hereunder is expressly conditional on Homeowner's giving written notification to Insurer within five days of any covered loss." Homeowner suffered a fire in the house on August 1. On August 2, he telephoned Insurer and said, "I have had a fire; please inspect the premises." Insurer agreed to send an adjuster to inspect the property. On August 10, Homeowner submitted a written notice of loss. Insurer refused to pay, on the grounds that Homeowner's written notification was not timely made. May Homeowner recover for his loss under the policy?

Not sure ☐

102. Author, a writer of best-selling novels, agreed to write a historical romance for Publisher. Their contract provided that Author would deliver her manuscript on or before January 1, 2011. The contract also provided that, to promote the book, Publisher would prominently announce the forthcoming book at the 2010 American Bookseller's Association Convention, to be held on December 1-2, 2010. The contract nowhere made any party's duty expressly conditional on any event. Due to poor office administration procedures by Publisher, Publisher failed to reserve exhibit space in time, and therefore did not exhibit (let alone announce Author's book) at the 2010 convention. Author then sent Publisher a letter saying, "I have finished the manuscript. However, due to your failure to announce the book at the 2010 ABA Convention as you contracted to do, I have delivered the manuscript to a different publisher for publication." If Publisher sues Author for breach of Author's promise to deliver the manuscript to Publisher by January 1, may Publisher recover damages? (For this question, disregard the issue of whether Author may have a claim for damages against Publisher for the failure to announce the book at the convention.)

Not sure ☐

103. Concrete Co. entered into a subcontract with Builder whereby Concrete Co. was to supply and install the concrete for a building as to which Builder was the general contractor. (Most of the expense of such concrete work is the work needed to pour and shape the concrete, not the cost of the raw materials.) The contract provided for a payment to Concrete Co. of $30 per cubic yard. The parties estimated that the job would take 1,000 cubic yards of cement. The contract said nothing about when payment would be due to Concrete Co., and there is no established custom in the industry regarding when payment for such services is to be made. Concrete Co. performed half the work (on schedule), and then said to Builder, "Pay me for the work I've done so far—$15,000—or I won't continue." Builder said, "I'll pay you at the end of the job." Concrete Co. refused to continue. May Concrete Co. recover $15,000 against Builder in a suit brought on the contract?

Not sure ☐

104. Seller agreed to sell and Buyer agreed to buy Blackacre, with the closing to take place on July 1. As Buyer was aware, Seller did not yet hold title to Blackacre, but promised in the contract that he would obtain it from its present owner (Owen) prior to July 1. The purchase price was $100,000, and the closing was to take place at the office of Law Firm, which represented Seller. The contract provided, "Time will be of the essence, because of Buyer's need to immediately commence construction of his new house on the property." On July 1, both parties showed up at the office of Law Firm. Seller said, "I have not been able to acquire the property from Owen. Maybe I'll be able to do so in the future, but I'm not very optimistic." Unbeknownst to Seller, Buyer had not arrived with $100,000; indeed, Buyer had been unable to raise any part of the purchase price. Buyer cleverly remained silent about this fact and immediately instituted a breach of contract suit against Seller. May Buyer recover the difference between the purchase price and the (higher) market value of the property?

Not sure ☐

105. Farmer was in the business of raising both chickens and pigs. Farmer agreed with Packer that on July 1, Farmer would deliver 1,000 chickens and 100 pigs to Packer, and that Packer would simultaneously pay Farmer 40 cents per pound of chicken and 50 cents per pound of pork. On July 1, Farmer delivered the 1,000 chickens but unjustifiably refused to deliver any of the pigs. Packer was immediately able to make up the shortage by buying 100 pigs from another supplier at the same price. However, Packer refused to pay anything for the chickens when the payment date (30 days after delivery) arrived. If Farmer brings suit on the contract for 40 cents per pound of chicken delivered, may he recover this amount?

Not sure ☐

106. Same basic fact pattern as in the previous question. Now, however, assume that the initial chickens-plus-pigs deal due on July 1 was part of a larger contract in which Farmer was to deliver 1,000 chickens and 100 pigs every month for the next year (with the July 1 shipment being first). Farmer delivered the 1,000 chickens on July 1, but delivered no pigs. He explained to Packer that the failure to deliver the pigs was a onetime event that would not reoccur. (Assume that a reasonable person in Packer's position would believe Farmer.) Packer said, "I don't care about your explanations—I'm terminating our contract, so don't bother with the August 1 delivery." Packer was a sufficiently large processor of meats that Farmer's failure to deliver the July 1 pigs did not require Packer to make any significant new supply arrangements, either for July 1 or thereafter. Is Packer liable for breach of contract on account of his refusal to accept shipments for August 1 or later?

Not sure ☐

107. Builder contracted to build a house for Owner on a lot owned by Owner at a cost of $200,000. The contract called for construction to start on July 1, and required Owner to have certain trees removed from the property prior to the start

of construction, since it would be impossible to do the work efficiently on a treed site. (The contract did not indicate that time was of the essence for the tree clearing or for the start date of the construction.) On July 1, Owner had not removed the trees, so Builder refused to start work. On August 1, Owner notified Builder that the trees had been removed. Builder had not yet picked up a substitute job, but he nonetheless responded, "Sorry, it's too late, I just don't want to do business with you anymore because of the delay." Owner was forced to hire a substitute contractor, who charged Owner $50,000 more than Builder would have charged. Builder suffered a loss of $5,000 during the month of July (measured by payments he had to make to his men at a time when he had no money coming in from the job with Owner). If Owner and Builder sue each other for breach, what damages will be owed by either or both parties?

Not sure ☐

108. Same basic fact pattern as in the previous question. Now, however, assume that had Owen cleared the site by July 1 as agreed, Builder could (and would) have performed all of his work in July, and would have earned $25,000 net of expenses. Further assume that on July 30, Builder had the opportunity to take a huge construction project that would last a full year, a project that he could not complete while at the same time building Owner's house on a reasonable schedule. Builder took the July 30 contract without realizing that Owner was about to finish clearing the trees. On August 1, Owner notified Builder that the site was now ready, but Builder said, "I'm sorry; I've taken a major job and will not be able to do your job." If Owner and Builder each sue the other for breach, what will be the result?

Not sure ☐

109. Customer wanted to have some brochures printed for a trade show that was to take place on July 1. He contracted to have Printer design and print 2,000 brochures, with delivery to take place on or before June 29. Printer delivered the 2,000 brochures on June 28. Due to a clerical error on Printer's part, the brochures were printed in the wrong color, thus clashing with all of Customer's other printed materials. Customer immediately complained about the error, and both Printer and Customer realized that there was not enough time before the trade show to reprint the job. The contract price was $5,000. A reasonable person would conclude that the "loss of value" to Customer from having the wrong-color brochures was approximately $2,000. Printer offered to give Customer a $2,000 discount on the job. Customer instead said, "No, the brochures as you printed them do not substantially conform to my specifications, so I'm not taking any of them and I'm not paying you a dime. You can pick up the brochures whenever you want." Instead, Printer has sued Customer on the contract for $5,000, but concedes in his papers that Customer may be entitled to a $2,000 offset for the wrong color. May Printer recover on the contract?

Not sure ☐

110. Same basic fact pattern as in the previous question. This time, assume that Printer delivered the brochures on June 15 printed in the wrong color. Printer called Customer the next day to ask about the job, and Customer said, "Everything seems to be fine." In fact, Customer had not had a chance to open the boxes, and did not do so until June 30, the day before the trade show. At that moment, Customer realized the color was wrong and panicked. Customer phoned Printer and said, "These brochures are totally unacceptable. Take them back, and I'm not paying you a

penny." Customer held the brochures for pickup by Printer. As in the previous question, Printer has sued for the purchase price less an allowance for the defect. May Printer recover on the contract (ignoring whether Customer may subtract damages for the wrong color)?

Not sure ☐

111. Buyer was a large business that owned hundreds of personal computers used in its own internal operations. Buyer contracted to buy from Seller a Model 100 computer made by Megabyte Corp. The contract called for delivery on July 1. On July 1, Seller delivered to Buyer a Model 200 computer made by Megabyte Corp. Seller delivered the Model 200 rather than the Model 100 because he was out of stock on the 100, and because he reasonably believed that the Model 200 (which differs from the 100 only in that it has a newer type of optical drive) would be acceptable to Buyer, since the Model 200 is a more advanced model that Seller was giving to Buyer at the lower Model 100 price. On that same day, July 1, Buyer told Seller, "This is the wrong model. We are not accepting it. Take it back. We're buying from someone else." In that same conversation, Seller offered to make delivery of the correct Model 100 machine the following day and demonstrated to the satisfaction of a reasonable person that he would be able to do so by procuring the machine from a distributor. Buyer said, "No, you've delivered us the wrong machine, so we don't want to do business with you anymore. Forget it." Seller picked up the machine and then sued Buyer for the profit he would have made on sale of a Model 100 at the contract price had he been permitted to deliver the Model 100 on July 3. Assuming that the state of the personal computer industry is such that Seller can get as many Model 100s as it has customers to buy them, may Seller recover this lost profit?

Not sure ☐

112. Same basic fact pattern as in the previous question. Now, however, assume that the contract itself contained a clause, inserted at the insistence of Buyer, that provided as follows: "Seller is aware that Buyer has standardized on the Megabyte Model 100 computer for all its internal needs so as to permit Buyer to maintain a uniform inventory of parts and to service its own machines. Therefore, Seller understands that no substitutions will be permitted." On July 1 (the last date for performance), Seller discovered that it did not have a Model 100 on hand, so it sent over a Model 200 to Buyer. Buyer refused to accept the machine, and then immediately so notified Seller. Seller said, "Just give me one more day—I can have a Model 100 to you by tomorrow." Buyer said, "No. Today was the last day for performance, and you've sent us the wrong model." Seller in fact sent over the proper model on July 2, but Buyer had already procured the machine it needed from someone else, so it refused to take delivery. May Seller recover for breach of contract from Buyer?

Not sure ☐

113. Builder was constructing a brick office building. Seller contracted to supply the necessary bricks to Buyer in lots of one ton per week, to be delivered to the construction site each Monday during construction. The first week, Seller did not deliver the bricks until Tuesday, so Builder's crews spent a mostly idle Monday. The following week, the bricks arrived on Monday, but they were the wrong color, and substitution was not made until Wednesday. After this second mistake, Builder said to Seller, "Our contract is off. Don't bother sending us any bricks next Monday." Seller said, "The first delivery problem was the fault of a supplier whom we've replaced. The second problem was the fault of a new employee who now knows what to do. I assure you that you'll get the right bricks next Monday." Builder said, "I can't afford to take chances, because each time you screw up it costs me idle time on the job having a value much greater than the bricks themselves [a true statement]. Sorry, the deal's off." If Seller sues Builder for breach of contract regarding the remaining installments, may Seller recover?

Not sure ☐

114. Contractor contracted to build a home for Owner on a lot owned by Owner. The contract called for Owner to make weekly progress payments. Three weeks into the job, on July 1, Contractor negligently destroyed several trees that, under an explicit provision of the contract, were to be left standing. Owner refused to make the next week's progress payment because of this act. However, Owner did not object to Contractor's continuing to work on the job between July 1 and July 21. Then, on July 21, Owner announced that he was canceling the contract because of the knockdown of the trees. Assume that the knocking down of the trees was a material breach of the contract. Was Owner within his rights in canceling the contract on July 21?

Not sure ☐

115. Same facts as in the previous question. Now, however, assume that Owner let Contractor continue until the end of the job, but withheld from the progress payments an amount equal to the value of the trees that Contractor wrongfully knocked down. Contractor has sued for the balance due represented by this holdback, on the theory that Owner, by permitting Contractor to continue with the work, waived the claim for damages for the knockdown. May Contractor recover this withheld amount?

Not sure ☐

116. Contractor contracted to build a house for Owner. The contract required all work to be completed by July 1. On June 20, at a time when Owner still owed Contractor the last $10,000 progress payment, Owner moved into the house. That same day, he gave Contractor a list of 17 defects to be cured (which Contractor promptly did), but omitted three other defects that he would have been aware of had he conducted a reasonably careful investigation of the house. On July 3, Owner discovered the remaining three defects, immediately notified Contractor of them, and said, "I'm not paying you the last $10,000, because these defects still exist and the time for performance has passed." Assume that the three final defects, viewed collectively, constituted a material breach of Contractor's obligations. Is Owner within his rights in withholding the final $10,000 payment?

Not sure ☐

117. Seller has contracted to supply widgets to Buyer on credit. The contract provides that Seller will extend such credit to Buyer only if, at the time of shipment, Buyer's credit is "in good standing." Seller and Buyer have done business together for years, and Buyer has always paid his bills within ten days to collect a 2 percent early payment discount. Under the current order, Seller is required to ship on July 1. Seller has previously shipped a different order (under a different contract) to Buyer on June 1, with terms "net 30." Buyer failed to pay by June 10 so as to take the 2 percent early payment discount and indeed has not yet paid the June 1 invoice (it is now June 28). Seller does not want to ship the July 1 order on credit, realizing that Buyer may now be in financial trouble. But Seller also does not want to breach the July 1 contract. What should Seller do?

Not sure ☐

118. Seller had a contract to custom-produce widgets for Buyer. There were no other buyers for this particular type of widget, and the cost of the parts and labor to be used by Seller represented a substantial portion of the purchase price that would be owed by Buyer. The contract called for delivery on July 1. It would (as Buyer knew) take Seller a minimum of two weeks to order the parts, receive them, and make the goods. On June 1, Seller heard from a third party that Buyer had told that party, "When the widgets come from the Seller, I'm going to refuse them because I lost the contract for which I needed them." On June 2, Seller sent Buyer a letter reciting this rumor, and stating, "Please respond immediately to let me know whether you intend to honor our agreement." Seller received no response by June 18, and on that date sent Buyer another letter stating, "Since you did not respond to my earlier letter, and the time within which I can buy the goods, receive them, and manufacture the widgets for July 1 shipment has now passed, I declare our contract terminated." Buyer now sues for breach, and in the lawsuit demonstrates that the rumor that Buyer would reject the goods was totally false. May Buyer recover against Seller for breach?

Not sure ☐

119. Stanley, a student in the New Jersey University (NJU) MBA program, accepted on February 1 of his last year of school a job offer with Search, Acquire & Destroy, Inc. ("Search"), an investment banking firm specializing in mergers and acquisitions. Stanley was given a one-year employment contract, to run from September 1 until the next August 31. One month after the contract was signed, on March 1, Search sent Stanley a letter that stated, "Due to the February 15 stock market crash, we will be unable to employ you as scheduled." On April 1, Stanley instituted a suit against Search for breach of contract. On May 1, Search objected that the suit was not yet timely. On that day, may the court immediately award damages to Stanley for breach of contract?

Not sure ☐

120. Same fact pattern as in the previous question. Now, however, assume that Search did not send any letter to Stanley on March 1, despite the tumultuous crash that had just occurred. However, Stanley heard that other MBA students who had received similar contracts from Search had been told that their contracts would not be honored. Therefore, on March 1 Stanley wrote to Search, "I've heard that you're canceling lots of contracts with my classmates. Are you still intending to go through with my contract?" Search did not respond. Three weeks after writing this letter, Stanley instituted a suit for breach against Search and took a job elsewhere at lower pay. At the trial of Stanley's suit (which took place in October), Search proved that the rumors that it had reneged on other contracts were false and that it had honored the contract of anyone who presented herself on September 1. May Stanley recover damages under his contract with Search?

Not sure ☐

121. Same basic fact pattern as in the previous two questions. Now, however, assume that Search sent the March 1 letter referred to in question 120, and Stanley took no immediate action except to say to himself, "I'll sue the bastards as soon as I finish my midterm exams next week." On March 5, before Stanley had filed suit, looked for another job, or communicated with Search, Search sent another letter saying, "We've reevaluated our position. Please disregard our March 1 letter; you're still welcome and expected to show up for work on September 1." Putting aside issues of timeliness of suit, may Stanley sue Search for breach of contract?

Not sure ☐

122. Same basic fact pattern as the previous question. Now, however, assume that Stanley responded to Search's March 1 contract cancellation letter by writing to Search on March 2, "Okay. I'll look for another job, and I'll sue you for the difference in wages, if any." On March 5, after receiving Stanley's letter, Search sent a letter saying, "Ignore our March 1 letter. The contract is reinstated." As of March 5, Stanley had not taken or even seriously looked for another job. Putting aside issues of timeliness of suit, may Stanley sue Search for breach?

Not sure ☐

123. Same basic fact pattern as the previous four questions. Now, however, assume that Stanley, immediately after getting Search's March 1 contract cancellation letter, wrote Search, "I do not accept your cancellation of our contract. I urge you to perform the contract as scheduled." Search never replied. On September 1, Search made an office available for Stanley and included his name on a sheet distributed to all employees listing new employees joining the firm that week. Stanley, not knowing of this, did not report to work on September 1 and instead sued Search for breach of contract on September 2. May Stanley prevail?

Not sure ☐

124. Seller and Buyer signed a contract in which Seller agreed to convey Blackacre to Buyer on March 1, 2010, in return for Buyer's payment of $10,000 on March 1, 2010, plus $100,000 the following January 1, 2011. On March 1, 2010, Seller conveyed the land, and Buyer paid the $10,000. On April 1, 2010, Seller learned that Buyer was insolvent. Seller wrote to Buyer, "Will you be able to make the January 1 payment?" Buyer never responded. On June 1, 2010, Seller sued for the $100,000 second and final installment. May the court, hearing the case in June 2010, award Seller this money?

Not sure ☐

125. On March 1, Seller contracted to deliver 1,000 widgets to Buyer for $10 apiece, with delivery to take place on July 1. On April 1, Seller notified Buyer, "We have gone out of the widget-making business and will therefore not be fulfilling our July 1 delivery to you." At the time Buyer received this notice, the market price of widgets was $11. Buyer decided not to buy substitute widgets, and instead revamped its business needs so that it would use gidgets instead. On July 1, the date for performance under the contract, the market price of widgets was $12. If Buyer brings suit against Seller for breach after July 1, what damages should it be awarded?

Not sure ☐

126. Steve wanted to buy a car from Dealer on credit. Steve did not yet have an adequate credit history. Therefore, Frank, Steve's father, orally said to Dealer, "Go ahead, sell him the car on credit. If he doesn't pay, I will." Steve signed a written contract promising to repay the purchase price. Steve failed to pay the debt, and Dealer has sued Frank. Is Frank liable?

Not sure ☐

127. Tycoon wanted to buy a new 2010 Stutz Bearcat from Dealer. However, Tycoon was afraid that Dealer would not be able to adequately service the vehicle. Dealer and Tycoon therefore entered into a purchase agreement in which Dealer said, "In the event that I am unable to satisfactorily service the car, Mechanic, an independent contractor, will do so." Simultaneously, Mechanic orally promised Tycoon that if Dealer did not fix Tycoon's car, Mechanic would do so for a reasonable fee. (Mechanic didn't really like fixing Bearcats, because it wasn't very profitable. He agreed to the arrangement with Tycoon mostly to help his friend Dealer make a sale.) Soon after, the car broke down, Dealer was unable to service it, Tycoon brought the car to Mechanic, and Mechanic said, "Sorry, I'm no longer in the business of servicing Stutz Bearcats." May Tycoon recover against Mechanic for breach of contract?

Not sure ☐

128. Same facts as in the previous question. Now, however, assume that Dealer promised to have Tycoon's car serviced as needed, but never told Tycoon about the service arrangement Dealer had made with Mechanic. At the same time, Mechanic orally promised Dealer, "If you can't fix Tycoon's car, I will fix it for a reasonable fee." Dealer was unable to fix the car, and sent Tycoon to Mechanic. Mechanic refused to try to fix the car. Dealer had to pay for Tycoon's car to be fixed by someone else. Dealer then sued Mechanic. May Dealer recover against Mechanic for breach of contract?

Not sure ☐

129. Amanda thought that her friend Barbara would enjoy reading the new nonfiction bestseller *The Way to a Man's Heart Is Through His Nose*. Amanda therefore called Bookstore and said, "Send *The Way to a Man's Heart* to Barbara. If she doesn't pay for it, I will." The book cost $29.95. Bookstore sent the book to Barbara, Barbara refused to pay for it (she instead held it for Bookstore to pick up), Amanda also refused to pay, and Bookstore sued Amanda for breach. May Bookstore recover?

Not sure ☐

130. Contractor was building a house for Owner on Owner's land. Contractor had fallen behind on the work, and every day of delay cost Owner $1,000 in indirect damages (e.g., costs of living elsewhere). Contractor informed Owner that Contractor needed a special pneumatic drill to continue with the work. The drill cost $400. Contractor went to his local building supply store, Emporium, and attempted to buy the drill on credit. Emporium refused unless Owner would guarantee payment for the bill. Owner orally said to Emporium, "Yes, if you sell the drill to Contractor, I'll be responsible if Contractor does not pay the bill." Contractor did not pay the bill, and Emporium sued Owner. Is Owner liable?

Not sure ☐

131. Buyer wanted to buy Blackacre from Seller. They entered into an oral option contract, by which Buyer paid Seller $10,000, and in return Seller agreed that Buyer could acquire Blackacre for $90,000 (plus the $10,000 paid for the option amount) at any time during the next six months. Within five months, Buyer tendered the $90,000, but Seller refused to accept it or to convey Blackacre. By now, the market value of the land is $130,000. May Buyer recover damages for breach of contract (putting aside whether Buyer may recover his option payment in an off-the-contract suit)?

Not sure ☐

132. Buyer and Seller orally agreed that Seller would convey Blackacre to Buyer on July 1 in return for Buyer's promise to pay $100,000 on August 1. Seller (stupidly) made the July 1 conveyance. Buyer refused to pay the money on August 1. May Seller bring a breach of contract action and recover the $100,000 August 1 payment?

Not sure ☐

133. Seller and Buyer orally agreed that Buyer would pay Seller $10,000 on July 1, and that on August 1, at a formal closing, Seller would convey Blackacre to Buyer in return for an additional $90,000. Buyer made the $10,000 July 1 payment. Seller declined to convey Blackacre on August 1, even though Buyer tendered the $90,000. May Buyer obtain a decree for specific performance, ordering Seller to convey to Buyer in return for $90,000?

Not sure ☐

134. Studio, a movie studio, orally contracted on July 1, 2010, with Star for Star to perform in a movie being made by Studio. Shooting was scheduled to begin on June 1, 2011, and was certain to take between four and six months. In March 2011, Star notified Studio that he would not appear in the movie. If Studio sues Star for breach of contract, will it be able to recover?

Not sure ☐

135. Boss and Employee orally agreed that Employee would work for Boss for the rest of Employee's life. Boss fired Employee after two years on the job. May Employee recover for breach of contract?

Not sure ☐

136. Boss and Employee orally agreed that Employee would work for Boss for five years. Their oral agreement also provided that either party could terminate the arrangement on 30 days' notice at any time. After two years on the job, Boss fired Employee without any advance notice. May Employee recover for breach?

Not sure ☐

137. Studio, a movie studio, orally agreed with Star that Star would perform in a movie to be made by Studio. The agreement was made on July 1, 2010, and provided that on June 1, 2011 (before the start of shooting), Star's entire fee of $1 million would be paid. The contract also provided that Star would be on location for 90 shooting days, beginning July 1, 2011. On June 1, 2011, Studio made the $1 million payment. On July 1, Star refused to show up for work. Studio has sued Star for breach of contract, and demonstrates that the movie probably would have made profits in excess of $2 million (whereas the movie lost money with the substitute actor that Studio was able to procure). May Studio recover $2 million from Star as damages for breach of contract?

Not sure ☐

138. Consumer visited a used-car lot operated by Dealer. Consumer and Dealer orally agreed that Consumer would buy a particular 1997 Ford Fiesta at a price of $1,500, with the actual purchase to take place within one week. Three days after this agreement, Dealer turned down a higher offer from someone else in reliance on the agreement. Consumer never came up with the money and therefore never consummated the purchase. May Dealer recover from Consumer for breach of contract?

Not sure ☐

139. Shopper and Jeweler (the owner of a jewelry store) orally agreed that Shopper would buy a particular antique gold ring for $399. The parties agreed that Shopper would return the next week with the purchase price and that they would then consummate the sale. The next day, Jeweler received an offer of $600 for the ring from another prospective purchaser, Buyer. Jeweler gave in to temptation and sold the ring to Buyer for this amount. Shopper has sued Jeweler for breach of contract. May Shopper recover?

Not sure ☐

140. Customer orally ordered 2,000 sheets of customized stationery to be printed for Customer by Printer. The parties agreed that the price would be $900. Printer set the type for the stationery and then made a "plate" (a metal representation of the type, which is used on the printing press and cannot be used for any other printing job). He was about to put the plate on the press when Customer called and canceled the order. Assume that the contract falls within the UCC. May Printer recover from Customer for breach of contract?

Not sure ☐

141. On July 1, Buyer telephoned Seller and ordered 1,000 widgets from Seller at a price of $6 per widget. The parties agreed that shipment would be made on July

15. No writing was ever signed or exchanged between the parties. On July 13, before Seller had shipped the goods, Buyer called up again and said, "Cancel my order." Seller sued Buyer for breach of contract. Buyer raised a Statute of Frauds defense. At trial, Seller's lawyer asked Buyer on cross-examination, "On July 13, did you cancel an order for 1,000 widgets you had made on July 1?" Buyer responded, "No. I did place an order on July 1, but it was only for 100 widgets, not 1,000. Anyway, my understanding is that all agreements for the sale of goods over $500 are not enforceable except by a signed writing." The trial judge has concluded that Buyer is lying and that Buyer actually ordered 1,000 widgets on July 1. May Seller recover any damages for breach of contract from Buyer? If so, based on what quantity of widgets?

Not sure ☐

142. On November 1, Toy Store ordered (by telephone) ten Wiz Bang home entertainment centers from Distributor, for sale during the Christmas season. The wholesale price to Toy Store was $80 per unit. The goods arrived on November 5. Toy Store put them in the basement, intending to put them up for display but never getting around to doing so. No writing was exchanged between the parties. On December 27, Toy Store discovered the goods in the basement and sent them back to Distributor with a note saying, "We never ordered these." Distributor has sued Toy Store for breach of contract. May Distributor recover?

Not sure ☐

143. Owner and Buyer orally agreed that Buyer would buy Blackacre from Owner at a total price of $100,000. Buyer made a $10,000 down payment. Owner wrote out and signed the following document: "Received from Buyer, $10,000 as down payment on Blackacre. Balance to be paid when deed and proof of marketable title are presented to Buyer. [Signed, Owner]" Owner then refused to consummate the transaction, and Buyer has sued for breach of contract. Owner raises the Statute of Frauds as a defense. May Buyer recover on the contract?

Not sure ☐

144. Toy Store orally ordered 100 Onion Patch dolls from Distributor at a price of $15 per doll. The only writing exchanged between the parties was a letter marked "Confirmation" sent by Toy Store to Distributor, which said, "This confirms our order for 50 Onion Patch dolls." Distributor received this letter only after Distributor had sent 100 dolls. Distributor billed Toy Store for all 100 dolls sent. Toy Store sent back the 100 dolls, saying, "We never ordered these." Assume that Distributor can get all the Onion Patch dolls it has customer orders for, and that it makes a profit of $2 per doll. May Distributor recover on the contract against Toy Store, and if so, how much?

Not sure ☐

145. Same basic fact pattern as in the previous question. Now, however, assume that Toy Store never sent any writing to Distributor. However, Distributor sent Toy Store a document marked "Confirmation," which said, "This confirms your order of 100 Onion Patch dolls from us at a price of $15 per doll." (The terms stated were the ones actually agreed to between the parties orally.) Toy Store received this confirmation on November 6, and received the dolls on November 10. On November 18, Toy Store orally asserted that it had never ordered the dolls, and sent them back to Distributor. If Distributor sues for lost profits on the dolls, may it recover?

Not sure ☐

146. On July 1, 2010, Salesman and Company orally agreed that Salesman would work for Company for six months at a stated salary and commission. Both parties signed a memorandum accurately setting out this understanding. On August 1, 2010, the two parties orally agreed to extend the contract (keeping all of its other terms the same) until August 30, 2011. On January 1, 2011, Company discharged Salesman, noting that their contract was over, according to the terms of the original written agreement. Assume that Salesman has not relied in any material way on the oral extension of the contract. May Salesman recover damages for breach of contract from Company?   Not sure ☐

147. Buyer and Seller agreed in writing that Buyer would buy Blackacre from Seller for $100,000, with closing to occur one week later, on July 7. The written document also required Seller to show Buyer written proof of marketable title no later than July 5. On July 3, Seller telephoned Buyer and said, "I can't get proof of marketable title any earlier than July 12. Can I give it to you then, and we'll close on July 14?" Buyer said, "Okay." On July 5 (before Seller had behaved any differently in light of the July 3 conversation), Buyer called Seller and said, "I've changed my mind. I want to insist on the original written conditions." Seller was unable to come up with the proof of marketable title by July 5, and Buyer has sued for breach. Seller shows that he could and would have come up with the proof of marketable title by July 12. May Buyer recover for breach?   Not sure ☐

148. Same basic facts as in the previous question. Now, however, assume that on July 3 Seller telephoned Buyer to say, "I could get proof of marketable title by July 5, but it would be much easier if I could get it by the 12th and we would then close on the 14th." Buyer orally agreed. Buyer then changed his mind, but did not inform Seller of his intent to insist on the July 5 date until the afternoon of July 4. By then, it was too late for Seller to get the proof. Had Buyer never agreed to the postponement of the date, Seller would have been able to get the proof of marketability by the originally required July 5 date. When Seller was unable to come up with the proof of marketability by July 5, Buyer canceled the contract. May either party recover from the other for breach? If so, which one may recover?   Not sure ☐

149. Buyer and Seller agreed in writing that Buyer would buy Blackacre from Seller for $100,000, with the closing to occur on July 7. On July 5, Seller told Buyer orally, "I don't want to go through with it. Will you let me out of the contract?" Buyer said, "Okay." The next day, Buyer had a change of heart and said to Seller, "I still want to close as originally scheduled." Seller said, "Sorry, you agreed to cancel our contract." Buyer now sues Seller for breach. May he recover?   Not sure ☐

150. Seller and Buyer agreed that Buyer would purchase 1,000 widgets from Seller at a price of $1 per widget. The parties both signed a memorandum listing the essential terms of the transaction. Before the date for delivery arrived, Buyer telephoned Seller and said, "Raise my order to 2,000 widgets." Seller shipped 2,000 widgets. Buyer, whose needs had decreased in the meantime, took 1,000 and sent the other 1,000 back to Seller. If Seller sues for damages based on Buyer's refusal to keep and pay for the second 1,000 widgets, may he recover?   Not sure ☐

151. Acme Corp. was a closely held corporation with two shareholders, Alfonse (who owned 51 percent) and Bernard (who owned 49 percent). Priscilla contracted to buy Alfonse's interest in Acme because she desired to have control over the company's operations, and because she wished to put her husband (who was currently

unemployed) in charge of the company. Just before the scheduled closing, Alfonse announced that he was not going through with the sale. Because Acme's operations are currently unprofitable and there is no ready market for the company's stock, Priscilla would find it hard to prove that the stock is worth more than the contract price. What kind of relief can Priscilla get that would satisfy her objectives of controlling the company and having her husband run the business?

Not sure ☐

152. Paul, age 61, was the only obstetrician in the Town of Ames (population 19,000). Paul wished to find a younger doctor who would gradually take over his practice. He therefore contracted with Deborah, a recent medical school graduate who wanted to specialize in obstetrics. The contract provided that Deborah would work for Paul on salary for four years, at which time Paul would retire; Deborah would then continue the practice by herself. The contract also provided that during the four-year phase-in period, if Deborah should leave the job in violation of the contract, she would not practice obstetrics in Ames for the balance of the four-year period. After one year of the arrangement, Deborah left Paul (without any breach of the contract on Paul's part, and in violation of the contract) and set up her own competing obstetrics practice in Ames.

(a) May Paul obtain a decree of specific performance ordering Deborah to return to the salaried position with him as provided in the contract?

Not sure ☐

(b) May Paul obtain an injunction ordering Deborah not to practice obstetrics on her own, or with any other doctor, in the Town of Ames for the rest of the four years?

Not sure ☐

153. Owner owned a painting by Van Gogh, *Irises*. Owner contracted to sell the painting to Collector for $10 million. After the contract was signed, but before the sale had been consummated, Owner orally accepted an offer of $15 million for the painting from Museum. Collector immediately sued Owner to enjoin the sale to Museum and to compel specific performance of the sale to Collector. Owner defended on the grounds that Collector's remedy, if any, should be the payment to Collector of $5 million (the difference between the contract price and the "value" as measured by Museum's offer). Collector retorted that he simply wants the painting. Should the court grant Collector's request for specific performance and an injunction against sale to Museum?

Not sure ☐

154. Builder contracted to build a house for Owner. The contract provided that the foundation would be sufficient to support a three-story structure in complete safety. Builder built the house, and Owner paid the full contract price. Owner then discovered that the foundation was cracked and that the house was no longer safe. To make the house safe, several walls will have to be torn down so that the foundation can be rebuilt; this will cost $100,000. If this strengthening work is done, the value of the house will increase by only $70,000 over what it is today. If Owner sues Builder for breach, how much will Owner recover?

Not sure ☐

155. Same basic fact pattern as in the previous question. Now, however, assume that the cracks are quite minor and decrease the value of the house by only $10,000. Tearing down the walls to rebuild the foundation would cost the same $100,000 as in the previous question. How much will Owner recover in a suit against Contractor for breach of contract?

Not sure ☐

156. Inventor desired to build a better mousetrap. Through careful market research, he became convinced that the single biggest problem with existing mousetraps was that they would "catch" household pets, most notably cats, as well as catching mice. He therefore invented the Smelly Mousetrap, which emits an odor that keeps cats far away. Inventor entered into an exclusive contract with Licensing Corp., whereby Licensing Corp. received the exclusive rights to manufacture and sell the product in return for paying Inventor a royalty of 6 percent of all sales of the product. The contract required Licensing Corp. to begin selling the product within six months and to make reasonable efforts to market it successfully thereafter. Licensing Corp. had trouble finding a plant that could produce the Smelly Mousetrap successfully, and therefore had not introduced the product a year after the promised introduction date. Assume that this was a material breach by Licensing Corp.

Inventor sued Licensing Corp. (at a time when the trap had still not been marketed) for breach of contract. Inventor introduces into evidence a business plan written for him by his brother-in-law, a recent MBA, in which the brother-in-law reasonably predicted first-year sales of 1 million units at $10 each, and a consequent royalty to Inventor of $700,000 for the first year. Inventor also shows that he spent $30,000 (including cash outlays plus the market value of the time he spent designing the product) in fulfilling his side of the contract. Which of the following amounts is a court most likely to award to Inventor in his breach of contract suit against Licensing Corp.?

(a) $700,000

(b) $730,000

(c) $30,000

Not sure ☐

Not sure ☐

157. Father promised Son that if Son would move onto Father's farm (Blackacre) and build a house on Blackacre in which Son would live, Father would leave Blackacre to Son in Father's will. (Father didn't actively want Son to move in or build the house; he was merely offering Son an opportunity he thought would benefit Son.) Son moved onto Blackacre, spent $20,000 in time and materials constructing a small house, and lived there for six months. Son would not have had money to live in a substantially better dwelling had he not lived on Blackacre. (The rental value of Son's six months of occupancy was nominal.) At the end of six months, Father died, and his will left nothing to Son. Son has sued Father's estate for breach of contract. Blackacre has a value of $200,000. (The small house has no value to the estate, because any buyer would knock it down to build a bigger one.) How much, if anything, will Son recover?

Not sure ☐

158. Contractor contracted to build a house for Owner for $100,000. After Contractor had bought $20,000 worth of materials, Owner repudiated the contract and Contractor stopped work. Contractor sold the supplies (making reasonable efforts to get the best price), but received only $7,000 for them. At a time when Owner had not paid Contractor anything on the contract, Contractor sued Owner for breach. Neither side produces any evidence of how much it would have cost Contractor to complete the contract. How much in damages, if any, should a court award Contractor?

Not sure ☐

159. Same basic fact pattern as in the previous question. Now, however, assume that at trial, Owner shows that had Contractor completed the contract, Contractor would have had to spend (in addition to the $20,000 already spent by Contractor on materials) an additional $90,000. How much should the judge award Contractor in damages?

Not sure ☐

160. Doctor and Patient agreed (in a single document) that Doctor would perform on two different days two operations on Patient, each of which was needed in order to save Patient's life. They agreed that there would be a single fee for this work of $5,000 (a low price because Doctor especially liked Patient). After Doctor had finished the first of the operations successfully, Patient decided to use a different doctor for the second operation. Patient refused to pay anything, and Doctor sued for breach. Doctor shows at trial that although the contract price for the two operations was only $5,000 total, the price charged by nearly all other surgeons in the community for the first operation alone would have been $7,000. Doctor also shows that partly as a result of the life-saving first operation, Patient now has a life expectancy of 20 years, during which time he will be likely to earn about $1 million (giving his life, at least for tort law purposes, a "value" of $1 million). Patient points out that the contract price for the two operations together is only $5,000. What should Doctor's measure of damages be?

Not sure ☐

161. Same basic fact pattern as in the in the previous question. Now, however, assume that Doctor performed both operations, and Patient refused to pay the bill. Doctor shows that despite his low original contract price of $5,000 for both operations, most surgeons in the community would have charged $9,000 for the two operations combined. What should Doctor's measure of damages be?

Not sure ☐

162. Contractor contracted to build a house for Owner for $100,000. After Contractor had incurred costs of $40,000 in partially performing, Owner repudiated the contract. Owner then used a different contractor to complete the work, to whom he paid $80,000. In the open market, it would have cost $50,000 to have someone else do the work initially performed by Contractor. Contractor has sued Owner for damages. Owner proves that to complete the contract, Contractor would have had to spend $70,000 above what he had already spent, so that Contractor would have lost $10,000 on the contract. What should Contractor's damages be?

Not sure ☐

163. Contractor contracted to build a house for Owner at a contract price of $100,000. The contract specified that all walls must be insulated with Apple brand insulation. Inadvertently, Contractor used Banana brand insulation, which cost him about the same but is generally considered to be slightly inferior. It would cost Owner $60,000 to replace the insulation with Apple brand, since doing so would require tearing down each wall. The market value of Owner's house, by contrast, is only $1,000 less than it would be had Apple brand insulation been used as specified. Owner has not paid any part of the contract price. The house (not counting the land on which it is built) has a market value of $90,000, because the price for such homes has dropped since the contract was made. How much (if anything) may Contractor recover in a suit against Owner for nonpayment?

Not sure ☐

164. On July 15, Seller orally agreed to convey Blackacre to Buyer for $100,000, to be paid on September 1. At the time of the oral agreement, Buyer gave Seller a $10,000 down payment. During the next several months, Buyer (with Seller's oral consent) moved onto the property and made improvements that increased the value of Seller's property by $15,000. The fair market rental value of Buyer's use of the property during these three months was $2,000. On September 1, Seller refused to convey Blackacre to Buyer, even though Buyer tendered the remaining $90,000 due on the contract.

(a) What kind of action, if any, can Buyer bring against Seller for relief?　　　Not sure ☐

(b) How much should Buyer be able to recover?　　　Not sure ☐

165. Contractor contracted to build a house for Owner. The contract provided that all walls would be insulated, and that asbestos-free insulation would be used. The contract price was $100,000. Contractor constructed the house according to plan in all respects, except that he inadvertently used insulation that had a significant asbestos content. It would cost $60,000 to open up every wall, remove the asbestos-based insulation, and replace it with asbestos-free insulation. The house as built is worth $20,000 less than had it not contained any asbestos. Because the housing market has declined since the contract was made, the house as-is is worth $70,000. Owner has made no payments to Contractor.

(a) Which theory of suit, if any, might allow Contractor to recover something against Owner?　　　Not sure ☐

(b) What damages, if any, should Contractor recover?　　　Not sure ☐

166. Same facts as in the previous question. Now, however, assume that Contractor intentionally used asbestos-based insulation rather than asbestos-free materials because it cost him $5,000 less and he wanted to increase his profit. How much, if anything, may Contractor recover from Owner?　　　Not sure ☐

167. Subcontractor, who was in the business of doing cement work, contracted with Contractor to put 1,000 cubic yards of cement into the foundation of a building being built by Contractor at a price of $100 per cubic yard. The parties agreed on a timetable. Subcontractor was continually and seriously (though unintentionally) late doing the work, and was discharged from the job after 60 percent of the concrete had been poured. Contractor suffered no out-of-pocket losses from the delays. Contractor has not paid Subcontractor anything so far. The market value of the 600 cubic yards laid by Subcontractor is $90,000.

(a) On what theory, if any, may Subcontractor recover against Contractor?　　　Not sure ☐

(b) What damages, if any, may Subcontractor recover?　　　Not sure ☐

168. Jeweler and Consumer agreed that Consumer would purchase a particular antique diamond ring from Jeweler for $3,000. Consumer signed a memorandum adequate to bind him under the UCC Statute of Frauds. As required under the contract, Consumer put down a deposit of 50 percent of the contract price ($1,500), and promised to return the next week with the balance, at which time Jeweler would give Consumer the ring. Consumer then telephoned Jeweler the next day and said, "I've changed my mind, and I want my deposit back." Jeweler said "No, I'm keeping your deposit as damages." Jeweler sold the ring to someone else the next week for $2,900. Consumer then sued Jeweler for a refund of the deposit. How much, if anything, is Consumer entitled to recover?　　　Not sure ☐

169. Seller carried for resale a particular kind of motor, the Model 123, that was carefully machined to be used in, and only in, a certain type of tin-can manufacturing machine. Buyer, whom Seller knew to be a tin-can manufacturer, ordered a Model 123 at Seller's standard price of $1,000. Since tin-can manufacturing machines are very expensive (costing more than $1 million on average), machine owners generally keep one or more 123s in stock as spares; alternatively, if a 123 is needed as a "live" replacement to get a broken machine running again, the machine owner usually orders the 123 to be sent by same-day messenger. Buyer ordered the 123 to be sent by the post office and received it in two days. Buyer then installed the motor, but it failed to work properly, costing Buyer an additional three days' loss of production. Buyer has sued Seller for consequential damages for the three days' lost production, and shows that those days have cost Buyer profits of $100,000. (This proof of what the plant would have earned in three days is quite certain, since it is based on the plant's recent past earnings, and on proof that Buyer can sell all the tin cans it can produce due to an industry shortage.) May Buyer recover the $100,000?

Not sure ☐

170. Boss hired Worker under a one-year contract, by which Worker was to serve as Boss's sales manager in the copy machine business at an annual salary of $40,000. After one day of work, Boss wrongfully fired Worker and paid her nothing. If Worker had read the local want ads, she would have discovered at least two other sales manager posts for which she probably would have been hired, each paying a salary of $35,000. Instead, Worker became depressed over the firing, did not work for the rest of the year, and her only employment-related income was $10,000 of unemployment benefits. If Worker sues Boss for breach of contract, how much will she receive in damages?

Not sure ☐

171. Contractor was a general contractor who maintained no staff of construction workers permanently on his payroll. Instead, Contractor hired "freelance" construction workers when and as he needed them for a particular project. Because the local economy was soft, he was always able to find such workers at the time he needed them. Contractor contracted to pave a parking lot for Owner for $100,000. If the contract had been fully performed, Contractor would have made a profit of $30,000. Instead, Owner repudiated the contract even before Contractor was able to begin. Contractor decided to retire immediately after this repudiation, so he did not look for any other contracts. Contractor has sued Owner for breach. Owner shows that had Contractor looked for a substitute parking lot paving job, he would have found one quite quickly at a similar $30,000 profit. May Contractor recover the $30,000 profit he would have made from full performance of the Contract with Owner?

Not sure ☐

172. Star, a well-known musical comedy actress, contracted with Studio, a movie company, to play the lead role in *Nebraska*, a musical in which Star was to sing and dance. After two weeks of shooting, Studio fired Star in breach of the contract and replaced her with another actress who Studio believed would do a better job. These facts quickly became public knowledge. Studio then offered Star a role in another musical comedy movie, *Kansas*, at the same salary. *Kansas* was expected to be an equally successful movie and would similarly have also showcased Star's singing and dancing talents. Star refused to accept this new role, saying (truthfully) that she had been sufficiently humiliated by her public discharge from *Nebraska* that she did not want to make another similar movie for Studio. May Star recover from Studio the contracted-for salary from *Nebraska*?

Not sure ☐

173. Landlord and Tenant contracted for Tenant to rent a store on Rodeo Drive in Beverly Hills from Landlord at a monthly rent of $5,000. Landlord agreed in the contract to perform various items of construction to make the store ready for Tenant, and agreed that this construction would be complete by July 1. The lease further provided that for every day after July 1 that the construction was delayed, Landlord would refund to Tenant $1,000 of the lease price. At the time of the lease, both parties believed that Tenant might earn as much as $350,000 per year from operating the store. The lease provided that the $1,000-per-day provision "shall be construed as a liquidated damages provision, not as a penalty." Landlord wrongfully failed to finish construction until August 1. Tenant withheld the first six months' rental payments ($30,000), claiming that the $1,000-per-day clause allowed him to do this. Landlord has sued for the $30,000, contending that the $1,000-per-day clause is invalid as a penalty. Landlord shows at trial that during Tenant's first year of actual operations, he has barely broken even. May Landlord recover the $30,000?

Not sure ☐

174. Bernard was in the business of buying personal computers, packaging them together with custom software he wrote, and reselling them as an integrated unit to an end-user customer. Bernard contracted to buy an IBM personal computer from Stacy, with delivery scheduled for July 1. Bernard simultaneously contracted with Zena to deliver to Zena custom software and the computer on September 1. The price in the Bernard-Stacy contract was $2,000 for the computer. On July 1, Stacy failed to deliver and said that she would not do so. On July 1, the price for a comparable IBM PC from other channels was the same $2,000. Bernard reasoned that he might as well wait a couple of weeks before buying a substitute personal computer to ship to Zena, since he would not be ready with the software until just before the September 1 date on which delivery of the whole system to Zena was due. On August 15, IBM announced a 15 percent price rise due to a shortage of microprocessor chips (an unusual event). Bernard immediately rushed to buy the PC from a third party and was forced to pay $2,300. Bernard has sued Stacy for $300 damages. Stacy contends that damages should be measured as of the difference between the contract price and the market price on the day of the breach, which would produce zero damages. May Bernard recover $300?

Not sure ☐

175. Same basic fact pattern as in the previous question. Now, however, assume that between the time the Bernard-Stacy contract was signed, and the time of Stacy's breach on July 1, the market price for computers dropped, so that it was $1,500 for the PC in question on July 1. Bernard nonetheless waited until July 25 to procure a substitute computer, because he did not want to lay out his cash until just before the scheduled redelivery date to Zena. By July 25, the price had rebounded to $2,000, and that is what Bernard paid. May Bernard recover from Stacy damages of $500 (the difference between the contract price and the market price on the date Stacy breached)?

Not sure ☐

176. Importer, who was in the business of importing coffee beans, contracted to sell 1,000 pounds of beans at $2 per pound to Wholesaler. The delivery was to take

place on July 1. Importer made the shipment, but Wholesaler unjustifiably sent the goods back to Importer (Wholesaler paid the freight both ways). At the moment when Importer got the goods back and learned of the rejection, the prevailing wholesale market price for coffee beans was still $2 per pound. It took Importer one week to find a substitute purchaser for the beans. Without saying anything to Wholesaler, Importer resold the beans to Grinder at $1.50 per pound; this was a reasonable price, since the wholesale market price of coffee had unexpectedly and suddenly dropped to this figure. Assuming that Wholesaler had no other means on hand with which to fill the order by Grinder, what damages may Importer recover from Wholesaler?

Not sure ☐

177. Same basic fact pattern as in the previous question. Now, however, assume that shortly after getting the beans back from Wholesaler, Importer resold them to Grinder at $2.50 per pound because of a sudden and unexpected upsurge in the market. Wholesaler, which had laid out $200 for round-trip freight, and which reasoned that Importer had gotten an unfair windfall profit, sued Importer for return of the $200 out of Importer's profits. May Wholesaler recover this amount?

Not sure ☐

178. At a time when the automobile market was soft and both dealers and car manufacturers had more inventory than they needed, Dealer contracted to sell a new 2012 Ford Fiasco to Consumer at a price of $10,000 (the market price for such a model). Dealer's cost was $8,000. Consumer failed to consummate the purchase and did not pay anything toward the purchase price. Dealer immediately sold that particular car to a different customer at the same $10,000 price. If Dealer and Consumer had consummated their arrangement, Dealer would have incurred $100 of out-of-pocket "dealer preparation" (e.g., cleaning and servicing) costs. How much, if anything, may Dealer recover from Consumer?

Not sure ☐

179. Manufacturer contracted to sell 1,000 metal rulers to Stationer at a price of $1 per ruler. Manufacturer instead sent 1,000 plastic rulers and billed Stationer the same $1 apiece. Stationer received the goods, paid for them immediately (without discovering the nonconformity), and then realized that they were plastic rather than metal. As an industry rule of thumb, plastic rulers are generally worth only 80 percent as much as metal rulers, and at the time Stationer received the rulers, the wholesale price of comparable plastic rulers was indeed 80 cents. The market price for both kinds of rulers then suddenly dropped due to an influx of cheap Asian imports, and by the time Stationer was able to resell the rulers to a local jobber, it received only 50 cents apiece for them.

(a) What damages, if any, may Stationer recover from Manufacturer?

Not sure ☐

(b) What, if anything, should Stationer have done differently?

Not sure ☐

180. Utility had for some time bought oil from Distributor, which in turn bought it from Refiner. On one occasion, Utility asked Distributor to quote a price for 10 million gallons of oil to be delivered within a given month, an unusually large amount. Distributor was able to combine this order with other orders and thereby get an extra 10 cents per gallon discount on a 20-million-gallon order from Refiner. Utility knew that Distributor was combining its 10-million-gallon order with other orders to get the cheaper price from Refiner. Before the date for delivering the

CONTRACTS SHORT-ANSWER QUESTIONS

oil to Utility arrived (and indeed, before Distributor had taken the 20 million gallons from Refiner), Utility unjustifiably repudiated the contract. Distributor would have made a profit of 10 cents per gallon on the 10 million gallons from Utility had Utility performed, as well as 10 cents per gallon on the contracts making up the other miscellaneous 10 million gallons ($2 million total profit). Instead, Distributor had to cut back its order from Refiner and had to pay 20 cents more per gallon on the other 10 million gallon contract, thereby suffering an out-of-pocket loss of 10 cents per gallon times 10 million gallons, or $1 million. How much, if anything, may Distributor collect from Utility in damages?

Not sure ☐

181. Insurer wrote a policy on the life of Father, a widower. Father paid the premiums and was therefore the owner. Father physically handed the policy to Daughter, saying, "I'm giving you this policy because I want you to receive the proceeds if I die." Six months later, Father married Stella. Father then sent written notice to Insurer, saying, "When I die, the policy proceeds should be paid to Stella, my wife, not Daughter." Father died, and both Stella and Daughter have made claim to the proceeds. Who is entitled to these proceeds?

Not sure ☐

182. Paula, a skilled bookkeeper, had long admired Susan, a major motion picture star. Motivated partly out of this admiration, Paula agreed to a two-year contract with Susan under which Paula was to be Susan's personal assistant and financial manager, taking care of all aspects of Susan's financial life. After one month, Susan tired of the arrangement, and handed Paula a letter that said, "I'm hereby assigning my rights under my contract with you to my good friend Tina," another movie star. Paula's hours, salary, and other general working conditions were to remain the same after the assignment. Paula objected to working for Tina because she found Tina much less lovable than Susan. Paula quit to take another job, and Tina sued her for breach of contract. May Tina recover?

Not sure ☐

183. Contractor contracted to build a house for Owner. The Owner-Contractor contract stated, "Any assignment by Contractor of any sums due hereunder is expressly prohibited." After Contractor had done about 20 percent of the work, he assigned his right to payment to Bank in return for an advance of 90 percent of the contract price. Bank notified Owner of the arrangement and said, "Make your payments to us, not to Contractor." Owner refused, and Bank has sued for an order compelling Owner to make payment to it rather than to Contractor. Is Bank entitled to the order?

Not sure ☐

184. Contractor and Owner signed a contract providing for Contractor to build a house for Owner. The contract said nothing about assignment. Contractor, wishing to divert some money from himself to his son Stewart, gave Stewart a letter stating, "I am hereby assigning to you all of my rights to payment under the contract between Owner and me." This letter was dated July 1, and was given to Stewart that day. On July 10, without knowing of the assignment, Owner paid a large sum due under the contract to Contractor rather than to Stewart. Contractor then died with more claims against his estate than there were assets. Stewart has now sued Owner, arguing that Owner must pay him the amount owed as of July 10, and that Owner's remedy is to recover the sum from Contractor's estate. Will Stewart be able to recover this money from Owner?

Not sure ☐

185. Same facts as in the previous question. Now, however, assume that Owner received notice of the assignment on July 8, but made the payment on July 10 anyway to Contractor rather than to Stewart. Contractor then died insolvent. Stewart now sues Owner for the amount due on July 10. May Stewart recover?

Not sure ☐

186. Contractor contracted to build a house for Owner. Contractor had long owed $1,000 to Creditor. Contractor assigned to Creditor the right to receive $2,000 in payment from Owner, in return for Creditor's discharging Contractor from Creditor's $1,000 claim against Contractor. Owner, before receiving notice of this assignment, made full payment on the contract to Contractor, who kept the money. Owner then received a demand from Creditor for payment, but Owner refused to pay twice. Creditor now sues Contractor for the full $2,000. May Creditor recover this money?

Not sure ☐

187. Same basic facts as in the previous question. Now, however, assume that before Owner paid anything on his contract with Contractor, Owner received notice from Creditor that Contractor had assigned to Creditor its rights under the Owner-Contractor contract. Owner, because of his own financial problems, defaulted, and never paid either Creditor or Contractor the $2,000 that he owed under the contract. Creditor has sued Contractor for $2,000. May he recover it?

Not sure ☐

188. Owner and Contractor contracted for Contractor to build a house for Owner. The contract price was $200,000. Contractor assigned his rights under the contract to Bank, in return for $180,000 in cash. Halfway through the construction, Owner asked for the house to be scaled down, in return for a reduction of the contract price to $170,000. Contractor agreed. Contractor then performed, and Owner paid $170,000 to Bank. Bank now contends that the modification was not binding on it, and that Owner therefore owes it an additional $30,000. May Bank recover this $30,000 from Owner?

Not sure ☐

189. Same facts as in the previous question. Now, however, assume that after Contractor assigned to Bank in return for a $180,000 payment, Contractor finished the work as called for in the original Owner-Contractor contract. After the work was done, Owner said to Contractor, "I'm short of funds. Can we reduce the contract price to $170,000?" Contractor (realizing that a fair price for the work would probably have been only about $170,000 anyway) said, "Sure. Anyway, it's not my money—just make your payment to Bank." Owner paid $170,000 to Bank, and Bank now sues Owner for the remaining $30,000. May Bank recover this $30,000?

Not sure ☐

190. Retailer contracted to buy 200 dozen men's dress shirts from Manufacturer. Manufacturer warranted the shirts' merchantability. Retailer was given 90 days after delivery to make payment. The contract also provided that if Manufacturer assigned his right to payment under the contract, Retailer would not assert against the assignee any claim or defense that he might have against Manufacturer. Shortly after the contract was signed, Manufacturer assigned his rights under the contract to Bank in return for an advance of 90 percent of the contract price. The shirts turned out to be defective and unmerchantable. Manufacturer then became insolvent, so that any claim by Retailer against him would be valueless. Retailer has declined to pay Bank, on the grounds that the goods were not merchantable. Bank asserts that it is not bound by any defenses that Retailer might have against Manufacturer. May Bank recover the entire contract price from Retailer?

Not sure ☐

191. Assembler, which is in the business of assembling electronics for customers, agrees in 2001 to take memory chips and circuit boards owned by Computer Corp and insert the chips into the boards. The contract calls for assembly of 10,000 boards at $10 apiece. Computer Corp supplies enough chips to assemble 15,000 boards in case some of the chips are bad. After the contract is signed, Assembler assigns all of its contract rights (including the right to be paid by Computer Corp) to Bank, in return for financing. Assembler does the work properly, delivers the completed boards to Computer Corp, and bills Computer Corp the contracted-for $100,000. However, Assembler does not return the 5,000 extra chips, for reasons unknown. Bank, as assignee of Assembler, demands payment of $100,000 and sues when Computer Corp doesn't pay. Assume the value of the missing chips is $60,000. Is Computer Corp entitled to set off the $60,000 against the $100,000 owed to Bank, so that any recovery by Bank will be limited to $40,000?

Not sure ☐

192. Same basic fact pattern as in the previous question. Now, however, assume that Computer Corp's claim against Assembler for missing computer chips arose out of a completely different contract between the two of them. Also, assume that Bank notified Computer Corp in January 2002 that Bank was now the assignee of Assembler's right to receive the $100,000 from Computer Corp. Lastly, assume that it was not until March 2002 that Assembler first failed to return the missing computer chips. Can Computer Chip assert the missing-chip claim against Bank?

Not sure ☐

193. Douglas was covered by a $100,000 life insurance policy with significant cash value. Douglas assigned the policy to Finance Co. as security for a $100,000 loan, but did not deliver the policy to Finance Co. Douglas then purported to assign the policy to Bank as security for an additional $100,000 loan; he gave the policy to Bank to hold as collateral. Douglas has since died, and both Finance Co. and Bank seek the policy proceeds. Who is entitled to the proceeds (assuming that the proceeds are not enough to cover either debt in full)?

Not sure ☐

194. Axle was the proprietor of a delicatessen. Axle contracted to deliver 100 pounds of roast beef and 100 pounds of turkey to Customer on July 1 for a buffet being held by Customer for its employees. The contract between Axle and Customer said nothing about assignment or delegation. On June 29, Axle realized that he did not have enough meat, nor did he have an appropriate delivery person. He therefore arranged for the meat to be supplied and delivered to Customer by Bart, who was also in the delicatessen business. Bart supplied poor-quality meat and delivered it late. Customer (which paid the contract price to Bart at the time of delivery because it didn't realize the meat was defective) has sued Axle for breach of contract. May Customer recover its damages from Axel?

Not sure ☐

195. Same basic fact pattern as in the previous question. Now, however, assume that Bart showed up at Customer's place of business on July 1 at the appropriate time, and with the contracted-for quality and quantity of meat. Customer said, "We ordered the meat from Axle, not from you. We're not going to accept it from you." Customer then sued Axle for breach of contract, in that Axle did not render the promised performance himself. May Customer recover?

Not sure ☐

196. Same fact pattern as in the previous two questions. Now, however, assume that the original Axle-Customer contract contained a provision stating, "This contract may not be assigned." The contract price was $1,000. Axle purported to assign to Bart the right to collect the $1,000 from Customer in return for Bart's promise to perform that contract and to pay Axle $200 of the price. Bart arrived on time with the required meat, and Customer refused to accept it from him. May Bart recover damages for breach of contract from Customer?

Not sure ☐

197. Same basic fact pattern as in the previous three questions. Now, assume that between the time the Axle-Customer contract was signed and the time for performance, Axle sold his business to Bart. As part of the contract for the sale of the business, Axle agreed that "all contracts between Axle and customers, including the Axle-Customer contract performable on July 1, are hereby assigned to Bart." Bart failed to show up on July 1 with the appropriate quantity of meat. Customer decided to ignore Axle and to sue Bart for breach of contract. Is Bart liable to Customer?

Not sure ☐

198. Alfredo, a famous tenor, contracted with the National Opera to perform the role of the Duke in *Rigoletto* for a production to be staged on July 1. The contract said nothing about assignment or delegation. Alfredo had an older brother, Alberto, who was an even more famous (and, according to most critics, better) tenor specializing in the same roles. Because Alfredo decided to go on vacation on July 1, and because Alberto especially wanted to perform the role, Alfredo delegated to Alberto the duty of making the July 1 performance. The National Opera's director objected to the substitution, but since it came at the last minute, had no choice but to allow Alberto to perform the part. Alberto performed creditably, and there is no evidence that his role was less well accepted by the public than Alfredo's performance would have been. National Opera now sues Alfredo for breach of contract. Putting aside the issue of the magnitude of damages, may National Opera recover from Alfredo for breach?

Not sure ☐

199. Archie owed $1,000 to Claire. Archie and Bonnie made a contract whereby Archie promised to paint Bonnie's house, and Bonnie agreed to pay $1,000 (the approximate value of Archie's services) to Claire. Archie painted the house in the manner called for in the contract, but Bonnie declined to pay Claire. May Claire, without first suing Archie, recover the $1,000 from Bonnie on a breach of contract theory?

Not sure ☐

200. Archie and Claire were boyfriend/girlfriend. Archie desired to give Claire a present. Therefore, he and Bonnie made the following agreement: Archie would paint Bonnie's house, and in return Bonnie would give Claire an antique ring that Bonnie inherited from her grandmother. Archie painted the house as called for by the contract, but Bonnie never gave Claire the ring. May Claire sue Bonnie for the value of the ring?

Not sure ☐

201. Owner contracted with Contractor for Contractor to build an office building for Owner. The contract provided for progress payments, including the payment of $100,000 to Contractor at the time the concrete work was finished. Contractor then subcontracted with Mason for Mason to do the concrete work for a price of $80,000. The Contractor-Mason contract provided, "Mason will be paid within 30 days of completion of his portion of the work, but in no event shall he be paid sooner than the day that Contractor is paid for the concrete work by Owner." Mason did the concrete work. Owner failed to make the progress payment to Contractor for the concrete work, and Contractor consequently failed to pay Mason the $80,000 owed to him. If Mason sues Owner for $80,000 of the $100,000 Owner-to-Contractor progress payment, may Mason recover, assuming that no statute applies?

Not sure ☐

202. The City of Griswold had a significant homeless population. No statute or court case had ever recognized a duty on the part of Griswold to give shelter to this homeless population. Nonetheless, the officials of Griswold, to alleviate suffering, contracted with a private company, Shelter, Inc., as follows: Shelter promised Griswold that any homeless person who presented himself to a shelter operated by Shelter before 8:00 P.M. on any evening would be given a bed for the night. The contract said nothing about direct actions by the homeless against Shelter. One evening, Ted, a homeless man, came to the shelter at 7:45 P.M. and asked for a bed. An official of Shelter told him, "I'm sorry, because of the cold we've had an unexpectedly high number of requests, and we simply can't give you a bed tonight." Ted was forced to spend the night outside and suffered injuries that required hospitalization. If Ted sues Shelter on a breach of contract theory for damages from not getting a bed, may Ted recover?

Not sure ☐

203. Owner, at the time he bought Blackacre, gave a mortgage on Blackacre to Bank in return for a loan of part of the funds to be used for the purchase. Some years later, with most of the mortgage still owing, Owner sold Blackacre to Buyer. In the contract of sale, Buyer promised Owner that Buyer would continue to make the payments on the mortgage held by Bank. Buyer took possession, but fell behind in the mortgage payments. Bank foreclosed, but even after the property was sold at foreclosure and the proceeds given to Bank, there was some money still owing on the mortgage. Bank does not want to bring a suit against Owner, who has left the jurisdiction. May Bank recover the balance due in a breach of contract action against Buyer?

Not sure ☐

204. Archie and Claire got married, the second marriage for each. Shortly after the marriage, Archie took out a $100,000 life insurance policy on his own life, issued by Insurer. Archie designated Claire as the beneficiary under the policy. The policy did not state whether Archie reserved the power to change the designation of the beneficiary. After one year, Archie changed the beneficiary on the policy (without Claire's consent) to Samantha, Archie's daughter by his prior marriage. Claire shortly thereafter received from Insurer notice of the change of beneficiary. Archie then died. Claire now sues Insurer to require Insurer to pay the $100,000 to her. Will Claire win?

Not sure ☐

205. Archie and Claire were boyfriend and girlfriend. Archie, desiring to make a gift to Claire, contracted with Bonnie as follows: Archie would make specified repairs to Bonnie's car, and in return Bonnie would give Claire an antique vase from her collection. Before doing the work, Archie told Claire about this. Claire, who was an antique dealer as well as a collector, realized that the vase in question would not fit into her collection, so she arranged to presell it to Donald for $300. Archie performed the work on the car. Before Bonnie gave Claire the vase, Archie and Claire had a fight and broke up. Archie and Bonnie then agreed that Bonnie would pay Archie $200 instead of giving the vase to Claire. Donald, when he didn't receive

the vase, sued Claire for breach of contract, but the suit had not yet been decided at the time Claire brought a breach of contract action against Bonnie. May Claire recover for breach of contract against Bonnie?

206. Archie and Claire were husband and wife. Archie desired to buy Blackacre (owned by Bonnie) and give it to Claire. Because Archie had many creditors who would attempt to seize any real estate to which Archie took title, Archie made the following contract with Bonnie: Archie would pay Bonnie $100,000 from a secret bank account that Archie had been maintaining, and in return Bonnie would convey Blackacre to Claire. The Archie-Bonnie contract was not put in writing. On the appointed closing date, Archie tendered the $100,000, but Bonnie said, "I've changed my mind and sold Blackacre to someone else." Claire has sued Bonnie for breach of contract. Assuming that the Statute of Frauds would prevent Archie from enforcing the promise against Bonnie, may Claire recover damages from Bonnie for breach of contract?

207. Same basic fact pattern as in the previous question. Now, however, assume that the Archie-Bonnie contract was in writing, so there is no Statute of Frauds problem. Archie paid Bonnie the $100,000, and Bonnie promised (in writing) to convey Blackacre to Claire the next week. The next day, Archie injured Bonnie in a car accident due to his own negligence, and Bonnie suffered $100,000 of medical bills. Bonnie therefore refused to convey Blackacre to Claire. Claire sued Bonnie for breach of contract. Bonnie now asserts (correctly, let us assume) that Archie owes her $100,000 for his negligence. Assuming that Blackacre is worth $100,000, may Bonnie decline to convey Blackacre to Claire?

208. Owner, at the time he bought Blackacre, gave Bank a mortgage in return for a loan of some of the purchase price. Some time later, Owner contracted to sell Blackacre to Buyer; as part of this contract, Buyer promised to make the remaining monthly mortgage payments to Bank. Buyer soon breached this promise, at a time when $100,000 was still owed to Bank. Bank foreclosed and received $50,000 in proceeds when Blackacre was sold at foreclosure.

(a) If Bank wants to collect the remaining $50,000, may it sue Owner before suing Buyer?

(b) Assume for this part only that the answer to part (a) is yes. If Owner pays Bank the $50,000, does he have the right to recover this amount from Buyer?

209. Archie owed Claire $1,000. Archie and Bonnie contracted as follows: Archie would paint Bonnie's house, and in return Bonnie would pay $1,000 (the approximate value of the house-painting) to Claire in satisfaction of Archie's debt to Claire. Archie painted the house satisfactorily, but Bonnie refused to make the payment to Claire. May Archie sue Bonnie for $1,000?

210. Producer, who was in the business of producing Broadway musicals, made the following contract with Theater Co., the owner of a Broadway theater: Producer would stage his next musical, *Zebras*, at Theater Co.'s theater for a minimum of one month at a daily rental of $10,000. The contract period included one week of rehearsals and three weeks of performances. After the week of rehearsals, just before the opening performance, the theater burned down; the fire was not the fault of either Producer or Theater Co. Producer incurred losses of $100,000 before he could arrange a substitute theater. Producer has sued Theater Co. for this $100,000 loss. May he recover?

Not sure ☐

211. Dealer, a store that sold personal computers, contracted with Buyer to sell Buyer ten ABC Corp. Model 5 personal computers. At the time of the contract, Dealer and Buyer both realized that Dealer did not have these computers in stock, and that it would have to order them from ABC Corp. Dealer immediately placed an order with ABC for the ten computers, which order ABC accepted. ABC then breached, failing to ship the computers to Dealer because ABC had received more orders than it could fill. Dealer made reasonable efforts to procure Model 5s from other dealers in the vicinity, but supplies were so short that no other dealer was willing to accommodate Dealer. Buyer has sued Dealer for breach. May Buyer recover?

Not sure ☐

212. Same basic fact pattern as in the previous question. Now, however, assume that the Dealer-Buyer contract was dated July 1 and called for delivery on September 1. Dealer waited until August 1 to issue a purchase order to ABC for the computers. Between July 1 and August 1, computer industry conditions tightened dramatically, so that on August 1 ABC rejected Dealer's offer. Dealer was unable to procure a substitute after making extensive efforts to do so. May Buyer recover damages for breach from Dealer if Dealer fails to supply the computers on September 1?

Not sure ☐

213. Manufacturer contracted to supply 1,000 pairs of men's gloves to Retailer. The contract contained a clause stating, "FOB Manufacturer's plant." Manufacturer packed the appropriate gloves into 50 boxes, then had the boxes picked up by Trucker, a common carrier, for delivery to Retailer. As Trucker's truck was en route to Retailer's store, the truck was involved in a major collision and all the boxes of gloves were destroyed in the resulting gasoline fire. By the time Retailer learned of the accident and was able to procure substitute supplies from another source, Retailer had missed several key weeks of the winter selling season and suffered losses of $2,000. May Retailer recover these losses in a breach of contract action against Manufacturer?

Not sure ☐

214. Same basic fact pattern as in the previous question. Now, however, assume that the Manufacturer-Retailer contract stated, "FOB Retailer's store at 1601 North Central Avenue, Chicago." Once again, the goods were destroyed while on the truck en route from Manufacturer's plant to Retailer's store. Assume that it was Retailer, not Manufacturer, who made the decision that Trucker should be used as the common carrier. May Retailer recover from Manufacturer Retailer's consequential damages from failure to receive the gloves?

Not sure ☐

215. Star, a movie star, and Devotee contracted for Devotee to serve as Star's personal assistant for one year. The two made the contract in large part because Devotee was a longtime admirer of Star's talents and was willing to work for below-market wages in order to bask in Star's glory. After six months, Star suddenly died of a quite unforeseeable heart attack. Star's executor immediately sent Devotee a letter saying, "I hereby reaffirm your contract. For the rest of the one-year contract, you will serve as my personal assistant to wrap up Star's affairs." Devotee refused, and went to work for Actor instead. Star's estate has sued Devotee for damages. May the estate recover?

Not sure ☐

216. Painter was in the business of painting houses. Owner, who wished to have his house painted, got competing bids from several house painters, including Painter. Solely because Painter's bid was the lowest, Owner awarded him the job. Halfway through the job, Painter died of a sudden heart attack. By this time, Owner had paid $5,000 of the $10,000 contract price. Owner was unable to find anyone to complete the job for the remaining $5,000, and was forced to spend $7,000 to have the job finished. May Owner recover $2,000 from Painter's estate?

Not sure ☐

217. In 2010, Distributor, a distributor of fuel oil, entered into a ten-year contract to supply oil to Utility Co. The contract provided that, for the first year, the price would be $1.20 (the prevailing market price), and that it would be adjusted each year thereafter by the amount of increases in the Consumer Price Index. During the next several years, the OPEC cartel regained power over the world's oil markets, and the price that Distributor had to pay for its supplies increased at twice the rate at which the Consumer Price Index increased. Consequently, at the end of four years, Distributor was required under the contract to resell oil for $1.35 that Distributor had to pay $1.60 for. If Distributor declines to continue performance on the grounds of impossibility and/or commercial impracticability, will it be allowed to do so?

Not sure ☐

218. Baker Brewing Co., a large beer brewer, contracted with the U.S. Broadcasting Co. (USBC), a TV network, for USBC to run a 60-second advertisement for Baker on Sunday, January 20, at 4:15 P.M. Although the contract did not so state, both parties understood that the advertisement would run during the first half of the Super Bowl football game. The day before the game was to be played in San Francisco, an earthquake decimated that city, and the game was canceled for that year. USBC offered to run the ad at the scheduled time and at a discount from the contracted-for rate, but Baker declined, pointing out that the advertisement prepared by it had a Super Bowl theme. If USBC sues Baker for damages based on breach of contract, will USBC prevail?

Not sure ☐

219. Same basic fact pattern as in the previous question. Now, however, assume that there was no earthquake and the game went forward as scheduled. By the time Baker's ad was due to be broadcast late in the second quarter, the score was 55-0 in favor of the home team, and audience telephone surveys showed that more than half the viewers had turned off the game in disgust. Baker immediately notified USBC by phone that it wanted to be discharged from the contract because its objective—reaching the typical large Super Bowl audience—had been nullified. USBC refused and broadcast the advertisement. If Baker refuses to pay, may USBC collect for the ad?

Not sure ☐

220. Painter, a housepainter, agreed to paint the outside of Owner's house for $10,000. All payment was due at the completion of the job, and no prices for individual parts of the work were contained in the contract. After Painter had painted approximately half the house, the house burned down, through no fault of either Owner or Painter. Owner collected the same insurance settlement as he would have collected had the house remained completely unpainted. On the open market, it would have cost Owner $5,000 to have someone paint that portion of the house that Painter actually painted before the fire. What, if anything, may Painter recover from Owner, and on what theory?

Not sure ☐

221. Same fact pattern as in the previous question. Now, however, assume that in addition to the paint actually used by Painter on Owner's house, Painter had bought an additional 200 gallons of an unusual shade of paint, at a cost of $1,000, which he anticipated using on the remainder of Owner's house. This paint, because of its custom mix and unusual shade, cannot be resold for any significant sum. May Painter recover from Owner for the $1,000 he spent on this paint?

Not sure ☐

222. Phillip, a young accountant, was given an employment contract by Dominant & Co., a large nationwide accounting firm. The contract provided that if Phillip were voluntarily to stop working for Dominant, then for three years thereafter, he would not work in the field of accounting in any city in which Dominant had an office. Dominant in fact has offices in the 20 largest American cities. Phillip worked for one year in Dominant's New York office, which employed 150 accountants. He spent his entire time working as a junior accountant on the Dominant auditing team that audited two of the ten largest industrial companies in America, and he did not develop close personal relationships with any one executive at either of these clients. He then decided to open up his own one-person accounting practice in his hometown of Cleveland (a city in which Dominant has an office). After Phillip began this Cleveland practice (at which he did not do work for any client whose matters he had worked on while at Dominant), Dominant sued Phillip for damages and/or an injunction against his new practice. Should a court award Dominant damages, an injunction, or neither?

Not sure ☐

223. Same basic fact pattern as in the previous question. Now, however, assume that the noncompete agreement between Dominant and Phillip said merely that for a period of two years following Phillip's departure from Dominant's employ, Phillip would not perform accounting work for any client on whose account Phillip worked while at Dominant. During Phillip's two years at dominant, his principal work was to be part of the tax advisory team for ABC Corp., a large Dominant client. After Phillip left Dominant, he immediately set up a practice (still in New York City) in which his principal client was ABC, and in which he gave ABC the same sort of tax advisory services as he gave them while working for Dominant (but at a lower price because of his lower overhead). Dominant has sued Phillip for an injunction against continuation of the services to ABC. Should the court grant Dominant's request?

Not sure ☐

224. Lucas held himself out to be a member of the California Bar. In fact, he had failed the bar exam three times and never passed it. Charles, a licensed plumber, had been carrying out his trade as an unincorporated sole proprietorship. After reading accounts in the business press about the benefits of incorporation, Charles asked Lucas to form a corporation, of which Charles would be the sole shareholder, to carry on Charles's plumbing business. Lucas agreed to do this work, and the parties agreed that Charles would pay $2,000 when the work was completed. Lucas properly performed the contracted-for work (filing of a certificate of incorporation; drafting of articles of incorporation, bylaws, etc.; issuing of stock) and then gave all the necessary paperwork to Charles along with a bill for $2,000. By coincidence, Charles then happened to discover that Lucas was never admitted to practice in California. Charles therefore refused to pay Lucas's bill. Lucas has sued Charles for $2,000. He shows in court that he, Lucas, did the work with the same standard of workmanship as a licensed California lawyer would have done and that Charles therefore has not suffered any disadvantage from Lucas's failure to have a license. Should the court award Lucas the $2,000 contract price?   Not sure ☐

225. Same fact pattern as in the previous question. Now, however, assume that Lucas did not do the incorporation work after repeatedly promising to do so. Charles performed work on a particular construction project (as an individual since Lucas had not yet set up the corporation) and failed to honor his own contract, leading to a judgment against Charles of $20,000. If the corporation had been set up as Lucas agreed to do, Charles would have been able to simply let that corporation default, and would have escaped personal liability. Consequently, Charles has now sued Lucas for $20,000 damages, representing the loss to Charles from the fact that Lucas did not perform the incorporation work. Assuming that the court is convinced that the $20,000 loss to Charles was a reasonably foreseeable consequence of Lucas's failure to perform the incorporation work, should the court award Charles his $20,000 damages?   Not sure ☐

226. Lawyer contracted to defend Client against a charge of murder. The parties agreed that Lawyer would be paid $100 an hour for his time throughout the trial. Lawyer spent nearly two years getting ready for trial, including extensive development of strategy and interview of witnesses. Client paid all bills promptly, and by the eve of trial had paid $100,000 in fees. Just before trial, Lawyer demanded that his hourly fee (including the fee for work already done, billed, and paid) be doubled to $200 per hour. Lawyer stated that he would not try the case unless this modification was made. Lawyer also pointed out to Client that the judge would probably not grant more than a one-month continuance to Client if Client wanted to change counsel, and that any newly hired lawyer would not be able to master the case in one month. (The request for an increased fee was not made because the work was harder than expected, but merely because Lawyer knew Client was rich, and believed Client would pay the extra money. $200 per hour, while high, was not unknown as a fee to be paid by a prosperous defendant to an attorney with skills like those of Lawyer.)

Client, feeling that he had no choice, very reluctantly agreed and signed a writing raising the hourly fee to $200; according to a local statute, a signed writing modifying a contract does not need consideration to be binding. Lawyer then tried the case and lost. Client refused to pay the amount represented by the increase from $100 to $200 per hour. Lawyer has sued Client for this increase.

(a) What defense should Client assert?   Not sure ☐

(b) Will this defense be successful?   Not sure ☐

227. Owner, who owned a house out in the country, had no reliable source of water. Owner therefore hired Driller to drill an artesian well on Owner's property. Both parties believed that the ground was relatively free of rock and that water would be found no more than 100 feet down. Therefore, the parties agreed on a flat fee of $1,000 for drilling the well. Driller began to drill, and almost immediately discovered that there was a huge slab of bedrock running throughout Owner's property. Driller therefore refused to keep drilling unless the price was raised to $10,000, a tenfold increase. Owner correctly realized that if he tried to hire any other drilling company now, that company would realize that there was rock and would charge the same $10,000 price, or more, as Driller. He therefore reluctantly signed a writing modifying the contract to provide for a $10,000 payment. (Under a local statute, a signed modification does not need consideration to be binding.) Driller completed the well and found water. Owner refused to pay anything more than $1,000. Driller has sued Owner for the other $9,000.

(a) What defense should Owner assert? Not sure ☐

(b) Will that defense succeed? Not sure ☐

228. Owner, who owned a five-story apartment building, sought to induce Buyer to buy the building for $1 million. During the negotiating process, Owner showed Buyer a pro forma income statement for the building, showing a net operating profit of $150,000. Unbeknownst to either Owner or Buyer, the actual profit for the building was only $100,000, the discrepancy being due to a mistake by Owner's bookkeeper as to the size of the building's utility and tax bills. Buyer, acting partly in justifiable reliance on the pro forma statement, contracted to buy the building. The contract did not refer to the pro forma or to the rent roll of the building, and did not contain a merger clause. After Buyer paid the purchase price, he discovered that the profit was really only $100,000.

(a) What contract theory, if any, should Buyer assert in an attempt to gain relief? Not sure ☐

(b) What relief, if any, is the court likely to grant Buyer? Not sure ☐

229. From time to time, Donald had bought business machines from Supplier. Since all sales were on credit, Donald furnished on July 1, 2010, a financial statement showing (truthfully) that his business had more assets than liabilities and was profitable. Shortly thereafter, Donald's business took a sharp unexpected turn for the worse and became unable to pay its bills as they came due. On October 1, Donald placed an oral order for $400 worth of equipment from Supplier, and Supplier agreed to send the order on credit. Just before shipping the order, Supplier learned (not through Donald) that Donald's finances were in trouble. Supplier therefore refused to ship the order unless Donald prepaid it. Donald refused and sued Supplier for breach of contract. May Donald recover for breach? Not sure ☐

230. "Crazy Foxy" was a dealer in stereos, TVs, and other electronic appliances. Rather than maintain a storefront, Crazy Foxy used door-to-door salesmen. One of these salesmen, Ed, went to the home of Brenda, in a middle-class neighborhood. Ed convinced Brenda to buy a Magnaview Model 350 19-inch color television, at a price of $500. Unbeknownst to Brenda (who was an invalid and therefore could not easily get out to shop), comparable TVs were routinely sold at the nearby shopping mall for $350 to $400. Ed made no statements about whether the price was a fair one and made (true) statements that the set was of fine workmanship. Brenda signed a contract to buy the set. She then discovered (by being told by her brother) that the $500 price represented an overpayment of at least $100, and perhaps $150. She refused to accept delivery or pay for the set. Crazy Foxy sued Brenda for breach of contract. What defense, if any, will enable Brenda to avoid having to pay the contract price or damages? Not sure ☐

231. Farmer, who was in the business of growing corn, frequently bought corn seed from Supplier. For the 2010 crop, Farmer ordered 300 pounds of seed at an agreed-upon price. Supplier confirmed the order by sending a "confirmation memo," which consisted of much boilerplate language, including the statement, "Farmer's only remedy for any breach of warranty shall be to return the merchandise within ten days of receipt thereof." The confirmation said nothing about any warranties. Farmer made no response to the confirmation and duly received the seed. He inspected the seed (which seemed fine) and then planted it. Alas, his entire crop failed because the seed turned out to be defective due to improper processing at Supplier's factory. Farmer has sued Supplier for return of his purchase price plus consequential damages representing the value that a proper crop would have had. Supplier defends by pointing to the ten-day right of return as the sole remedy. Will Farmer be able to recover damages for breach of contract against Supplier?   Not sure ☐

232. Greg was 17 but looked to be at least 19. (The age of majority in the jurisdiction is 18.) He purchased a new Corvette from Dealer by giving Dealer $2,000 and signing a note for the remaining $18,000. Dealer did not ask Greg his age before the transaction. Greg drove the car away without first procuring adequate insurance. He immediately wrecked the car, so that its salvage value was zero. Greg then missed his first payment (while still 17), and was sued by Dealer for that payment (plus all later-due payments, under an acceleration clause in the note). May Dealer collect the remaining payments from Greg?   Not sure ☐

233. Same basic fact pattern as in the previous question. Now, however, assume that Greg obtained the car on credit by falsely telling Dealer that he was 19. Greg put down a $2,000 deposit, with the understanding that he could pick up the car next week and pay the rest of the money in monthly installments. Before Greg was able to pick up the car, Dealer learned that Greg was only 17. Therefore, Dealer purported to cancel the contract and offered Greg back his $2,000. Greg refused, saying that he was thereby ratifying the contract. If Greg sues Dealer for breach of contract, will he prevail?   Not sure ☐

234. Carl, a hopeless alcoholic, had the ability to fool a casual observer into thinking that he was sober when he was in fact very drunk. One night, after Carl had had enough liquor to raise his blood alcohol well beyond the legally drunk threshold, Carl met Deborah, a stranger to him, in a bar. Deborah realized that Carl had consumed at least one or two drinks, but reasonably believed that he was not substantially impaired. Carl offered to sell Deborah his Rolex watch for $1,000. As Deborah realized, this was a cheap but not unheard-of price. Deborah agreed, and promised to pay $1,000 the next day; the parties signed a writing adequate to summarize the transaction on a cocktail napkin. The next morning, Deborah showed up at Carl's house with the $1,000. Carl said, "Sorry, honey, I was drunk as a skunk last night. Now that I've come to my senses, I'm not going through with the transaction." In fact, Carl had been sufficiently drunk at the time he made the transaction in the bar that he lost track of the fact that the Rolex was a gift from his late father; Carl would never have agreed to sell it for any price while sober. However, Carl had understood that he was making a contract. Deborah has sued Carl for damages and/or specific performance (at Carl's choice). May Deborah recover?   Not sure ☐

235. Patient checked into Hospital to have kidney stones removed. Hospital and the physician who attended Patient decided to let the stones pass naturally. To help Patient withstand the extreme pain of stones, a nurse (acting under the doctor's orders) gave Patient a dose of Coderol, a potent prescription-only painkiller. (Hospital billed Patient separately for the Coderol.) The Coderol was manufactured by Drug Co. Due to an error in the manufacturing process, the particular dose of Coderol given to Patient contained much too much of the active ingredient, a sedative, and Patient suffered a heart attack as a result. He recovered, and sued Hospital. (Drug Co. had become insolvent by the time of the suit and Patient therefore did not sue it.) Patient's suit against Hospital was not brought until two years and six months after the heart attack. The jurisdiction has a two-year statute of limitations for tort actions and a three-year statute of limitations for contract actions. Evidence at trial shows that no matter how carefully Hospital and its staff had inspected the Coderol or read the appropriate literature, they had no way of knowing that the particular dosage given to Patient, or any dosages for that matter, were defective. What contract theory, if any, should Patient assert, and may he recover?

Not sure ☐

236. "Big Bob" was in the business of selling used cars. In 2010, Consumer came to Big Bob's lot and asked for a four-door sedan that would be reliable. Big Bob pointed to a 2005 Igo Concerto, and said, "This is a top-notch little baby that should last you for a good ten years." Consumer paid Big Bob the $2,000 asking price and took the car. The parties did not exchange any writing. After six months, the entire transmission suddenly failed. The cost of repairing it is more than the value of the car. Consumer wishes to sue Big Bob for breach of warranty. Assuming that no implied warranty of merchantability has been breached, what type of warranty claim, if any, may Consumer make that has a good probability of success?

Not sure ☐

237. Dress Co. was a manufacturer of women's dresses. Retailer was in the business of reselling, among other things, women's dresses. A saleswoman for Dress Co. showed Retailer a sample of a new dress produced by Dress Co. The sample had bright red stripes, three inches wide, running vertically against a white background. This dress was shown in Dress Co.'s catalog as Model 123. Retailer placed an order for 15 Model 123 dresses in various sizes. (The written purchase order contained no description except "Model 123," and contained no language relating to warranties.) When the dresses arrived, Retailer discovered that the color of red was significantly lighter (tending toward pink) than on the sample, and that the stripes were only two inches wide. Retailer nonetheless attempted to sell the dresses, but they did not move well. Dress Co. has refused to accept a return of the dresses.

  (a) Can Retailer plausibly sue Dress Co. for breach of contract, and if so, on what theory?

Not sure ☐

  (b) What are Retailer's chances of prevailing in such a suit?

Not sure ☐

238. Law Firm desired to buy a new computer on which it could perform various office automation functions. Computer Co., a manufacturer of multiuser computer systems, learned of Law Firm's interest and began to solicit Law Firm. At one point in the discussion, a lawyer who worked at Law Firm told the representative of Computer Co., "We'll want to run the BestWord word processing program on this computer, since that's the program we're already using on our personal computers, and we don't want to retrain our people." The representative made no statement in response to this. After some time, Law Firm said to the representative, "Which model of yours do you recommend?" He replied, "We recommend our Model 431, 1 gigabyte, 16 megabytes RAM, 32-user system." Law Firm contracted to buy that model, partly relying on Computer Co.'s recommendation. The written contract did not recite any particular requirements held by Law Firm, made no relevant express warranties, and did not mention warranties at all. After the system was installed, Law Firm discovered to its horror that because of the system's unusual computer architecture, the BestWord software package did not then, and would probably never, run on the system. Does Law Firm have a contractual claim against Computer Co.? If so, identify that claim.

Not sure ☐

239. Same facts as in the previous question. Now, however, assume that Law Firm, based solely on research it had done through computer publications, said to Computer Co., "We want to purchase your Model 431 computer." Assume further that, as in the previous question, Law Firm indicated to Computer Co. that it planned to run the BestWord word processing package on the Model 431, but that Computer Co. made no express representation to Law Firm that BestWord would run on the 431. May Law Firm recover on the contract against Computer Co.? If so, identify the claim it should make.

Not sure ☐

240. Manufacturer was in the business of making automobile parts. Manufacturer bought a new drill press from Drill Press Co. In the negotiations, representatives of Drill Press Co. made no statements of any sort about the quality or merchantability of the press. The contract document contained no references to warranties, except for the following statement, printed in large type on the front of the contract: "ALL WARRANTIES, WHETHER EXPRESS OR IMPLIED, ARE HEREBY EXPRESSLY DISCLAIMED." The press, although new, failed to work in the way that a drill press would ordinarily be expected to work. Manufacturer, after fiddling with the machine for several weeks, gave up and sold the press to a used equipment dealer at a steep loss. Manufacturer has now sued Drill Press Co. for breach of the implied warranty of merchantability. Will Manufacturer prevail?

Not sure ☐

241. Dealer was in the business of selling used farm equipment. Farmer told Dealer that Farmer wanted a tractor for plowing and planting his soybean fields. Dealer recommended a used James Bear Model 2000 tractor. Farmer bought the tractor pursuant to a bill of sale that did not mention warranties at all but contained the words, handwritten by Dealer, "AS IS." The transmission broke the first day Farmer had the tractor, and Farmer spent more than the price of the tractor having the transmission fixed. Farmer then sued Dealer for breach of the implied warranty of merchantability, and for breach of the implied warranty of fitness for a particular purpose (soybean planting). Will Farmer prevail, and if so, on which of these theories?

Not sure ☐

242. Steve and Bob were both operators of used-car dealerships. They frequently sold used cars to each other for inventory. In general, they followed the practice of giving each other an implied warranty of merchantability on the cars they sold to each other. On one occasion, Steve offered Bob a 2007 Atoyot Capitalist. Bob asked to take the car for a test-drive. Bob spent 25 minutes driving the car but never drove the car in reverse. Had Bob driven the car in reverse, he would have immediately heard grinding sounds and would have known that the car's automatic transmission was badly damaged. (Most used-car lot operators in Bob's situation, when they test-drive cars offered to them, test how the car runs in reverse.) Bob bought the car for Steve's asking price and shortly thereafter discovered the broken transmission. Bob has sued Steve for breach of the implied warranty of merchantability. Will Bob recover?

243. Car Co. was a manufacturer of automobiles. Car Co. offered an express written warranty with each car, representing that the car would be merchantable and would perform according to certain published specifications. The writing containing the warranty also contained the following sentence, printed in large colored type: "Buyer agrees that Seller's liability under the foregoing warranties shall be strictly limited to the repair or replacement of defective parts. No other remedy (including, but not limited to, incidental or consequential damages for lost profits, or any other incidental or consequential loss) shall be available to Buyer." Consumer bought a new 2010 Model XZ9000T manufactured by Car Co. During his first six months of ownership of the car, nine different parts (including major parts, such as the transmission and the engine) failed and needed to be replaced. During these six months, the car was in the shop for 46 days. At the end of the six months, the car seemed to be working properly, but any person who was aware of the car's repair history would not have been willing to buy the car for anything close to the normal value of a six-month-old car of that model. Consumer has sued Car Co. for breach of the implied warranty of merchantability. Assume that the only applicable statute is the UCC. May Consumer recover?

244. Diane owed Pia $1,000, due on June 1. On that date, Diane said to Pia, "I can't pay you $1,000, and I will not be able to do so for quite some time. Would you be interested in taking my antique jade ring as satisfaction of the debt? It's in my mother's safe deposit box, but I can deliver it to you next Wednesday." Pia agreed to take the ring as satisfaction of the debt. Wednesday arrived, but Diane did not deliver the ring. One month later (after the market value of jade rings had dropped substantially), Pia sued Diane for $1,000. Diane now tenders the ring, but Pia refuses to accept it. May Pia recover the $1,000 from Diane?

245. Sam agreed in writing to work as Mary's personal assistant for two years at a stated salary. The agreement provided that it could not be modified or rescinded except by a writing signed by both parties. After one month, Mary said to Sam, "You know, Sam, this relationship really isn't working out very well. I think we'd both be happier if we went our separate ways and terminated the contract." Sam replied, "Yes, I agree." Mary wrote Sam a check for the time he had already worked, and Sam did not come in to work anymore. Five days after this discussion, Sam decided that he had made a mistake in agreeing, and demanded to be reinstated. Mary refused. Sam sued Mary for breach of the original written contract, claiming that the oral rescission was ineffective. Is Sam's assertion correct?

246. From time to time, Consumer bought goods from Storekeeper on credit. At the end of each month, Storekeeper sent Consumer a statement showing how much

Consumer bought and how much he owed. On July 1, Storekeeper sent Consumer a statement for transactions that took place in June, showing total transactions equaling $456 and a balance due of that amount. Consumer received and read the statement, but made no response (although he silently believed that there had been a computational error and that he really owed only $346). Consumer failed to pay the bill. Storekeeper has sued Consumer for the $456. Storekeeper does not show at trial any facts relating to the underlying purchases; he merely demonstrates that he sent the July 1 statement to Consumer and that Consumer did not respond.

(a) If the only evidence presented by Consumer is Consumer's statement that he does not remember how much merchandise he bought in June, may Storekeeper recover the $456?

Not sure ☐

(b) If Consumer introduces evidence, found by the trier of fact to be convincing, that the July 1 statement was the result of a clerical error and that it should have read $356, may Storekeeper recover the $456?

Not sure ☐

Contracts Answers to Short-Answer Questions

1. **Yes. By the** *objective theory of contracts,* **Alex's letter was an offer if Alex knew or should have known that a reasonable person in Barry's position would interpret it as such. See Rest. 2d, §19.** Since Alex certainly should have known that someone in Barry's position, reading the offer letter, would believe it to be an intentional offer, Alex's offer was valid despite his subjective desire not to enter into the contract. Therefore, Barry's acceptance was effective, and the two have a contract. (There is a small chance that a court might grant Alex's request to treat the contract as voidable on grounds of mistake if Alex can convince the court that he did not bear the risk of this kind of error and that enforcement would be unconscionable. But Alex is unlikely to prevail in such a quest for voidability.)

2. **Yes. It is irrelevant that one or both parties to an arrangement that takes place in a "business" context believe that the agreement is unenforceable. There is an exception to this rule if the parties** *explicitly* **manifest their understanding that the arrangement is not to be legally binding, but that did not happen here. See Rest. 2d, §21.** Therefore, the parties are bound.

3. **No. If one party intends not to be bound, and the other party** *knows* **this, then (at least according to most courts) there is no contract. See Rest. 2d, §21.**

4. No, probably. **Social engagements are generally treated as being presumed by both parties not to be binding. See Rest. 2d, §21.** (But if Alfred knew or had reason to know that Bertha viewed the prom date as a binding contract, then there will probably be an enforceable contract between them.)

5. Ava, probably. **Where the parties agree on the basic structure of a deal, but contemplate that there will be a subsequent formal and more elaborate writing, the issue of whether a contract existed prior to the writing is determined by looking at the** *intent of the parties.* If there is no direct evidence of the parties' intent, the court will look to circumstantial evidence of that intent. The size of the transaction, whether the agreement is of a type usually put in writing, and whether express agreement has been reached on all the terms, are some of the factors the court will consider. Here, most $20 million contracts for the sale of ten radio stations would be expected to be in writing. Also, the parties don't seem to have agreed on anything but the price; for instance, they have not agreed on the time for closing, the representations and warranties (if any) to be made by the seller, what to do if FCC approval is not given, etc.; see Rest. 2d, §27, Illustr. c.

   Therefore, the court would probably conclude from the circumstances that the parties did not intend to be bound. At the least, the court would probably hold that Ava did not intend to be bound and that Bridget knew or should have known of Ava's intentions. If either party doesn't intend to be bound, and the other party knows or should know of this, that's enough to prevent a contract from existing; see Rest. 2d, §27, Comment b.

   (Keep in mind that if the case is tried to a jury, and the judge decides that a reasonable jury could decide either way, it will put the question of whether a contract was intended to the jury. Thus in the mega-case of *Texaco Inc. v. Pennzoil Co.,* 729 S.W.2d 768 (Tex. App. 1987), the judge let the jury decide whether there was a contract between Texaco and Getty Oil for Texaco to buy Getty. Texaco and Getty had reached a one-page "agreement in principle" for a multibillion-dollar transaction. The jury decided that this was indeed intended to be a binding contract, even though such a contract would normally be embodied in a huge, carefully drafted, document. Consequently, Texaco—which induced

Getty to sell to it instead of to Pennzoil—was held liable for $10 billion for inducing breach of contract! The case illustrates that the "intent of the parties" is seldom directly ascertainable, and must be deduced from circumstantial evidence, as to which reasonable people may differ.

6. No. **Something that purports to be a "quotation" is rarely reasonably understood by the other party as being an offer—instead, it is usually properly understood as an** *invitation to the other party to make an offer,* **which the quotor will then accept or reject.** This is certainly the case where the quote does not specify the precise quantity (even if it specifies a minimum), and even more so the case where the quote is apparently addressed to numerous recipients. Here, since the quote did not specify the precise amount available (did Adlai have unlimited quantities of oil?), and since Bellamy should have known from the form-letter nature of the letter that it had been sent to many recipients, Bellamy should clearly have realized that Adlai did not intend to give Bellamy the power of acceptance. Therefore, there was no offer, and thus no contract, after Bellamy purported to accept.

7. No. **The legal effect of an offer is to create a power in the offeree to enter into a contract.** The letter from Adlai was sufficiently specific that it would constitute an offer if it were limited to the first sentence. But the second sentence—referring to approval by Adlai's office—makes it clear that Adlai was reserving to himself the power to consummate the deal. Therefore, Adlai did not give a "power of acceptance" to Bellamy, and Adlai's letter was therefore not an offer. Consequently, what Bellamy did was merely to make an offer, not give an acceptance.

8. No. **A mass-market advertisement, such as a newspaper ad, will rarely constitute an offer to sell. To be an offer, an advertisement must contain words of** *commitment to sell,* **and must be quite specific.** Here, the Piano Store did not indicate that it was committing to sell any particular number of pianos.

9. Yes, probably. **An advertisement can be an offer if it has specific terms and contains words of commitment to sell. See Rest. 2d, §26.** This ad would probably be found to have constituted a commitment by the Piano Store to sell that particular black piano for that price on that date to the first customer. Since Consumer met all of those requirements, his tender of the check constituted an acceptance, so a contract came into existence.

10. Yes. **An advertisement can be an offer if it has specific terms and contains words of commitment.** Arnold's advertisement constituted an offer that could be accepted by anyone who, knowing of the offer, brought the dog back.

11. No. **In general, an offer may not be accepted by one who does not know of the offer's existence. See Rest. 2d, §23.** Therefore, when a reward is offered for a particular act, a person who does the act without knowing about the reward cannot claim it. (But the rule is probably different where government offers a standard reward by statute.)

12. No. *The offeror is "master of his offer." That is, he may prescribe the method by which the offer may be accepted.* Since Buyer did not follow the clearly prescribed method of acceptance, he did not accept, and there was no contract.

13. Yes. **If no particular method of acceptance is insisted upon, the offeree can accept by any reasonable method under the circumstances. See Rest. 2d, §30.** Here, the offeror was not insisting that the signed and returned offer form was the only way to accept; he was merely suggesting (or was reasonably interpreted by Buyer as merely suggesting) this as one possible method of acceptance. Since no particular acceptance method was insisted upon, Buyer was justified in accepting by any method

reasonable under the circumstances (which the message on the answering machine would probably be held to be).

14. Yes. **The offeror is the master of the offer and may specify the method by which the offer may be accepted.** The purchase order, even though it was on a form prepared by Seller, became an offer by Buyer when Buyer signed it. Buyer, as "master of his offer" (even though the offer was on Seller's form), specified the terms under which a contract would be formed, and that offer specified that the signature by Seller's officer was all that would be required for acceptance. Therefore, Buyer's March 2 revocation was too late.

15. No. **Generally, if an offer is to be accepted by a promise, either (1) the offeree must use reasonable diligence to *notify* the offeror that there has been an acceptance, or (2) the offeror must in fact learn of the acceptance within a reasonable time (perhaps by other means). See Rest. 2d, §56.** Here, Seller did not use such diligence to notify Buyer, and Buyer did not learn of the acceptance by some other means. Therefore, the court would probably treat the lack of actual and attempted notice within a reasonable time as discharging the contract. (But if Seller had sent the signed form to Buyer promptly, and it had gotten lost in the mail, then the contract would be in force.)

16. Yes. **Since that offer did not specify whether acceptance was to be by promise or by performance, Seller was free to accept by either method, under UCC §2-206(1)(b).** Buyer's order was the offer. (The fact that Buyer's offer said, "Ship promptly," or words to that effect, will not be interpreted to mean that acceptance must be by shipment rather than by promise. See Official Comment 2 to §2-206.) Seller accepted by making a promise, as was his right. Therefore, a contract came into existence as soon as Seller sent his "thank you for your order" letter. At that moment, it became too late for Buyer to revoke his offer.

   NOTE: Citations to the UCC in this book refer to the pre-2003 UCC, since no state has adopted any of the 2003 Revisions. For further discussion of the 2003 changes, see *Emanuel Law Outlines: Contracts.*

17. No. **Some offers, either because of their express language or because of the circumstances, are clearly to be interpreted as only allowing acceptance by promise, or only allowing acceptance by performance.** The offer here is clearly one of the latter—Grandfather wasn't interested in having Grandson *promise* to attend and graduate from a law school, he was interested in the *performance*. Therefore, this was an offer for a unilateral contract, which could be only accepted by Grandson's performance. (Had Grandson begun to perform, for instance by entering law school, this would have been enough to make Grandfather's promise temporarily irrevocable for as long as Grandson stayed in school. See Rest. 2d, §45. But on our facts here, Grandson had not begun to perform, or even to make serious preparations to perform.) Therefore, there was no acceptance at the moment that Grandfather purported to revoke his offer, and the revocation was thus effective. See *Hamer v. Sidway*, 124 N.Y. 538 (1891).

18. Yes. **Normally, acceptance may not be made by silence. However, if because of the prior dealings of the parties it is reasonable that the offeree should notify the offeror if he or she does not intend to accept, then the offeree's failure to so notify the offeror will itself amount to an acceptance. See Rest. 2d, §69.** Here, the prior pattern of renewal followed by payment made it reasonable for Owner to notify Insurer that he was not renewing the arrangement, if indeed that was his intent. When Owner did not do so, he became liable for at least that portion of the premium attributable to the period during which Owner remained silent. (In theory, the two had a contract for all of 2010, but a court

would probably only make Owner pay for the first two months, on the theory that Insurer suffered no practical damages for the March-and-later period.)

19. **(a)** Yes, there is a contract, formed when Seller shipped the goods and Buyer kept them. **Conduct by both parties recognizing the existence of a contract establishes a contract even if the writings of the parties do not otherwise establish a contract. See UCC § 2-207.** No contract was formed by the exchange of Buyer's purchase order and Seller's acknowledgement form. Not only did Seller's form state a term "different" from one offered by Buyer (namely, the handling of warranties), but also Seller's form was expressly made conditional on assent to the additional or different terms. Therefore, this acknowledgement form did not operate as an acceptance.

    If Buyer had then told Seller, "Okay, we can live with your warranty disclaimer," that communication would have operated as an acceptance to Seller's acknowledgement form (which would now be the offer), and the parties would have had a contract with no warranty. But that is not what happened. Up until the moment Seller shipped the goods, there was no contract at all.

    (b) There is a warranty of merchantability. **The "contract by conduct" consisted of "those terms on which the writings of the parties agree, together with any supplementary terms incorporated under any other provisions [of the UCC]." See UCC §2-207.** Since the writings did not agree as to the warranty of merchantability, §2-314's implied warranty of merchantability, which is a supplementary term supplied by the UCC, became part of the contract. Therefore, Buyer can sue for breach of this warranty even though Seller never explicitly agreed to be bound by such a warranty (and indeed, indicated that it was not willing to perform if it had to honor such a warranty).

20. **(a)** Yes, the parties have a contract. **UCC §2-207 reverses the common law "mirror image" rule. That is, §2-207 provides that even if the document sent in response to an offer states terms that are additional to or different from those offered, the second document can constitute an acceptance** (assuming that this second document is not expressly made conditional on assent to the additional or different terms). Here, Seller's form was close enough to Buyer's form that it operated as an acceptance, even though it proposed an additional term (over/undershipment).

    (b) No. **Under §2-207(2)(b), the additional term does not become part of the contract if it "materially alters" the contract.** Consequently, the additional term—over/undershipment—did *not* become part of this contract. A clause allowing a 10 percent deviation either way in quantity would almost certainly constitute a material alteration. Therefore, the clause would not be part of the contract.

21. **(a)** Yes. **Under UCC §2-207, a definite and seasonable expression of acceptance can operate as an acceptance even though it states terms additional to or different from those offered or agreed upon, unless acceptance is expressly made conditional on assent to the additional or different terms.** The contract was formed when Seller sent its acknowledgement form. Although Buyer's purchase order and Seller's acknowledgement diverged on the subject of warranties, the forms agreed on all essential elements (e.g., price, description, delivery), so they were close enough to constitute offer and acceptance.

    (b) Yes, according to most courts. **If the acceptance contains a term that is "different from" (not "additional to") a term in the offer, most courts (but not all) have applied the "knockout" rule. By this rule, the acceptance's "different" term "knocks out" the conflicting term from**

the offer, and neither becomes part of the contract. However (and here is the trick), most courts also believe that any UCC-supplied "gap fillers" that would become part of the contract if neither form spoke on the issue also become part of the contract where the two forms conflict on the issue. Thus most courts would say that the warranty of merchantability automatically supplied by UCC §2-314 becomes part of the contract, just as it would if the two forms were silent on the whole issue of merchantability.

22. Yes, probably. **Most courts would hold that Buyer's purchase order, although silent on the subject of merchantability, implicitly included UCC §2-314's automatic "gap-filler" implied warranty of merchantability. Then, Seller's disclaimer of this warranty would be a term "different from" the implied term in Buyer's offer, the two conflicting terms would knock each other out, but the gap filler would** *come back in again* **just as it did in the prior question.**

23. No. **Where the "offer" and "acceptance" diverge materially on some negotiated term (e.g., price, quality, quantity, and delivery terms), the court will probably hold that the two forms are so different that the second is not a true acceptance at all.** In that event, no contract is formed by the exchange of documents, and neither party can be in breach. Therefore, Paper Co., by failing to ship on the appointed date, did not breach any contract.

24. (a) Yes. **Under the first sentence of UCC §2-207(3), "Conduct by both parties which recognizes the existence of a contract is sufficient to establish a contract for sale although the writings of the parties do not otherwise establish a contract."** Paper Co.'s shipment of the carload on the appointed delivery date, together with Buyer's use of the paper, was conduct that recognized the existence of a contract.

    (b) Forty-five cents. **In the case of a contract by conduct, the terms become "those terms on which the writings of the parties agree, together with any supplementary terms incorporated under any other provisions of this Act." (Second sentence of §2-207(3).) Since the writings did not agree as to price, the price term must be one of the "supplementary terms" incorporated under some other provision of the UCC. Under §2-305(1), if nothing is said in the contract about price, the price is "a reasonable price at the time for delivery."** That price is 45 cents (the market price).

25. No. **Most courts have held that if the parties have already reached an oral agreement (regardless of whether it is binding under the Statute of Frauds), a written confirmation sent by one will cause its "additional terms" to become part of the contract, if both parties are merchants, unless the additional terms materially alter the contract or buyer objects to these additional terms within a reasonable time. (This is not made clear by the text of UCC §2-207, but courts reach the result by noting §2-207(1)'s reference to a "written confirmation" that states terms "additional to or different from those . . . agreed upon. . . .")** Since Buyer did not object to the remedy limitation in Seller's confirmation, the only question is whether that limitation materially alters the contract. Comment 5 to §2-207 says that a clause that merely limits remedies "in a reasonable manner" does not materially alter the contract. That Comment also refers to §2-719, which says that consequential damages may be excluded where this would not be unconscionable (§2-719(3)), that limitation of damages where the loss is commercial is not unconscionable (*id.*), and that the buyer's remedies may be limited to return of the goods and repayment of the price (§2-719(1)(a)). Since return and repayment is what Seller's clause proposes, it is a reasonable remedy limitation and is therefore not a material alteration under §2-207(2)(b). Therefore, it was an "additional term" that became part of the contract when Buyer failed to object.

26. No. **A counteroffer normally terminates the offer.** Buyer's expression of willingness to buy at $180,000 was a counteroffer. (That is, it proposed a substituted bargain.) Since Buyer's power of acceptance terminated when he made his counteroffer, there was nothing for him to accept later, even though the original deadline had not yet passed.

27. Yes. **A counteroffer is an offer made by an offeree proposing a substituted bargain differing from that proposed by the original offer. See Rest. 2d, §39.** Buyer's inquiry concerning the $180,000 figure was not a counteroffer—it was too tentative to be one, since it did not indicate that Buyer was necessarily committing to pay the $180,000 price (merely that he was interested in knowing whether Owner would accept that price). Nor was Owner justified in interpreting the inquiry as being a rejection of his original offer. Therefore, that original offer stayed in place and was available to be accepted by Buyer before the deadline.

28. No. **An offer terminates if not accepted within the deadline set by the offer itself.** Owner's offer terminated on January 15, when Owner had not yet received any reply from Buyer. Buyer's January 16 letter was thus not an acceptance, but merely a new offer. Owner's silence in response to that offer did not act as an acceptance (since silence will generally not serve as an acceptance—there are exceptions to this rule, but none applies here). Therefore, even if Buyer thought that a contract was formed by his January 16 letter, and thus even if Buyer thought that he himself was trying to wriggle out of a contract, there was in fact no contract and Buyer has not breached.

29. Yes. **Two rules govern contracts by correspondence: (1) the rule that an acceptance is effective upon dispatch (the so-called mailbox rule); and (2) the rule that a revocation is effective only upon receipt by the offeree.** Here, Buyer's February 1 revocation letter was not yet effective on February 2 (since it had not yet been received by Seller). Therefore, the power of acceptance was still in force when, on February 2, Seller attempted to accept Buyer's original offer. Since by the mailbox rule Seller's offer was immediately effective when it was dispatched on February 2, a contract came into existence on February 2.

30. No. **As soon as Seller died, the offer made by him was terminated, since Seller had no further capacity to enter into the proposed contract. See Rest. 2d, §48.** It is irrelevant that Buyer did not know of Seller's death at the time he accepted the contract. (Observe that this is somewhat unfair to Buyer, especially since his acceptance would ordinarily have been effective "upon dispatch," that is, on February 3, when Buyer neither knew nor should have known that Seller was dead.)

31. No. **According to Rest. 2d, §87(1), an offer is binding as an option contract if it is "in writing and signed by the offeror, recites a purported consideration for the making of the offer, and proposes an exchange on fair terms** *within a reasonable time. . . ."* The offer here satisfies the requirements of being in writing and signed by the offeror, of reciting a purported consideration, and of being for an exchange on fair terms (since the facts tell us that $200,000 is a reasonable price). But two years is almost certainly not a "reasonable time" for the option to last—such options are more characteristically for six months or less. (By the way, at least under the Restatement view, the fact that the $1 consideration was never in fact paid is irrelevant, as long as it was recited to have been paid. But a modern court might not agree.)

32. Yes. **Under UCC §2-205, a "firm offer" is irrevocable, provided that it: (1) was made in a signed writing; (2) stated in its own terms that it would be held open; and (3) contained a period of irrevocability not exceeding three months.** Since the document here met all of these requirements, it became irrevocable as promised, even though Printer gave no consideration for this irrevocability.

Consequently, Paper Co.'s purported revocation was ineffective, Printer's acceptance was effective, and Printer may sue for breach.

33. No. **The UCC's firm offer provision applies only to merchants.** Consumer is *not a merchant*, and firm offers under §2-205 only bind merchants. Indeed, it was precisely to protect amateur buyers like Consumer that the requirement that the offeror be a merchant was inserted into §2-205.

34. Yes. **Under the modern view, once a person begins the invited performance under a unilateral contract, it cannot be revoked. See Rest. 2d, §45.** Arthur made an offer for a unilateral contract. (That is, he expected an acceptance to occur by performance, not by promise.) Once Brian began to perform, this offer became temporarily irrevocable. Thus once Brian started the trip westward, Arthur was bound (at least according to the Restatement and to most modern courts).

35. Yes, but just for $50. **Under Rest. 2d, §87(2), "An offer which the offeror should reasonably expect to induce action or forbearance of a substantial character on the part of the offeree before acceptance and which does induce such action or forbearance is binding as an option contract to the extent necessary to avoid injustice."** Brian's giving up of his ticket seems to qualify as "action of a substantial character." But a court would almost certainly hold that all that is required to "avoid injustice" here is to give Brian the market value of the ticket he gave up, not the "benefit of his bargain" (i.e., not the $500).

36. Yes. **Under Rest. 2d, §45, once a person begins the invited performance under a unilateral contract, it cannot be revoked.** Owner has clearly made an offer for a unilateral contract, not for a bilateral one, since Owner has made it clear that he doesn't want a promise, he wants a performance (i.e., the procuring of a willing and able buyer). Broker would probably be deemed to have begun to perform merely by virtue of having done his canvassing and locating Bertrand. (There is some chance that the court would take a strict view and hold that all of this was merely a preparation to perform, and that performance itself would not have begun until Broker introduced Bertrand to Owner.) Assuming that Broker is found to have begun to perform, he would be protected by §45, so long as he shows that Bertrand would in fact have bought the house.

37. Yes. **Rest. 2d, §87(2) states that "an offer which the offeror should reasonably expect to induce action or forbearance of a substantial character on the part of the offeree before acceptance and which does induce such action or forbearance is binding as an option contract to the extent necessary to avoid injustice."** This provision is often applied in cases where subcontractors prepare bids (which are offers) that the contractor relies upon in formulating his of her own bid. Here, Plumbing's bid was an offer. Plumbing knew that Contractor would rely on that bid if Plumbing's bid were the low one, and knew (or at least should have known) that Contractor would be bound once it incorporated Plumbing's bid and listed Plumbing's name. Therefore, it is fair to temporarily bind Plumbing.

38. Yes. **The accepted rule is that where a properly addressed acceptance is put into the mail, telegraphed, etc., the acceptance is *effective upon dispatch*.** (This is sometimes called the "mailbox rule").** Therefore, the parties had a contract on February 1. The fact that delivery of the letter was delayed beyond the time it would normally have been expected to arrive is irrelevant. Consequently, Seller's purported revocation of the offer on February 5 was ineffective. (But if Seller had waited a very long time, say two weeks, had heard nothing, and had then sold the stone to someone else, a court might hold that even though there was a contract between Buyer and Seller, Seller was "discharged" from the necessity of performing due to the passage of time without notice of the acceptance and due to the unavailability of the stone.)

39. No. The "acceptance effective upon dispatch" or "mailbox" rule only operates where the acceptance is properly addressed, or where an improperly addressed response gets to the offeree no later than a properly addressed one would have arrived. See Rest. 2d, §66. Here, Buyer's improperly addressed response was not effective upon dispatch, since it arrived two days after a properly addressed letter would have gotten there. Therefore, the acceptance was not effective until February 6 (its date of arrival). Seller's February 5 revocation was effective before that, so there was no offer left in force to be accepted on February 6.

40. Yes. A counteroffer terminates the offer, but a counteroffer (like a rejection) does not become effective until received by the offeror. Therefore, Buyer's later telegram of acceptance (which became effective when sent on the third), became immediately effective.

41. No. The general rule is that a counteroffer or rejection is not effective until received by the offeror, and an acceptance is normally effective upon dispatch. But by a special rule, a rejection that is both dispatched before and received before an acceptance prevents the ordinary "acceptance effective upon dispatch" rule from operating. Therefore, the rejection takes effect when it is received by the offeror, and by the time the acceptance arrives, the offer has terminated. See Rest. 2d, §40. Observe that this rule is necessary to protect one in Seller's position—otherwise, Seller would read Buyer's rejection, have no idea that the earlier-dispatched acceptance had not yet arrived, and therefore not be on notice that he is bound.

42. Yes. The special rule whereby a rejection or counteroffer that arrives before the acceptance changes the mailbox rule, and makes the acceptance effective only upon receipt does not apply where the acceptance is dispatched *before* the rejection or counteroffer. Here, the parties had a contract as soon as Buyer mailed his acceptance letter on February 1. The subsequently dispatched counteroffer (which would otherwise have had the effect of terminating the offer) was not effective at all, since at the moment it was dispatched there was already a contract, not merely an offer. The fact that this purported counteroffer arrived before the acceptance arrived is simply irrelevant.

43. Yes. Under §2-305(1), the court may supply a "reasonable price at the time for delivery" if nothing is said in the contract about price. Therefore, the court would probably supply a price that would typically be charged by a wholesaler to a restaurateur in Rest's city at that time. Similarly, §2-310(a) would make the time for payment the time when the merchandise was delivered to the buyer (except that the parties' prior course of dealing, that is, any previous orders, may establish that Rest was entitled to credit).

44. No. If the parties have omitted any attempt to express an intention regarding a particular term, the court will frequently fill the gap by supplying a "reasonable" term. Even though we have no way to know what poundage of each of the four vegetables Rest really needed or would have ordered, this is a contract that is subject to a complete concession by the party seeking enforcement (Produce Co.). That is, suppose that carrots, at 30 cents a pound, are the cheapest vegetable among the four. Produce Co. is free to say, "We'll assume that Rest would have performed by ordering the entire 2,000 pounds to be made up of the cheapest vegetable, carrots." The court would then award Produce Co. damages based on $600, less the cost of the carrots to Produce Co. and less quantities previously delivered.

45. No. There is no contract (because there is no "meeting of the minds") if the parties attach materially different meanings to the language of offer and acceptance that they use, and neither party knows or has reason to know the meaning attached by the other. Rest. 2d, §20. Since neither Owner nor Buyer was "at fault" in causing the confusion here, and since the color of the car would almost certainly be material to a collector of vintage automobiles, the misunderstanding has materially prevented a meeting of the minds, and there is no contract here. Thus either Owner or Buyer could, upon discovering the misunderstanding, refuse to consummate the transaction.

46. Yes, for the white car. **Even if the parties attach different meanings to their offer or acceptance language, a contract will be formed in accordance with the meaning of one of them if that party neither knows nor has reason to know of the misunderstanding, and the other does know, or has reason to know, of the misunderstanding. Rest. 2d, §20(2)(b).** Here, Owner had reason to know (though not actual knowledge) that Buyer was referring to the white car, and Buyer had neither knowledge nor reason to know that Owner intended the black car. Therefore, a contract was formed on the meaning attached by Buyer (the one "less at fault").

47. No. **The court in its discretion will allow a party who has made a unilateral mistake as to a material fact to escape the contract if the other party has not yet relied, and enforcement would be unconscionable.** The court might hold that there was a contract to sell the white car, on the reasoning explained in the answer to the prior question. (The court may avoid finding a contract, however, by concluding that the mere price discrepancy by itself gave Buyer reason to suspect that Owner did not intend to sell the white car, in which case the parties would be roughly equally at fault, and no contract would be formed.) But even if the court did find that a contract had been formed, it would almost certainly allow Owner to escape from the contract under the doctrine of unilateral mistake.

48. No. **A promise is not enforceable without consideration. There are two requirements for consideration: (1) a bargained-for exchange; and (2) the promisee suffers a "legal detriment"—that is, he or she gives up something of value, or circumscribes his or her liberty in some way.** Here, there was *no consideration* for Tycoon's promise to make the payment, and therefore, that promise is not enforceable.

49. No. **There are two requirements for consideration: (1) a bargained-for exchange; and (2) the promisee suffers a "legal detriment"—that is, he or she gives up something of value, or circumscribes his or her liberty in some way.** The transaction here satisfies one, but not the other, of the two requirements for consideration. It satisfies the requirement that the promisee undergo some legal detriment, because Stewart has gone through the bother of preparing the financial statement and submitting it to his father. But the facts indicate that the transaction does not satisfy the "bargain" requirement, despite Stewart's performance—the submission of the financial statement (and having a net worth less than $50,000) were merely conditions to the granting of the gift, not something actively desired by Tycoon. That is, there is no reason to believe that Tycoon actively wanted his son to be poor at age 21, or that Tycoon was "bargaining for" such poverty.

50. Yes. **There are two requirements for consideration: (1) a bargained-for exchange; and (2) the promisee suffers a "legal detriment"—that is, he or she gives up something of value, or circumscribes his or her liberty in some way.** Here, both requirements for consideration are met: (1) Stewart has suffered the necessary "legal detriment"—he has taken an act (actually two acts: marriage and procreation); and (2) this time, there is a "bargained-for" element. That is, the facts indicate that Tycoon actively desired a grandchild while he was still young enough to enjoy it, so he was bargaining for the child, not merely attaching a procedural condition to the gift.

51. Yes, probably. **If a transaction is cast in the form of a bargain, a court will probably not go below the surface to determine if the bargain was actually a gift. See Rest. 2d, §71.** Here, we have a mixture of bargain and gift. Since Stewart has actually given up something of value, and since the transaction is cast in the form of a bargained-for exchange, the court will probably not go behind the

surface to determine that the transaction really amounted to a promise by Tycoon to make a net gift of $500 to Stewart.

52. No. **The fact that a recited consideration was never paid is not dispositive as to whether there was consideration, but it is relevant evidence. See Rest. 2d, §71.** Here, that evidence would almost certainly convince the court that the whole arrangement was a sham, and that there was neither a bargain nor any legal detriment suffered by Stewart.

53. No. **The consideration doctrine only applies to *unexecuted* promises.** Once Tycoon actually made the payment, there was a completed gift, which remains in place despite the fact that Tycoon was not in the first instance bound to make it.

54. No. **Consideration requires that there be a bargain.** Employer did not bargain for any performance or promise by Peggy in return for his own promise. Although the 30 years that Peggy worked for him might be loosely termed "past consideration," those years are really not consideration at all because of this lack of a bargain.

55. Yes. **There are two requirements for consideration: (1) a bargained-for exchange; and (2) the promisee suffers a "legal detriment"—that is, he or she gives up something of value, or circumscribes his or her liberty in some way.** Here, there is consideration for Employer's promise of the pension. First, Peggy has undergone a legal detriment (she has promised to work for another year, thus limiting her right to work elsewhere or retire). Second, on these facts, Employer is pretty clearly bargaining to have Peggy work for him another year, rather than merely setting a neutral condition on Peggy's right to receive the pension.

56. No, probably. **As a general rule, a promise to pay for services received in the past is not supported by consideration. There are exceptions (e.g., when emergency services are supplied).** But here, given the fact that the services were not emergency, were not requested by Patrick, and were certainly not requested by the promisor (Fred), the court is unlikely either to find that consideration was present for Fred's promise or to find that that promise is enforceable without consideration. (Had Farmer come to New York especially in reliance on Fred's promise, then the promise would probably be enforceable without consideration, under the doctrine of promissory estoppel.)

57. Yes. **As long as there was a bargain, the court will not find a lack of consideration merely because of a gross disparity in what each party has given up or agreed to give up. See Rest. 2d, §79.** Parker might try to show that Denise used duress, but since Denise was in no way responsible for Parker's predicament (e.g., she wasn't in league with Loanshark), it's very unlikely that a duress defense will work.

58. No. **There was no consideration if someone was merely agreeing to perform a preexisting duty.** There was no consideration for Owen's promise to double Archie's fee—Archie merely agreed to do something he was already obligated to do (supervise the project).

59. Yes. **The court would recognize an exception to the preexisting duty rule here. According to Rest. 2d, §89(a), a promise modifying a duty under a contract not fully performed on either side is binding "if the modification is fair and equitable in view of circumstances not anticipated by the parties when the contract was made. . . ."** The unforeseen construction slowdown (doubling the amount of time Archie would have to put in on the job) would probably be found to be such an unanticipated circumstance. Even though, strictly speaking, there was no consideration for Owen's promise to double the fee (Archie was still merely agreeing to do what he was already bound to do), a modern court would probably regard this situation as involving an enforceable promise to modify a

contract. Thus Owen's promise to pay more would be binding even without consideration. (The difference between this fact pattern and the prior question—leading to a different result as to the enforceability of Owen's promise to double the fee—is that in the prior question, there were no changed circumstances making it fair to modify the contract, whereas in this question there were.)

60. Yes. **"A similar performance is consideration if it *differs* from what was [originally] required . . . in a way which reflects more than a pretense of bargain." Rest. 2d, § 73.** Here, in return for Owen's promise of a doubled fee, Archie agreed to an additional or different performance (trying to find a different contractor who would work faster). Since there is evidence that Archie's additional performance was at least in part bargained for by Owner in return for the higher fee, the additional performance is consideration for Owen's promise of a doubled fee.

61. Yes, in most courts. **If a creditor agrees to take partial repayment instead of full repayment, and *no other aspect of the deal has changed*, most courts regard the creditor's promise as lacking consideration.**

62. No. **A creditor's promise to forego part of his or her claim will be treated as supported by consideration if the debtor refrains from bankruptcy proceedings that he or she would otherwise employ, or otherwise suffers a legal detriment** (e.g., he or she increases the interest rate, gives extra security, etc.).

63. No. **Under UCC §3-311, a creditor who cashes a check thereby surrenders his or her underlying claim, provided that (a) the check or accompanying written communication contains a "conspicuous statement" that the check is being tendered in full satisfaction of the claim; (b) the claim is either unliquidated, or subjected to a bona fide dispute; and (c) the debtor acted in good faith.** Here, (a) is satisfied by the "paid in full" notation and the accompanying letter; (b) is probably satisfied, since we are told that E.T.'s reasoning is plausible, though not necessarily likely to prevail; (c) is also satisfied, since we're told in the facts that E.T. is acting in good faith. So when MCI cashed the check, this act released E.T., and nothing MCI wrote on the check would change this result.

64. No. **Where a plaintiff promises to waive an invalid claim, that promise is not consideration for the corresponding promise by the defendant, unless either (1) the plaintiff, at the time of settlement, had a good-faith belief that the claim was valid; or (2) the claim had in fact some possibility of being valid (some courts require both).** Pamela's original claim for damages for the back pains is clearly invalid (since these were definitely not caused by the accident). Here, Pamela surely did not believe that her claim was valid, and, viewed objectively, her claim was indeed invalid; therefore, her promise to waive that claim was not consideration for Derrick's promise to make payments, and Derrick's promise is thus invalid for lack of consideration.

65. Split of authority. **Where a plaintiff promises to waive an invalid claim, that promise is not consideration for the corresponding promise by the defendant, unless either (1) the plaintiff, at the time of settlement, had a good-faith belief that the claim was valid; or (2) the claim had in fact some possibility of being valid (some courts require both).** Some courts (and the Second Restatement) would allow Pamela to recover, on the theory that for Pamela's no-suit promise to constitute consideration, all that was required was that she have had a good-faith—even though unreasonable—belief that her claim might have merit. But other courts would hold that Derrick's promise is not enforceable, because it must have been the case *both* that Pamela had a good-faith belief that her claim might be valid and that that belief was reasonable (i.e., that the claim had some objective chance of prevailing).

66. **No. If a promise is an illusory promise, it is not sufficient consideration. See Rest. 2d, Sec. 77, Illustr. 2. An illusory promise is a statement that appears to be promising something but that in fact does not commit the promisor to do anything at all.** Here, Star did not in fact commit himself to do anything at all—he didn't commit to pay, and he didn't commit to keep the agency in force. Therefore, there was no consideration to support Agent's promise of full-time efforts. Consequently, Agent's promise was not binding.

67. Yes. **There is sufficient consideration if a promisor commits himself or herself to doing something.** This time, Star has bound himself to do something that, if done, would constitute consideration (to pay a "reasonable" commission); also, the notice provision is drafted in such a way that Star is obliged to leave the agency in force for at least 30 days. Therefore, Star has given consideration in return for Agent's promises, so Agent is bound.

68. **No. If a promise is an illusory promise, it is not sufficient consideration. See Rest. 2d, Sec. 77, Illustr. 2. An illusory promise is a statement that appears to be promising something but that in fact does not commit the promisor to do anything at all.** Customer has not in fact bound himself to anything—he has merely agreed that if he orders, the price will be $6, something quite different from agreeing that he will order. Since Customer's "promise" did not bind him in any way, it did not furnish consideration for Merchant's promise to sell as many widgets as Customer ordered at $6 per widget. Therefore, Merchant's promise was not binding.

69. Yes. **There is sufficient consideration if a promisor commits himself or herself to doing something.** This time, Customer really has bound himself to something—he has obligated himself not to buy widgets from anyone else for six months (a requirements contract). This constitutes consideration for Merchant's return promise to sell, so Merchant is bound.

70. Yes. **There is sufficient consideration if a promisor commits himself or herself to doing something.** A court would almost certainly find that the contract contained an *implied* promise by Buyer to use reasonable efforts to procure the needed financing. Such an effort (even if unsuccessful) would be consideration, so the promise to use such efforts was also consideration, and Seller's promise to sell was thus supported by consideration and is therefore enforceable. (But if the contract had stated something like, "Buyer may cancel this contract at any time for no reason, with no prior notice," then Seller's "lack of consideration" argument would probably have prevailed.)

71. Yes. **Promises to pay debts discharged in bankruptcy are enforceable *without* consideration. See Rest. 2d, §83.**

72. (a) Yes, based on the promissory estoppel doctrine. **"A promise which the promisor should reasonably expect to induce action or forbearance on the part of the promisee or a third person and which does induce such action or forbearance is binding if injustice can be avoided only by enforcement of the promise." See Rest. 2d, §90(1).** The promise is not supported by consideration, so under ordinary contract principles it would not be enforceable. (There is no evidence that Grandfather "bargained for" Grandson's building the house on Grandfather's property. For instance, Grandfather did not obtain the benefit of having Grandson live close to him, since Grandfather lived elsewhere.) But Grandfather should reasonably have expected that his promise of a deed would induce action by Grandson, and the promise did indeed induce that action (building a house and living on the premises). Since Grandson foreseeably relied to his detriment on the promise, the court will probably enforce it.

(b) $100,000. **Most courts, even when they apply the promissory estoppel doctrine, limit the remedy to what "justice requires." Typically, this means that the damages awarded are not** the full expectation "benefit of the bargain" measure, but merely reliance damages. Here, Grandson is only "out of pocket" $100,000, the amount he spent on building the house. Therefore, the court would probably only award him his $100,000, not the deed to the property or the $200,000 value of the property (which would be what was required to put him in the position he would have been in had the promise been kept).

73. Yes, probably. **Most modern courts, and Rest. 2d, §90(2), dispense with the requirement of detrimental reliance where the promise is a "charitable subscription" (i.e., a promise to make a charitable contribution).** This was a promise to make a gift, so it was not supported by consideration. (Deborah did not bargain for any return promise or performance by the university, as far as we can tell from the facts.) Nor did Deborah's promise induce detrimental reliance by the university, so the doctrine of promissory estoppel would usually not apply. However, Deborah's promise to the university falls into the "charitable subscription" category, so most courts would enforce it even though the University did not rely in any way up until the time Deborah reneged.

74. Yes, by use of the doctrine of mistake. **A contract can be avoided due to mutual mistake, if (1) the mistake was as to a "basic assumption" on which the contract was founded, (2) the mistake had a "material effect" on the parties' agreed exchange of performances, and (3) the risk was not allocated to the adversely affected party. See Rest. 2d, §§152 and 154.** As to (1), it seems to have been quite basic to the original release deal that Passenger was believed to have suffered only property damage. As to (2), clearly this assumption was material, since the actual damage suffered by Passenger was much greater than that which had been believed (and since Passenger's loss corresponded almost precisely to Driver's gain from the mistake). As to (3), the court would probably allocate the risk to Driver, since it is reasonable for the court to do so, especially in light of Driver's status as tortfeasor and Passenger's status as innocent victim.

75. No. **The doctrine of mutual mistake does not apply if the risk is allocated to the adversely affected party.** Here, a court would almost certainly allocate the risk of this mistake to Passenger, because Passenger failed to take advantage of the opportunity to learn of the possibility that she might have whiplash. The court might also classify this as a situation in which Passenger proceeded in "conscious ignorance" (i.e., that she knew her knowledge of possible injuries was incomplete, but elected to proceed anyway)—in this situation, a court will almost always allocate the risk to the consciously ignorant party.

76. No. **The doctrine of mutual mistake does not apply if the risk is allocated to the adversely affected party. See Rest. 2d, §154, Illustr. 5.** The court will almost certainly allocate the risk of this mistake to Builder. The reason is that Builder is a professional in the business of building homes, and Owner is not. Therefore, it is more reasonable for Builder than it is for Owner to have taken out drilling samples or to have otherwise protected against the risk of this sort of mistake.

77. No. **A contract can be avoided due to mutual mistake, if (1) the mistake was as to a "basic assumption" on which the contract was founded, (2) the mistake had a "material effect" on the parties' agreed exchange of performances, and (3) the risk was not allocated to the adversely affected party. See Rest. 2d, §§152 and 154.** Buyer satisfies the first two of the three requirements for the doctrine of mutual mistake: (1) the mistake was as to a basic assumption behind the contract, and (2) the mistake had a material effect on the parties' agreed exchange. But Owner cannot satisfy the third requirement that the risk of mistake not have rested upon her. The court will almost certainly allocate the risk of mistake to Owner, on the grounds that it is reasonable to do so because of people's common understanding that the seller of land always bears the risk that valuable minerals will unexpectedly be found beneath the land.

78. No, probably. **In general, it is even harder to avoid a contract for unilateral mistake than for mutual mistake. According to the Rest. 2d §153, one who wants to avoid a contract for his own unilateral mistake must make the same three showings as are needed for avoidance based on mutual mistake (see answer to prior question), plus must show either that enforcement would be unconscionable or that the mistake was known to, or due to the fault of, the other party.** Here, Owner probably still cannot make the initial showing that the risk of loss was not upon her; the common understanding of landowners is that if one sells one's property unaware that there are valuable minerals underneath it, that is simply one's own tough luck—probably the fact that the buyer is better informed would not change this. There is some chance, however, that a court would hold that Buyer's sneakiness in not revealing a basic fact changed what the reasonable allocation of risk would be in this situation (in which case the contract would be unenforceable, because the additional requirement— that Buyer must have known of the mistake—is satisfied here).

79. Yes, probably. **In general, it is even harder to avoid a contract for unilateral mistake than for mutual mistake. According to the Rest, 2d, §153, one who wants to avoid a contract for his own unilateral mistake must make the same three showings as are needed for avoidance based on mutual mistake, plus must show either that enforcement would be unconscionable or that the mistake was known to, or due to the fault of, the other party.** Contractor can probably make the basic three showings for avoiding a contract on grounds of either mutual or unilateral mistake (mistake as to basic assumption, material effect on the bargain, and allocation of risk). The more interesting question is whether enforcement would be unconscionable. A court would probably hold that where enforcement would result in a $100,000 loss on a $1 million contract, this would be unconscionable (especially since the town's position if Contractor were released would be no worse than if Contractor had never bid in the first place). See, e.g., *Elsinore Union Elementary School Dist. v. Kastorff*, 353 P.2d 713 (Ca. 1960).

80. No, probably. **A court would probably hold that Contractor's error was an error of "judgment" rather than a clerical error and that the whole idea behind the competitive bidding process is to place upon the bidder the risk of making such judgmental mistakes. See, e.g., Rest. 2d, §154, Illustr. 6.**

81. Yes, probably. **Assuming that Contractor can meet the basic three requirements for avoidance on grounds of mistake (mistake as to basic assumption, material effect, and risk of loss), Contractor will be able to avoid even though the mistake is unilateral if the other party had reason to know of the mistake. See Rest. 2d, §153.** Where one party's bid is almost 40 percent below the cheapest of the other bids, and all other bids are quite tightly clumped together, a court would probably find that the owner had "reason to know" that there had been a mistake. If so, Contractor would be allowed to avoid the contract. (Observe that this would happen even though requiring Contractor to perform would not be "unconscionable"—it's doubtful that a loss of $5,000 on a $1 million contract would amount to unconscionability.)

82. Yes, probably. **Under the parol evidence rule, a writing intended by the parties to be a full and final expression of their agreement (referred to as a "total integration") may not be supplemented or contradicted by any oral or written agreements made prior to the writing.** The court would probably first find that the note here was only a partial, not a complete, integration. That is, the note seems to represent the *final* agreement of the parties on the things that the note covers (e.g., due date, amount borrowed, who the borrower is, etc.), so it is an integration. But the note certainly does not seem to be a *"complete"* integration, because it does not cover a number of matters that are clearly part of the agreement (e.g., what the collateral is, the fact that Bank is relying on Borrower's submitted financial statement, etc.). The parol evidence rule provides (in part) that a *partial integration* may be *supplemented* but not *contradicted*, so Borrower will win if he can show that the oral promise only supplements the note.

Here, Borrower would probably prevail with his argument that the oral grace period term is a supplement to, not a contradiction of, the note, because the note says nothing about whether there will or will not be a grace period. If the court agrees with Borrower on this point (i.e., the court concludes that the absence of a grace period in the note is not the equivalent of a statement "there is no grace period"), then Borrower will get his grace period as long as he can convince the court that that is what the parties orally agreed upon.

83. No, probably. **The parol evidence rule provides (in part) that an integration (whether partial or total) may *not* be *contradicted* by a prior agreement.** On these facts, the oral promise of a grace period is in direct contradiction to the "no grace period" provision of the note. Since the note appears to be an integration (i.e., it represents the final deal of the parties on the terms that it covers), it may not be contradicted by a prior oral or written promise, even though the note is not a "complete" integration.

84. No, probably. **The fact that the prior promise or clause (giving a grace period) occurred in writing rather than orally makes absolutely no difference for purposes of the parol evidence rule—if the parties later sign an integration (i.e., a document that they intend to be their final agreement on at least some matters), all contradictory terms in prior writings or oral discussions are discharged (i.e., made inoperative).** (For this reason, the name "parol evidence rule," with "parol" having the sense of "oral," is misleading—the rule applies equally to prior written terms.)

85. No. **The parol evidence rule only applies to bar *prior* (or, according to some courts, contemporaneous) oral or written terms that contradict a partial integration, or that either contradict or supplement a complete integration.** Here, the facts clearly indicate that the Loan Agreement was intended not only as an integration, but also as a "*complete*" one—that is, it covered all of the points of the parties' deal for the loan. Not only may any integrated agreement not be contradicted by prior oral or written terms, but a complete integration may not even be *supplemented* by consistent additional terms. See Rest., §216. Since the oral grace period promise would supplement the written agreement, Borrower loses. (Of course, one of the factors that the court will consider in determining whether an integration is a complete one is whether the consistent additional term, had it been agreed upon, "might naturally be omitted from the writing." *Id.* Here, Borrower could argue that a grace period might naturally be omitted from the Loan Agreement, and the Agreement is thus a partial rather than complete integration. But as an issue of fact, Borrower will probably lose with this argument—the court would probably conclude that a grace period is so material, and so easily within the scope of the items normally covered by a comprehensive loan agreement, that it would not naturally be omitted.)

86. No, probably. **The parol evidence rule only applies to bar *prior* (or, according to some courts, contemporaneous) oral or written terms that contradict a partial integration, or that either contradict or supplement a complete integration.** The question boils down to whether the Loan Agreement is a complete integration. In the absence of the "merger" clause (the clause saying that there are no other agreements or representations except those in the document), the court would probably find that the Loan Agreement was not a complete integration (since it omitted a term that might naturally be omitted from the writing in these circumstances). But the merger clause changes this result—a merger clause generally disposes of the issue whether the agreement is completely integrated by indicating that it is. Consequently, even a consistent additional term (like the Corresponding Balance provision) will be excluded.

87. No. **The parol evidence rule only applies to bar** *prior* **(or, according to some courts, contemporaneous) oral or written terms that contradict a partial integration, or that either contradict or supplement a complete integration. The parol evidence rule says nothing about the enforceability of an oral or written term that is agreed upon** *after* **the integrated writing is signed.** Therefore, the parol evidence rule is completely irrelevant on these facts. (Under UCC §2-209, the extension agreement would be an enforceable modification even though Seller gave no consideration for it; however, there would probably be a Statute of Frauds problem if the contract were for more than $500.)

88. Yes, probably. **A no-oral-modifications clause is enforceable in contracts for the sale of goods; see UCC §2-209(2). However, the UCC recognizes that a party who orally agrees to modify the contract may be held to have** *waived* **his right to rely on the no-oral-modifications clause. See UCC §2-209(4). Generally, a party will be found to have waived the benefit of such a clause only if his oral agreement induces** *reliance* **by the other party.** Here, Buyer's assent induced reliance by Seller—Seller would have been able to finish the contract by the originally scheduled July 1 date, but stopped trying to do so based on Buyer's assent to the later date. Buyer will therefore almost certainly be held to have waived his right to rely on the no-oral-modifications clause, and Seller will get the benefit of the as-modified August 1 delivery date.

89. Yes. **Virtually all courts accept that evidence of fraud—at least, fraud of the sort that would permit the contract to be rescinded—is not excluded by the parol evidence rule or by a merger clause.** It is true that the agreement contained a merger clause, and such a clause will normally establish that the agreement was intended as a complete integration. However, Buyer is presenting his evidence pursuant to a claim of *fraud*, not merely breach of contract. Therefore, Buyer's evidence of fraud should be allowed into evidence.

90. Yes, probably. **Most courts would allow Buyer's evidence, on the theory that evidence of true fraud should not be kept out merely because the other party's lawyer has skillfully drafted a clause reciting that the very representation in question was never made, or that if made, was not relied upon.**

91. Yes. **Even if the contract contains a "merger" clause, the parol evidence rule will not keep out evidence that the parties did not intend their contract to become effective until the occurrence of some** *condition.* **See Rest. 2d, §217.** Here, that condition would be Owner's cancellation of his other siding contract.

92. Yes. **Virtually all courts agree that where the written document (even if it is a complete integration) is ambiguous on its face, the** *meaning* **that the parties intended for a term can be shown by "extrinsic evidence," including evidence of what they said to each other in their prior negotiations.** It is not clear from the face of the Computer-DOJ contract whether the reference to the GSA price schedule means the schedule in effect at the time of the Computer-DOJ signing, or the schedule as amended from time to time. Thus Computer Co. would be permitted to show through evidence of prior discussions, prior exchanges of draft agreements, etc., that both parties had in mind only the schedules as they existed at the time the Computer-DOJ contract was signed. Of course, DOJ would be permitted to use similar extrinsic evidence to prove the opposite.

93. (a) A trade usage. **UCC §1-303(c) defines "usage of trade" as "any practice or method of dealing having such regularity of observance in a place, vocation or trade as to justify an expectation that it will be observed with respect to the transaction in question."** Seller's evidence shows that there is a trade usage to the effect that used farm equipment sales are made without warranties.

94. No. UCC §2-306(1) says that a *"requirements contract"* (which is what we have here) sets a quantity equal to the buyer's "actual . . . requirements as may occur in good faith, except that no quantity unreasonably disproportionate to any stated estimate or in the absence of a stated estimate to any normal or otherwise comparable . . . requirements may be tendered or demanded." Here, Computer's new quantity ordered (half the prior total) may have been "disproportionate" to the prior estimate and expectations of the parties, but it was not "unreasonably" disproportionate, since it is reasonable for a buyer to chop his requirements to reflect loss of his largest customer. Similarly, there is no evidence that Computer has behaved other than in good faith.

95. Yes, probably. **If the buyer under a requirements contract changes his or her business plans solely to buy a cheaper substitute, the court is likely to find that this is the very sort of "bad faith" or "unreasonably disproportionate" change in requirements that UCC §2-306(1) is designed to forbid.**

96. No, probably. **Most courts that have considered the issue have agreed that if the buyer is able to take advantage of a major technological improvement demanded by its customers (and is not merely using this as a subterfuge for escaping from an otherwise unattractive requirements contract), the switch, and consequent elimination of requirements, will not be a violation of the contract.** Here, nothing in these facts suggests "bad faith" or "unreasonableness" on Computer's part.

97. Yes. **If a contractual provision is a promise, the nonperformance of that promise will entitle the other party to damages.** See Rest. 2d, § 225. The language regarding the bonus for low weight was a *condition* to the Mud Hens' duty to pay the bonus, but was *not* a *promise* made by Johnson. Therefore, Johnson had no obligation to achieve that weight, or even to try to achieve that weight. Consequently, he did not breach any promise, and the Mud Hens were not justified in withholding anything from his salary as damages. (The existence of a condition will often also represent a duty that the condition occur, but this is not always the case, and the present question is an illustration of how a condition might not be matched by a promise or duty.)

98. No, probably. **The majority rule is that where a person's duty is made conditional upon his or her "satisfaction," that person will be relieved if his or her satisfaction is honest, even if unreasonable.** This outcome is especially likely where there is no objective method of determining whether a reasonable person in the obligor's position would be satisfied (which is the case here, since the architecture of one's own house is such a matter of taste that it really cannot be said that Owner is being "unreasonable" or that a hypothetical "reasonable person" would like the plans).

99. Yes. **Even where the obligor's duty is phrased in terms of his or her "satisfaction," with no explicit requirement that he behave in good faith, the courts will *imply* a duty of good faith.** See Rest. 2d, §205. Here, Owner's assertion that he was not satisfied, when in fact the reason for his refusal to pay was that he didn't have the money, would almost certainly be found to be bad faith, and thus a breach of the contract.

100. No. **While courts will sometimes relieve the other party of the need for strict compliance with an express condition where a "forfeiture" would result, they will not do so where this would significantly alter the essence of the deal.** See Rest. 2d, §229. Receipt of a cashier's check for $200,000 on or before July 1 was an *express condition* of Farmer's duty to convey the property. Courts will ordinarily interpret an express condition *strictly*, and they would certainly do so here. Here, the very thing for which the parties bargained was Developer's right to "tie up" the property (i.e., to have an option on it) for exactly one year—granting Developer an extra two days to tie up the property would be significantly altering the very essence of the parties' deal, so the court would not do it.

101. Yes. **Courts will generally excuse noncompliance with even an express condition, if *"disproportionate forfeiture"* would otherwise result, and if the loss to the other party from nonoccurrence of the condition would not be material. See Rest.2d, §229.** Here, the reasons Insurer wanted written notice were to be able to inspect the property shortly after the alleged loss and to protect against false claims. Its interest was reasonably well protected by Homeowner's prompt oral notification. Since Homeowner would suffer an enormous "forfeiture" if the condition was strictly construed, and the loss to Insurer from not strictly enforcing the condition would be quite minimal, the court will relieve the condition. Alternatively, the court might hold that Insurer, by agreeing to send an adjuster, and by not saying to Homeowner, "Be sure to give us written notice within five days of the accident," *waived* its right to insist on the condition. (But if Homeowner had not given any notice at all until he gave written notice 60 days after the fire, and if the condition of the premises had changed materially in the interim, this might be enough to induce the court to deny contractual recovery to Homeowner.)

102. Depends. **While strict compliance with express conditions is ordinarily necessary before the other person's duty of performance arises, substantial performance is usually adequate to satisfy constructive conditions.** Here, the parties exchanged promises: Publisher promised to promote the book at the convention, and in return Author promised to deliver the manuscript by January 1. Since according to the agreement Publisher had to perform its promise before Author had to perform hers, it was a *"constructive condition"* of Author's duty to perform on January 1 that there not have been at that time an *uncured material breach* by Publisher. On these facts, Publisher certainly had an uncured breach as of January 1 (failure to announce at the convention), but the question remains whether that breach was *material*. (If it was not material, then Author must perform, but has a claim for damages against Publisher.) The fact pattern probably does not give us enough information to determine whether Publisher's breach was a material one—we simply don't know how important it was to Author to have the announcement made at the ABA meeting. If there are four major conventions per year, for instance, and an announcement at a meeting in early 2011 would be virtually as good, then probably the failure to announce at the ABA show was not material. If, on the other hand, the ABA show is the only major convention, and announcements made at the convention are materially more effective in promoting a novel like Author's than any other promotional mechanism available, then the failure to announce would probably be material. In any event, if Publisher's failure to announce *was* material, Author need not submit the manuscript (and since there is no opportunity to "cure" now that that show has already gone by, Author was within her rights to deliver the manuscript to whatever other publisher she wanted—her duty of performance under the Publisher-Author contract was discharged). If Publisher's breach was *not* material, then Author has breached by delivering the manuscript to someone else rather than Publisher, and Author can be liable for a full measure of damages (profits which would have been made by Publisher on the book). So you can see the importance to Author of having a lawyer who can correctly estimate whether Publisher's breach was "material"!

103. No. **Where two parties exchange promises under a contract, and the performance of only one party requires a period of time, his or her performance is due before the other party's performance unless the language or circumstances indicate otherwise. See Rest. 2d, §234(2).** Thus, in the typical construction contract—as we have here—the entire services must be performed before any payment is due, unless the contract or circumstances, such as industry customs, indicate otherwise. Since the parties made no arrangement regarding payment and there are no relevant industry customs, Concrete Co. was required to complete the entire job before receiving any payment. (His lawyer should have provided in the contract for progress payments.) Since Builder had no obligation to make payment after the work was half done, Concrete Co.'s duty of performance was not discharged by the nonoccurrence of any constructive condition, and Concrete Co. therefore breached by walking off the job. Since Concrete Co. did not substantially perform under the contract, it is not entitled to contractual recovery (though it may be able to recover the value of its services in a suit in quasi-contract).

104. No. **Both parties were to perform simultaneously (Seller to deliver the deed, and Buyer to deliver the purchase price). Therefore, it was a constructive condition of each party's duty that the other party "either render or, with manifested present ability to do so, offer performance of his part of the simultaneous exchange." Rest. 2d, §238.** Since Buyer did not have a manifest present ability to close the deal (he didn't have any money), Seller did not in fact have a duty to convey the property on July 1. Consequently, Seller's failure to convey the property or to offer to convey the property was not a breach, and Buyer cannot recover damages against him. (Of course, Seller can't recover damages against Buyer for breach either, for this same reason.) In colloquial terms, Buyer failed to *"tender performance."*

105. Yes, probably. **When a contract is *"divisible"* into corresponding pairs of part performances that can properly be regarded as agreed equivalents, a party who performs his or her part of one pair has the right to the other party's performance on that pair as if those were the only two pairs that had been contracted for. See Rest. 2d, §240.** Here, the stating of a separate amount per pound for the two types of product, and the lack of any apparent interrelation between the two (e.g., the chicken wasn't worth any less to Packer on account of Packer's not receiving the pork), suggest that the delivery of chickens and the payment of 40 cents per pound were properly viewed as agreed equivalents. Consequently, Farmer is entitled to the contract price for the chickens. (Packer would still be entitled to damages for Farmer's breach as to the pigs, but on these facts Farmer suffered no such damages.)

106. Yes. **Under UCC §2-612(3), whenever "nonconformity or default with respect to one or more installments substantially impairs the value of the whole contract, there is a breach of the whole." But the facts indicate that the value of the whole contract was *not substantially impaired* by Farmer's failure to deliver pigs on July 1. Comment 6 to §2-612 says, "If only the seller's security in regard to future installments is impaired, he has the right to demand adequate assurances of proper future performance but he has not an immediate right to cancel the entire contract."** Here, Farmer effectively gave Packer assurances of future performance (even though Packer didn't ask for them), so Packer was not entitled to cancel the whole contract.

107. Builder will owe Owner $50,000, but Owner will owe Builder an offsetting $5,000, for a net judgment of $45,000 in favor of Owner. **Since the contract did not indicate that time was of the essence, Owner had a reasonable time in which to *cure* his material breach. See Rest. 2d, §242.** Owner's failure to have the site ready, as promised, was a material breach of contract. Therefore, Builder was justified in not commencing work until this had been done. However, Owner cured the breach within a reasonable time, so that Builder's duty to perform was reinstated as of August 1. When Builder refused to perform on August 1, he was then in breach. Consequently, Owner may recover against Builder for damages for Builder's total breach. But Builder is entitled to an offsetting claim for partial breach against Owner for the one month of delay.

108. Builder will recover $25,000 in damages from Owner. **Normally, a party who has committed a material breach will get at least some time in which to cure that breach. But eventually, the material breach will no longer be curable. In determining whether that point of noncurability has been reached, the court will consider, among other factors, the degree of materiality of the breach, the importance of performance without delay, and the extent to which it appears to the injured party that delay may prevent or hinder him in making reasonable *substitute arrangements*. See Rest. 2d, §242.** On July 30, it reasonably seemed to Builder that any further delay by him in canceling the

contract with Owner would prevent him from getting a large substitute contract. Therefore, as soon as Builder, behaving reasonably, signed that substitute contract, Owner's material breach became noncurable. After that, Owner was liable for total breach, and Builder had no obligations and thus no liability for breach on his part. Builder can therefore recover his expectation damages (the $25,000 profit he would have made had the contract been performed).

109. No, probably. **Under UCC §2-601, "If the goods or the tender of delivery fail in any respect to conform to the contract, the buyer may . . . (a) reject the whole. . . ."** Here, the brochures certainly fail to conform to the contract. Therefore, Customer was within his rights in rejecting them (i.e., telling Printer that he didn't want them). Since Customer complied with the procedural requirements for rejection (e.g., he rejected "within a reasonable time after [the] delivery," as required by §2-602(1), and held them for the seller's disposition for a reasonable time under §2-602(2)(b)), Customer's liability came to an end. That is, Printer no longer had the right to bring an action for the price under §2-709. However, §2-508 gives the seller the right to *cure* for a reasonable time. The most difficult issue is whether Printer's "cure" could take the form of an allowance on the purchase price instead of correct goods. Section 2-508 says that cure must be by "conforming delivery," suggesting that a price allowance cannot be a cure. A price allowance for a *minor* defect might still be treated as a cure by courts, but where the defect is major (as here), the buyer probably has a right to refuse a price allowance and reject the goods.

110. Yes, probably. **Under UCC §2-606, acceptance of goods occurs after a reasonable opportunity to inspect the goods signifies to the seller that the goods are conforming.** Here, the passage of nearly two weeks after delivery of the job without any statement by Customer (except his statement that everything seemed okay) probably amounted to "acceptance" by Customer. Also, Customer's telephone call to Printer on June 30 probably was not effective to revoke his acceptance, because under §2-508, the buyer may revoke his acceptance only if he believed that the nonconformity would be cured and it has not been cured, or if his acceptance was reasonably induced by the difficulty of discovery or the seller's assurances—none of these conditions seems to have been met here. Therefore, Customer is stuck with his acceptance. Consequently, Customer has lost the ability to throw the goods back on Printer, and Customer is liable for the contract price (though he has an offsetting counterclaim for the difference between the value the goods would have had if they had been as specified and the value they have to him in their current wrong-colored state).

111. Yes, probably. **Under UCC §2-508(2), if the seller reasonably thought that the goods, though nonconforming, would be acceptable to the buyer, the seller gets additional time to cure after the time under the contract has passed.** Since Seller was shipping a "better" (i.e., more advanced and more expensive model), he probably had reasonable grounds to believe that the nonconforming tender would be acceptable. Therefore, Seller was entitled to a "further reasonable time" to substitute his conforming tender. In the circumstances, probably the taking of an additional two days (until July 3) to deliver the correct machine was a "reasonable time," so Seller was attempting to make a proper cure that he was entitled to make. When Buyer rejected Seller's attempts to make that timely cure, Buyer was therefore breaching the contract. Since Seller is a "lost volume" seller (i.e., he can get as many machines as he can get customers for and therefore lost one net sale when Buyer breached), Seller should be able to recover his lost profits under UCC §2-708(2).

112. No, probably. **When the time for performance is at an end (which was the case on July 1), the seller under UCC §2-508(2) may only get an additional reasonable time to cure if he or she had reasonable grounds to believe that his nonconforming tender would be acceptable to the buyer.** Here, Buyer, through the "no substitutes" clause inserted in the contract, had put Seller on

notice that strict compliance would be required. Therefore, Seller did not have reasonable grounds to believe that his nonconforming tender (the Model 200 instead of the 100) would be acceptable to Buyer. Consequently, Seller had no right to cure. Therefore, by a strict reading of the various clauses (including UCC §2-601's purported perfect tender rule), Seller has breached, may not cure, and may not recover anything on the contract. (But there is some chance that a court would hold that Buyer, by denying Seller even one additional day to cure, was behaving in bad faith; in that event, the court might hold that Seller did have a right to cure and may now recover for lost profits.)

113. No, probably. **Even where the seller makes a completely nonconforming and uncurable delivery of one installment, this fact does not by itself justify the buyer in canceling the rest of the installments. Under UCC §2-612(3), whenever nonconformity or default with respect to one or more installments substantially impairs the value of the whole contract, there is a breach of the whole.** Here, where Seller's breach had already cost Builder substantial lost-time damages, and where the risk of loss from future breaches was disproportionate to the value of the contract, a court would probably find that the "value of the whole contract" had been impaired. If so, Builder was entitled to cancel the remaining installments. (If the past damage to Builder, or the likely future damage from another breach, were less, Builder would probably have to be satisfied with Seller's assurances about future performance and would have to temporarily continue the contract.)

114. No. **If a person retains benefits under a contract after learning that a condition of the contract has not been met, he or she will be held to have waived the condition. See Rest. 2d, §246.** Since the tree knockdown constituted a material (and incurable) breach, Owner would have been within his rights in canceling the contract on July 1 or soon thereafter. But when Owner permitted Contractor to continue performance for a substantial time thereafter (and when Owner effectively accepted the benefits of Contractor's continued performance), this acceptance acted as a *waiver* of Owner's right to insist on Contractor's compliance with the condition that he not destroy the trees. Once Owner waived that condition, he was not permitted to reinstate the condition by changing his mind.

115. No. **It is true that Owner waived his right to cancel the contract when he allowed Contractor to continue with the work and accepted the benefits of that continued work. But by so doing, Owner waived only his right to cancel the contract (i.e., his right to treat the non-knockdown of the trees as a constructive condition of his own duty to go on with the contract). Owner did not thereby waive his claim to *damages* for breach of the promise that the trees would not be knocked down.** (But if Owner had expressly promised Contractor, "I won't even withhold money for the tree knockdowns," this explicit promise would probably be binding.)

116. Depends. **If Contractor can show that he would have been able to cure the three final defects by July 1 had he been notified of them at the same time (June 20) that he was told of the other defects, then Owner is not within his rights to withhold the final payment (because Owner's failure to give notice of all the nonoccurring conditions of which he was aware or should have been aware would have substantially contributed to Contractor's failure to cure).** But if Contractor cannot make this showing—that is, if Contractor would probably not have been able to fix the defects in time anyway even if he had known of them on June 20—Owner is justified in treating the three defects as the nonoccurrence of a condition to Owner's duty to make final payment. (Even then, Contractor might have a claim in quasi-contract for the value of the house as it existed on July 1, if that value is more than the progress payments already made by Owner. But if the contract price were higher than the value of the house with its defects, Contractor would lose the difference.)

117. Make a written demand upon Buyer for adequate assurance of due performance. **Under UCC §2-609(1), when reasonable grounds for insecurity arise with respect to the performance of either party, the other may demand adequate assurance of due performance, and until he or she receives such assurance, may, if commercially reasonable, suspend any performance for which he or she has not already received the agreed return.** Thus, Seller could make such a demand, and then hold up the July 1 shipment until receiving assurances from Buyer that Buyer's financial condition is in fact satisfactory. Official Comment 4 to UCC §2-609 states that a buyer's suspension of his previous practice of taking an early payment discount is by itself enough to create "reasonable grounds for insecurity."

118. No, probably. **Under UCC §2-609(1), when reasonable grounds for insecurity arise with respect to the performance of either party, the other may demand adequate assurance of due performance, and until he or she receives such assurance, may, if commercially reasonable, suspend any performance for which he or she has not already received the agreed return.** The rumor, even though it turned out to be false, was, when viewed from Seller's perspective, enough to constitute *"reasonable grounds for insecurity"* on Seller's part. Therefore, Buyer was required to respond to Seller's written demand for adequate assurance of due performance. Under UCC §2-609(4), Buyer had to make such assurances "within a reasonable time not exceeding 30 days." However, this clause did not give Buyer an absolute 30 days; instead, 30 days was merely the outside limit. Given Seller's time to order the parts and manufacture the goods, two weeks or so was all that was reasonable under the circumstances. Seller's failure to receive reassurances by the 18th allowed Seller to treat the silence as a repudiation of the contract. Consequently, Seller was permitted to suspend his performance, and did not become liable for breach on July 1, even though the original rumor was false.

119. Yes. **Generally, when a party anticipatorily repudiates a contract, the other party may bring an *immediate* action for breach, and may treat his own duties as being discharged. See** *Hochster v. de la Tour*, 118 Eng. Rep. 922 (Q.B. 1853).

120. Yes. **When Search failed to respond within a reasonable time, Stanley was entitled to treat that failure as itself constituting a repudiation. See Rest. 2d, §251.** It is true that Search never explicitly repudiated the contract. But when Stanley heard repeated rumors that Search was repudiating other similar contracts, reasonable grounds probably arose for him to believe that Search would repudiate his contract as well. Therefore, Stanley's March 1 letter was a demand by him (a demand that, in the circumstances, he was within his rights in making) for "adequate assurances of performance" by Search. Therefore, Stanley was entitled to bring an immediate action for breach.

121. No. **A repudiator's retraction is effective if it comes to the attention of the injured party before he or she materially changes his or her position in reliance on the repudiation or indicates to the other party that he or she considers the repudiation to be final. See Rest. 2d, §256(1).** Search's March 1 letter was a repudiation, but its March 5 letter was a *retraction* of the repudiation.

122. Yes. **A repudiation may be retracted only until the injured party either materially changes his or her position in reliance on a repudiation, or indicates to the other party that he or she considers the repudiation to be final. Rest. 2d, §256(1).** Here, Stanley's letter to Search constituted his statement to Search that he considered the repudiation to be final, so when Search received that letter, it lost its ability to retract. This is true even though Stanley had not materially changed his position in reliance on the repudiation yet.

123. Yes. **"The injured party does not change the effect of a repudiation by urging the repudiator to perform in spite of his repudiation or to retract his repudiation." Rest. 2d, §257.** (But if Stanley

could have found an equally high-paying job sometime during the March 1 to September 1 period, and refrained from looking until September 1, then he probably will be held to have failed to fulfill his "duty to mitigate," and he will lose those damages that could have been avoided through diligence. But he still has an action for breach of contract, and the only issue would be the avoidability of damages.) See also UCC §2-610(b), allowing the injured party to "resort to any remedy for breach . . . even if the aggrieved party has notified the repudiating party that it would await the latter's performance and has urged retraction." (This section is not applicable here, but would be applicable to a comparable situation involving the sale of goods, as where seller tells buyer that seller won't deliver, and buyer urges seller to continue with the contract.)

124. No. **Courts have generally refused to allow an immediate suit for breach based on anticipatory repudiation where the plaintiff owes no duties under the contract. See Rest. 2d, §253.** Buyer's insolvency (or even rumors of Buyer's insolvency) were sufficient to give Seller reasonable grounds for demanding assurances of performance from Buyer, which Seller did in his letter. When Buyer failed to reply, this failure to give the requested assurances amounted to a repudiation. However, Buyer had already received everything he was entitled to ever receive under the contract (conveyance of Blackacre), so a special rule was triggered: The injured party may not bring suit until the time for performance if he or she has already given all performance required under the contract. Therefore, Seller's suit for damages will not be timely until Buyer actually misses the January 1, 2011, payment. (But Seller might be entitled to a declaratory judgment stating that Buyer will owe the money on January 1.)

125. Split of authority between $1,000 and $2,000. **UCC §2-713(1) says that "the measure of damages for . . . repudiation by the seller is the difference between the market price at the time when the buyer learned of the breach and the contract price."** Most courts have held that "time when the buyer learned of the breach" means "time when the buyer learned of the repudiation" in cases involving anticipatory repudiations. By this majority view, Buyer would be entitled to damages of only $1,000 (since the market price would be judged as of April 1, when Buyer learned of the repudiation). But a respectable minority of courts (and the eminent commentators White and Summers) holds that the date for determining the market price should be the date for performance (here, July 1), which would give Buyer damages of $2,000. Still other courts measure the market price as of the date when the buyer learns of the repudiation plus a reasonable time to cover (here, presumably several days or weeks after April 1).

126. No. **A promise to** *pay the debt of another* **is within the** *Statute of Frauds* **and is therefore unenforceable unless it is in writing. See Rest. 2d, §112.** Here, Frank's promise to pay for the car if Steve did not pay was a promise to pay the debt of another (usually called a "promise of suretyship"), and therefore Frank cannot be bound since he did not sign any writing.

127. No. **Any promise to "answer for the duty of another" (not just a promise to pay the debt of another) falls within the "suretyship" provision of the Statute of Frauds.** Here, Mechanic has agreed to perform Dealer's obligation to Tycoon, so Mechanic is a surety who cannot be bound except by a writing signed by him.

128. Yes. **A promise of suretyship exists only where the promise is made to the person who is to receive the performance.** Here, Mechanic's promise to Dealer that he would fix Tycoon's car was not a promise of suretyship. The reason is that the promise was made to Dealer, not to Tycoon. Since Mechanic's promise to Dealer does not fall within the Statute of Frauds, it is enforceable even though oral.

129. Yes. **Amanda's promise does not fall within the suretyship provision of the Statute of Frauds. The reason is that a promise of suretyship exists only where another person's *legally enforceable debt* is being guaranteed.** Here, Barbara was not legally obligated to pay for the book (so long as she didn't keep it), since she never ordered it. Since Amanda was not guaranteeing the payment of someone else's legally enforceable debt, her promise was not a promise of suretyship. Amanda's promise is therefore enforceable though oral, just as is any other promise that does not fall within some provision of the Statute of Frauds. (If the book had cost more than $500, the special UCC Statute of Frauds governing contracts for the sale of goods, §2-201, would apply, however.)

130. Yes. **Under the "*main purpose*" rule, Owner's promise did not fall within the suretyship provision of the Statute, and that promise is therefore enforceable.** Here, the transaction was cast as a promise of suretyship. However, Owner's main purpose in entering the transaction was not to benefit Contractor, but to help himself (by getting the house built on schedule).

131. No. **Any promise to make a *transfer of land* is within the Statute of Frauds, and is therefore unenforceable unless in writing.** This applies to option contracts as well as to unconditional promises to transfer land. (But Buyer probably can recover his $10,000 option payment in quasi-contract.)

132. Yes. **At the time the oral contract was made, neither part was enforceable because both were within the Statute of Frauds. But a special rule provides that if the vendor fully performs, the vendee's promise is removed from the Statute. See Rest. 2d, §125(3).** Once Seller made the conveyance, this had the effect of removing Buyer's promise to pay the price from the Statute, and Seller may recover that price in an action on the contract.

133. No. **A contract for the sale of land must comply with the Statute of Frauds.** Here, the contract is for the sale of land, and it remains within the Statute even though Buyer has partly performed by paying the $10,000. Buyer's remedy is a suit in restitution for return of his $10,000 deposit.

134. No. **This contract falls within the "one year" provision of the Statute of Frauds, since it *cannot possibly be completed within one year*. See Rest. 2d, §130.** The one-year period starts from the *making of the agreement*, not from the beginning of performance. Therefore, the fact that from the beginning of performance until the end of performance will take less than a year is irrelevant.

135. Yes. **A contract is within the "one year" provision only if it *cannot possibly be performed within one year*. See Rest. 2d, §130.** At the time the contract was made, it was possible that Employee would die within a year. The fact that he did not in fact do so is irrelevant. (Also, courts generally take the view that if an employee under a lifetime contract dies, his death constitutes "performance" rather than mere "termination," so the possibility of death within a year means that there is a possibility of performance within a year, taking the contract out of the Statute.)

136. Split of authority. **Some courts reason that if a party ends a contract under a notice provision, this giving of notice constitutes "performance," thus taking the case out of the Statute (since it can possibly be performed within one year of its making). The Second Restatement §130 takes this approach. Other courts hold that the giving of such notice is merely a "termination," not a "performance," and thus is not enough to take the case out of the Statute.** Also, the fact that Employee might have died within a year does not take the case out, because if Employee were to die, the contract would not be "performed." (Distinguish this situation from the lifetime employment contract in the prior question—here, the primary purpose is not to give Employee lifetime employment, but rather to give him five years of employment. If he dies within a year, this primary purpose will not have been fulfilled, so the contract has not been "performed.")

137. Yes, probably. **Most courts hold that *when one side has fully performed, the contract is taken out of the one-year provision.* See, e.g., Rest. 2d, §130, Comment d.** It is true that when made, the contract could not be fully performed within one year of its making. But as of June 1, 1991, Studio had fully performed.

138. No. **According to UCC §2-201, "A contract for the sale of goods for the price of $500 or more is not enforceable by way of action or defense unless there is some writing sufficient to indicate that a contract for sale has been made between the parties and signed by the party against whom enforcement is sought. . . ."** Since Consumer did not sign any writing relating to the deal, he cannot be bound. The fact that Dealer relied on the oral agreement is irrelevant to the Statute of Frauds issue.

139. Yes. **Since the contract price was less than $500, the agreement did not fall within UCC's Statute of Frauds for the sale of goods, §2-201.** The fact that the item may have had a "value" of greater than $500 is irrelevant. Thus, Shopper will be permitted to attempt to prove in court by oral testimony that the agreement existed; if she carries this burden, she will be able to recover.

140. Yes. **Under UCC §2-201(3)(a), even without a writing, a contract for the sale of goods for a price of more than $500 is enforceable "If the goods are to be specially manufactured for the buyer and are not suitable for sale to others in the ordinary course of the seller's business and the seller, before notice of repudiation is received and under circumstances which reasonably indicate that the goods are for the buyer, has made either a substantial beginning of their manufacture or commitments for their procurement. . . ."** Here, the goods (the stationery) were clearly going to be specially manufactured for Customer by Printer, and Printer had made a substantial beginning of their manufacture. Nor could the goods be sold to anyone else, since they had Customer's name and address on them. Therefore, §2-201(3)(a) is applicable, and the oral agreement is enforceable.

141. Yes, but only as to 100 widgets. **If Buyer had kept his mouth shut in court, the contract would have been completely unenforceable due to the Statute of Frauds. But under UCC §2-201(3)(b), an otherwise unenforceable oral agreement will become enforceable "if the party against whom enforcement is sought admits in his pleading, testimony or otherwise in court that a contract for sale was made, but the contract is not enforceable under this provision beyond the quantity of goods admitted. . . ."** Since Buyer has admitted to having placed an order for 100 widgets, he can be sued for breach of contract with respect to 100. (It doesn't matter that the judge believes Buyer is lying and that Buyer really ordered 1,000.)

142. Yes. **This contract would ordinarily be unenforceable because of the Statute of Frauds. But under UCC §2-201(3)(c), an otherwise unenforceable oral agreement becomes enforceable "with respect to goods for which payment has been made and accepted or which have been received and accepted. . . ."** When Toy Store received the goods and kept them for seven weeks, through the Christmas season, it must be deemed to have "accepted" them: under §2-606(1)(b), acceptance of goods occurs when the buyer "fails to make an effective rejection . . . but such acceptance does not occur until the buyer has had a reasonable opportunity to inspect [the goods]." Under §2-602(1), "rejection of goods must be within a reasonable time after their delivery or tender. It is ineffective unless the buyer seasonably notifies the seller." So, by waiting seven weeks (especially when the Christmas season ended during this period), Toy Store failed to make a timely rejection, and therefore accepted the goods. Having accepted them, Toy Store was bound as if there had been a writing.

143. No. **Since this is a contract for the sale of land, it is enforceable against Owner only if Owner has signed an adequate memorandum. In non-UCC cases, the memorandum, to be sufficient, must**

normally state the *price* if it is to be enforced against the seller. See Rest. 2d, §131. (There is an exception when the price has already been completely paid, but that is not the case here.) If the receipt had cited the further fact that the balance "of $90,000" was to be paid upon the tender of a deed and proof of marketable title, then Owner would have been bound.

144. Yes, but only for $100 (50 dolls' worth of profits). **Toy Store's "confirmation" letter is sufficiently complete to serve as a memorandum under UCC §2-201(1). (The memorandum has to be a "writing sufficient to indicate that a contract for sale has been made between the parties and signed by the party against whom enforcement is sought. . . . A writing is not insufficient because it omits or incorrectly states a term agreed upon but the contract is not enforceable under this paragraph beyond the quantity of goods shown in such writing.")** Nearly all courts have held that the absence of a price term in the memorandum does not make the memorandum insufficient under §2-201. However, since the memo only refers to 50 dolls, not the 100 actually ordered, Distributor can only gain enforcement as to 50 dolls (even if the trial judge believes that the oral contract was for 100 dolls). This would give Distributor a recovery of 50 times $2 per doll profit, or $100.

145. Yes. **Normally, an oral contract will not be enforceable against a party who has not signed any writing indicating the contract's terms. But under UCC §2-201(2), "Between merchants if within a reasonable time a writing in confirmation of the contract and sufficient against the sender is received and the party receiving it has reason to know its contents, it satisfies the requirements [of the Statute of Frauds] against such party unless written notice of objection to its contents is given within 10 days after it is received."** Since both parties were merchants, and since the confirmation was sufficient to bind Distributor, it became sufficient to bind Toy Store when Toy Store did not give written notice of objection within 10 days of the November 6 receipt date.

146. No. **If the contract as modified falls within the Statute of Frauds, it has to be in writing (i.e., a memorandum containing all of its essential terms, including the new ending date, had to be signed by the party to be charged—here, Company). See Rest. 2d, §149.** To determine whether a contract as modified falls within the Statute of Frauds, we look at that contract as modified (including the originally agreed-upon terms). Viewed this way, the contract after the August 1 amendment was one that could not be fully performed within one year from its making (whether we regard it as having been made on July 1 or August 1—it is not clear which one the court would choose). Consequently, the modification was of no effect. The original contract remained in force, and expired on December 31, and Company did not act wrongfully.

147. Yes. **If the contract as modified falls within the Statute of Frauds, it has to be in writing.** The changes of the proof of marketability and closing dates were modifications of the contract. The contract as modified still fell within the Statute of Frauds (since it was for the sale of land). Therefore, the modification was not effective.

148. Yes, Seller may recover against Buyer for breach. **According to Rest. 2d, §150, if the parties to an enforceable agreement orally agree that all or part of the duty need not be performed, the Statute of Frauds does not prevent enforcement of the subsequent oral agreement "if reinstatement of the original terms would be unjust in view of a *material change of position in reliance* on the subsequent agreement."** Although the oral modification was not effective at the time it was made (since the contract as modified still called for the sale of land and thus was within the Statute of Frauds), Seller's subsequent *reliance* on Buyer's promise changed the equation. Since it would be unjust to allow Buyer to renege now (after Seller materially relied on the oral modification by not getting the proof of marketability on time), the court should enforce the oral promise as a waiver.

149. No. **Any contract not involving the sale of goods may be orally rescinded even though the original was (and had to be) in writing. See Rest. 2d, §148.** Even though the original contract was required to be in writing, that contract could be *rescinded* orally.

150. Unclear. UCC §2-209(3) states, "The requirements of the Statute of Frauds . . . must be satisfied if the contract as modified is within its provisions." This seems to mean that the modification must be evidenced by a memorandum, since the contract as modified is still for more than $500. However, §2-209(4) says, "Although an attempt at modification . . . does not satisfy the requirements of subsection . . . (3) it can operate as a waiver." A court might hold that Buyer's oral request for a higher quantity operated as a waiver of his right to insist on the original quantity (or to insist on the Statute of Frauds), in which case the court might award damages.

151. A decree ordering specific performance. **A court will grant equitable relief (including a decree for specific performance) as a remedy for breach of contract if damages are not adequate to protect the injured party, assuming that a couple of other conditions not here relevant are satisfied.** A controlling interest in a closely held business will generally qualify for a decree of specific performance, since damages are generally an inadequate remedy in this situation. (It will usually be hard to calculate the damages, since it is not clear how much the business is "worth," and money usually cannot purchase a substitute.) Therefore, the judge would probably order Alfonse to convey his shares to Priscilla at the contract price.

152. (a) No. **Courts will almost never order specific performance of a contract for personal services.** To grant such a decree would amount to imposing involuntary servitude on the defendant.

   (b) Yes, probably. **The court will grant an employer an injunction to enforce a noncompetition clause if the employee's services are unique or extraordinary.** Here, since obstetricians are scarce in Ames, the court would probably agree that Deborah was uniquely qualified to fulfill the contract. The court will not grant an injunction against competition where the probable result will be to leave the employee without any reasonable means of earning a living except returning to the old employer. But the noncompete here restricts Deborah only from practicing obstetrics in Ames—she is free to practice elsewhere. Therefore, the court will probably conclude that an injunction against competition within Ames will still leave Deborah with a reasonable means of making a living, and the court will therefore probably issue the injunction.

153. Yes. **Under UCC §2-716, "Specific performance may be decreed where the goods are unique or in other proper circumstances."** The classic illustration of a "unique" good is a one-of-a-kind work of art. Therefore, even though as a strictly economic matter Collector might be made "whole" by being awarded the $5 million difference between the contract price and the current market "value" of the painting, Collector is entitled to reject this economic compensation and receive the item itself.

154. $100,000. **The plaintiff in a breach of contract suit is normally entitled to recover "expectation" damages—that is, a sum sufficient to put him or her in the position he or she would have been in had the contract been completed. But there is an exception to this rule: Where a defendant has performed defectively (rather than failing to complete performance), the plaintiff is normally entitled to enough money to fix the work, even if this is somewhat greater than the loss in market value due to defendant's breach. See Rest. 2d, §348(1)(b).**

155. $10,000. **If remedying the defects in the defendant's performance would cost an amount that is *"clearly disproportionate"* to the loss in market value from the defects, the plaintiff may recover only the loss in market value. See Rest. 2d, §348(1)(b) and Illustr. 4; see also *Peevyhouse v. Garland Coal & Mining Co.*, 382 P.2d 109 (Okla. 1962).** The 10-to-1 ratio here between the cost

of remedying the cracks and the diminution of the market value of the home meets this "clearly disproportionate" test, so Builder will only be responsible for paying Owner a sum such that Owner will end up with a total economic package equal to the value that a properly constructed home would have had.

156. (c) **$30,000. Although as a general rule courts will award expectation damages (so as to put the plaintiff in the position he or she would have been in had the contract been fulfilled), courts are very reluctant to award damages for "lost profits" from a speculative or *new venture*.** The introduction of a "better mousetrap" certainly seems to qualify as a speculative venture whose profits are highly uncertain. This is especially true where the only proof presented by the plaintiff is somewhat arbitrary assumptions produced in a business plan (as distinguished from profits earned by similar enterprises in the past, or profits later earned by the plaintiff's own enterprise). Therefore, the court would probably award Inventor only his reliance damages (i.e., the $30,000 he spent in performing his side of the contract).

157. **$20,000, probably. Promises to make a gift are generally unenforceable, for lack of consideration. But where the promisee relies to his or her detriment on the promise, the promise will be enforceable *to the extent needed to avoid injustice* (promissory estoppel). See Rest. 2d, §90.** In such a promissory estoppel situation, a court will rarely award expectation damages (here, $200,000) or specific performance. Instead, the court will probably award *reliance* damages, in this case, the $20,000 that Son spent building the house. In other words, the court will put Son in the position he would have been in had the promise never been made, not the position he would have been in had the promise been fulfilled, since only the former is needed to avoid injustice.

158. **$13,000. A plaintiff who cannot prove his or her expectation damages (in the case of a construction contract, a party who cannot prove how much the contract would have cost to complete) may recover reliance damages without having to prove cost of completion.** In this case, Contractor's reliance damages are the amount he spent ($20,000) less any amount he received by way of avoidance or mitigation of damages (here, the $7,000 he got for selling the materials bought for the job).

159. **$3,000. A plaintiff's reliance damages are almost never permitted to exceed his or her expectation damages, but the burden of proof is on the defendant to demonstrate what these expectation damages would have been. To put it another way, if the defendant shows that the plaintiff would have suffered a loss on the completed contract, this loss must be subtracted from the plaintiff's reliance expenditures. See Rest. 2d, §349.** Here, Owner has shown that Contractor would have suffered a loss of $10,000 on the completed contract. Therefore, from Contractor's net reliance expenditures ($20,000 minus $7,000, or $13,000) must be subtracted the $10,000 loss, leaving $3,000 recovery. (To take advantage of this limitation, defendant will have to prove with *reasonable certainty* the loss that plaintiff would have suffered, just as a plaintiff must prove with reasonable certainty the profits he would have made, in order to recover those profits.)

160. **$7,000. A plaintiff who has *partly* performed and who has ceased performance only due to the other party's breach (as occurred here) is entitled to *restitution* damages, *even if these are greater than the contract price*. Restitution is the value of the performance conferred on the defendant; it is usually measured by the market value of plaintiff's performance, not the subjective "value" to the defendant.** Thus, although Patient's life may in some sense have been "worth" $1 million, Doctor cannot recover more than $7,000, the market value of the services he performed.

161. $5,000. **Where one party to the contract has *fully performed* and the other owes only money, the court will not award restitution damages where these exceed the contract price—the plaintiff**

is *limited to the contract price.* Observe that by performing the second operation, Doctor actually reduced his damages from $7,000 to $5,000!

162. **$50,000. A plaintiff who has partly performed and has not breached is entitled to restitution damages (the benefit conferred on the other party, as measured by market value) even though, had plaintiff fully performed, he or she would have *lost money* on the contract. See Rest. 2d, §373.** Thus, paradoxically, Contractor turns out better under the fact pattern in this question (he ends up making $10,000) than had he and Owner both fully performed (loss of $10,000).

163. **$99,000. On these facts, Contractor has clearly "substantially performed." That is, although Contract has breached the contract by installing the wrong type of insulation, Contractor's breach was not "material." Therefore, he is allowed to recover *on the contract.* Thus he can recover expectation damages, which in this case means the contract price.** Owner has a counterclaim for breach due to the use of the wrong type of insulation. Since the cost to remedy the nonconformance would be wildly disproportionate to the diminution of market value stemming from the nonconformance, Owner's claim will be limited to the change in market value. Thus, Owner has a counterclaim for $1,000, making a net recovery of $99,000 in favor of Contractor.

164. (a) A quasi-contract suit. **When the parties attempt to make a contract, but that contract is unenforceable or voidable because of the Statute of Frauds (the case here), mistake, illegality, impossibility, and so on, one party can bring a quasi-contract suit against the other to recover either the value of the services performed or the plaintiff's reasonable expenditures.**

   (b) **$23,000. Courts usually award the plaintiff the value to the defendant of the plaintiff's performance. See Rest. 2d, §375.** Here, Seller has received a $10,000 down payment and $15,000 worth of improvements. However, Seller would be entitled to deduct the fair value of the benefit Buyer has received under the contract ($2,000 worth of rent). Thus, Seller would owe a net of $23,000.

165. (a) Suit in quasi-contract (or *quantum meruit) for restitution damages.* **If a person is in material breach of a contract, that person cannot recover "on the contract," but may be allowed to recover in quasi-contract.** Here, Contractor has not "substantially performed." That is, his breach was a material one. Therefore, he cannot recover "on the contract," because contractual recovery is given to a breaching plaintiff only if he substantially performed. However, Contractor would be allowed to recover in quasi-contract (or *quantum meruit*—"as much as he deserves") for the value his performance conferred on Owner.

   (b) **$70,000. If a person is in material breach of a contract, that person cannot recover "on the contract," but may be allowed to recover in quasi-contract.** The key thing to note here is that Contractor is *not* allowed to recover the contract price minus the damages suffered by Owner due to the breach. (This amount, which would be $100,000 minus $20,000, or $80,000, is the expectation measure, which would only be allowed to Contractor if he had substantially performed.) Instead, Contractor may recover the market value of the house, which is $70,000. The fact that the house would cost $60,000 to repair would be viewed as irrelevant by most courts, since repair would be so disproportionate to the improvement in market value resulting from the repair as to constitute economic waste.

166. Nothing. **According to most courts, a plaintiff who breached "wilfully" (i.e., intentionally) cannot recover anything at all. See Rest. 2d, §374, Comment b.** However, Contractor would presumably be entitled to come onto Owner's land and demolish the house for its salvage value, as long as he left Owner's property in a state no less valuable than it was in when the contract was signed.

167. (a) **Recovery on a quasi-contract theory. If a person is in material breach of a contract, that person cannot recover "on the contract," but may be allowed to recover in quasi-contract.** As in Question 166, Subcontractor is a materially breaching plaintiff who is nonetheless permitted to recover in quasi-contract (i.e., off the contract) for the value that he has conferred on Contractor.

(b) **$60,000. Where a proportionate part of the total price can be easily calculated to match the portion of the work done by the plaintiff, the plaintiff's recovery in quasi-contract will never be allowed to exceed this pro rata contract price. See Rest. 2d, §374.** Since Subcontractor did 60 percent of the work, he cannot recover more than 60 percent of the contract price (i.e., 60 percent of $100,000, or $60,000). The fact that the market value of his performance (and thus the "benefit" to Contractor) was $90,000 is therefore irrelevant.

168. $1,000. **According to UCC §2-718(2)(b), a seller who justifiably withholds delivery of goods by virtue of the buyer's breach may not necessarily keep all payments made by the buyer. In the absence of a valid liquidated damages clause in the contract (which does not exist here), the seller may keep only 20 percent of the "value" of the contract (here, 20 percent of $3,000, or $600) or $500, whichever is smaller.** Thus in this case, Jeweler can keep only $500 of Consumer's money, and must refund the other $1,000. If Jeweler could show that he suffered actual damages greater than $500 (e.g., he resold the ring for less than $2,500), he could keep these damages instead. See §2-718(3)(a). But here, where Jeweler has lost only $100 on the resale, he is limited in keeping Consumer's money to 20 percent of the contract price or $500, whichever is less.

169. No. **UCC §2-715(2) allows the buyer to recover consequential damages from the seller's breach only to the extent of loss "resulting from general or particular requirements and needs of which the seller at the time of contracting had reason to know and which could not reasonably be prevented by cover or otherwise." This is essentially the rule of *Hadley v. Baxendale*, 156 Eng. Rep. 145 (1854).** Although Seller knew that most customers who buy the Model 123 are manufacturers for whom the motor plays a key role in a very large and expensive machine, the facts here do not indicate that Seller knew or should have known that time was of the essence. That is, Seller could quite reasonably have concluded that the motor was being bought as one of several spares, and that failure of that particular motor to operate would not normally cause Buyer's production to cease. Consequently, a court would probably hold that Buyer's immediate need for the machine was not a need that Seller had reason to know at the time of contracting, and Buyer would be limited to recovery of at most the $1,000 purchase price.

170. $5,000. **A party injured by breach of contract cannot recover for damages that he could have avoided by reasonable conduct. See Rest. 2d, §350.** This is the so-called *duty to mitigate*. Here, Worker could have found a reasonably similar job paying $35,000 if she had made reasonable efforts. Since she would have suffered a loss of $5,000 even had she made such efforts and gotten one of the substitute jobs, she can recover the $5,000. But she cannot recover anything beyond this.

171. Yes. **A lost-volume seller's failure to get "replacement" contracts does not diminish his or her recovery, because these contracts are not really replacements. See Rest. 2d, §350.** On the facts here, Contractor is a *"lost volume" seller*. That is, because of the essentially limitless availability of freelance construction workers, Contractor could have done the contract with Owner plus one or more additional parking lot contracts simultaneously. By losing the contract with Owner, Contractor has lost volume, and therefore lost profits.

172. Yes, probably. **Although an injured party generally may not recover damages that could have been avoided, that party will not be penalized for failing to take avoidance actions that would**

have involved undue risk, burden, or humiliation. See Rest. 2d, §350(1). Here, a court would probably find that Star would have been so humiliated by having to perform a similar role after having been fired by the same studio for her work in the *Nebraska* role that this was more than Star should have had to bear in order to collect her salary.

173. **No. A clause will be upheld as a liquidated damages clause, rather than being struck down as a penalty, if the amount is reasonable *either* when viewed from the time of contracting *or* from the time of the actual breach (at least according to the modern, and Restatement, view). See Rest. 2d, §356(1).** Since both parties believed that Tenant might make $1,000 per day from operating the store, the $1,000-per-day penalty for construction delay was reasonable when viewed as of the time of contracting, even though it later turned out to be grossly high. Therefore, the $1,000-per-day provision will be enforced, and Tenant may take the $30,000 as an offset against the rent.

174. Yes, probably. **Under UCC §2-712(2), the buyer may recover as damages "the difference between the cost of cover and the contract price. . . ." A buyer "covers" when "in good faith and without unreasonable delay [he or she makes] any reasonable purchase of or contract to purchase goods in substitution for those due from the seller." §2-712(1).** While Stacy may argue that Bernard "unreasonably delayed," the court would probably conclude that Bernard was justified in taking into account his own redelivery schedule in determining what kind of delay was "reasonable." Since the price of personal computers does not ordinarily jump sharply within a one-month period, Bernard probably behaved reasonably (especially since he was delaying his outlay of cash), so he would probably be entitled to the contract-cover differential.

175. No, probably. **UCC §2-713 states generally that "the measure of damages for non-delivery or repudiation by the seller is the difference between the market price at the time when the buyer learned of the breach and the contract price. . . ." This section, providing the so-called contract/market differential, does not specifically deny the covering buyer the right to use that section. However, Comment 5 to §2-713 says that this contract/market differential "applies only when and to the extent that the buyer has not covered."** Bernard covered, by buying the substitute computer. So Bernard is probably limited to the difference between the contract price and his cover price, which would produce zero damages.

176. None. **UCC §2-706(1) allows the seller to resell the goods, and to collect the "contract/resale differential" if the resale was made "in good faith and in a commercially reasonable manner." However, §2-706(3) says that "where the resale is a private sale the seller must give the buyer reasonable *notification* of his intention to resell."** Importer did not do this here. Therefore, he is limited to the contract/market differential (§2-708), which is zero on these facts.

177. **No. If the injured seller is able to resell the goods at a profit, nothing in the UCC or any common law principle requires him to account to the breaching buyer for this windfall, even if the buyer has sustained his own incidental losses in the transaction.**

178. $1,900. **Ordinarily, a seller's remedy when a buyer refuses to take or pay for the goods is either the contract/resale differential or the contract/market differential. But under §2-708(2), if neither of these measures would "put the seller in as good a position as performance would have done," then the seller is entitled to the profit which he would have made from full performance.** Here, Dealer is a "lost volume" seller to whom §2-708(2) is applicable—Dealer could sell as many cars as he could get his hands on, so the fact that he sold the car earmarked for Consumer to someone else doesn't really reduce Dealer's loss; he has still sold one fewer car during the course of the year than he would have sold if Consumer had honored the contract. Therefore, Dealer is entitled to the

difference between the contract price and the cost for the car, less the $100 expenses he saved by not having to fulfill the contract with Customer.

179. **(a)** $200. **A buyer who "accepts" goods that turn out to be defective generally must sue for breach of warranty. The usual measure of damages for breach of warranty, given by §2-714(2), gives the buyer "the difference at the time and place of acceptance between the value of the goods accepted and the value they would have had if they had been as warranted, unless special circumstances show proximate damages of a different amount."** By taking the rulers, not inspecting them within a reasonable time, and then reselling them, Stationer "accepted" them. Therefore, Stationer's damages are limited to the contract/value differential at the time of shipment, 20 cents per ruler times 1,000. The fact that the market price diminished further thereafter, and that Stationer took an additional $300 loss on top of the initial contract/value loss, is irrelevant and not compensable.

(b) Reject the goods by immediately sending them back to Manufacturer. **A buyer who receives nonconforming goods always has the right to "reject" the goods—that is, to return them to the seller and cancel the contract.** The seller will usually have a limited time to cure. But in any event, the buyer has a good chance of escaping from a bad bargain. Had Stationer immediately inspected the shipment, discovered the nonconformity, and returned the goods, Stationer probably would have avoided loss from the subsequent general market decline.

180. At least $1 million, and possibly $3 million. **Under §2-708(2), Distributor is clearly entitled to the $1 million profit it would have made directly from the contract with Utility (i.e., 10 cents per gallon times 10 million gallons). Additionally, nearly all courts hold that the seller may not recover consequential damages.** Nothing in the UCC expressly gives a seller the right to consequential damages (which the profits from these other contracts would probably be deemed to be). However, common law principles, unless expressly displaced by some specific code provision, enter the UCC through §1-103. Therefore, a court might hold that the ordinary principle of expectation damages (by which Distributor would get the full $3 million, including $2 million of "consequential" damages) should be applied here. Alternatively, a court might give a very broad reading to §2-708's grant to the seller of "profit . . . which the seller would have made from full performance . . . ," thus treating the profit from the contracts with third parties as being profits that Distributor would have made from "full performance" by Utility. However, cases in which sellers have been awarded any sort of consequential damages are exceptionally rare, perhaps nonexistent.

181. Daughter. **Generally, gratuitous assignments are revocable unless the assignment is "accompanied by delivery of a writing of a type customarily accepted as a symbol or as evidence of the right assigned." Rest. 2d, §332(1)(b).** When Father gave Daughter the insurance policy, he was making an assignment of his rights under the Insurer-Father contract. This was a gratuitous assignment, since Daughter gave no consideration. A gratuitous assignment is normally *revocable* at the will of the assignor, and Father's notice to Insurer would have been enough to constitute revocation. However, the insurance policy itself was probably a "symbol . . . of the right assigned," so delivery of that policy by Father to Daughter, together with the words of assignment, was enough to make that assignment irrevocable. Consequently, Father's notice to Insurer was of no effect, and Daughter is entitled to the proceeds.

182. No, probably. **A contract right may generally be assigned over the objection of the obligor. But there are several exceptions to this general rule. One of the exceptions is where the obligor's** *duties* **would be** *materially changed* **by the assignment, or the burden or risk imposed on him**

would be materially increased. See Rest. 2d, §317(2)(a). Paula can probably successfully argue that her duties involved such a close working relationship with Susan (and her willingness to enter the contract was so completely motivated by that relationship) that assignment would materially change her duties and/or materially increase her burdens.

183. **Yes. Normally, an anti-assignment clause in a contract will be enforced. But there are several important exceptions, one of which is that under UCC §9-406, an assignment of an "account" (that is, the right to receive money under a contract) is enforceable despite an anti-assignment clause.** Since what Contractor assigned to Bank was an "account," §9-406 makes the anti-assignment clause of the Owner-Contractor contract void. The reason for this Article 9 provision is to enable parties to a contract to raise money by borrowing against their contract rights.

184. **No. If an obligor (Owner) pays an assignor (Contractor) before he has received notice of the assignment, the obligor may use this as a defense against the assignee (Stewart).**

185. **Yes. Once an obligor receives notice of an assignment, he or she makes payment to the assignor rather than to the assignee only at his or her own peril—he or she will not be able to raise, as a defense against the assignee, the fact that he or she paid the assignor.**

186. **Yes. One who makes an assignment for value (which probably includes one who, like Contractor here, makes the assignment in return for past value) is normally held to *impliedly warrant* that he will do nothing to defeat or impair the value of the assignment. Rest. 2d, §333(1)(a).** Contractor, by pocketing the money from Owner that should have been paid to Creditor, would probably be held to have breached this implied warranty, and therefore be liable to make the payment.

187. **No. Although an assignor (Contractor) impliedly makes certain warranties about the assignment (e.g., that he or she will not do anything to defeat the value of the assignment, and that there are no hidden defenses that may be asserted by the obligor), the assignor does not impliedly warrant that the obligor (Owner) is solvent or that the obligor will perform. See Rest. 2d, §333(2).** Therefore, Contractor here has not breached any warranties and is not otherwise liable for Owner's performance.

188. **No. Even after the obligor (Owner) has received notice of the assignment, the obligor and the assignor (Contractor) are free to make good faith modifications without the assignee's (Bank's) consent, so long as the assignor has not yet fully performed. See Rest. 2d, §338(2); UCC §9-405(b).**

189. **Yes. Once the assignor (Contractor) fully performed his side of the bargain, he and the obligor (Owner) could no longer modify the contract without the assignee's (Bank's) consent. See UCC §9-405(b).**

190. **Yes. According to UCC §9-403(b), "an agreement between an account debtor and an assignor not to assert against an assignee any claim or defense that the account debtor may have against the assignor is enforceable by an assignee that takes an assignment: (1) for value; (2) in good faith; [and] (4) without notice of a defense or claim . . . ."** Here, Bank gave value, took in good faith, and took without notice of any claim or defense. Therefore, Bank gets the protection of the waiver-of-defenses clause signed by Retailer, and Retailer is out of luck.

191. **Yes. UCC §9-404(a)(1) incorporates the common law rule that an assignee of contract rights (Bank) "stands in the shoes of the assignor," and has no greater rights against the obligor (Computer Corp) than the assignor (Assembler) had.** Since Computer Corp (obligor) would have been able to asset the missing-chip claim against Assembler (assignor), it may assert that claim as

a recoupment against Bank (assignee). This right is dependent upon the fact that Computer Corp's claim arises out of the same contract as the contract right that Assembler has assigned to Bank.

192. **No. Under §9-404(a)(2), an assignee's claim is subject to a defense or claim by the obligor only if the defense or claim "accrues before the account debtor receives a notification of the assignment."** Here, the claim for the missing chips accrued in March 2002, which was after the time that Computer Corp received notice of the assignment to Bank.

193. **Bank. Normally, the first of two successive assignees is entitled to priority. But under the Restatement and the law of most states (see Rest. 2d, §342), there are four exceptions to this principle. One of the exceptions is that the second assignee will win if he or she takes the assignment in good faith, without knowledge of the prior assignment, gives value, and takes possession of a *writing* of a type customarily accepted as a symbol of the right assigned.** A life insurance policy is generally accepted as a symbol of the insurer's obligation to pay over the policy proceeds, so Bank has met the requirements for this part of this "four horsemen rule," and takes priority even though its assignment came after the one to Finance Co.

194. **Yes. As a general rule, the delegator remains liable even after the delegation.** Here, Axle delegated his duties to Bart. Thus, even if Bart (the delegatee) expressly promised to perform the duty owed by Axel (the delegator), Axle was still liable to Customer if Bart failed to perform.

195. **No. Contracts are ordinarily delegable even without the consent of the obligee. There is an exception if the obligee has a substantial interest in having the assignor perform personally, as where the promised performance requires unusual personal skill. See UCC §2-210(1).** But here, the timely delivery of a stated quantity of ordinary meat does not require personal skill, and Customer did not have a substantial interest in having Axle as opposed to Bart perform. Therefore, Axle was entitled to delegate, and the tendered performance by Bart caused Axle's duty to be discharged. Customer, by refusing to accept or pay, breached.

196. **No. Both at common law and under the UCC, a clause in the contract prohibiting assignment of "the contract" will normally be interpreted to bar delegation of the assignor's performance, but not to bar assignment by the assignor of his rights. See, e.g., UCC §2-210(3).** In this case, the prohibition on assignment of "the contract" meant that Axle had no right to delegate his performance to Bart without Customer's consent. Therefore, Customer had a claim for breach of contract when Axle did not personally perform. (But if Axle had personally performed, Customer would have been obligated to make payment to Bart instead of to Axle, since the assignment of rights would not be deemed to have been prohibited even though the "assignment of the contract prohibited" language prohibited delegation.)

197. **Yes. Unless the circumstances indicate otherwise, an assignment of "the contract" operates both as an assignment of the assignor's rights and as a delegation of the assignor's duties to the assignee, and *also amounts to a promise by the assignee to perform those duties*. See UCC §2-210(4); also Rest. 2d, §328.** This implied promise by the assignee is enforceable by *either* the assignor (Axle) or the obligee (Customer). Therefore, Customer may sue Bart for breach even though Bart never made a promise directly to Customer—Customer is viewed as a *third-party beneficiary* of the Bart-to-Axle promise.

198. **Yes, probably. Delegation is allowed except where the promisee has a substantial interest in having the promisor in particular supply the performance.** A contract in which the promisor is to make an artistic performance usually is held to fall within this special case. Thus a court would probably hold that the opera company had a substantial interest in having Alfredo, and only Alfredo,

perform; if the court so concluded, the opera company could collect at least nominal damages from Alfredo.

199. **Yes. The Restatement allows a third party to recover under a contract if he or she falls into the class of "intended beneficiaries."** Bonnie (the promisor) has promised Archie (the promisee) that Bonnie will satisfy an obligation owed by Archie to Claire (the third-party beneficiary). Claire is therefore a *"creditor beneficiary"* (to use the somewhat old-fashioned term) or an *"intended beneficiary"* (the modern term). Claire, as the creditor beneficiary or intended beneficiary, has the right to enforce the promisor's promise by a direct contract action. She does not have to sue her own obligor (Archie) first.

200. **Yes. The Restatement allows a third party to recover under a contract if he or she falls into the class of "intended beneficiaries."** Here, Claire is what was traditionally called a "donee beneficiary." Today, she would probably be put into the category of "intended beneficiary." In any event, since Archie's intent in reaching the contract with Bonnie was to make sure that Claire got the ring, Claire is entitled to bring a direct action against Bonnie to enforce the promise.

201. **No. The Restatement does not allow a third party to recover under a contract if he or she falls under the category of "incidental beneficiary." See Rest. 2d, §302.** Contractor bargained for the $100,000 progress payment from Owner on completion of the concrete work, Contractor was principally interested in making sure that he himself received money (and in any event, he had not yet engaged Mason). Therefore, it is very unlikely that a court would find that Mason was the "intended beneficiary" of Owner's promise to make the progress payment. Consequently, Mason is merely an *"incidental beneficiary,"* and as such has no contract rights against Owner. (But in many states, Mason could get a mechanic's lien against the property, and thereby effectively compel Owner to pay him directly to get the lien removed.)

202. **No, probably. In general, courts are reluctant to find that members of the public are intended beneficiaries of contracts between the government and service providers. Unless the contract expressly provides for liability to public beneficiaries, courts will generally allow a member of the public to recover on a contract theory only if (1) the government itself would be liable for those damages, and (2) a direct action against the private contractor would be consistent with public policy. See Rest. 2d, §313(2).** Since Griswold had no liability for failing to shelter the homeless, and the contract said nothing about direct actions by the homeless against Shelter, Inc., it is unlikely that a court would treat Ted as an intended beneficiary of the Griswold-Shelter contract, at least on a contract theory. (There is a small chance that he could recover on a tort theory if Shelter's undertaking caused Ted to decline other shelter opportunities in reliance).

203. **Yes. The Restatement allows a third party to recover under a contract if he or she falls into the class of "intended beneficiaries."** Owner's intent in extracting the mortgage payment promise from Buyer was to be sure that Bank would be paid so that Owner would have no residual liability. Therefore, Bank was an intended beneficiary (and, under the older terminology, a "creditor beneficiary") of Buyer's promise to Owner. Consequently, Bank can sue Buyer to enforce that promise.

204. **No. In the absence of a statement to the contrary, the promisor (Insurer) and the promisee (Archie) under a contract reserve the power to modify that contract until the beneficiary justifiably relies on it, brings suit on it, or manifests assent to it at the request of the promisor or promisee. See Rest. 2d, §311(3).** Since none of these three things happened here, Archie and Insurer had the power to modify the contract at the time Archie changed the beneficiary designation. Therefore, Claire is out of luck.

205. Yes, probably. **The power of the promisor and promisee to discharge or modify the agreement terminates when the beneficiary, without notice of the discharge or modification, materially changes his or her position in justifiable reliance on the promise.** Here, a court would probably conclude that Claire's making of a sale contract with Donald for the vase was a material and justifiable reliance on Bonnie's promise to give her the vase; therefore, at the moment of the Claire-Donald contract, Archie and Bonnie's power to modify their contract (at least as far as it concerned Bonnie's promise to give the vase to Claire) terminated.

206. No. **Any defense that the promisor could assert against the promisee *arising from the contract in question* may also be asserted against the third-party beneficiary.** Since Bonnie could assert the Statute of Frauds against Archie, and since that defense relates to the contract as to which Claire is the third-party beneficiary, Claire is equally barred.

207. No. **The promisor may not assert against the third-party beneficiary any claims or defenses held against the promisee except those arising out of the contract on which the beneficiary is suing. See Rest. 2d, §309.** Since Bonnie's tort claim against Archie is not a claim arising under the Archie-Bonnie contract, Bonnie must sue Archie, rather than using her claim as a setoff to cancel her obligation to convey Blackacre to Claire.

208. (a) Yes. **An intended beneficiary (Bank) has the right to collect on the promise from either the promisee (Owner) or the promisor (Buyer). In fact, he or she can sue each, though he or she can only collect once.** However, the beneficiary must be careful to ensure that at the time the promisor makes the promise to the promisee, the beneficiary does not grant a *"novation"* to the promisee. That is, it is possible for the beneficiary to say, either expressly or impliedly, "I agree to look solely to the promisor for performance, not to the promisee." If the beneficiary is found to have said this, he or she has given the promisee a novation (i.e., has agreed to discharge the promisee in favor of a claim against the promisor). See Rest. 2d, §280. Here, Bank did not consent to accept Buyer's promise to pay in substitution for Owner's promise to pay, so no novation took place and Owner is still liable.

(b) Yes. **The status of the promisee (Owner) is that of a "surety," or guarantor, of the promisor's promise to pay or give benefit to the beneficiary. As is the case for any surety, if the promisee is forced to make good on this guarantee (as Owner did when he paid Bank), Owner as surety is entitled to be reimbursed for his expenditure by Buyer as promisor. See Rest. 2d, §310.**

209. Yes. **The promisor (Bonnie) is obligated to both the promisee (Archie) and the intended beneficiary (Claire), and either may sue.**

210. No. **Ordinarily, contract liability is "strict"—that is, even if the party who fails to perform is not negligent or willful (and is thus in a sense "without fault"), he or she must still pay damages if he or she is unable to perform. But courts recognize the related defenses of "impossibility" and "impracticability." Under these defenses, if an event occurs the nonoccurrence of which was a basic assumption on which the contract was made, and that event makes a party's performance impossible or impracticable, the party will be "discharged" (i.e., freed from the contract). See Rest. 2d, §§261 & 263.** Here, it was a basic assumption of the Producer-Theater Co. contract that the theater would not cease to exist; when it did cease to exist, making Theater Co.'s performance impossible, this was sufficient to discharge Theater Co. from the contract.

211. **No, probably. According to UCC §2-615(a), "Delay in delivery or non-delivery in whole or in part by a seller . . . is not a breach of his duty under a contract for sale if performance as agreed has been made *impracticable* by the *occurrence of a contingency the non-occurrence of which was a basic assumption* on which the contract was made. . . ."** Here, both Dealer and Buyer contemplated that Dealer would be able to get the computers from ABC, the manufacturer. If Dealer had not made all reasonable efforts (including placing the order with ABC and then trying to find substitute supplies from other dealers), it might have remained liable. But having made all reasonable attempts at fulfilling the contract or getting substitute goods, Dealer would probably be released under §2-615(a)'s commercial impracticability provision.

212. **Yes. The "discharge for commercial impracticability" provision of UCC §2-615(a) applies only where the seller "has employed all due measures to assure himself that his source will not fail."** Here, by waiting a month, Dealer failed to use all appropriate measures to lock up his source of supply, so he will not get the benefit of §2-615.

213. **No. The phrase "FOB Manufacturer's plant" meant that Manufacturer's contractual obligation ended as soon as he delivered the goods to a common carrier. Under UCC §2-509(1)(a), since the contract did not require Manufacturer to deliver the goods at a particular destination, the risk of loss passed to Retailer once the goods were given to Trucker.** Retailer's only remedy is against Trucker.

214. **Yes. Under UCC §2-509(1)(b), since the contract required the seller to deliver the goods at a particular destination, the risk of loss would not pass to Retailer until the goods were delivered at Retailer's premises.** Since that never happened, the risk of loss never passed to Retailer, and Retailer has a claim for breach against Manufacturer. The fact that it was Retailer who chose to use Trucker is irrelevant.

215. **No. If the contract provides that performance shall be made by a particular individual who is a party, that person's death or incapacity will discharge both parties from the contract. This is true not only where the contract explicitly requires performance by the particular party, but also where the surrounding circumstances indicate that a personal relationship was intended. See Rest. 2d, §262.** Because of the close personal relationship between Star and Devotee, Star's continued existence was a basic assumption on which the contract was made. When Star died, Devotee was discharged under the doctrine of impossibility. (Observe that this close personal relationship also made Star's rights under the contract nonassignable, as discussed in question 182. Generally, the same test that determines whether a particular person's participation is so vital that his rights are not assignable or his duties not delegable will be used to determine whether his death discharges him and/or the other party.)

216. **Yes. If the contract provides that performance shall be made by a particular individual who is a party, that person's death or incapacity will discharge both parties from the contract. See Rest. 2d, §262.** Here, the painting of Owner's house was not the kind of job for which Painter had unique personal skills on which Owner relied. Therefore, Painter's death did not truly render performance of the contract impossible or impracticable—his estate could have hired someone else to finish the contract (albeit at a cost greater than the amount remaining to be paid under the Owner-Painter contract). Consequently, the estate was not discharged and must pay damages so as to put Owner in the position he would have been in had the contract been performed (i.e., pay $2,000 to bring Owner's total cost down to the originally contracted-for $10,000).

217. No, probably. **When a court decides whether a contingency has occurred, the nonoccurrence of which was a basic assumption on which the contract was made (UCC §2-615(a)), the court will look to whether the contingency was *foreseeable*, and whether the parties can be found to have explicitly or implicitly allocated the risk one way or the other.** By 2010, the possibility that oil prices might gyrate wildly, and that OPEC might regain control of the world's markets, was quite foreseeable. Furthermore, the parties carefully adopted a price escalator built on the CPI, thus showing their understanding of the risks of price increases. Therefore, a court would almost certainly hold that Distributor took the risk that oil prices would go up faster than the CPI went up, and Utility Co. took the risk that they would go up slower than the CPI.

218. No. **Where one party's purpose is completely or almost completely frustrated by events that destroy that party's purpose in entering the contract, most courts will discharge him or her from performing. See Rest. 2d, §265.** Baker will be able to successfully raise the defense of *frustration of purpose*. The contract is not impossible to perform—USBC could certainly broadcast the advertisement at the contracted-for time. But since Baker's primary purpose in broadcasting the ad at this particular time was to reach the Super Bowl audience with its Super Bowl–themed ad, and since that purpose has been completely frustrated by the earthquake (an unforeseeable event that occurred through no fault of Baker's), Baker will be discharged from the contract.

219. Yes. **For the doctrine of frustration of purpose to apply, the frustration must be substantial—"so severe that it is not fairly to be regarded as within the risks that [the party asserting the defense] assumed under the contract." Rest. 2d, §265, Comment a.** Unlike the risk of an earthquake, the risk of a "blowout" would almost certainly be regarded as within the risks that an advertiser takes when he or she books time on a sporting event. Also, the fact that a business deal turns out to be substantially less profitable (or even money losing) than the party asserting the defense expected will generally not be sufficient. See, e.g., Rest. 2d, §265.

220. Probably $5,000, on a restitution theory. **One who has been discharged by impossibility or frustration may recover for the benefit he or she has conferred on the other party.** The fire clearly discharged both Painter and Owner from the contract, under the doctrine of impossibility. However, the court would probably award Painter restitution for the value of the benefit he conferred upon Owner. Even though the one-half paint job was of no "long-term" benefit to Owner, courts generally determine the value of the partial performance as of the time *just before* the event that made performance impossible. Since Owner would have had to pay $5,000 to have one-half of the house painted (the performance rendered by Painter), the court would probably award Painter this sum.

221. No, probably. **Although in theory reliance damages are allowable in impossibility cases if justice requires (see Rest. 2d, §272(2)), courts almost never award them in practice.** For the court to give Painter recompense for the money he spent on this paint, the court would effectively be awarding Painter *reliance*, rather than restitution, damages—Owner received no benefit from this paint, since it was never used on his structure.

222. Neither. **Promises by an employee not to compete with his or her employer are strictly scrutinized by the courts, and will only be enforced if they are *(1) no greater than is required for the protection of the employer, (2) do not impose undue hardship on the employee, and (3) are not injurious to the public*. See Rest. 2d, §188.** Here, the harm to Phillip is extreme, since most accounting takes place in big cities, and Phillip is being deprived of his right to practice in his own hometown. On the other side of the scale, the noncompete is much broader than really needed to protect Dominant's interest, since Phillip is very unlikely to steal any clients (he hasn't really had significant client contact), and he is in any event practicing in a different city than where he worked for Dominant. Therefore, the court will almost certainly hold that as applied against Phillip's new Cleveland practice, the noncompete is illegal (or as it is sometimes put, "void as against public policy").

223. Yes, probably. **Promises by an employee not to compete with his or her employer are strictly scrutinized by the courts, and will only be enforced if they are** *(1) no greater than is required for the protection of the employer, (2) do not impose undue hardship on the employee, and (3) are not injurious to the public.* **See Rest. 2d, §188.** Here, the noncompete should pass muster: Dominant has a strong interest in not losing its existing clients to its own employees who have worked on the client's account, as has Phillip. Conversely, the burden to Phillip is not very great, since only the clients that he actually worked for while at Dominant are off limits, leaving him plenty of other opportunities to ply his trade.

224. No. **A contract in which a person is to do work for which a license is required will be unenforceable as illegal if the person does not have the license.** There are some exceptions where the requirement of a license is purely ministerial and has no strong protection-of-the-public element. But the prohibition on the practice of law without a license is strongly supported by the state's interest in protecting the public, so the requirement is far from merely ministerial. Consequently, the court will hold that Charles, as a member of the class that the state intended to protect by the licensing requirement, will be permitted to escape his obligation.

225. Yes, probably. **In general, if a contract calls for work to be done that can only be done with a license, and the licensing requirement is enacted for the purpose of protecting a class of which the other contracting party is a member, the court will allow that other (innocent) party to** *enforce* **the contract. See Rest. 2d, §181.** Since Charles was a client, and the licensing requirement for lawyers is designed to protect clients from incompetence, the court will almost certainly let him enforce the contract. Therefore, he will be permitted to recover damages for breach of contract.

226. (a) Duress. **If a party assents to a contract or a contract modification only because of an improper threat by the other party that leaves the victim no reasonable alternative, the contract will be voidable by the victim. See Rest. 2d, §175.**

(b) Yes, probably. **One of the things that can make a threat improper (leading to duress) is if the threat is itself a breach of the duty of good faith and fair dealing under a preexisting contract with the other party. See Rest. 2d, §176(1)(d).** Here, Lawyer and Client had a preexisting contract at $100 per hour, and a court would probably conclude that Lawyer's demand for a doubling of the fee, on the eve of trial, was a breach of Lawyer's duty of good faith and fair dealing. (But if the request for an increased fee stemmed from the fact that the work was much more difficult than either party reasonably anticipated when the contract was made, then Client's defense of duress would probably fail.) If the court does grant Client the defense of duress, it will do so by reducing the fee to the original $100 per hour, not by denying Lawyer any fee at all. In general, the remedy for duress is a restitutionary one (i.e., reducing the contract price or otherwise restructuring the deal so as to undo the unjust enrichment that the other party has obtained).

227. (a) Duress. **If a party assents to a contract or a contract modification only because of an improper threat by the other party that leaves the victim no reasonable alternative, the contract will be voidable by the victim. See Rest. 2d, §175.** Owner can raise the defense of duress (i.e., he can assert that he agreed to the modification only because halfway through the job and after discovery of the rock, he had no real choice and no ability anymore to get a better deal from anyone else).

(b) No, probably. **Even where a contract modification is induced by one party's threat to breach the preexisting contract, this does not automatically amount to duress. If the modification is induced by an unanticipated change in conditions, then the request for a modification is not a breach of the duty of good faith or fair dealing, and the agreement to modify will not be struck down on grounds of duress. See Rest. 2d, §176.** This seems to be the case here.

228. **(a)** Buyer should assert a claim for misrepresentation. **If one party's assent to the contract was induced by the other party's either fraudulent or innocent material misrepresentation, and the recipient was justified in relying on that misrepresentation, then the contract is voidable by the recipient. See Rest. 2d, §164.** Even though the misrepresentation was not made in the contract itself, it has a bearing on whether an enforceable contract is in place. So here, even though Owner's mistake as to the profit was an "honest" one, since the mistake was material (a one-third discrepancy in operating profit would almost always be considered material in a commercial real estate deal), and since Buyer was justified in relying on that misrepresentation (he was not required to carry out a full-scale examination of the underlying tax and utility bills; see Rest. 2d, §172), the contract is voidable at Buyer's option.

(b) The court will allow Buyer to void (i.e., rescind) the transaction if he wishes to do so. **If one party's assent to the contract was induced by the other party's either fraudulent or innocent material misrepresentation, and the recipient was justified in relying on that misrepresentation, then the contract is voidable by the recipient. See Rest. 2d, §164.** (But probably Buyer must either choose between giving up the deal entirely or paying the full $1 million purchase price—the court will not "rewrite" the deal to give the property to Buyer at a lower price.)

229. No, probably. **If a party knows that disclosure of a fact is needed to prevent some previous assertion from being misleading but doesn't disclose it, this will be actionable. See Rest. 2d, §161(a).** Ordinarily, a buyer, even one on credit, has no affirmative obligation to give details of its credit unless the other party requests them. But by submitting the July 1 statement, Donald was making a representation that his finances were sound; when the facts changed and Donald failed to correct what had now become a misleading statement, he effectively made a new misrepresentation. Therefore, the result is the same as if, just before the October 1 order, Donald had falsely stated, "My finances are sound."

230. None, probably. **There is no general duty to disclose information to the other party.** Brenda certainly does not seem to have a valid misrepresentation defense, because Ed did not make any affirmative misstatements, and his failure to disclose that the price was high relative to the prices of other sets probably does not fall within the narrow class of facts as to which the seller has an affirmative duty of disclosure (as would be the case, for instance, of a seller selling a termite-infested home). For instance, the fairness of the price was reasonably discoverable by Brenda despite her illness (e.g., by asking around or by reading the newspaper ads). Brenda has a somewhat better chance, but still not a very good one, of successfully asserting the defense of *unconscionability*. When goods have been sold to consumers at prices that are greatly excessive (two to three times the market price), courts have sometimes struck down the deal as unconscionable, especially where the buyer was poorly educated and did not understand the basic terms of the deal. But here, the overcharge was at most 50 percent, and there is no evidence that Brenda failed to understand the basic deal. It is very unlikely, therefore, that the court would strike down the deal for unconscionability.

231. Yes, probably. **UCC § 2-302(1) provides that "[i]f the court as a matter of law finds the contract or any clause of the contract to have been unconscionable at the time it was made, the court may refuse to enforce the contract, or it may enforce the remainder of the contract without the**

unconscionable clause, or it may so limit the application of any unconscionable clause as to avoid any unconscionable result." Even though Farmer is a businessman rather than a consumer, he will probably be able to get the "ten-day right of return is the sole remedy" clause knocked out of the contract on the ground that it is *unconscionable*. While it is ordinarily difficult for business people to get the court to find a clause to be unconscionable, here the right of return is so manifestly useless as a remedy (since this particular defect could not have been determined by inspection during the ten-day period) that a court will probably hold it unconscionable. The court can get additional guidance from UCC §2-719(2), which provides that "[w]here circumstances cause an exclusive or limited remedy to fail of its essential purpose," other Code-provided remedies (e.g., a suit for damages for breach of warranty) may be used.

232. No. **Until a person reaches the age of majority, any contract he or she signs is voidable. See Rest. 2d, §14.** (The age of majority varies from state to state, but it is 18 in most states—as here—and never less than 18.) Therefore, at the time Greg signed the contract, it imposed on him only voidable duties. If Greg still had the car, the court might require him to return it as a condition of disaffirmance. But since the car no longer exists (and Greg did not receive any cash or other value in exchange for it), he will be able to disaffirm—thereby defeating Dealer's suit—without giving Dealer anything in return.

233. No. **An infant may not ratify a contract until he or she reaches adulthood.** First, Greg has not reached the age of majority yet. Second, even if Greg had waited until after reaching 18 to ratify, the court would almost certainly hold that Greg's fraud entitled Dealer to avoid the contract on this ground (even though, had there been no fraud, Greg would by reaching 18 gain the right to ratify).

234. Yes, probably. **Where the intoxication is not enough to prevent a meeting of the minds, intoxication will only make the contract voidable if the other person knew (or had reason to know) of the intoxication, or the transaction is grossly unfair substantively. See Rest. 2d, §16.** If Carl had been so drunk that he was not capable of assenting to the proposed transaction, there would be no contract. But the facts do not indicate this. Here, Deborah did not have reason to know that Carl was seriously drunk, and the substantive terms were not grossly unfair. Therefore, the court will probably uphold the transaction (though it would probably let Carl pay damages equal to the difference between the market value of the Rolex and the purchase price, rather than issuing a decree of specific performance).

235. Yes, on a theory of implied warranty of merchantability. **A suit for breach of warranty is a type of contract action, and is therefore not time-barred here. Under UCC §2-314(1), "Unless excluded or modified . . . , a warranty that the goods shall be merchantable is implied in a contract for their sale if the seller is a merchant with respect to goods of that kind."** The fact that Hospital has billed Patient for the drug separately strongly suggests that when Hospital administered the dosage to Patient, it was making a "sale" of the drug to him, not merely supplying a service. Therefore, Article 2 and §2-314 would apply to the transaction. Since nothing in the transaction would have caused the implied warranty of merchantability to be excluded or modified, that warranty automatically came into effect. For goods to be merchantable, they must be at least "fit for the ordinary purpose for which such goods are used." §2-314(2)(c). A painkilling drug that is not manufactured according to specifications and causes a heart attack is clearly not "fit for the ordinary purposes for which such goods are used." Therefore, Hospital is liable for breach of the implied warranty of merchantability. The important thing to note is that even though Hospital and its employees were not the slightest bit negligent, and indeed could not possibly have discovered the defect, this fact is *irrelevant*—breach of warranty (whether the warranty is express or implied) is essentially strict liability; that is, liability imposed without regard to fault.

236. None, probably. **A seller can be held to have made an express warranty even though he or she never uses the word warranty, but if he or she is merely "puffing," or clearly expressing an opinion, he or she will not be held to have made a warranty.** Consequently, Consumer's best bet is to bring an action for breach of *express* warranty. That is, Consumer should claim that Big Bob's statement that the car was top notch and would run for ten more years was an express warranty that the car would indeed run for ten more years. However, the court would probably conclude that this statement was mere "*puffing*" by Big Bob. The fact that Big Bob said that the car "should" rather than "will" run for ten years, the relative lack of specificity in his statement, the notorious tendency of used-car salesmen to make loose claims, and the fact that the statement was oral rather than written would probably all indicate to a reasonable person in Consumer's position that this was not a promise meant to be legally binding. But the matter is not completely clear—a court might find an express warranty to have been made, especially in view of the fact that Big Bob was a "professional" and Consumer was not.

237. (a) Yes, on a theory of breach of express warranty. **According to §2-313(1)(c), "Any *sample* or *model* which is made part of the basis of the bargain creates an express warranty that the whole of the goods shall conform to the sample or model."** Here, what the saleswoman for Dress Co. showed Retailer was a "model" (as the term is used in §2-313(1)(c)) of what the contracted-for goods would look like. (It is a "model" rather than a "sample" because a sample is drawn from the bulk of goods that is the subject matter of the sale, and a model is not. See Comment 6 to §2-313.) Since Retailer bought in reliance on the appearance of the model dress, that model was "part of the basis of the bargain," and Dress Co. therefore will be held to have expressly warranted to Retailer that the delivered goods would match the model.

(b) Retailer's chances of winning are good. **According to §2-313(1)(c), "Any sample or model which is made part of the basis of the bargain creates an express warranty that the whole of the goods shall conform to the sample or model."** Since the deviations here between the model and the delivered goods were apparently substantial, the court will probably find that the express warranty was breached. There is therefore a very good chance that Retailer will be able to recover damages for that breach of express warranty. (The amount of damages will depend on the extent to which the court becomes convinced that the dresses failed to sell because of the deviation from the model, rather than for other reasons, such as Retailer's poor merchandising skills.)

238. Yes, a claim for breach of the implied warranty of fitness for a particular purpose. **According to UCC §2-315, "Where the seller at the time of contracting has reason to know any particular purpose for which the goods are required and that the buyer is relying on the seller's skill or judgment to select or furnish suitable goods, there is unless excluded or modified . . . an implied warranty that the goods shall be fit for such purpose."** Here, Computer Co. knew that Law Firm planned to use the BestWord product on whatever system it bought. Computer Co. also knew that Law Firm was relying in part on Computer Co.'s recommendation of a suitable model. Therefore, even though Computer Co. never expressly warranted that the BestWord package would run on the Model 431 computer, the sale contained an implied warranty that this special purpose or need of Law Firm's would be satisfied. This is so even though the computer may have been perfectly merchantable despite its inability to run the BestWord product.

239. Probably not. **According to UCC §2-315, "Where the seller at the time of contracting has reason to know any particular purpose for which the goods are required and that the buyer is relying on the seller's skill or judgment to select or furnish suitable goods, there is unless excluded or modified . . . an implied warranty that the goods shall be fit for such purpose."** Law Firm's insistence on a particular brand or model number strongly suggests that, in contrast to the prior question, here Law Firm was not "relying on the seller's skill or judgment to select or furnish suitable goods." In the absence of such reliance, no implied warranty of fitness for a particular purpose comes into play. Observe that the mere fact that it is the buyer who has mentioned a particular brand name does not by itself nullify the implied warranty of fitness for particular purpose. For instance, if Law Firm had said to Computer Co., "Would your Model 431 be suitable to run the BestWord word processing package?" and had Computer Co. avoided answering the question and let Law Firm buy the computer, there would probably have been an implied warranty of fitness for a particular purpose. But on the stated facts, Law Firm has actually insisted on the Model 431, and seemed not to be relying on the seller's judgment at all.

240. Yes. **The implied warranty of merchantability comes into effect under UCC §2-314, unless effectively excluded under §2-316. According to §2-316(2), "To exclude or modify the implied warranty of merchantability or any part of it the language must *mention merchantability* and in case of a writing must be conspicuous."** The disclaimer here met the requirement of conspicuousness, but since it did not mention merchantability, it is not effective to disclaim the warranty of merchantability. Therefore, Manufacturer gets the benefit of the implied warranty of merchantability, and will be able to recover for the clear breach of that warranty. (Since the drill press did not perform in the way that drill presses usually do, it failed to be merchantable under §2-314(2)(c)'s requirement that a merchantable product be "fit for the ordinary purposes for which such goods are used.")

241. No, Farmer will probably not prevail on either theory. **According to UCC §2-316(3)(a), "Unless the circumstances indicate otherwise, all implied warranties are excluded by expressions like 'as is,' 'with all faults' or other language which in common understanding calls the buyer's attention to the exclusion of warranties and makes plain that there is no implied warranty."** There is some chance that Farmer could prove that "the circumstances indicate otherwise." But the court is likely to conclude that the fact that the equipment was clearly used, the fact that there are frequently (probably usually) no implied warranties on used goods, and the fact that Farmer was a business buyer, all lead to the conclusion that the usual meaning of "as is"—that the buyer takes the risk—is applicable here.

242. Probably not. **Under UCC §2-316(3)(b), "When the buyer before entering into the contract has examined the goods . . . as fully as he desired . . . there is no implied warranty with regards to defects which an examination ought in the circumstances to have revealed to him."** Since Bob conducted the examination (and Steve did not restrict the scope of this examination), Bob will be held to be on notice of a defect that one in his position ought to have noticed, whether or not Bob in fact noticed it. Since a professional car buyer taking a test-drive would normally have driven in reverse and thus discovered the problem, Bob will be charged with knowledge of that problem, and there will be no implied warranty of merchantability with respect to that problem.

243. Unclear. **Under UCC §2-719(1)(a), a sale agreement "may limit or alter the measure of damages recoverable under this Article, as by limiting the buyer's remedies to return of the goods and repayment of the price or to repair and replacement of non-conforming goods or parts."** Based solely on this sentence, it would seem that limiting the buyer's remedies to repair or replacement would be enforceable, and that Consumer would be out of luck. However, §2-719(2) says that "where circumstances cause an exclusive or limited remedy to fail of its essential purpose, remedy may be had as provided in this Act." Consumer can make a plausible argument that the purpose of the repair-or-replacement remedy is to give Consumer, at least eventually, a car that is in the condition it was warranted to be in (i.e., a properly working car with an appropriate value). Here, Consumer can argue, this remedy has failed of its essential purpose, since Consumer has been denied use of the car for an unreasonably long time, and since there is reason to believe that the car is simply a "lemon" that will never really be made right. (Some states have passed so-called lemon laws giving car-buying consumers a right to return the car to the manufacturer for a refund, so the above analysis would only be needed if there was no lemon law or if the lemon law's terms were not satisfied.)

244. **Yes. An executor accord is an agreement by the parties to a contract by which one promises to render a substitute performance in the future, and the other promises to accept that substitute performance in discharge of the existing duty. See Rest. 2d, §281.** Since Diane's debt was undisputed, completely clear in amount, and already due, a court would almost certainly conclude that all that happened here was an *executory accord*, by which Pia would be obliged to take the ring instead of the debt only if Diane delivered the ring as agreed upon. When Diane failed to deliver the ring for a month and the market for jade collapsed, Diane's breach was a material one that relieved Pia of her obligation to take the ring in satisfaction of the debt. Therefore, Pia was restored to her original position as one entitled to receive $1,000. (Alternatively, Pia could have insisted on the ring or on damages for Diane's failure to deliver the ring—because the agreement was an accord, it was up to Pia to decide whether to sue for the $1,000 or the ring.)

245. **No. The parties are always free to agree to rescind their arrangement. So long as they discharge all of each person's remaining duties, the agreement does not have to be in writing, even if the original agreement says that any rescission must be in writing. See Rest. 2d, §283, Comment b.** (But if the oral agreement had merely been to modify rather than rescind the agreement, the clause in the original contract requiring a writing for any modification would have been enforced—thus a promise by Sam to take a lesser salary, or to extend the term of the contract, would not have been binding against him unless he signed that promise. Also, if the contract had been for the sale of goods rather than services, even a complete rescission would have had to be in writing—see UCC §2-209(2), stating that "a signed agreement which excludes modification *or rescission* except by a signed writing cannot be otherwise modified or rescinded.")

246. (a) **Yes. If a debtor holds a bill summarizing several transactions between the debtor and a creditor for an unreasonably long time without objecting to its contents, the creditor will be able to use the bill as the basis for a suit on an "account stated." See Rest. 2d, §282.** Storekeeper's sending of the statement, and Consumer's resulting silence, gave rise to an *"account stated."* This account stated was the equivalent of an *admission* by Consumer that there was a contract between Storekeeper and himself for $456, the amount shown. In the absence of any evidence by Consumer that the transactions did not really happen as shown on the statement, Consumer will be liable (even though Storekeeper does not produce direct evidence that the merchandise was actually sold).

(b) **No. Although Consumer's failure to respond in a timely manner to the statement will be treated as an admission by him, this admission is not binding—Consumer is still free to show, by independent evidence, that the computation was a mistake. See Rest. 2d, §282.** If Consumer does so, he will not be bound by the account (unless Storekeeper has relied to his detriment on Consumer's silence and the court applies promissory estoppel, or the state is one of the minority states that treats Consumer's silence as a promise to pay an antecedent debt, enforceable without consideration and without a writing).

Contracts Essay Questions

QUESTION 1:   Mary Frances wanted to restore her old Volkswagen. Her Uncle Daniel, who was a mechanic, came over on May 1 to visit, so she asked him how much he thought it would cost. He responded, "I could do it for between one and two thousand, but I don't know if I really have the time." That night, Mary Frances decided to hire Daniel. The next morning, May 2, she drove over to Daniel's house. Since neither he nor her aunt were home, Mary Frances left a note in the mailbox. The note said: "I will pay you $1,800 to fix up my car—just come on by to work on it. Love, Mary Frances." Daniel found the note and tried to call Mary Frances, but she wasn't home. He then went over to Acme Car Supplies and bought $100 worth of auto supplies that he could use for the job. The next day, May 3, Jimmy, another mechanic, drove by Mary Frances's house and saw the car. He told her he loved Volkswagens and would fix it "as good as new" for $1,500. Jimmy and Mary Frances signed a contract. That afternoon, Daniel came by to start the job. Before he could even open his car door, Mary Frances ran out onto the lawn and said, "I'm sorry, Uncle Dan. I already hired someone else to fix up my car." Daniel comes to you for advice. Assume the Statute of Frauds is not an issue.

QUESTION 2:   Job, who owned a bar, was a big sports fan and wanted to start a minor league hockey team in his town. To get funds for his new venture, he entered into a written agreement with Matt to sell his bar. Matt signed the agreement, but the sale was expressly conditioned on Matt obtaining a lease agreement for the nearby parking lot within three weeks. Job then contacted Kerry about buying her land, believing it to be a great place to set up an arena. Kerry was so excited that she immediately agreed to the sale and shook hands with Job, saying, "Since we're friends, we just need to shake on it!" That afternoon, she went out and signed a contract for a new house. Job then contacted Biz about making T-shirts and other merchandise for the team. Biz immediately signed a long-term contract and went out and bought new and expensive printing equipment. Finally, Job signed an agreement with Thunderbolt Lightning, a local hockey star, to be his announcer and "the voice of the team." Job figured Thunderbolt's enduring popularity would really help publicize the team. However, the next week, Thunderbolt called and said he couldn't be the announcer because he'd permanently lost his voice in an accident. At the same time, Matt called and said he had not been able to get the lease for the parking lot within the three-week period and the deal was off. However, he then admitted he'd never called the owners of the parking lot in the first place. Job, suddenly fed up with the situation, called Kerry and Biz and told them the deals were off. Biz panicked and pleaded with Job, saying she was desperate because of her gambling debts. Job then offered her a small cash settlement in exchange for her release of the contract. Biz signed the release. Job comes to you for advice regarding his rights and liabilities.

QUESTION 3:   Hannah is a famous reality television personality. She makes an agreement with Andy, a businessman, whereby Andy has the right to place Hannah's endorsement on fashion designs. Hannah agrees that Andy will be the only person to have this right, and Andy agrees to give Hannah one-half of any profits derived from the sale of such endorsed designs. Morgan, a traveling salesman for Andy, is 65 and has worked for Andy for 25 years. Believing that Hannah's endorsement will greatly increase sales, Andy suggests that Morgan retire, and tells Morgan that if he does so, he will pay Morgan a $20,000-per-year pension for the rest of Morgan's life. Morgan retires. The day after he does so, Morgan suffers a stroke that completely and permanently paralyzes him.

At the same time, Andy contracts to buy Willow Mall. Andy wants to line up a tenant so he can get bank financing to complete the mall purchase. Andy solicits and signs a letter of intent from Better, a large home improvement store, relating to a lease by Better of a store in the mall. The letter of intent provides that Andy will withdraw the store from the rental market, and that the parties will negotiate a lease. Andy goes to the bank and gets the financing. Better develops a marketing plan for the store and otherwise makes preparations to lease. Just before the lease is to be signed, Andy gets a better offer for the space from Best, one of Better's competitors. Andy calls Better and says the deal is off, and then leases the space to Best.

Feeling a bit nervous about a potential lawsuit from Better, Andy decides he needs a good television campaign for the new line of Hannah fashion designs (so he can increase his war chest if he has to fight Better in court). He decides to run a campaign in which one can obtain "Hannah points" for buying the endorsed clothing. The points add up to prizes, such as notebook computers and cash. Andy has a television ad made where a girl is shown with all the prizes she has collected through "Hannah points," including a famously handsome actor she won for 5,000,000 Hannah points and keeps in her room. A day after the ad comes out, Andy sees Hannah's endorsement on a third party's designs. Andy calls up Hannah, who says, "Hey, you never agreed to do anything, so I can do what I want! I went to law school, and I know you need consideration to enforce a contract!" The day after that, Pinkie, a girl who has collected 5,000,000 Hannah points, contacts Andy and demands the famously handsome actor. The day after that, Andy decides to stop paying Morgan's pension. Morgan calls up Andy and threatens to sue. The day after that, Better sends over notice of its lawsuit regarding the rental space. Andy comes to you for advice.

QUESTION 4:   George, despondent over the death of his dog, Mr. Barkypants, hires Washington to paint a portrait of the dog. The parties sign a contract agreeing that if the portrait is not completely satisfactory to George, he does not have to take it or pay for it. Alison, George's niece, calls up. Hearing how despondent George is, she asks if there is anything she can do to help. George (who is quite wealthy) states that if she names her day-old son "Mr. Barkypants," he will give the boy $20,000 on his 18th birthday. Alison agrees. A little less than a year later, Washington returns with the painting. George hates it and immediately tells Washington that he will not pay for it and that Washington has to take it back. Washington does so, and shows it to his friends at Famous Art Museum. They are overwhelmed by its beauty and pathos, and immediately hang it in the Museum's Great Hall. At the same time, Alison is facing some financial difficulties. She decides to sell her beloved harpsichord. Larry, a music lover, comes by her house and makes an offer of $2,000. She tells him she will accept no less than $4,000. Larry asks Alison if he can think it over for a while, and she agrees to give him a week. The next day, Harry comes to the house and buys the harpsichord for $5,000. Larry comes by later that afternoon with $4,000. Alison tells him, "Too bad—I just sold it!" Alison then calls up George and asks him if he would go ahead and give her the $20,000 owed to her son, as she doesn't think the $5,000 she got for the harpsichord is enough to help pay her bills for the next few months. George agrees to send her the money. What are the rights and liabilities of the parties?

QUESTION 5:   Melville, a manufacturer of diving equipment, used material produced and supplied by Toasty to insulate its diving suits. Melville would buy the material by sending a standard-form purchase order to Toasty. The form included an arbitration provision providing that a neutral arbitrator would settle any disagreement. In response to any order from Melville, Toasty would send an invoice stating that "any order is expressly conditioned on Buyer's assent to any conflicting terms in this invoice." Toasty would then send the material a few days later. There was no arbitration provision in Toasty's invoice. However, both the form and the invoice provided that "any modification or rescission has to be done in a writing signed by both parties." In 2010, Melville sent Toasty a purchase order, and Toasty responded with an invoice. Melville then called Toasty and told him he thought quality was going way down and he thought they had to go to arbitration to discuss problems with the past few orders. Toasty refused, saying he wanted to "fight it out in court." Toasty then says, "You know what? I rescind my agreement on this last bunch! I'm not sending you anything!" Melville had to fill a big order for the navy, and quality problems or not, he wanted the insulation from Toasty. However, Melville had never gotten anything in writing from the navy (he merely talked to the officer in charge of buying dive suits over the phone), and he has already made 200 dive suits for $500 a piece that say "U.S. NAVY" and are only suitable for sale to the navy (the suits' construction makes them incredibly impractical for civilian divers). He's now afraid that the navy might hear about Toasty rescinding the agreement and simply claim that they don't have to buy the suits because Melville never got anything in writing from them. Melville comes to you for advice.

Sample Answers to Contracts Essay Questions

ANSWER TO QUESTION 1:

Offer on May 1

The issue is whether the May 1 discussion was an offer for a contract or merely preliminary negotiations. **Normally, for a contract to come into existence, there must be an offer and an acceptance. An offer is a statement or act that creates a power of acceptance. Importantly, a party desiring to contract may make a statement that is not an offer, but rather a solicitation of bids. The test is whether a person in the offeree's shoes would reasonably have understood that the offeror was merely seeking to invite bids or start preliminary negotiations.** Here, Daniel's statement regarding how much he would charge for the job would reasonably be understood as merely preliminary negotiations. Importantly, he simply made an estimate of what he thought the job would cost, and stated he wasn't sure whether he had the time to do it. Consequently, no offer was made on May 1.

Offer on May 2

The issue is whether the note on May 2 was an offer. **An offer is a statement or act that creates a "power of acceptance." When a person makes an offer, he or she is indicating that he or she is willing to be immediately bound by the person's acceptance without further negotiation.** Here, Mary Frances's note ("I will pay you $1,800 to fix up my car—just come on by to work on it. Love, Mary Frances") evinces a clear intention to be bound without further negotiation. Consequently, her note was an offer.

Acceptance on May 2

Whether Daniel accepted the offer depends on whether this was an offer for a unilateral or bilateral contract. **If the offer created a unilateral contract, it could only be accepted by performance of the act requested. If the offer created a bilateral contract, it could be accepted by words or by actions if these actions fairly indicate to the offeror that the offeree intends to enter into the contract. Importantly, if it is unclear whether an offer seeks a unilateral or bilateral contract, the offer is interpreted as inviting the offeree to accept either by promising to perform what the offer requests or by rendering the performance, as the offeree chooses. Also, when accepting a bilateral contract by performance, courts look to whether the offeree's actions actually constituted the beginning of the performance.** Here, it seems more likely that this was an offer for a bilateral contract, as Mary Frances did not clearly state that Daniel could accept only by performance. Daniel first tried to accept by calling Mary Frances. When she was not home, he then went to the store to buy supplies. However, his actions in going to the store did not fairly indicate to Mary Frances that he intended to enter into the contract, since Mary Frances was unaware that he went to the store. Also, going to the store to buy $100 worth of auto supplies seems to be mere preparation for performance, not the requested performance itself. Importantly, there is no indication Daniel's purchases were unique in any way for Mary Frances's job. Consequently, it seems that Daniel did not validly accept the offer.

Did Mary Frances Revoke?

Mary Frances could also argue that she revoked the offer before Daniel had the chance to accept it. **The offeror is free to revoke his or her offer at any time before it is accepted. However, a revocation by the offeror does not become effective until it is received by the offeree.** Here, Mary Frances did not try to revoke her offer until Daniel came to her house to do the work. However, the question again revolves around whether Daniel validly accepted the offer. Since Daniel's actions in going to the store did not communicate to Mary Frances that he intended to accept, it is unlikely that a court would find that his actions in going to the store resulted in a valid acceptance. In addition, as stated above, it seems his actions in going to the store, did not constitute the beginning of the requested performance. Finally, the mere fact that he showed up for the job at Mary Frances's house (where he apparently went often enough that he was there to give advice in the first place) was likely not enough to constitute acceptance before he was informed of her revocation of the offer. Consequently, Mary Frances's revocation was likely effective.

Could Agreement Be Enforced Through Promissory Estoppel?

Finally, Daniel could try to enforce this through promissory estoppel. **A promise that the promisor should reasonably expect to induce action or forbearance on the part of the promisee or a third person and that does induce such action or forbearance is binding if injustice can be avoided only by enforcement of the promise.** Here, Daniel could argue that Mary Frances should have known that her offer would have induced him to begin work on the job. However, as stated above, his actions in going to the store or coming to her house to do the job do not appear to be the type of actions where injustice can be avoided only by enforcement of the promise (he does not seem to be out of a significant amount of money or time). Consequently, a court is unlikely to find promissory estoppel applies.

ANSWER TO QUESTION 2:

Job v. Matt

The issue is whether Job is required to return the deposit to Matt. **If a contract is subject to a condition subsequent, the contract is discharged if that condition subsequent fails to occur. However, every contract carries with it an obligation that the parties act in good faith in performing their obligations under it.** Here, the contract specifically stated the condition subsequent of Matt obtaining the lease for the parking lot within three weeks. However, Matt was required to act in good faith to satisfy that condition subsequent. Matt's failure to even contact the owners of the parking lot constitutes bad faith, which will prevent Matt from relying on the condition subsequent to terminate the contract. Job is entitled to damages in the amount of the difference between the contract price for the sale of the bar and its actual value at the time of the breach.

Job v. Kerry

The issue is whether there was a valid agreement between Job and Kerry. **An agreement to purchase land is unenforceable under the Statute of Frauds unless there is a writing signed by the party to be charged.** Here, the agreement between Job and Kerry is unenforceable, because they merely shook hands on the agreement and did not put any of it in writing. Additionally, she would not be able to recover any reliance damages she incurred by agreeing to buy a new house, because that agreement (to buy a home for herself) did not confer any benefit to Job.

Job v. Biz

The issue here is whether Job's contract breach was excused by Biz's signing of the release. **An executory accord is an agreement by the parties to a contract by which one promises to render a substitute performance in the future, and the other promises to accept that substitute performance in discharge of the existing duty. However, duress can void the agreement.** Here, Job and Biz agreed to an accord and satisfaction when Biz signed the release and took the cash payment from Job. While Biz agreed to the settlement under duress, that duress was not caused by any of Job's actions. Consequently, it is likely that a court will find the agreement valid, and Job's duties under it discharged.

Job v. Lightning

The issue is whether Lightning is in breach of contract with Job for not being the announcer for the team. **If a person is injured so that it is impossible for him or her to perform his or her contractual obligations, the contract is terminated and neither party has a cause of action against the other person for breach.** Here, Job and Lightning entered into a contract under which Lightning would perform personal and specialized services for Job's hockey team. When he permanently lost his voice, Lightning was no longer able to perform the required services. Therefore, under the doctrine of impossibility, the contract is terminated.

ANSWER TO QUESTION 3:

Andy v. Hannah

The issue is whether the agreement is enforceable even though, as Hannah claims, there was no consideration for the agreement since Andy did not bind himself to do anything. **An implied promise in a contract can be a sufficient detriment to constitute consideration.** Here, in signing the contract, Andy impliedly promised to use "reasonable efforts" to market Hannah's designs. The implied promise is a sufficient detriment to Andy to constitute consideration for Hannah's counterpromise that she would not place her endorsement upon anyone else's designs. Therefore, the contract is binding, and Hannah has breached it.

Morgan v. Andy

The issue is whether Andy is liable for Morgan's reliance on his promise. **Under the doctrine of promissory estoppel, a promise that the promisor should reasonably expect to induce action or forbearance on the part of the promisee or a third person and that does induce such action or forbearance is binding if injustice can be avoided only by enforcement of that promise. However, for promissory estoppel to apply, the promisee must actually rely on the promise.** Here, Morgan will probably not be able to use the promissory estoppel doctrine to recover on the promise of the pension. The reason is that Morgan has not significantly relied on the promise to his detriment—even without the promise, he still would have been forced to stop working as a traveling salesman because of his illness. Consequently, Andy is not liable for Morgan's reliance.

Better v. Andy

The issue here is whether the letter of intent was binding on Andy. **The letter of intent was not binding as a lease or as an agreement to enter into a lease. But it was binding as an obligation on both parties to negotiate in good faith.** The letter of intent was supported by consideration because Better's signature on the letter helped Andy get financing to acquire the mall. When Andy put the store back on the market and leased it to Best without ever pursuing the Better negotiations to completion, he violated his contractual obligation of good faith. Consequently, a court may find him liable to Better.

Pinkie v. Andy

The issue here is whether the television advertisement showing the handsome actor for Hannah points created an enforceable contract. **An offer that the offeree knows or should know is made in jest is not a valid offer, and even if it is purportedly accepted, no contract is created.** Here, Pinkie should have known that no matter how many Hannah points she collected, it was clearly a joke that she would then win the handsome actor and be able to keep him locked in her room. Consequently, she cannot claim any contract rights in the advertisement.

ANSWER TO QUESTION 4:

Washington v. George

The issue is whether George's personal dislike of the painting was enough to terminate the agreement. **A contract may make one party's duty to perform expressly conditional on that party's being satisfied with the other's performance. Importantly, when the object of a contract is to please the tastes of a person, on a matter for which there is no real objective standard (like art), courts will look at whether the person's own satisfaction was fulfilled.** It may be that the picture was an excellent one (Famous Art Museum seems to think so) and that George should have been satisfied with it, but under the agreement between him and Washington, his satisfaction was the only standard that mattered. Consequently, even though the painting itself was of fine quality, George was not required to accept it.

Larry v. Alison

The issue is whether Larry can hold Alison liable for her failure to sell him the harpsichord. **The UCC applies to the sale of goods for more than $500. Under UCC §2-205, an offer for the sale of goods is revocable at any time before acceptance unless it is supported by consideration or a merchant's offer in writing.** Here, the harpsichord is a good and not a service, so its sale is covered by the rules of the UCC. Alison made a counteroffer when she said she would not accept less than $4,000. Since Alison is not a merchant and the offer was not in writing, it was revocable at any time. When she told Larry she had already sold the harpsichord, she effectively revoked her offer, and he could no longer accept it even though she had said she would give him time to think about the purchase.

Mr. Barkypants v. Alison

The issue is whether Mr. Barkypants has rights against his mother for the $20,000. **A third-party beneficiary contract is created when two parties form a contract, the main purpose of which is to benefit a third person. An intended third-party beneficiary has a right to sue on the contract. For a third party to be an intended beneficiary, it must be the case that giving him or her the right to sue would be appropriate to effectuate the intentions of the parties. However, the original parties to the contract can rescind the contract and relieve one party's obligation to perform for the third party's benefit so long as the third party has not relied on the contract with knowledge of it.** Mr. Barkypants is the intended third-party beneficiary of this contract since Alison made the agreement in order to have George pay him the $20,000. Alison gave consideration by naming her child according to George's wishes, and Mr. Barkypants then had the right to $20,000. However, since Mr. Barkypants is still a toddler, there was no way he could have known of or relied on the contract. Consequently, his rights were terminated when George gave the money to Alison, and he has no right to recover the money from his mother.

Mr. Barkypants v. George

For the same reasons as above, Mr. Barkypants had a right as an intended third-party beneficiary to the $20,000. **However, the original parties rescinded the contract before Mr. Barkypants could have known of or relied on it.** Consequently, George is unlikely to be liable to Mr. Barkypants.

ANSWER TO QUESTION 5:

Arbitration

The issue is whether the arbitration clause is part of the contract. **Since this is a contract between merchants for the sale of goods over $500, the transaction is governed by the UCC. Under UCC §2-207, a definite and seasonable expression of acceptance or a written confirmation that is sent within a reasonable time operates as an acceptance even though it states terms additional to or different from those offered or agreed upon, unless acceptance is expressly made conditional on assent to the additional or different terms. The additional terms are to be construed as proposals for an addition to the contract. Between merchants, such terms become part of the contract unless (a) the offer expressly limits acceptance to the terms of the offer, (b) they materially alter it, or (c) notification of objection to them is given within a reasonable time after notice of them is received.** Here, both Melville and Toasty are merchants. By ordering and shipping material, Melville and Toasty entered into an enforceable contract for the sale of the insulation material. However, it is unlikely a court would find that the arbitration clause was part of the contract because Toasty specifically rejected it in the terms and conditions in his invoice by stating that "any order is expressly conditioned on Buyer's assent to any conflicting terms in this invoice," and that invoice failed to include an arbitration clause. Consequently, Melville will likely be unsuccessful in any attempt to force Toasty to arbitration.

Rescission

The issue is whether Toasty's oral rescission was valid. **Under UCC §2-209(2), an agreement that excludes modification or rescission except by a signed writing cannot otherwise be modified or rescinded.** Here, the no oral rescission clause is part of both forms, and thus part of the contract. Consequently, Toasty cannot rescind based simply on his telephone conversation with Melville.

Oral Contract with the Navy

The issue is whether the navy can get out of the agreement with Melville by claiming that there was no written agreement. **Under the UCC §2-201(3)(a), no writing is required "if the goods are to be specially manufactured for the buyer and are not suitable for sale to others in the ordinary course of the seller's business and the seller, before notice of repudiation is received and under circumstances which reasonably indicate that the goods are for the buyer, has made either a substantial beginning of their manufacture or commitments for their procurement." The reason is that the seller is highly unlikely to start producing custom-made goods for the buyer unless there has in fact been an oral contract.** If the navy tries to repudiate the contract, a court will likely hold the contract enforceable because the custom dive suits constituted a special manufacture of goods that are not suitable for sale to others (they say U.S. NAVY and are too impractical for regular divers) and, by making 200 of them, Melville has made a substantial beginning in the goods' manufacture.

CRIMINAL LAW

Criminal Law Table of Contents

ACTUS REUS AND MENS REA

CAUSATION

RESPONSIBILITY

JUSTIFICATION AND EXCUSE

ACCOMPLICE LIABILITY AND SOLICITATION

HOMICIDE AND OTHER CRIMES AGAINST THE PERSON

THEFT CRIMES

Criminal Law Short-Answer Questions

1. Nelson had always been intrigued by the outer limits of human ability. Having already run several marathons and completed two triathlons, Nelson decided to join the Polar Bear Society. This was an organization that takes a yearly swim in the ocean when the outside temperature is below freezing. Nelson took his first swim on January 2, and promptly sank as soon as he entered the deep water. Richie, who was a veteran Polar Bear, immediately dove in to rescue Nelson. Meanwhile, Nelson, due to the shock of almost drowning as well as the extremely cold temperatures, lost voluntary control of his limbs and started thrashing uncontrollably. As soon as Richie got near, Nelson (without consciously realizing what he was doing) wrapped his arms around Richie's neck and choked him. Richie lost consciousness and drowned. Another member of the Polar Bears rescued Nelson. May Nelson be held criminally liable for the death of Richie?

Not sure ☐

2. Same facts as in the previous question. Now, however, suppose that Peter, who was not affiliated with the Polar Bears, was watching Richie's attempt to rescue Nelson from ten feet away. Peter was a well-trained former lifeguard who could easily have rescued Richie without danger to himself once Nelson had released Richie. However, Peter intensely disliked Richie from a prior acquaintanceship (he thought Richie was unbearably macho and arrogant), so Peter declined to intervene or even to call for help. Had Peter called for help, it is very likely that another member of the Polar Bears would have jumped into the water in time to rescue Richie. May Peter be held criminally liable for the death of Richie?

Not sure ☐

3. Same facts as in the previous question. Now, suppose that the entire episode came about in part because Peter had talked Nelson into joining the Polar Bears and into jumping in the ocean that fateful day. (Based on Peter's knowledge of Nelson's swimming ability and level of conditioning, Peter was not negligent in persuading Nelson to participate, and Peter did not wish Nelson to come to any harm.) May Peter be held criminally liable for the death of Richie?

Not sure ☐

4. Paul and Jim were motorists in the State of Ames. The two approached an empty parking spot at the same time. After each yelled at the other about who was entitled to the spot, Paul left his car and walked over to Jim's car. Paul pulled a screwdriver from his pocket and touched it to Jim's throat, hoping that the touch would scare Jim away. In fact, however, Jim reacted by twisting his head, and in so doing, cut himself severely against the blade of the screwdriver. Paul did not intend to physically injure Jim. The State of Ames defines the crime of assault as occurring where one "purposely causes bodily injury to another." A decision of the Ames Supreme Court states that assault is a crime that requires "general intent." May Paul properly be found guilty of assault?

Not sure ☐

5. The City of Los Diablos was plagued with a series of frightening episodes in which motorists used explosives to blow each other up. To combat this problem, the city enacted a new statute, making "explosive murder" a crime. The statute provided

that any motorist who "purposely" killed another motorist with any explosive would be guilty and could be punished by death. (The jurisdiction follows the Model Penal Code's definition of the term "purposely.")

Dean, an explosives expert, was cut off by Marie on the highway during rush hour one day. In a rage, Dean stayed behind Marie until she came to a dead stop in traffic. Dean pulled his car off the road, walked to Marie's car, and threw enough dynamite inside to blow up Marie's car and any cars around Marie's car. Marie and two other motorists in adjacent cars, Fred and Lona, were killed. Dean desired to kill Marie, but did not desire to kill Fred or Lona (though as an expert he knew that they were practically certain to be killed, so strong was the explosive). The state now prosecutes Dean for three counts of "explosive murder." Of how many counts of explosive murder (none, one, two, or three) will Dean be convicted?

Not sure ☐

6. Same facts as the previous question. Now, however, assume that the statute defining "explosive murder" covers any motorist who "purposely or knowingly" kills another motorist with an explosive. Also, suppose the following: (1) Dean knew that Fred would almost certainly be killed by the explosion (though he did not affirmatively desire that Fred be killed); and (2) Dean was unaware that Lona would be killed but, as an explosive expert, should have known that Lona was almost certain to be killed by the explosion. The jurisdiction applies the Model Penal Code's definition of "knowingly."

(a) Can Dean be convicted of the explosive murder of Fred?

Not sure ☐

(b) Can Dean be convicted of the explosive murder of Lona?

Not sure ☐

7. The State of Langdell makes it the crime of "indecent exposure," a misdemeanor punishable by up to one year in prison, for a person "to expose his genitals in any public place." The statutory definition does not specifically mention any mental state as being required for the crime. Dennis was arrested while walking in front of the courthouse with a portion of his genitals clearly visible through a hole in his blue jeans. The case is being tried before a judge. Dennis concedes that the above facts are accurate but proves (to the satisfaction of the judge) that he, Dennis, was unaware that his pants were ripped and therefore unaware that his genitals were showing. In a jurisdiction following the Model Penal Code's approach to relevant matters, may Dennis be convicted of the crime of indecent exposure?

Not sure ☐

8. Harry and Bill, who did not know each other, met on the street one day and began to talk. Harry told Bill that he was late for an appointment in the building they were standing near and that he would pay Bill $250 to do him a favor. Harry explained that he had borrowed his friend's red Porsche and parked it down the street, but had lost the keys. Having learned that Bill was an auto mechanic, Harry asked Bill to break into the Porsche, hot-wire it, and deliver it to an address that Harry scribbled on a piece of paper. Bill accepted the offer and carried it out. The story later turned out to be false—in fact, the Porsche belonged to a stranger, and Harry was really a thief who had duped Bill into delivering the car to Harry's fence. Bill was charged with auto theft, defined in the jurisdiction as "knowingly or purposefully taking a vehicle belonging to another." The case is tried before a judge, who finds that Bill actually believed Harry's story, but that a "reasonable person" would

not have believed the story. If the state follows the Model Penal Code approach to mistake, can Bill be convicted?

Not sure ☐

9. Same basic facts as the previous question. Now, assume that (1) Bill not only actually but also reasonably believed Harry's story; (2) it is a crime to hot-wire a vehicle (i.e., to enter it without keys and to start it and drive it away without keys), even with the owner's consent; (3) Bill was unaware that hot-wiring was a crime; and (4) most adults in the jurisdiction do not know that hot-wiring is a crime, although the crime is part of the jurisdiction's criminal penal code, which can be found in any library. Can Bill properly be convicted of the crime of hot-wiring?

Not sure ☐

10. Cliff had been Hilda's personal servant for two years. Over those years, Cliff had developed an intense hatred for Hilda. Therefore, he concocted a plot to murder her: Each morning, Cliff had always walked into Hilda's room to deliver her morning paper. This time, he entered the room intending to place a lethal dose of cyanide in her coffee. However, while reaching into his pocket for the cyanide, Cliff accidentally knocked over the entire pot of boiling coffee onto Hilda. Hilda died two months later from complications relating directly to the burns she suffered from the spill. (It is not unusual for a person to die of burns of the seriousness usually found when boiling coffee is massively spilled on the body.) May Cliff be convicted of murder?

Not sure ☐

11. Desmond attempted to burglarize an apartment of which Virginia was the sole resident. (The jurisdiction defines burglary as "entry of a building with a purpose to commit a crime therein, unless the defendant is privileged to enter therein.") His plan was to take whatever jewelry or cash he could find. In his attempt to enter the locked apartment, Desmond used a crowbar. Not only was he unsuccessful in prying the door open, but he also destroyed the locking mechanism. He then abandoned his burglary attempt.

   Meanwhile, Virginia, who heard the noise, tried to leave her apartment by the front door, which was the only exit from the apartment. Desmond had so jammed the lock that Virginia was unable to get out for five hours, until police finally broke down her door. The jurisdiction defines kidnapping, in part, as "the intentional and unlawful . . . confinement of another for a substantial period in a place of isolation." Assuming that the ordinary common law approach to intent applies, and assuming that the "confinement," "substantial period," and "place of isolation" elements are satisfied, may Desmond be convicted of kidnapping?

Not sure ☐

12. Rena and Clare, who were strangers to each other, each spotted a taxicab in the city of Gotham at the same time. They both grabbed the door handle at once, and then began to argue over who should take the cab. Clare kicked Rena on the knee-cap. Clare's intent was to kick Rena lightly. However, Rena had just undergone knee surgery, and the kick did permanent damage to her knee. The state in which Gotham is located has two degrees of battery, simple and aggravated. Simple battery is defined as "the intentional causing of minor bodily harm." Aggravated battery is defined as "the intentional causing of serious or permanent bodily harm." May Clare be convicted of aggravated battery?

Not sure ☐

13. Cinderella had been tortured for many years by her wicked and ugly stepmother, Gretchen. Finally, Cinderella decided to end the problem by poisoning Gretchen's

soup. Cinderella put three milligrams of cyanide into a one-cup serving of Campbell's Hearty Beef Noodle. This was a sufficiently large dose that anyone who drank the entire cup, even a 300-pound football player, would have been 99.5 percent certain to die. Gretchen drank the entire cup, and then lapsed into unconsciousness. While Gretchen was unconscious but two or so hours away from death, Prince, Cinderella's lover, happened to walk into the kitchen and saw Gretchen with her head on the table as if she were sleeping. Prince had been planning and hoping for years for a way to free Cinderella from her bondage, so he quickly acted. He grabbed a cleaver from the knife rack and began to slash at Gretchen's neck. Just then, Alfred, Gretchen's faithful butler, appeared and tackled Prince after Prince had only produced a fairly minor stab wound. The wound would not have been fatal if Gretchen had not been in a seriously weakened condition. However, she was in a very weakened condition, and she therefore died of shock within 20 minutes (about an hour and a half earlier than she probably would have died from the poison alone). Assuming that Prince satisfies the intent requirements for murder, may he be convicted of murder?   Not sure ☐

14. Same basic fact pattern as in the previous question. Now, however, assume that Cinderella put only a small dose of cyanide in Gretchen's soup, and that Prince never came on the scene. Gretchen lapsed into a coma, but one that was not immediately life threatening. She was then hospitalized, where she remained for the next 14 months. As a result of a general weakening of her respiratory organs brought on by the cyanide, and also as a result of the fact that respirators had not yet been invented, Gretchen finally died of lung disease a little less than 15 months after the poisoning. The jurisdiction follows the common law approach to relevant matters. May Cinderella be convicted of murder?   Not sure ☐

15. Horton was a vigilante and a member of the Ku Klux Klan. He wanted to burn down a townhouse belonging to Frank, whom Horton considered to be a dangerous "bleeding-heart liberal." Therefore, Horton attempted to throw a lighted torch through the open window of the townhouse. Because of Horton's bad aim, the torch instead went into the open window of the next-door townhouse, belonging to Ben. Ben's unit was completely destroyed, but Frank's was unscathed. The jurisdiction defines arson, in part, as "the intentional destruction of a building or occupied structure of another by fire or explosion." May Horton be convicted of the destruction by arson of Ben's townhouse?   Not sure ☐

16. Keith and Neil were neighbors, and at one time had been friends. However, Neil became convinced (falsely and unreasonably) that Keith was having an affair with Neil's wife. Consequently, Neil, who was a chemist by profession, threw a bowl of acid at Keith's face, intending to disfigure Keith. Keith happened to be standing near his own swimming pool and immediately dove in. The water washed away the acid before it could do any damage. However, Keith had inadvertently dived into the shallow part of the pool and smashed his face on the bottom of the pool. As a result, Keith suffered a fractured nose and cheekbones, and his appearance was permanently disfigured. The jurisdiction defines the crime of "mayhem" as "the intentional infliction of life-threatening or disfiguring bodily injury." May Neil be convicted of mayhem?   Not sure ☐

17. Paul stabbed Jim in the chest. Because of the stress and fright brought on by the episode, Jim had a moderately serious heart attack. (The heart attack from the stabbing was minor, and Jim would have recovered even if not treated.) Jim was brought to the hospital immediately and treated by Dr. Bob. Dr. Bob treated the wound with a wonder drug that causes blood to coagulate rapidly to reduce bleeding. The packet containing the drug comes with stern warnings that the drug should never be used when the patient has had a recent heart attack. Dr. Bob was aware of this warning, but carelessly disregarded fairly clear (though not extremely obvious) signs that Jim had had a heart attack. The medication caused Jim's blood to thicken, putting a fatal stress on his already-burdened damaged heart. Paul has now been charged with murdering Jim. May Paul be properly convicted?

Not sure ☐

18. Klaus was caught shoplifting a flashy diamond bracelet worth $3,000 from a local jewelry store. At his trial for larceny, Klaus asserted an insanity defense. This defense showed the following: Klaus was highly intelligent and highly educated, and he knew on an intellectual level that it was morally wrong and against the law to steal. He was also extremely wealthy by inheritance, so the stealing was not from financial motives. However, Klaus had been a diagnosed kleptomaniac since the age of five, and had always been fascinated by bright, shiny objects. Despite years of psychotherapy, every time Klaus was in close proximity to a dazzling object, such as the diamond bracelet stolen here, he felt a powerful primeval urge to possess it, an urge that he was powerless to resist. (Police found dozens of similar shiny bracelets, some valuable and some made of cheap materials like glass and zirconium, stuffed under Klaus's mattress in his bedroom.) In a jurisdiction applying the *M'Naghten* test for insanity, may Klaus be convicted of larceny?

Not sure ☐

19. Same facts as in the previous question. Now, assume that the jurisdiction applies the Model Penal Code approach to insanity. May Klaus be convicted of larceny?

Not sure ☐

20. Same facts as in the previous two questions. Now, assume that the prosecution is made in a federal court under federal law, because the jewelry store was at a PX run by the United States on an army base. May Klaus be convicted of larceny?

Not sure ☐

21. Same facts as in the previous question. Assume that Klaus presents all of the evidence referred to in question 18. The federal prosecutor makes no attempt to rebut this showing, and merely argues that the showing, even if believed, does not establish the insanity defense. The trial judge instructs the jury that "the burden of coming forward with evidence of insanity is upon the defendant. Once the defendant presents such evidence, the burden shifts to the prosecution to prove, by a preponderance of the evidence, that the defendant was not insane at the time of the acts charged." Has the judge correctly instructed the jury as to the burden of proof in federal insanity cases?

Not sure ☐

22. Samson was charged with the serial murder of ten victims, all of whom were apparently strangers to him. Samson asserted an insanity defense. At trial, Samson introduced testimony by three eminent psychiatrists, all of whom agreed that Samson committed the murders because he believed "God told him to do it," and that Samson lacks the cognitive ability to recognize either that his conduct is morally wrong or that it is legally wrong. The court-appointed psychiatrist who examined Samson testified (to the prosecution's surprise and disgust) that he, too, believed

that Samson cannot tell right from wrong and is insane. The prosecution cross-examined each of the psychiatrists but with little apparent effect. The trial judge let the case go to the jury, and the jury convicted Samson. Should the appeals court overturn the verdict on the grounds that the jury's implicit finding of no insanity was against the overwhelming weight of the psychiatric evidence?

Not sure ☐

23. After the police received a 911 phone call, they entered Jim's apartment. They found him lying in a pool of blood on the floor. Seated across the room was Jane, Jim's wife, who was calmly holding a loaded .38 revolver in her right hand. Jane was arrested and charged with first-degree murder, which requires premeditation. You, as Jane's court-appointed defense lawyer, have discovered from talking to Jane that (1) she underwent a lobotomy 15 years ago, at the age of 10; (2) she has been undergoing psychiatric care ever since; and (3) according to her psychiatrist, since (and because of) the lobotomy, Jane has been incapable of forming or carrying out plans and is capable only of impulsive "spur of the moment" action. The jurisdiction imposes the *M'Naghten* test for insanity, and you have concluded that Jane is not insane by this definition.

(a) Assuming that Jane definitely fired the fatal shot, what defense should you assert on her behalf?

Not sure ☐

(b) Will you succeed with that defense?

Not sure ☐

24. Egor was a heavy drinker. He was also hopelessly in love with his former girl-friend, Kelly, a flight attendant who had dumped him because she couldn't stand his drinking any longer. One evening, when Egor knew that Kelly was away on a flight, Egor got himself quite drunk, then broke into Kelly's house. Egor's drunken intent was merely to sit in Kelly's house, listen to the radio, think back to the good old times when they were together, and then leave. While in the house, Egor had a few more drinks and listened to Kelly's Sony Walkman. When it came time to leave, Egor mistakenly believed that the Sony Walkman was his (he owned a similar one, and mistakenly thought he had brought his own with him to Kelly's house) and left the house with the Walkman.

Not sure ☐

Egor was arrested by a police officer immediately upon leaving Kelly's house and charged with burglarizing her house. (The jurisdiction defines burglary as "the unlawful entry to a building with purpose to commit a crime therein." The prosecution asserts that the "crime therein" was the larceny of the Walkman.) At trial, Egor shows that he intended to take the Walkman but only because he mistakenly believed that the Walkman was his own. The prosecution shows that no sober person would have made this mistake. May Egor's drunkenness prevent him from being convicted of burglary?

Not sure ☐

25. Seymour, a 22-year-old law student, went out on a first date with Beth, who was also a law student. After they saw a movie together, Beth invited Seymour to return to her apartment for a nightcap. Seymour then drank four beers and one vodka, enough to make him legally drunk and to substantially impair his ability to assess and respond to events around him. He began to kiss Beth, and she willingly returned his embraces. He then began to undress her. Beth responded, "No, I don't want to." Had Seymour been sober, he would have realized that Beth meant it. But in his state of drunkenness, he incorrectly believed that Beth was just teasing him,

and that she really wanted to have intercourse. He therefore had intercourse with her without her consent. Beth subsequently filed a complaint, and Seymour was charged with rape. The jurisdiction defines rape in such a way that it is committed only if the defendant knows that the woman has not consented, or recklessly disregards the possibility that she has not consented. May Seymour be convicted of rape?

26. Marlon was the head of an organized crime family. Matt, who had become a "soldier" in the family several years previously, went to Marlon and told him he wanted to leave the family. Marlon ignored Matt's demand and handed Matt a piece of paper. On this piece of paper was the name of a man, Joey, whom Marlon wanted killed. Matt told Marlon that he wouldn't commit the murder. Marlon replied, "We'll see about that." When Matt arrived home, he found his beloved poodle, Fifi, dead on the kitchen floor with her throat slit. Nearby was a note that read, "It's a shame that such a nice dog had to die to show her master what happens to people who don't obey orders." Matt, terrified, realized that he would certainly be killed if he did not obey Marlon's order. Therefore, he reluctantly murdered Joey. Matt has now been charged with first-degree murder.

    (a) You are Matt's lawyer. What defense do you think would have the best chance (however small) of success?

    (b) Will the defense you listed in (a) prevail?

27. Same basic fact pattern as in the previous question. Now, however, assume that when Matt told Marlon he wanted to leave the family, Marlon responded, "You knew when you applied for this job that it was a lifetime commitment. Now go rob the First National Bank, or I'll kill you." In the year since Matt had realized his ambition to become a soldier in Marlon's crime family, Matt had seen two instances in which Marlon had indeed ordered the execution of soldiers who wished to leave the family. Reasonably believing that he himself would be killed if he did not follow the order, Matt robbed the bank. May he successfully assert the defense of duress?

28. U.S. troops had been placed into the Middle Eastern country of Petrolia to defend the country (and its oil fields) against a threatened attack by the neighboring nation of Dictatoria. Private Callow and his commanding officer, Sergeant Macho, were out on patrol one day when they found and captured a prisoner hiding behind the bushes. Both reasonably believed that the man was a Dictatorian spy (which in fact he was). After they bound their prisoner's hands and feet, Sergeant Macho ordered Private Callow, "Burn the soles of his feet with your cigarette lighter so we can find out what he knows." Private Callow reluctantly did so. The spy lapsed into unconsciousness before he could give much useful information. Then the two soldiers brought him back to base camp. When their superiors found out what the men had done, they were both charged with the crime of torture. Private Callow defended on the grounds that all he did was to perform an act that he was directly ordered to do by his military superior. The prosecution shows that Private Callow was aware, from reading he had done, that U.S. military regulations allow for the questioning of spies but not for the physical torture of them. Will Private Callow's defense of obedience to military orders succeed?

29. Same basic fact pattern as in the previous question. Now, assume that Private Callow did not in fact know that it was against U.S. military regulations to torture a spy. Assume further that Private Callow had heard other soldiers speak about how they had performed such torture, with good results. The prosecution, however, proves that an American soldier of "average sophistication" would have known that torture of suspected spies was illegal. Will Private Callow's defense of obedience of military orders be accepted?

Not sure ☐

30. Darryn and Dexter were inveterate mountain climbers. One day, while they were in a sparsely settled mountainous region, a sudden and unexpected storm caught them by surprise. The two men reasonably believed that if they could not find shelter, they would probably freeze to death. After trudging blindly through the snow for two hours, they came upon a log cabin owned by Valerie, who was not present. The two men forced the lock of the cabin, went inside, built a fire, and (suffering from dehydration and cold) drank the only hot liquid available, coffee, which they brewed in Valerie's coffeepot. They returned to safety the next day. Dexter and Darryn were prosecuted for burglary, on the theory that they had intentionally entered an occupied building without permission and with intent to commit a felony therein (theft of the provisions).

(a) What defense should Darryn and Dexter assert?

Not sure ☐

(b) Will this defense succeed?

Not sure ☐

31. Same facts as in the previous question. Now, however, assume that the storm was not in fact nearly as serious as Darryn and Dexter thought and that most mountaineers with their experience would have realized this. Darryn and Dexter honestly (though unreasonably) believed that the situation was life threatening; in other words, they panicked. Assuming that the defense you listed in part (a) of your answer to the previous question would otherwise be applicable, will the defendant's unreasonableness deprive them of this defense?

Not sure ☐

32. Valjean, an unemployed father of two, broke into a grocery store late one night to steal a bottle of milk and a loaf of bread. Valjean's sole purpose was to be able to feed his two young children, ages three and one. Valjean knew that he could take the children to a city-run overnight shelter, where they would receive food. However, he believed that shelters are degrading, and he did not want to subject his children to one. (Valjean also realized that he might be eligible for welfare but knew that such an application takes more than a month to be approved.) If Valjean is prosecuted for burglary, may he successfully assert the defense of necessity?

Not sure ☐

33. Drew was a thief with a penchant for stealing clothes from outdoor clotheslines. One day, Drew was in the process of stealing Steve's favorite beach towel from Steve's backyard when Steve accosted him. Steve, who was taller than Drew and very angry, put Drew in a headlock and started pulling him off the property. (Assume that Steve was using an amount of force that seemed reasonably necessary to make sure that Drew did not come back and steal again.) Drew ducked out of the hold and punched Steve on the chin, causing Steve to become momentarily unconscious. Shortly thereafter, Drew was arrested for the crime of assault. (No larceny-related crime was charged.) Drew asserted the defense of self-defense. Will this defense succeed?

Not sure ☐

34. Jerome was walking down a deserted alley when he spotted a distinctive-looking woman wearing a cape. He recognized the woman from recent newscasts as being the Slapster. The Slapster had been eluding police for months. Her MO was to back each of her victims into a corner (she was quite tall and strong) and then remove a black leather glove from her pocket and slap the victim across the mouth with it. As Jerome knew, no victim had sustained more than mild injury from these attacks. All the victims gave the same description of her, and the police were able to publish a composite sketch of her that served as the basis for Jerome's recognizing her.

The Slapster approached Jerome, backed him into a corner, and removed a black leather glove from her pocket. Jerome feared (reasonably and correctly) being slapped with the glove. He therefore removed a knife from his coat and stabbed the Slapster in her cheek. Jerome intended to do as much stabbing as required to discourage the Slapster, and he assumed that he would have to gouge her fairly deeply on the face or neck to do so. In fact, he cut the Slapster's carotid artery, and she almost died (but was rescued by paramedics who happened to spot her). Jerome was arrested and charged with assault. He defends on the grounds of self-defense. Is Jerome entitled to the defense of self-defense?

Not sure ☐

35. Same basic facts as in the previous question. Now, assume that Jerome, to defend himself from the slap, swung at the Slapster with his knife with what the prosecution proves to have been an intent to kill the Slapster. However, since Jerome had poor aim and the Slapster had quick reflexes, Jerome merely gave the Slapster a one-inch gash on the wrist that required five stitches and caused no lasting injury to the Slapster. If Jerome is charged with assault, and if he asserts the defense of self-defense, will his defense be accepted?

Not sure ☐

36. Barry and Kelly were married but not happily. Kelly knew that Barry was capable of considerable violence, and in fact Barry had attacked and severely beaten her several times before. One Wednesday, at 2:00 in the afternoon, Barry told Kelly that at noon the following day (Thursday), he was going to kill her. Barry placed a large clock in the room and told Kelly to listen to the ticking, because each tick would bring her one second closer to noon and doom. At 10:00 P.M. Wednesday, Barry went to sleep after setting the burglar alarm on the front door of the apartment so that it would go off if anyone tried to enter or leave. Kelly realized that if she tried to run away, the alarm would probably wake Barry up, and he might kill her on the spot. At 10:30 P.M. Wednesday, Kelly pulled a gun from her drawer and shot Barry to death; her motive was to prevent him from killing her at noon the next day. Can Kelly successfully claim self-defense?

Not sure ☐

37. Bob and Ken, while sitting in a bar one night, got into a dispute about a girl who was the object of both of their affections. At a time when Ken had not used anything beyond mildly nasty words, Bob escalated the disagreement by rushing at Ken with his fists raised and starting to swing. Ken had known Bob for years, and he knew that Bob was not especially dangerous when using his fists in a barroom brawl. Nonetheless, Ken drew a pistol, which he pointed at Bob's right knee, saying, "Anybody who attacks me gets a piece of lead in the kneecap of his choice. Left or right?" Bob realized that he could not safely escape from the bar, since Ken would probably shoot him as he ran. Therefore, Bob quickly drew a pistol from his jacket pocket and aimed a shot at Ken's right hand, which held Ken's gun. The bullet went slightly wide and hit Ken in the heart, killing him instantly. If Bob is prosecuted for homicide, may he successfully assert self-defense?

Not sure ☐

38. While Spencer was trying to steal a TV from Martin's house, Martin suddenly accosted him. Spencer immediately dropped the TV, restrained Martin, tied Martin's hands behind his back, and ran from the house without the TV. The rope was weaker than Spencer thought, and Martin was able to break it almost immediately. Martin then, acting for the purpose of revenge (not to arrest Spencer), raced into the street, caught up with Spencer, and grabbed Spencer's arm. Martin started to punch Spencer, but before he could do so, Spencer punched Martin in the mouth, knocking out several of Martin's teeth. Spencer was charged with assault. Can Spencer successfully assert a claim of self-defense?

Not sure ☐

39. It was Friday night in the Yuppie Wallstreeter, a posh singles bar. Marla and Betty were both trying to get to know Stan, a handsome and apparently well-heeled young lawyer. Betty said to Marla, "Listen, sister, if I see you within 50 feet of Stan here, I'm gonna slice up that pert little face of yours." Betty then drew a razor blade from her purse to show she meant business. Marla realized that she, Marla, could simply leave the bar as Betty was requesting, and that there was no chance that Betty would follow her or attack her. But Marla also realized that handsome, young, well-heeled, and unattached male lawyers were becoming an increasingly scarce commodity. Therefore, she decided to stay and fight. She drew a knife from her purse and slashed at Betty, slicing off a piece of Betty's ear. Marla was charged with assault. In a jurisdiction following the Model Penal Code's approach to all relevant matters, may Marla successfully assert a claim of self-defense?

Not sure ☐

40. Same basic fact pattern as in the previous question. Now, however, assume that Betty's threat to Marla was that if Marla did not leave the bar, Betty would spray mace in Marla's face. Marla knew that mace is irritating but not seriously dangerous. Instead of leaving the bar, Marla sprayed her own mace at Betty before Betty could spray her. If Marla is charged with assault, may she successfully claim self-defense in a jurisdiction that follows the Model Penal Code view?

Not sure ☐

41. Same basic fact pattern as in the previous two questions. Now, however, assume that the setting was a party hosted by Marla at Marla's apartment. The actual encounter took place in Marla's spare bedroom, where Betty said to Marla, "I wanna talk to Stan here, and if you stay in this room with him, I'll slice you up." Marla realized that if she, Marla, left the room in compliance with this demand, Betty almost certainly would not attack her anywhere else at the apartment. But instead, Marla determined to hold her ground and attacked Betty with a knife, seriously injuring her. In a jurisdiction following the Model Penal Code approach to relevant matters, may Marla assert self-defense?

Not sure ☐

42. Mary was a prosecutor in the juvenile division of the state's attorney's office. She had been receiving threatening phone calls (apparently from a juvenile she was prosecuting), and so obtained permission to carry a pistol. One evening after work, she walked up the stairs of the stoop to her house. Just before she opened the door, she heard footsteps running down the sidewalk in front of her house. She turned toward the street with her gun drawn and saw a boy who looked to be about

14 years old pointing a black gun at her. In a panic, Mary shot the boy in the chest, killing him. It turned out that the boy was in fact a somewhat tall (for his age) 10-year-old, who was pointing a water pistol at Mary just to play a joke. Assuming that Mary's belief that the gun was real and that she might be shot was a reasonable (though mistaken) belief, may Mary assert a claim of self-defense?

Not sure ☐

43. Same facts as in the previous question. Now, however, assume that Mary's mistaken beliefs (that the gun was real and that she might be shot by it) were unreasonable, even though honest. May Mary assert a claim of self-defense?

Not sure ☐

44. The police suspected Karen of being a drug dealer, but they had no evidence against her. They decided to arrest her and thereby induce her to become an informant. Two uniformed officers went to Karen's house without an arrest or search warrant. One of them, Officer Smith, found Karen in her backyard, took out his pistol, pointed it at her, and shouted, "Freeze. You're under arrest." Unbeknownst to Smith, Karen was an excellent shot. She reached into her purse, drew out a small pistol, and shot Smith's pistol out of his hand, slightly injuring Smith's thumb. The other officer subdued Karen and arrested her.

Prosecutors later determined that the initial attempt to arrest Karen had been unlawful, because the police lacked probable cause and lacked a required arrest warrant. However, the prosecutors have charged Karen with the crime of assault, for shooting at and injuring Smith's hand. Assuming that Karen realized that Smith was a police officer, that Karen was not fearful that she would be seriously injured during the arrest, and that her only motive was to avoid what she knew to be an unlawful arrest, may Karen defend against the assault claim by asserting self-defense?

Not sure ☐

45. Same facts as in the previous question. Now, however, assume that Karen did not shoot at Officer Smith, but merely slapped him in the face in an attempt to distract him so that she could escape. Assuming that this slap is found not to constitute the use of deadly force, may Karen defend against an assault charge by asserting that she was using self-defense to prevent an unlawful arrest? Assume that the jurisdiction follows the Model Penal Code approach to relevant issues.

Not sure ☐

46. Martin knew that his son Charlie's classmates had been picking on him a lot recently. One day, as Martin was driving home from work, he saw Charlie standing on the sidewalk, being beaten up by George, a larger boy, who was wielding a baseball bat. Martin realized that if the beating were allowed to continue, Charlie might be seriously injured or even killed. Martin also realized that he could simply escort Charlie into the car and drive away. But he felt that this would indicate to George (and indirectly to the other boys in the neighborhood) that they could beat Charlie up with impunity. Therefore, instead of helping Charlie get away or urging him to flee, Martin got a baseball bat out of the trunk and began striking George. George died as a result of his injuries, and Martin was charged with murdering him.

(a) What defense should Martin assert?

Not sure ☐

(b) Will Martin succeed with this defense?

Not sure ☐

47. Bill was out taking an evening constitutional when he came upon a man attacking another. The attacker (whose name turned out to be Steve) was substantially larger than the victim (who turned out to be Kevin). Kevin was lying on the ground while Steve was kicking him with heavy boots in a way that seemed likely to lead to serious injury or even death. Bill had never seen either Steve or Kevin before. By this time, Kevin was so beaten that it did not appear that he could get up and run away even if Steve could be momentarily distracted. Bill was not very handy with his fists, but he happened to have a knife on him. After demanding (unsuccessfully) that Steve leave Kevin alone, Bill took his knife and plunged it into the back of Steve's neck. Steve bled to death. If Bill is charged with murdering Steve, may he successfully assert a claim of defense of others?

Not sure ☐

48. On his way to work one day by foot, Alex rounded the corner and suddenly saw his friend Carl engaged in a scuffle with Bert. Bert was the larger of the two men and appeared to be getting at least slightly the better of the few punches that Alex observed, though each was striking the other. Alex reasonably believed that Bert had initiated the fight, since he was bigger and since Alex knew Carl to be a basically peaceable person. Alex tried to persuade the men to stop fighting, but they disregarded him. Alex then jumped into the middle and delivered a hard punch to Bert's chin, knocking him to the ground, where he struck his head against the curb and was seriously injured. It ultimately became clear that Carl had attacked Bert without provocation and that Bert was merely (and properly) defending himself. If Alex is charged with assault of Bert, may Alex successfully assert a claim of defense of others?

Not sure ☐

49. Darnell was walking down a secluded street in Gotham one day when he was accosted by Rick, who was a stranger to him. Rick said, "Give me your wallet, and be quick about it. I won't hurt you unless you resist." Rick did not display any weapon. Darnell was upset, but believed Rick's statement that he would not be hurt if he complied. However, Darnell had more than $500 in his wallet, and he decided that he would rather resist. He therefore punched Rick in the jaw. Rick fell down, striking his head on the pavement, killing him instantly because of the freak angle of his fall. Darnell has been charged with manslaughter. Assuming that a court concludes that Darnell's use of his fists did not constitute use of deadly force:

   (a) What defense should Darnell assert?

Not sure ☐

   (b) Will this defense succeed?

Not sure ☐

50. Same facts as in the previous question. Now, however, assume that instead of punching Rick, Darnell pulled out a gun and shot Rick in the head. Assume further that Darnell was not good at boxing or any other form of self-defense, and that he was not a fast runner; therefore, Darnell's only choices were to surrender his wallet or to use the gun. Furthermore, assume that Darnell's wallet contained his entire life savings, $100,000 (which he was about to spend to purchase a house). May Darnell successfully assert the defense that you gave as your answer to question 49 (a)?

Not sure ☐

51. For several months, Pierre's neighborhood had been afflicted with burglaries believed to have been committed by "the Big Cat," a 6'2" burglar who stole only jewelry, and who seemed to be a gentlemanly sort who did not carry a weapon or threaten violence to those he was burglarizing. One night, at 2:00, Pierre awoke to find a man meeting the description of the Big Cat in Pierre's bedroom, going

through Pierre's dresser drawers. Pierre grabbed his revolver and pointed it at the burglar. The burglar said, "Cool it, man. Let me go, and I won't hurt you." The burglar turned to climb out through the window with Pierre's wallet (containing $10,000) in his hand. Pierre realized that the burglar would escape with the wallet if Pierre did not use the revolver, which was the only weapon at his disposal. Therefore, Pierre shot the burglar through the back, killing him instantly. Pierre was charged with the murder and now asserts that he was entitled to defend his property. Will the court accept this claim?

Not sure ☐

52. Same basic fact pattern as in the previous question. Now, however, assume that Pierre was not home on the night in question. Instead, in reliance on press reports about the prior burglaries, Pierre rigged a "spring gun"—that is, a gun with its trigger attached to the front door of Pierre's house. When the Big Cat pushed open the front door, he was immediately killed by a bullet automatically fired by the spring gun. It turned out that contrary to the press reports, the Big Cat was heavily armed and indeed had slain at least one prior burglary victim who accosted him. Assuming that the jurisdiction follows the "modern view" toward relevant matters, if Pierre is charged with murdering the Big Cat, may he successfully claim defense of property?

Not sure ☐

53. Same basic fact pattern as in the previous question. Now, however, assume that before Pierre left, he did not set up a spring gun but instead put barbed wire all around the perimeter of his property. No signs warning about the barbed wire were posted. The Big Cat never attempted to burglarize Pierre, but one of the children in the neighborhood tried to climb over the barbed wire fence to retrieve a ball, slipped at the top, and bled to death from a neck wound suffered as a result. If Pierre is charged with manslaughter, may he successfully defend on the grounds that he was defending his property?

Not sure ☐

54. While Officer Goodbar was on patrol one night, he spied coming out of a house a black-clad figure, whom he suspected of being Charlie, a locally prominent burglar. Goodbar stopped the suspect, who indeed turned out to be Charlie. Charlie was carrying a bag of loot, which seemed to have been stolen. Goodbar had Charlie drop the bag, and then frisked Charlie against a wall. Charlie was not carrying any firearm. In fact, Charlie had (to Goodbar's knowledge) been arrested and convicted of burglary on several prior occasions, yet had never been found to have carried a weapon or to have caused bodily injury to anyone. Shortly after the frisking, Charlie started to run away from Goodbar. Goodbar drew his service revolver, pointed at Charlie, and shouted, "Stop or I'll shoot." Charlie failed to stop. Goodbar shot at Charlie, aiming for his left leg. However, the shot went slightly high, hitting Charlie in the back and killing him instantly. If Goodbar is charged with murdering Charlie, may Goodbar successfully claim that he was privileged to behave the way he did as an adjunct of making an arrest?

Not sure ☐

55. Stanley was a law-abiding citizen. One afternoon, while walking down a street in Little Italy, Stanley observed a teenager running out of a store, holding a box. An old man chased the teenager, screaming in Italian (a language that Stanley recognized but didn't understand). Some of the other people in the street around him began speaking Italian and pointing toward the teenager. Stanley reasonably believed that the boy had just committed shoplifting (a felony in the jurisdiction)

from the man's store. Therefore, Stanley gave chase. As he got close to the boy, Stanley made a flying tackle, hoping just to bring the teenager down. Instead, the teenager, while falling, cracked his head and suffered serious injuries. It later turned out that the teenager was the grandson of the old man, and that there had not been any crime, merely a family argument. Assume that Stanley acted reasonably (at least given his lack of ability to understand Italian) in concluding that the teenager was a fleeing thief. If Stanley is charged with the crime of assault, will he be able to raise the defense of private arrest?

Not sure ☐

56. Epsilon Gamma Delta was a wild college fraternity. The members knew that other fraternities had been sued for personal injuries resulting from fraternity antics, so EGD tried to protect itself. On the first day of pledge period, the fraternity brothers told their pledges that the pledges would be hazed in order to become initiated, and that the pledges would have to sign a waiver consenting to the hazing and relieving the fraternity and its members of responsibility for injury or death. Barney, a pledge, signed such a waiver form. That evening, Riccardo (president of the fraternity) told Barney to climb up onto the roof of the frat, and to dive into a mattress that Riccardo and some of his fraternity brothers would hold below. Barney followed the instructions, missed the mattress, and was killed. Riccardo was charged with manslaughter. May Riccardo successfully defend on the grounds that Barney consented to the activity that led to his death?

Not sure ☐

57. Darnell was an active trader and investor in stocks. Petra was the president of a New York Stock Exchange–listed company and had business dealings with Darnell. Federal prosecutors caught Petra trading on inside information and induced her to become a government informant and cooperating witness. Before Petra's cooperation became publicly known, federal prosecutors convinced her to try to get evidence useful in a prosecution against Darnell, whom the prosecutors suspected of being an ardent insider trader. Therefore, one day, Petra phoned Darnell and said to him, "We're going to be selling the company to a large, rich multinational, and the price should skyrocket. You'll probably want to buy at least 100,000 shares." In fact, this information was true. Darnell immediately bought 1 million shares at $30 apiece; shortly thereafter, the acquisition was announced, and the price skyrocketed to $60, permitting Darnell to sell out at a large profit. Darnell was charged with insider trading. Darnell now asserts an entrapment defense. The prosecution shows at trial strong evidence that Darnell used information from Petra and other insiders to insider trade on at least four prior occasions. If the jurisdiction follows the "majority" approach to entrapment, will Darnell's entrapment defense be successful?

Not sure ☐

58. Same facts as in the previous question. After Petra made her initial disclosure about the pending acquisition, Darnell responded by saying, "Well, I've recently become a born-again Christian, and I realize that it is wrong to insider trade, so I'm not going to do it." Petra responded, "Come on, Darnell, everybody does it. Besides, if I think you're a wimp who's afraid of his own shadow, I won't have anything to do with you anymore." Darnell then insider traded. At Darnell's insider-trading trial, his lawyers show that nearly every person given inside information straight from the mouth of the president of a publicly held company would trade on that information if the president urged them to do so (even if the recipient of the information was an otherwise law-abiding citizen). Assume that the jurisdiction applies the minority "police conduct" test for entrapment. Will Darnell's entrapment defense succeed?

Not sure ☐

59. Phil was a resident of San Francisco. He loved to drive his car at high speeds up and down the hills of the city. One afternoon, he decided to attempt a "vehicular ski jump" (i.e., to drive very fast up to the top of hill, in the hopes that his car would sail at least a few feet off the ground when it crossed the top). Phil knew that if there was a pedestrian or other car on the other side of the hill, he would probably hit them, but he decided to take the chance. He started at the bottom of the hill, gunned the car, and made the jump. Dina was standing on the other side of the hill and was struck by the car. She was severely injured, but because of extensive and immediate surgery, did not die. The jurisdiction defines manslaughter as "criminal homicide that is committed recklessly." Phil is charged with attempted manslaughter. If the jury finds that Phil's actions were reckless, can Phil be convicted of attempted manslaughter?

Not sure ☐

60. Norman had a strong hatred of people rich enough to drive luxury cars. Therefore, he stationed himself on a bridge overlooking a busy highway and brought a stack of bricks with him. Each time Norman spotted a car whose market value was, in Norman's estimation, more than $30,000, he dropped a brick toward the car's front window. Each time Norman dropped a brick, he knew that the brick might not only break the driver's front window, but also cause him to lose control of the car, possibly killing him. Norman did not actively desire to bring about a vehicular death (he merely wanted to cause property damage and bodily injury); nor did Norman believe that death was substantially certain to result. One particular brick that Norman dropped struck the front window of a Rolls-Royce driven by Bernard. Bernard lost control of the car, smashed into a concrete abutment, and nearly died. Norman has been charged with attempted murder. Assume that Norman's mental state as to the possibility of killing Bernard was that Norman was reckless, and that in his jurisdiction one who recklessly endangers the life of another can be convicted of murder if death proximately results. May Norman be convicted of attempted murder?

Not sure ☐

61. Drew decided to rob First National Bank of Ames. His plan was to enter the bank shortly before closing, wearing a mask, and to point a gun at one of the tellers while delivering a note demanding money. In furtherance of his scheme, Drew purchased a .38-caliber revolver and ammunition. (In the state in which Ames is located, it is perfectly legal for an ordinary citizen such as Drew to purchase and possess such a gun and ammunition; such revolvers are frequently used by Ames residents for sport shooting, self-defense, and other lawful purposes.) Drew also purchased a Halloween mask, which he planned to wear to obscure his identity from the bank surveillance cameras he expected to encounter. Because Drew unwisely dropped hints of his plan to a neighbor, the police learned of the plot and arrested Drew the night before he intended to commit the robbery. They found the gun and the mask, but no other tangible evidence of the plot. Drew confessed to the police that he indeed planned to rob the bank the next day. Drew was charged with attempted bank robbery. May he be properly convicted?

Not sure ☐

62. Same basic fact pattern as in the previous question. Now, assume that when the police arrested Drew at his house, they did not find the gun and the mask. However, they found a note that said, "Mr./Ms. Teller: Take all the money in your cash drawer and put it into a bag. Do not shout or make any sudden movements, or I'll shoot." If the prosecution shows that Drew in fact wrote the note and that he intended to use it in robbing First National Bank the next day, may Drew be convicted of attempted bank robbery?

Not sure ☐

63. Norbert was a professional terrorist who specialized in explosions. Norbert used his bomb-making expertise to put together two pounds of plastic explosive, a container, and a detonator. He went to the airport and, using a curbside bellman, checked a bag containing the bomb onto National Airlines Flight 123. Norbert himself did not take the flight. Norbert intended for the bomb to explode in midair so that everyone aboard would be killed. Since the detonator contained an altimeter, the bomb could only explode (and indeed would have exploded) if present at an altitude of 25,000 feet or more. However, unbeknownst to Norbert, National's security personnel examined baggage checked via bellmen, and the bomb was discovered before Norbert's suitcase was placed on the plane. The bomb was then disarmed. Norbert was arrested while waiting in the airport restaurant and charged with attempted murder. May Norbert be properly convicted?

Not sure ☐

64. Harvey decided to assassinate the governor of Langdell. Using a German-made rifle that he had previously bought and used for sport purposes (legally), he went to the Langdell Outline Warehouse, a now-abandoned building that had once been used to store publishing materials. Harvey chose the site because he knew that the governor's inaugural-day motorcade would proceed down the street in front of the warehouse, affording him a perfect view and good chance of escape. Harvey placed himself in position in a small room at the Warehouse two hours before the motorcade was due. However, a police officer on the street below happened to look up, and saw activity in what was supposed to be an abandoned warehouse; the officer investigated and arrested Harvey. Can Harvey be convicted of attempted murder?

Not sure ☐

65. Bernard, a wealthy collector of coins, was in a short-term cash bind. He knew that his coin collection was insured for $1 million, whereas it would be worth only $600,000 if he had to sell it on short notice. Therefore, Bernard decided to fake a theft to collect the insurance. He moved his coin collection from his home to a hole in a field outside his country house. He then returned home, arranged furniture and paper to suggest a struggle, hit himself with a baseball bat to create a bruise, and tied his hands together with rope (using his teeth when necessary). He then phoned the police, saying that he had been robbed of his coin collection. The police took down his story and began to investigate. Simultaneously, Bernard filled out an insurance claim form, falsely stating that his collection had been stolen and asking for the $1 million policy proceeds. Before Bernard could mail the claim form to the insurance company, the police became sufficiently suspicious that they arrested him on a charge of attempted insurance fraud. May Bernard be convicted?

Not sure ☐

66. Donald had suspected (falsely) for some time that his wife had been going through the papers he brought home from his office, and that she had then been selling copies to competing companies. Donald finally resolved to kill her by poisoning her. He went to a drugstore, complaining of insomnia. The druggist gave him a bottle of nonprescription sleeping pills. Donald, mistakenly believing these pills to be lethal in quantity, placed 20 tablets into his wife's coffee. His wife drank the coffee. Because the pills were antihistamine-based, even ingesting 100 pills simultaneously would not have killed a person, and indeed, Donald's wife suffered no ill effects except mild drowsiness. Donald has been charged with attempted murder. May Donald be convicted?

Not sure ☐

67. Dwain was a drug-trade "mule" whose job it was to bring crack into the United States on his person. On one particular trip, Dwain did not have drugs on him, but because he met the profile of a drug smuggler, Dwain was taken into custody and interrogated by federal narcotics officials. Dwain falsely told the officers that he had never smuggled drugs; of course, he knew that this was a lie. Dwain believed that federal law defined the crime of perjury to include telling a lie to a police officer while in custody. In fact, the federal law of perjury is restricted to statements made in a courtroom under oath, and does not cover statements (even sworn ones) made to police officers. Federal prosecutors charged Dwain with attempted perjury. May he be properly convicted?

Not sure ☐

68. Dolores was a small-time drug dealer. After her previous supplier was arrested, Dolores changed to a new supplier, Evan. In their first transaction, Evan sold Dolores ten packets that he said were cocaine. Dolores went out on the street and began "advertising" the bags as cocaine and selling them. She sold one bag to Fred, who unbeknownst to Dolores was an undercover narcotics officer. Fred immediately arrested Dolores. Upon testing, the packet proved to contain only talcum powder, a substance that is not banned. Dolores was charged with attempting to distribute cocaine, and evidence at her trial shows that Dolores in fact believed that the substance was cocaine. May Dolores properly be convicted?

Not sure ☐

69. Karpov was somewhat mentally unstable, but had never done anything very harmful or dangerous to anyone else. Karpov believed that the moon was inhabited by living beings who had the ability to send fatal cosmic rays to particular destinations on earth. Karpov fervently desired to cause the death of his next-door neighbor, Sergei. To carry out his plan, Karpov installed a powerful light beam on his roof and flashed toward the moon, in Morse Code, the following message, "Please send your fatal cosmic rays to annihilate my next-door neighbor, Sergei." Sergei was not aware of Karpov's plot. The police, investigating the mysterious flashes, discovered the plot. Karpov has now been charged with attempted murder. May he properly be convicted?

Not sure ☐

70. Darren was a paroled rapist. He decided to resume the activities that had caused him to be imprisoned. He therefore set out one evening to find a suitable victim. After a short while, he spotted Jane, a young woman walking alone. Darren followed Jane for several blocks, knife in hand; Darren's plan was to accost her when they were in an especially secluded area, and to force her to have sex with him. Darren presumed that an alley just off of Ninth Avenue would be the best spot. When Darren was at Seventh Avenue, just two blocks away, a police officer in a patrol car happened to pass by, traveling slowly. Darren realized that his face had probably been spotted, and that if a rape occurred nearby shortly afterward, the

officer might be able to identify him. Therefore, Darren turned around, now walking away from Jane. Seeing Darren's somewhat suspicious behavior, the officer stopped him and questioned him. Darren's knife and his manner did nothing to assuage the officer's suspicions, and a check of his identity by radio turned up the information that Darren was a paroled rapist. The officer arrested Darren, and the prosecutor charged him with attempted rape.

(a) What is the best defense Darren can assert?

Not sure ☐

(b) Will this defense be successful?

Not sure ☐

71. Same basic fact pattern as the previous question. Now, assume that no police officer came on the scene. As Darren got to Eighth Avenue, he said to himself, "If I'm caught, I'll go back to jail for ten years. Probably not worth running that kind of risk." Darren turned around and walked away. If Darren was apprehended immediately after turning away and charged with the attempted rape of Jane, should he be convicted?

Not sure ☐

72. Same basic fact pattern as in the previous two questions. Now, assume that no police officer came on the scene, and that Darren finally caught up with Jane. Darren said to Jane, "Lie down and take your pants off; you won't get hurt if you obey." Jane said, "I'll do whatever you tell me. But you should know that my boyfriend was a junkie who died of AIDS. Are you sure you want to go through with it?" Darren thought for a few seconds, realized that he had no way of knowing whether Jane's story was true or false, and responded, "Forget it, babe." May Darren be convicted of the attempted rape of Jane?

Not sure ☐

73. Dorothy was a police officer who had walked the same foot patrol every night for 15 years, between Columbus Drive and Lincoln Avenue, from 7:00 P.M. to 1:00 A.M. Dorothy had been most reliable, and had never been known to leave her beat during the middle of a shift during the entire 15 years. However, on one particular night, she left her beat and returned to the station at 8:00 P.M., claiming she had a headache. At 8:05 P.M., the limousine of gangster Johnny Scuzball deposited Johnny at the corner of Columbus and Lincoln, where he spoke a few words (apparently as part of a prearranged meeting) with Fred Slimy, head of a rival crime family. Three seconds after Slimy walked away from their meeting, a hail of bullets from rooftop snipers and from a moving car ripped through the body of Scuzball.

Slimy and Dorothy (among others) were charged with conspiracy to commit murder. The prosecutor, in addition to proving the above facts, showed that Dorothy had deposited $10,000 into her bank account the day before the shooting, and another $10,000 the day after, both in the form of checks drawn on a company owned by Slimy. The prosecution produced no other evidence that Dorothy and Slimy had in fact agreed to cooperate on a plan to kill Scuzball. May Dorothy properly be convicted of conspiracy to commit murder?

Not sure ☐

74. Dave had married a wealthy older woman, but was now in love with a stunning young model. While browsing through *Soldier of Fortune* magazine one day, he saw an ad that read, "For quick service in sensitive areas, call 1-800-BIG-KILL. We're not problem solvers, we're problem eliminators." Dave called the number and said, "I wonder if you could permanently eliminate a problem I've been

having; the problem is my wife." The voice at the other end agreed that this was well within his firm's capabilities and arranged to meet with Dave. The next day, Dave met with the representative, whose name was George; Dave agreed to pay $10,000 upon the successful "elimination" of Dave's wife. Shortly thereafter, George whipped out a badge, stated that he was an undercover police officer, and arrested Dave. Dave was charged with conspiracy to commit murder.

    (a) What argument should Dave make about why he may not be convicted of conspiracy to murder his wife?

    (b) In a jurisdiction that takes a "modern" view of the relevant issues (such as the view of the Model Penal Code), will the argument you cited in (a) succeed?

75. Bonnie and Clyde were well-known bank robbers who had recently been paroled. Because of the sensational nature of their crimes, their photos had been on the front page of most newspapers. Shortly after their parole, both walked into a store specializing in blowtorches. They requested a super-high-temperature plasma torch, usable only on very durable substances. Doug, the store owner, recognized Bonnie and Clyde immediately. Because of Doug's expertise with metalworking torches and clues dropped by Clyde, Doug knew to a virtual certainty that the two purchasers would use the torch to break into a bank vault by melting a hole through it. Doug hated all savings institutions, so he gladly supplied Bonnie and Clyde with the torch at his standard price. The next day, Bonnie and Clyde were caught using the torch to burn a hole through the main vault of First City Bank. Doug, along with Bonnie and Clyde, was charged with conspiracy to commit bank robbery. May Doug be properly convicted?

76. Same basic fact pattern as in the previous question. Now, assume that Doug, after hearing what Bonnie and Clyde wanted, replied, "Listen, I know that the only reason these torches are used is to cut through heavy metal of the sort used in bank robberies. If you want me to keep quiet about what I know concerning your plans, pay me $2,000 a torch. That's three times the going rate for this kind of torch, but you guys will soon make that back 100-fold." Bonnie and Clyde agreed and bought one torch. If Bonnie and Clyde are caught using the torch to get into the bank, may Doug properly be convicted of conspiracy to commit bank robbery?

77. Arnold, Ben, and Casper were stars of the Langdell Lions professional football team. Liza was a professional sportswriter assigned by her newspaper to cover the team. In accordance with prevailing sportswriters' practice, Liza visited the Lions' locker room after each home game. After one game, Liza entered the locker room while Arnold, Ben, and Casper were all in a state of undress. The three players decided to have a little fun with Liza. They agreed, in whispered negotiations, that they would surround Liza while still naked, and would all at once shout, "Won't you please touch my member?" They then carried out this plan, causing Liza great mental distress. The statutes of the state of Langdell do not recognize any crime of sexual harassment, nor did the actual conduct (as opposed to planning) by the three players violate any other substantive statute of Langdell. However, an ingenious young prosecutor decided to charge the three players with conspiracy to commit sexual harassment. May the three players be convicted as charged?

78. Edward and Fred were the ne'er-do-well sons of Gertrude, a wealthy woman. Gertrude announced that she intended to disinherit the two young men. Edward and Fred then hatched a plan whereby Edward, while wearing a mask and gloves, would bludgeon Gertrude to death. He would then leave the house and return with Fred shortly thereafter, and they would both report the ghastly murder to the police, insinuating that it was the work of a demented burglar. Each would tell the police that they had been together at a movie when the murder took place.

  The men planned to carry out their act the next evening. However, they did not realize that their conversation was overheard by their maid, Maria, who warned Gertrude. Police arrested Edward and Fred before they took any concrete steps to further their plan. Edward and Fred have been charged with conspiracy to commit murder. May they properly be convicted?

79. Roger was the ringleader and mastermind of a cocaine distribution network. Roger had recruited 50 "retailers." Each retailer showed up at 6:00 A.M. each workday at a safe house supervised by Roger; each worker was given one or more packets of cocaine and assigned to a particular street location. Since all workers got together every morning, each knew most of the others by sight, and often spoke to others; all knew that all were involved in the same business of reselling cocaine supplied by Roger.

  In a sophisticated police undercover operation, 20 operatives were sent out to various street corners at the same time one morning; each made a "buy" of cocaine and arrested the seller. Through her good luck, Agnes was not one of the sellers arrested. However, one of the 20 operatives arrested, Brian, named Agnes as being one of the members of the ring. Agnes was charged with conspiracy to distribute cocaine. The prosecutor now seeks to have an out-of-court statement made by Brian to the police ("Agnes was one of the other resellers who got drugs each day from Roger and sold them on the street") admitted in evidence against Agnes. Under the rules of evidence, this out-of-court declaration can only be used against Agnes if the court concludes that Agnes and Brian were both part of the same larger conspiracy (so that it cannot be used against Agnes if Agnes and Roger were to be found to have been part of a smaller two-person conspiracy, Roger and Brian part of another two-person conspiracy, etc.). May Brian's out-of-court statement be admitted against Agnes?

80. Same facts as in the previous question. Now, however, assume that Agnes and Brian were both charged with not only conspiracy to distribute cocaine, but also the substantive act of selling cocaine. With respect to Agnes, the prosecution's theory was that Agnes was part of the conspiracy, knew of and approved of Brian's activities, and is therefore guilty of the substantive crime of heroine resale if Brian is guilty (since she was Brian's coconspirator). If the only evidence concerning Agnes's participation in the conspiracy is that Agnes received drugs each day from Roger, knew that Brian was doing the same, and knew that Brian was selling the drugs (but there is no direct evidence that Agnes herself sold drugs on the street), may Agnes be convicted of the substantive crime of cocaine sale?

81. Same basic facts as in the previous two questions. Now, assume that Roger masterminded the ring and distributed drugs to Brian (among others), but that Roger never actually sold drugs on the street. If the prosecution shows that Brian sold drugs on the street that he received from Roger, may Roger be convicted of the substantive crime of drug selling?

Not sure ☐

82. Agnes was an arson-fraud specialist. Any local property owner who was short of funds could arrange to have Agnes "torch" his home or place of business, so that insurance could be collected. Agnes got much of her business through word of mouth, with one satisfied customer telling another. Agnes was working on burning houses for both Barry and Cathy. Agnes had acquired each of these clients independently of the other, but Barry knew that Agnes was about to do some work for Cathy, and Cathy knew that Agnes was about to do work for Barry. Neither of them cared especially whether the other's project went successfully (except, of course, that each hoped that Agnes would not get caught in the act of burning the other's house, thus bringing suspicion on them all).

At Agnes's request, Barry purchased some gasoline for use in torching his (but not Cathy's) house. Shortly after this, Agnes was arrested on suspicion of arson. At this point, Agnes and Cathy had agreed that Agnes would burn Cathy's house, but neither Cathy nor Agnes had taken any overt act to carry out this plan. The prosecutor has charged Cathy with conspiracy to commit arson of Barry's house. The jurisdiction requires an overt act before one can be convicted of conspiracy, but permits an overt act by one member of the conspiracy to be attributed against all members. Therefore, the prosecutor's ability to convict Cathy depends entirely on whether Barry and Cathy were in the same, or different, conspiracies. Were Cathy and Barry in the same conspiracy?

Not sure ☐

83. Amos, Bill, and Carol agreed to buy a building, take out an insurance policy on it, and burn it down for the insurance proceeds. After they had bought the building and taken out the policy, but before they had caused the fire, Bill had a sudden religious reawakening and decided to leave the conspiracy. He thought about notifying the police, but he was afraid that Amos and Carol might kill him in revenge if he did so. So he notified Amos and Carol that he was no longer part of the conspiracy, told them that he hoped that they, too, would abandon the plan, and prayed that somehow the other two would fail. However, Amos and Carol disregarded his advice and burned the building down. Bill (together with the other two) was charged with conspiracy to commit arson.

(a) What defense should Bill raise?

Not sure ☐

(b) Will his defense be successful?

Not sure ☐

84. Same facts as in the previous question. Now, assume that in addition to the steps he took in the previous question, Bill also notified the police that sometime within the next week, Amos and Carol would attempt to burn down a building at 123 Main Street. However, because the police were overworked, they failed to act on Bill's warning promptly, and the building was in fact burned down. May Bill properly be convicted of conspiracy to commit arson?

Not sure ☐

85. Bob was married to Carol. Alice was married to Ted. Bob and Alice had been attracted to each other for several years, but had not done anything about it. Finally, one day, Bob telephoned Alice and asked her to meet him at the Ames Acres Motel,

where they would conduct an assignation. Alice agreed. Unbeknownst to them, Carol was listening on an extension. She arranged to have the police meet her at the motel at the appointed time. The police arrested Bob and Alice in their room while they were in a state of partial undress but had not yet committed adultery. In the state of which Ames is a part, adultery is a substantive crime. The prosecutor charged Bob and Alice with conspiracy to commit adultery. If you are defending Bob (or Alice), what defense should you assert?

Not sure ☐

86. Same basic fact pattern as in the previous question. Now, however, assume that the way Bob and Alice came to be together in the motel room was that Bob's friend Peter said to both Bob and Alice, "You know, you'd make a great couple. You should really try to get something going together." In a jurisdiction that would recognize the defense you asserted in your answer to the previous question, may Peter, Bob, and Alice all be charged with and convicted of conspiracy to commit adultery?

Not sure ☐

87. Same basic facts as in question 85. Suppose that the jurisdiction follows the Model Penal Code approach to relevant issues. Would the defense you asserted in response to question 85 succeed?

Not sure ☐

88. Barbara was 15 years old, and Rick was 19. Rick and Barbara had sex (Barbara wholeheartedly consented) in the state of Langdell. Langdell law defines statutory rape as the crime of having sex with a woman under the age of 16 (with or without her consent), provided that the defendant is over the age of 18. Neither Barbara nor Rick was charged with statutory rape. However, both were charged with conspiracy to commit statutory rape. Under Langdell's statutory rape laws, Barbara could not be charged with statutory rape (since according to the legislature, she is a member of the class that is to be protected). May Barbara properly be convicted of conspiracy to commit statutory rape?

Not sure ☐

89. Same basic fact pattern as in the previous question. Assume that Barbara may not, under Langdell law, be properly charged with conspiracy to commit statutory rape (or with statutory rape itself). Will this fact prevent the conviction of Rick for conspiracy to commit statutory rape?

Not sure ☐

90. Anthony, Bing, and Cathy were all charged with conspiracy to commit murder. The prosecution alleged that the three had conspired together, and there was no evidence that anyone else had been involved. The murder was never achieved. The three defendants were tried in a single proceeding. The jury acquitted Anthony and Bing and found Cathy guilty. Does the fact that Anthony and Bing were acquitted entitle Cathy to have her conviction overturned?

Not sure ☐

91. Same basic fact pattern as in the previous question. Now, however, assume that for evidentiary reasons, only Cathy is charged with conspiracy, and Anthony and Bing are never charged. Assuming that the prosecutor shows, in Cathy's trial, that Cathy reached the requisite conspiratorial agreement with Anthony and Bing, does the fact that Anthony and Bing have never been charged prevent the conviction of Cathy?

Not sure ☐

92. Burger was an accomplished burglar, but he had not pulled a score in a month or so. This had a somewhat negative effect on Fenster, the fence to whom Burger sold

most of the merchandise he burgled. Therefore, Fenster said to Burger one day, "Why don't you hit Homer's house? I hear that he's going to be away for the next two weeks, and he's got a valuable coin collection." Burger took Fenster's advice and entered Homer's house at night, looking for the collection. He found it, left the house, and was arrested by the police as he was driving away. May Fenster be convicted of burglarizing Homer's home? Give the reason for your answer.

Not sure ☐

93. Anita was the director of sales for the ABC Pen Company, a company in the business of selling pens in large volume to business customers. Anita's friend Brian was a clerk in the purchasing office of Langdell County. Anita asked Brian how she might go about selling pens to Langdell. Brian replied, "There's a lot of bribery going on in the department. If you want to sell pens, you've got to give a 5 percent kickback to Charlie, my boss, who's director of the purchasing office." (Brian did not care one way or the other whether Anita succeeded in selling the pens to Langdell, or in bribing Charlie, except that he had a very mild interest in having Anita succeed at her business because he liked Anita.)

Acting on Brian's advice, Anita contacted Charlie and agreed to pay him 5 percent of the value of any pens that Charlie's department bought for Langdell. Charlie placed a large order, and Anita gave Charlie $5,000 as his 5 percent kickback. Throughout the proceedings, Anita kept Brian abreast of what was going on. Shortly after the payment, Anita, Brian, and Charlie were all charged with commercial bribery (which in the jurisdiction is defined as paying or receiving a benefit as consideration for violating the duties of one's job). Assuming that Anita and Charlie may properly be convicted of bribery, may Brian also be so convicted?

Not sure ☐

94. Alex and Ben were roommates. One night, Ben had consumed eight beers and two whiskeys within a one-hour period and was quite obviously intoxicated. Alex had also consumed a few drinks. Ben wanted to go out for some cigarettes, so he asked to borrow Alex's car. Alex was aware that Ben was quite drunk, but nonetheless lent Ben his car keys so that Ben could make the trip. While Ben was driving, he struck and killed a pedestrian. Assume that Ben's conduct amounted to involuntary manslaughter, which in the jurisdiction is defined as recklessly causing the death of another. Assume further that Alex, by lending his keys to Ben, recklessly disregarded the possibility that Ben might injure or kill someone. May Alex be held liable for manslaughter on the theory that he was an accomplice to Ben's manslaughter?

Not sure ☐

95. Arnold and Bob had been in prison together, and therefore Arnold knew that Bob was a convicted rapist. After the two got out of jail, they decided to cooperate on a burglary. They picked a house belonging to Monica and decided to burglarize it at a time when there was some chance (but by no means a certainty) that Monica would be home. The plan was for Arnold to drive the car and function as a lookout, while Bob went into the house to steal whatever jewelry and other valuables might easily be carried away. Before Bob went into the house, he said to Arnold, "Boy, I hear that Monica's a good-looking woman; maybe my gun will help me get lucky." Arnold laughed and said, "Now, keep your mind on money, not sex." Arnold did not especially desire to have Bob rape Monica—he didn't care one way or the other as long as Bob got the valuables out with appropriate speed. Bob went into the house,

gathered up some jewelry, and then was accosted by Monica. At gunpoint, Bob raped Monica. May Arnold be properly convicted of rape on an accomplice theory in a jurisdiction following the majority approach to relevant issues?   Not sure ☐

96. Ashley and Brian decided to rob a bank. Each was to carry a loaded pistol, but each agreed not to use it unless there was no other way to avoid being caught. The two strode into the bank, pointed their guns at the tellers, and demanded money, which they received. As the two were walking out of the bank, Bob slipped, with his gun still in hand. The gun discharged; the bullet hit the marble floor of the bank and ricocheted off, striking and killing Ray, a guard. Assuming that under the felony murder rule Bob is guilty of murdering Ray, may Arnold be convicted of Ray's murder on an accomplice theory?   Not sure ☐

97. Dan and Pat were friends. They agreed to rob First Hibernia National Bank. Dan's role was to supply the necessary equipment (principally a gun), drive the getaway car, and serve as lookout. Pat's role was to enter the bank, perform the actual holdup, and come out with the money. The robbery proceeded according to plan, except that both men were arrested shortly after they drove away from the bank. Dan and Pat were both charged with bank robbery and tried in a single proceeding. Pat was acquitted, for reasons not specified by the jury. Dan, however, was convicted. Does the fact of Pat's acquittal entitle Dan to a reversal of his conviction?   Not sure ☐

98. Peggy and Daphne witnessed a drug deal. Both were enraged by this breakdown of law and decency. Daphne, who knew that Peggy owned a gun, said to Peggy, "Why don't you shoot that drug-dealing scum?" Peggy got her gun, and both women went onto a nearby rooftop, from which they could see (and Peggy could shoot) the offending dealer. Moments before Peggy was to shoot, Daphne changed her mind about whether this was a good idea. She didn't say anything to Peggy, but she quietly went downstairs to the ground floor. As Daphne was walking away, Peggy shot the drug dealer to death. Daphne was charged as an accomplice to murder.

   (a) What defense should Daphne assert?   Not sure ☐

   (b) Will this defense succeed?   Not sure ☐

99. Same facts as in the previous question. Now, however, assume that instead of just leaving the rooftop, Daphne said to Peggy, "On second thought, I think this is a bad idea. Please give me your gun." Peggy refused. Daphne ran to get a police officer, but by the time Daphne and the officer arrived, Peggy had already shot the dealer. If Daphne is charged with being an accomplice to murder, may the jury properly convict her?   Not sure ☐

100. The state of Pound makes it a crime to commit prostitution, which is defined as "the selling of sexual acts in exchange for money." The state has no statutory provisions making it a crime to purchase sex from a prostitute. After Holly performed sex with John in return for a payment from John, both were arrested. Holly was charged with prostitution, and John was charged with being an accomplice to the crime of prostitution. May John properly be convicted?   Not sure ☐

101. Dominique was a 15-year-old girl. She became infatuated with Larry, a 22-year-old man, whom she had met at work. Dominique repeatedly telephoned Larry, asking him to have sex with her. Finally, Larry did so. In the State of Ames, where this took place, it is statutory rape for any man over the age of 20 to engage in intercourse with any woman under the age of 16. Larry was charged with statutory rape, and Dominique was charged with being an accessory to statutory rape. Putting aside the issue of whether Dominique's youth prevents her from being tried as an adult for the crime, may Dominique be convicted as an accomplice to statutory rape?

Not sure ☐

102. Larry cold-bloodedly murdered his wife, Dolores, to collect insurance on her life. Larry then confessed his foul deed to his friend, Dwain. Larry asked Dwain to supply him with money to get out of the country, but Dwain refused. Larry also said to Dwain, "I've trusted you, Dwain. Don't tell the police, or I'll be ruined." Dwain was instinctively law abiding, but he agreed not to turn Larry in. Larry escaped to South America. What crime, if any, is Larry guilty of?

Not sure ☐

103. Same facts as in the previous question. Now, assume that Dwain, eager to help his friend (but not acting out of any monetary motive), drove Larry to the airport to catch his plane for South America and lent him $10,000 for travel and temporary living expenses. Larry's escape was thus successful. Because Larry had virtually no funds of his own and the police were already hot on his tail, Larry could not have escaped without Dwain's assistance. May Dwain properly be charged as an accessory to murder and thus convicted of murder?

Not sure ☐

104. Same facts as in the previous question. Assume for this question only that the answer to the previous question is no. Of what crime, if any, is Dwain guilty?

Not sure ☐

105. Denzil mailed to his friend Albert a letter stating, "If you'd like to get rich quickly, meet me at my house at 10:00 P.M. We'll both rob the Bank of Langdell. Your friend, Denzil." Albert read the letter, but did not respond to it or take any steps toward robbing the bank.

(a) If you are the prosecutor, what is the most plausible crime you could charge Denzil with?

Not sure ☐

(b) Is Denzil guilty of the crime you gave as your answer to (a)?

Not sure ☐

106. Darren, a resident of Langdell, was estranged from his wife, Estelle. One day, while doing his food shopping, Darren heard a local gossip talking about Estelle: "Well, I hear that she's three months pregnant, and she left Darren five months ago." Darren was enraged that his wife was pregnant by another man. He went to his wife's apartment and shouted, "I'm gonna punch it out of you," and repeatedly punched her in the stomach. A week later, the child was stillborn, with a fractured skull. Langdell has a standard murder statute, which does not specify any rule regarding the death of fetuses. May Darren properly be convicted of murder?

Not sure ☐

107. Same facts as in the previous question. Now, however, assume that the child was born alive, but then died of complications (stemming from the fractured skull) ten minutes later. Can Darren properly be convicted of murder?

Not sure ☐

108. Desmond had been having increasing strife with his wife, Vera, a wealthy heiress. Desmond was the beneficiary of a large insurance policy on Vera's life. One day, Vera simply vanished, and had not been seen again by the time Desmond was put

on trial for murder six years later. The couple had two children, to whom Vera was known to be devoted, yet the children never received any communication from Vera. At the time of Vera's disappearance, Desmond owned a wood-chipping machine that could reduce wood and other dense substances to tiny fragments. Shortly after Vera's disappearance, police inspected the wood chipper and found a couple of tiny white fragments that seemed to be bone, though it could never be proven that these were human bones, let alone Vera's bones. At his murder trial, Desmond has raised the defense that since no body was ever found, it has not been shown that Vera is dead, and he therefore cannot be convicted of murder. Should the trial judge accept Desmond's argument and dismiss the case before it goes to the jury?

Not sure ☐

109. Dominick, a diamond trader in New York City, was in deep financial trouble. Therefore, he bought a large number of valuable diamonds, insured them, and purported to send them to a California bank. However, what Dominick really did was to have a set of fakes made up and to sell the real ones for cash, which he sent to Switzerland. He then sent the fake set, via airplane, addressed to the California bank. Simultaneously, Dominick put a bomb in a different package, which he made sure was on the same plane. Dominick had no desire to kill anyone, but knew that if his plan succeeded, people would die. The bomb exploded in midflight, as Dominick planned. All passengers were killed. Dominick filed an insurance claim for loss of the diamonds. Dominick was charged with murder of the passengers. May he be properly convicted?

Not sure ☐

110. Same basic fact pattern as in the previous question. Now, however, assume that Dominick decided not to send the fake diamonds by plane. Instead, he sent them by Federal Express. Simultaneously, he sent via Federal Express a second parcel, this one containing a bomb. The bomb was set to go off sometime within the first three hours after shipment. The bomb was powerful enough that, as Dominick knew, it would probably destroy the truck and anyone in it. Dominick reasoned (and, indeed, hoped) that the driver would happen to be out of the truck at the time of the explosion—he realized that Federal Express drivers spend about half their time on their route out of the truck making pickups and deliveries to customers. In fact, however, the bomb exploded while Joe, the driver, was on his truck. Joe was instantly killed, and Dominick was charged with his murder. May Dominick be convicted of murder?

Not sure ☐

111. Frank was a professional loan shark. Norman, the owner of a struggling garment-district business, needed money desperately. He borrowed $10,000 from Frank, under an agreement to pay it a week later with 3 percent interest. When Norman did not repay, Frank became furious. He went to Norman's house and, using his fists, broke both of Norman's legs. He also put out his lit cigarette on Norman's cheek. Frank did not intend to kill Norman. In fact, Frank affirmatively desired that Norman *not* die, since if he did, he would not be able to pay Frank back. Frank's intent was only to cause Norman sufficiently serious bodily injury that Norman would be persuaded to do whatever he had to do to pay Frank back. However, due to the shock, Norman suffered a heart attack and died a day later. Frank was charged with murdering Norman. Putting aside the felony murder doctrine, may Frank be convicted?

Not sure ☐

112. Dwight, a former intravenous drug addict, was diagnosed as having AIDS. Dwight knew from reading the popular press that doctors estimated that a person suffering from AIDS who had sex with a particular partner, say, 100 times, had about a 70 percent chance of giving that partner the AIDS virus. Dwight also knew that given the limits of today's medical knowledge, a person who is infected with the AIDS virus almost always eventually develops AIDS, and that virtually everyone who develops AIDS eventually dies of it. Notwithstanding this, Dwight decided that he was not going to lead a celibate life and that his sexual partners would just have to fend for themselves. Soon after his diagnosis, he began an ongoing sexual liaison with Sheila and did not disclose his condition to her. Nor did he ever wear condoms, because they rendered sex less pleasurable for him. Dwight and Sheila slept together more than 200 times over the next two years. Sheila contracted AIDS and died. Dwight is still alive. Genetic tests of the AIDS virus taken from the blood of both Sheila and Dwight show beyond a reasonable doubt that Sheila contracted AIDS from Dwight. May Dwight properly be convicted of murdering Sheila, and if so, on what theory? Not sure ☐

113. Benny and Clark decided to rob a convenience store owned by Omar. Each carried a loaded pistol, but neither planned to shoot the pistol unless absolutely necessary. Benny demanded that Omar lie down. Benny then tied Omar's hands behind his back. Finally, Benny tapped Omar lightly on the forehead with his gun, intending to stun him briefly so that the two robbers would have a little extra time to get away before Omar could untie himself and phone the police. Unbeknownst to Benny, Omar had an unusually thin skull, and the blow with the butt of the gun caused Omar to burst a blood vessel, which resulted in his death. (At most, 1 person out of 100 subjected to this stress and blow, as Omar was, would have died from it.) Benny is charged with murdering Omar.

(a) If you are the prosecutor, what doctrine would you use to increase your chances of getting a murder conviction? Not sure ☐

(b) Will the doctrine you used in your answer to part (a) enable you to convict Benny of murder? Not sure ☐

114. Same facts as in the previous question. If the jurisdiction follows the Model Penal Code approach to all relevant matters, would Benny be convicted? Not sure ☐

115. Same facts as in question 113. Assuming that Benny may properly be convicted of murder on these facts, may Clark be convicted of murder? Not sure ☐

116. Same basic facts as in the previous three questions. Now, however, assume that after Benny ordered Omar to lie down, Omar grabbed his own gun, shot at Benny but hit Jean, a shopper who happened to be standing nearby. Jean died instantly. Benny is charged with murdering Jean. May he properly be convicted? Not sure ☐

117. Same facts as in the previous four questions. Now, assume that Omar complied with Benny's demand that he lie on the floor, but that Omar managed to signal the police. A police officer arrived, saw Clark holding a loaded gun, and shot Clark to death. May Benny be properly convicted of Clark's murder? Not sure ☐

118. Donald had just finished stealing, at gunpoint, $100,000 in cash from First National Bank. He drove away from the crime scene, being careful to stay within the 55 mph speed limit. However, he knew that the police were on his tail. One mile from the crime scene (en route to the hideaway where he planned to stash the loot), Donald struck and killed Peter, a pedestrian. Donald was negligent in not looking more closely, but his inattention did not rise to the level of recklessness. May Donald be convicted of murdering Peter?

Not sure ☐

119. Seymour returned home unexpectedly early from a business trip. Upon entering his apartment, he saw his wife, Ellen, in bed with a man whom Seymour immediately recognized as his own best friend and next-door neighbor, Fred. Seymour was seized with a fit of unspeakable rage. He grabbed the first object he could find, which happened to be a hammer he had been using for some home repairs. He attacked Fred with the hammer, pounding him repeatedly on the head. He intended to kill Fred, and that is exactly what he did. What is the most serious crime, if any, of which Seymour can be convicted?

Not sure ☐

120. Same facts as in the previous question. Now, assume that Seymour spotted Ellen and Fred in bed and then left the apartment before the other two realized that they had been seen. Seymour checked into a hotel, brooded for the next day, and then purchased a pistol. He went to Fred's house, waited outside Fred's door, and shot Fred (without exchanging any words) when Fred emerged. Fred died immediately. What is the most serious crime of which Seymour may be convicted?

Not sure ☐

121. For several months, both Sam and Victor had sought the affection of Terry, a waitress at the bar where both men worked. Finally, Sam and Victor agreed that they would have a street fight in an alley behind the bar, and that the loser of the fight would not pursue Terry any further. Early in the fight, Victor got the upper hand, punching Sam in the face. Sam realized that any time, he could call off the fight without being seriously hurt. However, Sam became enraged at losing the fight. With a burst of adrenaline, he managed to get Victor in a stranglehold and throw him to the ground. He then began to kick Victor in the head with his heavy boots, attempting to seriously injure or even kill Victor. In fact, Sam succeeded—Victor died two hours later of head injuries. What is the most serious crime of which Sam can be convicted?

Not sure ☐

122. Larry took his girlfriend, Lorraine, to a disco. As they were dancing, another patron, Ken, made numerous attempts to cut in on Larry, so that he could dance with Lorraine. Finally, Lorraine said to Larry, "Let me dance with this guy—don't be so possessive." Lorraine then began to dance with Ken and refused to come back to Larry. Larry had an unusually short fuse—he had always had a hair-trigger temper, and in fact in childhood had suffered from "irritable baby" syndrome. Although a person of ordinary calmness would not have been unduly provoked by Lorraine and Ken's conduct, a person of Larry's emotional makeup would generally have done exactly what Larry did—he flew into a rage, pulled out a knife, and slashed Ken's throat right on the dance floor, killing him. What is the most serious crime of which Larry can be convicted?

Not sure ☐

123. Kirk was an avid, and properly licensed, deer hunter. During one deer season, he decided to hunt in a region called Acadia, which had once been completely uninhabited, but which (as Kirk knew) was now immediately adjacent to a sizable development of homes. Kirk was standing at a point he knew to be about 300 yards away from the closest houses, when he saw a moving flash of brown and white in the direction where the houses lay. He thought this was a deer. He immediately pointed his rifle and shot. Unbeknownst to Kirk, the flash of brown was in fact Sally standing in her backyard at the edge of the woods, wearing a brown fox-fur coat trimmed in white mink. The shot struck Sally in the chest, and she died immediately. Assume that Kirk's actions (hunting so close to the houses, shooting in the direction of the houses, and not verifying that what he saw was a deer) constituted gross negligence, but that his actions did not manifest a depraved indifference to the value of human life. What is the most serious crime of which Kirk is guilty?   Not sure ☐

124. Same basic fact pattern as in the previous question. Now, however, assume that Kirk was new to the region and did not know that there were housing developments nearby in the direction at which he was pointing his gun. Assume further, however, that an ordinarily careful person would have asked questions of hunters who lived in the area, and would probably have discovered that houses were nearby. May Kirk on these facts be convicted of the same crime that you listed as your answer to the previous question?   Not sure ☐

125. Same facts as in the previous question. Now, assume that the case is tried in a jurisdiction following the Model Penal Code's approach to all relevant matters. What is the most serious crime of which Kirk may be convicted?   Not sure ☐

126. Dan was a construction worker who worked on the upper floors of skyscrapers. He took a very casual approach to his job, throwing around large pieces of concrete and steel without worrying too much whether they fell over the side, even though he knew that a piece that fell and hit somebody would almost certainly kill them. One day, he tossed a 30-pound bag of dry cement over the side of the building because he didn't need it and the freight elevator was busy. The bag fortunately did not hit anyone when it landed; however, when it hit the street, it burst open and created a huge cloud of dust. About 30 seconds later, a car driven by Chris went into the dust cloud. Chris's vision was distracted, causing her to veer to the side and strike Valerie, who was standing on the sidewalk. Valerie died instantly. May Dan be properly convicted of involuntary manslaughter in a jurisdiction that requires recklessness for that crime?   Not sure ☐

127. Leonard believed (correctly) that Marvin had flirted with Leonard's girlfriend at a dance the previous night. When Leonard met Marvin on the street, Leonard said, "Don't you ever even look at my girlfriend again," and then gave Marvin a gentle but clear shove. Leonard was not trying to kill, or even seriously injure, Marvin—he was merely trying to convince Marvin that he, Leonard, was someone whose girlfriend ought not to be flirted with. However, Marvin lost his balance from the shove, fell down, cracked his head on the edge of the curb, and died of brain injuries. In a jurisdiction following the majority approach to all relevant matters, what is the most serious crime that Leonard can be convicted of?   Not sure ☐

128. Same facts as in the previous question. Now, assume that the jurisdiction applies the Model Penal Code's approach to all relevant matters. May Leonard be convicted of involuntary manslaughter?   Not sure ☐

129. Tom was a notorious practical joker. One day, he stood at his second-floor window, waiting for Victor (whom Tom knew slightly) to pass by below. As Victor passed by, Tom dropped a balloon filled with pig's blood, which Tom had procured from a medical supply store. The balloon broke when it hit Victor's head and splashed the blood all over him. Victor was not hurt, but he was quite disgusted. What crime, if any, has Tom committed?

Not sure ☐

130. Tom decided that, as a practical joke, he wanted to frighten his friend Victor. Therefore, he took a beaker that had a label with both a skull and crossbones and the word "acid" written in large type on it. Tom filled the beaker with water. He went up to Victor on the street, said to him, "This is from your ex-wife," showed him the beaker, and tossed the water near (but not on) Victor's face. For a brief instant, Victor believed that his face would be scarred and that he might be blinded. What crime, if any, has Tom committed?

Not sure ☐

131. Same facts as in question 129. Assume, however, that Tom missed Victor with the balloon, and the balloon splashed into the street. Victor was looking down at the pavement and never sensed that he was in danger of being hit until after the episode was over. Also, the balloon contained harmful acid, which would have scarred Victor's skin if it had touched him. Putting aside attempt crimes, what crime, if any, has Tom committed?

Not sure ☐

132. Michael met Wanda at a singles bar. By the time they met, it was obvious to Michael that Wanda had consumed quite a few drinks and was seriously drunk. Michael did not buy Wanda any additional drinks. Instead, he asked her if she wanted to come to his apartment, and she nodded, somewhat dreamily. When they got to his apartment, Michael undressed her and began to make love to her. Wanda giggled and made slurred remarks, which Michael reasonably believed indicated that she was conscious and that she was not objecting. The next day, Wanda, now sober, relived the whole episode and made a complaint to the prosecutor that she had been raped. Assume that Wanda demonstrates to the satisfaction of the court that she would not have consented to sex had she not been drunk, and that Michael knew or should have known that the appearance of consent was due to Wanda's drunkenness. May Michael properly be convicted of rape in a jurisdiction following the Model Penal Code approach?

Not sure ☐

133. Rick met Kevin at a bar for gay men. Kevin accepted Rick's invitation to go to Rick's apartment for a drink. At the apartment, Rick, using his superior strength, forced Kevin to submit to anal intercourse. In a jurisdiction following a traditional approach to the definition of rape, may Rick be convicted of rape?

Not sure ☐

134. Howard and Wendy were married and living together. One night, Howard insisted that they have sex. Wendy said that she did not want to do so because she had a headache. Howard insisted and used force to have his way. In a state following the traditional definition of rape, may Howard be convicted of raping Wendy?

Not sure ☐

135. Same basic fact pattern. Now, however, assume that Howard and Wendy had been living apart according to a separation agreement that they both signed. Wendy then invited Howard over for dinner to see if they could reconcile. Howard forced Wendy to have sex against her will at the end of the evening. In a state following the traditional definition of rape, may Howard properly be convicted of rape?

Not sure ☐

136. Howard and Wendy were married. Howard had a prospective business associate, Ted, whom Howard was anxious to impress. Howard told Ted, "I will arrange for you to have sex with my wife tonight. Don't worry about whether she consents or not." Howard then stood by while Ted forced Wendy to have sex with him, over her strong protests. In a state following the traditional definition of rape, may Howard be convicted of rape?

137. The State of Langdell makes it the crime of "statutory rape" for a male over the age of 20 to have sex with a female under the age of 16, even with the latter's consent. Mark, who was 21, met Jill at a college basketball game. Jill said she was 18 and that she was a freshman at the university. Mark honestly, and reasonably, believed this. With Jill's consent, they had sex. Jill was in fact 15½ and was still in high school. Mark was charged with rape. If Mark shows at trial that he honestly and reasonably believed that Jill was at least 16, may he properly be convicted? Assume that the state follows the prevailing view toward all relevant matters.

138. Same facts as in the previous question. Now, assume that the jurisdiction follows the Model Penal Code approach. May Mark properly be convicted of rape?

139. Doug attacked Estelle in a deserted parking lot at night. He forced her to partially disrobe and attempted to have intercourse with her. He achieved partial penetration, but there was no emission of semen. May Doug properly be convicted of rape?

140. Dave accosts Vicki on the street and makes her walk 20 feet to her car, where he detains her. May he be convicted of kidnapping?

141. Ludwig was the president of Bavarian-American Motors (BAM), a company that manufactured cars that looked German but were in fact American. The company was publicly held, and Ludwig had only a very small minority stake, even though he was president. By resolution of the board of directors, Ludwig was entitled to use one of the company's most expensive models, the BAM 560sel, for his personal use, as long as he remained president. After several quarters in which the company's profits dropped precipitously, the board of directors fired Ludwig (as they had the legal right to do). They also asked Ludwig to return the car (as he was required to do under the terms of his employment agreement).

Ludwig refused to return the car, which had a market value of $80,000. Ludwig kept the car for six months and refused numerous requests that it be returned. Ludwig knew he had no legal right to retain the car, but decided to keep it as a way of getting revenge on BAM for unjustly (though not illegally) firing him. At the corporation's request, the prosecutor charged Ludwig with the crime of larceny. The jurisdiction maintains the traditional definitions of theft crimes. Is Ludwig guilty of the crime charged?

142. Megan was a lowly messenger for the large, establishment law firm of Rich, Rich & Richer. As one of her tasks one day, she was given a stack of "bearer bonds." These were bonds that had a value of $1 million and that could be negotiated by anyone who held them, regardless of whether that person had proof of ownership. Megan left the office with the intent to perform her job properly, and headed toward the bank where the bonds were to be delivered. However, in mid-trip she realized that this might be the big break she had been waiting for. She sold the bonds to a Wall Street–based dealer in stolen instruments and received $50,000 for them. She then booked a flight to Rio de Janeiro. She was arrested at the airport and charged with larceny. Is she guilty of this crime?

Not sure ☐

143. As he was sitting in the park one day, Stanley noticed a wallet on the park bench beside him. He picked it up and saw that it contained several hundred dollars, as well as the driver's license (with address) of the wallet's owner, Wilhelmina. Stanley picked up the wallet and put it in his pocket, thinking that he would return it to Wilhelmina, who, based on the address on the license, lived quite nearby. However, the next day, Stanley realized that he could use the money himself, and that if he used the money, he couldn't very well return the wallet in person. Therefore, he kept the money and put the wallet in a public wastebasket. What crime, if any, has Stanley committed:

(a) At common law?

Not sure ☐

(b) Under the Model Penal Code?

Not sure ☐

144. Same basic fact pattern as in the previous question. Now, assume that at the time Stanley found the wallet, he said to himself, "I think I'll keep this, since I really need the money." But several days later, Stanley had a change of heart. He therefore went to the address shown on the license, hoping to find Wilhelmina and return her wallet to her. However, Wilhelmina had moved and left no forwarding address. Stanley went home, and he kept the wallet and money. While Stanley's apartment was being searched on account of an unrelated search warrant, the police found the wallet with the money still in it. Of what crime, if any, is Stanley guilty:

(a) At common law?

Not sure ☐

(b) Under the Model Penal Code?

Not sure ☐

145. Jerome owned and ran a jewelry store. Jerome advertised a ring as containing a "flawless white three-carat diamond," and offered it for sale at a price of $5,000. In fact, as Jerome well knew, the stone in the ring was cubic zirconium and had a fair value of $50. Virgil, who knew almost nothing about jewelry, relied on Jerome's statement that the ring was a diamond and paid Jerome's asking price. What crime, if any, has Jerome committed at common law?

Not sure ☐

146. Ready Rentals, Inc., was in the business of renting cars. Timothy rented a car from Ready, supplying a false name and false credit card number. He intended to use the car for as long as he could until Ready finally tracked him down and reclaimed it; he did not intend ever to pay for this use. After Timothy had used the car for six months, a police officer spotted it on a list of stolen cars, reclaimed it, and returned it to Ready. What crime, if any, has Timothy committed at common law?

Not sure ☐

147. Benjamin owned a new 2012 Ferrari Testarossa worth $150,000. One day, he left it parked in his driveway, with his keys in it. Dennis, Benjamin's next-door neighbor, had always wanted to drive a Testarossa. He spotted the keys through the window and decided that this was his chance. He intended to drive the car for an hour and then return it to Benjamin. After he had driven it for about ten minutes, he made a wrong turn on a steep curve while going much too fast. The car slammed into a tree and was totally destroyed. May Dennis be convicted of common law larceny?

Not sure ☐

148. Sally was a clerk at the FloorMart Variety Store. One Friday, late in the afternoon, George, the manager of the store, informed Sally that she was being laid off because business was poor. When Sally asked how large a check she would get as her retirement-plan proceeds, George told her that she would get zero, because she had not been on the job for two years (required under the plan before a claim vests). Sally incorrectly but honestly believed that she was entitled to the $300 balance shown on a recent statement as being "in" her retirement account. When George refused to pay this amount, Sally took one of the store's ruby rings, on sale for $289, in her purse and walked out with it. The ring was found when store detectives searched her in the parking lot. May Sally properly be convicted of larceny?

Not sure ☐

149. Alan, an attorney, represented Veronica, the owner of Stanhope Hall, a large estate that had been in Veronica's family for generations. Veronica decided to sell Stanhope Hall, and retained Alan to carry out the transaction. The property was sold for $1 million, of which Veronica immediately received $900,000. Veronica agreed to let Alan keep the remaining $100,000 in Alan's escrow account, to be used to pay any claims that might be made relating to the property (e.g., real estate taxes). Alan then prepared phony invoices purporting to be for expenses incurred prior to the sale, such as phony tax bills. He transferred $20,000, purportedly in payment of such bills, to his own personal account, and then spent the money. At the time he took the money, Alan never intended to repay it and relied on his ability to escape detection. What common law theft crime, if any, has Alan committed?

Not sure ☐

150. Same basic facts as in the previous question. Now, assume that Alan did not resort to any phony invoices or other subterfuges. Instead, Alan developed a serious gambling habit and needed $50,000 to pay off his bookmaker. He therefore wrote a check on the escrow account for $50,000 and gave the proceeds to the bookmaker. At the time of this transaction, Alan intended to repay the money the following month, when he reasonably expected to receive a $200,000 legacy from his recently deceased maiden aunt. Indeed, the bequest came through as scheduled, and Alan repaid the $50,000 two months after "borrowing" it. Of what common law crime, if any, may Alan be properly convicted?

Not sure ☐

151. Ernest, the owner of a small business, offered each of his employees the opportunity to enroll in a "medical insurance payroll deductions plan." Under the terms of the plan, each employee could obtain group health insurance through Ernest's company, and the prorated amount of the premium would be withheld from that employee's weekly paycheck. Several employees, including Francis, accepted Ernest's proposal. From Francis's paycheck each week was deducted $30, which was the pro-rata cost of health insurance on Francis. Unbeknownst to Francis, Ernest never paid the premiums to the insurance company, because he wanted to collect the $30 per week to use in the business, which was financially troubled. Francis developed cancer, and then discovered that he had no insurance to cover the $100,000 in hospital and doctor bills. What crime, if any, has Ernest committed:

(a) At common law?

Not sure ☐

(b) Under the Model Penal Code?

Not sure ☐

152. Same facts as in the previous question. Now, assume that the plan proposed by Ernest did not involve a payroll deduction. Instead, Ernest simply promised every employee that, as an additional employment benefit, everyone would receive free health insurance to be paid for by a check written by Ernest directly to the insurance company. Ernest, without telling anyone, fails to make the promised payments because they were too costly. Under the Model Penal Code, is Ernest guilty of theft?

Not sure ☐

153. Chrysallis Motors was a manufacturer of automobiles. The company normally sold through dealers; however, on one occasion, the company announced that it would sell, as a promotion, a limited number of "brand-new" cars direct to the public, at discounted prices. Val bought one of these cars for $12,000 ($1,000 less than Chrysallis's suggested list price). In purchasing, Val relied on Chrysallis's representation that the car was new and on the further fact that the odometer showed only 1 mile driven. In fact, however, the car was a "test" car that had been driven 300 miles and had its odometer set back to 1 to fool the purchaser; it also had sustained serious damage to its chassis, which had been only partially repaired. The car was thus in reality a used and repaired car, with a market value of at most $9,000. The president of Chrysallis knew, and approved, of his underlings' attempts to sell this and other used/damaged cars as new. Assuming that Chrysallis may be convicted of crimes carried out by its high officials, of what crime, if any, may Chrysallis be convicted?

Not sure ☐

154. Same basic fact pattern as in the previous question. Now, however, assume that Chrysallis correctly advertised the cars as slightly used test models, indicated that some may have been repaired, and did not set back the odometers. Chrysallis did, however, advertise that the models being sold were "the best American-built cars on the market." In fact, however, nearly every automotive reviewer and public opinion survey had concluded that the cars in question were far from the best on the market. Val bought in reliance, in part, in Chrysallis's statement that these were the best American-built cars. What crime, if any, has Chrysallis committed?

Not sure ☐

155. Audrey borrowed $200,000 from Barnacle Savings & Loan. She promised that she would invest the money in a florist business that she ran, and that she would repay it in one year. Instead, Audrey immediately transmitted the money to a secret numbered Swiss bank account and failed to repay the money in one year. Since she had no American-based assets, the judgment that Barnacle got against her was valueless, and Audrey refused to disclose the identity of the Swiss bank where the funds were secreted, let alone the number of the account. The prosecutor now charges Audrey with theft by false pretenses. He presents testimony by Charles (Audrey's husband at the time, now her ex-husband) that immediately following the loan, Audrey said to him, "I'll never repay that—it'll be safe in Switzerland, where we'll retire to spend our easy gains." May Audrey properly be convicted of theft by false pretenses:

(a) In a state following the common law definition of this crime?

Not sure ☐

(b) In a state following the Model Penal Code approach?

Not sure ☐

156. Jeremy was the sole heir of his father, Peter, who died leaving, among other things, a baseball card collection put together in the 1940s and 1950s. Jeremy, who was not at all interested in baseball, believed that the cards were of only modest value. He brought the collection to Harold, a dealer in baseball cards, and asked Harold how much Harold would pay him for the collection. Harold examined the cards and immediately noticed that one of them was an extremely rare 1906 Honus Wagner card produced by American Tobacco Co. (one of only 11 such cards in the world, because Wagner abhorred tobacco and ordered all samples destroyed immediately after printing).

The Wagner card was in fact worth $10,000, as Harold knew. Harold made no comment on the quality of any individual card or the collection. He merely said to Jeremy, "I'll pay you $1,000 for the collection." This seemed like a pretty good price to Jeremy, so he agreed. Shortly thereafter, Jeremy learned the true value of the card and complained to the prosecutor. The prosecutor charged Harold with theft by false pretenses, in view of the enormous disparity between the amount Harold bought the collection for and the amount that (as Harold knew) the collection was worth, more than $10,000. May Harold properly be convicted?   Not sure ☐

157. Same basic facts as in the previous question. Now, however, assume that Jeremy knew of Harold's great expertise in valuing baseball card collections and asked Harold to act as Jeremy's agent in arranging the sale of the collection at auction for the highest amount possible. Harold then said to Jeremy, "It's not a very valuable collection; rather than my trying to arrange an auction, why don't you let me buy it from you for $1,000, and I'll add it to my general inventory." If, as Harold knew, the Honus Wagner card alone was worth $10,000, may Harold be found guilty of theft by false pretenses?   Not sure ☐

158. Marvin, a professional criminal, knew that Stewart would be away from home for several days. Therefore, at 1:00 A.M. on a Tuesday, Marvin went to Stewart's house, jimmied a lock on the rear door, and entered Stewart's house. At the time of his entry, Marvin's intent was to steal whatever cash and jewelry he might find. However, Marvin inadvertently set off Stewart's alarm. Police arrested Marvin before he had a chance to place any of Stewart's possessions into the sack that he had brought with him. What is the most serious crime of which Marvin may be convicted, at common law?   Not sure ☐

159. Same basic fact pattern as in the previous question. Now, however, assume that Marvin broke into Stewart's law office building at night, when he knew that neither Stewart nor anyone else was present. The building was a self-standing office building used exclusively for the practice of law. Marvin's purpose was to steal a valuable painting hanging on Stewart's office wall. Marvin in fact succeeded at carrying off the painting. Police recovered the painting sometime later, and Marvin was charged with burglary. Assuming the common law definition of burglary is in force, may Marvin properly be convicted?   Not sure ☐

160. Byron and Jenny had dated for several years, but Jenny had finally broken off the relationship. Byron remained hopelessly in love with Jenny, indeed obsessed with her. One evening, when Byron knew that Jenny was asleep in her house, Byron opened her rear window, climbed through it, went up the stairs, and stood beside her bed. His only purpose was to look at his beloved while she lay asleep. Jenny unexpectedly woke up, was terrified by Byron's uninvited presence, and

summoned the police. Byron was charged with burglary. Assuming that the common law definition of burglary applies, may Byron properly be convicted?   Not sure ☐

161. Tim, a professional criminal, knew that Sally maintained a valuable coin collection. Tim knew that Sally was away on business. He hired a couple of confederates, rented a large moving van, and drove up to Sally's house at 2:00 one Saturday afternoon. Tim picked Sally's front lock, entered the house with his henchmen, and removed several pieces of furniture as well as the coin collection. They did this all by successfully pretending to be moving men engaged by Sally. Eventually, Tim was caught trying to sell the coin collection to a fence. May Tim properly be convicted of common law burglary?   Not sure ☐

162. Felicia was walking down a crowded city street one day, wearing her brand-new $300 necklace. Tina came by on a motorbike, grabbed Felicia's chain, whisked it off her head, and sped off before Felicia could even react. Several hours later, Tina was caught and charged with robbery. May she properly be convicted if the crime is defined in the common law manner?   Not sure ☐

163. As Amanda was getting out of her driveway, Philip came up to her and said, "I've got a knife in my pocket. Give me your purse like a nice lady, and don't make me use the knife." Amanda was not sure whether Philip really had a knife, or whether he would use it, but she decided to take no chances and handed over her purse. In fact, Philip did not have a knife and would never have harmed Amanda. May Philip properly be convicted of robbery?   Not sure ☐

Criminal Law Answers to Short-Answer Questions

1. No. **All crimes include as one of their elements the "actus reus"—i.e., the requirement that the defendant's conduct include a *voluntary act*. An act performed reflexively or while in a state of unconsciousness does not meet this actus reus requirement.** Here, the facts make it clear that the choking action by Nelson was not a volitional one, so he will not be convicted.

2. No. **As a general principle, a person is *not liable* under Anglo-American law for *omissions to act*. There are a few exceptions to this general principle (e.g., where a statute explicitly imposes a duty to act), but none of these exceptions is present here.** Therefore, even though Peter could easily have prevented Richie's death, and even though Peter's failure to intervene resulted from his active dislike of Richie, Peter has no criminal liability.

3. Yes, probably. **There are several exceptions to the general rule that a party will not be criminally liable for mere omission to act. One of the exceptions occurs where the defendant caused the danger (innocently or otherwise).** Since Peter brought the entire episode about by inducing Nelson to jump in the ocean (even though Peter did so without negligence and without any desire to harm Nelson), a court would probably hold that Peter was sufficiently implicated that he then had a duty to aid Richie, whose peril was the foreseeable result of Nelson's peril.

4. Yes. **When courts hold that a crime requires merely "general intent," they usually mean that all that must be shown is that the defendant desired to commit the act that served as the actus reus.** Here, the act that served as the actus reus was placing the screwdriver against Jim's throat. Once the prosecution shows that Paul desired to unlawfully touch Jim's throat for the purpose of frightening him, the fact that Paul did not intend to injure Jim will be viewed as irrelevant.

5. One. **According to M.P.C. §2-02(2)(a), if a crime requires that the defendant "purposely" cause a particular result, it must have been the defendant's "conscious object . . . to cause such a result."** Here, Dean can be convicted of "explosively murdering" a particular person only if it was his conscious objective to kill that person by explosives. Dean had the conscious objective of killing Marie, so he is guilty of that crime. By contrast, even though Dean was an explosive expert and knew that his conduct was practically certain to kill Fred and Lona as well, Dean did not "purposely" kill them, so he cannot be convicted of explosively murdering them.

6. (a) Yes. **According to M.P.C. §2.02(2)(b)(ii), where the element of the crime relates to a result of the defendant's conduct, the defendant acts "knowingly" if "he is aware that it is practically certain that his conduct will cause such a result."** Since Dean knew that Fred was almost certain to die in the explosion, Dean acted "knowingly."

   (b) No. **The Model Penal Code (and most recent decisions) imposes a subjective test for determining whether defendant "knowingly" caused a certain result.** That is, the test is whether the defendant *actually* knew or believed something, not merely whether a reasonable person in the position of the defendant would have had or should have had that knowledge or belief. Since Dean did not know that Lona would be killed, he will not be convicted of her explosive murder.

7. No. **If "indecent exposure" is not a strict liability crime, then Dennis cannot be convicted because he had an "innocent" mental state. If it *is* a strict liability crime, then Dennis can be convicted, because the whole concept of a strict liability crime is that it is a crime for which no culpable**

mental state at all needs to be shown—it is enough that the defendant has performed the act in question, regardless of his or her mental state. The fact that the legislature has failed to specify any mental state is not dispositive—courts often infer a mental state requirement even where the statute is silent.

Two factors that make it much more likely that a court will find that a crime is a strict liability one are (1) that the penalty prescribed is small, and (2) that conviction does not gravely damage the defendant's reputation. Here, neither of these factors is present: The penalty prescribed is imprisonment of up to a year—not a small penalty—and conviction would substantially damage Dennis's reputation. The Model Penal Code makes it clear that this could not be a strict liability offense, since any offense that is defined as a "crime," or that is punishable by imprisonment, cannot be based on strict liability. See M.P.C. §§2.02(1) and 2.05.

8. **No. Some older cases contain broad statements to the effect that a mistake of fact cannot be a defense unless the mistake was "reasonable." But the Model Penal Code—and nearly all modern statutes—holds that if intent or knowledge is required as an element of a crime, then even an *unreasonable mistake* will block conviction if it negated such intent or knowledge. See M.P.C. §2.04(1)(a).** Thus here, Bill's belief in the truth of Harry's story prevented Bill from having the requisite intent to take another's property or the requisite knowledge that it belonged to another—the fact that Bill was unreasonably credulous is irrelevant. Of course, the more unreasonable Bill's belief in the truth of Harry's story is, the less likely the judge or jury is to find that Bill in fact believed that story. But the facts here tell us that Bill actually believed the story, so this by itself is enough to negate purpose or knowledge.

9. Yes. **The fact that the defendant honestly (and even reasonably) fails to realize that particular conduct is a crime does not constitute a defense. There are exceptions (e.g., where the statute defining the conduct as a crime has not been published), but none of the exceptions are available here.** The fact that most adults are unaware that the conduct is a crime is not sufficient to trigger this "crime not sufficiently published" exception.

10. No. **For a defendant to be guilty of a crime, not only must there be the requisite act and mental state, but these two must also be in *concurrence*. That is, the mental state (the "mens rea") must *cause* the requisite act (the "actus reus").** Even though Cliff had the mental state for murder (intent to kill), and even though he committed an act that led to Hilda's death, the mental state did not cause the act. The act must be done for the actual carrying out of the intent and not merely in preparation for its execution. (Note that the fact that Hilda died two months later has no bearing on the answer—if Cliff could have been convicted of murder had Hilda died instantly, a two-month hiatus would not relieve him of guilt.)

11. No, probably. **In general, the requirement of *"concurrence"* means that if the defendant intends to commit crime A and in fact produces a result that is the actus reus for crime B, the defendant is not guilty of crime B. In other words, there is generally *no doctrine of "transferred intent"* for crimes, especially crimes requiring intent. (There are two important exceptions to this "no transferred intent" doctrine when a death results, namely the felony murder and misdemeanor manslaughter rules. But outside of the situation where death results, transferred intent generally does not apply.)** Desmond did not intend to unlawfully confine Virginia, the mens rea for kidnapping. It is true that he had a further intent, namely, to enter Virginia's apartment with a further intent to commit a crime (larceny) once he got inside, but the "no transferred intent" rule means Desmond cannot be convicted of the kidnapping.

12. No. **In general, if the actual harm produced is of a higher degree than the intended result, there is no liability for the greater harm.** Although Clare had the requisite mens rea for simple battery, she did not intend the aggravated injury (permanent damage to Rena's knee). Since aggravated battery is of a higher degree than simple battery, Clare cannot be convicted of a crime requiring the unintended result.

13. Yes. **A person cannot be convicted of causing a result unless he or she is found to have been a "cause in fact" of that result.** The issue, of course, is whether Prince "caused" Gretchen's death. Prince is not a "but for" cause of the death—the facts tell us that even if Prince had not hacked away at Gretchen, she would have died eventually from the poison. But being a "but for" cause of Gretchen's death is not the only way Prince can be found to meet the "cause in fact" requirement. The other way is if Prince is found to have been a *"substantial factor"* in bringing about the death. Here, since Prince *materially speeded* Gretchen's death, he would be found to have been a "substantial factor" in bringing about that death, he would thus satisfy the "cause in fact" requirement, and he would thus be guilty.

14. No. **The common law imposes a *"year and a day"* rule. By this rule, a defendant cannot be convicted of homicide if the victim does not die until a year and a day following the defendant's act.** Since Gretchen survived for almost 15 months, Cinderella gets the benefit of this rule even though her act was the direct and "but for" cause of Gretchen's death, and even though there were no other significant intervening causes. (The "year and a day" rule survives in most states even today, but the trend is to abolish this rule.)

15. Yes. **Under the *"transferred intent"* rule, when a defendant intends to harm a person or property, and the type of harm is the one intended but the victim is different, courts find that the required connection between intent and result exists.** It is true that Horton did not intend to burn down Ben's townhouse. However, since Horton intended to burn a townhouse and in fact did burn a townhouse, the fact that it was a townhouse belonging to an unintended victim is deemed irrelevant.

16. Yes. **In most instances, if the *general type of harm* intended actually occurs, the defendant will not be absolved because the harm occurred in a somewhat different *way* than intended. In this situation, the defendant is still considered the proximate cause of the injury, even though the injury didn't happen in precisely the manner he or she intended.** Here, Neil intended to disfigure Keith, and set in motion a chain of events that indeed resulted in Keith's disfigurement. The fact that the precise mechanism for the harm was that Keith smashed his face on the bottom of the pool, rather than having had his face burned by acid, will be disregarded by the court. Even though Keith's jumping into the pool might be viewed as an intervening cause, that jumping was "foreseeable" and "normal" as a response by Keith to Neil's action, so the jumping will not be viewed as superseding.

17. Yes. **For an intervening act to be superseding and thus absolve the defendant, the intervening act must be not only unforeseeable but also *"abnormal."*** Medical treatment performed on the victim as a result of the defendant's act will generally not be superseding even if it is negligently performed, since negligence occurs often enough that it is not "abnormal." If Dr. Bob's treatment had been "grossly negligent" or "reckless," then it might be sufficiently abnormal to be superseding. But here, the facts strongly suggest that Dr. Bob's conduct was merely negligent, not grossly negligent or reckless, so Paul is not absolved.

18. Yes. **Under the *M'Naghten* test, the defendant will be deemed insane only if he or she had a mental disease that prevented him or her from knowing the "nature and quality" of his or her act, or that prevented him or her from knowing right from wrong.** Since Klaus obviously knew that he was stealing property that did not belong to him, and knew that this was both legally and morally

wrong, he was not insane under the *M'Naghten* test. The fact that he was unable to resist his impulses is irrelevant under *M'Naghten*.

19. No. M.P.C. §4.01(1) provides that "a person is not responsible for criminal conduct if as a result of mental disease or defect he lacks substantial capacity either to appreciate the criminality of his conduct or to *conform his conduct to the requirements of the law*." The facts make it clear that Klaus lacked "substantial capacity . . . to conform his conduct to the requirements of the law," even though he knew intellectually that stealing was wrong. Therefore, Klaus is insane under the "volitional" prong of the M.P.C. test.

20. Yes. 18 U.S.C. §17 essentially incorporates the *M'Naghten* test. The defendant will be acquitted by reason of insanity only if "as a result of a severe mental disease or defect, [he] was unable to appreciate the nature and quality or the wrongfulness of his acts." The fact that the defendant is unable to conform his conduct to the requirements of the law is irrelevant under the federal insanity standard.

21. No. Under the federal statute, the *defendant* bears the burden of proving his insanity by *"clear and convincing evidence."*

22. No, probably. Most courts hold that the jury is always free to disregard or disbelieve the witness's evaluation of the defendant's mental condition, and that even complete unanimity among the psychiatric experts does not require the jury to agree with them. See, e.g., *People v. Wolff*, 394 P.2d 959 (Cal. 1964).

23. (a) The defense of diminished responsibility. If a defendant who is not insane nonetheless suffers from such a mental impairment that he or she is unable to formulate the requisite specific intent for the crime charged, in many states he or she may prove this, and thus avoid conviction of that particular offense. A defense made on these grounds is generally called the defense of "diminished responsibility" or "partial responsibility."

    (b) Probably not. At least half of all American jurisdictions reject the doctrine of diminished responsibility. Usually, they do so by holding that the insanity defense "supersedes" the defense of diminished responsibility—that is, in these states no evidence that the defendant suffers from a mental disease or defect may be introduced, except pursuant to a formal insanity defense.

24. Yes, probably. As a general rule, voluntary intoxication is not an "excuse" for what would otherwise be criminal behavior. Thus voluntary intoxication is not a defense to crimes that have traditionally been called crimes of "general intent"—i.e., crimes where the only intent required is the intent to do the particular physical act that serves as the element of the crime. But most courts hold that if the defendant's intoxication made it impossible for him or her to have the *specific intent* required for the crime, the drunkenness can effectively exculpate him or her.

    This seems to be the case here. Egor can only be convicted of burglary if he had an intent to commit larceny or some other crime at the time he entered. The facts make it clear that he did not have such an intent. The fact that he took Kelly's property is irrelevant, since his drunkenness prevented him from knowing that it was hers, and larceny in nearly all states requires knowledge that the property belongs to another. So, to sum up, evidence that Egor's drunkenness prevented him from having the (specific) intent required for larceny would in turn absolve him of burglary.

25. Yes. Virtually all courts agree that intoxication will never be considered to negate the existence of recklessness. Thus, M.P.C. §2.08(2) provides that "[w]hen recklessness establishes an element of the offense, if the actor, due to self-induced intoxication, is unaware of a risk of which he would have been aware had he been sober, such unawareness is immaterial." Since Seymour,

a presumably intelligent law student, would have been aware of Beth's lack of consent had he not been drunk, and since his intoxication was voluntary, he will be deemed to have been "reckless" even though he was not in fact aware of her lack of consent. Indeed, the rule that intoxication will not negative recklessness is principally designed to forestall the very consent-regarding-intercourse defense that Seymour is asserting here, and the similar defense in assault cases.

26. (a) Duress. **A defendant may claim the defense of duress if he or she committed his or her crime in response to a threat by a third person that produced in the defendant a reasonable fear that he or she would suffer immediate death or serious bodily injury.** At least on its face, this defense seems to apply on these facts. (By contrast, the defense of *necessity* will not work, because it applies only where the defendant has been compelled to act criminally because of nonhuman events, and the defense of *self-defense* will not work because that defense may only be used when the crime is committed against the aggressor.)

    (b) No. **Courts generally do not allow the defense of duress where the defendant is charged with the intentional killing of another—i.e., murder or voluntary manslaughter.** This is true even though the defendant is threatened with his or her own death if he or she refuses.

27. No, probably. **Duress is generally available as a defense in cases of robbery, unlike homicide cases. Here, Matt satisfies the requirement that he reasonably believed that a threat of serious bodily harm would be carried out. However, virtually all courts deny the duress defense to a defendant who has *voluntarily placed himself or herself in a situation* where there is a substantial probability that he or she will be subjected to duress.** A court would probably find that by electing to become a soldier in an organized crime family, Matt knowingly and voluntarily put himself in a situation where he would be required to commit crimes and would not be free to leave the organization once he had learned its secrets.

28. No. **Even where a defendant is acting under direct military orders from a superior, he or she may be convicted of any crimes he or she commits provided that he or she knew that the act ordered was unlawful.**

29. Unclear. **Some cases (e.g., *U.S. v. Calley*, 22 U.S.C.M.A. 534 (Ct. Mil. App. 1973)) suggest that if a reasonable man would have known that the order was unlawful, the defendant cannot defend on the grounds that he did not realize the unlawfulness. But the Model Penal Code, in §2.10, provides that as to trials in nonmilitary courts, it *is* a defense that the defendant did not know that the order was unlawful even if an ordinary person would have realized the unlawfulness.**

30. (a) The defense of necessity. **The defense of necessity may be raised when the defendant has been compelled to commit a criminal act because of *nonhuman events*; the harm sought to be avoided must be greater than the harm committed, the harm must be imminent, and there must be no noncriminal alternative.**

    (b) Yes. **The defense of necessity may be raised when the defendant has been compelled to commit a criminal act because of nonhuman events; the harm sought to be avoided must be greater than the harm committed, the harm must be imminent, and there must be no noncriminal alternative.** The specific requirements all seem to be satisfied here: clearly the men's death by freezing was more serious than a burglary involving no lasting damage; there did not appear to be, on these facts, any less-illegal safe alternative; and the harm was quite imminent.

31. Split of authority. **The general common law rule is that the defense of necessity (like the defenses of duress and self-defense) will be negated by an unreasonable though genuine mistake. However, the modern trend, as exemplified by the Model Penal Code, seems to be less harsh: Under M.P.C.**

§2.10, a genuine but unreasonable belief by the defendant that an emergency exists will not deprive him or her of the defense, unless the crime is one that can be committed "recklessly" or "negligently," not just purposely. Since (according to the Model Penal Code) burglary is a crime that can only be committed purposely (§221.1(1) requires a "purpose to commit a crime" inside the structure), the defendants' unreasonableness, even if it amounted to recklessness, would not deprive them of the necessity defense.

32. No, probably. **Courts almost never accept the defense of "economic necessity."** If Valjean's children were literally starving, so that he was avoiding an imminent threat to their life that could not be avoided in any other way, his defense might succeed. But here, the noncriminal alternative of a shelter was available; the fact that such an alternative had drawbacks of its own will not be sufficient to overcome a requirement for the defense of necessity that there be no noncriminal or less-criminal alternative that would avoid the harm.

33. No. **The defense of self-defense is allowed only where the defendant is resisting force that is** *unlawful*. Here, Steve, as a property owner defending his property, was entitled to use a reasonable amount of force, and the facts tell us that he did so. Since Steve's use of force was lawful, Drew was not privileged to use force to defend himself against Steve's lawful force.

34. No. **The only time one may use "deadly force" in self-defense is to defend oneself against** *serious bodily harm*. **"Deadly force" is generally defined as force that is intended or likely to cause death or serious bodily harm.** Jerome's use of the knife in an attempt to disfigure the Slapster would almost certainly be considered deadly force, since disfigurement would be considered serious bodily harm. Yet Jerome did not believe he was protecting himself from serious bodily harm, since a slap with a leather glove would not create such harm (and indeed Jerome knew that no prior victim had been seriously injured from a Slapster attack).

35. No. **A defense will be treated as involving deadly force if it was** *either* **intended** *or* **likely to cause death or serious bodily harm, and intent to kill renders irrelevant the fact that no serious bodily harm or death actually occurred.** Here, Jerome was not entitled to use deadly force to protect against this nonserious threat. Since Jerome used his knife with intent to kill, that intent is deemed the use of "deadly force."

36. No, probably. **For the defense of self-defense, the harm being defended against must be reasonably** *imminent*. **The danger that one may be attacked tomorrow (even if the attack is virtually certain) will not suffice. Even the Model Penal Code, which is somewhat more liberal (to the defendant) on this subject, allows the use of force in self-defense only to a person who is protecting himself or herself against unlawful force that will be used "on the present occasion." M.P.C. §3.04(1).** Kelly might get a murder charge reduced to manslaughter, or might successfully plead that her fright had made her temporarily insane, but she is not entitled to self-defense, at least according to strict legal doctrine. (A judge's answer to Kelly's question, "What should I have done?" would probably be that she should have telephoned the police.)

37. Yes. **The general rule is that one who is the** *initial aggressor* **may not then claim self-defense. But there are two exceptions to this rule. One of these is applicable here: If the defendant provoked the exchanged but used only nondeadly force, and the other party responded with deadly force, the defendant may then defend himself or herself, even with deadly force if necessary. In this situation, the victim's use of force is unlawful because it is excessive, so the defendant is allowed to counter it.**

Here, Bob's initial attack by fists was nondeadly force (since Ken knew that Bob was not especially dangerous with his fists). When Ken answered by pointing his gun at Bob and making a nonconditional threat, this amounted to the use of deadly force against Bob, and thus represented an unlawful escalation of force beyond the self-defense to which Ken was entitled. (Ken was entitled to use matching nondeadly force, such as his own fists, but not to escalate to deadly force.) Once Ken unlawfully escalated to deadly force, Bob was then entitled to use deadly force in return if nondeadly force would not suffice. Since there is nothing in the facts to suggest that Bob could have countered Ken's gun with anything less than his own gun, Bob was merely matching deadly force with deadly force, and acted lawfully even though he was the initial aggressor.

38. Yes. **This question involves an exception to the general rule that one who is the aggressor may not claim self-defense. Here, the exception is that if the defendant-aggressor withdraws from the conflict, and the other initiates a second conflict, the defendant may use nondeadly force and may use deadly force if he or she is threatened with death or serious bodily harm.** Here, it is true that Spencer was the initial aggressor, since he unlawfully started the conflict by burglarizing Martin's house and tying Martin up. But by leaving the house without the TV, Spencer withdrew from the initial encounter. Therefore, once Martin chased him and tried to punch him, Martin was initiating a second conflict, by the use of nondeadly force. Spencer was then permitted to use equal nondeadly force to defend himself against this renewed attack, which he did.

39. No. **The M.P.C., like nearly half of all courts today (although still a minority), requires that if one could *safely retreat*, he or she must do so rather than use deadly force. See M.P.C. §3.04(2)(b)(ii).** Since Marla could have left the bar with complete safety, the Model Penal Code would require her to do so, even if that meant sacrificing her chance to get to know Stan better. (The M.P.C. section just cited requires a person who can do so safely not only to retreat before using deadly force, but also to de-escalate the encounter by "complying with a demand that he abstain from any action which he has no duty to take." Since Marla had no "duty" to get to know Stan, she was required to abstain from that action rather than use deadly force.)

40. Yes. **Even in jurisdictions requiring retreat, this rule applies only before the defendant uses *deadly* force. All jurisdictions agree that if one has the right to use self-defense at all, it is never necessary to retreat before using nondeadly force.**

41. Yes. **Even those states that require retreat do not require it where the attack takes place in the defendant's *dwelling* (so long as the defendant was not the initial aggressor).** Since the encounter took place in Marla's home, she was not required to "retreat from room to room," even under the Model Penal Code, which otherwise requires retreat.

42. Yes. **If a person mistakenly but reasonably believes that he or she is in imminent danger, he or she can act in self-defense.**

43. No, probably. **Most states hold that the defendant's mistake must be a *reasonable* one for self-defense to apply. But some courts, and the Model Penal Code, hold that even an unreasonable mistake does not *necessarily* deprive the defendant of the self-defense claim.** (Here, Mary is charged with murder, a crime that under M.P.C. §210.2 may only be committed "purposely or knowingly" or "recklessly under circumstances manifesting extreme indifference to the value of human life." Assuming that Mary's mistake amounted to mere "negligence," M.P.C. §3.09(2) provides that her mistake does not deprive her of the claim of self-defense; however, it would deprive her of that defense as to a crime that may itself be committed "negligently.")

44. No. **In the most general terms, a person is justified in using self-defense to protect against the unlawful use of force by another. But all jurisdictions have a special rule restricting the use of**

self-defense in response to an unlawful arrest: **As long as the defendant knows that the other person is a police officer trying to make an arrest, the defendant may *not* use deadly force to avoid arrest even if he or she knows that the arrest is *unlawful*.** Although Karen did not seriously injure Smith, she shot a gun at him, and a court would almost certainly conclude that this constituted the use of deadly force. (See, e.g., M.P.C. §3.11(2), stating that "purposely firing a firearm in the direction of another person . . . constitutes deadly force.")

45. No. **In a slight majority of states, Karen would succeed, since a narrow majority permits the use of *nondeadly* force to resist an unlawful arrest. But the Model Penal Code, like a substantial and growing minority of states, prohibits the use of even nondeadly force to resist an unlawful arrest. See M.P.C. §3.04(2)(a)(i).**

46. (a) Defense of others. **A person may use force to defend another if (1) he or she reasonably believes that the other person is in imminent danger of unlawful bodily harm; (2) the degree of force he or she is using is no greater than that which seems reasonably necessary to prevent the harm; and (3) he or she believes that the party being assisted would have the right to use in his or her own defense the force that the defendant proposes to use in his or her assistance.** Here, these requirements are at least superficially met.

    (b) No, probably. **Most courts would probably hold that the defendant (Martin) may not use deadly force if he or she has reason to believe that the person being aided could retreat with safety. Thus, M.P.C. §3.05(2)(b) requires that the defendant at least "try to cause" the person being assisted to retreat where this can be done safely (although the defendant may then use deadly force if his or her attempt at encouraging retreat fails).** Since Martin did not attempt to help Charlie escape or urge him to escape, even though this could have easily been done, Martin probably ran afoul of this rule.

47. Yes. **A person may use force to defend another if (1) he or she reasonably believes that the other person is in imminent danger of unlawful bodily harm; (2) the degree of force he or she is using is no greater than that which seems reasonably necessary to prevent the harm; and (3) he or she believes that the party being assisted would have the right to use in his or her own defense the force that the defendant proposes to use in his or her assistance.** These requirements are met here, since Bill had reason to believe that Kevin was in imminent danger of serious harm, that nothing less than deadly force would suffice, and that Kevin would be permitted to use such deadly force in his own defense. The principal issue is whether Bill was permitted to use force in defense of a stranger, as opposed to a friend or relative. But most courts and statutes today do permit the use of force to defend even a total stranger from the threat of harm from another.

48. Yes, probably. **As long as the defendant's belief in the need for defense of others is reasonable, the defendant may assert the claim of defense of others even if his or her evaluation turns out in retrospect to have been wrong.** Since Alex reasonably believed, on the facts known to him, that Bert was the aggressor and that Carl needed help, Alex will not be deprived of his defense-of-others claim merely because he was wrong.

49. (a) Defense of property. **One has a right to use force to defend one's property against a wrongful taking, if the degree of force used is not more than appears reasonably necessary to prevent the taking.**

    (b) Yes. **Even if one knows that one will not be hurt, one is still entitled to use nondeadly force rather than give up one's property.** The degree of force used must not be more than appears reasonably necessary to prevent the taking, but Darnell's single punch seems to satisfy that requirement here. (If there was reason for Darnell to believe that a "request to desist" would have worked, then he would have had to make such a request; but presumably a mugger on a city street represents a serious enough threat that one does not have to plead with the mugger to desist.)

50. No. **Virtually all courts hold that one** *may not use deadly force* **to defend personal property. Even if nondeadly force would not suffice, and even if the particular means chosen were the minimum that would have gotten the job done, one is simply required to give up one's property rather than use deadly force.** (There is an exception recognized in some courts, for defense of one's own *dwelling* against a violent felony, but this is not applicable here.)

51. No, probably. **Most courts today allow the use of deadly force, even in the defense of one's dwelling, only where the intrusion appears to pose a danger of a** *violent* **felony. Where a burglar is clearly not armed or dangerous, the homeowner must let him or her escape rather than use deadly force, even if nondeadly force would not suffice to prevent the loss of property.**

52. No, probably. **The modern view prohibits the use of deadly mechanical devices, even if they happen to go off in a situation where the owner himself or herself would have been justified in using deadly force. See M.P.C. §3.06(5)(a).** Even though Pierre could in person have used his revolver to kill the Big Cat (since the Big Cat turned out to be dangerous to life), Pierre was not permitted to accomplish by mechanical means what he would have been able to do in person.

53. Yes, probably. **Mechanical devices may be used to defend property as long as they are non-deadly—i.e., as long as they are not likely or intended to cause death or serious bodily harm.** Barbed wire is generally considered to fall within this "nondeadly" category, even though in this case through an unlucky series of events it did cause death. Probably Pierre would not be deprived of his defense merely because he did not post warning signs. For instance, the Model Penal Code states that as long as the device is one "customarily used for such a [protective] purpose," warnings do not have to be given. M.P.C. §3.06(5)(c). Barbed wire clearly fits within this category.

54. No. **The Supreme Court has held that if a fleeing suspect (even a suspect who has committed a felony) poses no immediate threat to the officer and no threat to others, the officer may not use deadly force to stop the flight. Use of deadly force to apprehend a nondangerous fleeing suspect constitutes an unreasonable seizure under the Fourth Amendment.** *Tennessee v. Garner*, **471 U.S. 1 (1985). Therefore, the criminal law will almost certainly not recognize a privilege to use force where the force used is "unreasonable" under this constitutional standard. See also M.P.C. §3.07(2)(b), allowing deadly force to be used only where the fleeing felon is dangerous.** Here, Goodbar knew that Charlie was not dangerous, based on his prior record and on the fact that he was not carrying any weapon this time. Even though Goodbar did not intend to kill Charlie, he intended to (and did) shoot at Charlie, and shooting a firearm at someone constituted the use of deadly force.

55. No. **A police officer gets a privilege to use force (at least nondeadly force) to make an arrest for any felony, and he or she does not waive this privilege by making a reasonable mistake. But when a** *private citizen* **uses force (even nondeadly force) to make an arrest, he or she does not get the benefit of a reasonable mistake, and acts** *at his or her own peril.* Since here, no felony was in fact committed, Stanley cannot escape liability based on his reasonable error. Nor does Stanley get any protection from the fact that he used nondeadly force—a private citizen may not use even nondeadly force based on a reasonable mistake (though Stanley would be protected if the teenager had in fact committed a felony for which Stanley was trying to arrest him).

56. No. **Consent will not bar liability, except where lack of consent forms an element of the crime (e.g., rape), or where the harm arises out of an athletic contest or competitive sport.** Here, the hazing was not an athletic contest or competitive sport, and it posed the risk of serious bodily harm.

Therefore, this is not a situation in which consent would negate the crime, so Riccardo cannot defend on the grounds of consent.

57. No. **The majority rule (as well as the rule followed by the U.S. Supreme Court for federal crimes) is that one who is *predisposed* to a crime cannot be entrapped. That is, the entrapment defense requires that both of the following conditions be satisfied: (1) the government originated the crime and induced its commission; and (2) the defendant is an innocent person—i.e., one who was not predisposed to committing this sort of crime.** Here, the government's evidence that Darnell insider traded on several prior occasions means that he is predisposed, and therefore cannot use the defense.

58. Yes, probably. **Under the minority "police conduct" rule, entrapment exists where the government agents originate the crime, and their participation is such as is likely to induce unpredisposed persons to commit the crime. The defense is valid if it meets these requirements, even if the defendant himself or herself is predisposed. See M.P.C. §2.13(1)(b), following this minority rule and thus recognizing the entrapment defense where the government agent induces the crime by "employing methods of persuasion or inducement which create a substantial risk that such offense will be committed by persons other than those who are ready to commit it."** The facts here indicate that unpredisposed persons would commit insider trading under these facts, so Darnell can successfully assert the defense even if he himself was an inveterate insider trader who was clearly predisposed.

59. No. **A crime of attempt generally requires that the defendant have intended to bring about a certain *result*. Therefore, there can generally be no attempt to commit a crime defined in terms of recklessness or negligence.** This rule clearly applies as to those crimes defined in terms of recklessly (or negligently) bringing about a certain result. Since the statute here defines manslaughter as the reckless causing of a death, there can be no such thing as attempted manslaughter (at least manslaughter of the "involuntary" variety)—either the defendant intended to bring about death, in which case he is liable for attempted murder, or he did not intend to bring about death, in which case he is not guilty of any sort of attempted homicide. Since Phil did not intend to cause the death of Dina or anyone else, he cannot be liable for attempted homicide of any variety.

60. No, probably. **For a defendant to be convicted of attempting a particular substantive crime, he or she must have had an *intent* to do acts that, if they had been carried out, would have resulted in the commission of that crime. Traditionally, it is not enough that the defendant had a mental state that would have sufficed for the substantive crime had the substantive act resulted. Under M.P.C. §5.01(1)(b), "A person is guilty of an attempt to commit a crime if, acting with the kind of culpability otherwise required for commission of the crime, he . . . (b) when causing a particular result is an element of the crime, does or omits to do anything with the *purpose* of causing or with the *belief* that it will cause such result without further conduct on his part."** Under the traditional rule, the fact that a mental state of recklessness would suffice to convict Norman of murder if Bernard had died does not mean that Norman is automatically guilty of attempted murder given Bernard's survival. Only if Norman had intended to kill Bernard (or, perhaps, had known that it was substantially certain that Bernard would die) would Norman be guilty of attempted murder.

Under the Model Penal Code, since Norman merely thought it possible that Bernard's death might result, and did not act with the purpose of causing that result or with the belief that that result would occur, Norman is not guilty of attempted murder under the M.P.C. formulation (which agrees with the common law rule previously stated).

61. No, probably. **Mere intent is not sufficient for attempt liability—the defendant must be shown to have committed some *overt act* in furtherance of his or her plan. M.P.C. §5.01(1)(c) creates attempt liability if the defendant does "an act or omission constituting a substantial step in a course of conduct planned to culminate in his commission of the crime." But §5.01(2) says that conduct will not constitute such a "substantial step" unless it is "strongly corroborative of the actor's criminal purpose," and goes on to say that this requirement will be satisfied by "possession of materials to be employed in the commission of the crime, that are *specially designed* for such unlawful use or that can serve *no lawful purpose* of the actor under the circumstances."** (§5.01(2)(e).) Here, a court would almost certainly conclude that Drew's purchase and possession of the gun and the mask were "mere preparation," not the sort of act that satisfies the "overt act" requirement. The main problem is that both the gun and the mask are items that a person could *lawfully and logically own.*

The gun and the mask were not "specially designed" for the purpose of bank robberies, and they could have served a lawful purpose for Drew. At least under the Model Penal Code approach, there is clearly no attempt liability here.

62. Yes, probably. **Under the Model Penal Code, offering of the note would probably constitute a "substantial step" toward the crime, since §5.01(2)(e) provides that the "substantial step" requirement is satisfied by conduct that "corroborates" the defendant's criminal purpose, including "possession of materials to be employed in the commission of the crime, that are specially designed for such unlawful use."** The note would probably be held to be "specially designed" for bank robbery. Obviously, the risk that the fact finder will inaccurately conclude that Drew intended a criminal purpose is a lot smaller in the case of this demand note than in the case of the gun and mask in the prior question, both of which have "innocent" uses.

63. Yes. **Almost no matter what test is used to determine whether Norbert's acts were sufficiently definite to give rise to attempt liability, he will be found to have satisfied the act requirement. For instance, the act satisfies the "equivocality test," since the placement of a fully armed bomb into luggage that is to be checked onto a plane is unequivocally criminal. Similarly, under the "dangerous proximity to success" or "last act" tests, the checking in of the bomb-equipped bag easily passes muster. Under the Model Penal Code, the requirement of a "substantial step" that is "strongly corroborative" of criminal purpose is satisfied here, since one of the ways of meeting the substantial-step test is by "possession . . . of materials to be employed in the commission of the crime, at or near the place contemplated for its commission" (§5.01(2)(f)), a standard clearly satisfied here.**

64. Yes, probably. **M.P.C. §5.01(2)(a) makes it a "substantial step . . . strongly corroborative of the actor's criminal purpose" for the defendant to be "lying in wait, searching for or following the contemplated victim of the crime."** Harvey's act of "lying in wait" at the warehouse probably meets the act requirement for attempt liability.

65. No, probably. **Mere intent is not sufficient for attempt liability—the defendant must be shown to have committed some *overt act* in furtherance of his or her plan. M.P.C. §5.01(1)(c) creates attempt liability if the defendant does "an act or omission constituting a substantial step in a course of conduct planned to culminate in his commission of the crime." But §5.01(2) says that conduct will not constitute such a "substantial step" unless it is "strongly corroborative of the actor's criminal purpose."** Again, the question is whether the acts taken by the defendant were sufficiently overt and unambiguous that they should give rise to attempt liability. Here, the essence of insurance fraud is making a false claim. Where the defendant has planned his or her misrepresentation (in this case, the false statement that there had been a theft) but not yet communicated it to the would-be victim, courts have generally held that the requisite act has not yet been committed. The staging of the robbery, tying of the hands, etc., would probably be held to be mere preparation. (But the result would probably be different, and Bernard would probably be convicted of the attempt, if he had filed the claim but not yet been paid.) See Comment 16 to M.P.C. §5.01.

66. Yes. **Courts almost always** *reject* **the defense of factual impossibility. The prevailing rule is that the defendant may be convicted of attempt** *if, had the facts been as the defendant believed them to be, there would have been a crime.* Here, if the sleeping pills had in fact been lethal (as Donald believed them to be), Donald would have committed murder. That being the case, Donald's defense of impossibility is not valid.

67. No. **Courts always acquit when the defendant correctly asserts the "true legal impossibility" defense. In other words, if it is the case that even had the facts (as opposed to law) been as the defendant supposed them to be, no crime would have been committed, then the defendant is entitled to acquittal.** Here, since the act Dwain was committing (and, indeed, even the act he thought he was committing) was simply not a violation of the perjury statute, he cannot be convicted of attempting to violate that statute.

68. Yes. **Dolores could assert a variant of the impossibility defense, namely, what might be called** *"factual impossibility related to legal relationships."* **But in general, courts today almost universally reject this defense, just as they reject garden-variety claims of factual impossibility. The issue for most courts is whether, had the facts been as the defendant supposed, the defendant would have committed a crime. See, e.g., M.P.C. §5.01(1)(a), making it an attempt to "purposely engage . . . in conduct which would constitute the crime if the attendant circumstances were as [the defendant] believes them to be."** Here, had the packet really contained cocaine rather than talcum powder, Dolores would have committed the crime of drug sale; therefore, she can be convicted of attempting to commit that crime. (In an analogous situation, defendants are convicted every day of "attempted purchase" of drugs, where they buy from an undercover officer what they think is an illegal drug but which is in fact a harmless substance such as sugar.)

69. No, probably. **Although the defense of factual impossibility is almost always rejected, most courts recognize a small category of situations where the type of conduct engaged in by the defendant was so** *unlikely* **to result in the commission of a crime, and the defendant is so inherently** *undangerous,* **that society does not need to punish him or her. Thus, M.P.C. §5.05(2) provides that "[i]f the particular conduct charged to constitute a criminal attempt . . . is so inherently unlikely to result or culminate in a commission of a crime that neither such conduct nor the actor presents a public danger . . . the Court shall exercise its power . . . to enter judgment and impose sentence for a crime of lower grade . . . or, in extreme cases, may dismiss the prosecution."** The Comments to this section give as an example of such inherently unlikely means the commission of murder by black magic. Certainly the M.P.C., and probably most courts, would acquit Karpov of attempted murder here, because of the extreme unlikeliness that this general type of conduct will culminate in a death, and because of the lack of any other evidence of Karpov's dangerousness.

70. (a) **The defense of renunciation. Most courts will acquit a defendant of an attempt crime if he or she shows that he or she changed his or her mind and abandoned his or her plan to commit the crime.**

    (b) **No. All courts require that the renunciation be voluntary. Where the defendant learns that if he or she goes through with his or her plans, he or she is likely to be immediately**

apprehended, all courts agree that this abandonment should be treated as "involuntary," and thus ineffective. Here, the facts make it clear that Darren abandoned his plan only because there was a police officer nearby who would be likely to apprehend him. Therefore, Darren's renunciation was involuntary and is therefore ineffective. Since Darren committed the necessary act in furtherance of his plan (almost all courts would treat the act of stalking a would-be victim for several blocks with knife in hand as being a sufficient act in furtherance of a plan of rape), Darren will be convicted.

71. No. **Most courts will acquit a defendant of an attempt crime if he or she shows that he or she changed his or her mind and abandoned his or her plan to commit the crime.** Here, Darren has satisfied the requirement for renunciation: He voluntarily abandoned his plan. The fact that he did so in response to a *generalized* fear of apprehension probably will not render his renunciation involuntary— only where the abandonment comes in response to a specific threat of being caught will that threat render the renunciation involuntary.

72. Yes, probably. **In general, if the defendant abandons his or her attempt because he or she concludes that it will be less worthwhile than he or she expected, this will not be treated as a "voluntary" renunciation; only a voluntary renunciation will be effective.** Here, Darren has concluded that raping Jane is likely to produce less desirable results than he had expected, so the court will probably conclude that he falls within this rule.

73. Yes. **In a conspiracy case, the prosecution must show that the defendant agreed with at least one other person to commit a crime. However, there does not need to be "direct" evidence of an agreement, such as testimony by one of the conspirators that there was an agreement. Instead, the existence of the agreement may be (and usually is) proved merely by** *circumstantial evidence.* Here, the fact that Dorothy happened to leave her beat with a headache just before the shooting, together with the otherwise unexplained bank deposits, would be (or at least, legally, could be) sufficient circumstantial evidence to prove that there was in fact an agreement between Dorothy and Slimy.

74. (a) Lack of agreement. **In a conspiracy case, the prosecution must show that the defendant agreed with at least one other person to commit a crime.** Dave should argue that since his would-be co-conspirator, George, never in fact had any intent of committing the crime, there was never an agreement and thus no conspiracy.

   (b) No. **Older cases sometimes accepted the argument that there was no agreement, and therefore no conspiracy, where the other party had no subjective intent to go through with the conspiracy. But the modern view is that regardless of the lack of subjective intent on the part of one of the two protagonists, the other may be convicted of conspiracy as long as that other intended to carry out the conspiracy. This modern approach is followed by the Model Penal Code, which makes an individual liable for conspiracy if he or she "agrees with [an] other person or persons," regardless of the subjective state of the other person. See M.P.C. §5.03(1)(a).** Since Dave intended to achieve the substantive result of murdering his wife, he can be convicted even though he was the only one who so intended.

75. No. **The mere knowledge on the part of a supplier that the goods he or she is supplying are to be used in some sort of crime is insufficient for a conviction of conspiracy to commit that crime.** If Doug had had some stake in the venture, or had known specifically that First City would be robbed, this might be enough to make him guilty of conspiracy. But his generalized knowledge that some sort of bank robbery would be committed is not sufficient.

76. Yes, probably. **A person may be convicted of conspiracy only if he or she had an *actual intent* to further the criminal objective, not just mere knowledge of that objective. But intent may be shown by circumstantial evidence. If a supplier charges his or her criminal purchasers an *inflated price* compared with what the item costs when sold for legal purposes, this is strong circumstantial evidence of his or her intent to further the criminal purpose.** Thus, Doug could be convicted on these facts.

77. No, probably. **Traditionally (and still today in England), one could be convicted of conspiracy to commit an objective that is "immoral" even if not unlawful. But nearly all U.S. states today allow a conspiracy conviction only if the defendants intended to perform an act that was explicitly criminal.** Since Langdell has not made it a criminal act to sexually harass someone, there can be no crime of conspiracy to commit such harassment.

78. Split of authority. **About half the states have statutes requiring that for someone to be convicted of conspiracy, some *overt act* in furtherance of the conspiracy must have been committed.** In these states, Edward and Fred could not be convicted, since there has been no overt act. (If they had, for instance, purchased a baseball bat that Edward was to use to bludgeon Gertrude, this would have sufficed in these states.) But the other states have no such requirement, and at common law no overt act is required. The Model Penal Code takes a middle position: An overt act is required except where the crime the defendant is conspiring to commit is a felony of the first or second degree; since murder is a felony of the first degree, Edward and Fred could be convicted under the M.P.C. approach. See M.P.C. §5.03(5).

79. Yes, probably. **A court would probably hold that the conspiracy here was a single *"wheel"* conspiracy, with Roger at the hub and Agnes, Brian, and the other 48 resellers as spokes. For a "wheel" arrangement to be considered a single conspiracy rather than a series of smaller ones, it usually must be the case that (1) each spoke knows that the other spokes exist; and (2) the various spokes have, and realize that they have, a "community of interest" (i.e., each spoke realizes that the success of the venture depends on the performance of the other spokes).** The conspiracy here seems to meet both of these requirements, since Agnes clearly knew that Brian existed and vice versa, and since Agnes should have understood that economies of scale (e.g., the need to maintain the safe house) would have prevented the arrangement from working if Roger was the ringleader and Agnes was the only reseller.

80. No, probably. **A 1946 Supreme Court decision, *Pinkerton v. U.S.*, states that each member of the conspiracy, by virtue of his or her membership alone, is liable for the substantive crimes committed by any colleague in furtherance of the conspiracy. But the modern view rejects the theory of *Pinkerton*, and holds that only where the defendant is shown to have "aided and abetted" the person who actually carried out the substantive crime may the defendant be held liable. In other words, the modern view is that *mere membership in a conspiracy, without proof of aiding and abetting, will not make the defendant liable for other co-conspirators' substantive crimes*.** See Comment 6(a) to M.P.C. §2.06(3).

     By this test, Agnes would not be liable: Although she received drugs from Roger and was thus part of the conspiracy, she did not do anything to assist Brian in his drug sales efforts. The fact that Agnes and Brian were, in a loose sense, coconspirators (that is, they were members of the same conspiracy even though they didn't interact very much) is *circumstantial evidence* that Agnes may have aided and abetted Brian. However, in this situation, this circumstantial evidence is very weak (though often, evidence that two people were in a conspiracy together will be much stronger circumstantial evidence that one aided and abetted the other).

81. Yes. **Even under the modern view concerning liability for substantive crimes, Roger is liable for the substantive crime committed by Brian because Roger "*aided and abetted*" Brian's sales on the street. This result is reached by general principles of "accomplice liability," and can be reached without reference to the laws of conspiracy.** Of course, the fact that Roger and Brian were co-conspirators furnishes useful evidence that Roger in fact aided and abetted Brian's sales, but the thing that makes Roger liable for Brian's substantive crimes is that he was Brian's accomplice (by aiding and abetting Brian), not the mere fact that they were co-conspirators.

82. No, probably. **The spokes in a "wheel" conspiracy will only be considered members of the same large conspiracy (rather than individual single-spoke conspiracies) if each spoke knows that the other spokes exist and the various spokes realize that they have a "community of interest."** Here, the second requirement is probably not satisfied: Cathy didn't especially care whether Barry's house got burned down and his insurance paid successfully, nor did Barry care how Cathy's project turned out. It is true that each hoped that Agnes wouldn't get caught on the other's job, thus implicating them all, but it is doubtful whether this generalized fear of detection creates a sufficiently powerful community of interest. (See *Kotteakos v. U.S.*, 328 U.S. 750 (1946), holding that where the "hub" helped numerous individuals fraudulently obtain FHA loans, there were multiple conspiracies rather than a single one since each person cared only about having his or her own loan go through; this seems to be what is happening here.)

83. (a) The defense of "abandonment" or "renunciation."

    (b) No. **At the very least, the abandoning conspirator must take affirmative steps to thwart the conspiracy.** Usually, this means that he or she must notify the police, something that Bill did not do here.

84. Yes. **Most courts (and the Model Penal Code) require that the defendant not only have attempted to thwart the conspiracy, but that he or she must have actually *blocked the crime* from being committed. See Comment to M.P.C. §5.03(6) ("Notification of the authorities which fails to thwart the success of the conspiracy because not timely or because of a failure on their part will not sustain a defense to the charge of conspiracy . . .").** Since Bill, through no fault of his own, failed to thwart the burning, he cannot use the renunciation defense.

85. Wharton's Rule. **Wharton's Rule provides that where a substantive offense is defined so as to necessarily require more than one person, a prosecution for the substantive offense must be brought, rather than a conspiracy prosecution.** The rule is commonly applied to adultery, and thus provides that where a man and woman would be guilty of adultery if they had intercourse, they may not be prosecuted for conspiracy to commit adultery (whether they have sex or merely prepare to have it). Many (perhaps most) states would follow Wharton's Rule in this circumstance.

86. Yes. **One well-established exception to Wharton's Rule is that there is no bar to a conspiracy conviction when there were *more participants* than were logically necessary to complete the crime.** Here, we have three participants, not merely the two who were logically necessary to commit the crime. Therefore, all three may be convicted even in a jurisdiction that recognizes Wharton's Rule.

87. No. **The Model Penal Code basically rejects Wharton's Rule. See Comment 3 to §5.04(2). The M.P.C. does bar "cumulative" punishment, so that if Bob and Alice had consummated their liaison, neither could have been punished for *both* adultery and conspiracy to commit adultery. But the M.P.C. does not prevent a conspiracy conviction merely on the grounds that both parties would be necessary to the substantive crime, had that crime been committed. "That an offense inevitably requires concert is no reason to immunize criminal preparation to commit it." *Id.*

88. No. **Nearly all jurisdictions hold that where the defendant could not be liable for the substantive crime because of a legislative judgment that the person is a member of a protected class, that person may not be convicted of conspiracy to commit the crime either.** Since Barbara, as an underage female, could not be convicted of statutory rape, she may not be convicted of conspiracy to commit that rape either.

89. No, probably. **Most modern courts hold that the inability to find one of two parties guilty of conspiracy does not prevent the other party from being guilty. In other words, there is today no general rule that there must be two guilty conspirators, rather than just one.** It is also irrelevant to most modern courts that the other party could not be convicted of the substantive crime (as is the case with Barbara here). The M.P.C. expresses this concept by saying that "It is immaterial to the liability of a person who . . . conspires with another to commit a crime that . . . (b) the person with whom he conspires is irresponsible or has an immunity to prosecution or conviction for the commission of the crime." §5.04(1)(b). (But Wharton's Rule might immunize Rick here.)

90. Yes, probably. **Nearly all courts hold that, at least where all the conspirators are tried in a single proceeding, it cannot be the case that one is convicted and the others are acquitted, since this result leaves the "plurality" rule (i.e., the rule that there must be more than one conspirator) unsatisfied. (The Model Penal Code takes no position on whether, as here, an inconsistent verdict in a single trial justifies overturning the one conviction.)**

91. No. **If some (even all but one) of the alleged conspirators are not brought to justice at all, this fact does not prevent conviction of the ones who are tried.** Obviously, the prosecution must show that the defendant indeed reached an agreement with the absent conspirators, but here the facts tell us that this was done.

92. Yes, because he is an accomplice. *One who aids, abets, encourages, or assists another to perform a crime will himself or herself be liable for that crime.* This is the fundamental principle of accomplice liability. Here, Fenster encouraged Burger to burglarize Homer's house, and intended to bring about the resulting burglary. Thus Fenster satisfies both the act and mental-state requirements for accomplice liability: (1) he rendered *assistance or encouragement* to one who committed a substantive crime (the act requirement), and (2) he *intended to bring about the crime* (the mental-state requirement).

93. No, probably. **Where the defendant knows that his conduct will encourage or assist another person in committing a crime, but the defendant does not particularly *intend or desire* to bring about that criminal result, most courts hold that the defendant is not liable as an accomplice to the crime.** Since the facts here suggest that Brian did not especially care whether Anita got the contract or succeeded in bribing Charlie, Brian would not be guilty.

94. Split of authority. **The Model Penal Code §2.06(4) says, "When causing a particular result is an element of an offense, an accomplice in the conduct causing such result is an accomplice in the commission of that offense if he acts with the *kind of culpability*, if any, with respect to that result that is sufficient for the commission of the offense." Other courts, however, hold that only an *intent* on the part of the defendant to produce the crime, not mere recklessness as to the risk of it, will suffice for accomplice liability.** In these courts, Alex would not be guilty since he did not intend for Ben to hurt or kill anyone.

95. Yes, probably. **If the defendant has assisted or encouraged his or her principal to commit a particular offense, and the principal commits not only this offense, but others as well, most courts will make the defendant liable for the additional crimes if they are the "*natural and probable*"**

consequences of the conduct that the defendant did intend to assist. **This is true even though the defendant did not intend for his or her principal to commit the substantive offense now in question.**

On this theory, since Arnold did intend to aid Bob in committing the crimes of burglary and larceny, and since on the facts known to Arnold, the rape by Bob was a "natural and probable" consequence of Arnold's assistance with the burglary/larceny, Arnold would be liable for rape as well. This is true even though Arnold did not desire that Bob rape Monica, and even though Arnold did not know to a substantial certainty that Bob would do so.

But Arnold would *not* be convicted under the Model Penal Code: The M.P.C. rejects the principle allowing an accomplice to be held liable for "natural and probable" crimes beyond those that he intended to aid or encourage. See Comment to §2.04(3).

96. Yes, probably. **The felony murder rule (at least in its strictest form) provides that if one is in the process of committing any of certain enumerated felonies (robbery usually being one), and one kills (even accidentally) a person during the course of that felony, the death is deemed murder.** So it is not farfetched that, on our facts, Brian is liable for murder. Now, we add to this the fact that Ashley is Brian's accomplice in the robbery. Since Ashley would have been guilty of felony murder had he accidentally killed Ray, it is not so unjust for him to be guilty of felony murder on an accomplice theory where the actual shooting was accidentally done by Brian rather than by Ashley. Holding Ashley guilty here does not run afoul of the general rule that the accomplice must have the mental state required for the crime the principal committed.

Under the Model Penal Code, which largely rejects the felony murder rule and merely makes the commission of certain felonies give rise to a rebuttable presumption of recklessness, the case might come out differently—if Ashley could show that he himself was not reckless even though he carried a loaded gun and accompanied Brian, who carried a loaded gun, then Ashley would escape liability since he would not have the "reckless" mental state required for murder (and would thus not satisfy the rule that an accomplice must have the mental state required for the substantive crime). See M.P.C. §2.06, Comment 7, and §210.2(1)(b).

97. Yes. **In general, if the principal and accomplice are tried at the same time, and the principal is acquitted, the accomplice must also be acquitted.** There are some exceptions (e.g., where the principal is the beneficiary of some special defense not applicable to the accomplice), but none of these apply here.

98. (a) The defense of withdrawal. **Just as one charged with conspiracy may sometimes raise the defense that he or she withdrew or renounced, so one who has given aid or encouragement prior to a crime may, if he or she changes his or her mind, be able to withdraw and thus avoid accomplice liability.**

(b) No. **It is not enough that the defendant had a subjective change of heart, and gave no further assistance prior to the crime.** He or she must, at the very least, make it clear to the other party that he or she is repudiating his or her past aid or encouragement. Daphne did not do this here, since she merely silently left the scene.

99. No. **Where the accomplice's assistance has merely been verbal, a verbal repudiation of the plan will usually suffice. Furthermore, if the defendant warns the authorities, this will almost always be enough, even if the defendant supplied more tangible help (e.g., a gun). What is *not* required for the withdrawal defense is that the crime actually be *thwarted*.** Consequently, the fact that Daphne did not succeed in blocking the crime is irrelevant. (Note that this is quite different from the

rule in conspiracy cases, where withdrawal will only be a defense if the conspirator actually thwarts the crime.)

100. No, probably. **In general, if a crime is defined so as to logically require participation by a second person (other than the one who commits the substantive offense), and the legislature has not authorized direct punishment of that second person, he or she will not be liable as an accomplice. The Model Penal Code expresses this idea by saying that the defendant is not liable as an accomplice if "the offense is so defined that his conduct is inevitably incident to its commission." M.P.C. §2.06(6)(b).** Since prostitution inevitably requires a customer, and the legislature has not made it a crime to patronize a prostitute, John cannot be convicted according to the prevailing view. (For this reason, some states have special "John laws," statutes making it a crime to patronize a prostitute.)

101. No. **Where a crime is defined mainly to *protect a certain class of victims*, the victim will not be convicted of being an accomplice to the crime, even if he or she actively helped cause the crime to be committed.** Since statutory rape statutes are universally designed to protect the minor child, the minor is never subjected to accomplice liability. Also, statutory rape, like prostitution, inevitably involves two people, so if the legislature has not expressly punished the second (here, the minor girl), accomplice liability will not be imposed.

102. None, probably. **Most states have a crime of "accessory after the fact" or "obstruction of justice." But neither of these typically applies where all the defendant has done is to fail to notify the authorities about a crime of which he or she is aware.**

103. No. **An accessory is one who aids or encourages the commission of a crime, and such an accomplice is guilty of the substantive crime just as if he or she had committed it himself or herself.** (Thus, if Dwain had supplied Larry with a gun with which Dwain encouraged Larry to kill his wife, Dwain would be guilty of murder as an accomplice.) But one who helps a criminal, even a felon, escape detection after the crime has been committed is not an accomplice, under modern law.

104. Obstruction of justice, or accessory after the fact. **The traditional phrase to describe the crime committed by one who helps another avoid apprehension is "accessory after the fact." Being an accessory after the fact does not make one an accomplice in the sense that one is guilty of the substantive crime that the other person committed. Instead, "accessory after the fact" is a type of obstruction of justice, and today, many statutes expressly call the crime "obstruction of justice." The penalties are typically much less severe than for the underlying substantive offense. The crime is committed only where the defendant knows that another person has committed a felony and gives *affirmative assistance* to hinder the felon's arrest.** (Refusal to tell the authorities about the crime is not sufficient.)

105. (a) The crime of solicitation. **The common law crime of solicitation occurs when one requests or encourages another to perform a criminal act.**

    (b) Yes. **The common law crime of solicitation occurs when one requests or encourages another to perform a criminal act, regardless of whether the latter agrees.** The fact that Albert declined Denzil's proposal does not give Denzil a defense—indeed, the main utility of the solicitation crime is in those cases where the person who is requested to commit the crime refuses (since if he or she agrees, both parties will generally be guilty of conspiracy and of the substantive offense).

106. No, probably. **Most courts do not classify fetuses born dead as being humans for the purposes of the murder statute.** Since the fetus was never "alive" (i.e., was never alive outside the womb), a court

would probably hold that no murder was committed. See, e.g., *Keeler v. Superior Court*, 470 P.2d 617 (Cal. 1970), holding D not guilty of murder on similar facts.

107. Yes. **Since the baby was born alive, it was a human for purposes of the murder statute.** The fact that the injury was done before the baby was outside the womb is irrelevant—as a result of Darren's acts, a human being who was alive outside the womb died, so Darren is guilty.

108. No. **The crime of murder requires, of course, that a death be proven. But a death can be proven without a body. The fact of a person's death can be proven, like any other fact in any criminal or civil case, by circumstantial (i.e., indirect) evidence. This is an issue of fact for the fact finder (the jury) to decide, rather than one of law for the judge.** Here, the unlikelihood that Vera would abandon her two young children without ever communicating with them again, the fact that Desmond stood to benefit from her death, and the fact that Vera was never seen again all would be enough to allow (though not require) a jury to find that Vera was dead and that Desmond killed her.

109. Yes. **Garden-variety murder requires an "intent to kill." But the requisite intent will be found not only where the defendant "desires" to bring about a death, but also where the defendant *knows with substantial certainty* that death will result, even if he or she does not desire the death. The Model Penal Code §2.02(2)(b) holds that a person acts "knowingly" with respect to a result of his or her conduct if he or she is "aware that it is practically certain that his conduct will cause such a result."** Here, Dominick knew with substantial certainty that a bomb sufficiently strong to destroy the airplane in midflight would be virtually certain to cause the death of anyone who was aboard. He therefore meets the intent requirement for murder. Since M.P.C. §210.2(1)(a) makes criminal homicide murder when the homicide is committed "purposely or knowingly," Dominick would be guilty of murder under the Model Penal Code.

110. Yes. **Nearly all courts hold that if the defendant realizes that his or her conduct poses a *very high risk of death* (even though not a substantial certainty), this will suffice for murder. The idea is usually put that a *"depraved heart"* or an *"extreme, reckless indifference to the value of human life"* will be a sufficient mental state for murder. See, e.g., Model Penal Code §210.2(1)(b) (D is guilty of murder if he or she has acted "recklessly under circumstances manifesting extreme indifference to the value of human life").** Here, unlike the prior question, it probably cannot be said that Dominick knew that death was "substantially certain" to result from his bomb. However, Dominick has certainly manifested a reckless and extreme indifference to the value of Joe's life, so he would almost certainly be convicted.

111. Yes, probably. **In most states, the mens rea requirement for murder is satisfied if the defendant intended not to kill, but to *do serious bodily injury* to the victim. A typical application of this principle is the case in which the defendant savagely beats the victim, with his or her intent limited to doing so, and the victim dies from his or her injuries.** This is what happened here, so in most states, Frank would be convicted. (But observe that under the Model Penal Code, Frank might not be convicted—intent to do serious bodily injury does not suffice as the mental state for murder under the M.P.C.; only if the prosecutor can show that Frank acted "recklessly under circumstances manifesting extreme indifference to the value of human life" may Frank be convicted. See M.P.C. §210.2(1)(b).)

112. Yes, probably, on a "reckless indifference to the value of human life" theory. **Nearly all courts are willing to hold the defendant liable for murder if he or she realizes that there is a very high risk of death from his or her conduct and goes ahead anyway. In most states, this result is accomplished by holding the defendant liable for murder if he or she acted "recklessly under circumstances manifesting extreme indifference to the value of human life" (the language of M.P.C.**

§210.2(1)(b)). **It does not matter that death was not substantially certain to result, and it does not matter that the defendant did not actually desire to bring about the death.**

Here, Dwight knew that if he slept with Sheila hundreds of times, there would be at least a 70 percent chance that she would develop AIDS, and he further knew that once she developed AIDS, it was only a matter of time before she died. Dwight's conduct here seems to manifest the required extreme and reckless indifference to the value of human life—it is not very different from shooting into a passing passenger train without intent to kill anyone but with knowledge that the odds are high that the bullet will strike someone.

113. (a) The felony murder rule. **The felony murder rule provides that if the defendant, while in the process of committing a dangerous felony, kills another (even accidentally), the killing is murder.**

   (b) Yes. **The felony murder rule provides that if the defendant, while in the process of committing a dangerous felony, kills another (even accidentally), the killing is murder.** The requirements for the felony murder doctrine appear satisfied here. The felony was certainly an "inherently dangerous" one, since armed robbery frequently results in death (even though the precise sequence that led to death here was unusual). Also, there was a causal relationship between the felony and the killing—the robbery quite directly gave rise to Omar's death. In general, the felony murder rule will apply if the felony is a robbery, the dead person is the victim, and the death occurs directly at the hand of the robber.

114. No, probably. **The Model Penal Code does not adopt the felony murder rule per se. However, M.P.C. §210.2(1)(b) establishes a *rebuttable presumption* of "recklessness . . . manifesting extreme indifference to the value of human life" where the defendant is "engaged or is an accomplice in the commission of, or an attempt to commit . . . robbery, rape . . . ." Thus, if an unintentional killing occurs during a robbery, the prosecutor can get a conviction without any additional showing of mental state, unless the defendant affirmatively shows that he or she was not reckless.** Here, if Benny can show (as he probably can) that he reasonably believed that the tap on the head with the butt of the gun would not even seriously injure Omar, let alone kill him, presumably the jury would find that Benny was not "reckless . . . manifesting extreme indifference to the value of human life." If so, Benny would be acquitted, even though he would be convicted under the usual felony murder approach (by which the defendant is guilty of murder even if he can show that the killing was not only unintentional but not even reckless).

115. Yes, probably. **Clark is clearly an accomplice to the armed robbery. If Benny is guilty under the felony murder doctrine, then Clark should have accomplice liability for that same death.** Since the mental state for Benny's conviction is not intent to kill but intent to commit a felony, and since Clark had that same felonious intent, he satisfies the requirement for accomplice liability that his mental state be the mental state required to commit the "substantive crime" (in this case, felony murder).

116. Unclear. **Some states would probably allow Benny to be convicted on these facts by using the felony murder doctrine. If the death of Jean can be seen as the "natural and probable consequence" of Benny's armed robbery, then he should be liable.** It is at least reasonably foreseeable that a shopkeeper might defend himself or herself against a robbery by trying to shoot the robber, and it is certainly foreseeable that if the owner did so, he or she might hit a bystander instead. On the other hand, the causal link between the felony and the death is clearly more attenuated than in the prior question, so not all states will apply the felony murder doctrine here. See, e.g., *People v. Washington*, 402 P.2d 130 (Cal. 1965), indicating that California will not allow felony murder in this situation, or in any situation where the fatal shot comes from the gun of a person other than the robber.

117. No, probably. **Where one robber is killed by the robbery victim or by police officers attempting to make an arrest, this is the weakest case for holding the other robbers liable under the felony murder doctrine.** First, Benny did not directly "cause" the death in the same way he would have if his own gun had, say, misfired. Second, to the extent that the felony murder principle is designed to protect only innocent persons, it would not be applicable to the death here of Clark, the co-felon. Few if any courts would convict Benny of murder here. See, e.g., *Commonwealth v. Redline*, 137 A.2d 472 (Pa. 1958), refusing to allow felony murder in this "police officer kills co-robber" situation.

118. Yes, probably. **The felony murder rule provides that if the defendant, while in the process of committing a dangerous felony, kills another (even accidentally), the killing is murder.** The felony murder doctrine probably applies in this situation, since Peter's death directly resulted from Donald's commission of the felony. Donald can argue that the actual felony was over at the time of the accident, but most courts have held that the requirement of a death that occurs "in the commission of" the felony is satisfied where the death occurs during the immediate post-crime escape. The fact that Donald was not behaving even recklessly at the time of the death should be irrelevant—the whole purpose of the felony murder doctrine is to make a death murder even though the felon's mental state was relatively innocent, apart from the fact that he or she was committing the underlying felony.

119. Voluntary manslaughter. **A defendant who kills while in a "heat of passion" is entitled to have the charges reduced to voluntary manslaughter, so long as his or her act was in response to a provocation sufficiently strong that a "reasonable person" would have been caused to lose his or her self-control.** The classic illustration of a provocation sufficient for voluntary manslaughter is where the defendant finds his wife "in flagrante delicto," as happened here.

120. Murder. **For voluntary manslaughter to apply, the defendant's act must be in response to a provocation sufficiently strong that a reasonable person would have lost his or her self-control. However, if the lapse of time between the provocation and the killing was so long that a reasonable person would have "*cooled off*," voluntary manslaughter does not apply.** Here, Seymour had 24 hours to cool off, and he was not in contact with either Ellen or Fred during this period (so that his passion was not rekindled). It won't matter whether Seymour himself was still enraged—as long as a reasonable person would not still have been completely enraged, Seymour loses the right to get the lesser charge.

121. Voluntary manslaughter, probably. **If the defendant and victim get into mutual combat in which neither one can be said to be the aggressor, most courts will reduce the defendant's liability to manslaughter.**

122. Murder. **The defendant's emotional makeup (including his or her hair-trigger temper) are not taken into account in determining whether the defendant was sufficiently provoked. The issue is always whether a "reasonable person" with an ordinary emotional makeup would be provoked to violence—the defendant's own emotional characteristics are ignored.** Here, Larry does not qualify for the lesser charge of voluntary manslaughter on these facts.

123. Involuntary manslaughter. **One form of manslaughter is "involuntary manslaughter," which is defined in most states as being the *reckless or grossly negligent causing of another's death*. It is not necessary for involuntary manslaughter that the defendant have desired to kill, or even that he or she desired to injure, the victim. It is enough that he or she behaved in a way that recklessly or grossly negligently disregarded the risk of serious bodily injury or death.** Since Kirk knew that there were houses nearby in the direction at which he was aiming, it would be quite plausible for a jury to find him guilty of involuntary manslaughter.

124. No, probably. **If the jurisdiction requires "gross negligence" or "recklessness" for involuntary manslaughter, as most jurisdictions do, Kirk's conduct here probably did not rise to that level.** Most courts hold that gross negligence or recklessness is only established where the defendant was *actually aware* of the danger, regardless of whether he or she *should* have been aware of it. Similarly, the Model Penal Code would acquit Kirk of manslaughter here. The M.P.C. requires "recklessness" for manslaughter, and under §2.02(2)(c), a person acts recklessly only when he or she "consciously disregards" a substantial and unjustifiable risk.

125. Negligent homicide. **M.P.C. §210.4(1) provides that "criminal homicide constitutes negligent homicide when it is committed negligently."** A person acts negligently, under the Code, when he or she "should be aware of a substantial and unjustifiable risk," and his or her failure to perceive that risk, under all the circumstances, involves a "gross deviation from the standard of care that a reasonable person would observe." The M.P.C. therefore does not require that the defendant be *actually* aware of the risk in order for him or her to act negligently, and thus be guilty of negligent homicide. Here, the facts tell us that Kirk should have asked questions to find out that there were homes nearby, so his failure to do so almost certainly constitutes negligence. Since Sally's death resulted directly from this negligence (that is, if Kirk had not behaved negligently, he would not have taken the shot and would not have killed Sally), Kirk can be liable for negligent homicide even though, strictly speaking, the shooting was an accident.

126. No, probably. **There must be a causal link between the defendant's act of negligence and the ensuing death. The defendant's conduct must not only be the "cause in fact" of the death, but also a "proximate cause" of the death (one whose relationship to the death is not bizarre or extraordinary).** Dan probably met the statutory requirement of recklessness. But reckless or not, his conduct must still be shown to have been the "*proximate cause*" of Valerie's death. Here, the chain of events that led to Valerie's death was quite hard to foresee, and probably abnormal. The main risk imposed by Dan's conduct (the risk that made his conduct reckless) was the risk that the bag would hit a pedestrian, or perhaps the risk that the bag would hit a car. There was relatively little risk that the bag would burst open, create a dust cloud, and distract the vision of a driver, who would then run over someone else. Because of the bizarreness and unforeseeability of the sequence that led to Valerie's death, Dan will probably escape guilt for manslaughter.

127. Involuntary manslaughter. **Nearly all jurisdictions apply the "*misdemeanor manslaughter*" rule, by which the defendant may be convicted of involuntary manslaughter when a death occurs accidentally as the result of the defendant's commission of a misdemeanor or other unlawful act. The unlawful act is treated as a substitute for negligence or recklessness.** Here, the shove constituted battery (a misdemeanor in most jurisdictions), and Marvin's fall and subsequent brain injury were the direct (and proximate) result of that shove. Therefore, Leonard may be convicted even though the death was an accident, and even though Leonard did not intend to do even serious bodily injury to Marvin.

128. No. **The Model Penal Code *rejects the misdemeanor manslaughter rule* in its entirety.** It is true that under the M.P.C., the fact that an act is unlawful may have an evidentiary bearing on whether it is reckless (the mens rea required under the Code for manslaughter). But here, it is very unlikely that Leonard's act would be found reckless, since he wasn't even trying to injure Marvin. So, the absence of the misdemeanor manslaughter rule actually changes the result.

129. Battery. **The crime of battery is defined in most states to cover the *intentional infliction of bodily injury or an "offensive touching."*** Being covered by animal blood is clearly offensive. A court would almost certainly conclude that Tom "touched" Victor here, even though he did so not directly, but by causing an object to touch Victor.

130. Assault. **In most states, one of the ways of committing assault is to *intentionally frighten another person into fearing immediate bodily harm.*** The fact that Victor was not actually injured is irrelevant, since he reasonably perceived that he was in danger.

131. Assault. **The prior question demonstrates one form of criminal assault, "intentional causing of fright." The present question illustrates the other form: *attempted battery assault.* One who unsuccessfully attempts to commit a battery (that is, one who attempts to injure or offensively touch another) is guilty of the crime of assault. For assault of the attempted battery type, it is not necessary that the potential victim be aware of the danger before it passes.**

132. No. **Nothing in the Model Penal Code makes it rape to have sex with a woman who has become drunk on her own volition but who remains conscious—the fact that the woman's drunkenness induces her to behave in a way that she might not if she were sober is treated by the M.P.C. as irrelevant.** Michael clearly has not used force or threats. However, under the M.P.C., Michael would be liable for rape if he had surreptitiously drugged Wanda or administered liquor to her without her knowledge. Similarly, if Wanda had been completely unconscious, Michael would be liable for rape, since M.P.C. §213.1(1)(c) makes it rape to have sexual intercourse where the female is "unconscious." (But some courts would convict Michael here, on the theory that there is no valid consent where the woman is drunk, even where the defendant did not induce this state.)

133. No, probably. **Rape is traditionally defined as unconsented-to sexual intercourse *by a male with a female.*** However, most states have revised their statutes to read in a gender-neutral manner both as to offender and victim; under such a statute, Rick would be guilty of rape.

134. No, probably. **Traditionally, rape is defined as having intercourse with a female who is not one's wife. Although a number of states have changed their rape laws on this point in recent years, many states have maintained this "spousal immunity."** Depending upon the state, Howard may have committed sexual assault, or ordinary assault, but he has not committed rape.

135. Yes, probably. **Although rape is still generally defined as nonconsensual sexual intercourse with a woman who is not one's wife, many states now treat a woman who is living apart from her husband under a separation agreement or decree as no longer being the wife of that person.**

136. Yes. **In most states, a husband may not commit direct rape of his wife, as principal. But nothing prevents a husband from being held to being an accomplice in the rape of his wife.** See, e.g., M.P.C. §213.6(2) ("Where the definition of an offense excludes conduct with a spouse . . . this shall not preclude conviction of a spouse . . . as accomplice in a sexual act which he . . . causes another person, not within the exclusion, to perform.")

137. Yes, probably. **Traditionally, statutory rape was a strict liability crime. Most jurisdictions hold that even a reasonable belief by the defendant that the girl was over the age of consent is not a defense.**

138. No, probably. **M.P.C. §213.6(1) provides that when "criminality . . . depends on a child's being below a critical age other than 10, it is a defense for the actor to prove . . . that he reasonably believed the child to be above the critical age."** So, Mark's reasonable mistake saves him from conviction under the Model Penal Code. (But if Mark were charged with the more serious M.P.C. crime of having sex with a girl under the age of ten, his reasonable but mistaken belief that she was older than ten would not save him.)

139. **Yes. First, the fact that Doug did not fully penetrate Estelle's vagina is not a defense—most statutes require penetration but also provide that penetration, "however slight," suffices. See, e.g., M.P.C. §213.0(2). Second, nearly all states agree that the crime is complete even if the male does not achieve orgasm.**

140. **Yes, probably. Kidnapping is generally defined as the unlawful confinement of another, accompanied by either a moving of the victim ("asportation") or a secreting of him or her. In many states the asportation need not be over a substantial distance.** Consequently, in many states, the requisite asportation for kidnapping will be found here despite the short distance.

141. **No. At common law, larceny is defined as the *trespassory taking and carrying away of the personal property of another with intent to steal*. The crime thus requires the wrongful taking of property *from another's possession*, so that if the defendant is already in rightful possession of the property at the time he or she appropriates it to his or her own use, he or she cannot be guilty of larceny.** Here, up until the moment he was fired, Ludwig was in rightful possession of the car, even though he did not hold title. Therefore, when he appropriated it by refusing to return it, he was not wrongfully taking it from the corporation's possession, so he is not guilty of larceny. (He is guilty of embezzlement, however.)

142. **Yes. At common law, larceny is defined as the *trespassory taking and carrying away of the personal property of another with intent to steal*.** Since Megan was a relatively low-level employee, a court would probably hold that she had been given only "*custody*" (a very temporary thing) rather than "possession," and that "possession" of the bonds remained in the law firm until Megan sold them to the dealer. Since Megan did not have possession of the bonds at the time she appropriated them, she has fulfilled the requirement for larceny: taking property out of the possession of another and carrying it away. Therefore, she committed larceny, not embezzlement. (Observe that the main difference between this question and the prior question is that here, the defendant was a low-level employee who was therefore deemed to have "custody," whereas in the prior question, the defendant was a high-level employee who would therefore be treated as having had "possession.")

143. (a) **No crime. The crime closest to which Stanley came to committing was larceny. But for larceny to exist at common law, the defendant must have intended to wrongfully appropriate the property *at the time he or she took possession of it*.** Here, Stanley's intent at the time he found the wallet was to return it, so this necessary concurrence of intent to steal with taking possession did not exist. The fact that Stanley changed his mind and took possession later on is irrelevant, since at common law the only intent that counts is the defendant's intent at the moment he or she takes possession.

   (b) Larceny. **Under M.P.C. §223.5, "a person who comes into control of property of another that he knows to have been lost . . . is guilty of theft if, with purpose to deprive the owner thereof, he fails to take reasonable measures to restore the property to a person entitled to have it."** Under this formulation, even if the defendant intends to return the property at the time he or she finds it, he or she will become guilty of larceny if he or she then intentionally fails to take steps to return the property. Here, once Stanley decided not to return the property, he became guilty of larceny even though he was not guilty at the time he first possessed the wallet.

144. (a) Larceny. **At common law, larceny is defined as the *trespassory taking and carrying away of the personal property of another with intent to steal*.** Here, Stanley had the requisite unlawful intent (to deprive the owner of the wallet) at the time he came into possession of it. Since he then

in fact kept the wallet, he is not saved by the fact that he ultimately changed his mind and took reasonable steps to return it.

(b) **No crime. Under the M.P.C., as long as the defendant, within a reasonable time after taking possession, takes reasonable steps to return the property, the fact that he or she may have had a wrongful intent at the time he or she first took possession is irrelevant. See M.P.C. §223.5.** Importantly, the purpose of the M.P.C. is to encourage the return of the property. Also, the fact that Stanley did not succeed in returning the property is irrelevant—all he was required to do was to take reasonable steps, which he did.

145. Obtaining property by false pretenses. **The crime of obtaining property by false pretenses occurs when the defendant makes a *false representation of a material present or past fact that causes the person to whom it is made to pass title to his or her property to the defendant*. The defendant must know that his representation is false, and must intend to defraud the other person.** Here, the property being transferred to Jerome was Virgil's money; since Jerome knew that he was making a false representation of a material fact (that the stone was a diamond when in fact it was not), and since that representation caused Virgil to pass title to his money to Jerome, the elements of false pretenses are satisfied. The crime was not larceny, because what Jerome obtained from Virgil was title to Virgil's money, not mere possession of that money, and one who obtains title from another is not guilty of common law larceny.

146. Larceny (by trick). **For a taking of property to be larcenous, the original possession by defendant must be wrongful. Possession will be wrongful if it is obtained by fraud or deceit. The larceny in this situation is said to be "by trick."** The principal question is whether, at the time Timothy rented the car, he took title or merely possession. If Timothy took title, then the crime would be theft by false pretenses; if he took mere possession, the crime would be larceny. Here, Ready kept title to the car and was merely entrusting Timothy with possession. Since at the time he rented the car Timothy intended not to return it, he meets the requirement that his possession have been "wrongful" at the time it occurred. "Larceny by trick" is not a separate crime from larceny; it is simply one way that larceny may be committed.

By the way, since Ready initially entrusted Timothy with possession (rather than having Timothy forcibly take and carry the property away), larceny did not occur until Timothy "converted" the property to his own use, which did not occur until he kept the car for a *substantial period of time*. Six months certainly satisfies this "substantial time" requirement, but one or two days would not have.

147. **No. First, larceny may only be committed intentionally, not negligently or recklessly. Also, the defendant must be shown to have had an *intent* to *permanently deprive* the owner of his or her property, or at least to deprive the owner of a significant portion of the item's *economic value*.** Dennis's planned one-hour trip would not have deprived Benjamin of a substantial portion of the car's economic value. It is true that as things turned out, the car was completely destroyed, but Dennis did not intend this to happen (even if he recklessly brought it about), so the requirement of intent rather than recklessness saves Dennis from a larceny conviction here. (But Dennis might be guilty under a statute making it a crime to "joyride." Such statutes exist in most states.)

148. **No, probably. Larceny exists only where the defendant intended to take property that he or she knew to belong to another. Where the defendant takes another's property with intent to collect a debt that the other owes him or her, this will generally negate intent to steal. Furthermore, as long as the defendant has an honest belief that the amount is due and takes property worth less than the amount believed to be due, the defendant will not be guilty even though the defendant is wrong about whether the debt is owed.** The fact that Sally was wrong about the terms of the

retirement plan will not defeat her "good-faith attempt to collect a debt" defense. Sally would also not be guilty under the Model Penal Code; see §223.1(3)(b), making it an affirmative defense to a theft prosecution that the defendant "acted under an honest claim . . . that he had a right to acquire or dispose of [the property] as he did."

149. Embezzlement. **Embezzlement is the** *fraudulent conversion of the property of another by one who is already in lawful possession of the property.* Here, Alan was already in lawful possession of Veronica's property (the $100,000), and fraudulently converted that property to his own use. What distinguishes embezzlement from larceny is that in larceny, the defendant is not in lawful possession at the time he or she converts the property to his or her own use. (For instance, if immediately following the sale Alan had refused to give the $100,000 to Veronica when requested to do so, this would be larceny, since Alan would never have obtained lawful possession of the money.)

150. Embezzlement. **Embezzlement is the** *fraudulent conversion of the property of another by one who is already in lawful possession of the property.* The issue, of course, is whether the defendant's *intent to return* the property constitutes a defense to an embezzlement charge. Where the property taken is money, and the defendant intends to repay the funds, virtually all courts hold that this is *not* a defense. The courts hold that even if the defendant shows that he or she had the wherewithal to repay the "loan," and in fact even where (as here) he or she succeeds in repaying it before being caught, this is no defense to embezzlement.

151. **(a)** No crime, probably. **Ernest comes closer to embezzlement than to any other crime, since it can at least be argued that Ernest held Francis's money and failed to use it for the agreed-upon purposes.** However, at common law, Ernest would probably succeed with the argument, "I was not really holding Francis's money. Instead, I agreed to make a payment out of my own funds on Francis's behalf, in return for his agreement to accept a lower weekly paycheck." Since one cannot embezzle one's own funds, most courts would hold Ernest not liable, any more than any other person who fails to make a contracted-for payment is liable for theft.

(b) "Theft by failure to make required disposition of funds received." **The Model Penal Code, precisely to avoid the result summarized in (a), has created the crime of "theft by failure to make required disposition of funds received." M.P.C. §223.8 provides that "a person who obtains property upon agreement . . . to make specified payment or other disposition, whether from such property or its proceeds or from his own property . . . in equivalent amount, is guilty of theft if he deals with the property obtained as his own and fails to make the required payment or disposition."** Since Ernest "obtained property" (i.e., the amount deducted from Francis's weekly paycheck) in return for his promise to pay an equivalent amount to the insurance company, he would be guilty under this section even though he was to make the payments to the insurance company out of his own funds, not out of any particular segregated funds that were the "property" of Francis.

152. No, probably. **M.P.C. §223.8 provides that "a person who obtains property upon agreement . . . to make specified payment or other disposition, whether from such property or its proceeds or from his own property . . . in equivalent amount, is guilty of theft if he deals with the property obtained as his own and fails to make the required payment or disposition."** However, this special Model Penal Code provision applies only to a person who "obtains property." Here, Ernest has not really obtained any property (as he did above by deducting from paychecks)—Ernest has merely made a general promise to confer a benefit, without extracting any direct quid quo pro such as a payroll deduction. On the facts here, a court would probably hold that Ernest was simply the breacher of a contract, not a thief.

153. Theft by false pretenses. **The crime of "false pretenses" is generally committed by (1) a false representation of a (2) material present or past fact, (3) which causes the person to whom it was made (4) to pass title to (5) his or her property to the misrepresenter, who (6) knows that his or her representation is false and who (7) intends to defraud.** Chrysallis has satisfied all of these elements here, since it falsely represented a material past fact (that the car was new and undamaged), this representation caused Val to pass title to his property (his $12,000 cash) to the misrepresenter (Chrysallis), and the misrepresenter knew that its representation was false and intended to "defraud" Val (in the sense that it intended to induce Val to give up his money in return for property that was not as described). This is false pretenses, rather than larceny by trick, because the victim gave title to his property (the money) rather than merely transferring possession of that property to the misrepresenter (Chrysallis). (In general, if the victim hands over money, it will almost always be the case that the crime, if any, is false pretenses rather than larceny by trick.)

154. None. **The closest Chrysallis came was to committing theft by false pretenses. But nearly all courts have recognized immunity to false pretenses prosecutions where the vendor engages in** *"puffing"* or *"seller's talk."* **A statement will be held to be puffing (and will thus not confer false pretenses liability) if the statement would be understood by most observers to be mere seller's talk, and would be** *unlikely to deceive an ordinary reasonable person in the group to whom it was addressed.* **See, e.g., M.P.C. §223.3, holding that "the term 'deceive' does not, however, include . . . puffing by statements unlikely to deceive ordinary persons in the group addressed."** Here, almost any person skilled in interpreting advertisements would understand that "best American-built car" was so vague that it was puffing rather than a precise promise or warranty. Therefore, even though Val himself may have been taken in, there would be no false pretenses liability.

155. (a) No, probably. **Most courts hold that the false representation on which a false pretenses prosecution is based must relate to a** *past or present fact,* **and that false** *promises,* **even when made with an intent not to keep them, are not sufficient.** (The rationale for this majority view is that a contrary rule might lead to imprisonment of debtors who borrow with an honest intent to repay, but later get into financial difficulties.) A minority of courts, however, now allow false promises to suffice for false pretense liability.

(b) Yes. **M.P.C. §223.3(1), which establishes the crime of "theft by deception" (roughly analogous to the common law crime of theft by false pretenses), makes a person guilty if he or she purposely "creates . . . a false impression, including false impressions as to . . . intention or other state of mind." However, the section goes on to provide that "deception as to a person's intention to perform a promise shall not be inferred from the fact alone that he did not subsequently perform the promise."** Thus, if the prosecutor could show only the fact that Audrey sent the money to Switzerland instead of repaying it, this would not by itself be enough to have the case go to the jury. But because of Charles's testimony that Audrey never intended to repay the money (i.e., that her statement to the bank that she intended to repay was false when made), Audrey could be convicted under the M.P.C. approach.

156. No, probably. **There can be no liability for theft by false pretenses unless there has been a false representation of a material present or past fact. In general, where one party simply** *remains silent* **even though he or she knows that the other party is under a false impression, the requisite false representation has not been made.** This is especially likely to be the case where it is the buyer,

rather than the seller, who has the expert information. (The result would be different if Harold knew that Jeremy was relying on Harold's expertise, or if Harold helped create Jeremy's false impression in some way, but neither of these facts is present here.)

157. Yes, probably. **One exception to the general rule that a person does not become liable for false pretenses by mere silence is that if the defendant is in a *fiduciary relationship* with the other party, he or she will have an affirmative duty to speak the truth rather than silently take advantage of the other party's mistake.** Here, Harold knew that Jeremy was relying on Harold's expertise in valuing baseball cards, and that Jeremy wished Harold to act as Jeremy's fiduciary. In this situation, Harold was probably not free to remain silent and offer an unfairly low price (even though in the prior question, where there was no fiduciary relationship between the two, Harold was entitled to make such an offer).

158. Burglary. **The common law crime of burglary is defined to be the breaking and entering of the dwelling of another at night with intent to commit a felony therein.** The "trick" here is that Marvin is guilty of burglary *even though he in fact did not carry out the crime he had intended* (larceny). That is, once Marvin broke into and entered Stewart's premises at night with intent to commit larceny, he had already completed the crime of burglary.

159. No. **At common law, burglary applied only where the defendant broke and entered the *dwelling* of another at night, with intent to commit a felony therein.** Here, Stewart's office was not a dwelling, so there could be no common law burglary. (Modern burglary statutes, however, have often been redrafted to include the entry of buildings in which no one resides, though even these statutes generally reserve heavier punishment for entry of a dwelling.)

160. No. **Burglary at common law requires not only the nighttime breaking and entering of the dwelling of another, but also the intent to *commit a felony within*. The breaking and entering cannot itself be the felony—there must be a separate felony (typically larceny) intended at the time of entry.** Here, Byron intended merely intended to look upon his beloved. This is not a felony (and, indeed, it is probably not even a misdemeanor or any other sort of crime). Therefore, Byron cannot be convicted of burglary, and is guilty of at most criminal trespass.

161. No. **The common law crime of burglary required the breaking and entering of another's dwelling *at night* with intent to commit a felony therein.** Here, the entry took place during the daytime, so it cannot be common law burglary. (All modern state statutes, however, would make this some form of burglary even though it occurred during the day, but in many states, it would be a lower degree of burglary than if it had taken place at night.)

162. No. **Robbery is generally defined as larceny committed with two additional elements: (1) the property is taken from the person of (or in the presence of) the owner, and (2) the taking is accomplished by using force or putting the owner in fear of immediate bodily injury.** Here, the property was taken before Felicia even knew what was happening to her, so there was neither force nor a placing of her in fear. The case is thus analogous to a pickpocketing, which is almost never considered a robbery.

163. Yes. **Robbery occurs where property is taken from the person of the owner, and the taking is accomplished by using force or placing the owner in fear.** Here, Philip made a threat that made Amanda fearful of bodily harm. The fact that Philip had no weapon and would not have used actual force even if Amanda had refused is irrelevant.

Criminal Law Essay Questions

QUESTION 1:   Kim rents a car from Ace Rentals. She tells Ace that she is going to drive out to the Grand Canyon and then return the car in two weeks. Ace tells her that is fine and that if she needs more time, she should just call them and they can extend the rental agreement. Before she heads out, she swings by her office at Crowley Computer to pick up a few things. Cecily, the office manager, sees Kim and asks her to sign a few checks for the company before she leaves. Kim goes into her office and signs the checks and then writes one out to herself on the company's account so she has a little extra spending money on the trip. As she writes out the check, she intends to repay the money as soon as she gets her next paycheck. As she's leaving, she sees Cecily's coat hanging off the back of her chair with her wallet sticking out of it. Kim grabs the wallet and drops it into her bag. She walks past a few desks and then decides she doesn't need the wallet, so she tosses it onto the floor, figuring Cecily will just think she dropped it. Kim then sees Parker, Crowley's CEO. Parker says, "Hey, I forgot my wife's anniversary—can you help me out?" Kim hates that Parker pulls this kind of thing all the time, so she decides to teach him a lesson. She shows Parker her earrings and says, "These are pure diamond. I'll sell them to you for $500." Parker says, "Thanks!" and pays her the money. Kim knows the earrings are glass and worth about $10. She then leaves for her trip. After two weeks, she decides she never wants to go back home, so she drives off into Mexico. What crimes have been committed? Assume this jurisdiction applies the common law.

QUESTION 2:   One day, Francine attempts to poison her husband, Jorge, by putting strychnine in his coffee. Jorge drinks the coffee and becomes dizzy. He takes two steps across the kitchen and then tumbles and hits his head against the oven. He dies from the blow to the head. When police arrive, they arrest Francine for Jorge's murder. An autopsy reveals that the poison was not enough to kill Jorge directly. At trial, Francine argues that the poison did not actually kill Jorge, so she is not guilty of his murder. She also pleads not guilty by reason of insanity. She claims she knew poisoning Jorge was morally wrong, but that she thought that the real Jorge had been replaced by an exact copy grown by the IRS in their secret lab. Because of that, she felt that she had to kill the fake Jorge to get the real Jorge back. Francine's estranged sister, Zooey, calls your office for advice. She tells you she hasn't spoken to Francine in years and has no idea what court Francine is in—she just got a message telling her about Jorge's murder. Before she spends any money to find Francine, she wants to know whether Francine's arguments would be successful.

QUESTION 3:   Jerry plans to rob First National Bank. He goes to the house of Lynette, the First National Bank president, hoping to steal her keycard while she is at the beach. Knowing Lynette is at the beach, he places a ladder against the side of her house so he can reach the second-story window. Jerry sees Jeff, a seven-year-old boy, walking by on the sidewalk. He tells Jeff he has locked himself out of his house, and asks if Jeff can go up the ladder and get his key ring inside (he knows Lynette keeps her keycard on her key ring, which she leaves at home when she goes to the beach). Jeff, who is a Badger Scout and always tries to be helpful, salutes Jerry, climbs up the ladder, and then returns down the ladder with the key ring. Jerry thanks him profusely and then goes home. At home, he shows the keycard to Diane and says that he has a plan to rob the bank, but he needs her help. Diane says she will help but makes Jerry promise not to hurt anyone during the robbery; he agrees. He tells her that they will need to use a gun but that she can be the one to hold it, and no one will have to shoot anyone (in fact, he truly doesn't want her to shoot anyone). The next day, Jerry and Diane go to the bank. Using Lynette's keycard, they sneak in the back door, where Teller confronts them. Before anyone can say anything, the gun in Diane's hand goes off accidentally and kills Teller. Jerry and Diane grab a bag of money, run from the bank, and flee down the street, where they see Toby. Toby asks, "What's going on?" Jerry tells Toby they just accidentally killed a bank teller and that they need to hide. Toby tells them to jump in his car. He then drives them out of town and drops them off at a secluded campsite, telling them, "I have no love for capitalists or police." What crimes have been committed?

QUESTION 4:   Marilyn was an angry young woman. She was fed up with "The Man" and decided to turn to a life of crime as a way to get revenge. Consequently, she went down to the street corner to buy heroin to sell. Dave, who in reality was an undercover police officer, sold her a bag of sugar, but told her it was heroin. She then went a little farther down the street and sold the bag, as heroin, to Perry, a drug user. With her money, she visited a local pet store and saw a rare Burmese chinchilla in the window. Believing it was illegal to own Burmese chinchillas, and also believing it was illegal to name a pet after an American president, she bought it and named it "President George W. Bush." In fact, neither owning a Burmese chinchilla nor naming it after a president is illegal. Finally, Marilyn saw Anthony, whom she knew was severely allergic to Burmese chinchillas. She brandished President George W. Bush at Anthony and said, "Give me your money, or I'll rub you down with this chinchilla!" Anthony simply rolled his eyes and walked away. Marilyn decided Anthony was not going to give her his money, so she gave up and started walking home. Officer Murphy, seeing all this, arrested Marilyn. What crimes could she be charged with?

QUESTION 5:   Officer Manly comes to Yiyun's house to arrest her for a murder committed five years before, for which the police have long suspected Yiyun. Officer Manly knocks on the door and says, "Yiyun! I don't have a warrant, but I'm taking you in!" Yiyun responds, "My constitutional rights say you need a warrant to come into my house to arrest me!" Officer Manly grabs her through the doorway and tries to cuff her. Yiyun punches and kicks Officer Manly. He finally subdues her and drives her to the stationhouse. Officer Manly tells his friend Officer Studly, "Hey, I might have made a mistake. We have to get Yiyun on some crime because I know she is a murderer." Officer Studly says, "Don't worry—I've got this." Officer Studly disguises himself as a fellow prisoner and sits next to Yiyun in the holding cell. He leans over to Yiyun and says, "Hey, I got some heroin if you want to have it. It'll take the edge off." Yiyun finds some money in her sock and buys the heroin. Officer Studly leaves the cell and finds Officer Manly. He says, "We got her for drugs! Let's throw the book at her!" Yiyun is eventually charged with resisting arrest and drug possession. At trial, she argues that her use of force in resisting Officer Manly was justified and that she was entrapped when Officer Studly sold her the drugs. Discuss the validity of her defenses.

Sample Answers to Criminal Law Essay Questions

ANSWER TO QUESTION 1:

The Rental Car

The issue is whether Kim committed any crime in taking the rental car to Mexico. **Common law larceny is defined as the trespassory taking and carrying away of the personal property of another with intent to steal. The requirement of a "trespassory taking" means that if the defendant is already in rightful possession of the property at the time he or she appropriates it for his or her own use, he or she cannot be guilty of larceny. Embezzlement is the fraudulent conversion of the property of another by one who is already in lawful possession of it.** The important question is what was Kim's intention when she rented the car? If she rented the car intending to return it within two weeks, she could not be guilty of common law larceny. This is because at the time she made the decision to appropriate the car, she was already in rightful possession of it under the rental contract. But if at the moment Kim rented the car she intended to steal it, this would be a "trespassory taking" and thus larceny. In that case, Kim would be guilty of "larceny by trick," since she gained possession of the property by fraud or deceit. If she did not intend to steal the car when she rented it, she likely committed embezzlement since she decided to steal the car after she had lawful possession (and Ace was willing to let her extend that lawful possession past two weeks). In that case, the issue becomes whether by taking the car to Mexico she "converted" it to her own use. Since Kim does not seem to have any intention of ever returning, it is likely a court would find this to be a sufficient conversion for the crime of embezzlement.

The Check

The issue is what crime Kim has committed by writing the company check to herself. **The rules for larceny and embezzlement are stated above. If an employee is one who has a high position, with broad authority, he or she will usually be deemed to have possession, not just custody, of the property he or she holds for the employer's benefit. Therefore, if he or she subsequently appropriates the property for his or her own use, he or she is guilty of embezzlement rather than larceny (larceny applies in the case of low-level employees, who are deemed to merely have "custody" rather than "possession"). If the defendant took money, it is no defense to an embezzlement charge that defendant intended to repay the money.** Since Kim is the one who signs checks on the company's account, it is likely she is a high-level employee. When she wrote the check to herself and used it for her trip, it is likely that she used the company's money in a way that was not authorized by her employment contract with the company. Ultimately, since Kim has possession of the contents of the company bank account, not mere custody, her use of the money for her own purposes is embezzlement rather than larceny. Her intent to repay later is no defense.

The Wallet

The issue is whether Kim moved the wallet far enough to result in a larceny. **The rule for larceny is stated above. To commit larceny, the defendant must not only commit a trespassory taking but also must carry the property away. As long as every portion of the property is moved, even a slight distance will suffice.** Here, although Kim only carried Cecily's wallet a few feet before deciding to drop it, this is likely a far enough distance to support a charge of larceny.

The Earrings

The issue is whether Kim committed a crime by selling her glass earrings to Parker while claiming they were diamond. **The crime of false pretenses has the following elements: a false representation, of a material present or past fact, that causes the person to whom it is made to pass title to his or her property to the misrepresenter, who knows that his or her representation is false and intends to defraud.** Kim knew her earrings were glass, and to get back at Parker, she told him that they were diamond. She then charged him 50 times their real value, not because she believed they were worth that much under the circumstances (since Parker was worried about getting in trouble with his wife), but because she wanted to defraud him. Consequently, since Parker passed title to his money by giving it to her in exchange for the earrings, Kim likely committed the crime of false pretenses.

ANSWER TO QUESTION 2:

Murder of Jorge

The issue is whether Francine is guilty of Jorge's murder even though the strychnine was not enough to kill him. **Murder is defined as the unlawful killing of another person. An "intent-to-kill" murder occurs when the defendant desires to bring about the victim's death. Importantly, the defendant's act is a direct cause of the victim's harm if the harm followed the defendant's act without the presence of any clearly defined act or event by an outside person or thing. Additionally, if the general type of harm intended actually occurs, the defendant will not be absolved because the harm occurred in a slightly different way than intended.** Francine intended to kill Jorge with the strychnine, and Jorge was in fact killed when he was made dizzy by the poison, fell, and hit his head. Consequently, even though Jorge died from the head injury and not the poison, Francine is guilty of intent-to-kill murder.

M'Naghten Test

If the court follows the *M'Naghten* test, it is unlikely Francine's insanity plea will be effective. **At least half the states apply the *M'Naghten* rule. Under that rule, the defendant must show that he or she suffered a mental disease that caused a defect in his or her reasoning powers, and that, as a result, the defendant did not understand the "nature and quality" of his or her act or did not know that his or her act was wrong.** Francine admitted she knew poisoning Jorge was morally wrong, even if she thought the IRS had switched his body. Consequently, she is not insane under the *M'Naghten* test, because she knew the nature and quality of her act, and she knew it was wrong.

Irresistible Impulse Test

Many states, including about half of those states that follow *M'Naghten*, have added a second standard by which the defendant can establish his or her insanity: that the defendant was unable to control his or her conduct. Here, Francine might claim that she felt she absolutely had to kill the fake Jorge, but this is probably not enough to count as an "irresistible impulse" (for example, if she were a kleptomaniac charged with larceny).

Model Penal Code Standard

The Model Penal Code allows the defendant to be acquitted if "as a result of mental disease or defect he lacks substantial capacity either to appreciate the criminality of his conduct or to conform his conduct to the requirements of the law." Thus, Francine would win if she satisfied either the *M'Naghten* test or the "irresistible impulse" test stated above. However, as already stated, she fails under both of these tests.

The Federal Standard

The modern federal standard states that the defendant wins only if "as a result of a severe mental disease or defect, [he] was unable to appreciate the nature and quality or the wrongfulness of his acts." As stated above, Francine knew she was poisoning Jorge and knew it was wrong.

ANSWER TO QUESTION 3:

Burglary—Jerry

The issue is whether Jerry can be found guilty of burglary even though he never went inside the house. **Under the common law, burglary is the breaking and entering into the dwelling house of another at night with the intent to commit a felony therein. However, no state now requires that the burglary occur at night. An accomplice is one who assists or encourages the carrying out of a crime, but does not commit the** *actus reus.* **A principal, by contrast, is one who commits the** *actus reus.* **While it is generally held that an accomplice cannot be convicted unless the principal is shown to have the required mental state to commit the crime, in cases where the accomplice uses an innocent dupe to commit the crime, the accomplice can in fact be found guilty as a principal.** Jeff, the principal (since he actually entered the house), had no intent to commit a crime—in fact, he simply wanted to help Jerry. However, Jerry, the accomplice, intended to trick Jeff into climbing into Lynette's window and stealing her key ring. Consequently, Jerry is guilty of burglary as a principal even though he himself never entered the house—he used an innocent agent to commit the breaking and entering. By contrast, if Jerry were charged as an accomplice, he'd be acquitted, assuming the jurisdiction follows the majority rule that an accomplice can't be convicted unless the principal is guilty.

Conspiracy—Diane and Jerry

Diane and Jerry are likely guilty of the crime of conspiracy. **Conspiracy is as an agreement between two or more persons to do either an unlawful act or a lawful act by unlawful means.** Jerry asked Diane to help him rob the bank, and she agreed, albeit after making him promise not to hurt anyone. Consequently, they are both liable for conspiracy.

Felony Murder—Diane

Although Diane did not intend to kill Teller, she is likely guilty of felony murder. **Under the felony-murder rule, the intent to commit a felony is sufficient to meet the** *mens rea* **requirement for murder. Importantly, the rule provides that if the defendant, while he or she is in the process of committing a dangerous felony, kills another (even accidentally), the killing is murder.** Although Diane did not intend to kill Teller, she did so while committing the dangerous felony of robbery. Consequently, she will be found guilty of the murder of Teller.

Felony Murder—Jerry

Jerry is likely also guilty of felony murder, although he never intended anyone to be killed. **Under the felony-murder rule stated above, if an accomplice helps a principal commit a dangerous felony and an unintended death directly results, the accomplice is guilty of the murder on the theory that the accomplice is guilty of the dangerous felony by operation of the accomplice-liability principles, and that guilt then makes the accomplice directly guilty of the felony murder. This result occurs even if the jurisdiction does not make an accomplice automatically liable for "natural and probable" consequences of other crimes by the principal.** Diane committed the *actus reus* of shooting Teller, and is guilty of murder under the felony-murder rule despite her intent. As a consequence, Jerry, who aided her in commission of the underlying felony, is also guilty of the murder of Teller.

Robbery—Diane and Jerry

Robbery is generally defined as larceny committed with two additional elements: (1) the property is taken from the person or presence of the owner, and (2) the taking is accomplished by using force or putting the owner in fear. Diane and Jerry went into the bank and took the money from the presence of those working in the bank (such as Teller). They also accomplished the larceny by using a gun (which, although they didn't want to use it against anyone, they clearly thought would place people in the bank in fear). Consequently, Diane and Jerry are likely guilty of robbery for taking the money.

Accessory after the Fact—Toby

One who knowingly gives assistance to a felon for the purpose of helping him or her avoid apprehension following his or her crime is an accessory after the fact. Under present law, the accessory after the fact is not liable for the felony itself, as an accomplice would be. Rather, he or she has committed a distinct violation, based on the obstruction of justice, and his or her punishment will not depend on the penalty attached to the felony committed. Jerry told Toby what happened, and Toby offered to help them escape. He then drove them to a secluded campground to hide. As such, Toby is guilty as an accessory after the fact for helping Diane and Jerry flee.

ANSWER TO QUESTION 4:

Attempted Drug Possession and Sale

The issue is whether Marilyn could be charged with attempted drug possession and sale even though the bag of heroin was actually sugar. **A claim of factual impossibility arises out of the defendant's mistake concerning an issue of fact. All modern courts reject the defense of factual impossibility. Impossibility is no defense in those cases where, had the facts been as the defendant believed them to be, there would have been a crime. Under these circumstances, the defendant is guilty of an attempt.** Here, although the heroin was actually sugar, Marilyn bought and sold it believing it was illegal drugs. Consequently, she could be found guilty of attempt for both the drug possession and sale.

Owning a Chinchilla and Naming It After a President

The issue is whether Marilyn could be found guilty of owning a chinchilla and naming a pet after a president if these were not in fact crimes. **If the defendant engages in conduct that he or she believes is forbidden by statute but is in fact not forbidden, the situation gives rise to the "true legal" impossibility defense.** Even though Marilyn consciously intended to violate the law, her actions were not in fact illegal. Consequently, under these facts, she could not be found guilty of any crime.

Attempted Robbery of Anthony

The issue is whether Marilyn could be found guilty of attempted robbery when Anthony didn't take the chinchilla threat seriously and simply walked away. **Robbery is generally defined as larceny committed with two additional elements: (1) the property is taken from the person or presence of the owner, and (2) the taking is accomplished by using force or putting the owner in fear. Renunciation is a defense to a crime; however, the defendant must show that he or she abandoned his or her attempt before completion of the substantive crime. However, if the defendant's renunciation is the result of dissuasion by the victim, it will probably be deemed involuntary.** Marilyn tried to take Anthony's money by putting him in fear of being rubbed with the chinchilla. When he walked away, she abandoned the attempt. However, her abandonment was only motivated by Anthony's conduct, so she could still be convicted of attempted robbery.

ANSWER TO QUESTION 5:

Resisting Arrest

The issue is whether Yiyun was justified in punching and kicking Officer Manly when she knew his arrest without a warrant was unlawful. **Virtually no state allows a suspect to use deadly force to resist an unlawful arrest. A substantial minority of states (and the Model Penal Code) now bar even the use of nondeadly force against an unlawful arrest. But the traditional view, probably still followed by a bare majority of states, is that a suspect may use nondeadly force to resist an unlawful arrest.** Here, Yiyun knew the arrest was unlawful and used nondeadly force (punching and kicking usually count as nondeadly force). Although it is unknown what rule this jurisdiction follows, in all probability, her use of force was likely unlawful.

Entrapment

The issue is whether Yiyun was entrapped when Officer Studly sold her the heroin. **The defense of entrapment exists where a law enforcement official, or someone cooperating with him or her, has induced the defendant to commit the crime. There are two distinct tests used to determine whether there has been an entrapment. The "predisposition" test, which is the majority test and the one used in federal courts, finds entrapment when (1) the government originates the crime and induces its commission, and (2) defendant is an innocent person who is not predisposed to committing this type of crime. The "police conduct" rule, the minority rule, finds entrapment when the government agent originates the crime, and his or her participation is such as is likely to induce unpredisposed persons to commit the crime, regardless of whether the defendant himself or herself is predisposed.** Here, the question becomes whether Yiyun is predisposed to heroin use. The facts do not state whether she is or not. If she is not normally a heroin user, she would probably pass the "predisposition" test (however, if the police showed she frequently purchased heroin from other sources, she would not be able to claim entrapment, even if the transaction between Officer Studly and Yiyun was entirely at Officer Studly's instigation). However, she would probably not pass the "police conduct" rule, since simply asking someone in a jail cell whether they would like drugs is unlikely to induce an unpredisposed person to commit the crime of buying drugs (although she could argue that the stress of being in jail would induce most people to try drugs).

CRIMINAL PROCEDURE

Criminal Procedure Table of Contents

CONSTITUTIONAL CRIMINAL PROCEDURE GENERALLY

ELECTRONIC SURVEILLANCE AND SECRET AGENTS

CONFESSIONS AND POLICE INTERROGATION

LINEUPS AND OTHER PRETRIAL IDENTIFICATION PROCEDURES

THE EXCLUSIONARY RULE

THE RIGHT TO COUNSEL

TRIAL PRACTICE

Criminal Procedure Short-Answer Questions

1. Until 2008, there had been no definitive answer to the "second interrogation" problem. This issue arises in the following kind of situation: The suspect is in custody, is given his *Miranda* warnings, and states that he does not want to talk to the police unless he can speak to his lawyer first. He is allowed to speak to his lawyer. The police then want to conduct another interrogation; they start asking questions, and the suspect does not ask to speak to his lawyer at that time. The issue is whether this "second interrogation"—done without the presence of counsel—violates *Miranda*.

   In 2008, the Supreme Court, deciding a case involving a federal prosecution and interrogation by FBI agents, held that this "second interrogation" violates *Miranda*, and that in federal prosecutions, the authorities may not initiate, without a lawyer present, a conversation with a suspect who has previously asked to have his or her lawyer present for questioning. *Smith v. U.S.* The Supreme Court, in *Smith*, referred to general *Miranda* principles and to cases decided under *Miranda*, but gave no indication of whether this principle would be binding on the states. In 2009, the Supreme Court of the State of Ames had to decide, on appeal, a case presenting precisely the same "second interrogation" issue, but this time one involving a state prosecution and state police officers. Assuming that the Supreme Court's 2008 *Smith* decision was based solely on the Fifth and Sixth Amendments, is the Ames Supreme Court constitutionally required to follow the decision in that case? Not sure ☐

2. Until 2010, the State of Langdell instituted all felony prosecutions by having a prosecutor present his or her case to a grand jury, which then issued an indictment. In 2010, the Langdell legislature passed a statute setting out a new procedure, to be applicable to all crimes committed after the date of the statute. Under this new procedure, a prosecutor, when he or she wished to bring charges, would issue something called an "information" setting forth the charges. The information would serve as the basis for an arrest warrant. Immediately after the defendant was arrested, a "preliminary hearing" would be held before a judge to determine whether there was probable cause to believe that the defendant had committed the crime charged. No involvement of the grand jury, and thus no indictment, would be needed.

   Applicable U.S. Supreme Court decisions make it clear that as a constitutional matter, no federal prosecution for a felony (that is, no prosecution for a crime punishable by more than one year in prison) may commence except by a grand jury indictment. Smith, charged by Langdell with the crime of murder committed in 2011, has challenged the proceedings against him; he asserts that it violates his federal constitutional right to a grand jury indictment for him to be prosecuted for a felony based on a method other than a grand jury indictment. Should the Langdell Supreme Court order that the proceedings be dismissed until Smith is indicted by a grand jury? Not sure ☐

3. A Pound state trooper stopped Brown. His car (including the trunk) was then searched without his consent. Marijuana was found in the trunk. Brown was charged with violating Pound's ban on the possession of marijuana. At a suppression hearing, Brown's lawyer argued (articulately and competently) that because Brown had been stopped without probable cause, the search of his trunk was not incident to a valid arrest, and was therefore itself illegal, so that the fruits of that search must be suppressed at the trial. The trial judge disagreed, holding the evidence admissible. Brown was convicted at trial. He appealed through the Pound system; he repeated his search and seizure argument before the Pound Supreme Court, but the court found against him and affirmed his conviction.

Brown has now brought a federal habeas corpus proceeding in federal court for the District of Pound. The federal district judge hearing the habeas corpus application is strongly convinced that the Pound courts misapplied applicable U.S. Supreme Court precedents; in the district judge's opinion, the stop of Brown's car and the subsequent warrantless search of his trunk were clearly in violation of the Fourth Amendment. May the district judge order that Pound give Brown a new trial, on account of the improper admission of the illegally obtained evidence?

Not sure ☐

4. The Empire Police Department received an anonymous and unsubstantiated tip that Dexter, an Empire resident, was buying and selling unlicensed handguns in violation of an Empire statute. This information did not, under applicable U.S. Supreme Court decisions, give the Empire Police probable cause to arrest Dexter for any crime. However, the police arrested Dexter anyway, and charged him with violating the state's handgun statute. Shortly after the arrest (before it had been at all publicized), Wendy, Dexter's ex-wife, came of her own volition to the Empire police station and furnished compelling evidence that Dexter had indeed been buying and selling unlicensed handguns. Wendy turned out to be the anonymous informant— she had not wanted to be deeply involved, but then had changed her mind.

Dexter is now being tried for the crime of buying and selling unlicensed handguns. He argues that because his arrest was made without probable cause and was thus a violation of his Fourth Amendment rights, he may not be tried for this crime. Assuming that Dexter is correct in asserting that his arrest was in violation of his federally guaranteed Fourth Amendment rights, must the prosecution against him be dismissed?

Not sure ☐

5. Law enforcement officials working for the Jefferson State Organized Crime Task Force suspected Johnny "the Cigar" Jordan of being the boss of a local organized-crime family. However, they had never been able to get any evidence of criminal activity conducted by Johnny. Johnny was known for never conducting business at his apartment, and for not maintaining any office. Instead, at 9:00 every evening, under cover of darkness, Johnny would take a walk through Central Park, accompanied by two or three people who police thought were his henchmen. Johnny and his companions would walk through the park, and only when no one was nearby would they say anything.

However, unbeknownst to Johnny, the task force had just acquired a new invention that was about to change the equation. The invention was an infrared telescope. From high up in an office building next to the park, the task force set up this device, which looked like an ordinary telescope. However, it was a telescope that worked on infrared light emitted by human bodies. Therefore, even though it was dark, officials could spot Johnny in their telescope, focus in tightly on his face, and have an experienced lip reader interpret what Johnny and his companion were saying. By the use of this method, they were able to learn that Johnny's organization was processing raw cocaine into crack at a "still" in downtown Jefferson City. (The police did not have a search warrant or probable cause to search or eavesdrop on Johnny.) Using the telescopically obtained information, they procured a search warrant, raided the still, and charged Johnny with various violations of state drug laws.

Johnny now argues that his initial words describing the drug operation were intended to be private, that the infrared operation was an illegal Fourth Amendment search of him, and that the search warrant thus obtained was illegal. Should the court accept Johnny's argument and rule that the search warrant was invalid? (For this question, assume that the answer is yes if by using the infrared device to read Johnny's lips the police were carrying out a Fourth Amendment search.)

Not sure ☐

6. Smith was a prosperous farmer who raised wheat and corn on his 100-acre farm. Smith had a fence around the outside of the entire 100 acres, and posted "No Trespassing" signs at many places on the fence. Greedy for a little extra revenue, Smith decided to devote a quarter-acre right in the middle of his parcel to the cultivation of marijuana. Police officers, acting on an anonymous and unsubstantiated tip, broke through Smith's fence and traipsed through his fields without a warrant, looking for signs of illegal drug growing. They found the marijuana and charged Smith with narcotics violations. Because of the small size of the parcel, it is doubtful that any method other than actual physical trespass on Smith's fields would have allowed the officers to spot the illegal plants; for instance, not even helicopter flyovers would probably have succeeded. May Smith have the results of the search excluded from his trial?

Not sure ☐

7. Police Officer Baker was walking her beat when she discovered a small cocker spaniel that appeared to be lost. The dog was wearing a collar that read, "My name is Rex. If I'm found, please return me to my home at 123 Maple Street." Baker decided to do just that. She took the dog to 123 Maple and rang the doorbell. A white-haired grandmotherly-looking woman who identified herself as Mrs. Jones, owner of Rex, answered the door. While the door was open, Baker happened to look past Jones into the center hall of the house, where she spotted what she instantly recognized (from reading *Soldier of Fortune* magazine) to be an Uzi submachine gun. Since Uzi submachine guns are illegal in every state, Baker knew that somebody was committing a felony. She kept her cool, did not give any hint about what she had seen, got a search warrant, and seized the submachine gun. Jones was prosecuted for illegal possession of the gun and defended on the grounds that Baker's act of spotting the gun, which began the whole episode, occurred without probable cause or a warrant and that the gun must therefore be suppressed.

(a) If you were the prosecutor, what doctrine or rule should you cite in opposition to Jones's suppression motion?

Not sure ☐

(b) Should the judge grant Jones's suppression motion?

Not sure ☐

8. Same basic facts as in the previous question. Now, however, assume that Officer Baker did not see any submachine gun, or anything unusual, while she stood in

the hallway returning the dog. Mrs. Jones invited her in to her living room to give her a cup of tea. When she went out of the room to prepare the tea, Officer Baker noticed a long, narrow case in the living room, which she knew to be of a type that often contains a gun; she had never seen such a container used for anything but a gun. She flipped open the top (which was not secured in any way) and discovered an Uzi submachine gun inside. Since Uzis are not permitted in private dwellings in the state under any circumstances, Officer Baker immediately confiscated the box and the weapon. At Jones's trial, if Jones moves to suppress the Uzi and the box, should her motion be granted?

Not sure ☐

9. Same facts as in question 7. Now, however, assume that at the start of the whole episode, Baker had received an unsubstantiated and anonymous tip that there might be some sort of illegal weapon stored at 123 Maple Street. Baker didn't know how she would get probable cause for a search warrant. She hung around the outskirts of Jones's house at 123 Maple for some time, hoping to catch some sort of break. Then, the dog (see question 7) emerged from a small dog-sized door at the side of the house and ran out to the sidewalk. Baker knew perfectly well that the dog was not lost. She seized upon this as a pretext, gathered up the dog, and rang the doorbell, hoping to get a glimpse into the house. Events later transpired as in question 7. Should the judge grant Jones's suppression motion?

Not sure ☐

10. Officer White was patrolling her beat. While she was standing on the sidewalk, she happened to look through the big picture window on the first floor of a house owned by Desmond. White could see through the window what appeared to be two large marijuana plants. She went up to the window (standing on Desmond's property to do so), opened the window, which was not locked, and stepped inside. There, she confiscated the two plants, which indeed turned out to be marijuana. Desmond was charged with violating state antidrug laws. He has moved to suppress the plants as the fruits of an illegal search.

   (a) If you were the prosecutor, what doctrine would you cite as your best chance to defeat Desmond's motion?

Not sure ☐

   (b) Would the argument you make in (a) succeed?

Not sure ☐

11. Town officials in the quiet suburban town of Crestwood had heard unsubstantiated but disquieting reports that Mercer, a homeowner, was keeping more than 100 dogs in his backyard, in unsafe, unsanitary, and cruel conditions. The entire property was obscured from view by ten-foot-high fences, and repeated attempts to reach the owner by either ringing the front bell or phoning the house were unsuccessful. From the sidewalk, police could hear what seemed like animal noises, but they didn't feel they had probable cause to believe that the local anti-cruelty-to-animals statute had been violated. They decided to use the local police helicopter, normally used for traffic control and the like. With two officers aboard, the copter pilot flew to a point over Mercer's backyard. Hovering at a distance of 500 feet, and using ordinary binoculars, they were able to see that there were at least 150 dogs being kept in appalling conditions. They returned to the station, got a search warrant, broke into the premises, took photographs of the conditions, and charged Mercer with the felony of cruelty to animals.

At his trial, Mercer moved to suppress virtually all evidence, arguing (correctly) that it all stemmed from what the police saw while they overflew his property, and contending that this was an illegal (because warrantless and without probable cause) search of his property. The prosecution has shown (without rebuttal by the defense) that helicopters, including those owned by private parties, frequently fly at 500 feet or even slightly below this, and that FAA Regulations permit civilian flights at this height. Assuming that the decision on the suppression motion turns on whether the police overflight constituted a search that violated Mercer's Fourth Amendment rights, should the suppression motion be granted?

Not sure ☐

12. Same basic fact pattern as in the previous question. Now, however, assume that the police were not looking for evidence of animal mistreatment but, rather, for evidence that a person might have been buried somewhere in Mercer's backyard. (However, they had no probable cause to believe that a search would find such evidence.) The police were looking for fairly subtle signs of recent burial, including small disturbances in the grass and shrubs. They knew that they would not be able to accomplish this from a 500-foot distance by using the naked eye or binoculars. Therefore, they brought with them a $50,000 automatic camera equipped with a computerized "ground cover anomaly detector," which used artificial intelligence principles to scan the ground cover, and to locate recent disturbances such as those that might be made by digging up ground and then replacing it.

This device scanned the entire backyard, zoomed into a particular four-square-foot area, and automatically photographed it in large magnification. Back at the police lab, the police developed and looked at the film, saw that it indeed looked as if a grave had been dug, and used this information to get a search warrant. They discovered while executing the warrant that there was indeed the body of a murder victim in a freshly dug grave at the site photographed. Were Mercer's Fourth Amendment rights violated by the helicopter procedure?

Not sure ☐

13. Police had probable cause to believe that evidence of a recent armed robbery might be found in the master bedroom of a house owned by Dubinski. They procured (using proper procedures) a warrant to search that room in Dubinski's house. Officer Piston rang Dubinski's bell, showed him the warrant, and immediately went to the bedroom. While in the bedroom, Piston (who had an unusually strong sense of smell) detected an odor that he believed was that of rotting meat or flesh. Since the kitchen was in an entirely different part of the house, Piston believed (assume reasonably) that this smell must belong to some fairly large organism that was dead, either a large pet or perhaps a human being. Piston followed his nose into the basement, where he discovered the partially decomposed body of a woman who turned out to be Dubinski's wife. The officer immediately impounded the body as evidence, and Dubinski was ultimately charged with murdering his wife. Dubinski has moved to suppress the body as evidence, arguing that Piston only found the body by going into a part of the house (the basement) where his warrant did not authorize him to be.

(a) If you were the prosecutor, what argument or doctrine might you cite to help defeat Dubinski's motion?

Not sure ☐

(b) Should Dubinski's suppression motion be granted?

Not sure ☐

14. After a terrorist was caught importing a suitcase-sized atomic bomb into the United States, federal and local authorities became very concerned about the possibility that other such bombs could be imported or produced inside the United States and used for terror or ransom. Fortunately, National Business Machines Corp. had developed, in 2010, an amazing portable neutron activator device (NAD), which could detect individual molecules of certain substances when present in the air. One of the trackable substances was tritium, a substance found only in nuclear weapons and a few other highly regulated items (none of which may be produced by private industry except under government contract).

Law enforcement officials in the town of Ames borrowed a NAD device and, purely as a precautionary measure, walked up and down the sidewalks of Ames, pointing the device at every open window. Lo and behold, they got a very strong reading while standing on the sidewalk outside a home belonging to Ezra, a recent immigrant whom the police had previously suspected (but without any tangible evidence) of harboring possibly violent views. Using this information, the police were able to get a warrant to search Ezra's house, and when they did so, they found a neutron bomb the size of a cassette radio, which could have destroyed all living organisms within the entire town of Ames. Assuming that there was no exception to the warrant requirement applicable at the time the officer initially stood outside Ezra's house with the NAD, may the ultimate fruits of the search (the bomb) be suppressed?

Not sure ☐

15. David properly addressed a package to "Joe Smith, 1100 Main Street [an office building], Suite 200." He sent the package overnight by National Express. Due solely to the negligence of a National Express employee, the package was instead delivered to Brown, who occupied Suite 300 of the same office building. Brown opened the package (without noticing that it was addressed to Smith instead of to himself), and saw that it contained five white plastic bags that held something that looked suspiciously like cocaine. Brown rewrapped the package into its original condition. He then notified federal drug authorities, who came to take the package. Without first getting a warrant, the officers immediately ripped open the package and saw that the plastic bags did indeed seem to contain something that looked like cocaine. They got a search warrant to allow testing of the contents, which turned out to be cocaine. At David's drug-sale trial, he has moved to suppress the evidence of what the package contained. Assuming that there were no exigent circumstances (or other exceptions to the search warrant requirement) at the time the police opened the box, should David's motion be granted?

Not sure ☐

16. Federal Treasury officials believed, without probable cause, that George was counterfeiting U.S. currency in his basement. They realized that it is almost impossible to counterfeit bills without producing some unsuccessful ones that must be burned or otherwise discarded. They therefore decided to stake out George's garbage. Twice a week, George put several sealed opaque large garbage bags on the curb in front of his house, to be picked up by Urban Carting (UC), the private sanitation company that supplied garbage-pickup service to George's neighborhood. Each morning, shortly before the UC truck came, the Treasury agents (acting without a search warrant) would open George's trash bags to see whether there was any evidence of counterfeiting inside. Eventually, they discovered a sheet of uncut

$20 bills, which turned out to be counterfeit. They arrested George and charged him with counterfeiting. He moved to suppress the evidence found in his trash as a violation of the Fourth Amendment. Should George's suppression motion be granted?

17. Same facts as in the previous question. Now, however, assume that George did not put his trash at curbside every day. Instead, he put the trash in his backyard inside two garbage cans. Twice a week, the UC workers would (with George's implied consent) go into George's backyard, bring the bags out to the street, and put them into the garbage truck. The Treasury officials did not want to go into George's backyard. Therefore, they arranged for the UC workers to pick up the garbage from the backyard in the usual manner, but then to show the agents the garbage at street-side before it was put onto the truck. In one such "viewing," the agents found the counterfeit bills referred to in the previous question. May George have this evidence of counterfeiting suppressed?

18. Same basic fact pattern as in the previous question. Now, however, assume that the Treasury officials did not want to tell the UC workers what they were doing, for fear that they would leak back to George that an investigation was in progress. Instead, the officials snuck into George's backyard shortly after he had put out the trash, took the bags out to the street, and viewed their contents. They then gave all the contents except the counterfeit bills to the UC collectors to put into the garbage truck. May the counterfeit bills be suppressed?

19. Ellen was in state prison on a narcotics possession charge. Inmates were allowed to have up to ten books in their cell at any time. One day, a guard who had taken a personal disliking to Ellen decided, for no reason other than to harass Ellen, that she wished to examine each of Ellen's books. The guard had no probable cause, and indeed not even any reasonable suspicion, of any wrongdoing by Ellen. While the guard went through one of the books, a postcard fell out detailing a plan by Ellen to escape from the prison. Ellen was charged with attempted escape, and she has moved to suppress the postcard as the fruit of an unlawful search. Should her suppression motion be granted?

20. Joe had been staying for several days in an apartment owned by his brother Bob while Bob was away. While in the apartment, Joe periodically smoked marijuana. Occupants of neighboring apartments had called the police to complain about the suspicious smells. The police could have obtained a search warrant, but they lazily declined to do so. Instead, they rang the doorbell of the apartment, ascertained that Joe was not the owner of the apartment, forced their way in, and looked over the apartment. They spotted marijuana in an open pouch on a coffee table and arrested Joe for possessing it. At Joe's trial for drug possession, can he have the marijuana suppressed on the grounds that it is the fruit of an unlawful search and/or seizure?

21. Agents of the Immigration and Naturalization Service (INS) apprehended Juan while he was walking down a path in Southern California, near the Mexican border. (The agents had the appropriate level of suspicion to stop him on possible immigration violations.) They ascertained that he was not in the United States legally and then found (legally) among his effects a postcard that led them to believe that Juan conducted a substantial cocaine processing operation in his hometown

of Oaxaca, Mexico. They put Juan into custody in a U.S. jail. They then, acting together with agents of the Drug Enforcement Administration (DEA) and Mexican authorities, raided Juan's house in Oaxaca. They did not get a warrant before doing so, and did not have probable cause to believe (merely a plausible suspicion) that they would find evidence of a crime. They found large quantities of raw cocaine and equipment to process it, seized all of this, and then introduced it in evidence in a U.S.-based prosecution of Juan for conspiring to import cocaine into the United States. May Juan have the fruits of the Oaxaca seizure suppressed?

Not sure ☐

22. Pierre, a Canadian, was an undocumented immigrant (i.e., one who entered this country without proper immigration papers and resided here illegally). Acting without a warrant and without probable cause, police officers forced their way into Pierre's apartment, looking for evidence linking Pierre to a terrorist group with which he was reputed to be affiliated. They found a bomb and other incriminating evidence. At his trial for attempted terrorism, Pierre has moved to suppress the evidence from the improper search of his apartment. Should his motion be granted?

Not sure ☐

23. The police in a small town are trying to solve a recent burglary. They know from local probation records that Robert, the most prominent and active burglar in the town over the past two years, was released from prison on parole just two days before the burglary they are now investigating. The police want to search Robert's apartment. They have presented themselves to a neutral and detached magistrate, and have asked for a warrant to search Robert's house, based on the information summarized above. Assume that the above information, taken in its entirety, would justify a reasonable magistrate in concluding that proceeds of the recent burglary probably would be found at Robert's apartment. Assume furthermore that if Robert were to be charged with and tried for the burglary, evidence of his prior burglaries and his recent release from prison (i.e., the items on which the request for the warrant is based) could not be admitted against Robert under the local rules of evidence. May the magistrate properly issue a search warrant?

Not sure ☐

24. Officer Brady submitted to a neutral and detached magistrate a request to search the home of Kaplan for evidence of drug possession. In support of the request, Brady submitted an affidavit written by him, stating that according to one Longo, a confidential informant who had previously been reliable, Kaplan was a drug user who kept large quantities of cocaine at his home. It was true that Longo did in fact give this information to Brady, and Brady honestly believed the information. However, in reality, the information was false—Kaplan was not a drug user, and (unbeknownst to Brady) Longo was Kaplan's archenemy and was merely trying to harass Kaplan. Brady was negligent in not quizzing Longo further about his information, but Brady did not behave recklessly in believing Longo's story or in submitting the affidavit.

The magistrate issued the warrant. Brady executed the warrant. He did not find any drugs, but he did find an illegal gun. At Kaplan's trial for unlawful possession of the gun, he has moved to suppress all the fruits of the search on the grounds that the warrant was improperly procured. Assuming that he demonstrates all of the above facts (including particularly that had the true facts been as stated in Brady's affidavit, there would not have been probable cause to search his premises for drugs), should the judge order the fruits of the search suppressed?

Not sure ☐

25. Same basic fact pattern as in the previous question. Now, however, assume for purposes of this question that the factual assertions made to the magistrate, even had they been true, did not amount to probable cause to search Kaplan's apartment for drugs, and that this fact should have been obvious to the magistrate. Assume further that Officer Brady knew that Kaplan had an illegal weapon at his apartment, but Brady did not bother to put this in his affidavit or tell the magistrate about it. Kaplan now moves to suppress the weapon. The prosecution argues that what Brady knew but didn't tell the magistrate (that the weapon was present) may be considered in determining whether there was probable cause for the warrant. Is the prosecution's contention correct?

Not sure ☐

26. Officer Carter is seeking a warrant to search a garage in the back of a house owned by Marvin. In support of his warrant request, Carter has given an affidavit in which he says, "A confidential informant who has given me information before, which has always proved reliable, has told me that proceeds of a recent burglary are likely to be found in this garage. I cannot identify my informant because his life might then be endangered." The affidavit does not describe how the informant has come to know this information. Assuming that the magistrate believes that Carter is honest, should the magistrate conclude that there is probable cause to issue the warrant?

Not sure ☐

27. Authorities suspected that Desmond, an insurance broker, was defrauding his clients by taking premiums from them and then not paying the money to the insurance companies. An affidavit from a police officer described with adequate particularity why the police believed that Desmond was doing this. The principal reason for suspicion of Desmond was a complaint by Edward, a client of Desmond's, that the insurer had canceled Edward's coverage for nonreceipt of premiums. The police officer requested, and the magistrate issued, a warrant authorizing a search of Desmond's office and the seizure of "all business books and records relating to Desmond's insurance business." Authorities raided Desmond's office and seized virtually every piece of paper in it, including a diary in which he wrote statements making Desmond seem to be guilty of tax fraud in a transaction unrelated to Desmond's dealings with Edward. In Desmond's tax fraud trial, may he have the diary suppressed on the grounds that the warrant was issued in violation of the Fourth Amendment?

Not sure ☐

28. Same basic fact pattern as in the previous question. Now, assume that Desmond also contends that the seizure of his diary, and its submission into evidence, violates his Fifth Amendment privilege against self-incrimination. Should the court at his trial exclude the evidence on this basis?

Not sure ☐

29. Gangster Paul Castel was assassinated while sitting in an Italian restaurant. Local police believed that competing mobsters carried out the murder under the direction of John Gotcha, Castel's rival. As it happened, a camera crew from a local TV station, WLCN, had been photographing Castel moments before the shooting. Prosecutors thought that the photographic film might show the faces of the assailants. However, the prosecutors believed that if they asked the station to submit the footage, or even tried to subpoena it, the footage might well be destroyed because the station was known for not helping law enforcement efforts. Instead, the prosecutors sought, and received, a search warrant authorizing them to search WLCN's offices and to seize "any photographic negative or positive or videotape relating to the shooting of Paul Castel." The search took place, and many materials referred to in the warrant were carried away. The station attacked the search and seizure as a violation of its Fourth Amendment rights. Which of the following arguments made by the station, if any, is correct?

Not sure ☐

(a) Because the station was not a suspect in or in any way connected with the wrong-doing, its premises could not properly be searched and its property seized.

(b) Where a nonsuspect is involved, prosecutors must try a subpoena first unless they bear the burden of showing that a subpoena would not be as effective.

(c) Because the materials were gathered by a professional news organization and had strong First Amendment value, a stronger-than-usual showing had to be made before it could be the subject of a search warrant.

30. The police had probable cause to believe that a particular convenience store was also used as a numbers betting operation. The police obtained a warrant entitling them to search the premises and to seize any evidence of illegal betting. The officers went to the store to execute the warrant. First, however, they frisked all persons present, including the owner of the store and Doug, a customer who was standing with a dollar bill and a quart of milk at the counter. When they frisked Doug, they found drugs. May Doug have the drugs suppressed on the grounds that they are the fruits of an unlawful search?

Not sure ☐

31. Armand Chisel, noted tycoon and art collector, suffered a terrible burglary in his collection. Chisel explained to the police that two valuable Van Gogh paintings had been stolen from him, one entitled *Irises* and the other entitled *Lilies*. He showed them color photographs of each. Later, the police developed probable cause to believe that both of these paintings might be found in the home of Frank, a notorious local fence. Because of their desire to do the least possible work, the police prepared an affidavit that listed these facts, but that requested a warrant to search for and seize only *Irises*, without mentioning that *Lilies* might also be found at Frank's premises. The warrant was issued. The officers went into Frank's one-room studio apartment, saw (and seized) *Irises* right away, and then noticed *Lilies* on the wall right near where *Irises* had been. They seized *Lilies* as well. At Frank's trial for receiving stolen goods, may he have *Lilies* suppressed as the fruits of an unlawful seizure?

Not sure ☐

32. Same basic fact pattern as in the previous question. Now, assume that the police found *Irises* as soon as they walked into Frank's studio. They nonetheless continued looking in other areas of the apartment to see if there was anything else they might find that was incriminating. In a closet, they found *Lilies*. May Frank have *Lilies* suppressed from his trial for receiving stolen goods?

Not sure ☐

33. The police had probable cause to believe that Wilson, who lived at a known address in the community, had carried out a particular recent burglary. There was no reason to believe that Wilson would flee the jurisdiction. The police considered getting a warrant for Wilson's arrest. But before they got around to doing so, one officer saw Wilson walking down the street. The officer went up to Wilson and arrested him

for the robbery. The officer then searched Wilson incident to the arrest, and found in Wilson's pocket proceeds from the robbery (namely a ring). At Wilson's trial for the robbery, he seeks to suppress the ring, on the grounds that it was the unlawful fruit of an arrest that was made without a warrant where a warrant could have been obtained. Should Wilson's suppression motion be granted?

Not sure ☐

34. Same basic fact pattern as in the previous question. Now, however, assume that the police decided that, without getting a warrant, they would go to Wilson's house and arrest him. They rang his doorbell, but he did not answer the door. The police knocked down the door after Wilson didn't answer and arrested him right inside the hallway. They informed him that he was under arrest, and he did not resist. During a search of Wilson's person they made incident to this arrest, they found the ring in his pocket, as in the above question. May the ring be suppressed on the grounds referred to in the previous question?

Not sure ☐

35. Same facts as the previous question. Now, assume that the police learned that Wilson knew that they were on to him, and the police were reasonably worried that Wilson might flee. It was a small town, and after hours, so no magistrate was available. The police rang Wilson's bell, saw that there was no answer, knocked down his door, and went into his bedroom, where they found him. They then searched the area around his immediate control and found underneath his pillow a gun that turned out to have been used in the robbery. May the gun be suppressed as the fruit of an unlawful arrest?

Not sure ☐

36. The police procured a validly issued warrant for the arrest of Fred on an armed robbery charge. Two officers went to his house to execute the warrant. When Fred did not answer the doorbell, they broke down the door. (Assume that the police acted properly so far). They found Fred asleep in bed in one of the two bedrooms. The two officers handcuffed Fred to the wrought-iron bed. They then searched the rest of the premises, including the other bedroom. In the other bedroom, in a box the size of a cigarette package, they found five vials of crack. The robbery charge against Fred was ultimately dismissed, but he was tried for crack possession. At this trial, may he have the crack vials suppressed as being the fruits of an unlawful search?

Not sure ☐

37. Same basic fact pattern as in the previous question. Now, however, assume that only one officer was making the arrest. He handcuffed Fred's two hands together, but did not handcuff him to the bed. The officer then searched the drawers of a nightstand that was located right next to the bed. There, he found the crack. Is Fred entitled to have this crack suppressed as the fruit of an unlawful search?

Not sure ☐

38. The police had probable cause to believe that Gerald committed a particularly vicious murder. They therefore obtained a warrant to arrest Gerald. They knew that Gerald lived with his brother, Harold, who was also thought to be a pretty nasty character (but who was not directly implicated in the murder for which they were about to arrest Gerald). The three arresting officers rang Gerald's doorbell but received no answer. They broke into the house. In the basement, one of the officers found Gerald waiting with a knife in his hand; that officer disarmed Gerald and handcuffed him.

After this, another officer inspected the second floor of the house, calling out, "Harold, or anybody else who's there, come out with your hands over your head."

He then looked in every room and in every closet large enough to hold a human being. In the closet of one of the bedrooms, he found a cache of weapons, which included what was eventually shown to be the murder weapon. It turned out that no one else was home—Harold was away on vacation. At his murder trial, Gerald has sought to suppress the murder weapon found in the closet, on the grounds that it was the fruit of an unlawful search. Should Gerald's suppression motion be granted?

Not sure ☐

39. Two state troopers, Ginn and Cannon, who were sharing a single patrol car, spotted a car traveling 80 mph on a road where the speed limit was 55 mph. The officers pulled the car over, and ordered the driver, John, to get out. State law allowed officers to make a full custodial arrest of any driver driving more than 15 mph over the speed limit. Officer Ginn formally arrested John, put handcuffs on him, searched his body (finding nothing incriminating), and placed him in the squad car, where Ginn remained with him. Officer Cannon then searched the entire passenger compartment of John's car. At the time of the search, Cannon did not have any cause to believe that contraband or evidence of crime would be found. In the backseat of the car, Cannon found John's windbreaker. In the zippered pocket of the windbreaker, Cannon found a vial of crack. At his trial for crack possession, John has moved to suppress the vial of crack as the fruit of an unlawful search. Should this motion be granted?

Not sure ☐

40. Two police officers, Genson and Hingham, received word that a warrant had just been issued for the arrest of Jim, a local resident, on charges of selling from his car vials of heroin, disguised in prescription-drug vials. The warrant mentioned that Jim customarily drove a late-model white Mercedes-Benz E350. Genson and Hingham happened to be passing Jim's house, and noticed a white Mercedes E350 pull into the driveway. While the driver was still inside, Genson and Hingham approached the vehicle, saw that the driver was Jim (whom they knew personally), told him he was under arrest pursuant to the warrant, asked him to exit the vehicle, handcuffed him, and placed him in the patrol car. Genson then asked Jim, "Do you have any drugs in the car—legal or illegal—or any prescription-drug bottles?" Jim responded, "I don't have any drugs, but in the trunk I've got a couple of empty vials that used to contain Valium." Genson asked for permission to search the trunk, and Jim said, "No way—go get a warrant if you want to do that." While Genson stayed with Jim in the patrol car, Hingham opened the trunk and saw inside it two apparently empty vials whose labels said that they contained Valium (assume that before Hingham opened the trunk, a reasonable officer in Hingham's position would have had a reasonable suspicion—not amounting to probable cause—that he might find prescription-drug vials there, and that the vials might contain trace evidence of heroin). Hingham opened the vials, and saw tiny amounts of white powder inside. He submitted the vials for testing; they proved to have trace amounts not of heroin, but of methamphetamine, the sale or possession of which Jim had never previously been suspected. Jim was prosecuted on both the heroin charge covered by the warrant and an additional possession of methamphetamine charge. Jim moved to suppress the vials as evidence on the meth charge. Should the court grant the motion?

Not sure ☐

41. The police obtained a validly issued warrant to arrest Arlene for fraud. They did not obtain any search warrant. Officers arrested Arlene as she was walking out of her office. They confiscated her purse and then escorted her to the police station. Two hours after the arrest, the purse was submitted to the police station's property department, where pursuant to the department's usual "inventory" procedure, the contents were inspected and itemized. In the purse, the officer performing the inventory procedure found a letter that implicated Arlene in the crime with which she had been charged. The police had time to apply for a warrant to search the purse (since they could have kept it impounded without inspection until the warrant was obtained), but chose not to do so because they did not want to be bothered. Nor did the police have probable cause for the search. Arlene has moved to have the letter suppressed as the fruit of an unlawful search.

(a) What exception to the warrant and probable cause requirements should the prosecutor cite as a reason for denying Arlene's suppression motion?

Not sure ☐

(b) Will this exception be found applicable here?

Not sure ☐

42. While Officer Griswold was cruising in his patrol car, he spotted a car that had apparently just crashed into a tree at the side of the road. He found the occupant, Denker, seriously injured but alive. There were several empty liquor bottles in the car, and Griswold thought he smelled liquor on Denker's breath. Because of the serious injuries, Griswold immediately called an ambulance and rode with the ambulance to the hospital. Griswold did not attempt to arrest Denker for driving while under the influence, even though he had probable cause to do so; Griswold reasoned that Denker wasn't going anywhere, so nothing would be served by a formal arrest.

At the hospital, Griswold realized that Denker's blood alcohol level would steadily recede, and it would become harder and harder to make a case for drunk driving against Denker. Therefore, without Denker's consent, and without procuring a search warrant (which would have taken too long at that time of night), Griswold took a blood sample from Denker's finger. This blood sample showed that Denker was well past the point of intoxication. Denker was charged with drunk driving. He seeks to have the blood sample excluded from evidence as the fruit of an illegal warrantless search and seizure. Should his suppression motion be granted?

Not sure ☐

43. Officer Henkle was an undercover "decoy" agent; it was her job to appear prosperous and relatively helpless so as to induce muggers to attack her. Eugene, a mugger, tried to steal Henkle's purse and necklace. Henkle announced that she was a police officer, and Eugene immediately fled. Henkle followed him on foot until she saw him disappear into a private house. She went up to the front door of the house and, without knocking or ringing the bell, opened the door and went looking for Eugene. Before she found him, she noticed an open cardboard box filled with miscellaneous jewelry and purses, apparently the result of prior (more successful) muggings. She arrested Eugene in his bedroom and then seized the cardboard box. Eugene was charged with one of the prior muggings, and a purse found in the cardboard box was introduced as evidence. If Eugene tries to have the purse suppressed as the fruit of an unlawful search, should his motion be granted?

Not sure ☐

44. Officer Johnson, while in his police cruiser, received a radio report that a robbery of a 7-Eleven store had just occurred, and that the robber was now believed to be escaping in a blue Ford two-door sedan. Near the scene of the crime, Johnson saw a car meeting that description traveling at a high rate of speed. He stopped the driver, Fred, on suspicion of being a robber, and arrested Fred for the robbery.

(Assume that he had probable cause to do so.) Johnson did not search the car at that time for evidence of the crime. (Assume that he had probable cause to do so.) Johnson had the police department tow truck deliver the car to the police station, where it was impounded. There, the next day, Johnson (without first having gotten a search warrant) searched the car's passenger compartment and trunk. In the trunk, he found a stocking mask and holdup note, both of which turned out to have been used in the robbery. Fred has now moved to have these two items suppressed from his robbery trial. Should this motion be granted?

Not sure ☐

45. For some time, the Ames police department had believed that George carried out the recent murder of his wife, Karen. An informant notified the police that he believed George transported Karen's dead body in the trunk of his maroon 2006 Pontiac. The police could have gotten a search warrant; they had probable cause to seize and search the car in connection with the murder investigation. However, they had not gotten around to procuring a warrant when Officer Karloff spotted George driving the car. Karloff had probable cause to arrest George for the murder. Karloff stopped George, arrested him for the murder, and took him and the car to the police station. At the station, Karloff opened the trunk and searched its contents for bloodstains, which he found. These bloodstains turned out to be the same type as Karen's blood, and they were introduced against George at his murder trial. May George have the bloodstains suppressed as the fruit of an illegal search?

Not sure ☐

46. Officer Jackson learned from a trusted informant that a white 2008 Buick, license plate number JRZ970, driven by Harold, would be passing by a particular location at a particular time and that it would contain heroin that Harold was planning to sell at retail. Jackson stationed himself at the appointed place and, sure enough, a white 2008 Buick with the correct license plate number drove by at the expected time. Jackson stopped the car (assume that he had probable cause to do so) but discovered that Leonard, not Harold, was the driver. Jackson did not arrest Leonard, because he had no probable cause for an arrest. He did, however, search the car, and found a zippered pouch in the trunk. He opened this pouch and found heroin. The police eventually became convinced that Harold, not Leonard, was the owner of the drugs in the trunk, and Harold was charged with possession of illegal drugs. At his trial, he moved to suppress the zippered pouch as the fruit of a search that was unlawful because it was warrantless. Should Harold's suppression motion be granted?

Not sure ☐

47. Police towed a car belonging to Marvin because Marvin had put insufficient coins in the parking meter, and time had expired. No search warrant was obtained, and the police did not have probable cause to perform a search. Once the car was in the police lot, the police unlocked and searched the car pursuant to a standard police procedure by which all towed cars are searched, and made a list of all valuables in the car. The purpose of this procedure was to guard against theft by police employees, as well as to prevent the owner of the car from making a false claim of theft by a police employee. When the police searched Marvin's car, they looked in the unlocked glove compartment and found illegal drugs there. At his drug trial, may Marvin get the drugs suppressed as the fruit of an unlawful search?

Not sure ☐

48. Officer Baines was the head of the Empire City Art Fraud Detection Bureau, a division of the Empire Police Department. Baines had heard rumors that Norma, a citizen of Empire, was forging and selling fake lithographs purporting to be by Salvador Dali. Baines knew that he did not have probable cause either to arrest Norma or to search her premises. Therefore, Baines decided to see if a more consensual approach would work. He rang Norma's doorbell, and when she answered, said to her, "Ma'am, we've heard that some fake Salvador Dali prints may be being made in your apartment. May I have a look around?" Baines did not tell Norma that forging art prints was a crime, and Norma believed that this was not a crime. Norma responded, "Sure, officer."

Baines at no time gave Norma *Miranda* warnings or otherwise suggested to her that anything he might find could be used against her. Also, Baines did not tell Norma that she had a right to refuse consent, and that if she refused he would not conduct a search at that time because he had no warrant. After Norma approved, Baines took a look around the apartment and immediately spotted a fake Dali print being manufactured; he left to get an arrest and search warrant, then came back and seized the fake print. At Norma's trial for art forgery, she moved to suppress all fruits of Baines's initial search, on the grounds that it violated the Fourth Amendment. Should her motion be granted?

Not sure ☐

49. Same facts as in the previous question. Now, however, assume that when Baines came to Norma's door, he was not wearing his police uniform. He said, "Ma'am, I'm a local art dealer, and I've heard that you've got a supply of fake Salvador Dalis that I could sell at a nice profit to tourists who don't know the difference between fake and real ones. Mind if I come in and take a look at your inventory?" Norma said, "Why, of course." At this time, she never dreamed that Baines was really a police officer working undercover. Baines spotted a fake print and then used this as the basis to get a search and arrest warrant. May the print be suppressed from Norma's ultimate trial?

Not sure ☐

50. Same facts as in question 48. Now, however, assume that Baines (in his police uniform) said to Norma, "Ma'am, we've heard reports that someone in this building is keeping a pet orangutan, which is illegal. I have no reason to believe that you in particular are doing this, but we're trying to check with everyone in the building. Would you mind if I looked around?" Norma said, "Go ahead." If Norma had known of Baines's true purpose—to look for fake prints of exactly the sort that she was producing—she would not have given consent. Baines spotted the fake and seized it. The prosecution now seeks to use it against Norma at her trial for art forgery. May she get it suppressed as a violation of the Fourth Amendment?

Not sure ☐

51. Same basic facts as in the previous three questions. Now, however, assume that Baines, wearing his uniform, went to Norma's door, rang the bell, and stated, "I have a search warrant. Will you consent to let me search your premises for fake Dali prints?" Norma responded, "Okay." In fact, Baines did not have, and had never applied for, a search warrant. Baines searched the apartment, found the fake print, and seized it. May Norma get it suppressed as the fruit of an unlawful search?

Not sure ☐

52. Henry and Wanda were a married couple living together reasonably happily. Officer Lemon had a vague suspicion (but not probable cause to believe) that a rifle owned by Henry had been used to fire the fatal shot in an unsolved murder. Acting without a warrant, Lemon came to Henry and Wanda's house. Henry was

not home, but Wanda was. Lemon asked whether Wanda or her husband had a rifle. Wanda replied that there was a rifle that she and her husband both owned and used from time to time. Lemon asked whether he could inspect the rifle and remove it for testing. Wanda, knowing that she herself was innocent of wrongdoing and believing that her husband was also, consented. Lemon looked at the rifle, took it away for testing, and discovered that it had indeed been used to fire the fatal shot. At his murder trial, may Henry get the rifle suppressed as the fruit of an unlawful search?

Not sure ☐

53. Same basic facts as in the previous question. Now, however, assume that Wanda was the sole owner of the rifle, which had been left to her by her father. However, she let Henry use it from time to time. The police had previously asked Henry to consent to a seizure and examination of the rifle, but he had refused. Now they asked Wanda to give a similar consent, and did not tell her about Henry's prior refusal. Wanda, not realizing that Henry had objected or that he had anything to hide, agreed to let the police examine and test the rifle. May Henry get the rifle suppressed from evidence at his murder trial?

Not sure ☐

54. The police 911 number received an emergency call from a woman identifying herself as Loretta, who said, "My husband has stabbed me with a kitchen knife. Please come help me; I live at 123 Main Street." Officer McGraw, accompanied by a paramedic, went to that address. Loretta answered the door and showed them her stab wounds. McGraw asked Loretta whether they could search the apartment. She responded, "My husband isn't home—he left after stabbing me, so I guess it's okay for you to look around." McGraw found a bloody kitchen knife underneath the bed in the sole bedroom of the apartment and seized it as evidence. It later turned out that Loretta and James were not married at all. Instead, Loretta was James's occasional girlfriend and did not live at 123 Main—she had in fact never stayed overnight at the apartment, and was just visiting at the moment of the stabbing. May James get the knife suppressed from his assault trial, on the grounds that McGraw's search for and seizure of the knife violated James's Fourth Amendment rights?

Not sure ☐

55. Same facts as in the previous question, but now assume James returns home just as Loretta is giving her consent. James tells the officer to get out and refuses to let McGraw search. May McGraw search the apartment over James's objections?

Not sure ☐

56. Troy rented one room (a bedroom) in a house owned by Larry. Their arrangement permitted Larry to keep a key to Troy's room and to enter that room to clean it once a week. The police suspected (without probable cause) that Troy possessed drugs. They came to the house and found Larry (but not Troy) present. They asked Larry for permission to search Troy's room. Larry agreed and let them use his key. In Troy's room, the police found illegal drugs. At his drug possession trial, may Troy get the drugs found in his room suppressed?

Not sure ☐

57. While Officer Noonan was patrolling his beat on foot one night, he saw a car with a broken window and the alarm blaring. When he looked inside the car's window, using his flashlight, he thought he could see that there was no radio in the spot where the radio would normally be. At about the same time, he noticed

a young woman (who turned out to be Marla) walking away from the car at a rapid clip, carrying a shopping bag. Noonan did not have probable cause to believe that Marla had broken into the car, taken the radio, or committed any other offense. However, based on Noonan's 20 years on the police force, on the very fast rate that Marla was walking, on the fact that the alarm had only recently gone off, and on the bag Marla was carrying, Noonan had what could best be described as a "solid hunch" that Marla might have done the break-in and taken the radio.

Therefore, Noonan accosted Marla, asked her to stop for a moment, and asked her whether she had anything to do with the car alarm's having gone off. Noonan blocked Marla's way in such a manner that it was clear to her that she would either have to answer his question or try to escape from him. Marla dropped the bag, apparently in a panic, and began to run. Noonan quickly looked in the bag, saw that it contained a car radio, and chased after Marla. He arrested her, and she was charged with burglary. At her trial, Marla has moved to suppress the radio, on the grounds that it is the fruit of a violation of her Fourth Amendment rights.

(a) What doctrine should the prosecutor cite in attempting to rebut Marla's suppression motion?

Not sure ☐

(b) Should Marla's suppression motion be granted, in light of the rebuttal you listed as your answer to (a)?

Not sure ☐

58. Officer Nelson, dressed in plain clothes, walked a foot beat around the neighborhood to try to spot criminal activity. His beat was a high-crime area in which there was an especially large amount of automobile theft. Nelson spotted a red Ferrari pull up and stop at a traffic light. Nelson could tell that the driver was a young black male. Nelson was quite prejudiced against blacks in general, and believed (in this case, quite irrationally) that few young blacks could afford Ferraris, and that this Ferrari was likely to have been stolen. (Not only did Nelson not have probable cause for this belief, but also his belief would not even qualify as a "reasonable belief based upon objective criteria.")

Nelson went over to the car, asked the driver to roll down the window, and asked, "Do you know where the nearest used-car dealer is?" Nelson was not in fact interested in getting an accurate answer to this question; he merely wanted to see whether the driver was nervous, whether there were lock-picking tools in the car, or whether there was any other sign of criminal wrongdoing. Nelson was prepared to let the car drive on if the driver didn't want to answer his question.

The driver had no idea that Nelson was a police officer. The driver (whose name was Vern) seemed extremely nervous; he tried to drive away, but the car stalled. Nelson saw through the rolled-up window that there did not seem to be a key in the ignition, but rather a series of loose wires hanging out. At that point, Nelson arrested Vern on charges of car theft. (Assume that by that time, Nelson had probable cause to believe that Vern had committed this crime.) At his trial, Vern has moved to suppress Nelson's testimony about what he saw, and any fruit of the subsequent search of the car, on the theory that all of this stemmed from an initial Fourth Amendment violation by Nelson in stopping Vern's car in the first place. Should Vern's motion be granted?

Not sure ☐

59. Same basic facts as in the previous question. Now, however, assume that (1) Officer Nelson was in his police uniform, rather than in plain clothes; and (2) Nelson, instead of asking for directions, asked Vern for his driver's license and registration. If the rest of the episode transpired as described above, may Vern obtain suppression of evidence stemming from this encounter (including Nelson's testimony about the loose wires sticking out of the ignition)?

Not sure ☐

60. Agent Oswald, of the federal Drug Enforcement Agency, was posted at the Denver Airport. His job was to determine which travelers seemed likely to be carrying illegal drugs and to catch them. One incoming passenger, Maria, attracted Oswald's suspicion because of the following: (1) she had arrived from Miami, an important place of origin of narcotics imported into the United States; (2) she arrived in the early morning (2:00), when relatively few DEA agents are on duty, a fact known to smugglers; (3) she had no luggage other than her shoulder bag, despite the fact that Miami to Denver is a fairly long trip; and (4) these three factors were among those listed on a "drug courier profile" form given to Oswald by DEA headquarters, as indicating that a person may be a smuggler. Oswald stopped Maria as she came up to the counter, took her aside, and asked her whether she was a smuggler. She was so nervous that she blurted out a confession. At her trial for drug smuggling, Maria has moved to suppress her confession as the fruit of a violation of her Fourth Amendment rights. Should her motion be granted?

Not sure ☐

61. Same facts as in the previous question. Now, assume that the factors for suspicion mentioned in the previous question did not exist, but the following factors did exist: (1) Maria had paid $2,000 for her round-trip ticket (originating in Denver) in the form of $20 bills; (2) the phone number on Maria's ticket was listed in the phone book under a different name than the name on Maria's ticket; (3) despite the long trip from Denver to Miami, Maria had stayed in Miami for only five hours; (4) it was July, a time when few people fly to Miami if they can avoid it; (5) Maria appeared nervous as she left the airplane, perspiring profusely and looking around her; and (6) Maria did not check any luggage. If Oswald stopped Maria based on these facts, and the rest of the episode transpired as in the previous question, may Maria's later confession be suppressed?

Not sure ☐

62. Officer Mulroney was walking the night beat in a downtown area where there were a lot of office buildings and few nighttime pedestrians. At 1:00 A.M., she spotted a teenager, Evan, who was carrying a heavy desktop computer. Mulroney thought it was strange that someone, especially a teenager, would be carrying a heavy and expensive desktop computer through an office district late at night. Therefore, Mulroney stopped Evan and asked what he was doing. He said that he was borrowing the computer from a friend and taking it to his apartment. Mulroney said, "Please come with me to the police station. I want to check the serial number of the computer to make sure it's not stolen." (Assume that at this moment, Mulroney did not have probable cause to arrest Evan.)

Mulroney then escorted Evan to the police station; he made no attempt to resist. Evan was required to wait for 45 minutes while the police checked the serial number against a statewide stolen property listing. It turned out that the computer was indeed stolen, and Mulroney so informed Evan. At that point, Evan confessed to being the thief. At his trial for burglary, Evan has moved to suppress his confession as the fruit of a Fourth Amendment violation. Should his motion be granted?   Not sure ☐

63. Officer Pasternak was an experienced cop who had followed the same inner-city neighborhood beat for many years and who knew almost everybody on that beat. In particular, he knew that Fiona sometimes used drugs (and even occasionally sold them), but he also knew that Fiona was as meek as a church mouse and would never hurt anybody. One day, he spotted Fiona standing on a street corner, appearing to hand money to a stranger and to receive a package in return. Pasternak reasonably suspected (though he did not have probable cause to believe) that Fiona had just received drugs. He went up to Fiona, briefly detained her, patted the pocket of her coat, felt a soft parcel, and then reached inside. At no time did he suspect that Fiona was carrying a weapon; he did, however, suspect that the soft parcel he felt inside her coat pocket might well be drugs. The parcel did indeed turn out to contain cocaine, for which he arrested Fiona. At her drug possession trial, Fiona has moved to suppress the parcel as being the fruit of a Fourth Amendment violation. Should her motion be granted?   Not sure ☐

64. Same basic facts as in the previous question. Now, however, assume that Pasternak did not know Fiona, and reasonably believed that Fiona might be carrying either a knife or a gun. After stopping her, he patted her coat pocket and felt the soft parcel, which he deduced might be cocaine. He reached inside her coat and retrieved the parcel, confirming his suspicions. May Fiona get the parcel suppressed at her trial for drug possession?   Not sure ☐

65. Every member of the Langdell Police Department had been told to be on the lookout for a blue car (make unspecified) with a license plate number beginning with the letters JQ. This was based on a description from a witness to a bank robbery, who had reported that a car having those characteristics was driven away by the bank robbers. Since the robbers had fired a shot (which did not hit anybody) during the bank robbery, the advisory said that the robbers may be armed and presumed dangerous.

     The day after the robbery, Officer Quarles spotted a blue Ford with a license plate number that began with JQ. The officers waved the car over to the side of the street and saw that it contained a driver (Gerard) and a front-seat passenger (Howard).

     (a) Officer Quarles asked the driver, Gerard, to get out of the car. He then asked Gerard whether Gerard had had anything to do with the bank robbery the other day. Gerard denied this but did so in a manner that did not allay Quarles's suspicion that this might indeed be the bank robber and the getaway car. Quarles then did a pat-down of Gerard but did not find any weapons. He asked Gerard to put his hands on the front hood of the car and looked inside the passenger compartment, to which Gerard might gain access during their encounter. Underneath the rear seat, Quarles found a bag of marijuana. It later turned out that Gerard was not the bank robber, but he was charged with marijuana possession. At his trial, Gerard moved to suppress the marijuana as the fruit of an unlawful search. Should his motion be granted?   Not sure ☐

     (b) Simultaneously with Quarles's encounter with Gerard, Officer Ramon asked the passenger, Howard, to exit the car on the passenger side. After Howard exited, Ramon noticed that he had a distinctive tattoo marking him as a member of the Tweets, a gang whose members were well known for (1) usually carrying electronic devices with which they could use Twitter to arrange street crimes and (2) nearly always carrying switchblades. Although at the moment Howard exited the car, Ramon had no probable cause to suspect Howard of wrongdoing, he patted down Howard's pockets to see if he was carrying a weapon. Ramon found something hard that he thought might be a switchblade; he removed it from Howard's pocket and discovered it was a box cutter, the possession of which by Howard was illegal in light of Howard's status (unknown to Ramon at the time of the encounter) as a convicted felon. At Howard's trial for illegal possession of the box cutter, he has moved to suppress the cutter. Should his motion be granted?

Not sure ☐

66. Drug Enforcement Administration agents at O'Hare Airport received a tip from an informant that a particular piece of brown luggage, registered to Harold Smith, would arrive on a particular United Airlines flight and would contain cocaine. (Assume that this tip did not give the DEA probable cause to search the bag, but that the informant was known to be a reasonably reliable source.) The agents waited for the flight in question to arrive. They then intercepted a brown bag registered to a Harold Smith before it arrived at the baggage carousel. The agents then had a trained dog sniff that particular bag (and no other luggage); the dog indicated that drugs were present. At that point, the agents left to get a warrant to open the bag. (From the time the agents first took possession of the bag until they left to get a warrant, less than five minutes elapsed.) The agents got the warrant and opened the bag. The bag turned out to contain heroin. From the baggage tag, the agents were able to find the address and phone number of Harold Smith. Therefore, they did not bother to detain or question Smith when he came to the baggage carousel. (Smith left when his bag wasn't on the carousel.) At Smith's trial for drug possession, he has moved to suppress the bag and the cocaine as the fruits of a Fourth Amendment violation. Should his motion be granted?

Not sure ☐

67. Federal immigration officials made a practice of stopping every car entering the United States from Tijuana, Mexico, into San Diego. The inspectors stopped each car, briefly questioned its occupants, and occasionally—often based merely on whim or very slight suspicion—decided to inspect a certain piece of luggage or the contents of a particular car. Charles was stopped in his car at this checkpoint, and seemed to the agent to be slightly nervous under questioning. Without any other basis for suspicion (and without a search warrant), the agent searched Charles's luggage. In it, he found marijuana, for which Charles was prosecuted. May Charles have the marijuana suppressed as the fruit of an unlawful search?

Not sure ☐

68. Immigration and Naturalization Service (INS) officials in the El Paso, Texas, area were concerned about the large numbers of Mexican citizens who were entering the United States illegally through the border near El Paso. Since there was no single road crossing the border, it was not practical to set up a fixed checkpoint at the border. Therefore, the officials began a program of "roving patrols." Each INS officer was given a vehicle and told to roam around the whole El Paso metropolitan area. Upon seeing a car whose occupant(s) appeared to be of Mexican

origin, the officer was permitted, at his or her discretion, to stop the car and briefly question the occupant. The officer could then ask for proof of citizenship or residency. On one occasion, an officer stopped a car driven by Jose, solely on the basis that Jose had Hispanic features and the agent guessed that he was probably of Mexican ancestry. After Jose could not produce a green card or other entitlement to residence, the officer arrested him and then searched his car. In the glove compartment, he found marijuana. At Jose's marijuana possession trial, may he suppress the marijuana on the grounds that it was the fruit of a search that violated his Fourth Amendment rights?

Not sure ☐

69. Police in the town of Langdell were concerned that a substantial number of drivers were driving without being properly licensed, and were driving unregistered vehicles. The department embarked on a program of occasional random "spot checks" to discover and deter this conduct. Each officer was told that approximately twice per day, he or she should pick a car at random, stop it, and ask to see the driver's license and registration. All officers were scrupulously careful to perform this task quite randomly, and thus did not discriminate against blacks, teenage males, or any other recognizable subgroup. Officer Turner randomly selected Donald for a stop; Turner had no objective basis for believing that Donald was especially likely to be driving without a license, driving an unregistered car, or otherwise committing any traffic violation. After Turner asked Donald for his license and registration, he observed that Donald's speech was somewhat slurred and smelled liquor on Donald's breath. Donald indeed turned out to be driving while drunk, and was prosecuted for this offense. May Donald suppress all evidence resulting from the stop (and thus the entire case), on the grounds that it stemmed from a violation of his Fourth Amendment rights?

Not sure ☐

70. Police in the town of Pound were concerned about an unusual spate of drunk-driving accidents. They therefore instituted a secret program of "sobriety checkpoints." The first such checkpoint was set up on a Friday night. Without any preannouncement, officers set up a roadblock on North Avenue, a fairly heavily traveled street. All vehicles passing through the checkpoint were stopped, and the police examined each driver for signs of intoxication. Edmund was one such driver. When the officer questioned him, he answered with slightly slurred speech. Edmund was then directed out of the traffic flow to the side of the road. There, a second officer asked him to walk a straight line. Edmund failed to do so satisfactorily. A Breathalyzer test was then performed, which Edmund failed. Edmund was then arrested for drunk driving and prosecuted. Did this procedure, or any part of it, violate Edmund's Fourth Amendment rights?

Not sure ☐

71. The FBI had been trying to put away organized-crime kingpin Lewis "Fat Louie" Lenkowitz for a number of years, without success. Finally, the federal agents decided that the right kind of electronic "bug" might be just the thing. The agents knew that Louie often transacted business at a neighborhood social club. With the help of local police officials, a phony fire scare was arranged at the club, and all patrons were temporarily evicted. Federal agents disguised as firefighters went into the club and clipped a bug on the wall of the room where Louie was known to transact business. This bug transmitted sounds in the room out to the local FBI

office one block away. No permission of any judge or magistrate was sought or received for this operation.

Shortly thereafter, Louie mentioned in passing, while at the club, "You remember when we put the cement shoes on old Jimmy Boffa?" Federal agents immediately charged Louie with the murder of Boffa, which had occurred some years earlier. They then sought to introduce Louie's statement against him at his trial. Louie has moved to have the statement suppressed on the grounds that it was obtained in violation of his Fourth Amendment rights. Should his motion be granted?

Not sure ☐

72. Langdell police were convinced that Melvin had murdered his wife, Wanda, who had disappeared one night after the two had been overheard arguing. However, the police had no direct evidence that Melvin did it. Harriet, an attractive young member of the Langdell force, volunteered for an undercover assignment to try to get evidence against Melvin. She arranged to "run into" Melvin at a local singles bar and to become romantically involved with him. He soon invited her to move in with him. She did but only after placing a "bug" under his bed that transmitted to the police station everything spoken in the bedroom. Several nights later, after a particularly passionate interlude, Melvin mentioned to Harriet that he had murdered Wanda. The police's tape of this statement, recorded at the police station via the bug, was introduced against Melvin at his subsequent murder trial. Can Melvin have this tape suppressed on the grounds that it was obtained in violation of his rights?

Not sure ☐

73. One night in Central Park, police officers in a roving patrol car suddenly heard muted cries that sounded like they were coming from an animal. They discovered a young woman lying beaten by the side of the path, her head terribly bloody. The officers immediately scouted around the area. They found a young man who was carrying a baseball bat, which appeared to have some dark, sticky substance on it. The officers arrested the young man, whose name was Claude, and took him to the police station. The officers did not say anything to Claude, either at the time of the arrest or during the trip, except, "Come on, guy, we're gonna have to take you into the police station."

At the station, Claude was booked on charges of committing the beating and put in a temporary holding cell until he could be arraigned. Shortly after Claude was put in the cell, a police detective walked in, and without any preamble said, "We know you beat that girl in the park. Did you rape her, too?" Claude responded, "No, I only hit her on the head once with the bat to try to stun her." Claude was tried on aggravated assault charges, and the prosecution sought to introduce his confession as the main part of their case against him. May the confession be admitted? Why or why not?

Not sure ☐

74. The police had long believed that Dennis had murdered his wife, but they had no proof. One day, an officer happened to catch Dennis driving through a red light. Local law permitted a prison term for that offense. Dennis was arrested, taken to the station house, arraigned, and held in a cell pending trial because he couldn't make the $200 bail. The police wanted to take advantage of this happy situation, so they put Alan, an undercover police officer, into Dennis's cell. Alan was dressed in regular prison garb and was coached to tell Dennis that he, Alan, was in for car theft.

Alan hoped that Dennis would incriminate himself in his wife's murder without any prompting, but this did not happen. Therefore, during their second day as cellmates, Alan said to Dennis, "You know, once I get out again—and I'm sure I'm gonna beat this rap—I'd love to have a partner to do bank robbery jobs with, which are what I'm really good at. But I can't have a wimp as a partner; I could only use somebody who would kill if the need arose. Did you ever kill anybody?" Dennis had always dreamed of getting a chance to commit a lucrative crime or two with an expert as mentor. So he replied, "Well, as a matter of fact, about two years ago, I murdered my wife, and they never pinned anything on me."

Dennis was then charged with murdering his wife, and Alan was called to testify about what Dennis had told him in the cell. Dennis asserts that admission of this testimony would violate his rights, since he never got any *Miranda* warnings before he made his incriminating statement to Alan. Should Alan's testimony be suppressed on this ground?

Not sure ☐

75. The police suspected (reasonably and accurately, as it turned out) that Elvira had committed a recent burglary of a valuable diamond-and-pearl necklace. The police decided to take a direct approach. Bess, one of the better detectives on the local force, was sent to Elvira's house. When Elvira answered the door, Bess inquired whether she could ask Elvira some questions about "a burglary that took place the other night, involving a necklace." Elvira invited Bess in. Bess questioned Elvira for nearly an hour and a half about the burglary and about Elvira's movements on the night of the burglary. At no time did Bess give Elvira any *Miranda* warnings.

About 45 minutes into the interview, Elvira said, "I've really got to get to the grocery store before it closes in ten minutes." Bess replied, "No, I think we really have to get to the bottom of this." Elvira reluctantly agreed to stay, in part because she wasn't sure she had any choice. Near the end of the interview, Elvira said, "Anyway, I'd never bother to steal a necklace if the largest diamond was only one-quarter carat and the total weight was only two carats." Since the police had never released these details about the necklace, and Elvira had claimed that she did not know the owner and had never seen the necklace, this remark was incriminating. At Elvira's trial for burglary, the prosecution tried to introduce the statement against her. Elvira has objected, on the grounds that the statement was obtained from her in violation of her *Miranda* rights. Should the statement be allowed into evidence?

Not sure ☐

76. While the USS *Nebraska* was docked in San Diego, her officers discovered one of the sailors dead in his bunk, cause unknown. The police were immediately called, and the gangway was sealed off so that no one could leave or enter the ship. At the time, there were 15 men aboard. The police then said, "We're not sure whether this death was murder, accident, or natural causes, but nobody leaves the ship until you've answered our questions." Each seaman was then taken privately to a cabin where one of the police officers questioned him about what, if anything, he knew concerning the death. No seaman was given *Miranda* warnings.

One of the seamen, Frank, when asked, "Did you have anything to do with the sailor's death?" answered, "Well, he was being mean to me all the time, so I put a pillow over his face while he was asleep till he stopped breathing." At Frank's trial for murder, prosecution seeks to introduce this confession into evidence against him. The prosecution argues that since at the time of Frank's questioning it was not known whether there even had been a crime, and the investigation certainly had not focused on Frank, *Miranda* warnings should not be applicable. Should Frank's confession be excluded from evidence against him?

Not sure ☐

77. Officer Nelson was on traffic patrol. He spotted a car driving with one taillight missing. (It was part of Nelson's job to stop and warn motorists of even minor infractions—he usually just warned them and let them go on their way.) Nelson flashed his lights and pulled the car over. Jermaine was driving the car. Nelson asked Jermaine for her driver's license and for the car's registration. Jermaine produced both. Nelson noticed that the owner of the car, according to the registration, was John Jones, not Jermaine. He asked Jermaine, "How do you come to be driving a car registered to John Jones?" Jermaine, suddenly very nervous, replied, "Well, I borrowed it from him. I was going to bring it back pretty soon." Nelson asked, "Does he know you have the car?" Jermaine said, "No, but I'm sure he wouldn't mind." This was enough to make Nelson quite suspicious. He radioed headquarters and found that Jones has reported the car as stolen 12 hours before. Jermaine was charged with car theft, and her earlier statement to Nelson was admitted against her to show that she knew that she did not have authority to take the car. Jermaine has moved to have her statement excluded from evidence as rendered in violation of *Miranda*. Should the statement be excluded?

Not sure ☐

78. In the middle of a crowded dance floor in a trendy nightclub, one of the patrons, Kathy, was suddenly found dead of one violent stab wound. The club's owners immediately prevented anyone from leaving and called the police. The police took the name and home phone number of everyone present. One of these was Harold, who had come to the club with Kathy as her escort, a fact known to the police. Two days after the murder, the detective in charge of the case, Detective Parsons, phoned Harold at his office and asked, "Would you mind coming down to the police station for an interview? We're interviewing everybody who was there to see if any of them spotted the killer." In fact, the investigation had already focused on Harold, who was known to have a violent streak, but Parsons gave no hint of this fact when he spoke to Harold.

Harold obligingly went down to the police station and was interviewed by Parsons in Parsons's office. Parsons did not give Harold his *Miranda* warnings. Parsons asked whether Harold had seen who did the killing and received a negative response. He then asked Harold, "Did you do it?" Harold blurted out, "I didn't mean to do it, but she was making me crazy with jealousy." At Harold's murder trial, he has sought to suppress the use against him of this incriminating statement made to Parsons. Should Harold's motion be granted?

Not sure ☐

79. Ike was getting into a parked car when Officer Quentin, of the Arbortown police, noticed that the registration on the car's front windshield had expired. As Ike drove away, Quentin stopped him and arrested him for driving with an expired registration sticker. (Driving with an expired registration sticker is, under local law, punishable by at most a $200 fine, and a jail term may not be imposed for it. Normally, a driver would not be arrested for this offense, but merely given a citation; however, local law did permit an arrest in this situation.) Quentin was known as an

especially tough "law and order" type. Therefore, he took Ike back to the police station, where he was booked and then held for several hours pending arraignment. During this time, the police ran a routine ID check on Ike and discovered that he was wanted by the police of another town (Elmont) for a burglary at 123 North Avenue in Elmont.

Officer Quentin went up to Ike and asked, "Did you commit a burglary at 123 North Avenue in Elmont two weeks ago?" Ike responded, "Hey, officer, I didn't go in the house, I just drove the getaway car on that one." At no time during this exchange (or prior to it) did anyone give Ike any *Miranda* warnings. Elmot police charged Ike with being an accomplice to the North Avenue burglary. His statement to Quentin was introduced against him. Ike protested that the statement was made in violation of the *Miranda* rules. The prosecutor argued in rebuttal that *Miranda* warnings need not be given when a person is in custody for a misdemeanor or other nonfelony crime. Must Ike's confession be excluded from evidence against him?   Not sure   ☐

80. Police were investigating a murder in which the victim, Molly, was found dead of stab wounds in her apartment. It turned out that Molly had been having an affair with Herb, a married man. Herb's wife, Jill, was known to the police to be a jealous sort who had become enraged in the past when Herb had carried on affairs with other women, though the police did not know whether Jill had been aware of the Herb-Molly affair. Finally, the police got a break—they found a couple of red hairs embedded in the carpet near Molly's body; since Molly was a brunette and Jill was a redhead, they were able to persuade a judge that this constituted probable cause for issuing a warrant for Jill's arrest. (Assume that the arrest warrant was properly issued.) They then arrested Jill for Molly's murder and brought her to the police station.

The detective in charge of the case, Detective Reynolds, went into Jill's holding cell. Reynolds did not give Jill any *Miranda* warnings. Reynolds said, without preamble (and without Jill's saying anything to him first), "Look, we know you did it. We know all about the affair between Herb and Molly, and we've got evidence that you knew about that affair too. Furthermore, we've got several red hairs found from the crime scene, embedded in the carpet right near where the body was found. It would make life a lot easier for everybody if you would just confess." Jill responded, "Well, I went to Molly's apartment that night and had a drink with her while I tried to talk her into stopping the affair. But I didn't kill her."

At Jill's murder trial, the prosecution, as part of its case in chief, introduced this statement to show that Jill was present at the murder scene. By then, Jill had changed her story and claimed that she was never at the apartment. Therefore, Jill's lawyer objected to the introduction of the statement, on the grounds that it was obtained in violation of Jill's *Miranda* rights.

(a) What argument should the prosecutor make for holding that *Miranda* is inapplicable to Jill's station-house statement?   Not sure   ☐

(b) Will this argument be successful?   Not sure   ☐

81. Same basic fact pattern as in the previous question. Now, assume that shortly after Jill made her statement to Reynolds, her husband, Herb, showed up at the police station. Normally, the police would not have allowed a suspect in custody to confer

with her spouse while a detective was present. But this time, Reynolds decided that he would let the meeting go forward while he, Reynolds, remained in the room, on the theory that you never knew when an emotionally distraught suspect might say something incriminating. Herb said, "Tell me you didn't do it, baby." Jill blurted out, "But I did it for you, Herb—she had her hooks in you, and she was ruining both our lives." At Jill's murder trial, she moves to exclude this statement from evidence against her, on the grounds that it was rendered in violation of her *Miranda* rights. Should the trial court exclude the statement on this basis?

Not sure ☐

82. Nell, a wealthy businesswoman, disappeared suddenly one day. Shortly thereafter, her family received a ransom demand for $1 millon, together with instructions about where and when the money should be delivered. Nell's husband, Lee, decided to pay the money, but to bring the police in on the ransom payment. Lee showed up at the ransom drop at the appointed time with the money. Police staked out the area.

Soon thereafter, Ken picked up the ransom and began to drive away. The police, led by Officer Stone, stopped him, handcuffed him, and put him in the back of the police cruiser. There, Stone, said to him, "If anything happens to Nell, you'll get the chair under the Lindberg law. Tell us where she is and save your life. Where is she?" Ken replied, "I've got her tied up in an apartment I've rented," and took the police there. At Ken's later kidnapping trial, the prosecution anticipated that Ken might claim that his only involvement was to pick up the ransom, not to participate in capturing or holding Nell. Therefore, the prosecution sought to introduce Ken's statement to Stone in order to show that Ken was the main or sole criminal. Ken has objected on the grounds that his statement to Officer Stone was taken in violation of his *Miranda* rights.

(a) What doctrine should the prosecution assert in opposition to Ken's objection?

Not sure ☐

(b) Will this doctrine apply to render *Miranda* inapplicable and the confession thus admissible?

Not sure ☐

83. Leonard was a somewhat incompetent burglar. Police stopped him outside a mansion late one night, holding a pillowcase filled with silver and jewelry, while the mansion's burglar alarm blared. He was arrested on burglary charges and taken to the station house. There, Detective Turner read him the following statement: "You have the right to remain silent. Anything you say can be used against you in a court of law. You have the right to the presence of your attorney during questioning. You have the right to the advice and presence of a lawyer even if you cannot afford to hire one. We have no way of giving you a lawyer now, but one will be appointed for you, if you wish, if and when you go to court." Leonard said, "It's okay— you've got me dead to rights, so let's skip the lawyer stuff. I did it."

At Leonard's burglary trial, the prosecution sought to introduce Leonard's stationhouse confession as part of its case in chief. Leonard argued that the confession must be excluded, because he reasonably interpreted the warning to mean that he could have an appointed lawyer only at trial, and that the police could and would interrogate him without appointed counsel present if he could not afford to have a hired lawyer of his own present. Should Leonard's confession be excluded on this ground?

Not sure ☐

84. Melvin was an eminent white-collar criminal defense lawyer whose clients included a number of financiers accused of serious securities-law crimes. One day, federal postal inspectors, acting on behalf of a federal prosecutor, arrested Melvin in his office for insider trading and took him in handcuffs to the federal courthouse for arraignment. While on the trip, Inspector Vincent, without reading Melvin his *Miranda* warnings, asked him, "How did you know to buy Dianetic stock the day before the takeover?" Melvin responded, "My brother-in-law is the president, and he told me." At Melvin's insider-trading trial, the prosecution sought to introduce his statement made to Vincent in order to show that Melvin acted on insider knowledge. Melvin has moved to exclude this statement on the grounds that he did not receive his *Miranda* warnings. The government argues that since Melvin, as a lawyer, knew his rights (a point not disputed by Melvin), the Inspector was not required to give the warnings. Must Melvin's confession be excluded?

Not sure ☐

85. Same basic fact pattern as in the previous question. Now, however, assume that (1) Inspector Vincent knew beyond a doubt that Melvin was rich enough to hire his own lawyer, since he had read a profile on Melvin in a recent *People* magazine stating that Melvin earned more than $1 million per year; and (2) Vincent gave the basic *Miranda* warnings to Melvin (that he had the right to remain silent and the right to have an attorney present), and omitted only the part about the right to have a court-appointed lawyer if he couldn't afford one. Must Melvin's incriminating statement be excluded?

Not sure ☐

86. Nestor was arrested on armed robbery charges and taken to the station house. He was read a complete set of *Miranda* warnings. Nestor made no statement or even gesture indicating that he understood the warnings and was waiving his rights. The police immediately began questioning him. Nestor answered their questions, thus incriminating himself. May his statements be introduced against him at trial as part of the prosecution's case in chief?

Not sure ☐

87. Omar was a 21-year-old man who lived at home with his parents. A well-documented facet of his personality was that he was very much influenced by any older man in whose company he happened to be at the time. Police arrested Omar on charges of participating in a burglary, in that he drove the getaway car for the principal burglar, Bob, an older man. The police arrested Omar at his house, in front of his mother. Omar was taken to the station and given his *Miranda* warnings. Simultaneously, Omar's mother (unbeknownst to Omar) arranged to have the family lawyer, Ralph, go to the station house.

Ralph arrived at the station house while Omar was being read his *Miranda* warnings. The officers at the front desk did not let Ralph see his client; nor did they inform Omar that Ralph had been retained for him by his family or that Ralph was there waiting to see him. Omar was read the *Miranda* warnings and said, "I don't want to hide anything." He proceeded to answer questions concerning his role in the burglary. At Omar's burglary trial, his lawyer seeks to suppress statements made at the station house. The defense demonstrates that because of Omar's impressionable nature, there is a very high probability that had Ralph been permitted to see Omar, Omar would have taken Ralph's advice to remain silent. Must Omar's statement be excluded from the case against him?

Not sure ☐

88. Same basic fact pattern as in the previous question. Now, however, assume that (1) no lawyer had been retained for Omar and thus none was waiting at the station;

and (2) the officer interrogating Omar said to Omar (after giving him his *Miranda* warnings), "The guy you pulled the burglary with, Bob, has already confessed that you were in it with him. So you have nothing to lose by confessing, and it may even shorten your sentence for having cooperated with us." The officer knew that this was a complete lie (Bob had not even talked to the police about anything), and the sole purpose of the officer's statement was to induce Omar to waive his *Miranda* rights. Omar agreed to answer questions and confessed. Must Omar's confession be excluded from evidence as a violation of his *Miranda* rights?

Not sure ☐

89. Two burglaries had recently been committed in New Ames. In the first, of a house on North Avenue, only property was taken and no one was injured. In the second, on Main Street, the elderly owner of the home was shot dead, presumably by the burglar. Police detectives noticed several similarities in the modus operandi of the two burglaries, and the police therefore concluded that the same burglar had committed both crimes; however, this conclusion was not public knowledge. The police learned from a reliable informant that Paul had been boasting about carrying out the North Avenue burglary. They therefore obtained a warrant for his arrest for that crime and arrested him at his house. While doing so, they stated that they were arresting him for the North Avenue burglary and made no reference to any other crimes.

After bringing Paul to the police station and keeping him in custody pending arraignment, Detective Wagner read Paul his *Miranda* warnings and then said, "I'd like to ask you some questions." Wagner did not say what crime the questions would be about, but Paul assumed (reasonably) that the questions would concern just the North Avenue burglary, since that was the only crime he had been arrested for and the only crime the policed had mentioned thus far. Paul said that he would be willing to answer Wagner's questions without counsel present.

Wagner began by asking about the North Avenue case, and Paul denied any involvement. Wagner then suddenly switched to asking about the Main Street burglary, and said, "We know you did that one, too—we found your fingerprints there." Paul was so stunned to find out that he was suspected in the Main Street case (which, as he of course realized, was really a murder case) that he blurted out an incriminating remark. At his later trial for murder in the Main Street case, Paul sought to exclude this remark from evidence, on the grounds that he was never given *Miranda* warnings as to the Main Street case, and his agreement to answer questions was predicated on his actual and reasonable belief that he would only be asked questions about the North Avenue case. Should Paul's remark be excluded from evidence?

Not sure ☐

90. Same basic facts as in the previous question. Now, however, assume that before giving his waiver, Paul asked, "Will I only be questioned about the burglary you've arrested me for?" Detective Wagner responded, "Yes," even though he secretly intended to switch the questioning to the Main Street case as soon as it seemed like Paul was off his guard. Must Paul's incriminating remark concerning the Main Street murder be excluded on *Miranda* grounds?

Not sure ☐

91. The police arrested Quentin on a murder charge, booked him, and put him in jail because he could not make bail. Shortly after he was first jailed, Detective Angstrom

read Quentin his full *Miranda* rights, and asked if he would answer some questions regarding the murder with which he was charged. Quentin responded, "I don't want to talk to no cop." The next day, a different member of the force, Detective Butts, repeated the warnings to Quentin, and asked if he would answer some questions regarding the murder. Butts was unaware of the prior day's discussion between Quentin and Angstrom, or of the fact that Quentin had asserted his right to remain silent. This time, perhaps because Butts was simply a more simpatico kind of guy, Quentin said that he would answer a few questions. He then did so, implicating himself. If Quentin asserts that the statements he made to Butts must be excluded from Quentin's murder trial because they were obtained in violation of *Miranda*, must the court exclude the statements?

Not sure ☐

92. Same basic fact pattern as in the previous question. Now, however, assume that after getting his first set of *Miranda* warnings, Quentin did not assert that he wanted to remain silent. Instead, he said, "I want a lawyer, and I might talk to you after I talk to the lawyer." Over the weekend, while Quentin was still in jail, a court-appointed lawyer visited him and discussed the charges. (The lawyer did not anticipate that Quentin would be questioned again, so he did not tell Quentin that he should remain silent if questioning resumed.) On Monday morning, Detective Butts came into Quentin's cell, ascertained that Quentin had met with the lawyer, gave Quentin his *Miranda* warnings again, and asked him if he would now discuss the case. Quentin agreed to do so. In response to questions by Butts, Quentin implicated himself. May these incriminating statements be introduced against Quentin at trial?

Not sure ☐

93. Raymond was arrested on suspicion of having committed a burglary in New York City on March 10. At the station house, the detective stupidly forgot to give Raymond his *Miranda* warnings and interrogated him. In response to the detective's questions, Raymond confessed that he had indeed done the burglary. (This questioning did not take place in a particularly coercive manner, and under the circumstance, a court would conclude that Raymond gave the confession "voluntarily.")

At Raymond's trial on the burglary charges, he took the stand in his own defense. Under questioning by his lawyer, Raymond asserted an alibi defense—he claimed that he had been in Chicago on the day and time when the burglary took place. On cross-examination, the prosecutor showed Raymond a transcript of his confession, and asked him, "If your alibi defense is true, how come you confessed to the crime, instead of either remaining silent or telling the police about your alibi defense?" Over an objection by Raymond's lawyer, the judge let the question stand. Raymond replied, "The confession is phony—I just gave it to get the police off my back. In fact, I was in Chicago that day, as I've just said."

The trial judge instructed the jury that they should consider this material only for purposes of evaluating Raymond's credibility as a witness, and not as bearing directly on the substantive issue of whether Raymond committed the crime. The jury found Raymond guilty. On appeal, should the appeals court order a new trial on the grounds that the material was admitted in violation of Raymond's *Miranda* rights?

Not sure ☐

94. Same basic fact pattern as the previous question. Now, however, assume that after Raymond's arrest, while he was at the station house, he was read his *Miranda*

warnings properly. Raymond elected to remain silent. Then, at trial, he took the stand and asserted his alibi defense as described in the previous question. On cross-examination, the prosecutor asked him, "If you really were in Chicago on the day of the burglary, then why didn't you tell the police that when they were questioning you in the station house?" Over an objection by Raymond's lawyer, the judge let the question stand. Raymond responded, "I just didn't want to talk to the police at that point." The jury convicted Raymond after being instructed by the judge not to consider the question and answer regarding Raymond's silence for any issue other than Raymond's credibility as a witness. Should the appeals court order a new trial on the grounds that the question and answer violated Raymond's *Miranda* rights?　Not sure ☐

95. The Ames Police Department received a call from an unidentified male caller, who stated, "You'd better evacuate the courthouse building. It will be blown up at 2:00 P.M." This call was automatically recorded, as are all incoming calls to the department. The police evacuated the courthouse, as urged, and tried (but failed) to find a concealed bomb. There was one, and it went off at 2:00 P.M., destroying the courthouse. Based on an informant's tip, the police focused their investigation on Stan. They arrested Stan for the bombing and asked him to give them a "voiceprint"—they wanted him to speak into a telephone the same words that the unidentified caller had spoken, so they could have an expert produce a printout of the sound waves from the two recordings and determine whether they were made by the same person. Stan refused, and the police got the court to order that he give the voiceprint or else be held in contempt. Stan reluctantly complied. At Stan's trial, the prosecution seeks to introduce the voiceprints from the two recordings, together with the expert's testimony that the same voice appears on both recordings. Stan objects on the grounds that use of this information would violate his Fifth Amendment privilege against self-incrimination. Should the court exclude the evidence on the basis urged by Stan?　Not sure ☐

96. Same basic fact pattern as in the previous question. Now, however, assume that there was no unidentified caller. Instead, the police received a letter stating, "Evackuate [sic] the courthouse by 2:00 P.M. At that time, a bomb will explode there." The police arrested Stan and sought a court order for a "dictation test." The court ordered this test, by which the police were to dictate to Stan the words of the warning letter, and Stan was to write them on a piece of paper. The point was both to analyze Stan's handwriting to see if it was the same as that on the letter and to see whether Stan misspelled the word "evacuate" the same way. Stan took the test and wrote "evackuate." At Stan's trial, the prosecution introduced the test note. Also, an expert testified that the handwriting on the test note seemed to be the same as on the real note. Stan conceded that use of the test note to show similarity of handwriting was not objectionable, but argued that its use to show the similarity of misspelling of "evacuate" was a violation of his Fifth Amendment privilege against self-incrimination. Is Stan's objection correct?　Not sure ☐

97. Based on the testimony of an accomplice, Tom was indicted for carrying out a particular burglary. He was then arrested and brought to the police station. Because Sheila, the owner of the burgled house, had gotten a brief look at Tom as he ran out of the house, the police decided to perform a lineup. They put Tom together with five other people (nonuniformed police officers) who approximately resembled Tom in terms of age, race, height, etc. Sheila was asked to look at the six men through a one-way mirror, and to state whether she could identify the burglar. She quickly picked Tom out of the lineup. At no time prior to or during this transaction did any police officer or other government officer say anything to Tom. At Tom's burglary trial, the prosecution offered into evidence the fact that Sheila had picked Tom out of the lineup. What, if any, constitutional right of Tom's would be violated by the admission of this evidence?

Not sure ☐

98. Same basic fact pattern as in the previous question. Now, assume that the court ruled the results of the lineup to be inadmissible. Assume further that at the trial, Sheila took the stand and was asked, "Can you identify the burglar as being somebody in this courtroom?" Over the defense's objection, the court permitted Sheila to answer, and she said, "Yes, it's the defendant." Sheila did not refer to the fact that she had made an earlier identification of Tom in the lineup. Neither side presented any evidence showing the reliability (or unreliability) of Sheila's in-court identification of Tom as being the burglar. Has the trial judge erred in permitting Sheila in court to identify Tom as the burglar?

Not sure ☐

99. First National Bank of Ames was robbed at gunpoint by a dark-haired woman wearing sunglasses. One of the tellers stepped on the "panic button," sending an alarm to police headquarters, so the police got an early jump on the case. One officer who rushed to the scene saw a car traveling away from the bank at a suspiciously high speed, so he stopped the car. Ursula, who wore sunglasses and was dark-haired, was driving the car. The officer made a warrantless arrest of Ursula. (Assume that the officer did not violate Ursula's Fourth Amendment rights in doing so.) The officer then took Ursula to the police station. It was now too late in the day to have Ursula brought before a magistrate, so she would have to stay in jail for the night. The police decided, however, that they should conduct a lineup while witnesses' memories were fresh.

Therefore, the police put Ursula in a lineup with five other women of approximately similar appearance, and asked two of the bank tellers if they could pick the robber out. Ursula protested prior to and during this lineup that she wanted to have her lawyer present during the lineup, but the police refused, telling Ursula that her lawyer would only delay the proceedings and make trouble. One of the tellers, Arlene, picked Ursula out of the lineup. At Ursula's bank robbery trial, she seeks to have this lineup identification excluded from evidence against her, on the grounds that the police's refusal to allow her attorney to be present violated her right to counsel. Should the lineup identification be excluded on this ground?

Not sure ☐

100. Same basic fact pattern as in the previous question. Now, however, assume that Ursula was formally charged with the bank robbery, given a preliminary hearing, and then arraigned (at which time she pled not guilty). Shortly thereafter, detectives working on the case interviewed Bruce, another teller who had been present during the robbery. The detectives showed Bruce six photographs, each of a different woman, and asked him whether he recognized any of them as being the robber. Bruce picked out Ursula's photograph immediately. (Neither Ursula nor her lawyer knew that this photographic identification session was going to take place, and

the lawyer was not present during it.) At Ursula's trial, the prosecution has offered into evidence the fact that Bruce picked Ursula's picture out of the bunch. Ursula objects, on the grounds that the photo ID session was carried out in the absence of her lawyer and thus violated her right to counsel. Should the fact that Bruce identified Ursula from the photos be excluded on this ground?

Not sure ☐

101. Tina was brutally raped one night in a poorly lit parking lot. Shorty after the crime, she told police that the rapist was not someone she recognized, that he was Asian, that he was about six feet tall, and that he wore a New York Mets jacket. Because Vincent was found wandering near the scene of the crime several hours later and had a previous conviction for rape under similar circumstances, he was arrested, charged, and arraigned.

   Two days after the crime, the police asked Tina to come to a lineup. There were six men in the lineup; Vincent was the only Asian, and he was taller than any of the others by at least five inches. The police made Vincent wear a New York Mets jacket, and none of the other men in the lineup had any kind of sports jacket. Vincent was given a court-appointed lawyer, who was present at the lineup. Tina stated that she could not be sure whether her assailant was one of those in the lineup.

   Three days later, the police asked Tina to come to another lineup. This time, there were six men, including two Asians; Vincent was the only person who was in both lineups. Vincent's lawyer was again present, and the lawyer protested several ways in which the lineup was unduly suggestive (e.g., that Vincent was the only one who was in both lineups, that there were only two Asians, that Vincent was taller than everyone else, etc.). The police disregarded his complaints. This time, Tina picked Vincent out as her assailant. At Vincent's rape trial, the prosecution sought to introduce into evidence the fact that Tina picked Vincent out of the second lineup.

   (a) What argument should Vincent's lawyer make about why this lineup identification should be excluded from evidence?

Not sure ☐

   (b) Will the argument you recommend in part (a) succeed?

Not sure ☐

102. Same basic fact pattern as in the previous question. Now, however, assume that the rapist, in addition to raping Tina, seriously stabbed her several times. Tina was rushed to the hospital, and although she was conscious, doctors were not sure that she would survive the night. Vincent had been arrested near the scene of the crime almost immediately but had not yet been formally charged. To get a prompt identification, and in view of the small size of Tina's hospital room, the police dispensed with a lineup. Instead, they used a "show-up"—that is, they brought Vincent (and only Vincent) into the hospital room in handcuffs and asked Tina, "Is this the man who did this to you?" Tina said, "Yes." Tina then recovered and testified at trial that Vincent was the man who attacked her. The prosecution also sought to introduce into evidence the fact that Tina identified Vincent in her hospital room. Vincent moved to exclude this prior identification from evidence. Should Vincent's motion to exclude be granted?

Not sure ☐

103. While jogging one night, Upton was struck and seriously injured by a car; the driver drove away rather than render assistance. Upton told the police that in the split second before the impact, he had gotten a very brief glimpse at the driver,

who was a young blonde woman. Based on an informant's tip, the police came to believe that Wendy was the hit-and-run driver. They procured Wendy's photo from her license application at the Department of Motor Vehicles. They then went to Upton's hospital room and showed him the picture of Wendy. They did not show him any pictures of other possible suspects (i.e., they did not conduct any photo array). As the detective handed Upton Wendy's picture, he said to Upton, "We think this is the woman. Can you identify her from this photo?" Upton replied, "Yes." At Wendy's trial for leaving the scene of an accident and vehicular negligence, the prosecution has sought to introduce into evidence the fact that Upton recognized Wendy from her photo in her hospital room. Upton seeks to exclude this evidence. Should the court find that the evidence would violate Upton's constitutional rights, and therefore exclude it?

Not sure ☐

104. Two masked gunmen robbed First National Bank of Pound, and for two months the police had no useful clues. Then, in an episode unrelated to the bank investigation, Officer Jackson of the police department learned from an informant that Albert possessed some illegal weapons in his apartment. The informant had proved unreliable in the past, so this tip did not give Jackson probable cause to obtain a warrant to search Albert's apartment or to arrest Albert. Jackson decided to set forth without a warrant, since he knew he couldn't get one. At a time when he knew Albert was not home, he broke into Albert's apartment and began ransacking the place. In a closed box underneath Albert's bed, Jackson found a batch of letters, which he started reading more out of voyeuristic curiosity than for any other reason. The first letter, written by Bertha to Albert, contained one sentence that read, "When Carter and I robbed First National Bank of Pound last month, we got away with $89,000 in loot, so I'd like to spend some of this money on one of the weapons you're selling."

Jackson immediately realized that this was probably the key to the bank job, so he took the letter and left Albert's apartment. Solely because of the letter, Bertha was charged with doing the bank job. At her trial, the prosecution sought to introduce the letter into evidence. Bertha objected, on the grounds that the letter was seized in violation of the Fourth Amendment. Must the judge exclude the letter from evidence?

Not sure ☐

105. Bart was a master drug smuggler who specialized in importing cocaine from Colombia. Bart was smart enough never to smuggle the cocaine in himself. Instead, he used various "mules." On one occasion, Bart recruited Karen to serve as a mule—Bart attached a kilogram of cocaine (owned by Bart) to the inside of Karen's thigh. Bart and Karen traveled on the same plane from Colombia to Miami. (They took the same flight so that Bart could retrieve the cocaine and market it at retail.) At Miami Airport, Drug Enforcement Administration (DEA) agents focused their attentions on Karen not because of any objective grounds for suspicion, but merely because one of them thought that Karen "looked shifty and nervous." In violation of the Fourth Amendment, the DEA agent stopped Karen, took her into a private room, and performed a strip search on her. There, the agent found the cocaine. Bart was implicated because he showed up on the airline's computer reservation system as having been Karen's traveling companion.

At Bart's trial for cocaine smuggling, the prosecution plans to offer the cocaine into evidence against him. At a suppression hearing, Bart has moved to exclude the evidence on the grounds that it is the fruit of the detention and searching of Karen, in violation of the Fourth Amendment; Bart also points out that the cocaine belongs to him. Should Bart's suppression motion be granted?

Not sure ☐

106. Officer Katz had many prejudices, especially concerning blacks and women. One day, he spotted Danielle, a black woman, driving an expensive late-model Porsche. Katz believed that no black woman could possibly have come to drive such a car except by stealing it, earning it through prostitution, or otherwise behaving unlawfully. Because of this belief and not because of any other objective clues, Katz pulled Danielle over and asked to see her license and registration. Both seemed in order, but Katz nonetheless believed that Danielle must be lying when she said she owned the car and had paid for it with honestly earned money. Therefore, Katz arrested her on charges of prostitution (thinking that she had paid for the car through this means), even though there was not a shred of evidence to support this.

At the station house, Katz questioned Danielle, after first reading Danielle her *Miranda* warnings. Under questioning, Daniel suddenly admitted that a large part of the money to buy the car had come from cocaine smuggling done by her and her boyfriend. Danielle was then charged with drug smuggling. At her trial, the prosecution sought to introduce her confession against her. Danielle has moved to suppress the confession on the ground that it is the fruit of a violation of her Fourth Amendment rights. Should Danielle's suppression motion be granted?

Not sure ☐

107. Federal prosecutors were trying to make an insider trading case against Gordon and Ivan, both wealthy and famous arbitrageurs. They began by breaking into Ivan's office at night and seizing all of the records in his office, which they then carted to a warehouse. They did this without probable cause and without a warrant. Buried among these documents (and not seen by authorities until much later) was a copy of a July 1 letter from Ivan to Gordon concerning trading in the stock of ABC Corp.; the letter made it clear that Ivan and Gordon were both guilty of insider trading in that transaction. The federal authorities were so busy building their case that they did not go through the documents seized from Ivan's office, and merely kept them boxed in a government warehouse.

Shortly thereafter, federal agents arrested Gordon without a warrant and without probable cause, and then questioned him without first giving him his *Miranda* warnings. Under the questioning, Gordon broke down, confessed to the ABC transaction, and gave police a copy of the July 1 Ivan-to-Gordon letter. The agents realized that they had gotten the letter from Gordon by violating his Fourth and Fifth Amendment rights, and that they might have a hard time introducing the letter into evidence against him. However, since they now knew about the letter, and saw that it was from Ivan to Gordon, they went back into the warehouse and discovered Ivan's copy of it in one of the boxes.

At Gordon's trial for insider trading, prosecutors offered into evidence against Gordon the copy Gordon had given them of the Ivan-to-Gordon July 1 letter. Gordon has moved to suppress this document on the grounds that it was obtained as the fruit of an unlawful search and interrogation of him.

(a) What doctrine should the prosecution cite in opposing Gordon's suppression motion?

Not sure ☐

(b) If the prosecution uses the doctrine you recommend in (a), should Gordon's motion be granted?

Not sure ☐

108. The police received a tip from a reliable informant that cocaine was being processed at a warehouse at 481 Main Street. The informant explained that he knew this because he had been a member of the operation until he quarreled with the other principals. The police went to the 481 Main address and discovered a locked warehouse that could plausibly have been a cocaine-processing factory. At this point, they knew they had probable cause to get a search warrant, and would normally have done so. Normally, they would have staked out the building while they got the warrant (so that no one could remove or destroy evidence). But to save time and to eliminate the need for a stakeout, they decided to see if they could break in first. They successfully broke into the building, and saw that it was indeed a cocaine-processing factory.

At that point, without touching anything, they relocked the premises, applied for a warrant (using only the information that they had had prior to the break-in), received the warrant, went back to the building, broke in again, and seized the cocaine and other evidence. This evidence was introduced against Jerry, one of the principals, in his trial for drug-related offenses. Jerry has moved to suppress the evidence, on the grounds that it was obtained in violation of his Fourth Amendment rights (since he was the owner of the building, as well as one of the owners of the processing operation). Should Jerry's motion be granted?

Not sure ☐

109. Harry, a wealthy industrialist, was on his way to work in his chauffeured limousine when two masked gunmen suddenly attacked the vehicle, spewing bullets into its tires. The gunmen then opened the door and forcibly abducted Harry. Shortly thereafter, Harry's family received a ransom demand, with which the family complied. Harry was released unharmed; however, since his captors had blindfolded him while they transported him to their hideaway, and kept masks on at all times, Harry was not able to help the police determine who had committed the crime. Starting shortly after the kidnapping, the police ballistics lab analyzed the bullets found in the car and discovered that these had come from a Smith & Wesson .38 revolver, of a type manufactured between 2000 and 2010.

The police immediately began examining the records of every gun dealer and pawnshop in the metropolitan area, figuring that there was a good chance that the owner (or at least original purchaser) of the gun used in the abduction would be listed in these records. The police then began to interview each Smith & Wesson .38 gun owner shown in the records, and to test each of his or her guns. After the police had checked about 10 percent of the listed guns, they happened to get a call from an anonymous informant, who said, "You'll find evidence of a serious crime at 1025 South Avenue."

The police realized that this did not furnish them with probable cause to obtain a search warrant for that address. Therefore, they decided to wing it. They went to 1025 South Avenue, rang the bell, and broke in when there was no answer. They ransacked the house, and in so doing, found a Smith & Wesson .38 revolver. Just on a hunch that this might have been the gun used in the Harry kidnapping case, they seized the gun and took it back to the police station. (They did not find any other evidence of criminality.) The department ran a ballistics test on the revolver, and it turned out to be the gun that had fired the bullets into Harry's car. The police went back to 1025 South Avenue, staked it out, and eventually arrested the owner, Kent, when he entered. Meanwhile, it turned out that Kent was the registered owner of the gun, and that his name appeared on the records of a local pawnshop as being the owner of that gun. The 1025 South Avenue address was listed as Kent's address in the pawnshop records.

At Kent's trial for kidnapping, the prosecution seeks to enter the gun into evidence and to tie it to the kidnapping by showing that it fired the bullets found in the car. Kent moves to suppress, on the theory that the police's possession of the gun stems directly from their illegal break-in of 1025 South Avenue at a time when they did not have probable cause or a warrant.

(a) What doctrine should the prosecution cite in support of its opposition to Kent's suppression motion?

Not sure ☐

(b) If the prosecution cites the doctrine you referred to in part (a), should the court grant Kent's suppression motion?

Not sure ☐

110. Leslie reported to the Ames police that her apartment had been burglarized. Officer Kaplan was sent to investigate the complaint. Leslie showed Kaplan into her home office, and had him sit in front of her desk. At one point during the interview, Leslie excused herself to go to the bathroom. Kaplan, with no evil purpose in mind, just curiosity, picked up a stack of letters from Leslie's desk. In the middle of the stack was a letter to Leslie stating, "Sis, I know you poisoned our mother to get her insurance money, but so far I can't bring myself to turn you in. I want you to know that I know, though. [signed] Morton." Kaplan deduced that this might be a clue to a murder case.

After leaving Leslie's apartment, Kaplan ascertained that Leslie indeed had a brother named Morton, and that their mother had died the month before; no one outside the family suspected foul play. Kaplan contacted Morton, who said, "Well, now that you're here, yes, I'd be happy to talk about why I think Leslie murdered our mother." Morton then described facts that made the police believe that Leslie had indeed killed her mother. Leslie was tried for this murder. At the trial, the prosecution relied heavily on Morton's testimony as to incriminating actions by Leslie. Leslie has moved to suppress Morton's testimony, on the grounds that the prosecution learned of Morton's existence only through Kaplan's illegal ransacking of Leslie's mail. Should Leslie's motion be granted?

Not sure ☐

111. Nelson's wife, Marie, disappeared without ever being heard from again. The police were convinced that Marie had been murdered, and that Nelson had done it. However, they did not have a shred of hard evidence to prove this. They therefore decided that they would have to play hardball to get anywhere with the case. Without probable cause and without a warrant, they arrested Nelson at his home and took him down to the police station. They dutifully read him his *Miranda* warnings. He agreed to listen to their questions, though not necessarily to talk. After two hours of grilling, Nelson finally confessed that he had done it, and described the method used. A videotape was made of this interrogation session, and it is clear that Nelson's confession was voluntary. Nelson was tried for murder, and the prosecution sought to introduce the videotape of Nelson's confession. Nelson has moved to suppress this confession, on the grounds that it was the fruit of the police's prior illegal arrest of him. Assuming that the arrest was indeed a violation of Nelson's Fourth Amendment rights, should Nelson's suppression motion be granted?

Not sure ☐

112. Officer O'Brien was irrationally prejudiced against young males with long hair, and against anyone who looked like a "hippie." O'Brien spotted Peter and Rachel walking hand in hand down the street and developed a hunch, based solely on their long hair and style of clothing, that the two were probably in possession of drugs. He arrested them both on drug charges and escorted them to the station house. There, each was subjected to a "clothing search," which was done to every arrestee in order to inventory their possessions and to protect against concealed weapons. The two were searched simultaneously. In Rachel's purse, five marijuana cigarettes were found. Rachel looked imploringly at Peter when this occurred. Peter then said, "I can't let Rachel take the rap for this—those cigarettes are mine." Peter was charged with marijuana possession, and the prosecution sought to use his station-house confession against him. Peter objected on the grounds that this statement was a direct fruit of his unlawful arrest. Should the court grant Peter's suppression motion?

Not sure ☐

113. The police had probable cause to arrest Stuart for the gangland-style murder of his rival, Ted. The police did not bother to get an arrest warrant, because they erroneously thought that one was not necessary under prevailing legal principles. They went to Stuart's apartment, and arrested him there and handcuffed him. (An arrest warrant was required because the arrest was made at the defendant's residence, and there were no exigent circumstances justifying dispensing with a warrant.) While still at the apartment, they read Stuart his *Miranda* rights and began questioning him about the murder. Stuart, figuring the game was up, agreed to talk and incriminated himself. At Stuart's murder trial, he argued that his confession was the direct result of the illegal arrest (illegal because there was no arrest warrant when one was required), and the confession was therefore the tainted fruit of the arrest. Should Stuart's suppression motion be granted?

Not sure ☐

114. The police had probable cause to believe that Veronica was the masked gunman who had recently robbed the local branch of First National Bank. They properly procured a warrant for her arrest, and arrested her at her house. They handcuffed her and brought her to the police department. There, Detective Usher questioned her about the robbery, without first giving her *Miranda* warnings. (He had learned from his personal experience that suspects often clammed up when read their *Miranda* warnings, and were somewhat more likely to speak if not given the warnings.) In response to Usher's questions (but not in response to any overt coercion or trickery), Veronica confessed that she was the robber. Usher left the room briefly to get a police stenographer, then returned. At this point, he read Veronica her *Miranda* warnings, and did not mention to her that her earlier confession would be inadmissible because unwarned. He then started asking the same questions that had led to the first confession.

Veronica, reasoning that she had already "let the cat out of the bag" by confessing, decided that there was no point in refusing to answer the same questions again, this time before the stenographer. Therefore, she agreed to answer Usher's second set of questions. Veronica again confessed to being the robber, and the stenographer recorded these answers. Veronica then signed the confession. At Veronica's bank robbery trial, the prosecution seeks to enter the signed transcript of the second confession into evidence against Veronica. (The prosecution concedes that the first confession is inadmissible.) Veronica has moved to suppress that second confession as the fruit of the earlier, non-*Mirandized* confession. Should Veronica's suppression motion be granted?

Not sure ☐

115. The police had probable cause to believe that Wilbur had rubbed out Xavier, a gangland rival. Xavier's body had been found with a distinctive rifle slug in his brain. While Wilbur was walking down the street, the police arrested him (they did not have a warrant, but they did not need one) and took him to the station house. At the station house, they questioned him, without first giving him his *Miranda* warnings. Wilbur admitted that he had done the shooting, and at the urging of the police told them that the murder weapon was at the bottom of a pond 200 miles away. Using the information furnished by Wilbur, the police located and dredged the pond, and recovered a rifle, which ballistics tests established to have indeed been used in the murder. (The police would never have had any reason to dredge that pond except for Wilbur's telling them that the rifle was there.)

At Wilbur's murder trial, the prosecution concedes that Wilbur's confession is inadmissible against him, but seeks to use the rifle (which independent records show was registered to Wilbur) in its case in chief against him. The police are willing not to bring out before the jury how they happened to dredge that pond—they merely want to show that a rifle registered to Wilbur was used to commit the murder. Wilbur objects that the police would never have found the rifle without his confession, so the rifle is the direct tainted fruit of the poisonous confession. Should Wilbur's suppression motion be granted?

Not sure ☐

116. Over the course of a year, three coeds at Ames State University were found, each in her own off-campus apartment, each stabbed to death. The police believed that a single killer was at work. Detective Johnson of the Ames police force received an anonymous tip that Bernard, who the caller said lived at 141 West Street in Ames, was the killer. This information did not amount to probable cause to arrest Bernard or search his house. Nonetheless, Johnson felt that he had to act. After telephoning Bernard and ascertaining that he was out, Johnson broke into Bernard's house and carefully searched it from corner to corner. He happened upon three separate snapshots, which he recognized instantly as being of the three dead girls. He immediately seized these photos and left the house. Based in part on other evidence not illegally obtained, the police were eventually able to charge Bernard with the murder of one of the girls, Kelly.

At Bernard's murder trial, the prosecution did not use the snapshot of Kelly (or anything else derived from Johnson's illegal search of Bernard's house) as part of its direct case. The defense then put on its case. Its only witness was Bernard. On direct, Bernard denied committing the murder of Kelly and said nothing more. On cross-examination, the prosecutor asked, "Did you ever meet

Kelly?" Bernard responded, "No." The prosecution asked, "Did you ever obtain a photograph of Kelly?" Again, Bernard answered, "No." Then, the prosecutor showed Bernard the snapshot and asked, "Isn't it true that this photo of Kelly was found in your house?" Bernard's lawyer objected to the prosecution's use of this photo, on the grounds that the photo was the direct fruit of an illegal search, and must thus be barred by the exclusionary rule. Should the trial judge sustain this objection?

Not sure ☐

117. The police suspected that Egon was the person who had killed Gerald, a business associate of Egon's. However, they did not have probable cause to arrest Egon or to search his premises. Instead, they simply broke into Egon's house one day while he and his wife were away, and seized the most interesting item they found, a Remington .33 revolver. This gun was of interest to the police because they had already determined, from ballistics tests, that Gerald had been shot with a Remington .33. Ballistics tests later showed that the seized pistol was indeed the murder weapon. The police knew that their seizure of the gun was illegal, and they had no other way to prove that Egon had owned the murder weapon. However, they had enough other circumstantial evidence of Egon's guilt that Egon was prosecuted for the murder anyway.

In the prosecution's direct case, only this circumstantial evidence, not the fact that Egon owned the murder weapon, was introduced. During the defense case, Egon did not take the stand. However, Fran, Egon's wife, did take the stand. She stated on direct examination, "So far as I know, Egon never kept a gun at our house." The prosecution, on cross-examination, then showed Fran the Remington seized from the house, and asked, "Don't you recognize this gun as one that was in your house up until several months ago?" Egon's lawyer immediately objected to this evidence on the grounds that it was the fruit of the unlawful entry into Egon's house. Must the court sustain Egon's objection?

Not sure ☐

118. Detective Lawrence of the Langdell police force received an anonymous call, in which the caller stated, "The occupant of apartment 3B in my building is selling drugs from that apartment. I live at 1865 Center Street." The caller did not say how he came by this information. Lawrence believed that this information was enough to establish probable cause to search apartment 3B at the 1865 Center Street address. He went before a neutral and detached magistrate, and presented the above facts to her in an affidavit. Lawrence did not conceal any relevant facts. The magistrate agreed with Lawrence that the facts here established probable cause, and the magistrate therefore issued a warrant to search apartment 3B of 1865 Center Street "for drugs or any paraphernalia associated with drugs." Lawrence executed the warrant by its terms (breaking into the apartment when there was no answer) and strictly confined his search to the scope of the warrant. He found cocaine that seemed to be held for resale, and seized it.

The occupant of the apartment turned out to be Herb. Herb was tried for a variety of drug charges. The prosecution offered the seized drugs as part of its case-in-chief. Herb moved to suppress the seized drugs, on the grounds that they were the fruit of an illegal search, since there was in fact no probable cause to support issuance of the search warrant. The trial judge has agreed with Herb that the warrant was issued without probable cause, because there was no indication that the informant was either generally reliable or reliable in this case, so that by the "totality of the circumstance" test (*Illinois v. Gates*), probable cause for the warrant did not exist. However, the trial judge has also concluded that Lawrence reasonably believed, on the facts known to him, that probable cause existed; the judge also believes that the magistrate similarly made a reasonable mistake as to the existence of probable cause. Must the trial judge order the drugs suppressed from Herb's trial?

Not sure ☐

119. Kathy was charged with shoplifting. Under state law, shoplifting, where the amount involved is less than $100, is classified as a misdemeanor. A jail sentence of up to six months is authorized. Kathy was indigent, and requested a lawyer for her trial. However, because of a shortage of funds, the county declined to provide one. Kathy was convicted and sentenced to one night in jail. She has appealed her conviction (and has not done the one night in jail, pending the outcome of the appeal). She argues on appeal that the county's refusal to provide her with a lawyer for the trial, in these circumstances, violated her Sixth Amendment rights. Is Kathy's contention correct?

Not sure ☐

120. Same basic fact pattern as in the previous question. Now, however, assume that because of the relatively large ($250) amount involved, Kathy was charged with petit larceny, a felony. The maximum sentence authorized for petit larceny is two years in prison. Because she was indigent, Kathy requested a court-appointed lawyer. The county declined to provide one due to budget constraints. Kathy was tried and convicted. The judge decided not to sentence her to jail, but sentenced her to pay a $100 fine. Have Kathy's Sixth Amendment rights been violated?

Not sure ☐

121. Lester was arrested for burglary, a felony, late one Friday afternoon. He was taken to the station house, booked, and then held in a cell at the county jail because no magistrate was available. Lester's confinement lasted from Friday afternoon until Monday morning. The police did not give Lester his *Miranda* warnings or make any attempt to question him. On Friday evening, Lester stated that he was indigent (which was true), and demanded that the authorities furnish counsel for him. They refused to do so. (Lester wanted a lawyer over the weekend because he believed that a lawyer might be able to get him released. In fact, there were some special emergency procedures available, under which a knowledgeable lawyer might indeed have gotten Lester released over the weekend.) On Monday morning, Lester was taken to an initial appearance before a magistrate, at which time the charges were read to him, he entered a nonbinding plea of not guilty, and counsel was appointed for him. Did Lester's confinement without counsel over the weekend violate his Sixth Amendment rights?

Not sure ☐

122. Marvin was charged with terrorism, a crime under state law. For political reasons, Marvin wanted to conduct his own defense, and petitioned the court to be allowed to do so. The judge verified that Marvin understood the consequences of self-representation—that his defense might well be less effective, in terms of the likelihood of conviction. The judge also ascertained that Marvin knew almost nothing about the law (for instance, he did not know about the rule against hearsay), and that Marvin was therefore extremely unlikely to conduct his own representation in a manner that would satisfy the minimum competency required of a practicing

lawyer. The judge therefore concluded that Marvin would be extremely unwise to represent himself. Must the judge, as a matter of federal constitutional law, allow Marvin to represent himself in this case?

Not sure ☐

123. Norman was charged with murdering his second wife. While he was under arrest and kept at the police station, he was given his *Miranda* warnings, and he made an extensive confession that was videotaped. In the confession, Norman disclosed facts that only the killer could have known. Since Norman was indigent, he requested and was given a court-appointed lawyer, Larry. The prosecution's case at trial rested mainly on the videotaped confession, which was shown to the jury. Larry presented a defense for Norman that fell far below the usual standards of competence. For instance, he put Norman on the stand without warning Norman that Norman's past criminal record could be used to impeach his testimony; as a result, Norman's prior conviction for murdering his first wife was brought out on cross-examination to impeach Norman. Nor did Larry object to the use by the prosecution of the videotaped confession; a more competent lawyer would probably have objected (though it is unlikely that the court would have excluded the confession from evidence even had the best available arguments been presented for exclusion). Needless to say, Norman was convicted on the murder charge. On appeal, he has argued that his lawyer's performance was so bad as to deny him the effective assistance of counsel, as guaranteed by the Sixth Amendment. Should the appellate court agree with Norman, and grant a new trial?

Not sure ☐

124. Osmond and Paula were co-indicted for bank robbery by a state grand jury, and arrested by local police. Since Osmond claimed to be indigent, the court appointed counsel for him. Osmond and Paula were then released from jail on their own recognizance. While both were out of jail, Osmond asked Paula if the two of them could meet to discuss their defense, without any lawyers present. Unbeknownst to Osmond, Paula had in fact already turned state's evidence. At the request of prosecutors, Paula wore a concealed transmitter to the meeting with Osmond. At that meeting, Paula said, "Don't you think we might be better off pleading guilty—you and I both know that we pulled this heist, and a jury's gonna believe we did, too." Osmond replied, "You and I may know we did it, but a jury doesn't have to know. I want to plead not guilty and defend this thing all the way." Shortly thereafter, Paula pled guilty. At Osmond's trial, the tape of his statement to Paula was played before the jury. Osmond argues that the use of this tape violated his Sixth Amendment rights, since his lawyer was not present at the meeting where Paula elicited the statement from Osmond. Should the court exclude the tape on this ground?

Not sure ☐

125. Same facts as in the previous question. Now, however, assume that Osmond had not been arrested or charged on the bank robbery charges, but he knew that the police regarded him as the principal suspect. The police knew that Osmond had consulted his longtime attorney about the charges that seemed likely to be filed against him. The police sent Paula to Osmond's house so that they could discuss what to do if charges were in fact filed. Unbeknownst to Osmond, Paula had already turned state's evidence, and was wired for sound. The conversation described in the previous question then occurred. Would it be a violation of Osmond's Sixth Amendment rights for his incriminating statement on the tape to be played before his jury?

Not sure ☐

126. Same basic fact pattern as in the previous two questions. Now, however, assume that Osmond was already indicted, and had retained a lawyer. Both Osmond and his lawyer, Loretta, believed that Paula was a true co-defendant; that is, neither realized that Paula had secretly turned state's evidence and was planning to plead guilty and testify against Osmond in return for a lighter sentence. Loretta asked Paula to come to a strategy meeting with herself and Osmond. Paula came to the meeting. At the meeting, Osmond volunteered several self-incriminating statements. Paula did not report these statements to the prosecution. At Osmond's trial, Paula testified against Osmond, but did not report any statements made at the strategy session. Osmond was convicted. On appeal, he argues that Paula's presence at the meeting between Osmond and Loretta constituted a violation of Osmond's Sixth Amendment rights, thus requiring a new trial. Should Osmond's new trial motion be granted on this ground?

Not sure ☐

127. Rafael was arrested for robbing First Bank, a crime that the police believed was committed by at least two perpetrators. No one other than Rafael was initially charged. Rafael was arraigned, and because he was indigent, the arraignment judge appointed Lawt, a legal aid lawyer, to represent him. Rafael was then released on his own recognizance. The day after the arraignment, the police visited Rafael at his house. They asked him whether he had consulted with Lawt yet, and he said that he had not. They then said to him, "We know you weren't the only robber. If you tell us who helped you, we'll ask the prosecution to go easy on you." Rafael thought about this proposition for a while, and agreed to talk to the police. They asked him to sign a waiver of his right to consult counsel, a document that he understood and signed. They then emphasized to him that he was not in custody, that he was free to discontinue the questioning at any time, and that if he did so the police would immediately leave. Rafael answered the police's questions about the robbery, explaining how he and his friend Justin had carried it out. Later at his trial, the prosecution offered these statements as evidence against him. Rafael sought to have the statements excluded as fruits of a violation of his Sixth Amendment right to counsel. Should the court grant his suppression motion?

Not sure ☐

Criminal Procedure Answers to Short-Answer Questions

1. Yes. **The Fifth Amendment privilege against self-incrimination and the Sixth Amendment right to counsel have both been held binding on the states (via the Fourteenth Amendment's Due Process Clause) just as they are applicable to the federal government.** The prosecution here might try to argue that merely because these guarantees are in a general sense binding on the states, this does not mean that the precise *contours* of each are binding on the states in the same way as on the federal government. But the Supreme Court has consistently rejected this argument—the Court has always held that once a particular Bill of Rights guarantee is binding on the states, it is binding in *precisely the same way* as on the federal government. See, e.g., *Malloy v. Hogan,* 378 U.S. 1 (1964). Since the 2008 *Smith v. U.S.* decision held that the interrogation there violates the suspect's Fifth and Sixth Amendment rights, and since the facts here are virtually indistinguishable, the Ames Supreme Court is constitutionally bound to find in favor of the defense.

2. No. **It is true that in the vast majority of situations where the Supreme Court has found that a particular Bill of Rights guarantee exists as against the federal government, the Court has also found that guarantee binding on the states via the Fourteenth Amendment's Due Process Clause (the "*selective incorporation*" doctrine). But there is one notable exception to this general rule: The Supreme Court has never found the right to a grand jury indictment to be binding on the states.** Therefore, any state may (and indeed most states do) commence a felony prosecution against the defendant based on some method other than a grand jury indictment, even though a defendant would have the right not to have a *federal* felony prosecution commenced against him or her without a grand jury indictment.

3. No. **The Supreme Court has held that "where the state has provided an opportunity for *full and fair litigation* of a Fourth Amendment claim, a state prisoner may not be granted federal *habeas corpus* relief on the ground that evidence obtained in an unconstitutional search and seizure was introduced at his trial." *Stone v. Powell,* 428 U.S. 465 (1976).** In other words, once a state prisoner gets a fair chance at his or her trial to argue that evidence should not be introduced against him or her because it was the fruit of an illegal search or seizure, he or she may not make this argument in a federal habeas corpus petition, even if the federal court is convinced that the state court reached a constitutionally indefensible conclusion.

4. No. **In all but the most unusual and shocking cases of violent police misconduct, the unconstitutionality of an arrest does not itself serve as a defense to charges.** That is, a defendant may be tried and convicted regardless of the fact that his or her arrest was made in violation of the Fourth Amendment. (The legality of the arrest is, however, important in determining whether evidence obtained pursuant to a search that was incident to the arrest must be suppressed, an issue not present on these facts.) The fact that Dexter was illegally arrested is of absolutely no value to him here—the prosecutor may proceed anyway, without even having to rearrest Dexter or recharge him.

5. Yes, probably. *Katz v. U.S.,* 389 U.S. 347 (1967), **establishes that even communications that in some sense occur in "public" may be protected under the Fourth Amendment. Basically, if (1) the defendant had an actual (subjective) expectation of privacy about the communication, and**

(2) that expectation was one that society recognizes as reasonable, then the communication will be protected by the Fourth Amendment, even if it occurred outside of a private home or office. Here, Johnny's communication probably satisfied this test: (1) he certainly showed an actual or subjective expectation that his words were not being overheard, and (2) in private everyday life, one's words are not overheard by such specialized devices, so that society ought to regard an expectation of privacy in these circumstances as being "reasonable."

Therefore, even though the communication occurred in a public place, the Fourth Amendment probably protected it. Since the police did not have a warrant or probable cause to monitor the conversation, Johnny will probably be entitled to have the conversation suppressed, and the search warrant therefore thrown out. (The facts are roughly analogous to those of *Katz* itself, where eavesdropping done from the outside of a public phone booth was found to violate the Fourth Amendment rights of the defendant who used the booth to make calls.)

If the police had merely been using a conventional device, such as an ordinary telescope, to get the information, then there would not have been a Fourth Amendment violation, because the "*plain view*" doctrine would have been applicable. But because the information here was obtainable only by use of equipment that was not generally available, plain view probably does not apply, and Johnny's Fourth Amendment rights are probably violated. (See, e.g., *Dow Chemical Co. v. U.S.*, 476 U.S. 227 (1986), stating that "an electronic device to penetrate walls or windows so as to hear and record confidential discussions . . . would raise very different and far more serious questions" than would the ordinary, generally available aerial camera used in *Dow*.)

By the way, *U.S. v. Leon*, 468 U.S. 897 (1984), might save the prosecution here. That case holds that if a search warrant is issued by a detached and neutral magistrate but is ultimately found to be unsupported by probable cause, the search and its fruits are nonetheless valid and admissible. So even if the task force relied on improperly obtained materials (the conversation) to get their search warrant, they might be able to get the fruits of the warrant admitted under *Leon*. That is why the facts tell you to ignore all issues except whether the Fourth Amendment protected the conversation in the park.

6. **No. A private dwelling, and the "curtilage" around it, are protected by the Fourth Amendment. The "curtilage" is the area closely surrounding a house, and will typically include a small backyard, a garage, and the like. But *open fields* beyond the curtilage are *not* protected by the Fourth Amendment. See *Oliver v. U.S.*, 466 U.S. 170 (1984).** Almost certainly, a 100-acre farm would be found to be open fields, especially a parcel in the middle of the 100 acres (as opposed to an area just outside of the farmhouse). Since the plants were in the open fields beyond the curtilage, it does not help Smith that officers trespassed on his property to get the evidence—he will simply be deemed to not have had a reasonable expectation of privacy with respect to such a field. Nor does it matter that Smith had a fence around the property or "No Trespassing" signs throughout—once something is found to be an open field beyond the curtilage, that is the end of the matter for Fourth Amendment purposes.

7. **(a)** The "plain view" doctrine. **Under this doctrine, "objects falling in the plain view of an officer who has a right to be in the position to have that view are subject to seizure and may be introduced in evidence."** *Harris v. U.S.*, 390 U.S. 234 (1968). More precisely, when an officer standing where he or she has a right to be spots something in plain view, no "search" is deemed to have taken place. Therefore, even if the officer got to that spot without having probable cause, there has been no Fourth Amendment violation. (The view does not necessarily entitle the officer to go in and seize the item; it merely assures that the view will not be deemed an unreasonable and thus illegal search.)

(b) No. **Under the "plain view" doctrine, "objects falling in the plain view of an officer who has a right to be in the position to have that view are subject to seizure and may be introduced in evidence." Harris v. U.S., 390 U.S. 234 (1968).** The plain view doctrine is applicable on these facts. Baker obviously did not violate any law by gathering up the dog and returning it to its home. Baker was certainly standing where she had a right to be when she stood at the door and looked in after it was opened. Therefore, her spotting of the weapon was not a Fourth Amendment search at all, so her lack of probable cause before the moment where she spotted it is irrelevant. The view itself then supplied probable cause to obtain the warrant, thus making the seizure legal as well.

8. Yes. **Under the "plain view" doctrine, "objects falling in the plain view of an officer who has a right to be in the position to have that view are subject to seizure and may be introduced in evidence." *Harris v. U.S.*, 390 U.S. 234 (1968).** It is true that Officer Baker was lawfully in the living room, which was where the gun was located. But the plain view doctrine does not apply here. Jones did not consent to Officer Baker's opening of the closed container, so the contents of that container will not be deemed to have been in plain view. The question is whether one in Jones's position would reasonably have expected a casual social guest to open closed containers, and the answer is almost certainly no. Since Jones will thus not be found to have consented to Officer Baker's opening of the container, Baker will be deemed to have overstepped her invitation, and the plain view doctrine will not apply. See, e.g., *Walter v. U.S.*, 447 U.S. 649 (1980) (the fact that police were legitimately in possession of a closed package did not mean that they were entitled to open it to see that it contained obscene films).

9. No. **Under the "plain view" doctrine, "objects falling in the plain view of an officer who has a right to be in the position to have that view are subject to seizure and may be introduced in evidence." *Harris v. U.S.*, 390 U.S. 234 (1968).** As long as the officer did not violate any laws or engage in shocking conduct, the fact that she was standing in a place where she had a right to be at the time she got the view is dispositive. The fact that Baker used a *pretext* to ring the bell and get her glimpse will not prevent the plain view doctrine from applying.

10. (a) The "plain view" doctrine. **According to the plain view doctrine, a defendant has no reasonable expectation of privacy, and thus no Fourth Amendment interest, in anything that is seen by a police officer "in plain view" while the officer is standing in a place where he or she has a right to be.** When Officer White, standing on the public sidewalk where she had a right to be, saw the marijuana plant, no search occurred.

(b) No. **As noted above, White did not commit a Fourth Amendment search by standing on the sidewalk and spotting the marijuana plant, since at the time she did so she was standing in a place where she had the right to be. But spotting the plant did not automatically give her the right to seize the plant without a warrant.** Once she went onto Desmond's property, entered his house without a warrant, and confiscated the plant, she was then committing a seizure. This seizure, because it was warrantless and did not occur under exigent circumstances, was a violation of the Fourth Amendment's ban on unreasonable seizures. Therefore, Desmond is entitled to get the plants excluded from evidence against him. (Obviously, White should have gone to get a search warrant once she spotted the plants from the sidewalk. If she was worried about the plants being destroyed, she should have had a colleague stand on the sidewalk and look in the window while she went to get the warrant.)

11. No. **In *Florida v. Riley*, 488 U.S. 445 (1989), the Court held that even a view taken by the police from a helicopter flying only 400 feet above the ground still fell within the "plain view" doctrine, and was therefore not a search.** Certainly the overflight here, at 500 feet, should not be considered

a search. The idea behind the *Riley* decision seems to be that since flights at that height are legal and are frequently engaged in by private people, a property owner should understand the risk that such overflights might occur, and therefore has no justifiable expectation of privacy as to anything that could be seen from such an overflight perspective. Nor should the police's use of binoculars change this result, since a person flying an ordinary helicopter for pleasure might well look out on the ground below using such binoculars.

12. Yes, probably. **In *Dow Chemical Co. v. U.S.*, 476 U.S. 227 (1986), where a $22,000 camera was used from a plane overflying a factory, the Court held that there was no reasonable expectation of privacy that was violated, and thus no search. However, in *Kyllo v. U.S.*, 533 U.S. 27 (2001), the Court found that when the government obtains special high-tech devices that are not in general civilian use and employs them from public places to gain "views" that could not be had by the naked eye, the use of such devices will be considered a search.** Here, the "ground cover anomaly detector" sounds like such a device.

    Importantly, the use of the extremely sophisticated, expensive, and unusual device here, coupled with the fact that a private home was involved, would probably lead the Supreme Court to hold that there was a Fourth Amendment search. Since there was no probable cause, Mercer's Fourth Amendment rights were violated, and he would probably be able to suppress the fruits of the later search pursuant to warrant.

13. (a) The "plain odor" doctrine. **The Supreme Court has at least implied that the "plain view" doctrine can apply where items are discovered through the use of *senses other than sight* (e.g., smell). See *U.S. v. Place*, 462 U.S. 696 (1983) (use of dogs to perform a canine "sniff test" on luggage in an airport does not constitute a Fourth Amendment search of the luggage).**

   (b) No, probably. **The "plain odor" analogy to the "plain view" doctrine likely applies here.** If plain view were being relied upon, the fact that the officer followed his line of sight into a place where he was not previously authorized to be would probably not be fatal—thus an officer who is entitled to stand in the foyer (perhaps because the owner of the house has consented to his being there), and who then sees an item in plain view in the living room, almost certainly has the right to go into the living room to inspect it more closely. By analogy, one who smells an odor while standing in a place where he has the right to be (the bedroom), probably has the right to "follow his nose" to get to the source. (The right to smell and thus find the body does not by itself automatically give the officer the right to seize the body, but since Officer Piston was already on the premises with a validly issued warrant, he probably had the right to impound the body as yet another piece of evidence of crime.)

14. Yes, probably. **Any "plain odor" doctrine would probably not apply where the police are employing high-tech "sense enhancing" technology. See *Kyllo v. U.S.*, 533 U.S. 27 (2001). The *Kyllo* decision suggests that if the police were to use a machine to detect odors, this would constitute a search, at least if it were directed at a home and if the device was not one generally used by the public.** Here, a court might analogize the detection of individual molecules with smelling a scent.

15. No. **The Supreme Court has held, on almost exactly identical facts, that if a government agent performs a search or seizure of the same material that has already been subjected to a private search or seizure, the government will be deemed to have intruded upon the owner's privacy interests only to the extent that the governmental search or seizure exceeds the scope of the private one. See *U.S. v. Jacobsen*, 466 U.S. 109 (1984).** Since here the agents were only opening the same package, in the same way, that Brown had already done, and since Brown's opening was a purely

private action not taken under color of law, the federal agents were not further disturbing David's privacy and thus conducted no search.

16. No. In *California v. Greenwood*, **486 U.S. 35 (1988), the Court held that trash (as well as other abandoned property) will normally not be material to which the owner has an objectively reasonable expectation of privacy.** Therefore, when a person puts trash on the curb to be picked up by the garbage collector, the police may search that trash without a warrant.

17. No, probably. **In *Greenwood*, the Court relied on the fact that the defendant was putting his trash into the custody of the trash collector, and that the collector could have gone through the contents, so a police inspection of the garbage was not a greater intrusion on the defendant's privacy than that to which he had already implicitly consented.** This reasoning ought to be applicable in this situation as well. That is, George was already consenting to having the UC collectors go into his backyard and bring the trash bags to the street. Once the bags were in the street, the UC workers could have gone through the bags, so they were not worsening the invasion of George's privacy by allowing Treasury officials to do the same thing.

18. Yes, probably. **The Court in *Greenwood* seemed to be limiting its holding to trash left at curbside or gotten by the actual garbage collector and brought to curbside.** Probably the Court would hold that George, by consenting to have the UC workers come into his backyard, was not thereby consenting to have government agents come onto his property to inspect his (admittedly abandoned) trash. After all, suppose that George's arrangement for trash disposal was that his day maid would come inside the house each morning and take the trash to the street—this would almost certainly not constitute consent by George to have government agents come into his house and take the trash away. The area right outside George's house in his backyard is within the "curtilage," and thus has a legitimate expectation of privacy associated with it, so the agents were presumably unlawfully infringing George's privacy by going there even if the ultimate result of their actions was to look at trash that they could have legally looked at had it been in the street.

19. No. **The Supreme Court has held that a prisoner has no legitimate expectation of privacy in his or her prison cell. *Hudson v. Palmer*, 468 U.S. 517 (1984).** Therefore, there are no Fourth Amendment limitations at all on prison officials' right to conduct searches of cells and to seize anything they find.

20. Yes. **The Supreme Court has held that an overnight guest normally has a legitimate expectation of privacy in the home where he or she is staying. *Minnesota v. Olson*, 495 U.S. 91 (1990).** Therefore, the police were required to get a search warrant, just as if Joe had owned the apartment. When they did not do so, they violated the warrant requirement, and the marijuana will be deemed the fruits of an illegal search.

21. No. **The Supreme Court has held that the Fourth Amendment does not apply to actions by U.S. officials that take place in a foreign country and involve a foreign national (at least one who does not yet reside in the United States or have substantial connections with the United States). Property owned abroad by a foreign national may normally be searched for and seized by U.S. officials without probable cause and without a warrant. This is true even if the information is used against the foreigner in an American criminal trial. *U.S. v. Verdugo-Urguidez*, 494 U.S. 259 (1990).**

22. Yes, probably. **It appears to be the case that a foreign national who is present in the United States has Fourth Amendment rights with respect to searches done in the United States. The Supreme Court assumed that this was the case (though it did not expressly so hold) in *INS v. Lopez-Mendoza*, 468 U.S. 1032 (1984).**

23. **Yes. Any trustworthy information may be considered in determining whether probable cause to search or arrest exists, even if the information would *not be admissible* at trial.** Thus, the police may use hearsay information, or even a prior criminal record of the suspect, as part of their showing of probable cause.

24. **No. In general, the issue is whether the *magistrate* acted properly—that is, whether detailed assertions making out probable cause are presented to the magistrate—not whether the officer acted properly.** It will normally not matter that false information is supplied to the magistrate. This is true even where the officer acted negligently in not catching the error. (But if the officer intentionally perjured himself in the affidavit, or acted recklessly in not catching the error, the result will probably be different.)

25. **No. Probable cause for the issuance of a warrant must be judged only by reference to the facts originally *presented to the magistrate* who was to issue the warrant.** If the police don't present to the magistrate evidence sufficient to establish probable cause, but the warrant is issued anyway and is later challenged in a suppression hearing, the warrant cannot be retroactively validated by police testimony that they had other facts not presented to the magistrate.

26. **Yes, probably. It used to be the case that where a warrant was sought on the basis of information from an informant, the magistrate had to be told the facts showing the "basis of knowledge" of the informant—that is, the particular means by which he came upon the information which he supplied to the police. But as the result of *Illinois v. Gates*, 462 U.S. 213 (1983), the "basis of knowledge" is no longer necessary—so long as the informant's information, viewed under the "*totality of the circumstances*," seems reliable, this will be sufficient. In particular, if there is evidence that the informant has been reliable in the past, neither the fact that the officer seeking the warrant will not identify the informant nor the fact that the informant's basis of knowledge is not disclosed will be fatal.** A magistrate might nonetheless conclude on these facts that there is such a scarcity of information that under the totality of the circumstances it cannot be said that it is more probable than not that proceeds from the burglary will be found in Marvin's garage. But if the magistrate did issue the warrant, and the proceeds were found in the garage, probably those proceeds would not be suppressed as fruits of an unlawful search.

27. **Yes, probably. The Fourth Amendment provides that no warrant shall issue except one "*particularly describing* the . . . things to be seized."** Probably the warrant here was so broad as to violate this requirement. Clearly the warrant could have been limited to records relating to Desmond's dealings with Edward, or in the worst case, records dealing with payments remitted to insurance companies on behalf of customers. The warrant here was utterly unparticular—it asked for all books and records, yet there is very little in an insurance office except books and records. Also, where the items seized have First Amendment value (like the diary), the requirement of specificity is usually enforced somewhat more strictly.

28. **No. Even though the diary entries contained incriminating statements made by Desmond, the seizure of these items and their introduction into evidence does not violate his Fifth Amendment rights. The seizure of preexisting items under a search warrant will never violate the Fifth Amendment, because the person against whom the search is directed is not required to aid in—that is, incriminate himself by—the production or authentication of the incriminating evidence.** (By contrast, Desmond might be able to resist a *subpoena* for his diary on the grounds that this would violate his Fifth Amendment rights.)

29. **None. Nonsuspects' premises may be searched and their property seized just as readily as those of suspects. The fact that a subpoena would be just as effective (perhaps more effective), and less

intrusive, is irrelevant. **News organizations, whatever their First Amendment rights may be in the abstract, are not entitled to any special protection when it comes to the issuance of search warrants.** In a case involving somewhat similar facts (search of a news organization for photographs of wrongdoing), *Zurcher v. Stanford Daily*, 436 U.S. 547 (1978), each of these arguments was made by the news organization and rejected by the Supreme Court.

30. Yes, probably. **The police may protect themselves while performing a search, in the sense that they may check any person in control of the premises who is likely to be dangerous. But where a person simply happens to be on the premises to be searched, and appears not to have any connection with the criminal activity that gave rise to the warrant, that person may not be searched or frisked. See *Ybarra v. Illinois*, 444 U.S. 85 (1979) (warrant to search a bar and its bartender did not allow the police to frisk each patron).** Since Doug seemed to be an ordinary patron unconnected to any illegal betting that may have been occurring on the premises, the police probably did not have the right to stop and frisk him.

31. No. **It is not required, for application of the plain view doctrine, that the police's discovery of an item in plain view be "inadvertent," so the fact that the police knew in advance that they were just as likely to find *Lilies*, not named in the warrant, does not matter. See *Horton v. California*, 496 U.S. 128 (1990).** Thus, even though *Lilies* was not mentioned in the warrant, the police were entitled to seize it because it was in plain view while they were carrying out their lawfully issued warrant for *Irises*.

32. Yes. **The police are not permitted to go beyond the scope of the warrant.** They may seize items that they find in plain view while they are properly executing the warrant (as happened in the prior question), but once they have found what they came for, they must stop. Similarly, if they are looking for something large, like a human body, they may not look in places that could not possibly hold the item they are looking for (e.g., small closed containers).

33. No. **Arrest warrants are, as a general rule, not constitutionally required. This is true even where the police have sufficient advance notice that procurement of a warrant would not jeopardize the arrest. See *U.S. v. Watson*, 423 U.S. 411 (1976).**

34. Yes. **The only situation in which an arrest warrant may be constitutionally required is where the police wish to *enter private premises* to arrest a suspect. If there are no exigent circumstances (e.g., a serious threat that the suspect will flee or will destroy evidence), the police may not enter a private home to make a warrantless arrest.**

35. No, probably. **The police may enter even private premises to make a warrantless arrest if there are *exigent circumstances* that make it impractical for the police to delay the entry and arrest until they can obtain a warrant.** Since the crime was a serious one, and there was reason to believe that Wilson might flee at any moment, the requisite exigent circumstances seem present. If the police were entitled to enter Wilson's premises at all for this purpose, they were entitled to go throughout the house until they found him, so the fact that they intruded further than in the prior question is irrelevant. Once they arrested him, they were entitled to search the area around his control as a search incident to arrest (at least for purposes of protecting themselves), and were entitled to seize any weapon they found as a result of that limited search.

36. Yes, probably. **The police will, of course, argue that the search took place incident to a valid arrest, and that the fact that there was no search warrant is therefore irrelevant. But the search-incident-to-arrest exception to the normal requirement of a search warrant (an exception that stems from *Chimel v. California*, 395 U.S. 752 (1969)), covers only the area within the arrestee's**

possible control. Since there were two officers, and since Fred was already handcuffed to the bed, it was very unlikely that Fred could get into the other bedroom to seize any weapon that might have been present there. Also, it was quite unlikely that any weapon would be in something as small as the container. Therefore, it seems very unlikely that the search of that container aided the police's interest in protecting their safety or protecting against the destruction of evidence, the two reasons for the search-incident-to-arrest exception.

37. No, probably. **The search-incident-to-arrest exception to the normal requirement of a search warrant (an exception that stems from *Chimel v. California*, 395 U.S. 752 (1969)), covers only the area within the arrestee's *possible control*.** The drawers sound like they were within Fred's control—even though he was wearing handcuffs, he might have been able to open the drawer and grab a weapon from that drawer. With only one officer present, it would have been hard for that officer to prevent such a desperate grab. Consequently, the court would probably find that this was a valid search incident to arrest.

38. No, probably. **The search of the closets here cannot be justified as a search incident to the arrest of Gerald, since the area of search went far beyond any area to which Gerald could possibly have had ready access once he was handcuffed. But the Supreme Court has held that once an arrest takes place in the suspect's home, the officers may conduct a *protective sweep* of all or part of the premises if they have a "reasonable belief" based on "specific and articulable facts" that *another person* who might be dangerous to the officer may be present in the areas to be swept. *Maryland v. Buie*, 494 U.S. 328 (1990).**

    While doing such a protective sweep, the police may not make a detailed search of the premises but merely give them a cursory look to make sure that there is no one else around who may be dangerous. This seems to be what the officer was doing, since Harold was known to live at that address and thought to be possibly dangerous; also, the degree of risk was magnified by the fact that Gerald was found in the basement holding a knife, indicating that he had somehow learned of the possibility of the arrest (so that he could have tipped off Harold as well). Since weapons were found in a closet large enough to hold a man, and thus large enough to be a proper subject of the protective sweep, the officer probably acted legally in opening that closet. Once he rightfully opened the closet, he had the right to seize anything that was in plain view, including the murder weapon.

39. Yes. **If the police make a custodial arrest of a driver, if they are able to secure the driver so that he or she cannot gain access to the passenger compartment, the police may not then use the search-incident-to-arrest rationale to search the compartment. See *Arizona v. Gant*, 129 S. Ct. 1710 (2009).**

    When the arresting officers had handcuffed John to the patrol car, they did not have to worry that he could gain access to the passenger compartment. Consequently, the officers could not search the passenger compartment incident to John's arrest, even though the arrest was proper. Nor was there any other exception justifying a warrantless and without-probable-cause search of the compartment; for instance, at the moment the police started the search they had no probable cause to suspect drugs or contraband would be found.

40. No. **The 2009 decision in *Arizona v. Gant*, 129 S. Ct. 1710 (2009), says that it is no longer the case that when the police make a valid custodial arrest of a driver and ensure that he or she has no further access to the passenger compartment, they have the automatic right to search the entire compartment incident to that arrest. However, *Gant* also says that if the police who are making the arrest "reasonabl[y] believe that evidence relevant to the crime of arrest might be found in the vehicle," they may use the search-incident-to-arrest rationale as authority for searching**

any part of the vehicle (and any containers found in the vehicle) where such evidence might be found, even though the vehicle is no longer within the immediate control of the arrested driver. The "reasonable belief that evidence might be found" standard is clearly less demanding than probable cause.

The police qualify under this rule. The facts tell us that Officer Hingham had a "reasonable suspicion" that the trunk might contain prescription-drug vials, and that those vials, if they were found, might contain trace evidence of heroin. Since Jim was being arrested for selling heroin from prescription-drug vials, Hingham's suspicions related to the "crime of arrest." Therefore, even though Hingham did not have full probable cause to believe the vials would contain contraband or evidence of crime, he was entitled to make a search incident to arrest of the trunk, and then to make a search of any containers in the trunk if such suspected evidence of the crime of arrest (heroin sales) might be found in those containers. Once he found the vials, any contraband they turned out to contain could be the basis for criminal charges as to a crime (meth distribution) different from the crime of arrest to which the reasonable suspicion pertained.

41. (a) The "routine inventory procedure" exception. **If a police department routinely inventories all personal effects found on an arrested suspect, and does so to prevent police department employees from committing theft and to prevent arrestees from making false claims of theft, the procedure does not need to be supported by a warrant or by probable cause. See *Illinois v. Lafayette*, 462 U.S. 640 (1983).**

    (b) Yes. **If a police department routinely inventories all personal effects found on an arrested suspect, and does so to prevent police department employees from committing theft and to prevent arrestees from making false claims of theft, the procedure does not need to be supported by a warrant or by probable cause. See *Illinois v. Lafayette*, 462 U.S. 640 (1983).** The procedure here followed the requirements for a routine inventory procedure.

42. No, probably. **The taking of the blood sample clearly constituted a Fourth Amendment "seizure." The Supreme Court has recognized that where probable cause to search exists, and where *exigent circumstances* make it impractical to take the time to procure a search warrant, an exception to the warrant requirement will be recognized. See, e.g., *Cupp v. Murphy*, 412 U.S. 291 (1973) (holding that dried blood could be taken from under D's fingernails, where D was suspected of strangling his wife and it was thought that D would immediately clean his nails).** Because Denker's blood alcohol level was declining moment by moment, the court would almost certainly apply the "exigent circumstances" exception.

43. No. **Normally, a police officer may not enter a private home to make a search, even with probable cause, unless a warrant has been procured. One of the common exceptions to this rule is for a search incident to arrest, but the police may ordinarily not enter a private dwelling to make an arrest without an arrest warrant. However, there is an exception to both the search warrant and arrest warrant requirements where the police enter a private dwelling in *"hot pursuit"* of a suspect. See *Warden v. Hayden*, 387 U.S. 294 (1967).** Since Henkle was in hot pursuit of Eugene at the time she entered the house, the exception applies. Since she was entitled to be in the house while looking for him, anything she saw there could be seized without a search warrant under the plain view doctrine.

44. No. **In a series of cases, the Supreme Court has recognized a *"vehicle impoundment"* or "stationhouse search" exception to the warrant requirement: When the police have probable cause to both search and seize the car, and they exercise the right to seize it by taking it to the police**

station, they need not get a warrant before later searching the car's contents. See, e.g., *Chambers v. Maroney*, 399 U.S. 42 (1970), allowing a warrantless station-house search of the impounded car under similar circumstances. This exception to the warrant requirement for an impounded vehicle seems to stem from the Supreme Court's perception that "one has a lesser expectation of privacy in a motor vehicle because its function is transportation and it seldom serves as one's residence or the repository of personal effects. . . ." *U.S. v. Chadwick*, 433 U.S. 1 (1977). The search-incident-to-arrest rationale cannot apply, since the search took place a significant time after the arrest. Nor does the "routine inventory search" exception apply, since there is nothing in the facts to suggest that the car's contents were being subjected to a routine inventory itemization.

45. **No, probably. The Supreme Court has recognized a *"vehicle impoundment"* or *"station-house search"* exception to the warrant requirement: When the police have probable cause to both search and seize the car, and they exercise the right to seize it by taking it to the police station, they need not get a warrant before later searching the car's contents. See, e.g., *Chambers v. Maroney*, 399 U.S. 42. *Florida v. White*, 526 U.S. 559 (1999), strongly suggests that the failure to get a warrant when there is time to do so does not make the eventual warrantless seizure unlawful.**

46. **No, probably. For the police conduct to be valid, two different rules must be combined. First, the doctrine of *Carroll v. U.S.*, 267 U.S. 132 (1925), holds that when the police stop a car and need to perform a search to preserve evidence (because the car can quickly be driven out of the jurisdiction), they may search the car without a warrant even though no arrest has been made. (They must have probable cause to make the search, however.) Second, the Court held in *U.S. v. Ross*, 456 U.S. 798 (1982), that where a warrantless search of a lawfully stopped vehicle is allowed (i.e., the *Carroll* doctrine applies), the police may also open any *closed container* that they find during the search, on the theory that the intrusion is not materially greater.** Since Jackson had probable cause to stop the vehicle, and then probable cause to search it, he was also entitled to open containers that he found in it. This was true even though he had not arrested Leonard, so that the search-incident-to-arrest rationale does not apply.

47. **No. If a car is impounded because it has been towed for some kind of traffic or parking violation, the car may be subjected to a warrantless *"inventory search."* This is true even though the police do not have probable cause at the time they make the search. *South Dakota v. Opperman*, 428 U.S. 364 (1976).** (In fact, the police may even open closed containers found in the vehicle, if they do so as part of standardized procedures that apply to every towed or impounded car. *Colorado v. Bertine*, 479 U.S. 367 (1987).)

48. **No. This is a classic situation demonstrating that when a person *voluntarily consents* to a search, any Fourth Amendment objections he or she might have are waived.** Nothing in the facts suggests that Norma's consent was other than voluntary—there is no sign, for instance, of coercion or deception by Baines. The fact that Baines did not give Norma her *Miranda* warnings or otherwise advise her of the possible consequences of the search is irrelevant—there was no arrest, so *Miranda* warnings were not required, and the Supreme Court has never held that anything like the *Miranda* warnings must be given before permission to search is requested. Nor does it make any difference that Norma thought she had not committed a crime.

49. **No. "When an individual gives consent to another to intrude into an area or activity otherwise protected by the Fourth Amendment, aware that he will thereby reveal to this other person either criminal conduct or evidence of such conduct, that consent is not vitiated merely because**

it would not have been given but for the non-disclosure or affirmative misrepresentation which made the consenting party unaware of the other person's identity as a police officer or police agent." L&I, p. 207. Norma knew, at the time she let Baines into the house, that she would thereby expose her art fraud to him. The fact that she didn't know he was a police officer should make no difference. Her consent will be deemed voluntary and thus effective.

50. Unclear. **Courts are split about the proper result when the police officer admits that he or she is a police officer, but gains consent to search by misstating the purpose of the search. Where the purpose is such that the consenter knows that his or her evidence of criminality will be revealed to the person (even though he or she is confused about whether the discovery of that criminality is the purpose of the search), a strong argument can be made that there has been no real privacy violation, and that the consent should be regarded as voluntary.** By this standard, the consent here should be binding, since Norma knew that Baines would or at least might spot her in-process forgery efforts. But other courts have held that when the police intentionally lie about the purpose of their search, the consent has been fraudulently procured and should not be binding.

51. Yes. **Where the consent to search was procured after the officer falsely stated that he had a search warrant, the consent will be deemed to be invalid.** *Bumper v. North Carolina*, 391 U.S. 543 (1968). In this case, it is easy to see that the person's consent is not really voluntary—the person is or may be responding to the fact that a refusal to consent will be meaningless because the officer has a warrant.

52. No. **If the third person and the defendant have joint authority over the premises or over an object, the third party's consent to a search will be binding on the defendant.** When a husband and wife live together, they will almost always be presumed to have joint control over the premises, and the facts here tell us that Henry and Wanda both had ownership and control over the rifle. Therefore, Wanda had authority to consent to the search of premises and the search and seizure of the rifle, so her consent will be binding on Henry. The fact that Wanda was mistaken about her husband's guilt or the danger from consenting to a search is irrelevant.

53. No. **Where an object is the sole property of the consentor, the fact that the defendant has not or would not consent to a search (and even the fact that this lack of consent is known to the police) will not invalidate the effectiveness of the property owner's consent.** The fact that Henry had previously denied consent to the police makes no difference—Wanda owned the rifle and was therefore entitled to let the police examine it.

54. No. **A search will be valid if consent to it is given by a person who the police *reasonably but mistakenly believe* has joint authority over the premises. See *Illinois v. Rodriguez*, 497 U.S. 177 (1990), involving similar facts.** The basic idea is that the Fourth Amendment bars only "unreasonable" searches and seizures, and where the police reasonably but mistakenly believe there is joint authority, the search is a "reasonable" one.

55. No. **As a result of a 2006 decision, the third party's consent will not be binding on the defendant, at least where it appears that the third person and the defendant have equal claim to the premises.** *Georgia v. Randolph*, 547 U.S. 103 (2006). The fact that James is present and objecting at the time of Loretta's consent—rather than absent without the chance to object—makes all the difference.

56. Yes. **Larry did not have joint authority over the room, or even "apparent" authority (since it should have been clear to the police that Larry was merely a landlord, not a joint occupant, of the bedroom). Therefore, Larry's consent was not effective vis-à-vis Troy. See *Stoner v. California*, 376 U.S. 483 (1964) (the management of a hotel may not consent to a search of a guest's room).**

This is not a case in which the two parties, Troy and Larry, had "joint authority" over the premises. Instead, Troy had a vastly greater right of access to, and expectation of privacy in, his bedroom.

57. **(a)** The "stop and frisk" doctrine. **By this doctrine, an officer may stop and briefly detain a person, even without probable cause for an arrest, if the officer has an** *articulable reason, based on objective facts,* **for suspecting that the person may have committed a crime.** (The officer may also do a superficial frisk of the suspect if he or she has reason to believe the suspect dangerous, an aspect not at issue on these facts.)

(b) No. **Under the "stop and frisk" doctrine, an officer may stop and briefly detain a person, even without probable cause for an arrest, if the officer has an articulable reason, based on objective facts, for suspecting that the person may have committed a crime.** The stop of Marla was certainly a Fourth Amendment "seizure," since it was reasonably apparent to Marla that she was not free to leave without answering Noonan's questions. However, this is a situation in which the "stop and frisk" doctrine makes the Fourth Amendment seizure a "reasonable" one even though there was not full probable cause for an arrest. Noonan certainly had a number of objective reasons for suspecting that Marla might have something to do with the break-in. The fact that the break-in had just occurred, that the alarm had just started, that Marla was walking more rapidly than a person usually would, and that she was walking away from the car holding a bag that might easily contain a radio—all of these factors were, when taken together, enough to raise the kind of "reasonable hunch" that would justify at least a brief stop. Once Marla refused to answer the questions, ran away, and left a bag holding a radio, then, of course, Noonan had probable cause to arrest her.

58. No. **This question, at first glance, seems to involve the question of whether Nelson had enough suspicion to make a "stop" of the** *Terry* **"stop and frisk" variety. However, in reality, no stop (or other Fourth Amendment seizure) occurred at all. In deciding whether a Fourth Amendment seizure has occurred, the Supreme Court uses a "reasonable person" test, by which a seizure has occurred only "if, in view of all of the circumstances surrounding the incident, a reasonable person would have believed that he was not free to leave."** *U.S. v. Mendenhall,* **446 U.S. 544 (1980).**

Vern did not know, initially, that Nelson was a police officer, or that he was anything other than what he purported to be, which was a civilian who wanted directions. Therefore, a reasonable person in Vern's position would have believed that he was free to disregard the request for information and to drive on. Since Vern's freedom of motion was not circumscribed, there was no Fourth Amendment "seizure" of his person or of his vehicle, up until the moment where Nelson saw the hot-wiring and made the arrest. Therefore, it didn't matter that Nelson had absolutely no rational grounds for suspicion at the time he walked up to the car and requested the information.

59. Yes, probably. **Here, there was a true "seizure" within the meaning of the Fourth Amendment— Vern knew he was dealing with a police officer, and a reasonable person in his position would have understood that he was not free to disregard Nelson's request and drive away. Therefore, the "stop" violated the Fourth Amendment unless Nelson had a "reasonable suspicion, based on objective facts, that the [suspect] is involved in criminal activity."** *Brown v. Texas,* **443 U.S. 47 (1979).** The facts tell us that he did not—for instance, the fact that Vern "looked suspicious" and was seen driving in a high-crime area will not suffice to justify a stop. Since Nelson would not have gotten his "plain view" through the window if he had not made the stop, and since the stop was an unreasonable seizure (even though it did not amount to a full arrest), presumably the fruits of that plain view will be suppressed.

60. Yes, probably. **By taking Maria aside and questioning her, Oswald undoubtedly committed a "stop," since it should have been clear to a reasonable person in Maria's position that she was not free to leave. Therefore, the question is whether Oswald had "reasonable suspicion, based on objective facts, that [Maria] was involved in criminal activity."** *Brown v. Texas*, **443 U.S. 47 (1979).** Almost certainly, the facts here do not meet the standard. Indeed, the factors here were among those relied on by the prosecution in *Reid v. Georgia*, 448 U.S. 438 (1980), yet the total "suspicious" facts there were found not to justify a stop. The problem here is that a large number of completely innocent passengers might meet some or all of the three factors relied on here. Also, the fact that these factors are listed in the "drug courier profile" does not help the prosecution—a reviewing court will make its own determination of whether the facts justified reasonable suspicion. Since the stop of Maria was a violation of her Fourth Amendment rights, the resulting confession will almost certainly be excluded as fruit of the poisonous tree.

61. No, probably. **The facts here are similar to those of** *U.S. v. Sokolow*, **490 U.S. 1 (1989) (though that case involved a trip from Honolulu to Miami). There, the Court held that the DEA agents had sufficient grounds for a stop (though not for a full arrest), because although each of these facts taken by itself was completely consistent with noncriminal behavior, taken together they created a plausible scenario of drug smuggling.** Since Oswald was justified in conducting a stop of Maria, no Fourth Amendment violation occurred as long as the stop was not so long or so intrusive as to constitute a full-scale "arrest." If Oswald had taken Maria into a private room and confronted her one-on-one, this might have been an arrest, but his single question to her near the counter, even though it was probably part of a stop, was not so intrusive or lengthy as to go beyond the bounds of a stop.

62. Yes, probably. **The initial stop probably did not violate the Fourth Amendment—the facts suggest that Mulroney had "reasonable suspicion, based on objective facts" that the computer may have been stolen and that Evan either stole it or knew that it was stolen. She was therefore entitled to detain him briefly and to question him briefly. But she was almost certainly not entitled to require him to come to the station house to answer additional questions—this was such a more intrusive procedure, and of such greater duration, that it probably raised the episode from a "stop" to a full-fledged arrest, for which probable cause was required. See** *Hayes v. Florida*, **470 U.S. 811 (1985), holding that a station-house detention, even though brief and unaccompanied by interrogation, is "sufficiently like [an] arrest to invoke the traditional rule that arrests may constitutionally be made only on probable cause."**

There is some chance that the prosecutor can succeed with the argument that the police worked as rapidly and unintrusively as possible, consistent with their need to discover whether a particular computer with a particular serial number was indeed stolen. But this argument will probably be rejected on the grounds that the time and distance were simply too great to constitute a stop. Since Evan confessed only after the police learned that the computer was stolen, he has a very good chance of having his confession ruled the fruit of the illegal pseudo-arrest.

63. Yes, probably. **Pasternak was acting properly when he detained Fiona, since his suspicions were sufficiently reasonable and objective that they justified a "stop," even though not a full-fledged arrest. An officer, once he has made a lawful stop, is entitled to do a protective two-part frisk (first a pat-down and then reaching under the surface if the pat-down discloses something), provided that the pat-down is for a** *weapon*. **Even where an officer has made a legitimate stop, he may not perform a frisk with the sole purpose of finding contraband or evidence.** *Ybarra v. Illinois*, **444 U.S. 85 (1979).** Since Pasternak did not suspect that Fiona was armed or dangerous, and he was merely frisking her to find the contraband, this frisk was unlawful since he did not have

probable cause to arrest her or probable cause to believe that he might find contraband. Because the frisk went beyond the bounds of the Fourth Amendment, the fruits from that frisk (the packet) must be suppressed.

64. **Yes, probably. On these facts, as opposed to those of the prior question, Pasternak was at least justified in conducting the initial pat-down to discover whether Fiona carried a weapon. But since Pasternak was looking for a knife or a gun (and certainly knew that virtually any dangerous weapon would have to be hard), he could not have believed that the soft object he was feeling could be a weapon.** Consequently, Pasternak was not entitled to reach into Fiona's pocket to retrieve the soft parcel.

65. (a) **No. Where the officer makes an investigative stop of a vehicle and believes that the driver may be dangerous, the officer can not only perform the pat-down but also check the inside of the passenger compartment (even if the driver has been asked to exit). See *Michigan v. Long*, 63 U.S. 1032 (1983). (And nothing in *Arizona v. Gant*, 129 S. Ct. 1710 (2009), eliminating the police's automatic right to search the passenger compartment incident to a driver's arrest, changes this fact, since the search here was an officer-safety check, not a search incident to arrest.)** Since Quarles had the right to look for weapons (although not to look for the purpose of finding contraband or evidence), he was entitled to seize any contraband he found in plain view while performing this weapons scan. Therefore, the marijuana should be admissible.

(b) **No. Once a proper investigative stop of a vehicle occurs, the police are entitled to do a patdown of any passenger—even one whom they have no suspicion of wrongdoing—as long as the police have a reasonable suspicion that the passenger may be armed and dangerous. *Arizona v. Johnson*, 129 S. Ct. 781 (2009).** Once Officer Ramon saw Howard's tattoo and understood that it marked Howard as a member of the Tweets, Ramon's knowledge that Tweets members typically carry switchblades gave him reasonable suspicion that Howard might be armed and dangerous.

66. **No. The informant's tip, although it did not amount to probable cause, certainly was specific enough and objective enough that it would have allowed a *Terry*-like stop of Smith. The Supreme Court has held that in these circumstances, the police may instead *briefly* detain the luggage without detaining the suspect/owner. See *U.S. v. Place*, 462 U.S. 696 (1983), allowing a brief detention and canine sniffing of luggage on similar facts, but holding that a 90-minute delay between initial seizure and conducting of the sniff was too long.** The agents might not have been justified in detaining the bag for a long time, or in opening it, but they were justified in keeping possession of it for the brief five-minute period to conduct the nonintrusive canine sniff. Once the sniff proved positive, they certainly had probable cause to get a warrant, and were thus justified in keeping the bag until a warrant could be procured.

67. **No. The Supreme Court has repeatedly held that travelers may be stopped as they enter the United States and their possessions checked for contraband. The agent may do so based on mere suspicion, or in fact no suspicion at all, and may do so without a search warrant.** Some types of intrusion may be so severe that they need a higher degree of suspicion (e.g., a strip search or a rectal search for drugs), but the mere inspection of baggage does not fall within this "extremely intrusive" category, so neither objective grounds for suspicion nor a warrant is required.

68. **Yes. Immigration officials may conduct such a "roving patrol" in the interior, so long as they merely briefly question the occupants rather than conducting a full-scale search. The officers do not need probable cause to do this. However, the official must have a "*particularized and**

objective basis" for suspecting that the people in the vehicle may have committed an immigration violation. The Mexican appearance of the car's inhabitants is not by itself sufficient to allow even a brief stop for questioning, like the one that happened here. *U.S. v. Brignoni-Ponce*, 422 U.S. 873 (1975). (But attempts by the driver to evade the officer, the presence of an extraordinary number of passengers in the car, or a Mexican mode of dress or haircut are each additional factors that, when added to Mexican ancestry, might be sufficient to justify a stop. See *Brignoni-Ponce*.)

69. Yes. The Supreme Court has held that the police may not follow a practice of randomly stopping cars to check such things as licensing and registration. *Delaware v. Prouse*, 440 U.S. 648 (1979). Only if the officer has some objective suspicion that the particular driver has committed an offense may he or she stop the car. (A checkpoint scheme where *every* car is stopped would pass muster; the problem comes where each officer is given discretion about which cars to stop randomly.)

70. No. The prior question establishes that police may not randomly stop cars to check for traffic violations. But the police may set up a fixed "*sobriety checkpoint*" to check for drunk driving. The stop at such a checkpoint is a "seizure" for Fourth Amendment purposes. Nonetheless, each driver may be stopped even though the police have no particular suspicion about any one driver. The police may then engage in brief questioning to spot signs of intoxication, and may use further procedures (including giving a Breathalyzer or walk-the-line test) when they have particular and objective reasons to believe that the driver is drunk. *Michigan Department of State Police v. Sitz*, 496 U.S. 444 (1990).

    It appears that such a sobriety checkpoint will be allowed only when the police stop every car (or perhaps some mathematically determined selection of cars, such as every fourth car). If the police use their own discretion about which cars to stop, the scheme probably fails in the same way that random traffic stops failed in *Delaware v. Prouse* (cited in the prior question). Here, the procedures used were satisfactory, since all cars were stopped, and since the intrusion on Edmund was very minimal until he showed signs of drunkenness.

71. Yes. Bugging and wiretapping are "searches," as the term is used in the Fourth Amendment. Therefore, absent exigent circumstances, bugging and wiretapping may not occur except on probable cause and with a warrant. In fact, a federal statute, so-called Title III (18 U.S.C. §§2510-20), prohibits all eavesdropping and wiretapping without a court order. The bugging here clearly violates both Title III and the Fourth Amendment, and Louie can keep his bugged statement out of evidence.

72. No. The Supreme Court has held that "*secret agents*"—that is, people who engage in conversations with a suspect without the suspect's knowing that the other party is a police officer or informant—are not conducting "searches," and thus cannot violate the Fourth Amendment. This is true whether the agent is "bugged" or "unbugged." See, e.g., *U.S. v. White*, 401 U.S. 745 (1971). Furthermore, the prohibitions against bugging and wiretapping contained in Title III expressly exclude (and thus permit) interceptions made by or with the *consent of a party to the conversation*. Even though Harriet was a police officer, and Melvin did not know this, recording Melvin's statement does not violate either the Fourth Amendment or Title III. (However, if the bug had been used to record a conversation between Melvin and someone else, at which Harriet was not present, then Title III would apply and the statement could not be used; the difference here is that Harriet was a party to the communication being intercepted.)

73. No, because Claude was not given his *Miranda* warnings. This is a classic illustration of when *Miranda* warnings must be given: The suspect was in custody, and he was questioned by the police; therefore, the police were required to tell him (1) that he had the right to remain silent,

(2) that anything he said could be used against him in a court of law, (3) that he had the right to have an attorney present before any questioning, and (4) that if he could not afford an attorney, one would be appointed for him before questioning, if he wished. Since Claude was not given these warnings, nothing he said may be used against him. It doesn't matter that Claude's confession was in a sense "voluntary," rather than "coerced"; *Miranda* is a "bright line"—i.e., automatic—rule.

74. **No. It is true that Dennis was in "custody" at the time he made his statement, and that his statement was in response to a question asked by someone who was in fact a police officer. Thus the formal requirements for *Miranda* (custody and police interrogation) seem to be met. However, the Supreme Court has held that where the defendant talks to an undercover agent or a government informant, and the defendant does not *know* that he is talking to a law enforcement officer, no "custodial interrogation" will be deemed to have taken place, even if the exchange occurs while the defendant is in jail. Therefore, *Miranda* warnings do not have to be given in this situation. See *Illinois v. Perkins*, 496 U.S. 292 (1990), involving facts similar to those in this question.**

75. **No, probably. The issue, of course, is whether Elvira was "in custody" at the time she made the statement. The Supreme Court seems to follow an "objective" standard for determining whether somebody is in custody for *Miranda* purposes: The suspect will be deemed to have been in custody if a *reasonable person* in the suspect's position would have *understood that he or she was not free to go*. See *Berkemer v. McCarty*, 468 U.S. 420 (1984), establishing this test.**

    Here, the situation amounted to custody by this standard—a reasonable person in Elvira's position, after being told that she could not (or at least should not) go to the grocery store, would probably have felt that she was not free to leave or to evict Bess whenever she wanted. Since Elvira was in custody, and since Bess was a police officer interrogating her (and Elvira knew that Bess was a police officer), the requirements for *Miranda* warnings were satisfied. Since *Miranda* warnings were not given, Elvira's statement may not be introduced against her as part of the prosecution's case in chief.

76. **Yes. The requirement of *Miranda* warnings is triggered wherever the police conduct a custodial interrogation of someone who they think may have something to do with or know something about a possible crime. The fact that the police are not certain that a crime has been committed, or the fact that the investigation was not "focused" on the person being interrogated, does not make a difference. See *Stansbury v. California*, 511 U.S. 318 (1994).** Since Frank was clearly in custody (in the sense that a reasonable person in his position would have known he was not free to leave without answering the questions), and since he was clearly being interrogated by a police officer, *Miranda* warnings needed to be given.

77. **No, probably. The Supreme Court has held that ordinary stops of a driver for minor traffic violations normally will not constitute a taking into custody for *Miranda* purposes. See *Berkemer v. McCarty*, 468 U.S. 420 (1984), holding that since such stops are generally temporary and brief, and the motorist knows that he will probably be allowed to go on his way, *Miranda* warnings do not have to be given.** Here, Jermaine had no reason to believe (at least, no reason apart from her own knowledge that she had committed a crime) that this was anything other than a routine traffic stop that would allow her to go on her way when she promised to get the taillight fixed. She had no reason to believe that she had been arrested or would be arrested. Therefore, the coercive element usually associated with custodial interrogation was not present here, and it is unlikely that the court would find that *Miranda* warnings had to be given.

78. **No, probably. The fact that the defendant was at a police station or in jail at the time he made the incriminating statement is certainly a factor making it more likely that he was in custody than**

if the statement had taken place at some other, more neutral place (e.g., the defendant's home). But presence at the station house does not automatically make the situation custodial—if the defendant was present at the station house *"voluntarily,"* in response to a request by the police for cooperation rather than in response to an arrest, there is a good chance that the court will find the situation noncustodial. See *Oregon v. Mathiason*, 429 U.S. 492 (1977) (D came to station in response to officer's message that officer would "like to discuss something with you"; no custody was found to exist, and thus no *Miranda* warnings were required). Here, where Harold did not believe that the investigation had focused on him, and where the police said that they were requesting his help rather than arresting him or demanding that he come in, custody will probably be found not to exist.

79. Yes. **There is no *"minor crimes"* exception to the *Miranda* requirement—if an interrogation meets all of the standard requirements for *Miranda* warnings (especially the requirement that the suspect be "in custody"), these warnings must be given no matter how minor the crime, and regardless of the fact that no jail sentence may be imposed for it.** *Berkemer v. McCarty*, 468 U.S. 420 (1984).

80. (a) That Jill's statement was not in response to any "interrogation." **It is not enough that the suspect makes an incriminating statement while in custody—*Miranda* only applies where there is "interrogation" during the custody.** The prosecutor should argue that Detective Reynolds may have made statements, but he did not ask questions, so that there was no interrogation.

    (b) No, probably. **The Supreme Court has held that there can be "interrogation" even though there is no direct questioning. The Court has held that "the term 'interrogation' . . . refers not only to express questioning, but also to any words or actions on the part of the police (other than those normally attendant to arrest and custody) that the police should know are reasonably likely to elicit an incriminating response from a suspect."** Rhode Island v. Innis, 446 U.S. 291 (1980). Reynolds, by going into such detail about the evidence the police had against Jill, and by mentioning how desirable it would be if Jill were to confess, should probably have known that some incriminating response was likely to be made by Jill in response. The fact that Reynolds volunteered the information on his own, without stating it in response to a question by Jill, further reinforces the argument that Jill must have understood Reynolds's statements as an attempt to get her to talk.

81. No, probably. **In a somewhat similar situation where the police set up a meeting between the suspect and his spouse in front of the police, the Supreme Court held that no interrogation took place when the suspect made a statement to the spouse.** *Arizona v. Mauro*, 481 U.S. 520 (1987). The court in *Mauro* held that "officers do not interrogate a suspect simply by hoping that he will incriminate himself." This would seem to render Jill's statements ones not made under interrogation, and thus ones not covered by *Miranda*. (However, the Court found in *Mauro* that the police officer there had not *intended* to try to use the encounter to elicit incriminating information from the suspect; here, the facts tell us that this *was* part of Reynolds's intent. But since *Rhode Island v. Innis* tells us that what really matters is the probable effect on the suspect—whether the police conduct is reasonably likely to elicit an incriminating response from the suspect—and since most suspects do not blurt out admissions in front of police officers merely because they are speaking to their spouses, a court would probably hold that the likelihood of any incriminating statement was sufficiently small that no interrogation should be found to have existed, whatever Reynolds's intent may have been.)

82. (a) The "public safety" exception to *Miranda*. **The Supreme Court has recognized a "public safety" exception to the *Miranda* rule: *Miranda* warnings are simply unnecessary prior to**

questioning that is "reasonably prompted by a concern for the public safety." *New York v. Quarles*, 467 U.S. 649 (1984).

(b) Yes. **The Supreme Court has recognized a "public safety" exception to the *Miranda* rule: *Miranda* warnings are simply unnecessary prior to questioning that is "reasonably prompted by a concern for the public safety." *New York v. Quarles*, 467 U.S. 649 (1984).** Ken was certainly in custody at the time he made the statement, and he certainly made the statement in response to interrogation. But since it was quite possible that other accomplices were holding Nell, and that time might be of the essence in saving her from further harm, the court would almost certainly find that the "public safety" exception applied.

83. No. **The Supreme Court held that a warning virtually identical to the one here was sufficient, in *Duckworth v. Eagan*, 492 U.S. 195 (1989).** The Court held that such a warning should reasonably have suggested to the suspect that although he couldn't have a court-appointed lawyer until he went to trial, the police would not interrogate him before then if he asked for a court-appointed lawyer and they couldn't get him one.

84. Yes, probably. **In *Miranda* itself, the Court stated that "the Fifth Amendment privilege is so fundamental to our system of constitutional rule and the expedient of giving an adequate warning as to the availability of the privilege so simple, we will not pause to inquire in individual cases whether the defendant was aware of his rights without a warning being given."** Subsequent lower-court cases have held that even where the defendant is a lawyer who almost certainly knew his or her rights, this will not excuse a failure to give the warnings.

85. No, probably. **The Supreme Court has never expressly dealt with the issue of whether a subject known to be wealthy enough to afford his own lawyer must nonetheless be given the "court-appointed lawyer" portion of the *Miranda* warnings. But lower courts have generally agreed that if the defendant was actually able to afford his own lawyer, and the police were aware of that ability, their failure to give this portion of the warning is not fatal.**

86. No. **The defendant's silence and his subsequent answering of questions, without anything more, will never be held to be a valid waiver of the right to remain silent or of the right to have a lawyer present.**

87. No. **In a case involving similar facts, the Supreme Court held that the defendant's waiver was "knowing and voluntary," and thus effective. *Moran v. Burbine*, 475 U.S. 412 (1986). Even though the defendant might have reached a different decision about whether to waive his rights if he had known that a lawyer had been retained and was trying to reach him, the *Moran* Court felt that this was irrelevant—the defendant knew his rights and made a conscious decision to waive them; this was all that mattered.** Omar will be held to have knowingly waived his rights, and the confession will be admitted against him.

88. No. **The Supreme Court has never dealt with whether police trickery regarding the strength of their case voids a *Miranda* waiver. However, almost certainly the decision in *Moran v. Burbine* (see prior answer) would be binding in this situation as well, since the fact that the police have a strong or weak case has no bearing on whether the defendant understands his or her rights and has consciously chosen to waive them. Lower courts that have considered this "trickery regarding the strength of the police case" issue have generally held that the waiver is nonetheless effective.**

89. No. **On similar facts, the Supreme Court held that a confession to another, more serious crime need not be suppressed. *Colorado v. Spring*, 479 U.S. 564 (1987). The fact that the suspect believes**

that he or she is being interrogated only about Crime 1 (a minor crime), and gives his or her *Miranda* waiver on that assumption, does not prevent his or her being questioned about, or his or her confession being admissible as to Crime 2, even if that crime is much more serious. (This assumes that the police have not affirmatively misrepresented the likely scope of the questioning; *Spring* deals only with the situation where the police are silent about the possibility of questioning on the second crime. Since Detective Wagner did not say one way or the other what the questioning would be about, and it was merely the situation that led Paul to presume that the questions would relate only to the North Avenue case, the rationale of *Spring* is applicable here.)

90. Unclear. In *Colorado v. Spring* (see prior answer), the Supreme Court carefully declined to consider whether an affirmative misstatement by the police as to the nature of their questioning would produce a different result than where the police were merely silent concerning what they planned to ask about. So, where (as in this question) the police tell a suspect that the interrogation will involve Crime 1 while they intend to ask him about Crime 2, this may well be police "trickery" sufficient to invalidate the *Miranda* waiver.

91. Unclear. The only Supreme Court case involving the rights of the police to reinitiate questioning after the defendant has asserted his right to remain silent is *Michigan v. Mosley*, 423 U.S. 96 (1975). There, the second questioning was considerably later, by a different officer, and about a *different crime* than the subject of the first questioning. On those facts, the Court held that D's *Miranda* rights were not violated by the resumption of questioning. Here, most facts are similar to those in *Mosley*: A substantial time passed between the two questioning sessions, and a different officer did the second questioning. But the same crime was involved in both situations, so the issue becomes whether this makes the decisive difference; lower courts have disagreed about whether the police may resume questioning without any change in subject matter.

92. No. On almost precisely these facts, the Supreme Court has held that the resumption of questioning without the suspect's lawyer present violates *Miranda* and the post-*Miranda* case of *Edwards v. Arizona*, 451 U.S. 477 (1981). See *Minnick v. Mississippi*, 498 U.S. 146 (1990) ("When counsel is requested, interrogation must cease, and officials may not reinitiate interrogation without counsel present, regardless of whether the accused has consulted with his attorney.") Observe that Quentin does better by asking for a lawyer than he does by merely asserting that he wants to remain silent.

93. No. The Supreme Court has held that where the defendant takes the stand and makes a statement, the prosecution may use a confession obtained in violation of *Miranda* to *impeach the defendant's credibility* as a witness. *Harris v. New York*, 401 U.S. 222 (1971). (But if the statement was not only obtained in violation of *Miranda*, but also was coerced or was involuntary, then it cannot be used even for impeachment purposes. See *Mincey v. Arizona*, 437 U.S. 385 (1978). However, there is no evidence of coercion or involuntariness on the facts here.)

94. Yes. Where the defendant remains silent after being given his *Miranda* warnings, this fact may not be used to impeach the defendant at trial. *Doyle v. Ohio*, 426 U.S. 610 (1976).

95. No. The privilege of self-incrimination applies only to responses by the suspect that are essentially "*testimonial.*" A wide variety of physical identification procedures have been held not to be testimonial, and thus not subject to the privilege against self-incrimination. For example, the suspect may be ordered, against his will, to furnish a blood sample. *Schmerber v. California*, 384 U.S. 757 (1966).

96. No, probably. The privilege of self-incrimination applies only to responses by the suspect that are essentially "*testimonial.*" Again (as in the prior question), the issue is whether Stan's response on

the test was essentially "testimonial." Stan can argue that it is—he can contend that by misspelling "evacuate," he is essentially telling the court, "This is the way I spell the word 'evacuate.'" The prosecution can argue that his response is not really testimonial but is rather more of a simple identification device. The usefulness of his response, for instance, does not depend on whether the court believes the "truth" of what Stan says when he writes the note (thus distinguishing this situation from one in which Stan writes out a confession, and the confession is offered in court to prove the truth of the statements contained in that confession). The prosecution's position will probably win, in light of *Pennsylvania v. Muniz*, 496 U.S. 582 (1990), holding that requiring a drunk-driving suspect to answer questions to test his mental acuity (e.g., "In what year did you have your sixth birthday?") did not violate his self-incrimination rights.

97. The Sixth Amendment right to counsel. **The Supreme Court has held that a suspect has an absolute right to have *counsel present* at any pretrial confrontation procedure (e.g., lineup or show-up) if "adversary judicial criminal proceedings" have commenced against him (e.g., an indictment).** *U.S. v. Wade*, 388 U.S. 218 (1967); *Kirby v. Illinois*, 406 U.S. 682 (1972). Since Tom had already been indicted, and thus "adversarial judicial criminal proceedings" had commenced against him, he had an absolute right to have a lawyer (a court-appointed lawyer if necessary) present to advise him and to make sure that the proceedings were not unduly suggestive. Because the police did not honor this right, the fruits of the lineup will be excluded, even though nothing in these facts suggests that the lineup was in fact unduly suggestive or otherwise unfair to Tom.

98. Yes. **Where a lineup is held without the presence of counsel, and thus violates the rule of *U.S. v. Wade*, 388 U.S. 218 (1967), not only may the prosecution not introduce at trial the fact that the defendant was picked out of a lineup, but the prosecution will even have to make a special showing before the witness who made the lineup identification will be allowed to testify in court that the person sitting in the dock is the person observed by the witness at the crime scene. The prosecution must show by "clear and convincing evidence" that the in-court identification is not the "fruit of the poisonous tree" (i.e., not the product of the improper lineup identification).** The prosecution has made no showing that Sheila's in-court identification does not stem from her lineup identification. (That is, the prosecution has not shown that Sheila had a long time to identify Tom during the burglary, that she correctly described Tom before the lineup, or anything else to dispel the possibility that Sheila may be remembering Tom's face from the lineup and not from the earlier burglary). The prosecution therefore loses.

99. No. **The right to have counsel present in lineup proceedings only attaches when "adversary judicial criminal proceedings" have commenced against the defendant.** An indictment, a formal charge, a preliminary hearing, an arraignment—any of these would constitute the initiation of adversary judicial criminal proceedings. But the mere making of a warrantless arrest, even when coupled with taking the defendant to the police station and holding her in custody, does *not* amount to adversary judicial criminal proceedings, according to nearly all lower courts that have considered the issue (though the Supreme Court has never decided this point). So, even though Ursula actually requested her lawyer, and even though the risk to her of unfairness from the lineup was arguably just as great as if she had already been, say, arraigned, she is deemed to have no right to counsel. Therefore, the lineup results may be admitted against her (at least if the way the lineup was carried out was not grossly unfair judged by the "totality of the circumstances").

100. No. **Even after adversary judicial criminal proceedings have begun against the defendant, the defendant has no right to have counsel present where witnesses view still or moving pictures of the suspect for ID purposes. See *U.S. v. Ash*, 413 U.S. 300 (1973).** In other words, picking Ursula's

photo out of a "photo array" is deemed to be something quite different from picking Ursula herself out of a lineup—in the former situation, there is no right to have counsel present, whereas in the latter there is.

101. (a) That the identification violated Vincent's right to due process. **If a lineup identification (or other confrontation) is so "*unnecessarily suggestive* and conducive to irreparable mistaken identification" that it denies the suspect *due process of law*, that identification will not be admitted into evidence. Whether the identification procedure was so unfair as to amount to such a due process violation is determined by looking at the "totality of the circumstances" surrounding it.** *Stovall v. Denno*, 388 U.S. 293 (1967).

(b) Yes, probably. **It is very hard for the defendant to show that the lineup procedure was so suggestive and unfair that it amounted to a violation of his due process rights. But one of the very rare cases in which the Supreme Court so held involved facts quite similar to these (and in fact, the lineup here was probably even more suggestive, since Vincent was the only Asian the first time). See Foster v. California, 394 U.S. 440 (1969).** In *Foster*, the Court concluded that the procedures were so suggestive that an identification of the defendant as the perpetrator was "all but inevitable"—this seems to be an accurate description of the procedures here as well. (Also, courts take into account the likely *reliability* of the identification, not just the degree of suggestiveness. Here, since the place where the crime took place was very poorly lit, Tina's ability to clearly perceive the rapist and thus later correctly identify him was somewhat impaired, making it more likely that the court would find a due process violation.)

102. No, probably. **It is true that a show-up is an extremely suggestive and unreliable form of identification, compared with, say, a lineup or even a photo array. But the Supreme Court has held that where the exigencies of law enforcement demand very prompt action, and a show-up is more easily arranged than a lineup or a photo array, the show-up may be used despite the risk of undue suggestion.** A prime example of the need for rapid action is where the victim is in the hospital and may soon die. In fact, the fact pattern here is somewhat similar to that of *Stovall v. Denno*, 388 U.S. 293 (1967), where the Supreme Court held that the hospital room show-up, although very suggestive, did not violate the defendant's due process rights. (Also, observe that Vincent had no right to have counsel present, since he had not yet been formally charged.)

103. Yes, probably. **Just as a lineup or show-up may be excluded on the grounds that it is so suggestive that it violates the defendant's due process rights, so a photographic identification may be that suggestive.** Here, the photo ID was equivalent to a one-person show-up—the police did not see whether Upton could pick out Wendy's picture from among a group of photos, but rather, handed him just one photo and said, "We think this is the woman." In that situation, it was almost certain that Upton would identify Wendy. Also, given the short period of time that Upton had to glimpse the driver, there is additional reason to doubt the reliability of his identification.

But such due process issues are determined by the "totality of the circumstances," and there are no hard-and-fast rules. A court might conclude that the photo ID, although suggestive, was not so unfair as to be a due process violation. See, e.g., *Simmons v. U.S.*, 390 U.S. 377 (1968), finding that a photo ID did not violate the defendant's due process rights, even though he appeared, together with others, in all six of the photographs shown to the victim.

104. No. **It is true that the exclusionary rule allows evidence seized in violation of the Fourth Amendment to be suppressed ("excluded") from criminal trials. However, the defendant may only obtain suppression of materials that were seized in violation of *his or her own* expectation of privacy. This is the rule of "*standing.*" See *Alderman v. U.S.* 394 U.S. 165 (1969).** The break-in by

Officer Jackson, made without probable cause and without a warrant, was clearly illegal and a violation of Albert's Fourth Amendment rights. But that break-in did not violate *Bertha's* rights, since she had no possessory interest in Albert's apartment, was not present there, and did not "own" the letter once she had sent it. Since no reasonable expectation of privacy on Bertha's part was violated by the search, the illegality cannot serve as the basis for suppression of the letter in her trial.

105. **No. Bart's problem is that he lacks standing to object to the unlawful seizure and search of Karen. The fact that Bart had a possessory interest in the cocaine seized is not by itself enough to allow him to challenge the constitutionality of the seizure. Only if Bart's possession of the cocaine gave him a legitimate expectation of privacy with respect to that item will Bart be allowed to protest.** *Rawlings v. Kentucky*, **448 U.S. 98 (1980).** Once Bart put the cocaine on Karen's person, where any customs agent might look at it, and where Karen might have shown it to third parties (e.g., her friends), Bart almost certainly lost any expectation of privacy he had regarding that cocaine. The facts here are similar to those in *Rawlings* (D put his drugs in X's handbag, which was then illegally searched; D was held to have no right to object to the search and seizure of the drugs).

106. **Yes. Where evidence is indirectly derived from a violation of the defendant's constitutional rights, that evidence will often be suppressed—this is the *"fruit of the poisonous tree"* doctrine, by which an initial constitutional violation (the "tree") will be deemed to "taint" the evidence that is indirectly found because of it (the "fruit").** Danielle's confession would almost certainly be found to be tainted fruit from the "tree" of the stop made without probable cause, and the arrest made without probable cause. If Katz had never made his illegal stop of Danielle's car, and his illegal arrest, she never would have been in a position to confess at the station house.

   In cases where the confession derives from an illegal arrest or stop, the prosecution can sometimes show that the taint was *"purged"* by intervening events. But the mere giving of *Miranda* warnings, and the suspect's "voluntary" decision to confess, are generally held not to be the kind of intervening events that will purge the taint. So, here, the relation between the confession and the prior illegal stop/arrest is so strong, and the police wrongdoing so great, that the "fruits of the poisonous tree" doctrine will almost certainly be applied. See, e.g., *Wong Sun v. U.S.*, 371 U.S. 471 (1963) (illegal arrest of D was followed by his confession; the confession must be suppressed because it was the fruit of the illegal arrest).

107. (a) The "independent source" doctrine. **If a particular piece of evidence comes from two sources, only one of which derives from the illegality that the defendant complains of, the exclusionary rule does not apply.**

   (b) No. **Since the government has an "independent source" for the contested evidence, the illegality is not the "but for" cause of the evidence's availability, and the illegality is thus ignored.** The prosecution already had the July 1 letter in its possession, so this constituted an "independent source" for that letter. The fact that the government did not focus on the document, and learned of the document's significance only due to the illegal questioning of Gordon, will probably not prevent the independent source doctrine from applying here. Also, although the government acted illegally in getting Ivan's copy of the letter, Gordon does not have standing to object to the violation of Ivan's rights. Even though every step taken by the federal agents was grossly illegal, they end up with evidence they can use to convict Gordon.

108. **No. Here, as in the prior question, the "independent source" exception saves the prosecution. On very similar facts, the Supreme Court held that since the police ultimately seized the evidence based on a properly issued warrant, the fact that they first viewed the evidence by an illegal**

break-in was irrelevant—the subsequent with-warrant seizure was an "independent source." See *Murray v. U.S.*, 487 U.S. 533 (1988).

If the court believed that the police would not have bothered to get a warrant had they not first broken in and seen the evidence, the result might be otherwise. But here, the facts tell us that if the police had been unable to break in, they would have taken the extra trouble to get a warrant anyway. That being the case, the second entry is viewed as an independent source. The fact that the first break-in made life easier for the police (in the sense that had they not discovered anything wrong, they would not have bothered to get the warrant) is viewed as irrelevant.

109. (a) The "inevitable discovery" doctrine. **Under this exception, evidence may be admitted if it would "inevitably" have been discovered by other police techniques had it not first been obtained through the illegal discovery. The prosecution bears the burden of showing, by a preponderance of the evidence, that the information would inevitably have been discovered by lawful means.** *Nix v. Williams*, **467 U.S. 431 (1984).**

(b) No. **Under this exception, evidence may be admitted if it would "inevitably" have been discovered by other police techniques had it not first been obtained through the illegal discovery. The prosecution bears the burden of showing, by a preponderance of the evidence, that the information would inevitably have been discovered by lawful means. Nix v. Williams, 467 U.S. 431 (1984).** This is a situation in which the "inevitable discovery" rule should apply. The police were in the process of examining the records of every local pawnshop and gun shop to check on anyone who had bought a Smith & Wesson .38. Although they had not yet found Kent's name, the police would inevitably have gotten to that particular pawnshop, and would then have found Kent's name and address. Therefore, they would have looked for Kent until they found him, and would have then either discovered the gun or become increasingly suspicious of Kent if he couldn't produce it. A court would probably be satisfied that the police really would have inevitably discovered the gun even had no illegality taken place.

110. No, probably. **The courts are extremely reluctant to find that a** *"witness lead"* **is the tainted fruit of a poisonous tree. As the Supreme Court has put it, "The exclusionary rule should be invoked with much greater reluctance where the claim is based on a causal relationship between a constitutional violation and the discovery of a live witness than where a similar claim is advanced to support suppression of an inanimate object."** *U.S. v. Ceccolini*, **435 U.S. 268 (1978).** It is true that the police's lead to Morton as a witness (and, indeed, the entire police knowledge that a crime was committed) stemmed directly from Kaplan's illegal look at Leslie's mail. (Kaplan may have had the right to sit at Leslie's desk, since he was there to investigate a burglary reported by her, but this consent clearly did not extend to Kaplan's ransacking through a stack of letters on Leslie's desk, so what he did went beyond the scope of the consent and constituted an illegal search.)

Since Kaplan was not actively looking for evidence against Leslie when he stumbled upon it, and since Morton was in fact anxious to testify (and thus was a most "voluntary" witness), it is unlikely that the court will view Morton's testimony as the tainted fruit of the admitted poisonous tree (the illegal search). (The facts here are somewhat similar to those of *Ceccolini*, where the witness's testimony was admitted.)

111. Yes. **Where evidence is indirectly derived from a violation of the defendant's constitutional rights, that evidence will often be suppressed—this is the** *"fruit of the poisonous tree"* **doctrine, by which an initial constitutional violation (the "tree") will be deemed to "taint" the evidence that is indirectly found because of it (the "fruit").** This is a classic illustration of the "fruit of the poisonous tree" doctrine. The confession derived directly from the arrest—without the arrest, Nelson would not have been subject to station-house questioning by the police and would therefore not have confessed. Furthermore, there was a quality of "purposefulness" in the police's conduct—they knew they were violating Nelson's right to be free of unreasonable seizures, yet they violated that right precisely to have the chance to question him and thus the chance to get a confession. In this situation, a court is very unlikely to hold that the taint of the illegal arrest was "purged" by any subsequent event. The giving of the *Miranda* warnings, and the fact that the confession was "voluntary" rather than "coerced," will almost never by themselves be enough to purge the taint of an illegal arrest. See *Brown v. Illinois*, 422 U.S. 590 (1975), excluding a confession derived from a similar illegal arrest.

112. **No. On very similar facts, in *Rawlings v. Kentucky*, 448 U.S. 98 (1980), the Supreme Court concluded that the spontaneous outburst was not the tainted fruit of the admittedly illegal arrest.** Clearly, there was some connection between the illegal arrest and Peter's self-incriminating statement, but this does not automatically mean that the statement is the tainted fruit of the illegal arrest. The issue is always whether there have been intervening events sufficient to "purge" the taint. The fact that Peter's statement was somewhat voluntary and was not in response to any questioning is a factor strongly tending to purge the taint.

113. **No. The Supreme Court has announced a *per se* rule that where an arrest is made with probable cause, but the arrest is unconstitutional because it is made without a required arrest warrant, the "fruit of the poisonous tree" doctrine will *never* be used—any resulting confession, no matter how directly it stems from the arrest, will not be tainted by the illegal arrest. *New York v. Harris*, 495 U.S. 14 (1990).**

114. **Yes, probably. In this "two-confession" scenario, the second confession will not normally be deemed to be the tainted fruit of the earlier poisoned confession. If the second confession was "knowingly and voluntarily made," it will not be invalidated merely because there was a prior, illegally obtained confession having the same substance. *Oregon v. Elstad*, 470 U.S. 298 (1985). But the post-*Elstad* case of *Missouri v. Seibert*, 542 U.S. 600 (2004), says that where the police make a conscious decision to follow a two-step process with the purpose of undermining *Miranda*—performing unwarned questioning until they get a confession, then giving the *Miranda* warnings, then asking the suspect to repeat the confession—there will be a presumption that the warnings were not effective as to the second confession.** That's what happened here, so *Seibert* means that the warnings will probably be found to be ineffective, in which case the second confession will be found inadmissible.

115. No. When a confession obtained in violation of *Miranda* furnishes the police with leads to additional evidence, such as physical evidence (e.g., stolen property or a murder weapon), such additional evidence will virtually never be treated as tainted fruit merely because the evidence derived from a non-*Mirandized* confession. See *U.S. v. Patane*, 542 U.S. 630 (2004).

116. No. The Supreme Court has held that illegally obtained evidence may always be used to *impeach* statements made by the defendant. This is true even if the illegal evidence is used to impeach statements elicited by the prosecution from the defendant on cross-examination. See *U.S. v. Havens*, 446 U.S. 620 (1980). This is what happened here. Even though it was only in response to the prosecution's questions on cross-examination that Bernard denied having the photo, the prosecution is able to impeach Bernard's testimony by presenting that illegally seized photo. (Of course, Bernard is entitled to a jury instruction stating that the snapshot should only be considered as evidence of Bernard's trustworthiness as a witness, not as direct evidence of whether he committed the crime, but it is questionable whether the jury will truly disregard the snapshot when deciding Bernard's guilt.)

117. Yes. **The prosecution may use illegally obtained evidence to impeach the defendant on cross-examination. But illegally obtained evidence may *not* be used to impeach the testimony of *defense witnesses* other than the defendant himself or herself.** *James v. Illinois*, 493 U.S. 307 (1990). Since the testimony being impeached was that of Fran, not the defendant, *James* means that Egon may successfully object to use of the gun to impeach the testimony. (If the prosecution can convince the judge that the "inevitable discovery" exception, or some other exception to the exclusionary rule, is applicable, then the result would be different, but there is nothing on these facts to suggest that the prosecution can make such a showing.)

118. No. **The Supreme Court has held that the exclusionary rule does not bar the use, even in the prosecution's case-in-chief, of evidence obtained by officers who acted in *reasonable reliance* on a search warrant that was issued by a detached and neutral magistrate but that was ultimately found to be unsupported by probable cause.** *U.S. v. Leon*, 468 U.S. 897 (1984). Since the facts tell us that Lawrence reasonably believed that he had probable cause, furnished an affidavit stating everything he knew, and got the affidavit approved and the warrant issued by a neutral and detached magistrate, the requirements for the special "good-faith" exception of *Leon* are satisfied. The net result is that the prosecution gets to use evidence in its case-in-chief that was seized in direct violation of the Fourth Amendment's prohibitions on warrants issued without probable cause.

119. Yes. **An indigent person must be given court-appointed counsel for his or her trial if he or she is to be sentenced to prison for any length of time upon conviction. It does not matter that the offense is classified as a "misdemeanor" under state law or that the jail term actually imposed is very brief.** *Argersinger v. Hamlin*, 407 U.S. 25 (1972).

120. No. **As long as an indigent defendant is not sentenced to imprisonment, the state is not required to appoint counsel for him or her, even if the offense is one that is punishable by imprisonment. This rule seems to apply even where the offense charged is a felony under state law, so long as the judge does not in fact impose a jail sentence.** *Scott v. Illinois*, 440 U.S. 367 (1979).

121. No. **The Sixth Amendment right to appointed counsel applies only at "critical stages" in the prosecution.** The fact that Lester was confined over the weekend because of the unavailability of a magistrate did not make this confinement a "critical stage," so he was not entitled to counsel during that time. Typically, the earliest "critical stage" in the prosecution will be the arraignment, at which the defendant enters a plea. Usually, counsel does not have to be appointed for a defendant prior to the arraignment. The fact that a lawyer might have been of some use to Lester—for instance, by getting him released over the weekend—is irrelevant to whether Lester had a Sixth Amendment right to counsel at that time.

122. Yes. **So long as the defendant is mentally competent to waive his or her right to counsel, he has a Sixth Amendment right to proceed *pro se*.** *Faretta v. California*, 422 U.S. 806 (1975). This is true even though the court is convinced that the defendant will almost certainly do a poor job of self-representation.

123. No. It is true that the Sixth Amendment does not merely entitle the defendant to have a lawyer, but rather, entitles him or her to the "effective assistance of counsel." However, a defendant whose lawyer has actually participated in the trial must make two showings to sustain his or her "effective assistance" claim: **(1) that the counsel's performance was "deficient," in the sense that it was not a "reasonably competent" performance; and (2) that these deficiencies were *prejudicial* to the defense, in the sense that there was a "reasonable probability that, but for**

[the] unprofessional errors, the *result of the proceeding would have been different.*" *Strickland v. Washington,* 466 U.S. 668 (1984).

Norman can make the first of these showings easily, but he cannot make the second—the proof of his guilt is so overwhelming that he cannot show a reasonable probability that if he had a competent lawyer, he would have been found not guilty. (All Norman has to do is to show that with competent counsel, there was a reasonable probability that the fact finder would have had "reasonable doubt" as to Norman's guilt. But Norman almost certainly cannot make even this limited showing.)

124. **Yes. An indicted defendant who already has a lawyer has a Sixth Amendment right not to have the police elicit statements from him or her in the absence of that lawyer. Since Paula was acting as a government agent, and deliberately elicited the incriminating statement from Osmond, Osmond's Sixth Amendment rights were violated. See *Maine v. Moulton,* 474 U.S. 159 (1985), finding a Sixth Amendment violation on similar facts.** The fact that it was Osmond, not Paula, who requested the meeting will be irrelevant so long as Paula went out of her way to elicit the incriminating statement. (But if Paula had merely listened passively to remarks volunteered by Osmond, there would be no Sixth Amendment violation even though Paula was acting as a government agent and went to the meeting wired in the hopes of hearing such a statement. See *Kuhlmann v. Wilson,* 477 U.S. 436 (1986).)

Observe that Osmond wins with his Sixth Amendment argument, even though he loses with both a Fourth Amendment argument and a *Miranda* argument. There is no Fourth Amendment violation, because the bugging was done with the consent of one of the participants, and the fact that the participant was a "secret agent" makes no difference. The *Miranda* "self-incrimination" argument loses because Osmond was not in custody. The Sixth Amendment argument is the difference for Osmond between keeping the damaging evidence out and having it come in.

125. **No. The Sixth Amendment right to counsel does not attach until formal judicial proceedings have been commenced against the defendant (e.g., by indictment, arraignment, formal charge, etc.). The mere fact that the police have already focused their investigation on the defendant and expect to bring charges against him or her is not enough. *Hoffa v. U.S.,* 385 U.S. 293 (1966).** This is true even though the police know that the suspect has a lawyer with whom he is consulting on the matter. The fact that Paula was in effect a police agent, and deliberately elicited incriminating material from Osmond, still does not violate Osmond's Sixth Amendment right to counsel.

126. **No. The presence of an undercover agent at a conference between a suspect and his lawyer will be a violation of the suspect's Sixth Amendment right to counsel, but only if material from the conference is somehow used by the prosecution. Since the prosecution made no use of the material, Osmond has no Sixth Amendment claim. See *Weatherford v. Bursey,* 429 U.S. 545 (1977), finding no Sixth Amendment violation on similar facts.**

127. **No. The 2009 decision in *Montejo v. Louisiana,* 129 S. Ct. 2079 (2009), holds that no automatic Sixth Amendment violation occurs when a suspect who is represented by counsel voluntarily submits to a noncustodial police-initiated interrogation outside the presence of that counsel.** Rafael's decision to speak to the police will be treated as a valid waiver of his Sixth Amendment right to counsel.

Criminal Procedure Essay Questions

QUESTION 1:   Officers Friendly, Stone, and Holmes are sitting in a coffee shop at around 9 P.M. when they hear a nearby pawnshop alarm go off. They look across the street and see Kevin running from the shop. Officer Friendly leaps up and goes after Kevin. As he runs across the street, Officer Friendly is almost hit by Mags, who is swerving all over the road in her car. Realizing that Kevin is getting away, Officer Friendly draws his revolver and shoots Kevin in the leg. Kevin falls to the sidewalk, and Officer Friendly immediately places him under arrest. In Kevin's pockets, Officer Friendly finds several gold watches and rings. At the same time, Officers Stone and Holmes get up and run after Mags. At the next stoplight, they tell Mags to step out of the car. Mags gets out of the car and apologizes profusely—it's clear that she is absolutely sober, and she only swerved while driving because she was looking for a particular address on the street. Officer Stone asks Mags for her license, and she says that she had it suspended several months ago. While Officer Stone tells Mags she is under arrest for driving without a license, Officer Holmes searches the car's passenger compartment. Under the passenger-side floor mat, he finds several baggies of cocaine. Larry is walking by and shouts, "Hey, leave that lady alone!" Officer Holmes yells at him to stop. Larry says, "I don't want to! I'm going home!" Officer Holmes then walks over and tells Larry to empty his pockets. Larry says, "No, I know my rights!" Officer Holmes reaches into Larry's jacket pocket and pulls out a bag of marijuana. Officer Holmes then arrests Larry for drug possession. Kevin, Mags, and Larry all sue the police department, arguing that their arrests were unlawful. The police department comes to you for advice.

QUESTION 2:   Jojo drove to the sheriff's department to retrieve a set of tools from his impounded truck (Jojo is well known in town for being an honest and trustworthy guy, but he is sometimes forgetful—in this case, his truck was impounded for unpaid parking tickets). As a matter of procedure, Deputy Ringo checks with his own county and a nearby one to see whether there are any outstanding warrants for Jojo's arrest. A clerk in neighboring Revolver County tells Deputy Ringo that her database shows that there is an active arrest warrant out for Jojo. Deputy Ringo is surprised, but realizes he has no reason to question the clerk. As Jojo is driving out from the impound lot, Deputy Ringo arrests him on the Revolver County warrant, searches his person, and finds several bags of illegal drugs. Deputy Ringo arrests Jojo for felony possession of narcotics. Jojo tells Deputy Ringo he wants a lawyer, but he is indigent and can't afford one. Deputy Ringo responds that the county can't afford to give him a lawyer, so he'll just have to "wing it" himself. Also, Deputy Ringo says, "Even if we could give you a lawyer, you're only entitled to one when you appeal your conviction in a higher court."

After spending the night in jail, Jojo goes before Judge George. Judge George hates drug users, so he sets Jojo's bail at $1 million. Jojo, who doesn't have access to this kind of money, spends the next week in jail. At Jojo's trial for drug possession at the end of the week, the court discovers that there was no outstanding warrant for Jojo's arrest—the warrant was recalled six months earlier, but this fact was never entered by the Revolver County Sheriff's Department into its database. Based on the mistake, Jojo argues the drug evidence found as a result of Deputy Ringo's search cannot be used against him. Judge George disagrees, and allows the drug evidence to be admitted. At a break in the trial, Paul, the prosecutor, tells Jojo that he'll make a deal—if Jojo pleads guilty, Paul will recommend that Judge George impose the minimum sentence. Jojo figures there is no way he can win, so he agrees and is sentenced to one year in jail. After sentencing, he overhears Judge George say to his clerk, "I was just hoping to scare the guy straight. I think he would have gotten probation if he pushed the trial the whole way." Jojo starts to think he made a bad deal with Paul. Please discuss the issues raised by Jojo's arrest and prosecution.

QUESTION 3: Officer Westerberg comes to arrest Stinson (a well-known hermit and recluse) at his house for the recent robbery of a valuable Mercado painting, *Unicorn Girl*. Officer Westerberg has an arrest warrant, but no search warrant. As they are arresting Stinson, the officers hear a noise in the adjoining room. They draw their weapons, and Mr. Whiskers, Stinson's cat, comes trotting out. The officers ask Stinson if anyone else is in the house, and he says, "No! I never allow people in my house!" Even though they believe Stinson, Officer Westerberg and several other officers conduct a full-scale search of Stinson's three-bedroom house to look for any evidence. In the back bedroom, they find the missing Mercado under a bed. Officer Westerberg takes Stinson to the station. He puts Stinson in an interrogation room and says, "You have the right to keep your yap shut. Also, you can get one of those high-priced weasels to lie for you if you would like." Stinson shouts, "Whatever! I did it! You know I did it! I stole the Mercado from the Mars Museum!" At Stinson's subsequent trial for the robbery, he shows up with the best criminal lawyer in town, "No-Lose" Bob, to represent him. The judge, mistakenly believing that Bob has violated a local court rule in a different case, refuses to consent to the representation. "Sometimes-Lose" Slim takes on Stinson's representation. Stinson is convicted. Stinson immediately appeals, arguing that the government violated his rights by refusing to allow Bob to represent him. The government argues that even if Stinson's Sixth Amendment right to be represented by a paid attorney was violated, this violation should be deemed harmless error unless Stinson can show that Slim's representation of Stinson so adversely affected the outcome as to constitute "ineffective assistance of counsel." Please discuss the issues concerning Slim's arrest and trial.

QUESTION 4: Prestonwood Police set up a fixed checkpoint at the corner of Willowbrook and Champions. They decided to randomly stop ten cars every hour. When each car was stopped, they walked around the car to see if they could spot any evidence that the car contained narcotics. They also used Pogue, a drug dog, to conduct a canine sniff. Mick drives through the checkpoint and is stopped. During the stop, Pogue alerts to Mick's trunk. Inside, the police find several pounds of marijuana. After arresting Mick, the sheriff calls the officers at the checkpoint and tells them to move the checkpoint several blocks east to Jones's Bowling Emporium. He tells the officers to stop any car leaving the local bowling alley and to give them a flier seeking witnesses of a shooting that had occurred a week before. Councilman Bowler, who is in a hurry to get home, takes a flier and says, "You know, what you're doing is totally illegal. I read a law book once, and you need probable cause to stop someone. I think you might end up getting the town sued. I'm going to ask Sheriff Ron about this." At the same time, Officer Keith sees Bill get into his car down the street. Officer Keith is pretty sure that Bill might be involved in the shooting. He follows Bill on his motorcycle and watches Bill fail to use a turn signal, which is a violation of the local driving law. He pulls over Bill, and notices several air fresheners hanging from the rearview mirror. Officer Keith then notices the strong smell of marijuana smoke and sees a burning marijuana cigarette in the car's cup holder. He seizes the marijuana cigarette and places Bill under arrest. Please discuss the issues raised.

QUESTION 5: One night, as Officer Miriam was walking down the street during her routine patrol, she heard a strange noise coming from a nearby house. While standing on the sidewalk, she used her flashlight to look inside the house's dark basement window (she wouldn't have been able to see inside without it). In the window, she saw what looked like marijuana plants growing inside. As she was standing there, she saw Amy walk out of the house and get into her car. Since Officer Miriam was on foot, she quickly walked by the car and secretly stuck an electronic beeper on the back bumper so police could track Amy's car. Amy drove out to the freeway, and then on to her friend Jean's farm. The next day, the police flew over the farm with a helicopter and took several pictures of the farm's fields (using Officer Miriam's digital camera). The pictures were then blown up (at a cost of $22,000) so that officers could clearly identify marijuana plants growing on the property. Officer Miriam then drove out to the farm with another officer and used a thermal imaging device to take a picture of the farmhouse. The imaging device detects invisible infrared radiation and converts it into a visible image showing relative warmth, with cool areas in black and hot areas in white. The device indicated that the basement was much warmer than it should have been, convincing the officers that Jean was using heat lamps to grow marijuana in the basement as well as out in the fields. This information was enough to convince a judge to issue a search warrant for the house. During the subsequent search, the officers discovered that Jean is indeed growing marijuana in her basement. At trial, Amy and Jean argue that any evidence against them was the result of several illegal searches. Discuss.

Sample Answers to Criminal Procedure Essay Questions

ANSWER TO QUESTION 1:

Kevin v. Officer Friendly

For a warrantless arrest to be lawful, it must be supported by probable cause. For there to be probable cause to arrest a person, it must be reasonably likely that a violation of the law has been committed and that the person to be arrested committed the violation. However, even if there is probable cause for an arrest, the Fourth Amendment places limits on how the arrest may be made. The main rule is that the police may not use deadly force to make an arrest if the suspect poses no immediate threat to the officer and no threat to others. After a lawful arrest is made, the police may search the area within the arrestee's control. Seeing Kevin run from the pawnshop at night with the alarm going off likely gave Officer Friendly probable cause to arrest him. Once he arrested Kevin, he then could conduct a fairly full search of Kevin's person. Consequently, he could validly empty Kevin's pockets to look for weapons, contraband, or stolen property from the pawnshop. However, Officer Friendly will likely be liable to Kevin for use of excessive force in making the arrest. Kevin was running away when Officer Friendly used deadly force to shoot him in the leg. There was no indication that Kevin posed any immediate threat to anyone (in fact, he was merely trying to flee). While Officer Friendly could argue that burglars like Kevin often had weapons, such an argument is unlikely to justify Officer Friendly's use of force.

Mags v. Officer Stone

If a police officer sees a driver commit a traffic violation, that officer may lawfully stop and arrest the driver depending on the severity of the traffic violation. However, in most driver arrests for traffic violations, the police will not be entitled to search the passenger compartment incident to that arrest. More precisely, a warrantless search of the passenger compartment is lawful only if (1) the arrestee has access to the passenger compartment at the moment of the search, or (2) the police reasonably believe that the passenger compartment might contain evidence of the offense for which the arrest is being made. After watching Mags swerve along the road, the officers had reasonable suspicion to stop her car to investigate whether she was driving while intoxicated. Once she admitted she didn't have a license, they had probable cause to arrest her for driving without a license. However, the search of the passenger compartment was likely not a proper search, because Mags was out of the car and had no access to the passenger compartment at the moment of the search. Also, Mags was arrested for driving without a license—thus, it was unlikely a search of the passenger compartment would lead to the discovery of necessary evidence relating to that offense. Consequently, while the arrest was lawful, the search of the car was not.

Larry v. Officer Holmes

The issue is whether Officer Holmes could lawfully stop and frisk Larry. Where a police officer observes unusual conduct that leads him or her reasonably to conclude that criminal activity is afoot, he or she may briefly detain the suspect to make inquiries. Probable cause is not required—reasonable suspicion, based on objective facts, that the individual is involved in criminal activity, will suffice. Once the officer conducts a lawful stop, then assuming nothing in the initial encounter dispels his or her reasonable fear for his or her or another's safety, the officer may conduct a carefully limited search of

the outer clothing in an attempt to discover weapons. Nothing Larry did would lead a reasonable officer to conclude he was engaged in criminal activity. He just yelled that the officers should leave Mags alone, which is not indicative of any crime. Thus, the initial stop was unlawful. Additionally, once Officer Holmes stopped him, Officer Holmes had no right to reach into Larry's pockets. While Officer Holmes could argue that this was a lawful search for weapons, Larry seemed to pose no threat, Officer Holmes would only have been allowed to search the outside of Larry's clothing, and once he felt the bag of marijuana, it should have been clear to him that the bag was not any kind of weapon. Thus, the search was unlawful as well.

ANSWER TO QUESTION 2:

Deputy Ringo's Search

The issue is whether Deputy Ringo's search incident to arrest of Jojo is valid since he was mistaken regarding the existence of the arrest warrant. **If the police reasonably (but mistakenly) believe that there is an arrest warrant outstanding for a particular suspect and arrest him or her, evidence found during a search incident to this wrongful arrest will be admissible, at least where any police conduct consists of "nonrecurring and attenuated negligence."** Here, the search is still valid as one properly made incident to arrest. Deputy Ringo acted in good-faith reliance on the existence of the apparent warrant. When an arrest and incident search arises from "nonrecurring and attenuated negligence" by the police department, rather than from "systemic error or reckless disregard of constitutional requirements," the error will not invalidate the search incident to the invalid arrest. Since there is no indication that the failure to enter the recall of the arrest warrant into the Revolver County database is recurring and systemic, the evidence discovered during the search of Jojo does not need to be suppressed.

Jojo's Right to a Lawyer

Deputy Ringo is wrong regarding Jojo's right to legal representation. **The Sixth Amendment says, "In all criminal prosecutions, the accused shall enjoy the right . . . to have the Assistance of Counsel for his defense." The Sixth Amendment right means that an indigent defendant has the right to have counsel appointed for him or her by the government in any prosecution where the accused can be sent to jail. Thus, in any felony prosecution, and in any misdemeanor prosecution for which the sentence will be a jail term, the indigent has the right to appointed counsel. In addition to the trial itself, a defendant has a right to counsel during any "critical stage" of the proceedings, which may include trial, initial appearance, preliminary hearing, and arraignment (but if local procedures make it clear that nothing done by the defendant at a particular stage binds him or her, then presumably counsel does not need to be appointed at that stage).** Here, Jojo has stated that he is indigent, and he has been arrested for felony drug possession. Thus, he is entitled to a court-appointed attorney. Also, he is entitled to the attorney for any proceeding that could bind him—clearly, this would include the trial itself, but it might include other parts of the prosecution (such as the bail hearing). Deputy Ringo was incorrect when he stated Jojo could only have an attorney for the appeal.

$1 Million Bail

The issue is whether the amount set by Judge George was lawful. **The Eighth Amendment (applicable in both state and federal proceedings) provides that "excessive bail shall not be required." However, the Bail Clause does not give the defendant right to affordable bail in all situations—it merely means that when the court does set bail, it must not do so in an unduly high amount, judged on factors such as seriousness of the offense, the weight of the evidence against the defendant, defendant's financial ability, and his or her character.** Here, it's likely that $1 million bail for an indigent defendant accused of the nonviolent crime of drug possession might be found to be excessive. While the fact Jojo cannot pay does not automatically make the bail excessive, the fact that he is known as a trustworthy but forgetful guy should be taken into account by the judge. Finally, while the facts do not state what drugs Jojo was carrying, there was no indication he was engaged in any drug sales or drug dealing. Consequently, it's likely the bail was unlawfully excessive.

The Plea Bargain

Most criminal cases are resolved by plea bargain rather than by trial. To give the defendant an incentive to "settle" the case rather than fight through the trial, the prosecution normally gives the defendant an inducement of a lighter sentence than what he or she would get if he or she were con- victed at trial. Plea bargains are generally enforceable, even if the defendant later has a change of heart. Paul offered a minimum sentence if Jojo simply pled guilty to the charges. Since Jojo agreed, the bargain (which is essentially a contract) is enforceable even if Jojo later has a change of heart and thinks he made a bad deal.

ANSWER TO QUESTION 3:

Miranda

The issue is whether Stinson's confession has to be suppressed. *Miranda* **holds that when the police question a suspect in custody, his or her confession will be admissible against him or her only if he or she has received *Miranda* warnings. Before *Miranda* will apply, three requirements must be satis- fied: (1) the suspect must be taken into custody, (2) the confession has to come about as the result of questioning, and (3) the questioning and custody must be done by the police or other law enforce- ment authorities. Once *Miranda* applies, the suspect must be warned that (1) he or she has the right to remain silent; (2) anything he or she says can be used against him or her in a court of law; (3) he or she has a right to an attorney; and (4) if he or she cannot afford an attorney, one will be appointed for him or her prior to any questioning if he or she desires.** Stinson was clearly in police custody. Although Officer Westerberg's statement ("You have the right to keep your yap shut. Also you can get one of those high-priced weasels to lie for you if you would like.") seems to be referencing a right to remain silent and a right to an attorney, this is unlikely to be a good enough statement of Stinson's *Miranda* rights (and it fails to address the fact anything he says could be used against him and that he could have a court-appointed attorney). However, it is unlikely Stinson's confession needs to be suppressed as it was not the result of any questioning. Stinson spontaneously admitted stealing the Mercado. Since this was not a result of question- ing, Stinson cannot claim the confession should be invalidated as the product of a violation of *Miranda*.

Search of Stinson's House

The issue is whether the police could search Stinson's house based only on the arrest warrant. **In general, when the police are making a lawful arrest, they may search the area within the arrestee's control. This is known as a search incident to arrest. Only the area that is at least theoretically within the suspect's immediate control may be searched incident to the arrest (the basic idea is that only the area that the suspect might get to in order to destroy evidence or gain possession of a weapon may be searched). However, when the arrest takes place in the suspect's home, the officers may conduct a protective sweep of all or part of the premises if they have a reasonable belief based on "specific and articulable facts" that another person who might be dangerous to the officers may be present in the areas to be swept.** Here, the search of the entire house was likely unnecessarily widespread. Though the officers may have lawfully searched the room they discovered Stinson in, they were not justified in searching the entire three-bedroom house for evidence. However, the officers could argue that the noise they heard in the other room might have been another person who could put the officers in danger. But when they saw Mr. Whiskers trot into the room, a court could find that their suspicions should have been dispelled (in fact, their suspicions did in fact seem dispelled since they believed Stinson when he said no one else was in the house). Also, since Stinson was a "well-known hermit and recluse," they should not have thought that anyone else was in the house. Consequently, the search of the entire house for evidence was likely unlawful.

Representation by Bob

The Sixth Amendment guarantees the right of a criminal defendant who does not need appointed counsel to hire private counsel of his or her own choosing to represent him or her. If the private counsel chosen by the defendant is qualified, the court's denial of permission for the lawyer to conduct the defense is an automatically reversible error—the defendant does not have to demonstrate on appeal that the denial of counsel of choice is likely to have affected the outcome. There is no indication in the facts that Bob is not a qualified attorney (in fact, he is the best one in town). Since the court violated Stinson's right to have counsel of his choosing, Stinson's conviction should be reversed without any showing of whether Bob's presence as a lawyer would have made any difference.

ANSWER TO QUESTION 4:

The Drug Checkpoint

The issue is the lawfulness of the checkpoint checking for drugs. **The police may set up a fixed checkpoint on the highway to test for compliance related to driver safety. Thus, they can stop to check for drunkenness, and can probably check to see that the driver is licensed and the vehicle is registered. However, the police may not set up a fixed checkpoint to pursue general crime-fighting objectives, such as narcotics detection.** A court is likely to find that the warrantless stops during the drug checkpoint were unreasonable and a violation of the Fourth Amendment, because they were being done for general crime-fighting purposes, not administrative concerns relating to road safety. Thus, the stop of Mick was unlawful.

The Bowling Alley Checkpoint

The police may set up a fixed roadblock or checkpoint to find witnesses to a recent crime if that is a reasonable method of finding such witnesses. Based on the facts, it seems that the police were searching for witnesses to the shooting, not suspects, and that they were doing so in a minimally intrusive way by simply handing out a flier seeking witnesses to the crime. Consequently, the stops were lawful.

Stop of Bill

The issue is whether the stop of Bill for the turn signal is unlawful because Officer Keith had other motives for stopping him. **If the police have probable cause to believe that a traffic (or other) law has been broken, they may stop the perpetrator, even if their motive in doing so is to seek evidence of some other crime for which they do not have probable cause or even reasonable suspicion.** Here, since Officer Keith saw Bill fail to use his turn signal (a violation of local law), he was justified in stopping him. Importantly, it did not matter that Officer Keith had another secret reason for the stop, as there is no pretext exception to the general rule that police may make a warrantless stop of a vehicle when they have probable cause to believe that an offense has been committed. Thus, the stop of Bill was lawful.

Seizure of Marijuana

It was well settled that if police find evidence in plain view in a vehicle, they may seize the evidence. Here, from the smell and looks of the marijuana cigarette, it was plain to Officer Keith that the cigarette was evidence of a drug crime. Consequently, he was justified in seizing it. Additionally, once he saw and smelled the marijuana, Officer Keith had sufficient probable cause to arrest Bill.

ANSWER TO QUESTION 5:

Officer Miriam's Search with the Flashlight

The issue is whether Officer Miriam's use of her flashlight to search Amy's basement window violated her constitutional rights. **When police stand on public property, but use mechanical devices to obtain the view of the defendant or his or her property, the "plain view" doctrine often applies. Importantly, the use of a flashlight by a policeman in the nighttime does not prevent an observation from falling within the "plain view" doctrine.** Officer Miriam was standing on the public sidewalk. Though she used her flashlight to illuminate the window, the use of her flashlight does not take the marijuana evidence out of the "plain view" exception to the search warrant requirement. Consequently, the evidence could be used against Amy.

The Beeper

The issue is whether the beeper constituted an unlawful search. **Even where the device used to gain view of the defendant's property is more sophisticated than a flashlight, the use of the device will be upheld under the "plain view" doctrine if two conditions are met: (1) the view takes place from a location where the police have a right to be, and (2) the information obtained could have been gotten from "plain view" surveillance executed without the special device. Importantly, courts have specifically held that the use of an electronic beeper to trail a vehicle on public roads does not violate the driver's reasonable expectation of privacy.** Here, since Officer Miriam could have lawfully followed Amy's car along the public roads if she were not on foot, the use of the beeper to track Amy's movements to Jean's farm is likely constitutional. Thus, the fact the police discovered Amy's and Jean's activities at the farm through the use of the beeper is unlikely to invalidate the evidence discovered at the farm.

The Aerial Search

The use of sophisticated aerial equipment did not prevent the "plain view" doctrine from applying, as long as the equipment was generally available to the public. Importantly, the Fourth Amendment does not protect open fields. Despite the fact that the police used a significant amount of money to blow up the pictures, a digital camera is widely available to the public. Also, from the facts, it appears that the marijuana that the police saw was growing in the farm's open fields. As such, Jean did not have an expectation of privacy regarding those fields, and the police did not engage in an unlawful search (although this might have been different if Jean had made some effort to protect herself against aerial surveillance).

The Thermal Imaging Search

When the government obtains special high-tech devices not in general civilian use and employs them from public places to gain views that could not be had by the naked eye, the use of such devices will be considered a search. Thus, the use of such equipment will require a search warrant. Here, the police used a special thermal imaging device that is not in general civilian use to get a look at the inside of Jean's farmhouse's basement. Although the police could argue that they were simply measuring "heat" given off by the home, this argument is likely to be unavailing since the officers were using specialized equipment. As such, since they did not have a warrant to search at the time they used the thermal device on the farmhouse, the evidence found in Jean's basement should be suppressed as the fruits of an illegal search.

PROPERTY

Property Table of Contents

POSSESSION AND TRANSFER OF PERSONAL PROPERTY

ADVERSE POSSESSION

FREEHOLD ESTATES

FUTURE INTERESTS

MARITAL ESTATES

CONCURRENT OWNERSHIP

LANDLORD AND TENANT

EASEMENTS AND PROMISES CONCERNING LAND

ZONING AND OTHER PUBLIC LAND-USE CONTROLS

LAND SALE CONTRACTS, MORTGAGES, AND DEEDS

THE RECORDING SYSTEM AND TITLE ASSURANCE

RIGHTS INCIDENT TO LAND

Property Short-Answer Questions

1. While walking down Main Street, Paul found a very distinctive antique ring containing valuable stones. He quickly picked it up and pocketed it, and he at no time made any effort to find the true owner. The day after the discovery, he inadvertently left the ring on a table at a restaurant run by Donna. Donna picked up the ring and put it in her safe. Two days later, Paul realized that he must have left the ring at Donna's restaurant, so he asked her whether she had it. Donna replied, "Yes, I have it. Is it yours?" Paul answered, "Well, I guess it's mine now, because I found it on the street." Donna refused to give Paul back the ring, saying that Paul was not the true owner. In a suit brought by Paul against Donna for possession of the ring, who will win?

Not sure ☐

2. Oscar was the owner of a very valuable painting, *Rosewood*. In 1980, *Rosewood* was stolen from Oscar's home. Oscar reported the theft to the police, collected insurance proceeds, and made no further efforts to locate the painting. (For example, he did not report the theft to a national information bank that lists stolen paintings, nor did he notify local art dealers.) In 1983, unbeknownst to Oscar, Anita, an art collector, bought *Rosewood* from a private gallery for $10,000. (This price was approximately the fair market value of the painting at the time, on the assumption that there was clear title.) The gallery showed Anita documents indicating that the gallery had the right to sell the painting, and Anita had no reason to believe the painting to be stolen.

Anita proudly displayed the painting at her house for the next 25 years. Even though Anita and Oscar lived in the same town, Oscar did not learn of Anita's possession of the painting until 2008, when a friend happened to mention it to him. The local statute of limitations on actions to recover personal property is ten years. Assuming that the state follows the "modern" rule regarding when the statute of limitations on stolen personal property begins to run, if Oscar sues Anita in 2008, may he recover the painting from her?

Not sure ☐

3. Same facts as in the previous example. Now, however, assume that Oscar promptly made all feasible efforts to recover the painting, including listing it with an information bank and notifying local art dealers of the theft. Despite all of these steps, Oscar did not learn until 2008 that Anita had been proudly showing the painting as her own for the past 25 years. If Oscar sues Anita in 2008 to recover the painting, will he succeed?

Not sure ☐

4. Olivia's 2005 Subaru was stolen while parked on the street in front of her house. Six months later, Arnold purchased from Dealer a used 2005 Subaru to which Dealer appeared to have good title. Arnold paid the full fair market value for the car. In fact, the car was the one that had been stolen from Olivia, though there was no way Arnold could reasonably have known that the car was stolen property. Through a random check of vehicle identification numbers by local police, the police discovered that the car Arnold was driving was stolen property and so notified Olivia. Olivia has now sued Arnold in 2009 for return of the car. Arnold defends on the grounds that he is a bona fide purchaser for fair value. Assume that there are no relevant statutes. May Olivia recover the car?

Not sure ☐

5. After Dan's lawnmower broke, Dan asked Jerry if he could borrow Jerry's mower. Jerry agreed. Dan used the mower and then left it out in the front yard for one hour while he went to do an errand. During this hour, an unknown person stole the mower. The neighborhood is a relatively safe one in which the theft of a mower during broad daylight is rare, but not completely unforeseeable. Assume, therefore, that Dan's conduct in leaving the mower out for the hour that he was away does not constitute common law negligence. If Jerry sues Dan for the value of the mower, will Jerry recover?

Not sure ☐

6. In 1990, Sidney, a wealthy industrialist, said to his son Norman, "I am hereby giving you my valuable Monet painting, *Ballerinas.*" Sidney did not, however, at any time give Norman possession of the painting; nor did he give him any document indicating any transfer. The painting continued to hang on Sidney's wall for the next 15 years. In 2005, Sidney died. His will bequeathed all of his personal property to his daughter, Denise. Who owns the painting, Norman or Denise?

Not sure ☐

7. Same facts as in the previous question. Now, however, assume that in 1990, following their conversation, Sidney handed Norman a sheet of paper that stated, "I, Sidney, hereby transfer to Norman title to my Monet painting, *Ballerinas.* Despite this transfer of title, I reserve the right to maintain physical possession of the painting until my death, since I love looking at it." Sidney then died, leaving all of his personal property by will to his daughter Denise. Who owns the painting, Norman or Denise?

Not sure ☐

8. Stanley owned 1,000 shares of AT&T stock. Stanley was diagnosed as having pancreatic cancer, an invariably fatal disease. He then said to Rose, his longtime mistress, "Because I'm going to die soon, I want you to have my 1,000 shares of AT&T as a token of my esteem." He handed her the stock certificate for these shares, and she thanked him profusely. One month later, Stanley consulted another specialist, who told him that the earlier diagnosis of pancreatic cancer was incorrect, and that he was suffering from the painful but nonfatal disease of pancreatitis. Two hours after receiving this good news, Stanley was struck and killed by a car while crossing the street. He never had a chance to speak to Rose after receiving his reprieve from cancer. Stanley's will leaves all his personal property to his estranged wife, Karen. Who owns the shares, Rose or Karen?

Not sure ☐

9. Albert, an elderly widower, placed $100,000 in a bank savings account bearing the designation, "Albert in trust for Bertha." Bertha was Albert's girlfriend. During the next two years, Albert made no withdrawals, nor did Bertha. Albert then died, leaving all of his personal property by will to his son Steven. Steven and Bertha each now claim the proceeds of the bank account. Neither produces any evidence of Albert's intent in creating the bank account. What part, if any, of the proceeds should be awarded to Bertha?

Not sure ☐

10. Same facts as in the previous question. Now, however, assume that Albert withdrew $80,000 from the account shortly before his death. Of the remaining $20,000, what part, if any, should be awarded to Bertha?

Not sure ☐

11. Same facts as in the previous two questions. Now, assume that in 2009, Albert withdrew $60,000 from the account. Bertha objected on the grounds that this money, once it was deposited into this type of account, immediately belonged to her. She has therefore sued for an injunction preventing Albert (who is still alive) from making further withdrawals and requiring him to return the funds. Neither side has produced any evidence as to Albert's intent in creating the account. What, if any, portion of the relief sought by Bertha should be awarded by the court?

Not sure ☐

Assume for questions 12-21 that the applicable statute of limitations on actions to recover possession of real property is 20 years.

12. In 1960, Beck purchased valid title to Blackacre, located in Ames. That same year, Warren purchased valid title to Whiteacre, the adjoining parcel. Both parties reasonably but mistakenly believed that the boundary line between Blackacre and Whiteacre was a large oak tree, so in 1961, both fenced their property accordingly. In reality, the proper boundary between the two parcels is 30 yards to the south of the oak tree, so that the existing fencing has been depriving Warren of the use of land that belongs to him. In 2008, Warren discovered the error, and has brought an action to recover the 30-yard strip. May Warren recover the strip?

Not sure ☐

13. Otto was the owner of Greenacre. In 1985, Otto said to his son, Samuel, "I hereby give you a gift of Greenacre." However, Otto did not deliver any deed to the property, as was required by the Statute of Frauds. Samuel lived on the property for the next 23 years. In 2008, Otto died, leaving all of his real and personal property to his second wife, Wanda. Who has title to Greenacre?

Not sure ☐

14. In 1960, Osmond, the owner of Blackacre, left the property "to my son Steve and my daughter Deborah in equal shares." Steve moved onto the property and lived there for the next 40 years. Deborah never liked the property and made no attempt to live there at any time. In 2008, Deborah died, leaving all of her personal and real property to her son Frank. If Frank now seeks a judicial declaration that he is the owner of a one-half interest in Blackacre, will he succeed?

Not sure ☐

15. Same facts as in the previous question. Now, however, assume that in 1990, Frank demanded that Steve let Frank move into the premises with Steve. Steve refused, claiming that he was now, by the doctrine of adverse possession, in sole ownership of the premises. Frank never took any further action. In 2011, if Frank sues for a declaratory judgment that he is a one-half owner of Blackacre, will he succeed?

Not sure ☐

16. In 1980, Owen bought Blackacre, which at the time was rural property suitable mainly for hunting and fishing. Owen never visited the property and held it as an investment. That same year, Baker began making extensive use of the property during the hunting and fishing season (which runs from April through November). For 15 consecutive years, Baker camped out on the property during hunting season for at least 60 nights, and hunted and fished during the day. In 1995, Baker brought his friend Carter to the property, and they hunted and fished together extensively that season. At the end of the season, Baker died. Carter used the premises in the same manner as Baker did for the next seven years (bringing us to 2002). In 2002, who is the owner of Blackacre?

Not sure ☐

17. In 1980, Omar purchased Greenacre, undeveloped land that he held as an investment. That same year, Botnick, a would-be farmer, began to plant corn on the property. He planted and harvested the crop (the only crop that could be economically cultivated on the property, and the crop cultivated by neighboring farmers on their land) for 23 consecutive seasons. Meanwhile, Omar never visited the property, and conveyed it to Alan for value in 1991. In 2003, who owns Blackacre?

Not sure ☐

18. Orlando acquired Blackacre in 1960. In 1970, Alice acquired Whiteacre, the adjacent parcel. Alice built a fence on what she thought was the border between the two properties. In fact, her fence encroached 40 yards into Orlando's property. Alice actively, openly, and continuously occupied this 40-yard strip for the next 35 years. In 2005, Orlando discovered the error and informed Alice that she had been using his property. Alice said, "Okay, I now recognize that this strip is your property." She also moved the fence. Shortly thereafter, Alice died, leaving Whiteacre to her son Stokes. Who owns the strip, Stokes or Orlando?

Not sure ☐

19. In 1980, Ara received a deed to Blackacre, a ten-acre parcel, from Xavier. Unbeknownst to Ara, Xavier did not in fact have good title to the property. Rather, legal title to Blackacre at that time was in Benton. After receiving his deed, Ara moved onto one acre of the property, which he used as his homestead. The entire ten-acre parcel was known in the community as "the Blackacre Farm." In 2010, Benton sued Ara. Benton concedes that the one acre on which Ara actively resided has passed to him by adverse possession, but Benton asserts that the other nine acres still belong to him. Is Benton's contention correct?

Not sure ☐

20. Same facts as in the previous question. Now, however, assume that Ara never received a deed from Xavier or from anyone else; instead, Ara was simply a squatter who moved onto the property and began to use it. If Benton sues for a return of the nine acres not physically occupied by Ara, will he win?

Not sure ☐

21. Beginning in 1990, Ali was the record owner of Whiteacre. In 2000, Ashley moved onto the property and began occupying it in an open, continuous, and hostile manner. In 2010, Bates threatened to kill Ashley if Ashley did not move off the property. Ashley complied, and Bates moved onto the property. After Bates had occupied the property continuously, openly, and hostilely for three years, Ashley brought an ejectment action against him. Should the court order Bates evicted in favor of Ashley?

Not sure ☐

22. O'Malley was the owner in fee simple of Blackacre. As a gift, O'Malley delivered to Abel a deed to Blackacre; the deed read, "to Abel and his heirs." Abel recorded the deed as required by local statutes. Abel then delivered a deed to Blackacre to Barbara, who recorded it. Abel then died, leaving as his sole heir his son, Callaway. Who owns Blackacre?

Not sure ☐

23. In the State of Ames, there is a one-year statute of limitations on actions to enforce a right of entry for condition broken. Ames also has a statute barring any possibility of reverter 50 years following the creation of a fee simple determinable. In Ames, O held a fee simple absolute in Blackacre. Because O had watched his daughter's marital prospects become ruined by her early involvement as a pornography star, O sold Blackacre to A, a nightclub operator, under a conveyance, "To

A and his heirs as long as the premises are not used for topless or erotic dancing, and if they are so used, then the premises shall revert to O." This conveyance took place in 1980. A complied with this restriction. In 1988, O died, leaving all his real and personal property to his son S. In 1990, A conveyed, "To B and his heirs, in fee simple absolute." That same year, B began to use the premises as a topless bar, and continued doing so for the next 19 years. In 2009, S asks the court for a determination that the property now belongs to him because of B's operation of the topless club. Should the court grant S's request?

Not sure ☐

24. Same facts as in the previous question. Now, however, assume that the deed from O to A stated, "To A and his heirs, provided that no topless or other obscene dancing ever takes place on the premises. If such dancing does take place, Grantor or his heirs may reenter the property." All other facts remain the same, except that in 2009, S files suit for a decree authorizing him to reenter the property. Should the court grant S's request?

Not sure ☐

25. In a state following common law rules of property without modern statutory modifications, O conveyed Blackacre "to A and the heirs of his body." A then conveyed "to B and her heirs." (B was A's girlfriend.) A then died, leaving as his sole heir a son, S. What is the state of title to Blackacre?

Not sure ☐

26. A, the owner of Blackacre, left the property by will to B, his second wife. The bequest read, "To B for so long as she remains unmarried. If she remarries, the property shall revert to my heirs." B died ten years later without ever having remarried. She left as her sole heir her niece, N. At A's death, he left one heir, S, a son by his first marriage, who is still alive. What is the state of title?

Not sure ☐

27. O conveyed Blackacre "to A for life, remainder to B." One year later, A quitclaimed all of his interest in Blackacre to C. After this quitclaim deed, what is the state of title?

Not sure ☐

28. O held a fee simple absolute in Blackacre. He conveyed "to A for life." After this conveyance, what interest, if any, does O hold in Blackacre?

Not sure ☐

29. O conveyed Blackacre "to A for life, then to B and his heirs." Immediately after the conveyance, what interest, if any, does B have in Blackacre?

Not sure ☐

30. O conveyed Blackacre "to A for life, then to B's children and their heirs." At the time of this conveyance, B had one child, C. Immediately following the conveyance, what interest, if any, does C have in Blackacre?

Not sure ☐

31. O conveyed Blackacre "to A for life, then to B and his heirs. However, if B dies without issue, then to C and his heirs." Immediately following this conveyance, what interest, if any, does B have in Blackacre?

Not sure ☐

32. O conveyed Blackacre "to A for life, then, if B is living at A's death, to B in fee simple." Immediately after this conveyance, what interest, if any, does B have in Blackacre?

Not sure ☐

33. O conveyed Blackacre "to A for life, then to B and his heirs, but if B dies before A, to O and his heirs." Immediately after this conveyance, what interest, if any, does B have in Blackacre?

Not sure ☐

34. O devised Blackacre "to A for life, then to A's heirs." Assuming that the Rule in Shelley's Case is not in force, what interest in Blackacre, if any, do A's heirs have immediately after this conveyance?

35. O conveyed Blackacre "to A for life, remainder to the first daughter of A who produces a child while married." A then died. At A's death, he has one daughter, D, who has not yet married or had a child. O is still alive. Immediately after A's death, what is the state of title to Blackacre? Assume that all common law doctrines are in force without statutory modification.

36. O conveyed Blackacre "to A for life, remainder to A's oldest daughter for life if she has a child while married, remainder to B and his heirs." At a time when A's oldest daughter, D, had not yet married, A conveyed his life estate to B. After that conveyance, what is the state of title? Assume that all common law doctrines are in force without statutory modification.

37. O, in his will, left Blackacre "to A for life, remainder to A's heirs." A then issued a quitclaim deed (giving whatever interest A had, without specifying or warranting what that interest was) to B. Two years later, A died, leaving as his sole heir at law S, a son. What is the state of title to Blackacre?

38. In a state with no statutes modifying the relevant common law rules, O conveyed Blackacre "to A for life, remainder to O's heirs." Shortly thereafter, O quitclaimed any interest he might have in Blackacre to B. O then died, leaving as his sole heir a son, S. A then died. What is the state of title?

39. The same facts as in the previous question. Now, however, assume that all transactions occurred in the late twentieth century, in a state that follows the usual twentieth-century approach to conveyances of the ones described in the question. Assume further that in O's initial conveyance to A, he added the sentence, "I mean for this gift to take effect in exactly the manner that I have expressed." What is the probable state of title?

40. O is the fee simple owner of Blackacre. He wishes to convey title to his son, S, but only from the time that S graduates from law school. But he wants S to know that S will definitely get the land if he does graduate from law school. What conveyance should O make to S to accomplish this result? (Assume that the Statute of Uses is in force.)

41. O owned Blackacre in fee simple. He bargained and sold it "to A and his heirs, but if liquor is ever served on the premises, then to B and his heirs." Immediately after this conveyance, what is the state of title?

42. What is the state of title after each of the following two conveyances?

(a) O bargains and sells Blackacre "to A for life, then to B and his heirs if B survives A, otherwise to C and his heirs."

(b) O bargains and sells "to A for life, then to B and his heirs, but if B should die before A, then to C and his heirs."

43. O conveyed Blackacre "to A for life." At the time of the conveyance, Blackacre had always been used as farmland, and O knew that A was a farmer. However, the parties made no agreement concerning the use to which A would put the property.

A took possession and began farming. Shortly thereafter, oil was discovered on an adjacent parcel. A immediately drilled an oil well on the property and struck a gusher. A sold the resulting oil and put the proceeds of the sale in his bank account. Has A's conduct violated O's rights?

For questions 44-53, assume that the common law rule against perpetuities is in effect.

44. O conveys "to A for life, remainder to A's oldest son who survives A for life, remainder to B and his heirs." A and B are alive at the time of the conveyance, but A does not yet have a son. Is the remainder to B and his heirs valid?

45. In 1980, O conveys "to A for life, remainder in fee simple to the first son of A who has a child while married." At the time of this conveyance, A has no son who has had a child while married, but does have an unmarried childless son, B. In 1985, B has a child while married. In 2005, A dies. Is the remainder to B valid?

46. O conveyed Blackacre "to the Sierra Club, so long as it maintains the property in a state of wilderness. If the property is not in such a state, then to A and his heirs." A was alive at the time of this conveyance. Ten years after the conveyance (while both O and A were still alive), the Sierra Club allowed the property to be developed instead of used as a wilderness. A has brought suit for a declaration that he is now the owner of the property. Will A win?

47. In 1980, O, the owner of Greenacre, gave to A Corp. (in return for a payment of $20,000) the following document: "I, O, hereby grant to A Corp. an option to purchase Greenacre at any time during the next 30 years for a price equal to $100,000 plus an additional sum equal to the compounded interest, at 10 percent, on $100,000 from the date of this option." O died in 1990, leaving all his real and personal property to B. In 2009, A Corp. seeks to exercise its option. Does it have a right to do so?

48. Same facts as in the previous question. Now, however, assume that A Corp., on the date it purchased its option from O, simultaneously leased Greenacre from A for a 30-year period. If A Corp. tries to exercise the option in 2009, will it succeed?

49. O bequeathed Blackacre "to A for life, then to A's oldest surviving child for life, then to the oldest surviving child of B." B was a woman who at the time of O's death was 70 years old, and her two children (C and D) were 50 and 45, respectively. Eighteen years after O's bequest, both A and A's only surviving child died. C also died in the interim, but D is alive. Does D take Greenacre?

50. In 2000, O bequeathed Blackacre "to A for life, then to A's widow." At the time of this bequest, A was not yet married. In 2002, A married B, a 30-year-old woman. A died in 2008. Does B get Blackacre?

51. Same facts as in the previous question. Now, however, assume that A was already married to B by the time O made his bequest. Does B get to take the property upon A's death in 2008?

52. In 1980, O bequeathed Whiteacre "to A for life, then to A's first son to reach the age of 21." A was a man who, in 1980, had no sons. In 1982, a son, B, was born to A. In 2004, A died. Does B take the property on A's death?

53. In 1980, O bequeathed Whiteacre "to A for life, then in equal shares to those of A's children who survive him, but only when each attains the age of 30. I want to be sure that children born to A after my death are included in this bequest." In 1980, A had one child, B, who was 10. In 2005, A died, without ever having had any other children, and with B still alive. Does B take the property?

Not sure ☐

54. Same facts as in the previous question. In a state following the most common statutory modification to the Rule Against Perpetuities, would the gift to B be valid?

Not sure ☐

55. O conveys Blackacre "to A and his heirs, but in the future, title shall pass solely by inheritance, not by will or inter vivos transfer." A purports to convey a fee simple absolute to B for fair market value. Is the conveyance to B valid?

Not sure ☐

56. In 1980, O conveyed Blueacre, a 900-acre farm, to H. In 1985, H married W. In 1990, H, in return for reasonable consideration, delivered to A a deed in fee simple for Blueacre. In 2005, H died. What is the state of title in Blueacre? (Assume that the common law is in force in all relevant particulars.)

Not sure ☐

57. H and W live in a community property state. If H and W are divorced, which of the following items will be community property? (Assume that H and W's divorce is no-fault.)

Not sure ☐

    (a) Blackacre, which W bought before the marriage, and which has remained in her name before the divorce.

    (b) Whiteacre, which W inherited from her father after the marriage, and which has remained in her name until the divorce.

    (c) $20,000 in a bank account entitled "H and W jointly," representing net rental proceeds paid by a tenant of Whiteacre; all of these payments were made after W inherited the property as described in (b) above.

    (d) $100,000 in a bank account in H's name alone; this represents money earned by H from his salary during the years following the marriage while working for ABC Corp., a large company.

    (e) Stock in ABC Corp. held in H's name, which he received as part of ABC Corp.'s stock ownership plan.

    (f) A summer home purchased by H, in his own name, from which the down payment and all subsequent mortgage payments have been made out of H's earnings.

58. O conveyed Blackacre "to A and B as co-tenants." A then died, bequeathing all of his real and personal property to his son, S. B is still alive. What is the state of title to Blackacre?

Not sure ☐

59. O conveyed Blackacre "to A and B as joint tenants." B then conveyed to C, by a quitclaim deed (conveying whatever interest B had in the property). Subsequently, A died, bequeathing all of his real and personal property to his son, S. What is the state of title?

Not sure ☐

60. O conveyed Blackacre to his three children, A, B, and C, as joint tenants. A fell upon hard times and sold whatever interest he had in the property to B. B then died, leaving all of his personal and real property to his two children, daughter D and son S. C is still alive. What is the state of title?

Not sure ☐

61. O owned Blackacre in fee simple. O died intestate, leaving as his sole heirs a son, S, and a daughter, D. The intestacy statute provides that, "When the decedent dies with no spouse and one or more children, the children shall share equally in any real and personal property owned by the decedent at his death." One year after O's death, S died, leaving all of his real and personal property by will equally to his two sons, X and Y. What is the state of title to Blackacre?

62. O, the fee simple owner of Whiteacre, died, leaving the property by will to his three children, A, B, and C, "as tenants in common." A purchased C's interest. The property is a single-family home. A moved in and used the property as his principal residence. B, a bachelor, has now demanded to live in the home as well. If A refuses, will a judge order A to share the house with B?

63. Henry and Wanda were husband and wife. Using funds supplied entirely by Henry, the two purchased Blackacre from Oscar. (The deed from Oscar to Henry and Wanda read, "To Henry and Wanda in fee simple," without further elaboration.) Shortly thereafter, Henry became infatuated with a younger woman, Georgia. To celebrate the six-month anniversary of their affair, Henry conveyed to Georgia his interest in Blackacre. (Assume that the land is located in a state that permits such a conveyance.) For the next five years, Henry continued to be married to Wanda, but carried on his affair with Georgia. Then, Wanda died, leaving all of her real and personal property to her and Henry's daughter, Denise. Shortly thereafter, Henry died. What is the state of title? (Assume that the common law approach to all relevant matters is in force, unmodified by statute or case law.)

64. Herb and Wendy, husband and wife, were the owners of Blackacre, which they held by tenancy of the entirety. In 2007, Herb and Wendy were divorced. They intended to sell the property, but before they could do so, Herb died suddenly. Herb's will leaves all of his real and personal property to Stan, his son by a prior marriage. What is the state of the title to Blackacre?

65. Arthur and Bertha, after inheriting Blackacre from their father, held it as tenants in common. Originally, Arthur lived in the premises, and Bertha had no interest in doing so. After a few years, Arthur moved out and sent Bertha the following letter: "I am moving out of Blackacre. You have the right to live on the property. If you do not do so, I will rent it out." Bertha made no response. Arthur, after advertising for a tenant, rented the property to Xavier, who responded to the ad. Xavier paid $20,000 of rent during the first year. (Xavier paid all operating costs, such as utilities.) At the end of the first year of this rental, Bertha learned of the arrangement and sent Arthur a letter stating, "You owe me one-half of the rent paid by Xavier." Is Bertha correct?

66. Omar, the owner of Whiteacre, left the property, in equal parts, to his daughter Carol and his son Dan. The will said nothing about who should occupy the property. The property was a single-family home. Dan already had a home of his own, suitable for his family. Carol did not. Therefore, Carol moved into the house and has since occupied it. The estimated fair market rental value of the house is $18,000 per year. Dan has demanded that Carol pay him one-half of this amount to compensate for her use of the premises. Carol has responded, "You are free to live here with me, but I'm not paying you any money for my use of the premises." If Dan sues for one-half of the fair market rent represented by Carol's occupancy of the premises, will Dan prevail?

Not sure ☐

67. Edward and Felicia, brother and sister, received Whiteacre as a bequest in their mother's will. Edward, who had been living on the property while his mother was still alive, continued to do so after her death. Felicia has never had any interest in living on the property. The property is presently worth approximately $800,000, and has a rental value of $50,000 per year. However, Edward has rejected all suggestions by Felicia that the property be sold or rented out to third parties (though Edward has always indicated that Felicia is welcome to live on the property with him). What sort of action, if any, may Felicia bring to accomplish her goals?

Not sure ☐

68. On July 1, 2009, L and T orally agreed that T would lease L's premises for one year, the lease to commence on August 1 of that same year and run until July 31, 2010. T gave a deposit as called for in the oral agreement. On August 1, when T tried to take possession, he discovered that L had rented the premises to someone else. Does T have a valid cause of action against L for breach of the lease?

Not sure ☐

69. L and T agreed that T would rent an apartment from L for $800 per month. No specific term was set. T took occupancy on July 1 and paid the rent for that month.

   (a) What type of tenancy have the parties created?

Not sure ☐

   (b) Suppose that after approximately two years, T wants to terminate the arrangement. If T gives notice of termination on July 15, what is the date on which his termination will be effective, under the common law view?

Not sure ☐

70. Larry, who has large holdings of agricultural land, rented a particular parcel to Tom for one year, from January 1, 2009, through December 31 of that year. The lease called for an annual rental of $30,000, to be paid in a lump sum immediately following the harvest, on October 1. The parcel also included a residential structure, which Tom planned to occupy. Tom took possession as scheduled, farmed for the year, and planned to leave on December 31. On December 30, he was stricken by a severe virus. He therefore has remained in residence through January 3, and has kept his farm machinery on the premises as well. During Tom's year of occupancy, farm prices fell. Therefore, Larry would like to keep Tom as a tenant, especially if he can do so at the same rent. Assuming that the traditional common law approach to relevant matters is in force, what should Larry do on January 3, and with what result?

Not sure ☐

71. Same facts as in the previous question. Now, however, assume that the court takes the more modern view toward the issues. Would the course of action you recommended for Larry in your answer to the previous question work?

Not sure ☐

72. Leonard leased a store to Terry, for a lease term ending August 30, 2009. In July 2009, Leonard signed a lease with Tina for the premises, to commence September 1, 2009. Leonard knew that Tina planned to operate a new retail store, and that it would be important to Tina to be selling her fall clothing inventory starting promptly in September. When Terry's lease term ended, he refused to vacate the premises, and was still there on September 20, at which time he moved out. May Tina sue Leonard for damages for failing to make the premises available to her on September 1?

Not sure ☐

73. Leroy was in possession of a house and represented himself to be the owner of it. Leroy then leased the house to Tony for three years, ending in 2003. After Tony moved into the house, he discovered that Leroy does not in fact own the house, but rather, has rented it from Peter under a one-year lease that will end at the end of 2001. (It is now mid-2000.) Peter has not said anything to suggest that he will move to evict Tony at the end of the Peter-Leroy lease, but Peter has also not indicated that he will let Tony stay. Tony would like to move out and stop paying rent, on the grounds that Leroy does not have valid title to the premises for the full period of the Leroy-Tony lease. May Tony do so?

Not sure ☐

74. Same facts as in the previous question. Now, however, assume that Tony discovered Leroy's duplicity before he, Tony, took possession of the house. May Tony cancel the lease?

Not sure ☐

75. Lester, the owner of an apartment building, rented a first floor apartment to Tess. Shortly thereafter, Lester rented ground-floor space (immediately below Tess's apartment) to the proprietor of Heavy Metal Heaven, a rock and roll club. The lease between Lester and Heavy Metal provided that Heavy Metal would conduct its activities so as not to materially inconvenience any tenants of the apartment building. But Heavy Metal set its loudspeakers to the maximum level, so that every night, Tess was unable to sleep until the club closed at 2:00 A.M. Tess decided that she could no longer tolerate the noise and moved out. She then delivered to Lester a notice stating, "I consider our lease at an end." Lester relet the premises at a lower rate. May Lester recover from Tess the difference between the rent paid by Tess and the lower rent he is now receiving?

Not sure ☐

76. Same facts as in the previous question. Now, however, assume that it is a tight housing market, and Tess has not been able to find another apartment at the same (relatively affordable) rate she is paying to Lester. Tess has therefore remained a resident in the apartment, but has gone on a rent strike, notifying Lester that she will not pay any rent until he makes the noise stop. Assuming that Tess continues to withhold the rent, may Lester have her evicted?

Not sure ☐

77. Lou is the owner of a freestanding commercial property (a store) together with a parking lot that can hold 50 cars. Lou leased this property to Ted, who operates a grocery store on the premises. In early 2008, the state seized by eminent domain the front half of the building's parking lot to use for widening the roadway. Since Ted can now provide parking for only half as many cars as before, his business has dropped precipitously.

(a) May Ted declare the lease canceled and move out if the common law approach to this question is followed?

Not sure ☐

(b) At common law, may Ted remain but pay a lesser rent, reflecting the diminution in the value of the premises to him as a result of the condemnation?

Not sure ☐

(c) Assume that Ted continues to use the premises (whether voluntarily or involuntarily) after the condemnation. Assume further that in 2011 (after Ted's lease has terminated), Lou receives a $100,000 condemnation award from the state, representing the lost value of the premises. Does Lou owe Ted any portion of this award, under the common law approach?

Not sure ☐

78. L leased a storefront to T, knowing that T intended to use the premises to sell crack to neighborhood residents. T was then convicted and sent to prison on drug charges relating to his conduct on the premises. Therefore, T folded up his operations and stopped paying rent. L, knowing that T probably has a hefty bank account, has sued T for back rent. If the court is aware of all of the above facts, will the court order T to pay back rent to L?

Not sure ☐

79. Lila, a notorious slumlord, rented a one-bedroom apartment to Terence for $400 per month. The lease made no explicit warranties regarding condition of the premises. Unbeknownst to Terence at the time the lease was signed, the apartment was (and still is) infested with rats, and the toilet did not and does not work. Terence is quite poor and cannot pay moving expenses or a security deposit to move to a different apartment. He would like to be able to withhold the rent until the rats are exterminated and the toilet fixed. In a jurisdiction following the unmodified common law rule on relevant issues, may Terence withhold rent on the grounds that the apartment is not habitable?

Not sure ☐

80. Same facts as in the previous question. Now, assume that the jurisdiction takes an approach toward the relevant issues that is fairly typical of the way most states now approach the issues. May Terence withhold rent?

Not sure ☐

81. Same facts as in the previous two questions. Now, assume that Terence knew, prior to signing the lease, that there were rats and that the toilet was broken. In a "modern" jurisdiction, will Terence be found to be entitled to withhold rent until the conditions are fixed?

Not sure ☐

82. Same facts as in the previous three questions. Now, assume that the lease between Lila and Terence was a standard form of lease, and provided in its "boilerplate" that "Tenant hereby waives any implied warranties, including specifically the implied warranty of habitability. If the premises are not habitable, it shall be the duty of Tenant to perform any needed repairs." Terence was aware of this clause at the time he signed the agreement and made a perfunctory attempt to have Lila modify the clause, but she refused. Assuming that Terence did not know of the particular defects (rats and stuffed toilet) before moving in, may he withhold rent in a jurisdiction following the "modern" view toward the warranty of habitability?

Not sure ☐

83. In a small New England town where winters are fierce, Developer built a small "strip mall" (i.e., a structure designed to house several retail stores). Developer leased part of the structure to Retailer, who (as Developer knew) intended to operate a women's clothing boutique on the premises. The lease was silent about Developer's obligation to maintain any particular level of comfort or habitability in the premises. (Bad lawyering by Retailer's lawyer!) On December 1, the center's boiler broke, and Developer did nothing to fix it for the next two and a half months. Retailer attempted to heat the premises with electric space heaters, but was only partly successful. Fewer customers than expected have tried on or bought clothes because of the lack of heat. If Retailer withholds the rent for the months of December, January, and February, will a court find that Retailer was within his rights?

Not sure ☐

84. Lena is a professional landlord who owns a number of apartment buildings in the city of Ames. She rented an apartment in one of these buildings to Troy. The lease provided for a one-year term, with no renewal options. After Troy moved in, he discovered that the heat was inadequate, the locks did not work, and other things were wrong. He therefore lodged a complaint with the City of Ames Housing Agency, which is in charge of seeing that landlords obey their statutory obligations concerning residential housing. At the agency's demand, Lena reluctantly fixed the problems. At the end of the one-year lease, Lena notified Troy that she would not renew his lease. Lena customarily renews residential leases and gave Troy no explanation of why she would not renew his, though he suspects that this is due to his complaint to the agency. If Troy refuses to move out at the end of the lease term, and Lena sues to evict him, what defense should Troy raise? What is the likely result if he does raise it?

85. Lana, a homeowner, rented her home to Tully in 2009 under a one-year lease, since she was to be abroad on an academic sabbatical for that year. The lease said nothing about the parties' obligations in the event of sudden destruction of the premises. Tully agreed to pay a rent of $500 per month. (The house had a fair market rental value of $1,000 per month, but Lana charged less because she liked Tully and thought he would take good care of the house.) After Tully had occupied the house for four months, the house was struck by lightning, and its upper floor (of two) was destroyed. The house is still "habitable" in the sense that Tully could live there, but only under much less pleasant circumstances (including the lack of a formal bedroom) than he had anticipated.

    (a) May Tully terminate the lease and stop paying rent?

    (b) May Tully recover damages from Lana for his "loss of bargain"? If so, in what amount?

86. Lamar, the owner of several residential buildings, rented an apartment to Tomas. As Lamar knew at the time he signed the lease (and as Tomas did not know), the shower door in the bathroom was cracked, leaving a jagged edge. On Tomas's first night in the apartment, he reached to open the shower door and badly slashed his wrist, permanently losing sensation in three of his fingers. If Tomas sues Lamar for personal injury damages, and the jurisdiction follows the traditional common law approach to all relevant issues, will Tomas recover?

87. Same facts as in the previous question. Now, however, assume that (1) Lamar was not aware of the broken glass, but if he had conducted an inspection of the premises sometime in the previous year (as a reasonable landlord would have done), he would have discovered the danger; and (2) the jurisdiction follows the "modern" view toward all relevant issues. If Tomas cuts his hand in the manner described in the previous question, will he be able to recover against Lamar?

88. Lehman leased a building to Tuttle for ten years. Under the terms of the lease, Lehman was not required to keep the heating plant in working order, and Tuttle had the right (but not the obligation) to make any reasonably necessary repairs or replacements of that unit. After two years, the boiler broke, and Tuttle (behaving reasonably) installed a new boiler. This boiler is attached to the cement floor of the basement, and is also attached to the ductwork that begins in the basement. With four months remaining on his lease, Tuttle has decided not to renew. Tuttle realizes

that the relatively new boiler has substantial market value and can be moved to a new site. If Tuttle removes the new boiler and reattaches the old (broken) boiler, thus putting the premises in the condition they were in shortly before he did the boiler replacement, may Lehman recover damages from Tuttle?

Not sure ☐

89. Ludlum rented a suite in an office building he owns to Trotta. As part of the lease, Trotta gave Ludlum a two-month security deposit. The lease was for five years. After three years, Trotta moved out without cause and stopped paying rent. Because the real estate market was a tight one, Ludlum almost immediately found a new tenant. Ludlum therefore sent Trotta a letter stating, "I am hereby terminating our lease because of your abandonment of the premises. You will be held responsible for all damages I suffer." Ludlum then relet the premises to the new tenant at the same monthly rent, so that his only losses are the loss of one month's rent ($1,000). Ludlum would like to be able to keep the entire security deposit until the expiration of the original five-year Ludlum-Trotta lease term. May he do so?

Not sure ☐

90. Same facts as in the previous question. How could the party to whom your answer was unfavorable have altered the result, either by a drafting change or by subsequent conduct?

Not sure ☐

91. Lockhart leased a suite in an office building he owned to Terhune. Terhune gave Lockhart a $5,000 security deposit at the commencement of the lease. Halfway through the lease, Lockhart sold the building to Pribble. Lockhart kept possession of all security deposits after the sale transaction. At the expiration of Terhune's lease, Terhune left the premises in their original condition. Terhune requested that Lockhart return his security deposit, but Lockhart had by then gone bankrupt. May Terhune recover the security deposit from Pribble?

Not sure ☐

92. Logan rented a house to Tierney. The lease provided that (1) the rent was to be due promptly on the first of each month; (2) prompt payment was "of the essence" of the lease; and (3) if the rent was more than 14 days past due, Logan would have the right to terminate the lease effective immediately. There were no other relevant lease provisions. On three occasions, Tierney paid the rent between 15 and 25 days late, and Logan took no action and made no response. Then, Tierney paid a particular month's rent 15 days late, and Logan sent a letter stating, "I hereby exercise my contractual right to terminate the lease effective immediately." Will a court enforce this termination letter?

Not sure ☐

93. Lombard leased office space to Toland, for a two-year term. At the end of the lease term, Toland attempted to renew the lease, but Lombard refused. One week after the lease expired, Toland still had his furnishings on the premises. Summary proceedings were available to Lombard to evict Toland, but these would have taken approximately two months, and Lombard had a tenant who wanted to take occupancy immediately. Therefore, over a weekend, Lombard entered Toland's premises, moved his furniture into the hall, and changed the locks. When Toland arrived Monday morning, he found his furniture in good shape, but he was effectively out of business until he could arrange to move into new quarters; this took him two weeks, during which time he lost $10,000 worth of business. If Toland sues Lombard for $10,000 in damages, will Toland recover?

Not sure ☐

94. Same facts as the above question. Now, however, assume that Lombard did not change the locks or remove Toland's furniture, but instead resorted to summary proceedings. Toland was finally evicted by this means two months after the lease expired. The rent Toland paid under the lease was $1,000 per month, but he did not pay anything for the two holdover months. However, the new tenant, once he entered, paid a rent of $2,000. There is no other evidence on the issue of damages. What damages, if any, may Lombard recover from Toland?   Not sure ☐

95. Link leased an apartment to Taylor. With two years to go on the lease (which was for $1,000 per month), Taylor fell far behind on the rent and was nowhere to be seen. (In fact, he was vacationing in Europe.) On August 1, Link entered the premises and removed Taylor's furniture to a warehouse for safekeeping. Link also began efforts to relet the premises. The market value of such premises for lease was approximately $1,000, the amount Taylor had been paying. Because Link was not very efficient at advertising, it took him six months to find a substitute tenant, who then signed for $1,000 a month and moved in. (Had Link been efficient at advertising the space, he could have rented it in one month.) Taylor's security deposit exactly covers the rent accrued prior to August 1. How much, if anything, may Link recover from Taylor?   Not sure ☐

96. Same facts as in the previous question. What should Link have done differently?   Not sure ☐

97. Same facts as in the previous two questions. Now, assume that Link did not reenter the premises or move Taylor's furniture out. Instead, Link allowed the premises to remain vacant and notified Taylor that he was doing so. Link made no effort to relet the premises. After the term expired (with 24 months of rent unpaid), Link sued Taylor for the cumulative unpaid rent. May Link recover this amount?   Not sure ☐

98. Lillian, the owner of an apartment building, leased an apartment to Tracey for two years at $1,000 per month. After one year of the lease had expired, Tracey wanted to travel in Europe for ten months. She therefore transferred to Stuart the right of occupancy for the next ten months, reserving to herself the right to occupy the premises for the final two months of her lease with Lillian. Rent payments (at the same $1,000 per month) were to be made by Stuart to Tracey, and Tracey would pass them on to Lillian. Tracey went off on her trip and failed to make any payments to Lillian. Lillian has now learned that Tracey has become insolvent. Meanwhile, Stuart, after occupying the premises for four months, has moved out, and is apparently not sending rent payments to Tracey. The premises are currently unoccupied. Lillian would like to sue Stuart for the four payments he owes Tracey covering the time he actually occupied the premises, plus the six payments that became due after he left the premises. Which, if any, portion of this money may Lillian recover from Stuart?   Not sure ☐

99. Same facts as in the previous question. Now, however, assume that Tracey transferred to Stuart the right to occupy the premises for the full one year remaining on the Lillian-Tracey lease. As in the previous question, assume that Stuart is to make payments to Tracey, not to Lillian. All other facts are the same as in the above question. Of the ten months for which Stuart owes rent to Tracey (four months that Stuart occupied the space and six months that elapsed after he moved out), for how many can Lillian recover from Stuart?   Not sure ☐

100. Lewis rented a house to Theresa. In the lease, Theresa promised to pay $1,000 monthly rent for the three-year lease term. After one year, Lewis sold the house to Paul. The sale documents did not mention who would be entitled to any rent. Meanwhile, Theresa moved out and has stopped paying rent (though she has paid for all of the months in which she actually used the premises). If Paul sues Theresa for rent for the time when the house was empty, may Paul recover?

Not sure ☐

Questions 101-109 below relate to the following fact pattern:

Lloyd, the owner of Blackacre, leased the property to Thelma for a five-year term. In this lease, Thelma promised to pay Lloyd rent of $1,000 per month. Three years into the lease, Thelma assigned her remaining interest in the lease to Tim. In the Thelma-Tim transaction, Tim did not expressly promise Thelma to perform Thelma's obligations under the master lease, but merely accepted from Thelma a document stating, "I hereby assign to you all my rights under my lease with Lloyd." Tim then moved onto the property.

101. After Tim moved in, he made the first six monthly $1,000 payments directly to Lloyd, and Lloyd made no objection. Then, Tim did not make any payments for the next three months. If Lloyd sues Thelma for the three months during which Tim did not make payments, may Lloyd recover?

Not sure ☐

102. Same facts as in the previous question. Assume, now, that Lloyd does not sue Thelma for the missed three months, but instead sues Tim for this period. Assume further that Tim was in residence during the three months for which no rent was paid. May Lloyd recover the three months rent from Tim?

Not sure ☐

103. Same facts as in the previous two questions. Now, assume that after missing three months of rent, Tim assigned to Theo any interest that Tim had in the premises. Tim moved out. Theo took possession and failed to pay the next six months rent. If Lloyd sues Tim for this six-month period, may Lloyd recover?

Not sure ☐

104. Same basic fact pattern as in the previous three questions. Now, assume that in the original Lloyd-Thelma lease, Thelma promised to keep the premises insured, with Lloyd named as the loss payee. Assume that this promise is deemed not to "touch and concern" the land (the majority rule regarding promises to insure). Also assume, as in the previous questions, that Tim merely took an assignment of Thelma's rights and made no express promises. Neither Thelma nor Tim paid the insurance premium. The property burned down. If Lloyd sues Tim for failing to keep the premises insured, may Lloyd recover?

Not sure ☐

105. Now, assume that at the time Tim took possession from Thelma, he promised Thelma that he would carry out all duties that Thelma was required to perform under her lease from Lloyd. As in the previous question, assume that Tim did not pay the insurance premium. Lloyd sues Tim for damages due to this failure. May Lloyd recover?

Not sure ☐

106. Now, assume that at a time when Tim was in possession (having received an assignment from Thelma of Thelma's rights, but having not made any promises of his own), Lloyd sold the property (and assigned all of his rights in the property) to Leon. In the sale documents, Leon did not make any promises to Lloyd, and merely gave Lloyd the purchase price. Assume further that in the original Lloyd-Thelma lease, Lloyd promised to keep the premises in repair. During Tim's occupancy, Leon has not made required repairs. May Tim sue Leon for damages?

Not sure ☐

107. At a time when Tim was in possession (having taken an assignment from Thelma but not having made any promises), Lloyd sold the property to Leon, as in the previous question. Tim failed to pay rent for six months while he was in possession. Leon has sued Tim for this rent. May Leon recover from Tim?

Not sure ☐

108. Assume that the original Lloyd-Thelma lease stated, in a negotiated term, that Thelma would not sublet or assign without Lloyd's written consent. Also, assume that when Thelma assigned to Tim, Thelma (as required under the lease) asked Lloyd's consent, and Lloyd consented because he felt that Tim was at least as responsible a tenant as Thelma. Now, Tim seeks to assign to Theo, but Lloyd objects because he feels (reasonably) that Theo is irresponsible. If Theo takes possession, may Lloyd have Theo evicted?

Not sure ☐

109. Same facts as in the previous question. Now, assume that the anti-assignment clause in the Lloyd-Thelma lease was continued in the fine print "boilerplate" of the standard residential lease prepared by Lloyd, and that at the time that lease was signed, the residential housing market was sufficiently tight that nearly all landlords insisted on imposing similar no-assignment provisions. Thelma now wishes to assign her remaining rights to Tim. Tim is willing to assume all of Thelma's obligations, and is a financially responsible and otherwise good tenant. Lloyd refuses to consent to the assignment, solely because he wishes to raise the rent to $2,000 per month (now the prevailing market rent for such an apartment because of a rise in real estate prices since the Lloyd-Thelma lease was signed). May Lloyd prevent Tim from taking occupancy?

Not sure ☐

110. Orin owned a large country estate, Country Oaks, which contained a trout stream. Orin's friend and neighbor Norman, owner of an adjacent parcel, fished in the stream for several years with Orin's consent. Orin decided to sell Country Oaks to Alfred, but wanted to protect Norman's fishing rights. Therefore, with Alfred's consent, Orin's deed to Alfred contained an easement granting Norman and his successors the right to fish in the stream in perpetuity, as well as the right to get to the stream by a path running through the estate. Five years later, Alfred conveyed Country Oaks to Barbara. The Alfred-to-Barbara deed did not contain any easement for fishing.

(a) If the jurisdiction follows the traditional common law approach to relevant issues, may Norman continue to fish in the stream?

Not sure ☐

(b) In a jurisdiction following a contemporary approach to the relevant issues, may Norman continue to fish in the stream?

Not sure ☐

111. Angela is the owner of Auburnacre. Burt is the owner of Blueacre. The two parcels are adjacent, and have never (at least as far as property records go back, which is 200 years) been under common ownership. A lake, located on public land and open to the public, borders the eastern edge of Auburnacre; the Auburnacre-Blueacre border is on the west side of Auburnacre. For many years, the lake had been useless because it was algae-infested. However, in 1995, the state dredged and reclaimed the lake so that it is now usable for fishing. Beginning in 1995, Angela allowed Burt to cross Angela's property to get to the lake for boating. (Because the land is out in the country where few roads exist, Burt would have to drive 25 miles to get to the lake if he were not permitted to cross Auburnacre.) No written agreement between Angela and Burt regarding Burt's right to cross Angela's land ever existed.

In 2008, Burt conveyed Blueacre to Carter. Shortly thereafter, Carter attempted to cross Auburnacre to get to the lake. Angela objected, and thereafter put a road-block across the path, in the middle of Auburnacre, that Burt had formerly used. May Carter compel Angela to remove the roadblock so that Carter can cross over to use the lake?

Not sure ☐

112. Helen owned a parcel of land in a mountainous region. Helen was the owner of a hang gliding shop, and stored five hang gliders on each of her two trucks for use in lessons. Helen then sold the eastern half of her property to Ingrid. The deed to Ingrid did not specify any easement. The portion sold to Ingrid is situated near the driveway to Helen's portion, so that the rear five feet of each glider hangs over Ingrid's property when Helen parks her trucks (on her own portion) in the most convenient fashion. The only way Helen can avoid having the gliders hang over Ingrid's property is to park her trucks in the street (which would be legal, but very unsightly and inconvenient), or to build a costly garage. If Ingrid seeks an injunction to prevent Helen from parking her trucks in a way that causes the gliders to hang over Ingrid's property, will Ingrid be successful?

Not sure ☐

113. For many years, Daphne owned a ten-acre parcel of waterfront land known as the Overlook. The westernmost five acres of the property (called West Overlook) contained a house and a driveway leading to Main Street, a public road. The easternmost five acres (called East Overlook) consisted of a little-used summerhouse located on a peninsula jutting out into the western side of Lake Moon, a two-mile-wide lake; East Overlook had a dock on the lake. The only land-based way to exit East Overlook would have been to use the driveway across West Overlook to get to Main Street. However, Daphne never left East Overlook by crossing West Overlook in this manner. Instead, if she wanted to leave East Overlook, she always sailed from her dock in a small motorboat across Lake Moon; at the opposite shore of the lake, she used a car that she parked adjacent to Smith Avenue, a public street.

In 2001, Daphne sold East Overlook to Frederika. The deed made no mention of any easement across West Overlook. As Daphne knew, Frederika was buying East Overlook to use it as a waterfront summerhouse; Frederika was happy with the limitation that she would have to enter and leave by some sort of boat crossing the lake between Smith Avenue and East Overlook. But then, in 2009, Frederika suffered a stroke that made it extremely dangerous for her to travel the two miles by boat. She asked Daphne to permit her to enter and exit by use of a van that would use the driveway over West Overlook to connect East Overlook with Main Street. Daphne refused. Frederika has now sued for a judicial declaration that she has an easement to cross West Overlook by van. Should the court find for Frederika?

Not sure ☐

114. Xavier and Yentil were neighbors who lived on adjacent parcels in the state of Skidmore. On Xavier's property was a tennis court. For a period of 11 years,

Xavier extended to Yentil a standing invitation to use the tennis court whenever Yentil wished (whether Xavier was present or not). Yentil took advantage of this invitation, using the court at least once a week for the entire 11-year period. Then, Xavier and Yentil had a falling out, and Xavier refused to allow Yentil to use the court any further. The statute of limitations to recover real property in state of Skidmore is 10 years. Does Yentil now have a right to use the court over Xavier's objections?

Not sure ☐

115. Astrid and Ben were adjacent landowners. Astrid's property was valuable beach-front property. Ben's property adjoined Astrid's on the side away from the ocean. From 1990 to 2007, Ben and his family continually (at least once a week in nice weather) traveled to the beach by walking along a beaten path crossing Astrid's side yard. (They could have driven to a public beach four blocks away, but preferred walking directly to the beach area behind Astrid's house.) Astrid never gave permission to Ben to use this path in this way, but she did not voice any objection either. Then, in 2007, Astrid sold her property to Charles. Charles immediately barred the path so that Ben could no longer use it. The statute of limitations for actions to recover real property in the jurisdiction is 15 years. Does Ben have a right to continue using the path to the beach?

Not sure ☐

116. David owned a home, with a large yard, in the state of Earl. Earl has a 20-year adverse possession statute. Frances lived in a large lot down the street. Every year or so, David had his huge oak trees trimmed. Since his yard was large and heavily wooded, the trimming always generated a huge pile of branches that needed to be dumped somewhere. Frances regularly dumped her grass trimmings and branches in a secluded spot on her property. Without Frances's permission (but with her knowledge), David dumped his oak tree branches in Frances's pile most autumns, over a 30-year period. Then, Frances sold her house to Grant, who was much less laid-back. Grant informed David that he could no longer dump branches on his (Grant's) property. Is David entitled to continue dumping?

Not sure ☐

117. Darwin owns a parcel of land located behind a public high school in the state of Kent. Kent has a 15-year adverse possession statute. The children in the neighborhood have been riding their bicycles daily to school for more than 20 years via a path that cuts through Darwin's property. They have done so even though Darwin has never given children permission to use the path. Recently, a number of the children have purchased four-wheel motorized all-terrain vehicles (ATVs). The children cross Darwin's path on these ATVs at speeds up to 40 mph, making a lot of noise and digging up the path much more severely than standard bicycles do. If Darwin brings a suit to prevent the use of the ATVs on his path, will he succeed?

Not sure ☐

118. Paula is in the business of breeding rare walk-swim cats. At any time, she has approximately ten such cats. These cats need to walk and swim extensively each day. For a number of years, Paula has bred these cats on Blackacre, a parcel she owns, and has kept them in a small kennel on that property. Daniel is the owner of Whiteacre, adjacent to Blackacre, which contains a pond and plenty of unused land. Therefore, Paula purchased from Daniel an easement for her cats to walk from Blackacre to Whiteacre, and to roam and swim on Whiteacre. Two years

after negotiating this easement, Paula bought Greenacre, located on the other side of Blackacre from Whiteacre. Paula built a larger kennel on Greenacre, and now breeds and keeps her cats there. She now walks her cats from Greenacre to Blackacre, then to Whiteacre, where they roam and swim just as they did before Paula bought Greenacre. Although the kennel is larger, Paula has not increased her cat population beyond the original ten. Daniel objects that the easement he sold Paula is in favor of Blackacre only, and may not be extended to benefit Greenacre as well. (Indeed, the original easement mentions Blackacre as being the benefitted parcel, and of course does not mention Greenacre since Paula at the time did not own it.) Is Daniel entitled to block Paula from her present use of the easement?

        Not sure ☐

119. From Dunes Development Co., George purchased a house just off the 16th fairway of Sandy Dunes Country Club. Dunes Development Co. constructed the club. The deed from Dunes stated that George would have the right to free use of the Sandy Dunes Golf Course indefinitely, but was silent on whether the golf rights that George received were transferable. Two years later, George sold the house to Henry. By then, the course was no longer being operated by Dunes Development Co., but rather, by Ian, who bought it from Dunes. When Henry attempted to use the golf course for free, Ian refused. If Henry brings suit against Ian to enforce the free-golf provision of the deed, will Henry prevail?

        Not sure ☐

120. Frookie owned a 2,500-acre parcel of land, which was heavily wooded with pine trees. Winnie was a local artist who specialized in making handmade wreaths to be sold during the holiday season. To secure a steady supply of pine branches for the wreaths, Winnie obtained from Frookie a nonexclusive right (for a single annual flat fee) to take as many pine branches from Frookie's farm as she needed to make the wreaths. This continued for three years, during which Winnie made between 500 and 600 wreaths per year. Then, Winnie assigned her right to take the pine branches to two large corporations in the business of making wreaths. Combined, these corporations plan to take enough pine branches to make 50,000 wreaths per year. Upset over losing so many pine branches, Frookie brought suit to enjoin the corporations from coming on his property. Will Frookie prevail?

        Not sure ☐

121. Same facts as in the previous question. Now, however, assume that Winnie's right to take pine branches from Frookie's parcel was "exclusive"—i.e., that Frookie could not also remove pine branches from the property or permit anyone else to do so. Also, assume that the Frookie-Winnie contract called for Winnie to pay Frookie $4 for every 100 branches removed from Frookie's property. Can Frookie block the two corporate assignees from succeeding to Winnie's rights and taking 50,000 wreaths per year?

        Not sure ☐

122. Quince owned a limestone quarry and a manufacturing plant in which he worked the limestone into gravestones and monuments. A parcel owned by Pierce lay between the quarry and the manufacturing plant. Therefore, Quince purchased from Pierce an easement to drive his trucks along a ten-foot-wide strip of Pierce's land so the stone could be taken from the quarry to the manufacturing plant. Quince's business grew over the years, and in 2005, Quince shuttered the plant, and built a newer, larger plant some miles away. At the time the old plant was shuttered, Quince told Pierce by telephone, "I won't be needing the easement across your land anymore."

Shortly thereafter, Quince sold the quarry, as well as the shuttered plant and the land it stood on, to Raymond. Raymond immediately started driving his trucks from the quarry to the plant. If Pierce brings suit to stop Raymond from crossing Pierce's property, will Pierce be successful?

Not sure ☐

123. Abbott and Bingham were adjacent landowners and fanatical tennis players. Abbott, the richer of the two, built a clay tennis court on his property. At the time of construction, he said to Bingham, "For as long as you own your property, you are free to use the court whenever you wish, so long as I am not playing on it." Bingham immediately sent Abbott a letter stating, "I want to thank you for your generosity in allowing me to use your tennis court whenever I want (assuming you are not using it, of course) for as long as I stay in the house. I regard this as significantly enhancing the value of my own property." For ten years, the arrangement worked well. Then, Abbott discovered one day that Bingham was having an affair with Abbott's wife. Abbott angrily wrote to Bingham, "I am hereby revoking your right to use my tennis court. Never set foot on my property again, under pain of prosecution for trespass." Bingham now sues for a declaratory judgment that he is entitled to use Abbott's court. The state where the land is located has a 25-year statute of limitation on adverse possession actions.

(a) What property interest, if any, did Abbott grant to Bingham at the time the court was constructed?

Not sure ☐

(b) Should the court hold that Bingham has the right to use Abbott's court now?

Not sure ☐

124. Same facts as in the previous question. Now, however, assume that at the time the court was originally constructed, Abbott said to Bingham by phone, "If you'll pay half the cost of constructing the court, you'll be able to use it forever." No document was ever signed or exchanged between the parties, but Bingham in fact paid half the cost of constructing the court (one-half of the $40,000 cost).

(a) Should a judge hold that Bingham has the right to use the court as long as he lives in the house?

Not sure ☐

(b) Is there some alternative judgment that the court might sensibly render?

Not sure ☐

125. Allison and Bertrand were neighboring landowners who owned fee simples in adjacent parcels of land. The parcels were separated by a fence that lay on Allison's property. Since proper maintenance of the fence was important to Bertrand's property as well as to Allison's, both parties agreed that when the fence needed repairs and painting from time to time, Allison would cause this to be done, and Bertrand would then reimburse Allison for half the cost. The agreement also provided that if Bertrand did not pay a debt that was properly owing, Allison could get a lien on his land for the unpaid debt. The agreement was embodied in a document signed by both parties, and filed in the local real estate records indexed under both Allison's and Bertrand's names. The document did not specifically give Bertrand any right to come upon Allison's land to make the repairs if Allison declined to do so.

Two years after this agreement, Bertrand conveyed his parcel to his daughter, Claire, in fee simple. Claire never explicitly or implicitly promised to pay for repairs to the fence. Five years after this conveyance, Allison spent $1,000 to have the fence extensively repaired and repainted. (Intervening repairs had occurred while

Bertrand still owned his parcel, and he paid for them. The $1,000 was for work done to repair wear and tear that occurred after Claire took title.) Allison now seeks to recover $500 from either Bertrand or Claire. If both refuse to pay, will Allison's suit be successful against Claire, assuming that there is no special statute in force relevant to this question, and assuming that the common law approach applies?   Not sure ☐

126. Same basic fact pattern as in the previous question. Now, assume that Bertrand never made the conveyance to Claire. Assume further that Allison, five years after her deal with Bertrand, conveyed her parcel to her brother Doug. If Doug sues Bertrand for enforcement of the promise, may Doug recover?   Not sure ☐

127. Same basic fact pattern as in the previous two questions. Now, assume that the original Allison-Bertrand document also contained a promise by Allison that she would not replace the wooden fence with a structure made of any other material (because Bertrand liked the look of natural wood). (This promise was contained in the document that was filed in the land records.) Assume that as in the previous question, Allison conveyed the property to Doug, and further assume that Bertrand conveyed his property to Claire. If Doug begins to replace the wooden fence with a shiny metal one, may Claire get an injunction against Doug?   Not sure ☐

128. Harry and Isadore were adjacent landowners in a residential area. Each believed that swimming pools were tacky. They therefore agreed, in a writing signed by both, that neither would ever permit his property to have a swimming pool placed upon it. Three years later, Isadore sold his parcel to James. At the time of purchase, James did not have actual knowledge of the Harry-Isadore agreement. A check by James of the real estate records failed to disclose the Harry-Isadore agreement (because it had never been filed by either party). If James had asked Isadore, Isadore would have told him about the agreement, but James never asked, and Isadore never thought to mention it. James has now begun work to prepare his site to contain a swimming pool. If Harry sues to enjoin the construction by James, should the court grant Harry an injunction?   Not sure ☐

129. Same facts as in the previous question. Now, however, assume that just before Isadore sold his parcel to James, he orally stated to James, "I've promised Harry never to build a pool upon my property, and he's made the same promise to me. However, I don't think this agreement, even though it's in writing, would be binding on you as a purchaser, since you didn't sign the agreement." Should a court now enjoin James from building the pool?   Not sure ☐

130. Developer, a residential real estate developer, purchased a farm and set about creating Happy Farms, a planned residential community. Developer prepared a subdivision map (or plat) for Happy Farms, which showed that all 36 lots on Happy Farms were to be used for residential purposes, showed where roads and sewers were to run, and contained other details indicating that the property would be a residential community. Developer then sold Parcel 1 at Happy Farms to Kathy. In the deed from Developer, Kathy agreed that her parcel would be subject to the restrictions contained in the plat, which was filed in the real estate records. Developer did not state in the deed that other parcels later sold by him would be subject to similar restrictions, though Developer orally told Kathy, "Other buyers will be subject to the same limitations, so you'll be sure that you'll have a purely residential community with high standards."

Developer then sold Parcel 2 to Lewis. Due to Developer's administrative negligence, the deed to Lewis omitted the restrictions contained in Kathy's deed. However, there is evidence that Lewis knew that a general residential plan had been prepared by Developer and filed in the real estate records. Several years later, Lewis attempted to open a candy store on part of his property. (Local zoning laws allow this because the area is zoned mixed use.) If Kathy sues Lewis to enjoin him from using his property for nonresidential purposes, will the court grant Kathy's request?

Not sure ☐

131. Same basic fact pattern as in the previous question. Now, assume that Developer then sold the remainder of the lots (40 in all) making up the Happy Farms Development; each lot was sold with a deed restricting the buyer to residential uses of the property. Fifteen years passed. During this time, the area surrounding Happy Farms went from farmland to robust commercial (office and retail) development. A corner lot in the development, which belongs to Michael, now has an office building across the street from one side of Michael's house and a large store across the street from the other side. As a private house, Michael's property is worth $200,000 (less than the $300,000 average value of homes within Happy Farms, because Michael's has more traffic, more noise, a commercial rather than residential view, etc.). Michael, who happens to be a developer of office buildings, would like to tear down his house and erect a small office building instead. Kathy (one of the other Happy Farms owners) has sued to enjoin Michael from proceeding with this plan. Michael argues that the character of the surrounding area has so changed that it is unfair to force him to keep his property residential. Should the court grant Kathy's request for an injunction?

Not sure ☐

132. For 20 years, Dexter has operated a private dump in the town of Hampshire. The dump now receives approximately 500 tons of garbage per year, about the same annual amount that it has always received. The only negative environmental effect from operation of the dump is odor, and the odors are no more serious than they have always been (i.e., a mildly disturbing garbage smell that depending on wind condition can be perceived as far as one-half mile away from the dump). As the town has become more affluent, the citizens have become increasingly unhappy about the dump. Finally, the Hampshire Town Council recently passed a zoning ordinance providing that no dump may be operated within the town, and further providing that any existing dump must be discontinued within two years following passage of the ordinance. Because Dexter's property now has a huge pile of unsightly garbage on it, its value has declined to $200,000 (versus an approximately $1 million value as an operating dump). Dexter has brought an inverse condemnation suit against Hampshire, arguing that the ordinance amounts to a "taking" of his property and that he must therefore be compensated for the $1 million value it has (though he is willing to give the town a credit for the $200,000 that the property will be worth after it is no longer a dump). Should the court award Dexter the $800,000 relief he seeks?

Not sure ☐

133. Same facts as in the previous question. Assume that the two-year phase-out period passed while Dexter was challenging the Hampshire ordinance, and that for one year after that Dexter was effectively put out of business while a court hears his Fourteenth Amendment claim. (Assume for purposes of this question that the

phase-out period is long enough to satisfy case law requiring a substantial "amortization" period when a previously allowable use is banned.) Assume further that the court decided that the ordinance went beyond the scope of reasonable land use regulation, and amounted to a temporary taking of Dexter's property for one year. If Hampshire is willing (as it must be) to suspend its ordinance henceforth, must it pay Dexter damages for the one-year period during which he was unable to operate the dump?

Not sure ☐

134. Herbert, a multimillionaire industrialist, moved into the exclusive community of South Fork. A validly promulgated ordinance of South Fork provides that the plans for any residential structure must be examined and approved by the town Planning Commission before construction starts. The ordinance further provides that no plans will be approved unless the proposed structure is "in architectural consonance with nearby residences." Herbert bought a vacant parcel on an exclusive street on which all existing houses were either brick Georgian colonials or Tudor-style mansions. Herbert submitted plans for a very large residence patterned after a fourteenth-century French castle with 16 turrets. The Planning Commission agreed that Herbert's design was architecturally meritorious in the abstract, but rejected it on the grounds that it was not in architectural harmony with other houses on the block. If Herbert sues to have the Planning Commission's judgment overturned, on the grounds that as a matter of common law, zoning commissions may not pursue aesthetic objectives, is Herbert likely to succeed?

Not sure ☐

135. Jones operates a car dealership along a highway located in the town of Nordstrom. For 20 years, Jones has had a billboard on the edge of his property extolling his dealership's virtues to passersby on the highway. Then, the Nordstrom Town Council enacted a comprehensive zoning ordinance, which among other things bars all billboards anywhere in the town. The "preexisting uses" section of the ordinance provides that any nonconforming use must be phased out within five years of the ordinance. Jones has sued to overturn the ordinance as applied to him, arguing that while Nordstrom has the right to ban billboards prospectively, it may not require him to remove an existing billboard because this constitutes a taking of his property without due process. Will Jones prevail?

Not sure ☐

136. The town of Twin Peaks is a long-established wealthy community whose residents include almost no blacks or other minorities, and almost no poor people. Twin Peaks never had a comprehensive zoning ordinance until 2005. That year, it enacted an ordinance that, among other aspects, provided that no home may be built on a parcel of land containing less than two acres. Prosser, a local developer, acquired a ten-acre parcel on a quiet street in Twin Peaks. He proposed to build 20 single-family residences on the parcel. Prosser realized, of course, that he would not be permitted to build the development unless he could either have the two-acre minimum removed from the ordinance or obtain a variance for his development. The Town Council refused to do either. Prosser was reluctant to sue the town, because he did not want to alienate it.

However, Twin Peaks is sued by Prince, a black resident of nearby Glendale, who argues that if the two-acre minimum were lifted, he would be able to afford, and would choose, to live on Prosser's development. Prince contends that Twin Peaks' refusal to lift the minimum violates his equal protection rights. At trial,

Prince is able to prove that the two-acre minimum has the effect of dramatically reducing the number of black residents in Twin Peaks, since most nearby blacks are insufficiently wealthy to afford the two-acre parcels. However, neither side produces any evidence as to whether the Town Council of Twin Peaks was motivated by a desire to keep out blacks, either at the time the ordinance was originally enacted or at the more recent time when the Council refused to lift the two-acre minimum. On these facts, will the court find that Twin Peaks has violated Prince's equal protection rights?

Not sure ☐

137. Same facts as in the previous question.

    (a) What statutory action, if any, could Prince bring that would have a good probability of success?

Not sure ☐

    (b) Will Prince succeed with such an action?

Not sure ☐

138. Same facts as in the previous three questions. Now, however, assume that there is convincing evidence that the Town Council of Twin Peaks was *not* motivated by any racially discriminatory intent, and that the two-acre minimum zoning rule was enacted for the purpose of maintaining the "uncrowded" and "pastoral" nature of the town. Assume that Twin Peaks is located in the state of New Jersey. No relevant statutes have been enacted.

    (a) What theory might Prosser use to attack the two-acre rule?

    (b) If the court agreed with Prosser's suit, what remedy would the court be likely to award?

Not sure ☐

139. The State of Pound has enacted a landmark designation–enabling statute that permits any city to designate certain buildings as landmarks, in which case the city may prevent the landmark from being destroyed or altered. Designations must be based on the recommendation of an impartial committee of architectural or historical experts. The City of Acropolis, located in Pound, appointed such a committee, and then designated a building at 120 Main Street as being such a landmark. The building, by the renowned architect Mies van Wright, was built in 1930, and was the first skyscraper to use the modern and then-revolutionary glass-and-anodized-aluminum technique. Because the building is only 18 stories high, and local zoning permits a building of up to 90 stories, the building's owner, a developer named Darwin, wishes to tear it down. Acropolis's regulations prohibit the destruction of any landmark building. If Darwin attacks the designation and/or the antidestruction rules that accompany that landmark designation, will a court overturn the designation and permit Darwin to demolish the building? If so, on what theory?

Not sure ☐

140. The downtown portion of the city of Blue Haven was economically depressed. The town elders decided that one way to revitalize the area would be to use the city's eminent domain powers to put together a parcel of existing residential structures and convert this to a shopping mall. The city therefore instituted proceedings (as authorized by state law) to take title by eminent domain to 40 single-family residences in the heart of the downtown area. The city planned to demolish the structures after taking title, and to turn the property over (for a nominal fee) to Developer. Developer, in turn, agreed to construct a major shopping center on the parcel. Homeowner filed suit to block the eminent domain proceedings against his house, on the theory that the taking here would be for private, not public, use (since the shopping center would end up being owned by Developer), and that it would thus violate the Fifth Amendment of the U.S. Constitution. Will Homeowner's suit succeed?

Not sure ☐

141. By telephone, Simon agreed to sell, and Bryant agreed to buy, Blackacre for a price of $200,000, with the closing to take place on April 1. On March 15, the day after this conversation, Simon sent Bryant a letter confirming all of the relevant terms of the agreement. The letter stated, "I will assume that this letter accurately states our arrangement, and will bind us both, unless I hear from you to the contrary by March 20." Bryant received the letter, but sent no response. On April 1, Simon arrived with a marketable deed at the time and place that his letter specified for closing. Bryant did not show up at all. If Simon sues Bryant for breach of contract, may he recover damages?

Not sure ☐

142. Same facts as in the previous question. Now, however, assume that Bryant arrived at the time and place designated in the letter for closing with a certified check in the amount specified in Simon's letter. Simon did not show up. If Bryant brings an action for specific performance against Simon, will the court grant Bryant's request?

Not sure ☐

143. Tycoon, a wealthy industrialist, has for many years owned a 100-acre parcel of undeveloped, heavily wooded land, called Twin Oaks, in the state of Bates. Grandson, Tycoon's daughter's oldest son, wished desperately to become a farmer. Tycoon therefore orally proposed to Grandson the following arrangement: If Grandson would move onto the property, construct a permanent dwelling, and clear at least 50 acres, he could keep whatever crops (or their proceeds) he could grow on the property. Furthermore, if Grandson did all this and then continued to farm for at least five years, Tycoon would leave the property to Grandson in Tycoon's will. Grandson moved onto the property, built a small cabin, cleared 75 acres, and farmed them for the next seven years, keeping all proceeds as agreed. Tycoon then died, but his will made no mention of the arrangement. (Instead, the will left Twin Oaks to Tycoon's niece, Edna.) If Grandson sues Tycoon's estate for an order of specific performance directing the estate to convey Twin Oaks to Grandson, will Grandson prevail? Assume that Bates follows the majority approach to all relevant matters.

Not sure ☐

144. Same basic fact pattern as in the previous question. Now, however, assume that Tycoon's proposal to Grandson was that if Grandson would move onto the farm with Tycoon (into an already existing structure), and would care for Tycoon during the latter's declining years, the property would be left to him by will. Grandson would meanwhile receive free room and board. Grandson did move onto the property and cared for Tycoon until the latter's death seven years later. However, Grandson did not clear any trees or build any structures (though he did do some maintenance on the property as well as taking care of Tycoon). If Tycoon's will did not leave Twin Oaks to Grandson, will a court grant Grandson's request that the estate be ordered to convey Twin Oaks to him?

Not sure ☐

145. Shelby, the owner of Blackacre, contracted to sell the property to Bennett. The contract document, dated March 1, provided that the closing was to take place on

April 1. The contract did not contain a "time is of the essence" clause, and did not specify the consequences if either party was unable or unwilling to close on the appointed day. On March 25, Bennett said by telephone to Shelby, "My bank loan hasn't gone through yet. I won't be able to close on April 1, but I will be ready on April 10." Shelby replied, "Either close on April 1 or the contract is off." On April 1, Shelby showed up at the appointed place with a deed, but Bennett did not appear. Bennett tendered a check for the purchase price on April 10, but Shelby refused to take it. There is evidence that Shelby was trying to get out of the contract not because the delay was material in light of the surrounding circumstances, but because someone had unexpectedly come along and offered Shelby a higher price. If Bennett sues Shelby for a decree ordering Shelby to convey the property to Bennett for the contract price, will a court grant Bennett's request?

Not sure ☐

146. Sherwood contracted to sell Blackacre to Bridges, with the closing to take place on April 1. The contract called for Sherwood to convey the property "by warranty deed," and specified nothing further about the nature of the title that Sherwood was to convey. The property was a ten-acre hunting preserve in a sparsely settled remote rural area. A title examiner retained by Bridges's lawyer examined the real estate records and found the following items concerning the property: (1) a deed covering the relevant area, from Rosen to Sherwood, issued and recorded in 2005; and (2) no entry in the records that Rosen ever became a record owner of the property. Bridges's lawyer called Sherwood's attention to these facts. Sherwood, prior to the closing date, presented an affidavit from Rosen stating that Rosen first entered the property in 1970, and that Rosen believes he became the owner by adverse possession in 1990. The record owner of the property, Peters, could not be located. On the scheduled closing date, Bridges informed Sherwood that Sherwood was in default because he had not tendered appropriate title. Sherwood insisted that he was tendering title as called for in the contract. If Bridges declines to close, and Sherwood sues for an order of specific performance directing Bridges to close, will Sherwood prevail?

Not sure ☐

147. Squires contracted to sell Whiteacre to Brady, with the closing to take place on June 1. The purchase price was to be $200,000, in the form of a cashier's or certified check. The contract required Squires to convey a marketable title. On June 1, both Squires and Brady turned up at the appointed place for the closing. Squires tendered a deed, together with an abstract of title showing that Squires had good title. The contract also required Squires to have a Certificate of Occupancy for a newly constructed deck attached to the house. Brady demanded the Certificate of Occupancy, and Squires said, "I don't have it." Brady responded, "Well, I refuse to close." Squires asked Brady to show him the certified check for the purchase price. Brady said, "I don't have it. I didn't bother going through with my bank loan because I knew you didn't have the Certificate of Occupancy." (This assertion is true.) Squires refused to return Brady's 10 percent deposit, paid to Squires at the time the contract was signed. (The deposit is returnable, according to the contract, only if seller is in default and buyer is not, on the closing date.) If Brady sues Squires for the return of his deposit, will Brady win?

Not sure ☐

148. Same basic fact pattern as in the previous question. Now, however, assume that the abstract of title that Squires proffered on June 1 showed that the house on the property (an important part of the overall value of the property) encroached ten feet onto the property of Squires's easterly neighbor. If Brady sues Squires for return of his deposit, and Squires asserts the defense that Brady did not tender his own performance (because Brady did not bring a check to the closing), may Brady recover the deposit?   Not sure ☐

149. Sherman contracted to sell Greenacre to Bruce. The contract was signed on June 1, 2009, and called for closing to occur on August 1, 2009. On July 1, 2009, Sherman died. His will (executed in 2008) left all of Sherman's personal property to his daughter Deirdre, and all of his real estate to his niece Nell. The closing took place as scheduled on August 1, with the sale proceeds paid to Sherman's estate. Who should receive the sale proceeds, Deirdre or Nell?   Not sure ☐

150. Spratt contracted to sell a house to Booth. After the contract was signed, but before the scheduled closing date, the house burned down. Spratt was not at fault. Neither Spratt nor Booth had any insurance in force on the property. On the closing date, is Booth obligated to pay the purchase price to Spratt in return for a deed to the now much less valuable property?   Not sure ☐

151. Same facts as in the previous question. Now, assume that Spratt carried $100,000 of insurance on the property, that the contract price was $300,000, and that the land with charred remnants on it instead of a house is worth $100,000. What are the rights and obligations of the parties?   Not sure ☐

152. Spence sold a house and lot to Bagley under an installment sales contract. The contract provided for the $200,000 purchase price to be paid at the rate of $5,000 per month for 40 consecutive months (with interest on the unpaid balance also being payable each month). The contract further provided that if Bagley ever became more than 30 days in arrears on any payment, Spence could, at his sole option, declare the contract forfeited and reclaim the property. Bagley moved in and made the first 20 payments without incident. He then lost his job and fell 90 days behind in the payments. The fair rental value of the property is $2,000 per month. Spence sent Bagley a letter stating, "Because you have violated the terms of our agreement, I am hereby exercising my right to declare the agreement terminated. Please vacate immediately." If Spence seeks an order declaring the contract terminated and decreeing that Bagley leave the premises, will Spence succeed?   Not sure ☐

153. Steel contracted to sell Greenacre to Boswell. The contract stated that Steel would convey marketable title to Boswell, and that the deed would be a warranty deed free of all easements and other encumbrances. On the appointed closing date, Steel tendered to Boswell a warranty deed that stated the property is "subject to an easement on behalf of a parcel located to the northwest of the subject parcel, enabling the beneficiary of the easement to use the subject parcel's driveway." Boswell and Boswell's lawyer did not carefully read the deed. Instead, they accepted it and paid the purchase price without realizing that the deed was subject to the easement. Several days later, when Boswell's neighbor used Boswell's driveway, Boswell realized that he had been given a deed that did not conform to the contract. Boswell now sues to recover damages under the contract for breach of the representation concerning lack of easements. Assuming that Boswell shows that the property is less valuable because the easement exists, may Boswell recover under the contract?   Not sure ☐

154. Fred was the owner of Greyacre, located in the state of Cabot. Cabot law requires all deeds for the transfer of real property to be witnessed by two people. Fred, who was getting on in years, decided to make a gift of Greyacre to his son, Stewart. He therefore prepared a deed giving Stewart the property, signed it, and had it witnessed by two people (thus fulfilling all of the requirements for a deed in Cabot). He handed the deed to Stewart, saying, "You are now the owner of Greyacre." The next day, Fred had a change of heart, realizing that he might live another 15 years and wanting the satisfaction of knowing that he was still the owner of Greyacre. He therefore asked Stewart to return or rip up the deed. Stewart was upset, but he was also a dutiful son. He therefore ripped up the deed (first making a photocopy, however), and told Fred that he had done so. Shortly thereafter, Fred died, leaving all of his personal and real property to his daughter, Denise. Who owns Greyacre, Stewart or Denise?   Not sure ☐

155. In 1980, Spitzer conveyed Blackacre to Butler under a standard warranty deed. In 2009, as Butler was preparing to resell the property, he discovered that Spitzer's predecessor in title had lost his title through adverse possession before ever conveying to Spitzer. The present holder of title by adverse possession is Adolf, who is not in possession of the property (Butler is), and who has never actively asserted rights to the property. Butler realizes that he will not be able to convey a marketable title to any subsequent purchaser because of Adolf's superior title. Butler therefore wishes to sue Spitzer for breach of some or all of the covenants of title. The statutes of limitation on actions for breach of the covenants of seisin, right to convey, and against encumbrances are all five years in the jurisdiction. The statutes of limitation on the covenants of quiet enjoyment and warranty are both three years. If Butler brings suit in 2009 against Spitzer for breach of all of these covenants, on which, if any, may he recover? For each covenant on which he may not recover, state the reason.   Not sure ☐

156. Same facts as in the previous question. Assuming that Butler can locate Adolf, what action would you advise Butler to take?   Not sure ☐

157. Same facts as in the previous two questions. Now, assume that Butler, without disclosing the fact that Adolf has a superior title, conveys the property by warranty deed to Capshaw in 2000. In 2009, while Capshaw is still the record owner of the property and in possession of it, Adolf brings an action for a declaration that he is the legal owner of the property. If Capshaw immediately brings suit against Spitzer for violation by Spitzer of the covenant of quiet enjoyment, may Capshaw recover? (Assume that nothing in the Butler-to-Capshaw deed refers to any covenants made by Butler's predecessor(s) in title.)   Not sure ☐

158. Schneider conveyed a house and lot to Block under a general warranty deed. The deed did not list any encumbrances or encroachments. At the time Block received (and paid for) the deed, he was aware that a garage built and belonging to Schneider's eastern neighbor, Jones, was located half on Jones's property and half on Schneider's property. (Block closed the transaction anyway, because he thought he was getting a price that was good enough to overlook this problem.) Several years later, Block decided that he had made a mistake in tolerating this state of events. He therefore instituted a suit against Schneider for breach of covenant.

(a) For breach of which covenant should Block sue? Not sure ☐

(b) Will Block be found to have waived the benefit of that covenant by agreeing to close with knowledge of the problem? Not sure ☐

159. Developer was in the business of buying large parcels, subdividing them, and building new houses on each. Developer sold a newly built house and the lot on which it stood to Benjamin, a would-be homeowner. The transaction was done by warranty deed. Both the sale contract and the deed contained the following statement in capital letters: "DEVELOPER MAKES NO OTHER WARRANTIES, EXPRESS OR IMPLIED, REGARDING THE STATE OF THE LAND OR STRUCTURES BEING TRANSFERRED." Unbeknownst to either Developer or Benjamin, Developer's employees, because of their ignorance, had failed to use the proper mix of sand and gravel in the cement employed for the building's foundation. Hairline cracks began to appear shortly after the closing, and within one year the house was structurally unsafe and unsalable.

(a) What action, if any, should Benjamin bring against Developer? Not sure ☐

(b) What is the probable result of the action you advised bringing in (a)? Not sure ☐

160. Same facts as in the previous question. Assume that during his first and only year of ownership, Benjamin did not become aware of the cracks in the foundation. At the end of a year, he sold the house to Carter, and Carter moved in. If Carter sues Benjamin on the same theory as you gave in your answer to part (a) of the previous question, will Carter succeed against Developer? Not sure ☐

161. Same basic fact pattern as in the previous question. Now, assume that Carter brings a suit against Developer on the same theory that you gave in your answers to the previous two questions. Assuming that the jurisdiction is one that recognized the validity of the action by Benjamin against Developer, would Carter succeed against Developer? Not sure ☐

162. Same facts as in the previous three questions. Now, assume that at the time Benjamin sold the property to Carter, Benjamin knew that the foundation was cracked and that the building would be nearly worthless to a buyer who knew of this defect. However, Benjamin did not disclose this fact to Carter, and Carter thus bought in ignorance of the problem. May Carter recover against Benjamin? Not sure ☐

163. In 2000, Oliver conveyed Whiteacre to Arkin. Arkin did not record at the time. In 2002, Oliver conveyed the same property to Beacon. Beacon took the property without knowledge of the earlier conveyance to Arkin, paid fair value for it, and promptly recorded. Arkin recorded his conveyance in 2004. In a jurisdiction that has a pure race recording act, who owns the property as between Arkin and Beacon, and why? Not sure ☐

164. Same facts as in the previous question. Now, however, assume that Beacon did not record his deed until 2004, and that Arkin recorded in 2003. At the time Arkin recorded, he knew of Oliver's conveyance to Beacon, and knew that Beacon had through negligence failed to record. In a pure race jurisdiction, who has priority, Arkin or Beacon, and why? Not sure ☐

165. Oliver conveyed Whiteacre to Arkin in 2000; Arkin did not record at the time. Oliver then conveyed to Beacon in 2002. Beacon did not know about the deed to Arkin at the time he took possession. In 2003, Arkin recorded, without knowledge of the conveyance by Oliver to Beacon. In 2004, Beacon discovered the conveyance to Arkin by doing a title search, and immediately recorded. If the jurisdiction has a race-notice statute, who has title as between Arkin and Beacon, and why?   Not sure ☐

166. Oliver conveyed Whiteacre to Arkin, for value, in 2005. Through negligence, Arkin did not record at the time. Oliver, who was aware of Arkin's failure to record, sold the property to Beacon in 2007. Just before the conveyance to Beacon, Oliver told Beacon, "I conveyed to Arkin in 2005, but Arkin has not recorded. As long as you record before Arkin can, you'll be safe." Beacon paid almost full value for the property and immediately recorded (still in 2007). In 2008, Arkin suddenly realized, with panic in his heart, that he had failed to record, and that Beacon had recorded. Arkin immediately recorded. In a race-notice jurisdiction, who has priority, Arkin or Beacon, and why?   Not sure ☐

167. Oliver conveyed Whiteacre to Arkin in 2005. At the time, Arkin did not record. Oliver then conveyed Whiteacre to Beacon in 2007. Beacon did not record. Beacon, at the time he took, did not have actual knowledge of the conveyance to Arkin. In 2008, Arkin recorded. Beacon has never recorded. In a "pure notice" jurisdiction, who has priority, Arkin or Beacon, and why?   Not sure ☐

168. Oakley conveyed Blackacre to Adler on September 1. Oakley then conveyed Blackacre to Bowles on September 10. Bowles recorded on September 10. Adler recorded on September 14. At the time Bowles received his deed, he was not aware of the earlier conveyance to Adler, and he paid fair value. In a jurisdiction with a race-notice statute and a 15-day grace period, who has title to Blackacre, as between Adler and Bowles (and why)?   Not sure ☐

169. What could the losing party in the previous question have done to protect himself?   Not sure ☐

170. Same basic fact pattern as in question 170. Now, however, assume that Adler did not record his deed until September 18. As between Adler and Bowles, who owns Blackacre, and why?   Not sure ☐

171. In 1980, Odell conveyed Blackacre to Arias. Arias did not record at the time. In 1990, Odell conveyed to Beck. At the time of the conveyance, Beck had actual notice of the earlier conveyance to Arias. Beck recorded immediately after receiving his deed. In 2000, Beck conveyed to Cabbott. Cabbott had neither actual nor constructive notice of the conveyance by Odell to Arias, and Cabbott paid Beck fair value. In 2005, Arias finally recorded. In 2007, Cabbott recorded. The jurisdiction has a race-notice statute. Between Arias and Cabbott, who has title?   Not sure ☐

172. In 1980, Osborn gave a gift of Whiteacre to Abrams. At the time, Abrams did not record the deed. In 1990, Osborn purported to give Whiteacre as a gift to Boone. At the time Boone received his deed, he had no knowledge of the earlier gift to Abrams. Boone immediately recorded. In 2005, Abrams recorded. The jurisdiction has a race-notice statute. Between Abrams and Boone, who has title?   Not sure ☐

173. In 1960, Orcini conveyed Blackacre to Arlen for value. Arlen never recorded his deed. In 1970, Arlen conveyed to Bishop. Bishop paid fair value and promptly recorded. In 1980, Orcini conveyed Blackacre to Chavez. Chavez had no knowledge of the earlier Orcini-Arlen conveyance, or of the Arlen-Bishop conveyance. Chavez paid fair value and immediately recorded. The jurisdiction has a race-notice statute. In a dispute between Bishop and Chavez, who has superior title to Blackacre?

Not sure ☐

174. Same basic facts as in the previous question. Now, however, assume that (1) Chavez knew of the Orcini-Arlen conveyance and the Arlen-Bishop conveyance at the time Chavez took, and (2) the jurisdiction has a pure notice statute. In a dispute between Bishop and Chavez, who wins?

Not sure ☐

175. In 1980, O'Neill conveyed Blackacre to Arens. At the time, this deed was not recorded. In 1990, Arens conveyed to Burrows. This deed was not recorded at the time. In 2000, O'Neill conveyed to Craft. This deed was never recorded. In 2005, Craft conveyed to Dempsey. Dempsey promptly recorded his deed from Craft. Neither Craft nor Dempsey, at the time each took his conveyance, had any actual knowledge of the O'Neill-to-Arens-to-Burrows line of conveyances. In 2009, Burrows recorded the O'Neill-to-Arens and the Arens-to-Burrows deeds. The jurisdiction has a race-notice statute. In a contest between Burrows and Dempsey, who has priority?

Not sure ☐

176. In 1995, Oakley conveyed Blackacre to Andrews for value. Andrews never recorded the deed. In 2005, Oakley conveyed the same property to Burns for value. Burns promptly recorded. At the time Burns took, Andrews was in possession of the property (as, indeed, he had been since 1995), and the property (a farm) contained a mailbox with Andrews's name prominently displayed on it. Burns lived far away from the property and never visited it before he took. If he had visited it, he would have seen signs of Andrews's possession. If he had spoken to Andrews, Andrews would have explained that he was the owner. The jurisdiction has a pure notice statute. In a contest between Andrews and Burns, who has superior title?

Not sure ☐

177. In 1980, Olivia conveyed Blackacre to Albright. At the time, Albright did not record his deed. In 1990, Olivia conveyed Blackacre to Brown. Brown took without any notice (actual or record) of the earlier conveyance to Albright. Brown promptly recorded. In 1995, Albright belatedly recorded. In 2005, Brown conveyed to Crystal. Crystal bought for value. Brown, being an honest sort, disclosed to Crystal before the sale that there was an earlier conveyance by Olivia to Albright, and that that conveyance had been subsequently recorded. (Crystal paid a somewhat lower price to reflect the possible uncertainty about title.) Crystal promptly recorded her deed. The jurisdiction has a race-notice statute. In a contest between Albright and Crystal, who wins?

Not sure ☐

178. Barnes contracted to purchase Blackacre from Selish. As part of the contract, Selish provided Barnes with a metes-and-bounds survey of the property, which was in fact an accurate description of the property that Selish intended to sell and Barnes intended to buy. The survey did not disclose that the garage located principally on the property encroached three feet onto the neighboring property; in fact, the survey did not show the garage structure at all. However, if Barnes (or his lawyer) had measured the distance from the house to the garage, and compared this with the distance from the house to the rear property line, they would have seen by looking at the survey that the garage must encroach on the neighbor's property. In any event, Barnes bought the property without being aware of the encroachment.

At the time of the closing, Barnes purchased from Title Co. a standard title insurance policy on the property. The policy excluded any "any facts that an accurate survey of the property would disclose." The title report that accompanied the policy did not refer in any way to the fact that the garage encroached or might encroach on the neighbor's property. Three years after the purchase, the neighbor sued Barnes and obtained a court order compelling Barnes to remove the encroaching garage, at a cost of $40,000. If Barnes sues Title Co. for $40,000, will Barnes recover?   Not sure ☐

179. Plotnick and Duffy were adjacent property owners. Plotnick's land contained a six-story building, built in conformity with applicable building codes (including ones governing the depth and strength of the foundation). Duffy's property was undeveloped. Duffy decided to build his own building. He was a very conservative sort. Therefore, he dug an unusually deep foundation (15 feet). Duffy dug only up to his property line. He proceeded without negligence and in conformity with all codes dictating how to excavate and build a foundation. However, because of the geography of the land and the unusual nature of Plotnick's foundation, Plotnick's foundation cracked and his building was severely damaged once there was no longer supporting soil on the Plotnick-Duffy border. Plotnick sued Duffy for the damage. Duffy proved at trial that if there had been no building on Plotnick's property, Plotnick's land would not have caved in. May Plotnick recover?   Not sure ☐

180. Phillips and Decker each own a parcel that abuts the Bountiful River in the state of Ames. Decker is upstream from Phillips. Since 2006, Decker has operated a private hydroelectric plant. To maintain the necessary pressure, Decker has built a dam on the river, which has the effect of diverting the water through the hydroelectric plant's turbines, and then out into a pond at the rear of Decker's property. Beginning in 1975, Phillips, a farmer, had been irrigating a five-acre parcel of his property. This worked well until Decker built his dam in 2006; since then, so little water has been present in the Bountiful River by the time it reaches Phillips's property that the pressure needed to perform useful irrigation is not present. Assuming that Ames follows the common law approach to relevant matters, if Phillips sues Decker for improperly using the water, will Phillips prevail?   Not sure ☐

181. Same facts as in the previous question. Now, assume that Decker's use (for hydroelectric power) commenced in 2006, and that Phillips did not begin trying to use his property for irrigation until 2009. Ames follows the common law approach to relevant matters. May Phillips recover against Decker for improper use of water?   Not sure ☐

182. Same facts as in the previous question. Assume, however, that Ames is one of the 17 states that have abolished the common law riparian rights doctrine, and that Ames has replaced that doctrine with the most common alternative. Would Phillips win in a suit against Decker for improper water use?   Not sure ☐

183. Pringle and Delaney are adjacent landowners. At the time Pringle bought his property in 1970, a six-story office building was already present on that lot. This building nearly reaches the eastern property line (and does not violate any zoning rules). Delaney has owned his lot (which is to the east of Pringle's property) since 1990. The land has been vacant. Now, Delaney proposes to build a 12-story office building on the western side of his property. This building would conform with all applicable zoning laws; however, the effect of this building will be to deprive Pringle's tenants (at least those in the eastern side of the building) of nearly all of the sunlight and view that they have always had, since the two buildings will only be three feet apart. If Pringle sues Delaney to enjoin Delaney from placing the building so close to the property line that Pringle's tenants' light and view will be cut off, will the court grant Pringle's request?

Not sure ☐

Property Answers to Short-Answer Questions

1. Paul. **A finder of lost property has rights superior to those of everyone except the true owner. As a corollary of this general rule, courts hold that a possessor who loses the property after finding it may nonetheless recover it from the third person who subsequently finds it or takes it.** Therefore, although Paul will for a reasonable time be treated as holding the ring in trust for the true owner, he has the right to recover possession of it from Donna.

2. No. **To begin with, anyone whose chain of title includes a thief cannot prevail over the "true" owner. But the true owner's right to recover the property can become time-barred. The modern rule on the running of the statute of limitations is sometimes called the "*discovery*" rule. By that rule, the statute of limitations on an action to recover stolen property normally does not begin to run against the record owner until the owner knows, or should know, the identity of the possessor. But the rule assumes that the owner has made prompt** *reasonable efforts* **to find the possessor or to put the world on notice of the stolen property.** Here, Oscar did not do this; for instance, he failed to list the painting in the information bank, a step that a reasonably diligent owner would normally take. Therefore, a court will probably hold that the statute began to run against him immediately. In that event, Anita became the owner by adverse possession in 1990.

3. Yes, probably. **Under the modern "discovery" rule, the statute of limitations did not begin to run against Oscar until he knew (or, with the exercise of reasonable diligence, should have known) the possessor's identity.** That did not happen until 2008, so Anita is not yet the owner by adverse possession, and Oscar can recover the painting.

4. Yes. **As a general rule,** *a seller cannot convey better title than that which he or she holds.* This is true of the unknown thief. Therefore, Dealer never got good title (regardless of whether he thought he did), and could not in turn give good title to Arnold. Consequently, even though Arnold paid full value and was completely innocent, he will lose the car. (Statutes in most states set up a certificate of title program, which would have protected Arnold in this situation.)

5. Yes, probably. **The loan of the mower was a** *bailment*, **and the duty of the bailee depends on the purpose of the bailment.** Here, the bailment was solely for the benefit of the bailee (Dan). In this situation, the bailee is required to use *extraordinary care* to protect the goods from loss. Dan is not an insurer of the goods (Jerry can win only if he shows that Dan was at least partially at fault). But leaving another person's property out for an hour while unsupervised probably constitutes some level of fault, so Jerry can probably recover (even though Dan's conduct does not rise to the level of common law negligence).

6. Denise. **There are three requirements for the making of a valid gift: (1) delivery, (2) intent to make a gift, and (3) acceptance by the donee.** Here, the delivery requirement was not satisfied, since Sidney did not give Norman either physical possession of the painting or possession of any symbolic or written instrument representing the gift.

7. Norman, probably. **The delivery requirement can be satisfied in most states by a written instrument given to the donee, even if the instrument is not under seal.** See *Gruen v. Gruen*, 496 N.E.2d 869 (N.Y. 1986).

8. Karen. **Stanley's "gift" to Rose was a gift *"causa mortis"* (i.e., a gift in contemplation of death). Most courts hold that if the donor fails to die from the *contemplated* peril, the gift causa mortis is automatically revoked.** Since Stanley died from a car accident, not the contemplated cancer danger, this rule means that the gift was revoked and was part of his estate at death.

9. All, probably. **The account here is a "Totten Trust" (the name commonly used to describe an account of the form "A in trust for B"). Most courts, and the Uniform Probate Code, hold that where the trustee of a Totten Trust (here, Albert) dies before the beneficiary (here, Bertha), the beneficiary is *presumed* to be entitled to all funds left in the account.** This presumption is rebuttable by a showing that the trustee intended a different result, but there is no such evidence here.

10. All. **The trustee under a Totten Trust generally has the right of withdrawal during his or her lifetime, but the fact that he or she has this right (and the fact that he or she uses it as to some of the proceeds of the account) does not by itself rebut the presumption that the surviving beneficiary takes the balance remaining in the account at the trustee's death.**

11. None, probably. **In the case of a Totten Trust, the courts generally presume that during the depositor's lifetime, he or she has the right to withdraw all funds.** Unless Bertha comes forward with evidence that Albert intended a gift to her, she will lose.

12. No, probably. **Beck obtained title to the 30-yard strip by the doctrine of *adverse possession*, 20 years after he first fenced in the property (i.e., in 1981). One of the requirements for adverse possession is that the possession be *"hostile."* But most courts hold that one who possesses an adjoining landowner's land under the mistaken belief that he or she has only possessed up to the boundary of his or her own land meets the requirement of hostile possession.** (But a minority of courts would disagree with the result, and would hold that Warren may recover possession because Beck's possession was not hostile.)

13. Samuel. **Most courts hold that where a person takes possession of land under an oral gift, the possession meets the hostility requirement even though it is technically with the owner's consent.** Consequently, Samuel has taken by adverse possession.

14. Yes. **Steve and Deborah held the property as co-tenants. As a general rule, co-tenants each have equal access to the premises. If Steve had refused Deborah's attempt to live on the premises, then Steve's occupancy for the statutory period would have been hostile, and Steve would have taken Deborah's half interest by adverse possession.** But since Deborah never asked to live on the premises, and Steve never said that she couldn't, Steve's occupancy was not hostile, so he does not take her interest by adverse possession even though he was in sole occupancy for more than the statutory period. Consequently, Deborah still owned her one-half interest at the time of her death, and that interest passed to Frank.

15. No. **Steve's refusal to let Frank move into the premises made Steve's possession of the premises thereafter hostile to the Deborah/Frank interest.** Therefore, when Steve possessed the property for the next 20 years after this statement of hostility, he got the benefit of the adverse possession doctrine, and in 2010 he will be the sole owner.

16. Owen. **Two successive adverse possessors may "tack" their ownership (i.e., the holding period of the former can be added to that of the latter) in some circumstances. But tacking is allowed only where the two possessors are related by *"privity."*** Because the property is suitable only for hunting and fishing, Baker's and Carter's use of it for this purpose probably met the requirement of continuous and hostile possession (whereas possession for 60 days per year would not suffice for

more highly developed property, such as a private house in a suburb). Therefore, had Baker continued his use for 20 consecutive seasons, he would have taken title by adverse possession. But he lasted only 15 seasons. However, since Baker and Carter did not have any formal contractual relationship as to Blackacre, they were not in privity. Therefore, Carter cannot take advantage of Baker's 15 years of occupancy, and Carter's time started to run only in 1995. By 2002, Carter is not yet the owner.

17. Botnick. **First, Botnick's cultivation of corn qualifies as continuous and hostile, since it is the only use for which the premises are suitable. Second, the fact that two different record owners held title during Botnick's first 20 years of occupancy does not harm Botnick's case: There is, in a sense, "tacking" on the owner's side.** Therefore, in 2000, Botnick gained title to Blackacre.

18. Stokes. **In 1990, Alice became the owner of the strip by adverse possession. Once she gained title by adverse possession, her title was of the same quality, and subject to the same rules, as if she had gotten title by deed. Therefore, she could not convey that title to anyone else except by compliance with the Statute of Frauds.** Her oral "grant" to Orlando was ineffective because it was not in writing as required by the Statute of Frauds. Therefore, Alice owned the strip at her death, and it passed to Stokes.

19. No. **Normally, the adverse possessor must actively possess the entire parcel he or she is claiming. But where a person enters property under *"color of title"* (i.e., under a written instrument that is defective for some reason), the possessor gets title to the entire acreage described in the instrument, even if he or she "actually" possesses only a portion of it. (For this constructive possession doctrine to apply, the parcel must be one recognized in the community as a single parcel.)** Therefore, Ara constructively possessed the entire ten-acre parcel even though he actively lived on only one parcel. Thus, he became owner of the whole ten acres in 2000.

20. Yes. **This case falls within the general rule that a person can gain by adverse possession only title to the portion he or she *actually* occupies.** In other words, the doctrine of "constructive possession" (applied in the prior answer) does not apply here, because Ara did not take under "color of title."

21. Yes. **In general, the first possessor has priority over any subsequent one. Thus, a person who possesses land, and who is ousted from that possession by another, may bring an ejectment action to regain possession.** (Thus, Bates is not permitted to say, "You don't own the property, Ali does." Even though Ali could defeat Ashley, Bates may not defeat Ashley.)

22. Barbara. **The gift "to Abel and his heirs" does not mean "to Abel for life and then to his heirs." Instead, "to Abel and his heirs" means "to Abel in *fee simple*."** Therefore, Abel had the right to do whatever he wished with the property, and his deed of it to Barbara was effective. Thus when Abel died, he had no interest in Blackacre to leave to his son and heir.

23. Yes. **The original grant from O to A was a *fee simple determinable*. We know this because of the phrase "as long as" and the word "revert." Therefore, after the conveyance, O was left with a *possibility of reverter*.** When O died, his possibility of reverter passed to his son S. When A purported to convey a fee simple absolute to B, he really conveyed only a fee simple determinable subject to S's possibility of reverter. When B began using the premises for the forbidden purpose in 1990, title *automatically* reverted to S, without S taking any formal action. Therefore, S remained the owner of the property in 2009 and is entitled to a judicial decree to that effect. (If more than 50 years passed after O's original creation of the fee simple determinable, then S or his successors would lose their right to this decree, since they would be barred by the 50-year statute of limitations on possibilities of reverter.)

24. No. **Now, the O-to-A conveyance established a** *fee simple subject to a condition subsequent.* **(The phrases "upon condition that" or "provided that," when taken with a clause providing for reentry, establish that a fee simple subject to condition subsequent, rather than a fee simple determinable, was created.)** This left O (and, after his death, S) with a right of entry, not a possibility of reverter. By the statute of limitations, S was required to bring his suit for reentry within one year of B's commencement of the illegal use (i.e., by 1991). When S did not do so, his right of entry was extinguished. By comparing this question with the prior one, you can see the importance of distinguishing between a fee simple determinable and a fee simple subject to a condition subsequent.

25. Fee tail in S, reversion in O and his heirs, nothing for B. **The phrase "A and the heirs of his body" creates a** *fee tail.* **Under medieval common law, the effect of a fee tail to A was to "entail" the estate—that is, to require that upon A's death, the property would go to A's oldest surviving son, thence to that oldest son's oldest surviving son, etc., down the generations. A fee tail at common law could not be conveyed to someone outside the family.** Therefore, the purported conveyance by A to B was ineffective. (Today, in all American states, the fee tail is not given its common law effect; most states transform it into a fee simple absolute, in which case the conveyance to B would have taken effect and B would hold a fee simple absolute.)

26. Fee simple in N, probably. **The bequest to B was ambiguous; it may have created a life estate defeasible, or it may have created a fee simple determinable. The ambiguity stems from the fact that there was no explicit gift ever specified to occur on B's death if she dies unmarried. The modern trend is toward treating such a bequest as creating a fee simple determinable, because of the absence of any instructions for handling the property if B dies unmarried. See** *Lewis v. Searles,* **452 S.W.2d 153 (Mo. 1970), finding a fee simple determinable on similar facts.** Therefore, B's fee simple determinable passed to N, and at that point became a fee simple absolute (since the event of defeasance—B's remarriage—could no longer occur). The possibility of reverter possessed by S was divested at the moment B died without having remarried.

27. Life estate *per autre vie in C, remainder in fee simple in B.* **After the initial conveyance by O, A was a life tenant. In all states, a life tenant may convey the interest that he or she holds, or a lesser one (but not a greater one).** Therefore, A was capable of conveying his life estate to C; once that conveyance took place, C had a life estate *per autre vie* (life estate measured by another person's life), since C's interest would end when A died, not when C died. B continued to hold the fee simple remainder that he got when O made the initial conveyance.

28. A reversion. **When the holder of a vested estate transfers to another a smaller estate, we call the interest that remains in the grantor a "reversion."** Since the estate created by O is smaller than the one he held (i.e., a life estate is smaller than a fee simple absolute), what O was left with was a reversion.

29. Indefeasibly vested remainder. **A remainder is a future interest that can become possessory only upon the expiration of a prior possessory interest created by the same instrument.** Since B's interest was created by the same instrument that created A's life estate, and since B's interest will become possessory when that prior life interest expires, B has a remainder. This remainder is a vested remainder, because it is not subject to any condition precedent, and an identified already-born person (B) holds the remainder. The remainder is "indefeasibly" vested because it is certain to become possessory at some future time (even if B dies before A does, the remainder will pass by will or intestacy to B's heirs, and there is certain to be somebody who will be there to take possession when A dies).

30. Vested remainder subject to open. **C's interest is some sort of vested remainder. The vested remainder is "subject to open" because if another child (let's call him D) is born to B, C's remainder "opens up" to give D a half interest in it. The remainder will stay open until either A dies (in which case only the then-living children of B will take anything), or B dies, in which case he can have no further children.**

31. Vested remainder subject to divestment. **B has a remainder vested subject to divestment. If A died immediately, B's interest would become possessory. But if B died without issue (either before or after A's death), B's interest would be completely defeated or "divested."** (C's interest, which cuts short B's vested interest, is called an executory interest.)

32. Contingent remainder. **A remainder is contingent rather than vested if it is either subject to a condition precedent, or created in favor of a person who is unborn or unascertained.** Here, the remainder to B is subject to a condition precedent (the condition that B survive A for his remainder to become possessory). If B does survive A, his remainder will become vested at the same time it becomes possessory.

33. Vested remainder subject to divestment. **Notice that the grant here is functionally indistinguishable from that in the prior question, yet the remainder here is vested (subject to divestment), whereas the one in the prior question is contingent. This relates solely to the words: Here the clause creating the remainder in B does not contain any limit, and the limit is introduced by a separate clause containing the phrase "but if." As a matter of interpretation, the separate clause beginning with "but if" indicates that the remainder is being "taken away," and this indicates a condition subsequent rather than a condition precedent (thus a remainder subject to divestment rather than a contingent remainder).**

34. Contingent remainder. **One of the two ways a remainder will be contingent rather than vested is if it is held by a person who is at the time of the conveyance either unborn or not yet ascertained.** Here, since A is still alive, we don't know who his heirs will be. Therefore, the remainder is contingent. As soon as A dies, the remainder will both vest and become possessory (since we will know who A's heirs are, and they will take possession).

35. Fee simple in O. **After the initial conveyance by O, D had a contingent remainder. But at the time A died, D did not meet the contingency (having had a child while being married). By the common law doctrine of** *destructibility of contingent remainders*, **a contingent remainder was deemed "destroyed" unless it vested at or before the termination of the preceding freehold estates.** Since D had not met the contingency by the time the prior estate (A's life estate) expired, D's contingent remainder was destroyed. Therefore, O's reversion became possessory, giving him a fee simple absolute. (Today, most states have, by case law or statute, abolished the doctrine of destructibility of contingent remainders.)

36. Fee simple in B. **By the doctrine of** *"merger,"* **whenever** *successive vested estates are owned by the same person*, **the smaller of the two estates is absorbed by the larger.** When A conveyed his life estate to B, B then had two successive vested estates (the life estate and the previously received vested remainder in fee simple). Consequently, the smaller estate (A's life estate) was merged into the fee simple and disappeared. Then, by the doctrine of destructibility of contingent remainders (see prior question), the destruction-by-merger of A's life estate caused D's contingent remainder dependent upon it to also be destroyed, since that contingent remainder did not vest at or before the termination of the preceding freehold estates.

37. Fee simple absolute in B. **Under the *Rule in Shelley's Case*, if a will or conveyance creates a freehold in A, and purports to create a remainder in A's heirs, and the estates are both legal or both equitable, the remainder becomes a fee simple in A.** Thus, by operation of the Rule, A received both a life estate and a remainder in fee simple. Then, by the doctrine of merger, A's life estate merged into his remainder in fee simple, and A simply held a present fee simple. A's quitclaim deed to B transferred this fee simple to B. A had nothing left at the time of his death, therefore, so S took nothing.

38. Fee simple absolute in B. **The *Doctrine of Worthier Title* provides that if the owner of a fee simple attempts to create a life estate (or fee tail estate), followed by a remainder to his or her own heirs, the remainder is void. The grantor thus keeps a reversion.** After the initial conveyance by O, A had a life estate and O had a reversion (with the remainder to O's heirs being void). Therefore, O's quitclaim deed to B was effective to pass O's reversion to B. Once A died, the reversion held by B became a possessory fee simple absolute. Since the initial remainder to O's heirs never took effect, S (O's heir) took nothing.

39. Fee simple absolute in S. **Today, most states make the Doctrine of Worthier Title a rule of construction, rather than an absolute rule of law as it was at common law. In other words, the doctrine applies only where the grantor's language and surrounding circumstances indicate that he intended to keep a reversion.** Here, O's statement that he wants the gift to take effect exactly as written rebuts the presumption that a reversion rather than remainder was intended. Consequently, the gift will take effect as written, which means that O's quitclaim deed to B was of no effect. Consequently, O's heirs held a contingent remainder before O's death, and that remainder vested in S when O died. When A died, S's remainder became possessory.

40. O should bargain and sell Blackacre "to S and his heirs from and after the date on which S graduates from law school." **The bargain and sale will raise a use in S. That use will then be executed under the Statute of Uses, becoming a fee simple in S to commence upon the graduation date.**

41. Fee simple in A subject to an executory limitation, and a shifting executory interest in fee simple in B. **The bargain and sale raises a use in A in fee simple subject to condition subsequent, and a use in B. The Statute of Uses executes both of these uses.** The net result is that if A or his heirs serves liquor on the property, then the gift over to B will take effect.

42. **(a)** B and C each have contingent remainders. **The limitation on B's interest is stated in the same clause as the gift to B. Therefore, C's interest is not "cutting off" B's interest, but is instead merely awaiting the natural termination of B's interest.** B and C each have equitable contingent remainders that are executed by the Statute of Uses into alternate legal contingent remainders.

     (b) B's interest is a vested remainder subject to divestment, and C's interest is an executory interest. **Here, the language that limits B's interest ("but if") comes in a separate clause following the clause that gave the gift to B. Therefore, C's interest cuts off B's interest, rather than merely awaiting the natural termination of B's interest.** Since an interest that cuts off a prior interest is generally an executory interest rather than a remainder, C has an executory interest.

43. Yes. **A life tenant may not normally remove earth or minerals from the property.** (There are two exceptions: (1) if the property was used for mining prior to the commencement of the life estate, the tenant may continue this use; and (2) the tenant may mine if this is the only way of accomplishing the purpose of the life estate. But neither of these exceptions applies here.)

44. Yes. **The remainder to B is a vested remainder, which vested in interest (though not in possession) on the day of the original conveyance by O.** Therefore, the remainder to B vested less than 21 years after some life in being at the creation of the interest (e.g., A's life).

45. No. **We always analyze the Rule Against Perpetuities as of the date of the conveyance, not by reference to how things actually work out.** Viewing the matter from the date of the conveyance, it is possible to imagine a situation in which B would die, an additional son—call him C—would be born to A after the conveyance, A would die, and C would marry and have a child more than 21 years after the death of A and B. Under this scenario, however unlikely, the remainder would vest in C more than 21 years after all named lives in being at the creation of the interest.

   Because of this possibility, the gift to B (which is a contingent remainder) will fail, *even if it actually turns out that B marries and has a child.* Observe that the key difference between this question and the prior question is that here, the remainder to B is contingent (we don't know at the time of the conveyance which child, if any, of A will marry and have a child), whereas in the prior question, the gift to B and his heirs was a vested remainder. Since the contingent remainder won't vest until it becomes possessory, and this might (however unlikely) be more than 21 years after lives in being at the time of the conveyance, the gift to B fails (whereas the gift to B in the prior question succeeds because it is a vested remainder, which vests at the moment of creation).

46. No. **The gift over to A was an executory interest, and was thus subject to the Rule Against Perpetuities. An executory interest is not vested at its creation, and vests only when it becomes possessory. See *City of Klamath Falls v. Bell*, 490 P.2d 515 (Ore. Ct. App. 1971).** Since there was a possibility, at the time of the gift, that the Sierra Club might continue to maintain the property in a wilderness state indefinitely, it was possible that the gift over to A would not become possessory (and thus vest) until after lives in being plus 21 years. Therefore, the gift to A was void. Instead, O kept a possibility of reverter, and that possibility now becomes possessory.

47. No. **What A Corp. has purchased here is an option "in gross." (That is, the option is not granted in connection with a present lease of the property.) An option in gross is subject to the Rule Against Perpetuities—it will be unenforceable if it could be exercised beyond the end of the Perpetuities period, even if the optionee paid real money for it in the belief that it would be exercisable.** Since there is no measuring life in being at the time of the option's creation (A Corp. is a corporation, not an individual), the option violated the Rule by being scheduled to last more than 21 years. (But a judge might order B to refund A Corp.'s $20,000 option purchase price.)

48. Yes. **Where an option to purchase property is granted in connection with a lease of that property (i.e., the option is not "in gross") and is exercisable only during the lease term, then the option is not treated as being subject to the Rule Against Perpetuities.**

49. No. **Viewed as of the time of O's bequest, it was "conceivable" (at least in the eyes of the common law) that B could have another child, despite her advanced age.** If A's oldest surviving child was one who was not born until after O's bequest (so that A's child is not a measuring life), and if C and D had also died by the time A and A's oldest surviving child died, and then this hypothetical child born to B in B's old age (let's call this child E) took more then 21 years after the death of A and A's oldest surviving child, then E would have taken later than lives in being at the time of O's conveyance plus 21 years. The gift over to E, in that event, would violate the rule.

   This is the so-called *fertile octogenarian* rule. Under the common law, it does not matter that in fact D is to take the gift, and that D was himself a measuring life—the mere possibility that there might have been someone like E who would take in violation of the rule is enough to ruin the gift to D. (Today, most states have "wait and see" statutes; under these statutes, we would look at the fact that it is now D who is to take, and since D was a life in being at the time of the bequest, the gift would be valid.)

50. **No. As of 2000, it was possible that A would live a long time more, would marry someone born after 2000, and would then die after 2021.** That person would thus be a life not yet in being at the time of O's bequest and would be taking more than "lives in being plus 21 years" after 2000. Thus the bequest to "the widow" is invalid. This is true (at least at common law) even though the person who actually takes (here, B) was someone who was in fact born by 2000. This is the "*unborn widow*" rule. (But again, a modern "wait and see" statute would cause the gift to be valid, since the recipient, B, turns out to be someone born before the date of the original conveyance.)

51. Yes, probably. **Most courts would accept evidence that by the term "widow," O intended to refer to A's existing spouse.** If such evidence were presented, the conveyance would be read as meaning "to A for life, then to B, provided that she is A's widow." Since B is a person in being (and identified) at the time of the conveyance, she can be a measuring life, and the gift to her is valid.

52. **Yes. Even under the strict common law approach, the *period of gestation* may be added to the "lives in being plus 21 years," so the gift to this hypothetical child born after A's death would be valid.** That being the case, the gift to B (born well before A's death) is also valid. You might think that the gift would be ruined by the possibility that A might have died without any living children, but with a pregnant widow. It would thus take the unborn child 21 years plus up to nine months to reach the age of 21, making his or her interest invalid.

53. **No. It was possible, viewed as of 1980, that another child (let's hypothetically call him C) would be born to A after 1980. It was also possible that A and B might also die prior to C's ninth birthday. If both of these events happened, C's interest would then vest too remotely (more than 21 years after the deaths of the measuring lives—i.e., A and B). Because of this theoretical possibility, not only was the gift invalid as to children born after 1980, but it was also invalid as to the rest of the *class* of children (i.e., B).** (If O had not included the remark about specifically covering later-born children of A, then the court might have saved the bequest by viewing the class as closing at the time of O's death, or by viewing the class as referring only to those members who could take without violating the Rule Against Perpetuities. But with the bequest as written, the common law approach would be that since there might be a member of the class who could not take without violating the Rule, no member of the class may take.)

54. **Yes. The most common statutory modification today is the "*wait and see*" approach, by which if the interest *actually* vests within lives in being at the time of creation plus 21 years, the fact that things might have worked out differently is irrelevant.** Since here, B was a life in being at the time of O's bequest, the gift to him is valid even though it might have turned out that the later-born C took later than lives in being plus 21 years.

55. **Yes. The limitation in O's grant to A is an illegal "*restraint on alienation*"—restraints upon the alienation of a fee simple are void.** (But use restrictions are not deemed invalid restraints on alienation. If O's conveyance had read, "To A and his heirs, provided that the property not be used for the sale of alcohol," this would have been a valid fee simple subject to condition subsequent.)

56. Fee simple in A for 600 acres; life estate in W for 300 acres, with remainder in A. **The common law estate of *dower* entitles a widow, on her husband's death, to a life estate in one-third of the lands of which he was seised at any time during their marriage, provided that the husband's interest was inheritable by the issue of the marriage (if any).** Since H was seised of Blueacre at some point during the marriage (from 1985 through 1990), W held the estate of dower inchoate. On H's death, this became the estate of dower consummate. The husband cannot, by conveying his property during his life, defeat the right of dower. If he purports to make such a conveyance, his widow may

subsequently make her claim for dower against the present holder of the property. W is entitled to have 300 acres set aside for her for life by A; after her death, A can once again take possession of them. (Observe that A's lawyer should have had W join in the deed from H before allowing A pay money for the property.)

57. (d), (e), and (f) are all community property. **They are all either H's earnings during the marriage or things purchased from those earnings. (a), (b), and (c) are separate property, because property received by a spouse before marriage, and property received by gift, inheritance, or bequest after marriage, are separate, and income from separate property is separate property.**

58. B and S hold as tenants in common. **Today, all states establish a presumption that an ambiguous conveyance creates a tenancy in common rather than a joint tenancy.** Therefore, O's ambiguous conveyance made A and B hold as tenants in common. Consequently, when A died, there was no right of survivorship on the part of B. Instead, A's undivided one-half interest in Blackacre passed to S. S and B now hold as tenants in common.

59. S and C as tenants in common. **When B conveyed to C, this had the effect of *severing* the joint tenancy between A and B.** Therefore, A and C held as tenants in common, not joint tenants, immediately after the conveyance by B to C. Therefore, when A died, C had no right of survivorship. S inherited A's share of the tenancy in common.

60. C, D, and S hold as tenants in common, with C having a two-thirds interest, and D and S each having one-sixth. **The conveyance by A to B severed the joint tenancy, but only as to the one-third possessed by A. After the A-to-B conveyance, B and C held two-thirds as joint tenants, and B separately held the remaining one-third as tenant in common. When B died, C took the entire two-thirds by right of survivorship. D and S each took only a one-half interest in the one-third that B had held as tenant in common. See *Jackson v. O'Connell*, 177 N.E.2d 194 (Ill. 1961), involving similar facts.**

61. D owns an undivided one-half interest, and X and Y each own an undivided one-quarter interest, as tenants in common. **When people "share" under the intestacy statute, all courts interpret them as taking as tenants in common, not as joint tenants.** Therefore, D had no right of survivorship in S's undivided one-half interest in Blackacre, so S was able to leave his one-half interest to X and Y, who each then held a quarter.

62. Yes. **Each tenant in common is entitled to *possession of the whole property*, subject to the same rights in the other tenants.** It does not make any difference that one of the tenants in common has a larger undivided interest than the other—the relative size of the interests matters only when the property is sold and the proceeds are allocated.

63. Fee simple absolute in Georgia. **Oscar's original conveyance to Henry and Wanda created a tenancy by the entirety in them, since at common law any conveyance to two persons who are husband and wife necessarily results in such a tenancy.** (In fact, in the 22 states that retain tenancy by the entirety, there remains a presumption that a husband and wife who take property take it by the entirety.) When Henry conveyed his interest to Georgia, this did not have the effect of destroying the tenancy by the entirety, since such a tenancy is *indestructible* while both parties are alive and remain husband and wife. But the conveyance did have the effect of passing to Georgia whatever Henry's rights were. When Wanda died before Henry, her interest was extinguished, and there was nothing for her to pass to Denise. Since Henry would have taken the entire property had he kept his interest, Georgia steps into his shoes and takes the entire property.

64. Wendy and Stan each have an undivided one-half interest as tenants in common. **When husband and wife are divorced, the tenancy by the entirety automatically ends. In most states, the property is then deemed to be held as tenants in common (i.e., without right of survivorship).** Thus, when Herb died, his undivided one-half interest as tenant in common passed to Stan.

65. Yes. **Although a co-tenant is normally entitled to occupy the premises himself or herself without accounting for their reasonable rental value, the same is not true if he or she leases the premises to a third person. Once he or she does this, and collects rent, he or she is required to share these rents with his or her co-tenant.**

66. No. **Each co-tenant is entitled to occupy the entire premises, subject only to the same right on the part of the other tenant. But the occupying tenant has, in general, no duty to account for the value of his or her exclusive possession.** If Carol refused to let Dan live in the property, then Carol would be liable to pay Dan one-half of the rental value of the premises. But as long as Carol holds the premises open to Dan, she does not have to pay Dan any part of the imputed value of her own occupancy.

67. She should bring an action for partition. **Any tenant in common or joint tenant (but not a tenant by the entirety) may bring an equitable action for partition. By this means, the court will either divide the property or order it sold and the proceeds distributed. Normally, each tenant has an absolute right to partition, even over the objection of the other.** Since the property probably cannot be readily divided, the court will order it sold. Felicia will get half of the sale proceeds.

68. Yes. **The issue, of course, is whether the L-T lease must satisfy the *Statute of Frauds*. In most states, the Statute of Frauds does not cover a one-year lease, even if the lease is to commence in the future (and thus even if more than one year is to elapse between the date the lease contract is made, and the date on which the lease itself would terminate).** Even though more than one year elapsed between July 1, 2009 (the date the lease was orally agreed to), and July 31, 2010 (the last day of the lease), the contract did not need to be in writing, according to the majority view.

69. **(a)** Periodic tenancy. **A periodic tenancy is a tenancy that continues from one period to the next automatically, unless either party terminates it at the end of a period by notice. One way a periodic tenancy is created is where the parties make a lease without setting a duration; in this situation, the period stated for rental payments is usually the period for other purposes.** Since L and T stated the rent on a monthly basis, the tenancy will be a month-to-month tenancy.

    (b) August 30. **When a month-to-month tenancy is terminated, the last date of the lease is generally the end of a period, but not less than one period later than the notice date.** Thus, T was required to give L 30 days notice, and the lease terminated at the end of the period that was in progress on the 30th day (i.e., the end of the calendar month in which the 30th day after notice occurred).

70. Give Tom notice that he is binding Larry for another one-year term. **The traditional common law view is that if the tenant holds over for even one day, the landlord could bind the tenant for an additional term. This was true even where there were extenuating circumstances. Most courts held that such a holdover creates a periodic tenancy and that the length of the period is determined by the way rent was computed under the former lease.** On this basis, Larry could bind Tom for a full additional year, since the prior rent was computed on an annual basis.

71. Probably not. **Modern courts generally recognize extenuating circumstances on the part of the holdover tenant, especially where only a very short holdover period is involved.** Accordingly, a modern court would probably not allow Larry to bind Tom to another year based on a three-day

holdover (especially one that did not involve an agriculturally significant part of the year), where the holdover was due to illness and thus was involuntary.

72. Split of authority. **Under the so-called American view, the landlord has a duty to deliver only "legal" possession, not actual possession. Under the so-called English rule, the landlord does have a duty to deliver actual possession. American jurisdictions are approximately split between the two rules.** In a court following the American view, Tina would not be able to sue for damages (and probably would not be able to cancel the lease either). In a state following the English rule, Tina would be able to recover damages from Leonard, and would probably also be allowed to cancel the lease. (But Tina's damages would probably be limited to the difference between the amount specified in her lease and the fair market value of the space; she would probably not be able to recover profits she would have made during the holdover period, since she is establishing a new venture whose profits are speculative.)

73. No. **A tenant, as a general rule, is "estopped to deny his landlord's title to the leased property."** That is, once a tenant (Tony) takes possession, he may not cancel the lease or refuse to pay rent on the grounds that his landlord (Leroy) does not have valid title to the premises. If Peter actually evicts Tony, obviously Tony may stop paying rent. But until actual eviction occurs, Tony must live with Leroy's fraud and the resulting uncertainty. (Of course, Tony has the right to sue Leroy for damages for breach of contract, but this is not the same thing as the right to cancel the lease or withhold rent payments.)

74. Yes. **The rule that the tenant may not deny his landlord's title applies only after the tenant takes possession.** Before the tenant takes possession, he or she may, upon discovering the "paramount title" (here, Peter's) terminate the lease if he or she did not know of the paramount title at the time he or she signed the lease.

75. Probably not. **Older cases hold that the landlord generally has no duty to control the conduct of other tenants. But the modern trend is to impute the acts of other tenants to L where these acts are in violation of the relevant leases, and L could have prevented the conduct by eviction or otherwise. See Rest. 2d, §6.1, Comment d.** Especially where, as here, Lester had reason to know before he made the lease with Heavy Metal that a significant chance of inconvenience to others existed, the court will probably hold against Lester.

76. Yes. **Here, Tess can only claim to have been *"constructively,"* rather than *"actually,"* evicted. Where the eviction is merely constructive, the tenant is not entitled to terminate the lease, or to stop paying rent, unless he or she abandons the premises. If he or she stays on the premises, his or her only remedy is to sue for damages (i.e., the amount by which the premises are worth less to him or her because of the breach).** Even assuming that Lester had a contractual duty to prevent Heavy Metal from making excessive noise, Tess did not have the right to remain on the premises without paying rent.

77. (a) No. **Under the common law approach, a lease is not deemed terminated where only a portion of the premises is taken, even if a majority, or a part necessary to the operation of the rest, is taken.** (But the modern view, exemplified by the Second Restatement is to allow the tenant to cancel the lease, and stop paying rent, so long as the condemnation significantly interferes with the use contemplated by the parties, and the tenant moves out.)

(b) No. **At common law, the partial condemnation doesn't even relieve the tenant from paying the full rent.**

(c) Yes. **The tenant is entitled to that portion of the award representing the loss of value to the tenant.** If Ted can show, say, that the premises were worth $300 per month less to him because of the parking lot seizure, and that this occurred when the lease had two years to run, Ted would be entitled to $7,200 of the condemnation award.

78. **No. If the landlord knows that the tenant will use the property for illegal purposes (but does not actively assist the tenant in the illegality), the enforceability of the lease depends on the seriousness of the offense.** Where the crime to be committed is a very serious one (such as the drug distribution here), all courts will make the lease unenforceable. This will mean that either party may cancel the lease with impunity. Also, neither party to an illegal contract is generally entitled to recover anything from the other; the court will leave the parties as it finds them, and will, for instance, not order T to pay back rent to L.

79. **No. At common law, the landlord was not deemed to have made any implied warranty that the premises were habitable, even in the case of residential property.**

80. **Yes. More than 40 states now impose some sort of implied warranty of habitability on residential dwellings.** In most or all of these, infestation of rats and/or nonworking toilets would render the premises uninhabitable, and in nearly all, the tenant would be justified in not paying the rent (or at least in depositing the rent into a court-administered escrow fund pending the repairs).

81. Split of authority. **The defect here is a "patent" (obvious) one, rather than a "latent" one. Some courts hold that there is no implied warranty against any defect that the tenant knew about (or should reasonably have known about through inspection) at the time he or she signed the lease. But other courts hold that the warranty does generally cover even patent defects. Under the Second Restatement, the tenant is generally held to have waived any preexisting defects, but there is an exception for those defects that would make the premises unsafe or unhealthy. See Rest. 2d, §5.3, Comment c.** Since the presence of rats and a nonworking toilet would almost certainly make the premises unhealthy, Terence would not under the Restatement approach be found to have waived his right to object to these defects, so he could withhold rent.

82. Yes, probably. **Those states imposing an implied warranty of habitability generally make it difficult for the landlord to establish a waiver by the tenant of that warranty. For instance, the Restatement bars waivers of this warranty where they are "unconscionable or significantly against public policy," and lists as factors for determining whether the waiver runs counter to public policy the following: whether the waiver resulted from conscious negotiations, whether it was part of a "boilerplate" lease, whether the tenant had significantly less bargaining power than the landlord, and whether the parties were each represented by counsel.** Each of these factors favors Terence's argument that enforcement of the waiver would be unconscionable. Most courts would therefore probably refuse to enforce the waiver.

83. Unclear. **Only a few cases have held that there is an implied warranty of habitability in commercial leases. The Second Restatement takes no position on whether there is such a warranty in commercial leases; see Rest. 2d, §5.1, Caveat. Similarly, most statutes imposing implied warranties of habitability apply only to residential leases.** However, a court might hold that the failure here was so severe, and so devastating to Retailer's ability to use the premises for the purpose that (as Developer knew) Retailer intended, that the warranty should be implied.

84. The defense of retaliatory eviction, which will probably succeed. **Many courts and statutes (probably a majority) hold that even where the lease term is at an end, the landlord may not refuse to renew the lease when this is done for the purpose of retaliating against a tenant who has asserted his right to habitable premises. The doctrine of retaliatory eviction is most likely to be applied where the landlord attempts to terminate the tenancy in retaliation for complaints made to a**

housing authority about building code violations. See Rest. 2d, §14.9, recognizing the defense on the facts of this question. The retaliatory eviction doctrine is more likely to be applied where the landlord is a "professional" (i.e., one in the business of renting residential space) than where the landlord is an "amateur" (e.g., one who rents the second floor of his house). See Rest. 2d, §14.8(2).

85. **(a) Yes. In most states, either by statute or case law, the common law rule that required the tenant to keep paying rent for premises that were no longer usable has been reversed.** Thus, the tenant normally may terminate the lease and stop paying rent if the damage to the premises is substantial.

   (b) No. In most courts, termination and abatement of rent is the *sole* remedy available to the tenant where the premises are destroyed. See Rest. 2d, §5.4, Comment f.

86. **Yes. The traditional common law approach is that the landlord is generally not liable for physical injury to the tenant. But there have always been exceptions, including a rule making the landlord liable if he or she *conceals*, or fails to disclose, a dangerous defect he or she knows to exist at the start of the lease.** Since Lamar knew of the danger and failed to fix or disclose it, he will be liable even under the strict common law approach.

87. Yes, probably. **Since the jurisdiction follows the "modern" view, it imposes an implied warranty of habitability. Most courts that have considered the issue find that where the premises are not habitable, and where reasonable care on the landlord's part would have caused the defect to be discovered, the landlord is responsible in tort for any resulting physical injury. Rest. 2d, §17.6(1).** If there were nothing to indicate that Lamar was negligent (even though he failed to find and correct the defect), most courts would probably not make him liable (i.e., most would not impose strict liability for a breach of the warranty of habitability). But here, Lamar was clearly negligent.

88. **No. Where the tenant has the right to install a fixture, he or she generally also has the right, at the end of the lease term, to remove that fixture, provided that he or she restores the property to the condition it was in prior to the attachment. See Rest. 2d, §12.2(4), and Illustration 29 thereto.** The lease clearly gave Tuttle the right to install a new boiler. Therefore, Tuttle had the right to remove that boiler, even though the removal may have "damaged" Lehman (in the sense that it rendered the premises less valuable than they would have been had Tuttle left the new boiler there). The key aspect is that Tuttle restored the premises to the condition that they were in shortly before he made the original attachment of the new boiler.

89. **No. By terminating the lease and reletting for his own account, Ludlum also effectively terminated his right to keep the security deposit.** Therefore, he must return that deposit to Trotta (less his $1,000 damages).

90. Ludlum could have relet for Trotta's account rather than his own. **The event that caused Ludlum to have to return the security deposit was not Trotta's abandonment, but Ludlum's letter of termination and his reletting of the premises for his own account.** Instead, Ludlum should have sent a letter to Trotta stating, "I have no obligation to do so, but I will try to relet the premises for your account, not mine. I will hold you responsible for any shortfall between what I am able to get on the reletting and the monthly rent you will owe." By this technique, the Trotta-Ludlum lease would have remained in force, and Ludlum would remain entitled to the security deposit until the expiration of the five years.

91. Yes, probably. **In some states, the purchaser is liable only if he or she has actually received the deposit from the prior landlord. But the majority view (and the view taken by the Restatement)**

seems to be that the purchaser must account for the security deposit (even if he or she did not receive it from the prior landlord), on the grounds that this an obligation that "touches and concerns the land." See Rest. 2d, §16.1, Illustr. 13.

92. No, probably. **First, because forfeiture of the right to remain on the premises is a drastic remedy, courts will generally allow the landlord to cancel the lease only where the tenant's breach has been material. Second, courts will be quick to find that the landlord has *waived* the benefit of a forfeiture clause by failing to object to previous similar latenesses.** The 15-day lateness might be held not to be material. Also, the court will probably hold that when Logan failed to object to the three prior latenesses of approximately the same magnitude, Tierney was justified in believing that the termination clause would not be strictly enforced.

93. Split of authority. **The modern trend is to entirely prohibit a landlord from using self-help, so that the landlord must use judicial proceedings. But other courts, probably still a slight majority, permit the landlord to use at least some degree of self-help to regain the premises** (e.g., changing of locks or peaceable removal of furniture, but no touching of another human being). Lombard's conduct was probably acceptable in states following the latter approach.

94. $4,000 ($2,000 times two months). **Although the rent being paid under the prior lease is some evidence of the fair value of the premises, the amount of a new lease is better evidence. See Rest. 2d, §14.5.** Therefore, the court will probably conclude that Lombard could have started the new lease two months earlier and received $4,000 extra had Toland not held over.

95. Nothing. **Link's action in entering the premises and removing the furniture will probably be found to have amounted to a *termination of the lease* by Link.** Once the lease was terminated, Link had no more right to receive "rent" from Taylor. It is true that Link had the right to receive "damages" for the breach, but these damages are usually calculated by the difference between the lease amount and the fair market value of the premises. Since this difference is zero, Link probably will not recover anything. (Observe that this result is *not* due to any duty on Link's part to "mitigate" damages but, rather, to the mere fact that the lease was at market value and the measure of damages reflects only the landlord's surplus rent.)

96. Notify Taylor that he would attempt to relet for Taylor's account. **In most states, the landlord has the right to inform the tenant that he or she is attempting to relet on the tenant's behalf.** This way, Link's act of removing Taylor's furniture probably would not have counted as a termination of the lease (but rather, an attempt to make the premises relettable for Taylor's account). Taylor would then still have been liable for the difference between the monthly rent payments and the rent actually taken in by Link. Thus, Taylor would have been liable for the six months missed rent. (Probably Link would not be penalized for the inefficiency of his attempts to relet, since he had no "duty to mitigate.")

97. Yes, probably. **The traditional view is that a landlord has *no "duty to mitigate"* (i.e., no duty to try to find a new tenant), and that he or she may simply let the property stay vacant and recover rent from the tenant who has abandoned.** But a growing minority of courts hold that the landlord does have a duty to mitigate (especially in residential leases).

98. None. **A sublease by a tenant does not establish privity of estate between the sublessee (Stuart) and the lessor (Lillian).** Since Tracey transferred to Stuart only the right to occupy the premises for *part* of the time remaining on Tracey's lease with Lillian, the Tracey-Stuart transaction was a *sublease*, not an assignment. Consequently, the sublessee here is not liable to the lessor even on covenants running with the land. Thus, Stuart is liable only to Tracey, not to Lillian, and Lillian cannot recover anything from Stuart.

99. All 10. **An assignee (here, Stuart) is in privity of estate with the nonassigning original party (Lillian), so the assignee receives the benefit, and bears the burden, of any covenants running with the land.** Here, the Tracey-Stuart transaction was an *assignment*, not a sublease, since it was for the entire balance remaining on the Lillian-Tracey lease. Since the obligation to pay rent is a covenant running with the land, Stuart bears the burden of that covenant vis-à-vis Lillian. Thus Lillian can sue Stuart for the rent, including rent accruing after he moved out. (Of course, Stuart only has to pay once, so if he pays Lillian, this is a defense if Tracey later sues him.)

100. Yes. **Theresa's promise to pay money runs with the land, both as to benefit and burden. Since it runs as to benefit, it may be enforced by an assignee (Paul) on the benefit side.** When Lewis sold the property to Paul, he implicitly assigned his reversion to Paul. So Paul can sue Theresa for the rents, just as Lewis could have.

101. Yes. **Thelma, as the original tenant, had both privity of estate and privity of contract with Lloyd. When Thelma assigned to Tim, her privity of estate ended, but her privity of contract remained. Therefore, she was still liable on the original lease.** The fact that Lloyd accepted rent payments directly from Tim, without objection, was not sufficient to release Thelma from her contractual liability (even though this acceptance of rent may have constituted an acceptance by Lloyd of the validity of the assignment from Thelma to Tim).

102. Yes. **Since Tim never promised either Thelma or Lloyd that he would perform Thelma's obligations, he had no contractual liability to pay rent. But by taking possession of the premises, Tim entered into *privity of estate* with Lloyd. He was therefore liable for performances under the lease whose burden runs with the land.** Since the promise to pay rent is such a "running with the land" promise, Tim was liable.

103. No. **Since Tim never assumed contractual liability for Thelma's promises (see answer to prior question), his obligation was based only on privity of estate.** When Tim assigned to Theo and left the premises, that privity of estate ended. Therefore, there was no basis on which Lloyd could hold Tim liable for the period in which Theo, not Tim, was the occupant.

104. No. **Although Tim has privity of estate with Lloyd (see the answer to question 102), this privity imposes on Tim only the burden of covenants that run with the property.** Since the promise to keep the property insured is (according to our assumptions) one that does not "touch and concern" the land, the burden of that promise does not run with the land. Consequently, Tim is not bound by that promise even during the length of time he is in residence.

105. Yes. **Since Tim promised Thelma to fulfill all of her obligations under the master lease, Tim "assumed" the lease, and is in privity of contract, not just privity of estate, with Thelma. Accordingly, Lloyd is a *third-party beneficiary* of Tim's promises under ordinary contract principles.**

106. Yes. **A promise to make repairs runs with the land both as to benefit and burden.** Therefore, Tim gets the benefit of that promise, and Leon gets the burden of that promise (even though Leon never promised Lloyd that he would perform Lloyd's repair obligations, and even though Tim had no privity of contract with Thelma).

107. Yes. **Thelma's original promise to Lloyd to pay rent touched and concerned the land, and therefore ran with the land both as to benefit and burden. Tim, by taking the assignment and moving in, became in privity of estate with Lloyd, and therefore had a noncontractual duty to pay rent for the time of his occupancy** (see answer to question 102 above). Since the benefit of Thelma's promise to pay rent ran with the land, just as the burden did, Leon got the benefit of this running. Therefore, he can recover not just against Thelma but also against Tim.

108. No, probably. **Most American courts follow the rule in *Dumpor's Case*, by which a landlord's consent to one assignment destroys an anti-assignment clause completely, even though the initial consent was to a particular assignee.** (Lloyd could have avoided this problem by making his consent to the original Thelma-Tim assignment "expressly conditional upon there being no further assignments.") A substantial minority of American courts have rejected the rule in *Dumpor's* case; such courts would allow Lloyd to have Theo evicted here.

109. No, probably. **Most states now hold, either by statute or case law, that even where the lease prohibits assignment or sublease without landlord's consent, the consent *may not be unreasonably withheld*.** This is especially likely to be the case where the anti-assignment provision is a boilerplate clause imposed on a tenant who has little or no bargaining power (as was the case here).

110. **(a)** No. **At common law, it was not possible for an owner of land (Orin) to convey that land to one person and to establish by the same deed an easement in a third person. This was the rule against creating an easement in a *"stranger to the deed."***

(b) Yes, probably. **Most modern courts have abandoned the common law "stranger to the deed" rule, and allow an easement to be created by a deed in a person who is neither the grantor nor the grantee. This is especially likely where the easement relates to a use that existed prior to the conveyance.** Since Norman fished in the stream prior to the Orin-to-Alfred conveyance, a modern court would probably uphold the easement in the deed to Alfred. Once that easement is recognized as valid, *it burdened the land*, and therefore is still in force even though it was omitted from the Alfred-to-Barbara deed.

111. No, probably. **Normally, an easement may be created only by compliance with the Statute of Frauds, which did not happen here. Therefore, the only kinds of easement that might have come into existence are (1) an easement "by implication," (2) one by "necessity," or (3) one by "estoppel." But an easement by implication will only come into existence if (among other requirements) the owner of a parcel sells part and retains part, or sells pieces simultaneously to multiple grantees (the requirement of *"severance"*).** Neither Angela nor her predecessors ever owned what is today Blueacre and thus never sold any part of it; consequently, the requirement of "severance" is not satisfied. An easement "by necessity" doesn't exist, because the two parcels, Auburnacre and Blueacre, were never under common ownership. And an easement by estoppel doesn't exist because neither Burt nor Carter ever made any substantial or foreseeable reliance on the supposed easement. So Carter has no easement at all.

112. Yes, probably. **The only way Helen can avoid an injunction is to show that a valid easement exists. Since no express easement exists, Helen must show that an easement by implication exists. An easement by implication is created if three requirements are met: (1) land is being divided up so that the initial owner of the parcel (here, Helen) is either selling part and retaining part, or is subdividing the property (the "severance" requirement); (2) the use existed prior to the severance; and (3) the use is at least reasonably necessary (and in some instances strictly necessary) to the continued enjoyment of the land.** Here, the first two requirements are met: Helen sold part to Ingrid and kept the rest, and the hanging over of the gliders onto Ingrid's property occurred prior to the sale to Ingrid.

But most courts would probably hold that the third requirement, that of "necessity," is not met. When the implied easement is created by grant (i.e., in favor of the grantee, Ingrid in this case), most courts require only "reasonable" necessity. But where the implied easement is *"reserved"* (i.e., runs in favor of the grantor rather than the grantee), most courts require that the easement be *"strictly"* or *"absolutely"* necessary. Here, Helen has other ways, albeit inconvenient and/or expensive ones, of solving her problem, such as parking in the street or building a structure elsewhere on her property. Therefore, a court is unlikely to find that the easement is absolutely necessary. (In a court following the minority rule that only "reasonable" necessity is needed for an implied reservation, Helen might prevail, but even here her odds are not good since her need is not very strong.)

113. No. **Frederika's best hope for establishing an easement is to show that the requirements for an "easement of necessity" are satisfied. For such an easement, three conditions must be met: (1) the necessity must be "strict" rather than "reasonable"; (2) the parcels must have been under common ownership just before a conveyance; and (3) the necessity must come into the existence of, and be caused by, the conveyance that breaks up the common ownership.** Here, the first two requirements are satisfied, but the third one is not; Frederika's need to cross West Overlook was not created by the conveyance of East Overlook to her.

114. No. **The only way Yentil could possibly prevail would be to show that an easement by *prescription* came into existence. An easement by prescription is formed when a person uses another's land, in a manner similar to adverse possession, for more than the statute of limitations period. However, one of the requirements for the formation of an easement by prescription is that the use must be "*adverse.*" If the use of the property is granted through the permission of the owner, the use is "permissive," not adverse.** Here, Xavier clearly gave Yentil permission over the 11 years to use the court, so Yentil's use was permissive rather than adverse, and Yentil did not obtain any easement by prescription.

115. Yes. **Ben has obtained an easement by *prescription*. When one property owner uses another's property for more than the statute of limitations period applicable to adverse possession actions, and does so in an adverse manner (see answer to prior question), an easement by prescription results.** The requirement of "adverse" use is satisfied here by the fact that Ben never asked Astrid's permission, and Astrid never expressly consented, merely tolerated the use. The use must be reasonably continuous, which was the case here. The use need not be exclusive, since it is only an easement by prescription, not formal title, that is being granted by adverse possession. This easement by prescription, once it came into existence in 2005, became a burden on Astrid's land, so that Charles is bound even though he was not the owner while the easement was ripening.

116. No. **David's only hope is to show that an easement by prescription came into existence. But one requirement of such an easement is that the prior use must be reasonably *continuous*. If the use is so infrequent that a reasonable landowner would not be likely to protest and would view the matter as an occasional minor trespass, the continuity requirement is not satisfied.** A dumping that occurs at most annually, and sometimes not for two years, probably would not be found sufficiently frequent, in which case no easement by prescription would be found.

117. Yes. **If the present use significantly increases the burden on the servient tenement over what it was from the original use that led to the easement, the present use is not within the easement.** To begin with, the court will probably find that a prescriptive easement exists on Darwin's property—this is because the path was used without his permission for a period of time exceeding the state's adverse possession statute of limitations. However, even though a prescriptive easement exists, the court will probably find that the *scope* of this easement does not extend to the use of motorized ATVs. Here, the increase in noise, danger, and surface erosion caused by the use of the ATVs almost certainly exceeds the scope of the original bicycle path easement.

118. Yes, probably. **Paula's easement here is probably an easement *appurtenant*—that is, an easement for the benefit of a particular dominant estate (Blackacre). A holder of a dominant estate may normally not be allowed to extend his or her use of the easement so that *additional property* owned by him or her is benefitted. This is true even if the use for the benefit of the additional property does not increase the burden on the servient estate (Whiteacre).** Even though the number of animals, and the nature of their activities on Whiteacre, has not changed or increased, a court will probably hold that Paula cannot use the easement while housing the animals on Greenacre.

119. Yes. **Both the benefit and burden of an easement appurtenant pass with transfer of the property.** The original deed from Dunes to George created an easement appurtenant, since the free-golf rights were clearly intended to benefit a purchaser of the house in his capacity as owner of a house adjacent to the course. Thus, the benefit passed when George sold the dominant parcel to Henry, and the burden passed when Dunes Development sold the servient parcel to Ian. (This rule that both benefit and burden pass with the land is always subject to a contrary agreement; thus, if the original deed from Dunes to George had said that George's rights were not transferable to a subsequent purchaser of a house, Henry would be out of luck. But here, no such provision was present in the deed.)

120. Yes. **Winnie's right is not an easement but instead a *"profit in gross"*—i.e., the right to go on another's land and to remove timber, minerals, or other items from the soil. Most courts will generally allow the assignment of profits in gross, especially when they are commercial in nature. But courts are reluctant to permit *"division"* of a profit in gross, which is what Winnie has attempted to do here. This is especially so where the profit is nonexclusive (i.e., where the servient tenement retains the right to remove the same product). Where division of the profit would make the profit much more burdensome on the servient owner than originally intended, the courts will not allow the division.** Here, the servient owner (Frookie) probably did not intend for the profit holder to demand more than enough pine branches for a few hundred wreaths per year, so the court is likely to deny the division of the profit.

121. No, probably. **Here, the court is likely to uphold the division of the profit in gross. Courts are much more likely to uphold a division of a profit in gross when a royalty is paid to the servient owner based on the amount of use, and where the profit is exclusive—in such a situation, the burden on the servient owner stemming from the division is less severe than where there is a flat fee and/or the profit is nonexclusive.**

122. No. **An easement is like any other estate in land, in the sense that any extinguishment of it must normally satisfy the Statute of Frauds.** Therefore, Quince's oral statement, taken by itself, did not extinguish the easement, and that easement passed to Raymond when the dominant tenement (the quarry and manufacturing plant) were sold to Raymond.

123. (a) A license. **A license is a right to use the licensor's land that is revocable at the will of the licensor. A license is not required to satisfy the Statute of Frauds, and thus may be created orally.** This is what happened here: Abbott did not sign any writing, and Bingham's confirmatory letter did not satisfy the Statute of Frauds as is normally required for an easement (since it was not signed by Abbott, the only person who could create the easement); nonetheless, a license was created.

    (b) No. **The feature that distinguishes a license from an easement is that the license is *revocable at the will of the licensor*.** Therefore, Abbott had the right at any time to revoke the license, regardless of his motive.

124. (a) No, probably. **If a license would have been an easement except that it did not meet the Statute of Frauds, and the licensee makes substantial expenditures on the land in reliance on the**

licensor's promise that the license will be permanent, courts generally will give the licensee some protection against revocation. But usually they will not grant full enforcement of the license where there is some more limited method of protecting the licensee's interests, as there is here (see answer to part (b)).

(b) Award $20,000 plus interest. **Where the licensee makes substantial expenditures on the land in reliance on the licensor's promise of irrevocability, the court will generally protect the licensee's *reliance* interest—i.e., his investment in the improvements.**

125. No. Since Claire never promised to pay for repairs, the only way Bertrand's promise could be binding on Claire is if that promise was a "covenant running with the land." In particular, Claire will only be bound if the burden of the covenant runs with the land. There are several requirements in order for the burden to run. One is that the burden "touch and concern" the land. Here, this require-ment is satisfied, since nonpayment would result in a lien that would touch and concern the land. But a second requirement in nearly all states is that there must be "*horizontal privity*" between promisor and promisee. In particular, it remains the rule everywhere (except in four states that have modified it by statute) that the *burden of the covenant may not run with the land where the original parties to the covenant were "strangers to title"*—i.e., had no property relationship between them at the time of the promise. Here, this rule is not satisfied: Allison and Bertrand were strangers to title, and thus could not create a covenant the burden of which would run with the land (unless Allison gave Bertrand an easement to come onto Allison's land to make repairs if she did not do so herself; the facts say that this did not happen).

126. No, probably. **The vast majority of jurisdictions apply the same horizontal privity requirement for the running of a benefit as they do for the running of a burden, whatever that rule is in the particular jurisdiction.** Since the burden of the promise here would not run (see the answer to the prior question), nearly all states would refuse to allow the benefit to run either, so that Doug would not be permitted to recover.

127. Yes. **Since Allison's promise not to change fences is a negative promise, and the relief sought by Claire is an injunction, the question is whether we have a valid "*equitable servitude*" (not a "covenant at law," as we had in the two prior questions). An equitable servitude is a promise (usually negative in nature) relating to land that will be enforced by courts against an assignee of the promisor.**

The promise here satisfies the requirements for equitable servitudes, which are less stringent than for covenants at law. The promise must "touch and concern" both the promisor's land and the prom-isee's land; that requirement is satisfied here, since Allison (the promisor) has bound herself with respect to a structure on her property, and the appearance of Bertrand's property is directly affected by the promise. Horizontal privity (privity between Allison and Bertrand, the original promisor and promisee) is *not* required for an equitable servitude; therefore, the fact that Allison and Bertrand had no preexisting property relationship and were thus "strangers to title" does not prevent Allison's promise from being an enforceable equitable servitude, even though it prevented Bertrand's counter-promise to pay for repairs from being enforceable at law as to Bertrand's successor. Nor is there any vertical privity requirement for equitable servitudes, so Claire could enforce the servitude against Doug even if she only held, say, a lease on the property owned by Bertrand. Courts will not enforce an equitable servitude against an assignee of the promisor unless the assignee was on actual or constructive notice of the servitude at the time he took possession. But the fact that the Allison-Bertrand agreement was filed in the land records put Doug on such constructive notice.

128. No. **Harry is trying to enforce an equitable servitude against Isadore's property. But equity will not enforce an agreement against a subsequent purchaser unless the purchaser had *notice* of**

the restriction at the time he took. **This notice can be either actual or "constructive."** But the facts make it clear that James did not have actual notice at the time he purchased, and the absence of any valid recordation of the agreement means that James did not have constructive notice either. Therefore, the restriction is not binding against him, and he can build the pool.

129. Yes. **Here, James has actual knowledge of the Harry-Isadore agreement, so the usual rules allowing an equitable servitude to be enforced against an assignee of the promisor should apply.** The fact that Isadore made what turned out to be an incorrect statement of law should not be a defense for James—James was always free to inspect the Harry-Isadore agreement, discover that it was silent on the issue of whether it ran with the property, and consult a lawyer to learn that such an agreement runs with the land.

130. Yes, probably. **Most courts will apply the doctrine of *"implied reciprocal servitude"* in this circumstance. This theory holds that if the earlier of two purchasers (here, Kathy) acquires his or her land in expectation that he or she will be entitled to the benefit of subsequently created equitable servitudes, there is immediately created an "implied reciprocal servitude" against the developer's remaining land.** For this reciprocality doctrine to apply, a general development plan must be in existence at the time of the first sale, a requirement satisfied here. Courts frequently apply the doctrine even where the restrictions are not inserted in the later deed (here, the one to Lewis).

131. Yes, probably. **Most courts faced with this situation have realized that if they relieve a border lot from the restrictions, there will be a "domino" effect: The restricted owners whose lots are next inside the border will now be able to argue that enforcement of the restrictions is unfair against them, until finally the restrictions will no longer apply even in the center of the once-restricted area.** Also, when Michael bought his lot he obviously knew that it was on the outer corner of the development, and that there was a risk that the nonrestricted areas across the street might give rise to office buildings and other nonresidential use. He therefore probably paid less for the property than he would have for one in the protected center of the development. Putting the equities together, the court is unlikely to conclude that the restrictions are so unfair to Michael that he should be relieved of them.

132. No, probably. **Occasionally, a land-use control is sufficiently draconian that a court will conclude that it amounts to a "taking" for Fourteenth Amendment purposes, for which compensation must be given. But this is extremely rare, especially in the environmental regulation area. A land-use regulation is valid as long as the means chosen "substantially advance" a legitimate state interest, and do not "deny an owner economically viable use of his land."** *Nollan v. California Coastal Commission,* 483 U.S. 825 (1987). The town is certainly advancing its legitimate interest in not suffering the noxious odors associated with a dump. Furthermore, Dexter is not being deprived of all economically viable use of his property, but merely the most "valuable" use, so a court is extremely unlikely to hold that the ordinance constitutes a taking.

133. Yes, probably. *First English Evangelical Lutheran Church v. Los Angeles County,* 482 U.S. 304 (1987), **holds that where an owner is denied all economically viable use of his property, for a reasonably substantial time, compensation must be paid.** Since during the one-year period Dexter couldn't operate a dump, and probably couldn't use his property in any other remotely useful way (since he didn't know whether he would be permitted to use a dump later on), a court would probably hold that these requirements were satisfied. If so, Hampshire would have to pay Dexter damages equal to a reasonable "rental" value for the premises during the year.

134. No. **Nearly all states (which by statute give local zoning boards their powers) agree that aesthetic considerations may constitute at least one factor in the municipality's zoning decision.** Many

states do not allow such aesthetic factors to be the *sole* factor, but here, the commission's judgment is not based solely on aesthetics, but also, at least arguably, on the maintenance of property values by preserving architectural harmony.

135. No, probably. **The vast majority of states hold that such an "amortization" provision does not violate due process or constitute a taking, as long as the amortization period is sufficiently long for the owner to recover most of his costs and to arrange an alternative use or location.** Jones has already had the billboard for 20 years (plus the five-year phase-out), so he has had plenty of time to recoup its costs. Also, he can continue to run his business without the billboard, so the injury to him is not extreme. (But about five states hold, either as a matter of state statutory law or federal constitutional law, that nonconforming uses must be permitted indefinitely, rather than being "amortized.")

136. No. **Prince probably has standing to assert his claim, since he has been directly affected by the allegedly illegal zoning. However, the Supreme Court has held that a racially discriminatory *purpose*, not merely effect, needs to be shown before an ordinance will be subjected to strict equal protection scrutiny. Without strict scrutiny, the ordinance here merely has to be rationally related to a legitimate state purpose, which is almost certainly the case.** See *Arlington Heights v. Metropolitan Housing Development Corp.*, 429 U.S. 252 (1977). Unless Prince is able to bear the burden of showing that the town's ordinance was enacted (or maintained) for racially discriminatory purposes, the fact that the ordinance has a disparate negative effect on minorities is irrelevant to the equal protection claim.

137. (a) A federal Fair Housing Act suit. **The Fair Housing title of the 1968 Civil Rights Act makes it unlawful to "make unavailable, or deny, a dwelling to any person because of race, color, religion, sex or national origin."**

   (b) Yes, probably. **If Prince had been able to show that Twin Peaks intentionally tried to limit access by blacks, this would be a clear violation of the Housing Act. The Supreme Court has never decided whether a discriminatory purpose (rather than mere disparate effect) must be shown for a violation of the act, but most lower federal courts have held that the plaintiff in such a suit does *not* need to show that the defendant had a discriminatory intent. Instead, plaintiff merely has to prove that the defendant's land-use controls had a disparate effect on blacks or other racial minorities. The burden then shifts to the defendant town to show that it was acting in pursuit of a legitimate governmental interest, and that there was no less-discriminatory way of achieving that same interest.** See, e.g., *Huntington Branch NAACP v. Town of Huntington*, 844 F.2d 926 (2d Cir. 1988). Probably Twin Peaks could not meet this burden, so probably Prince would win his suit on this theory.

138. (a) A *Mount Laurel "fair share"* suit. **In *Southern Burlington County NAACP v. Township of Mount Laurel*, 336 A.2d 713 (N.J. 1975), the New Jersey Supreme Court held that exclusionary zoning practices that fail to serve the general welfare of the region as a whole violate statutory law and the state constitution. The court held that a municipality may not foreclose opportunities for low- and moderate-income housing, and must allow at least that town's "fair share" of the present and prospective regional need for such housing.** Since the two-acre minimum prevents even middle-class housing, let alone lower-class housing, from being constructed, the scheme would almost certainly be a *Mount Laurel* violation.

   (b) Grant a rezoning of the parcel. ***Mount Laurel* (and a successor case, *Mount Laurel II*) holds that where the trial court concludes that the project sought to be built by the developer is suitable for that specific site, the court may order the municipality to rezone the particular project. This is the so-called builder's remedy.** This would permit Prosser to go ahead with his project immediately, rather than merely watch as the town meets its "fair share" obligation by other means, such as allowing an apartment complex to be built in some other part of town. (But the New Jersey legislature has subsequently put a moratorium on the builder's remedy.)

139. No, probably. **If Darwin could show that the designation was "arbitrary" or "discriminatory," he might be able to convince the court that Acropolis and/or Pound had exceeded their police power. But there is no evidence of this in our facts. Alternatively, Darwin could argue that his ability to use the property has been so diminished that a taking has occurred. But this will almost certainly fail, in light of the Supreme Court's holding in *Penn Central Transportation Co. v. City of New York*, 438 U.S. 104 (1978), that the designation of Grand Central Terminal as a landmark, with the concomitant prohibition on building above it, did not constitute a taking.** Since Darwin can continue to use the building for its originally constructed purpose as an office building, the fact that he could derive, say, three or four times as much net revenue by demolishing it and constructing a larger building will probably not be enough to raise the landmark designation to the level of a "taking."

140. No. **The Supreme Court has construed the requirement of a "public use" quite broadly: It is satisfied as long as the state's use of its eminent domain power is "rationally related to a conceivable public purpose." See *Kelo v. New London*, 545 U.S. 469 (2005).** Here, revitalizing the downtown area is certainly a conceivable public purpose, and taking private residences to enable a developer to put up a shopping center is rationally related to achieving that purpose.

141. No. **The *Statute of Frauds* is applicable in all states to any contract for the sale of land, or for the sale of any interest in land. Therefore, either the contract itself, or a memorandum of it, must be in writing. Furthermore, the contract or memorandum must be signed by the "party to be charged."** On the facts here, the party to be charged is Bryant, and the contract is not enforceable against him because of the lack of signature.

142. Yes. **The *Statute of Frauds* is applicable in all states to any contract for the sale of land, or for the sale of any interest in land. Therefore, either the contract itself, or a memorandum of it, must be in writing. Furthermore, the contract or memorandum must be signed by the "party to be charged."** Simon's memorandum satisfies the Statute of Frauds as against him, even though it does not satisfy the Statute as against Bryant. This is because Simon signed the memorandum, and the memorandum thus contains the signature of the "party to be charged." Courts will almost always give a decree of specific performance against a defaulting seller, ordering him to convey the property to the buyer in return for the purchase price.

143. Yes, probably. **Most (but certainly not all) states recognize the "*part performance*" exception to the Statute of Frauds for land-sale contracts. Under this doctrine, a party (either buyer or seller) who has taken action in reliance on the contract may be able to gain enforcement of it at equity.** In most states, if the "purchaser" (here, Grandson, in the sense that he was "purchasing" the farm in exchange for his services) takes possession, makes improvements and changes his position in reliance, this will be the sort of part performance required. Courts generally require that the part performance be "unequivocally referable" to the alleged contract (i.e., that the part performance be clearly in response to the oral contract, and not explainable by some other facet of the parties' relationship). This requirement seems to be met, since Grandson has made permanent improvements to the property by building the cabin and cutting down the trees, and these improvements are not readily explainable by the mere Grandfather-Grandson relationship.

144. No, probably. **Even in the majority of states that recognize the part performance exception, courts require that the part performance be "*unequivocally referable*" to the alleged contract.** See *Burns*

v. McCormick, 135 N.E. 273 (N.Y. 1922). Since Tycoon and Grandson were relatives, the fact that Tycoon moved onto the property and took care of Tycoon was not necessarily associated with the alleged contract—Grandson might have been doing this just for love, or in return for free room and board. Also, the work done by Grandson was not in the nature of permanent improvements on the land, weakening his claim.

145. **Yes, probably. In a suit for specific performance of a land-sale contract, the general rule is that time is *not of the essence* unless the contract expressly so provides or the surrounding circumstances indicate that it is. Thus, generally, even though the contract specifies a particular closing date, either party may obtain specific performance although he or she is unable to close on the appointed day (as long as the defaulting party is able to perform within a reasonable time after the scheduled date).** Since the surrounding circumstances do not suggest that time was of the essence from Shelby's perspective, and since Bennett was able to perform within what a court would probably find was a reasonable time of the scheduled closing date (ten-day delay), the court will probably grant Bennett a decree of specific performance. (But a few courts, most notably the New York courts, hold that where the contract does not explicitly make time of the essence, either party, by a unilateral notification to the other that it will insist upon strict adherence to the contracted-for settlement date, may make time of the essence. In such a state, Shelby would win.)

146. **No, probably. If the contract is silent on the issue of the kind of title to be conveyed by the vendor, an obligation to convey a *marketable* title will be implied. Where the title is required to be marketable, the title will generally be considered insufficient if it is based on adverse possession. Unless the vendor can show beyond a reasonable doubt that the claim of adverse possession is valid, this will be treated as a defect.** The affidavit from Rosen would almost certainly not be sufficient to establish beyond a reasonable doubt the validity of Rosen's title by adverse possession. A court would therefore almost certainly conclude that Bridges was not required to "buy a lawsuit"—i.e., buy a property that he would have trouble reselling because his buyer could raise the same lack-of-marketability objection that Bridges is now raising (even though, if Sherwood were to bring a quiet title action, a court might well conclude that he does have valid title because Rosen did take by adverse possession).

147. **No, probably. The key to solving this question is that where the seller's duty to deliver the deed and the buyer's duty to pay the money are *concurrent*, then each party must be sure to *tender his or her own performance* to be able to hold the other party in default.** Therefore, Brady could hold Squires in default (and get a return of his deposit) only if Brady tendered his own performance. Since Brady did not have the certified check with him, or even have the funds readily available, Brady did not tender his own performance. Consequently, Squires's own "breach" is irrelevant, and Squires will probably be allowed to keep the deposit. (The result might have been different if Squires's failure to comply with the contract stemmed from an incurable problem, such as complete lack of title in Squires; it also would have been different if Squires had repudiated the contract ahead of time. But neither of these events happened here.)

148. **Yes, probably. The usual rule that each party must tender his or her own performance to hold the other in breach does not generally apply where a defendant's inability to perform is *incurable*.** On these facts, Squires's lack of marketable title (due to the encroachment) was so severe, and so impossible to cure, that Brady's failure to tender his own performance would probably be overlooked by the court, and Brady would get his money back.

149. **Deirdre. "Common sense" would suggest that the answer should be Nell, since Sherman died while still the technical owner of the real estate, so it would seem fair to give Nell the proceeds**

from the post-death sale of an asset that was earmarked for her. But instead, courts apply the doctrine of *"equitable conversion."* By this doctrine, the signing of the contract is deemed to vest in the purchaser equitable ownership of the land, and the vendor is treated as becoming the equitable owner of the purchase price at that time. As a result of the equitable conversion doctrine, the purchase price goes to the person to whom the personal property was bequeathed, and the person to whom the real estate was devised gets nothing.

150. Yes, probably. **Most courts adopt the rule that since the vendee acquires equitable ownership of the land as soon as the contract is signed, the risk of loss immediately shifts to him or her. This is true even though the vendee never takes possession prior to the casualty.** There is an exception if the vendor caused the loss negligently, but the facts indicate that this was not the case.

151. Booth must pay the purchase price, but receives a credit for the $100,000 insurance proceeds received by Spratt. **Courts following the majority "risk of loss passes to vendee" rule usually hold that the purchaser gets the benefit of the vendor's insurance. The vendor is deemed to hold the insurance proceeds in a "constructive trust" for the vendee, and the vendee gets an abatement of the purchase price equal to the amount of the insurance.**

152. No, probably. **When the purchaser under an installment sales contract has paid a substantial percentage of the purchase price, most courts try hard to avoid allowing the seller to make the buyer "forfeit" his or her rights under the contract.** The court might order Spence to use statutory foreclosure proceedings before evicting Bagley. In that event, Spence would have to put the property up for sale, and would have to pay to Bagley any amount that the property sold for less the $100,000 that Bagley still owes Spence. (In other words, the installment contract would be treated as if it had been a mortgage.) Or, the court might give Bagley the right to make the payments on which he had been in arrears ($15,000) and then continue with the contract. If the $5,000 monthly payments due from Bagley were no more than a fair rental price for the property, the court would probably not use either of these methods, since the situation would be analogous to a tenant who falls behind in his rent. But here, the monthly payments are much more than fair rental value, so the court would, as stated, take steps to avoid forfeiture.

153. No, probably. **Under the doctrine of *merger*, obligations imposed by the contract of sale are generally discharged unless they are repeated in the deed.** There is an exception where the contract covenant is "collateral" to (i.e., not directly related to) the promise to convey land. But here, the representation in the contract that there were no easements related directly to the transfer of title, and most courts would hold that that representation was merged out of existence when Boswell accepted the deed that did not repeat the obligation. (But the Uniform Land Transactions Act, if in force in the jurisdiction, would prevent merger from happening.)

154. Stewart. **If a deed is validly executed and delivered, title passes immediately to the grantee. Thereafter, return of the deed to the grantor, or even destruction of the deed, has no effect either to cancel the prior delivery or to reconvey the title to the original grantor.** The only way the title can get back to the grantor is if a new, formally satisfactory, conveyance takes place. Since Stewart never executed and delivered a valid deed to Fred, title remains in him.

155. None. **The covenants of seisin, right to convey, and against encumbrances are all "present" covenants. That is, they are breached at the moment the conveyance is made. Therefore, a breach of these can occur even though there was no eviction.** Consequently, Spitzer violated these at the time of the original conveyance (at least the covenants of seisin and right to convey were breached, though the covenant against encumbrances may not have been). However, Butler's problem is that these

covenants are time-barred: The five-year statute of limitations on each began to run at the time of conveyance, and the actions became time-barred in 1985. The covenants of quiet enjoyment and warranty, by contrast, are "future" covenants. That is, they are breached only when an eviction occurs. The covenants both promise that the grantee's possession will not be challenged. An action on either of these future covenants is not time-barred, since they have not yet started to run. However, there is no cause of action on these, either: Until Adolf starts eviction proceedings or otherwise actively asserts that his title is superior, Butler has not even been constructively, let alone actually, evicted. Therefore, Butler will have to wait until Adolf actively asserts his title before he may sue Spitzer. To the extent that the uncertainty renders Butler unable to convey a valid title, Butler is simply out of luck.

156. Negotiate to buy Adolf's interest and then put Spitzer on notice that Butler is about to make this purchase. **Butler can obviously "solve" his lack of title by buying Adolf's title (gained by adverse possession).** As long as Spitzer is on notice that Butler plans to do this, and Spitzer is given a chance to intervene and negotiate directly with Adolf, the onus is then placed on Spitzer: If Spitzer takes no action, and Butler pays a fair price for Adolf's interest, Butler can then recover this sum from Spitzer, according to most courts. (That is, negotiations between Adolf and Butler will constitute constructive eviction by Adolf; Butler will then be entitled to "settle" the case and charge Spitzer for the cost of this settlement, so long as Spitzer was given the chance to intervene and lessen his own damages.)

157. Yes. **The future covenants (warranty, quiet enjoyment, and further assurance) are universally held to *run with the land*.** Since these covenants are not breached until there is an actual or constructive eviction, they would be rendered almost useless if a subsequent transfer of the land cut them off. Therefore, Capshaw can sue Spitzer even though he had no privity of contract with Spitzer.

158. (a) Covenant against encumbrances. **The covenant against encumbrances is a representation that there are no encumbrances against the property.** The encroachment by Jones was such an encumbrance, so this covenant was violated.

(b) No, probably. **Most courts hold that even where the grantee is aware of a defect, his or her knowledge does not nullify the relevant covenant.**

159. (a) Suit for breach of the implied warranty of habitability. **Many courts today allow a home purchaser to sue a professional developer for the breach of this warranty in a way that is analogous to the landlord-tenant implied warranty recognized in nearly all jurisdictions.**

(b) Split of authority. **The strong emerging trend is to recognize an action for implied warranty of habitability in sales by professional developers of new homes.**

160. No. **Courts have nearly always refused to allow an implied warranty claim against one who is not in the business of building or selling homes.** The consequence is that the buyer of a used home, such as Carter, cannot sue the person who sold it to him (Benjamin).

161. Yes. **Most courts now allow a purchaser of a used home to sue the *original builder* for breach of the implied warranty of habitability if the defect was latent when the purchaser bought and appeared within a reasonable time after construction.** In other words, privity of contract is generally no longer required for implied warranty of habitability suits, where such suits are allowed at all.

162. Split of authority. **Traditionally, the seller has never been liable for merely failing to disclose material defects of which he or she is aware. But today, many states hold that the seller has an affirmative duty to disclose material defects of which he or she is aware, and that he or she will be liable in damages if he or she does not do so.**

163. Beacon, because he recorded first. **Under the pure race statute, Beacon wins automatically, without regard to whether he had actual knowledge of the earlier conveyance to Arkin (which the facts tell us he did not).** Beacon recorded his deed before Arkin did, so that is the end of the matter.

164. Arkin, because he recorded first. **The phrase "pure race" means exactly what it says: Whoever records first wins, regardless of his or her or the other party's state of knowledge.** Thus, Arkin wins because he recorded first, even though he delayed recording for even longer than Beacon did and knew of Beacon's interest at the time he (Arkin) recorded. Arkin wins, furthermore, despite the fact that at the time Beacon paid fair value and took his deed, Beacon had no way (at least from the public records) of discovering the conveyance to Arkin. The moral of the story is that in a pure race jurisdiction, a grantee must record immediately.

165. Arkin, because he recorded first. **Under a race-notice statute, the second grantee (Beacon) will prevail over the earlier grantee (Arkin) only if the second satisfies two requirements: (1) he or she records before the earlier purchaser records, and (2) he or she took without notice of the earlier conveyance.** Here, Beacon flunked the first of these requirements. (The fact that Beacon had notice at the time he recorded is irrelevant; what counts is whether Beacon had notice at the time he received his deed, which he did not on the facts here.)

166. Arkin. **A race-notice statute requires that the subsequent purchaser record before the earlier purchaser, and take without notice of the earlier conveyance.** Here, Beacon failed the second of these requirements, since he knew of the conveyance to Arkin at the time he, Beacon, took. Therefore, Beacon's having recorded first does not save him. (The fact that Oliver lied about the way the recording statute works should not insulate Beacon from his own failure to comply with the statute.)

167. Beacon. **Under a "pure notice" statute, the sole issue is whether the subsequent grantee had actual or constructive notice of the prior grant at the time the subsequent grantee took.** At the time Beacon took in 2007, he had neither actual nor constructive notice of the grant to Arkin (the facts tell you he did not have actual notice, and the lack of recordation means that he did not have constructive notice). Therefore, the fact that Arkin later recorded, and that Beacon never recorded, is irrelevant.

168. Adler. **A grace period statute protects the first grantee for the grace period, regardless of whether he or she records. If he or she still has not recorded at the end of this period, he or she loses this special protection.** Here, the 15-day grace period is joined with standard race-notice provisions. This means that as long as Adler recorded within 15 days following the date he took his conveyance, nothing Bowles did would deprive Adler of priority. (So that the fact that Bowles neither knew nor could not have known of the earlier transaction to Adler is not enough to save Bowles.)

169. Hold the deed and purchase price in escrow for 15 days. **Bowles (or his lawyer) should have known that for 15 days following September 10, some earlier conveyance from Oakley might suddenly be recorded, thus giving the earlier grantee priority. Therefore, Bowles should have insisted that his purchase price, and the deed, be held in escrow for 15 days following September 10.** At the end of that period, if no earlier conveyance from Oakley was recorded, the escrow agent would have recorded Bowles's deed on September 25 and given the purchase price to Oakley simultaneously. If (as in fact happened) some earlier conveyance was recorded between September 10 and September 25, the transaction would have been canceled, Bowles would have gotten back his purchase price, and the deed would have been ripped up.

170. Bowles. **Once the grace period expired (which happened on September 15), the problem was transformed into a conventional race-notice problem.** That is, Bowles, as the second grantee, could

prevail only if he met two requirements: (1) he recorded before Adler recorded, and (2) he took without notice of the conveyance to Adler. On these facts, Bowles satisfied both these requirements, so he wins.

171. Cabbott, probably. **Ordinarily, the second grantee under a race-notice statute must fulfill two requirements to take priority over a prior grantee: (1) he or she must record before the earlier grantee records, and (2) he or she must have taken without notice of the earlier grant.** Here, Cabbott has not fulfilled the first of these requirements, since Arias recorded before he (Cabbott) did. However, most statutes requiring a race require it only where the contest is *between grantees from a common grantor.* Since Arias and Cabbott are claiming under different grantors, Cabbott's failure to record before Arias probably will not be fatal. Allowing Cabbott to win fulfills the goal of encouraging reliance on the public record: at the time Cabbott took from Beck, paying full value, Cabbott had no practical way to know of the earlier conveyance to Arias, so there is a strong interest in protecting him even though he was negligent by waiting to record. (Obviously, Cabbott could have protected himself fully by recording immediately, so that he would have won the race-to-record with Arias, even though he never knew of Arias's existence.) So the court will probably find for Cabbott.

172. Abrams. **Boone appears to have fulfilled the two requirements for taking priority over a prior grantee under a race-notice statute: He took without notice of the prior grant, and he recorded before the prior grantee recorded. However, in the vast majority of states, a grantee receives the benefit of the recording act (i.e., he or she gets to take priority over an earlier unrecorded conveyance) only if he or she *gives value* for his or her interest.** Here, Boone did not give value, but rather received a gift. Therefore, he gets no benefit from the recording act, and the usual principle of "first in time, first in right" applies. This is true even though Abrams similarly received a gift and thus did not give value.

173. Chavez. **At first, Chavez appears to violate one of the two requirements for taking ahead of a prior grantee: Chavez failed to win the "race" to record before Bishop did. But in reality, Bishop will be deemed never to have recorded at all. A grantee records only when he or she *adequately* records. The mere fact that a deed is recorded somewhere in the public records does not mean that the recording is "adequate"—the document must be recorded *in such a way that a reasonable searcher would find it.* Here, only if a searcher would have found the document using the grantor and grantee indexes would Bishop's deed be adequately recorded.**

A searcher in Chavez's position would have started with a "root" of Orcini (or one of Orcini's predecessors in recorded title); Chavez would then never have found the Orcini-to-Arlen deed because that deed was never recorded. Thus he would not have known to look in the grantor index to find that Arlen later conveyed to Bishop, and he consequently would never have found the deed to Bishop. In other words, Bishop would be deemed to have adequately recorded only if Bishop made sure that not only was his own deed recorded, but also *the deed by which his grantor took* (the Orcini-to-Arlen deed), and so forth back in the chain at least 50 or 60 years. Since Bishop is in a position equivalent to not having recorded at all, Chavez is the first to "adequately" record, and he is thus the first grantee; it is Bishop who is the second grantee, and he loses because he did not adequately record first.

174. Bishop, probably. **Here, Chavez has not fulfilled the sole requirement for a subsequent grantee to take, since he was on actual notice of the prior conveyance.**

175. Burrows. **Dempsey's fatal mistake was that although he made sure that his own conveyance (Craft to Dempsey) was promptly recorded, he did not make sure that his whole chain of title was recorded.** That is, he failed to make sure that the O'Neill-to-Craft deed was recorded. The entire

line running from O'Neill through Arens through Burrows was then recorded (in 2009) at a time when Dempsey had still not "adequately" recorded. Therefore, Dempsey, as the second grantee, has not fulfilled one of the two requirements for a subsequent grantee to take under a race-notice statute: He did not win the race to record, because one wins that race only by "adequately" recording, which Dempsey has never done.

176. Andrews. **Under normal principles, Burns would get the benefit of the recording act because he took without actual or record notice of the prior grant (the unrecorded deed to Andrews). But Burns loses because of the doctrine of "*inquiry*" notice. Even if the subsequent purchaser has neither record nor actual notice of a prior unrecorded conveyance, he or she will be found to have been on inquiry notice of it if at the time he or she took he or she was in possession of facts that would have led a reasonable person in his or her position to make an investigation, which would in turn have advised him or her of the existence of the prior unrecorded right.**

   Most courts hold that the subsequent grantee has a duty to *view the property*, and if it is in possession of someone other than the record owner, he must inquire as to the source of the latter's rights in the property. Here, the facts tell us that if Burns had viewed the property, he would have discovered Andrews, and that if he had discovered Andrews, Andrews would have told him that he, Andrews, had an unrecorded deed. Therefore, Burns is charged with inquiry notice of Andrews's deed, and Burns is thus a grantee "with knowledge" of that deed (thereby removing him from the protection of the notice statute).

177. Crystal. **Brown, at the time he took, met the two requirements for a subsequent grantee to take priority in a race-notice jurisdiction: He won the race to record ahead of Albright, and he took without notice of Albright's deed.** That being the case, not only Brown's own "ownership" but also his ability to *resell* his property is protected by courts construing the recording acts. That is, once an interest is purged by its acquisition by one without notice of the prior unrecorded document, the interest remains "clean" when resold, *even if the new purchaser has actual or record notice.*

178. Yes, probably. **Title Co. will probably argue that it is exculpated by the clause in the title policy excluding facts that an accurate survey of the property would disclose. But even if Title Co. persuades the court that this exclusion covers the garage, Title Co. will probably be liable for *negligence* for not having called Barnes's attention to the encroachment. See, e.g., *Shotwell v. Transamerica Title Ins. Co.*, 558 P.2d 1359 (Ct. App. Wash. 1976), holding that the title insurer could be liable for negligence in the search even as to an item (an easement) that was excluded from coverage by the policy.**

179. No, probably. **Plotnick had an absolute right to "*lateral support.*" However, this absolute right exists only with respect to land in its *natural state*. If the owner has constructed a building, and the soil under the building subsides in part due to the adjacent owner's acts, but also in part because of the weight of the building itself, the adjacent owner is not liable in the absence of negligence.** Therefore, since Duffy's acts would not have caused Plotnick's land to cave in had the land been vacant, and Duffy behaved nonnegligently, Duffy does not have to pay for damage accruing to Plotnick's structure.

180. Yes, probably. **In a common law jurisdiction, each riparian owner has an absolute right to all or any part of the water for "natural" uses (regardless of the effect on downstream owners), but an owner may take for "*artificial*" uses only after all natural uses have been satisfied, and then only in parity with other artificial users.** Irrigation of small areas of farmland is generally considered "natural," whereas use for hydroelectric power is almost certainly artificial. Therefore, Phillips

has priority over Decker; Phillips can recover damages, obtain an injunction, or both. (The fact that Phillips was using the water first does not matter to the result.)

181. Yes, probably. **Courts following the common law approach do not grant any advantage based on priority of use.** The fact that a riparian owner has used stream water for a certain purpose for many years does not give him any greater rights than if he were making this use for the first time. Thus the problem is solved the way it is in the prior answer (with Phillips winning because his use is "natural" and Decker's is "artificial").

182. No, probably. **The 17 arid states that have abolished the common law riparian rights doctrine have generally adopted the *"prior appropriation"* doctrine instead.** In some of these states, a water user must apply for a permit to get priority; in these states, the issue would be decided based on who got a permit first (which the facts don't disclose). But in the remaining "prior appropriation" states, the right to appropriate is absolute (i.e., no permit is required), and the priority of the right dates from the time the appropriator began construction of the necessary works to take the water. In such a state, Decker, as the first user, would prevail.

183. No. **Generally, courts hold that an owner may build as tall as he or she wants, and as close to his or her property line as he or she wants, as long as he or she does not violate zoning rules.** In particular, courts almost never recognize an owner's right to sunlight or view. For instance, courts almost never recognize that a landowner has acquired an easement of "light and air" by implication or even by necessity. Pringle is almost certainly out of luck. (His remedy was to build his own building far enough in from his property line that even a neighboring building later built right up to that property line would not block his own light completely.)

Property Essay Questions

QUESTION 1:   George and Harry owned large adjoining ski cabins in the mountains. The boundary line between the properties was never clearly marked, and both men used the cabins only in the winter because of their proximity to Ski Valley, Idaho. However, 25 years ago, George did spend a summer up at his cabin when he was having his home in Boston remodeled. During the summer, he dug a water well on a section of the property that he thought was his, but in fact was Harry's. George connected water pipes to the well and used it to keep water in a large koi pond he had on the property. Because the well and koi pond were fairly far from the cabin, Harry never noticed that they were there (since the property was covered by snow whenever he was using it, he didn't walk around it very much). Harry was adjudicated mentally incompetent 15 years ago. He died recently, and his executor filed suit to eject George and quiet title. The jurisdiction's statute of limitations for adverse possession is 20 years.

When the lawsuit hit the local papers, Skippy came forward. Skippy had been using George's cabin every summer, unbeknownst to George. George's sister, Margaret, who mistakenly believed the cabin had been left to her by George and Margaret's mother, had "sold" Skippy's aunt the property 24 years ago as a summer mountain retreat. Skippy's aunt came to the property every summer for 10 years. When she died, she left it to Skippy, who came to the cabin every summer for the next 14 years. Although they (and George) had noticed that furniture had been moved around from time to time, they all thought it was merely due to ghosts.

George was really upset about the lawsuits, so his daughter bought him tickets to go see Del Devlin. During the concert, Del released a live bat. The bat flew over the crowd in confusion. George jumped for it. George grabbed the bat, but he was soon tackled and trampled by the crowd. The bat was stripped from him.

While George was in the medical tent, he saw Jimmy walk by him with the bat. George yelled, "Hey, that's my bat!" Jimmy ran, with George fast on his heels. Jimmy had a head start on George, but George was catching up. Jimmy found a rock and stuck the bat under it. He then ran a few hundred yards more until George caught up and grabbed him by his shirt. Jimmy sat on the ground and held up his hands, exclaiming, "I don't see any bat here!"

Sally, who had been in the original scrum for the bat, saw Jimmy stick it under the rock. While Jimmy and George were talking, she grabbed the bat and yelled, "He's my pet now, and I'm naming him Edward!"

Please discuss the issues.

QUESTION 2:   Rick owns Padanaram Acres in fee simple absolute. Every Tuesday, he plays poker with his friends Andrew and Alex. One Tuesday, low on chips, he tells Andrew and Alex that he will go all in and bet his ownership of Padanaram Acres on winning the next hand. When the players show their cards, Andrew has two aces, Alex has two aces, and Rick has nothing. Consequently, since Andrew and Alex both won, Rick takes out a piece of paper and conveys Padanaram Acres to Andrew and Alex. While he's writing, all three of them throw in comments, which Rick tries to incorporate as he goes. Both Alex and Andrew want some definite time period on their ownership; both Andrew and Alex owe money to Meghan, Kerry, and Amie; and all three of them think the town could use an annual rock festival. Finally, the deed reads:

"I, Rick, having the poker-playing skills of a dead fish, convey my estate, Padanaram Acres, to Andrew and Alex for Andrew's life, then to Meghan and Kerry jointly, provided that they use it annually for a Salute to Padanaram Rock Festival. If they fail to use Padanaram Acres as provided, then to Amie and her heirs."

Describe fully the interests created by this deed.

QUESTION 3: Rafael owned a large parcel of undeveloped land along Interstate 12. The land was zoned for commercial use, and Rafael was interested in selling it to Carl, a real estate developer. Nancy owned a small farm directly behind Rafael's land. Nancy's land was on a point that stuck out into the middle of the ocean, so the only access to it was over a gravel road passing through the edge of Rafael's land. Nancy had been using the access point since she first bought the land 25 years before. She'd never asked for Rafael's permission to use the road—in fact, she'd never met Rafael. Rafael showed up one day and told Nancy about his development plans. Nancy sold him her farm by a quitclaim deed, which was recorded in the registry of deeds. Immediately thereafter, Rafael decided to give the farmland he had just purchased from Nancy to his daughter (who lived out of state) as a wedding present. He executed a quitclaim deed in favor of his daughter, Kendra. The deed was recorded in the registry of deeds. Neither deed mentioned the gravel road. A few months later, without Kendra's knowledge, Rafael gave John permission to come onto the land to hunt muskrats. A year later, Rafael finally sold the land near the interstate to Carl. This deed was recorded in the registry of deeds. After being fired from her job and divorcing her husband, Kendra decided she wanted to move onto the farm. She showed up and saw John shooting muskrats. She told him he was trespassing. John said he got Rafael's permission and wasn't going anywhere. Then he shot another muskrat. At the same time, Kendra noticed a building crew for Carl erecting a fence across the gravel road. Kendra comes to you for advice.

QUESTION 4: Landlord owns a small strip mall along Route 2. There are three different shops in the mall, and Landlord decides to rent them out to tenants. Toby rents the first shop, planning to open a new location for his restaurant, Toby's Treats. To make the new space look like the old restaurant, he installs specialty lighting in the ceiling; an elaborate bar that is carefully designed to fit a particular alcove, and that is attached to the wall and floor by strong weight-bearing bolts; and a custom refrigeration system that is attached to the building's ductwork. The lease is silent on whether Toby may remove the items at the end of the lease. Landlord leases the second shop to Bookie to use as a bookstore. Bookie signs a one-year lease. Two months later, Bookie realizes she hates books and stops paying rent. She calls up Landlord and tells him that she has a friend, Curly, who would lease the shop, and then asks to get out of the lease. Landlord refuses, and demands that Bookie keep paying the rent due under the lease. Landlord rents the third shop to Drinkie, who wants to open a beer distributor. Landlord runs a liquor shop two blocks away, so he asks Drinkie to agree not to sell wine or liquor along with the beer. Drinkie does so, but three months later, he signs the remainder of his lease over to Drunkie, who immediately adds wine and liquor sales to the shop. A short time later, a new megamall opens up in a much better location. Sixty days before the end of any of Toby's lease, Landlord learns that Toby is not planning on renewing. Landlord sends Toby a letter warning him not to remove the items that he installed. Toby removes them anyway, fixes up the holes, and takes them with him to the new megamall location. Landlord comes to you for advice.

QUESTION 5: The Town of Really Awful decides it needs an image change to attract new residents and businesses. Consequently, it changes its name to the Town of Really Quite Pleasant. The town council then decides to enact several new plans to clean up the area and improve the town. First, it decides to move Piggy's hog farm out of the town limits, since it smells fairly terrible. The town council passes a zoning ordinance stating that no hog farm may be operated within the town limits, further providing that any existing hog farm must be discontinued within two years of passage of the ordinance. Piggy comes to the town council meeting to complain, and the council tells him they actually like the idea of a "pretty" farm, just not a hog farm, and maybe he should think about raising something nice, like petunias. Piggy then tells the council that he is going to file a lawsuit because he should be "paid for his hardship!" At the same time, the town council decides it really wants to remove a billboard within town limits that sits along the main interstate. The billboard is operated by Ted's Auto Sales; plastered across it is the slogan "This Town Is Really Awful, but Our Prices Are Great!" The billboard has been in the same location for 20 years. The town council passes another zoning ordinance that bars any billboards within town limits. However, it includes language that says, "Any nonconforming billboard use must be phased out within three years of this ordinance." Ted calls the council and threatens to sue to overturn the ordinance, as it applies to him. Finally, the town council decides to pass a zoning ordinance for any new development in the town. The ordinance states that no new home can be built on fewer than five acres of land. Morello, a black resident of the Town of Not So Bad, which is three towns over, claims that the new ordinance in the Town of Really Quite Pleasant unjustly discriminates against minorities, who he claims are unlikely to be able to afford such a large parcel of land. In fact, he argues that if he could buy a smaller piece of land, he would move to the Town of Really Quite Pleasant. The town council comes to you for advice.

Sample Answers to Property Essay Questions

ANSWER TO QUESTION 1:

George—Adver\se Possession

George will likely get title to the land where his well was by adverse possession. **A person gains title to land through adverse possession if he or she engages in use that is hostile, exclusive, open and notorious, continuous, and actual for the statutory period.** George's use was hostile because he did not have Harry's permission to put the well on his property; it was exclusive to the portion of the property containing the well since Harry never went over there; it was open and notorious because Harry would have seen it if he had looked; it was continuous since he used it without interruption for longer than the statutory period of 20 years; and it was actual in that he did use that portion of the property covered by the well (although simple use of the well would not allow him to claim title to the entire piece of property, since he only used a small portion of it). Though Harry could claim that George's adverse possession initially began during a time when neither party was using the land (the summer), this is irrelevant since, once built, the well was in place the entire year. Also, although Harry was adjudicated mentally incompetent 15 years ago, courts only look at whether the landowner was competent at the time adverse possession began. It appears that Harry was competent then, so his later incompetence does not affect the statutory period. George should retain title to the well.

Skippy—Adverse Possession

Skippy is unlikely to get title to George's land through adverse possession. **The elements of adverse possession are stated above.** Skippy's use was hostile, because he did not have permission to use the property (Margaret's permission didn't count since she did not actually own the property); it was open and notorious because George would have seen Skippy if he had looked; and it was actual because he was using the entire cabin during the summer. However, Skippy's use was not exclusive, since George came every winter to use the property. Also, Skippy's use was likely not continuous for the statutory period. While seasonal use can be good enough for adverse possession, courts look at the nature and condition of the land and how a true owner would use the land. Here, it looks like the nature and condition of the land (snow-covered mountains near a resort) is conducive to ski cabins, and owners of these properties use them for skiing at Ski Valley (as both George and Harry do). Consequently, he does not seem to be using the land as an actual owner would. Also, he did not hold the land himself for the entire statutory period. While the uses of different owners can be tacked together if the owners are in privity, courts look at some reasonable connection between the owners and a good-faith transfer of the property between them. Although there seems to be such a reasonable connection, the fact that things were moved around in the house should have alerted either Margaret or Skippy to the fact that George was also using the property—in such a situation, they should have investigated and would have likely discovered the fact that Margaret didn't own the property. Ultimately, because of the issues concerning exclusivity and continuous possession, a court is unlikely to find that Skippy gained title to the land by adverse possession.

George Captures Bat

George did not get title to the bat. **Under the rule of capture, to gain title to the bat (a wild animal, since it is not commonly kept as a pet or used for work), George must show that he intended to deprive the animal of its natural liberty, did indeed do so, and gained control over the animal.** While he intended to grab the bat, and did so for a moment, the issue here revolves around control. If he actually had control of the bat when he had his hands around it, the bat would be his even though it was later stripped away by other people in the crowd. If he did not actually have control, the bat was not his. In similar situations (such as when a baseball goes into the stands), custom often applies as to who ultimately controls and gains title to the ball. George only seemed to have the bat for a moment, and most concertgoers in a situation like this would expect a "scrum," with the last person to have complete control to gain title to the animal, object, or whatever was thrown into a crowd. Since the rule of capture was created with the intent to avoid fights and litigation, and it was likely the bat passed through many hands before someone gained final control over it, it seems likely a court would rule that the last person to have clear and unequivocal control of the bat should get title (otherwise 50 people might be arguing over title to the bat).

Jimmy Abandons Bat

Jimmy likely still has title to the bat. Since Jimmy didn't lose the bat by intentionally hiding it under a rock, the issue here is whether Jimmy abandoned the bat. **To abandon a piece of property, the person must show that they have decided to relinquish title to the property.** Although Jimmy hid the bat under a rock and ran away, he did so with the express purpose of *keeping* the bat by throwing George off. Consequently, Sally (who saw Jimmy hide the bat and likely understood his intentions) could not gain title to the bat by swooping in and claiming it was lost or abandoned property.

ANSWER TO QUESTION 2:

Rick

The issue is whether Rick retains any interest in Padanaram Acres. **Rick had a fee simple absolute, the biggest parcel of ownership interest. No future interest attaches, and duration could be infinite. However, Rick is assumed to convey all of what he owns, as there were no words of limitation in the conveyance.** Consequently, Rick has no remaining interest in Padanaram Acres.

Andrew and Alex

The issue is what interest Andrew and Alex have in the land. **The most common phrase for creating a life estate is "to B for life." A life estate is one of the freehold estates, and is always accompanied by a future interest. It terminates at the death of the life tenant. Usually, a life estate is measured in terms of the life of the grantee, but it is possible to create a life estate that is measured by the life of someone other than the grantee. Such a life estate is called a life estate *per autre vie*.** Here, the grant creates a life estate that terminates naturally at the end of Andrew's life, which is the measuring life. Consequently, Alex has a life estate *per autre vie*; Alex can use and possess the property for Andrew's life. As owners of a life estate, Andrew and Alex can only convey the rights they have, and they can't commit waste. Although they have concurrent ownership under the deed, they are unlikely to be anything more than co-tenants. The deed does not indicate that they are tenants by the entirety or joint tenants—there are no rights of survivorship, and no indication they are married. In cases of ambiguity, co-tenancy is presumed, so it needs to be explicit (which is a reversal of the common law rule). As co-tenants, they each have a right to occupy the entire premises, subject only to each other's right to occupy.

Meghan and Kerry

The issue is what interest Meghan and Kerry have in the land. **A vested remainder subject to divestment is created when no condition is attached to the clause giving the grantee his or her interest, but a second clause is added to take the interest away if a condition fails to occur. It is vested at the time**

of conveyance, but can be lost. At the death of Andrew, the interest in Padanaram Acres will immediately transfer to Meghan and Kerry. However, if they fail to hold the annual rock festival, their interest will then transfer to Amie and her heirs. Although Meghan and Kerry share concurrent ownership, for the reasons stated for Andrew and Alex's ownership, they are unlikely to be more than co-tenants.

Amie

The issue is what interest is held by Amie and her heirs. **A shifting executory interest is a future interest in one other than the grantor but that usually takes effect by cutting short a prior interest before its natural termination.** The deed gives Amie and her heirs a shifting executory interest that will cut short Meghan and Kerry's interest if they fail to hold the rock festival every year. If they fail to hold the festival, Amie will receive a fee simple absolute in the property.

ANSWER TO QUESTION 3:

Kendra v. Carl

The issue is whether the parties' use of the gravel road created an easement. **An affirmative easement is one that entitles its holder to do a physical act on the land of another. An easement by prescription can be created in the same way a person gains title to land though adverse possession (continuous, open, notorious, hostile, and actual use of the land for the statutory period). Easements can also be created by necessity. Easement by necessity does not require that there have been an actual prior use before severance. However, three requirements must be met: (1) the necessity must be strict rather than reasonable; (2) the parcels must have been under common ownership just before a conveyance; and (3) the necessity must come into existence at the time of, and be caused by, the conveyance that breaks up the common ownership. Such an easement need not be in writing or recorded.** Although Nancy likely gained use of the gravel road through easement by prescription, that use was likely extinguished when Rafael gained title to both the commercially zoned land and the farm. However, when Rafael then transferred the farm to Kendra, an easement by necessity was created since there was no way to access the farm except by crossing the commercially zoned land. Carl could argue that she could swim or use a boat, but courts find that strict necessity means that the property must not be able to be effectively used without disproportionate effort or expense. Making Kendra swim or boat to her farm property seems to fit this standard. Consequently, she will likely still be allowed to use the gravel road across Carl's property. However, if Carl has some particular issue with the road's location, he can likely block the road as long as he provides a reasonable alternative access point.

Kendra v. John

John has no rights to continue hunting on the land. **A right to come onto the property to engage in a recreational activity like hunting will typically constitute only a license, and a license is revocable at the will of the licensor. A license does not require a writing and can be created orally.** At most, John had a license to enter the property from Rafael, but since Rafael no longer owns the property, Kendra is well within her rights to tell John to leave.

ANSWER TO QUESTION 4:

Landlord v. Toby

Toby was not required to leave any of his improvements. **"Trade fixtures" are items specially adapted for use in the tenant's trade or business. Such trade fixtures may be removed regardless of how deeply embedded they are, as long as the premises are restored to their original condition.** As long as Toby has restored the premises to their original condition (e.g., by repairing the ceilings, walls, and floors to remove any holes where the items were attached), Toby will win any suit filed by Landlord regarding the fixtures, because he acted properly.

Landlord v. Bookie

The issue is whether Bookie will have to keep paying her rent even though Curly is willing to rent the premises. **The traditional view—and probably still the majority one—is that landlord has no duty to try to find a new tenant. The landlord may simply let the property stay vacant and recover rent from the tenant who has abandoned, even if a perfectly suitable tenant requests the right to lease the premises. However, an increasing minority of courts hold that the landlord does have a duty to mitigate by finding a suitable replacement.** It's unclear whether Curly is a suitable replacement for Bookie. Even if she is a suitable replacement, under the majority rule, Landlord could just leave the property vacant and continue to collect rent from Bookie. Consequently, it's likely that Bookie still owes rent under the lease.

Landlord v. Drunkie

The issue is whether Landlord has any rights against Drunkie. **An assignment is the transfer by the lessee of his or her entire interest in the leased premises. An assignee has the benefit and the burden of any covenants that were made by the original lessee and that run with the land. A promise by the tenant not to compete with the landlord's use of other property the landlord owns or rents runs as to the burden on the land, thus it can be enforced against the assignee of the tenant.** Here, Drinkie has signed over the rest of his interest in the leased premises to Drunkie, so it is an assignment. Consequently, since Drinkie's promises can be enforced against Drunkie, Landlord can sue for damages and an injunction to stop Drunkie's wine and liquor sales.

ANSWER TO QUESTION 5:

Piggy v. Town Council

The first issue is whether Piggy would have any rights against the town. **A land-use regulation is valid as long as the means chosen substantially advance a legitimate state interest and do not deny an owner economically viable use of his or her land. Occasionally, a land-use control is sufficiently harsh that a court will conclude that it amounts to a taking for Fourteenth Amendment purposes, for which compensation must be given. However, that is extremely rare, especially in the environmental regulation area.** The town is advancing its legitimate interest in not suffering the noxious odors associated with a hog farm. Furthermore, Piggy is not being deprived of all economically viable use of his property (in fact, the council would like him to continue to use it), but merely what might be the most "valuable" use (although that is not clear on the facts). Consequently, a court is extremely unlikely to hold the ordinance constitutes a taking for which compensation must be paid.

Ted v. Town Council

Ted is unlikely to overturn the ordinance. **Most states hold that an "amortization" provision does not violate due process or constitute a taking, so long as the amortization period is sufficiently long for the owner to recover most of his or her costs and to arrange an alternative use or location. However, a small minority of states do hold that nonconforming uses must be permitted indefinitely.** Although the three-year period is not particularly long, Ted has already had the billboard for 20 years, so he has likely already recouped its costs. Also, since he can continue to sell cars without the billboard, any injury to him is unlikely to be extreme. Assuming this state follows majority law, the ordinance is likely valid.

Morello v. Town Council

It's unlikely that Morello would be able to win any suit against the town council. **The U.S. Supreme Court has held that a racially discriminatory purpose, not merely effect, needs to be shown before an ordinance is subjected to strict equal protection scrutiny. If an ordinance does not trigger strict scrutiny, it simply has to be rationally related to a legitimate state purpose.** Morello likely has standing to challenge the ordinance since he claims he was directly affected by the allegedly illegal zoning. However, assuming that Morello would be able to prove that the five-acre minimum has the effect of dramatically reducing the number of minorities in the town, there is no evidence that the ordinance was enacted for racially discriminatory purposes (the town council's main goal seems to be simply to make the town more attractive to newcomers). Consequently, the ordinance likely passes the rational basis test despite the fact that it might have a disparate impact on minorities.

TORTS

Torts Table of Contents

INTENTIONAL TORTS AGAINST THE PERSON

INTENTIONAL INTERFERENCE WITH PROPERTY

DEFENSES TO INTENTIONAL TORTS

NEGLIGENCE GENERALLY

ACTUAL AND PROXIMATE CAUSE

JOINT TORTFEASORS

DUTY

	Short-Answer Question Numbers	Essay Question Numbers
II. MENTAL SUFFERING	**57-62**	
A. Mental suffering without impact	58-62	
1. No recovery without physical symptoms	59	
2. Minority rule	60	
3. Fear for safety of others	61, 62	
4. "Zone of danger" rule	58	

OWNERS AND OCCUPIERS OF LAND

	Short-Answer Question Numbers	Essay Question Numbers
I. TRESPASSERS	**63-65, 70**	**2**
A. Trespassing children	63-65	2
II. LICENSEES	**66, 67, 71, 73**	
A. Social guests	66	
1. Duties to licensee	67	
III. INVITEES	**68, 69, 72**	
A. Who is invitee	68, 69	
1. Business visitors	68, 69	
IV. LESSORS AND LESSEES	**74**	
A. Lessor	74	

DAMAGES

	Short-Answer Question Numbers	Essay Question Numbers
I. DAMAGES GENERALLY	**75**	
A. Reimbursement by third persons	75	

DEFENSES IN NEGLIGENCE ACTIONS

	Short-Answer Question Numbers	Essay Question Numbers
I. CONTRIBUTORY NEGLIGENCE	**76-81**	
A. Avoidable consequences	76	
1. Seat belt defense	76	
B. Claims against which not usable	77	
1. Intentional torts	77	
C. Last clear chance	78-81	
1. Plaintiff helpless, defendant inattentive	79	
2. Plaintiff inattentive, defendant doesn't discover	81	
3. Antecedent negligence of defendant	80	

NUISANCE

MISREPRESENTATION

DEFAMATION

MISCELLANEOUS TORTS: INVASION OF PRIVACY, MISUSE OF LEGAL PROCEEDINGS, AND INTERFERENCE WITH ADVANTAGEOUS RELATIONS

Torts Short-Answer Questions

1. Jerry Joker, a notorious practitioner of pranks, wanted to play one on his friend, Frank Friendly. Jerry took a real gun and loaded it with blanks. He put a stocking cap over his head so that he could not be identified. At 11:00 P.M., he rang Frank's doorbell. When Frank answered, Jerry put the gun two inches from Frank's temple, said, "Greetings from the Godfather," and pressed the trigger. Jerry intended that Frank merely be startled by the loud noise. Frank was not startled. However, a small piece of the casing from the blank broke loose and caused a small scratch on Frank's face, which healed quickly. What tort(s), if any, has Jerry committed? Not sure ☐

2. Same basic facts as in the previous question. Now, however, assume that when Jerry pressed the trigger, no bullet escaped, and there was no touching of Frank's body. For a split second, Frank thought that the bullet would hit him, but he then quickly realized that it was a joke when Jerry pulled off his mask. What tort(s)? Not sure ☐

3. Driver, while driving his car, saw Pedestrian, his enemy, standing at the side of the road. Driver drove his car through a muddy puddle for the purpose of splashing Pedestrian. Some dirty water hit Pedestrian, but he suffered no bodily harm. What tort(s)? Not sure ☐

4. Driver saw Pedestrian standing near the side of the road. Driver drove through a muddy puddle, knowing that the water would probably (but not certainly) splash Pedestrian. However, Driver did not actively desire the splashing to occur. Pedestrian was indeed splashed. What tort(s)? Not sure ☐

5. Patient agreed to have Surgeon remove Patient's gallbladder. While Patient was under general anesthetic, Surgeon fondled Patient. The operation then proceeded normally. Patient was revived, and learned about the fondling only later. What tort(s)? Not sure ☐

6. Dexter, intending to frighten Paul, fired from behind Paul a pistol loaded with blanks. Unbeknownst to Dexter, Paul was completely deaf. Paul therefore did not realize what had happened until afterward (at which time he was highly offended). What tort(s)? Not sure ☐

7. Loan Shark warned Peter, a compulsive gambler, that if Peter did not pay up, Loan Shark would injure Peter's wife, Molly. One day, as Molly was about to get into the family car, Peter spotted one of Loan Shark's henchmen running away from the car. Peter yelled out to Molly, "Don't turn the ignition!" At the time he yelled out his warning, Peter was desperately frightened that he was too late and that Molly would be blown to bits. Fortunately, Peter's warning came in time, and Molly complied. Peter then discovered a car bomb placed at Loan Shark's instructions and disarmed it. May Peter recover for assault? Not sure ☐

8. Detective, a department store detective, honestly but unreasonably believed that Paula had been shoplifting in the store that Detective was guarding. He did not attempt to stop Paula himself. Instead, he waited until she had left the premises and then summoned a police officer, requesting that the officer arrest Paula. Detective did not tell the officer any particulars; he merely asserted that Paula was a shoplifter who must be arrested. The officer arrested Paula, took her to the station house for two hours, and then released her after becoming convinced that she was innocent. What tort(s), if any, has Detective committed?

                                                         Not sure ☐

9. Timid owed money to Mobster, a loan shark. When the money was overdue, Mobster sent his henchman, Hulk, a large and scary-looking man, to try to collect the debt from Timid. Hulk went to Timid's house, and while standing in the foyer, said to Timid, "If you don't have the money back by next Thursday, with the 2 percent per week vigorish, next Friday I'm gonna shoot out both your kneecaps. Think about what it'll be like for a young man like yourself to spend the next 30, 40 years on crutches." Tina, Timid's wife, watched this conversation, and Hulk knew she was watching. Both Timid and Tina became extremely terrified and went into hiding where Hulk was unable to find them. What tort(s) have been committed by Hulk, and against whom?

                                                         Not sure ☐

10. Pilot was flying a recently built, apparently properly maintained aircraft. Through no fault of Pilot, something suddenly went terribly wrong, and Pilot completely lost control of the aircraft. The aircraft spiraled down, finally striking a farmhouse owned by Owner. In the impact and resulting fire, the farmhouse was completely destroyed. Pilot was able to eject just before impact, and parachuted down safely on someone else's land. Has Pilot committed trespass against Owner?

                                                         Not sure ☐

11. Cable Co. wanted to supply cable TV service to Customer. Because of the layout of the land, the only way Cable could do this was by stringing an aboveground wire from the street, across Peter's property, and into Customer's house. The wire never touched Peter's property and has caused no harm to his land or loss of economic value to him. Has Cable Co. committed trespass against Peter?

                                                         Not sure ☐

12. Auto Maven, an aficionado of fine cars, spotted Owner's brand-new Lexus convertible parked on the street, with the keys left in the ignition. Maven took the car for a three-minute joyride, during which time he drove it one mile. He then brought it back to the same spot, with no damage to the physical condition of the car. What tort, if any, has Maven committed?

                                                         Not sure ☐

13. Owner left his watch with Jeweler for repairs. Jeweler did the repairs and then shipped the watch, properly addressed to Owner, via American Parcel Service (APS). APS mistakenly delivered the package to Neighbor, who lived next door to Owner. Before the watch could be returned to Owner, it was destroyed in a fire in Neighbor's house. What tort, if any, has APS committed against Owner?

                                                         Not sure ☐

14. Same basic facts as in the previous question. Now, however, assume that APS learned of its mistake one day after making it, immediately retrieved the watch from Neighbor, and delivered it to Owner. What torts, if any, has APS committed against Owner?

                                                         Not sure ☐

15. Surgeon believed that Patient was suffering from a noncancerous growth in his esophagus. Patient agreed to have Surgeon perform surgery for the limited purpose of removing the polyp. After Patient was under a general anesthetic, Surgeon opened him up and discovered that the polyp was in fact a malignancy that had

spread to the stomach. If the malignancy had not been removed, Patient's life would have been in danger. It would have subjected Patient to material (though not extreme) extra risk to sew him up, bring him out of anesthesia, get his consent to the extended operation, and then do the operation. Instead, Surgeon simply removed the cancerous growth from the stomach. Unbeknownst to Surgeon, Patient had always told friends and relatives, "If I ever get cancer, I don't want them to cut it out of me—I just want to be left alone to die." Patient recovered and sued Surgeon for battery. Does Patient win?

Not sure ☐

16. Same basic facts as in the previous question. Now, however, assume that Surgeon discovered, in addition to the polyp, a set of inflamed tonsils. Surgeon removed the tonsils. According to standard medical practice it is wise to remove inflamed tonsils to prevent additional minor illnesses; however, failure to remove such tonsils does not seriously threaten a person's life or health. Patient awoke, discovered that Surgeon had taken out the tonsils without consent, and sued Surgeon for battery for the tonsillectomy. Will Patient win?

Not sure ☐

17. Drug Lord (not his real name) was in the business of selling crack. He had heard rumors in the neighborhood that a man nicknamed Scarecrow was a hit man for a rival drug gang, and that Scarecrow had been given a contract on Drug Lord's life. As Drug Lord was finishing a sale of crack, he saw Scarecrow come up to him and draw and aim his pistol at Drug Lord. As Scarecrow was about to say something, Drug Lord shot him in the hand to disable him. Scarecrow turned out to be an undercover police officer who wanted to arrest Drug Lord (an arrest that would have been legal in the circumstances). Has Drug Lord committed battery against Scarecrow?

Not sure ☐

18. Peter and Dan had been enemies for years. One day, as Dan was standing on the street corner, he saw Peter approaching him brandishing a knife. Peter yelled out, "This time, I'm really gonna carve you up." Dan knew that he, Dan, was a faster runner due to an old football knee injury suffered by Peter, and that he, Dan, could therefore run home and lock himself in his house. Instead, Dan chose to stand his ground, drew his own knife, and when Peter attacked him, stabbed Peter (though not fatally) in the heart. Once the struggle began, no lesser use of force by Dan would have permitted him to maintain his own safety. Is Dan liable to Peter for battery?

Not sure ☐

19. Same facts as in the previous question. Now, however, assume that Peter came to Dan's dwelling and made his threat while standing in Dan's front hallway. As above, Dan then knifed Peter in the heart. Is this battery?

Not sure ☐

20. Homeowner was about to go away on a one-month vacation. His home was a farmhouse in a sparsely settled area where the police could not be relied upon to respond to burglar alarms. Therefore, Homeowner installed a "spring gun," which was set to fire a bullet at about knee height if anyone tried to enter through the front door. Shortly after Homeowner left, Burglar attempted to enter the house with the intent of stealing some of its contents. The gun went off and shot Burglar in the knees, paralyzing him. Is Homeowner liable to Burglar, and if so, for what?

Not sure ☐

21. Master had been faithfully served for years by Valet, his domestic servant. One day, Master's expensive antique Audemars Piquet watch disappeared. The following

day, Valet unexpectedly quit and disappeared. Master tried to locate Valet but was unsuccessful. One week after Valet's disappearance, Master saw him in the street. Master noticed that Valet was wearing what appeared to be (and in fact was) the missing watch. He asked Valet to return it, and Valet refused. Since Valet was much bigger and stronger than Master, Master knew that he would not be able to recapture the watch without using a weapon. Master realized that if he left to get a police officer, Valet was likely to disappear again. Master therefore pulled out his knife and said, "If you don't give me the watch, I'm going to have to take it from you." A scuffle broke out (with Valet unarmed), and Valet was stabbed and seriously wounded. Valet now sues Master for battery. May Valet recover?

Not sure ☐

22. Same facts as in the previous question, except that (1) Master reasonably but incorrectly believed that the watch being worn by Valet belonged to Master; and (2) Master, instead of using a knife, put a headlock on Valet to recover the watch, and Valet was unexpectedly injured. May Valet recover against Master for battery?

Not sure ☐

23. Clerk, who worked for Store, observed Customer behaving in a somewhat suspicious manner, leading Clerk to reasonably believe that Customer had hidden an item belonging to Store in Customer's purse. When Customer tried to leave Store without paying for any merchandise, Clerk prevented her from leaving and told her that he thought she had shoplifted. Customer denied this, and Clerk required her to remain seated in Store while Clerk summoned Detective, who also worked for Store. Detective arrived within four minutes and asked to see the contents of Customer's purse. Customer showed Detective the purse, and no items belonging to Store were found in it. Detective then let Customer leave. Customer has sued Store for false imprisonment. Will Customer recover?

Not sure ☐

24. Pilot was flying his two-engine private jet from New York to Boston. Suddenly, one engine stopped working, and Pilot was unable to restart it. Pilot knew that there was a good, but not 100 percent chance that he would be able to continue on just the other engine until Boston. However, he decided that it would be more prudent to make an emergency landing sooner. There were no commercial airfields around, so he landed in a meadow owned by Farmer. There was no measurable economic harm done to the meadow. Farmer has sued Pilot for trespass. May Farmer recover anything?

Not sure ☐

25. Same basic facts as in the previous question. Now, however, assume that when Pilot's plane landed, it caused $1,000 worth of damage to Farmer's crops, damage that could not have been avoided no matter how carefully Pilot had landed on Farmer's property. May Farmer recover this $1,000 in a trespass action?

Not sure ☐

26. Same basic facts as in the previous two questions. Now, however, assume that when Farmer saw that Pilot was planning to land, he drove his pickup truck at the last second into the meadow, in such a way that Pilot could not use the meadow as a landing strip. There were no other places nearby on which Pilot could make an emergency landing. He ended up crashing into a nearby forest and dying. Pilot's estate has sued Farmer in tort. Will the estate win?

Not sure ☐

27. Officer, a police officer, received a report that a home at 125 Main Street had just been burglarized. Officer had no reason to believe that the burglar was armed. As Officer's police car pulled up to the house, Officer saw Suspect, a man with a

stocking cap on his head, leave the back of the house and start to climb a fence. Officer yelled, "Stop or I'll shoot!" but Suspect did not stop. Officer realized that he could not run as fast as Suspect, and that his only way to stop Suspect was by using his revolver. He therefore aimed at Suspect's left leg. Because of wind conditions, the bullet went slightly but tragically awry, hitting Suspect in the spine and paralyzing him. Suspect had in fact just burglarized the house. Suspect sues Officer for battery. May he recover?

Not sure ☐

28. Same facts as in the previous question. Now, however, assume that the report received by Officer was that the burglar had raped one of the inhabitants. Also, assume that although Officer reasonably believed that Suspect was the burglar, in fact Suspect: (1) was a homeless man who was not the real burglar/rapist; (2) was wearing a stocking cap because he wanted to protect himself from the cold; and (3) started to flee because he saw Officer approach with a drawn gun. Suspect has sued Officer for battery. May he recover?

Not sure ☐

29. Driver had suffered for years from periodic epileptic seizures. His doctor instructed him to take a daily dose of Dilantin, an antiepilepsy medicine. Normally, Driver took his medicine as prescribed. One particular Tuesday, however, Driver accidentally dropped the bottle on the floor, breaking it, before he could take his daily dosage. Driver then drove to the drugstore to get a replacement bottle. While en route, he suffered an epileptic seizure, lost control of the car, and injured Pedestrian. There is evidence that a typical dose of Dilantin remains effective for just one day, and that if Driver had taken his Dilantin that day, he would probably not have had his seizure. Pedestrian has sued Driver for negligence. Can Pedestrian recover?

Not sure ☐

30. Teen, who was 13 years old, was permitted by his parents to operate the family's 30-foot motorized cabin cruiser while the parents were away on vacation. (Assume that no statute or ordinance prohibits this.) On a slightly foggy day, Teen ran the boat at 35 knots. A reasonable adult pilot would have known that 35 knots, while a safe speed under good visibility, was not safe under the slightly foggy conditions. However, a reasonable 13-year-old would not normally have had such knowledge. While cruising at 35 knots, the boat came unexpectedly upon another vessel, was unable to turn aside in time, and smashed the other vessel, owned by Priscilla. Priscilla has sued Teen for negligence. May Priscilla recover?

Not sure ☐

31. In the trucking industry, it is customary to use only a side-view mirror, not a rear-view mirror, on tractor-trailers, since a rear-view mirror is impractical. In recent years, a video camera device has become available that can be mounted at the rear of the trailer and that transmits the view from the rear of the truck to a monitor next to the driver. Because of the device's substantial cost ($3,000), only about 10 percent of large trucks have been outfitted with the new device. Trucker, an individual who owned his own large rig, had not installed the new camera device and therefore had no ability to see the view from the rear of his truck. Trucker sideswiped Driver, who was driving a small car near the rear of Trucker's truck. Even a very careful driver in Trucker's position could not have avoided the accident without the rear camera device. However, if Trucker's truck included the camera device, a reasonable driver would almost certainly have seen the danger and avoided the accident. Driver has sued Trucker for negligence.

(a) May the availability and growing usage of the camera device be admitted as part of Driver's case on the question of whether Trucker was negligent?

Not sure ☐

(b) Assume for this part only that the answer to (a) is yes. May Trucker introduce evidence that the widely followed custom in the industry is not to install the cameras because of their high cost?

Not sure ☐

(c) May a jury properly find that Trucker was negligent?

Not sure ☐

32. Owner lent his new Mercury Speedster sports car to Driver for a day. Owner knew that Driver's license had recently been revoked for reckless driving. Driver drove the car fast and recklessly, and hit Pedestrian. Pedestrian has sued Owner (since Driver is judgment proof). May Pedestrian recover in negligence against Owner?

Not sure ☐

33. A statute requires railroads to fence in their tracks except at official crossings. The statute's legislative history shows that its purpose is to prevent children and animals from wandering onto the track, where they may be hit by trains. Railroad failed to fence in a particular section of track. Child, who was two, wandered near the track, ate wild berries growing right next to the track, and was seriously poisoned. In a suit by Child against Railroad, should the judge instruct the jury that Railroad's violation of the fencing statute constituted negligence per se?

Not sure ☐

34. A city ordinance provides that all homeowners shall keep their sidewalks free of snow "at all times," and provides that failure to do so is a misdemeanor. The purpose of the ordinance is to make sidewalks safe for pedestrians. After a particularly heavy snowfall, Owner, who was 68 years old, attempted to shovel the walk but strained his back and stopped before the job was finished. Owner lived alone and was unable to find anyone else to finish the shoveling. Later that day, Pedestrian slipped and fell on the unshoveled portion of Owner's walk; the accident would not have occurred had the walk been shoveled. Pedestrian has sued Owner. Will Owner's failure to keep the walk free of snow constitute negligence per se?

Not sure ☐

35. The federal Food and Drug Act provides that any poisonous substance must be marked with the word "poison" and with a skull and crossbones at least one-half inch high. Cleaner Co., a manufacturer of various household cleaners, sells DeClog, a very powerful chemical for unclogging drains. Cleaner sells DeClog in a clear plastic bottle that exposes the substance's attractive cherry-red color, similar to the color of Hawaiian Punch. On the bottle, Cleaner includes the required "poison" and skull and crossbones markings but takes no other childproofing precautions. Child, who was two years old, found a bottle of DeClog underneath the kitchen sink, drank it, and was horribly wounded. Child has sued Cleaner, and Cleaner defends on the grounds that it complied with all applicable warning statutes (a correct assertion). Does Cleaner's statutory compliance bar Child's negligence suit?

Not sure ☐

36. Passenger was aboard an airplane operated by Airline. The airplane disappeared over the Mediterranean Sea in clear weather, and no trace was ever found. Passenger's estate has sued Airline. Passenger has not come forward with any evidence of Airline's negligence. Airline has produced testimony that some otherwise unexplained plane crashes turned out to have been caused by plastic bomb devices that even very close security inspection could not have detected. However, Airline has not produced any evidence directly suggesting that this is what happened here. There is no other evidence as to the cause of the accident. Should the judge:

(a) Direct a verdict for Passenger;

(b) Direct a verdict for Airline; or

(c) Send the case to the jury?   Not sure ☐

37. Same facts as in the previous question. Now, however, assume that Airline has come up with detailed testimony and documents tending to show that (1) the pilot was an extremely careful person who followed all safety precautions with utmost attentiveness; (2) Airline itself conducted every possible safety precaution prior to each flight, including meticulous checking for bombs; and (3) a hostile nation's jets were in the area at the time the plane disappeared. Should the judge:

(a) Direct a verdict for Passenger;

(b) Direct a verdict for Airline; or

(c) Send the case to the jury?   Not sure ☐

38. A state statute provides that whenever a municipality constructs a dam for the purpose of maintaining a reservoir, the dam must be high enough to control rains from a rainy season that is as heavy as the heaviest rainy season that has ever occurred during the ten years prior to construction. (Assume that a city that builds a dam to this standard is conclusively deemed nonnegligent.) City built a dam and reservoir next to Farmer's land. Five years prior to construction, a rainy season produced 30 inches of rain; in every other year in the past 10, there was no more than 20 inches. However, the dam constructed by City was capable of withstanding only 25 inches of rain during a season. A year after the dam opened, an unprecedented rainy season occurred, yielding more than 40 inches of rain. Fifteen inches of this rain suddenly flowed over the dam, flooding Farmer's land and destroying his crops. (Even 10 inches of rain, if it had flowed suddenly onto Farmer's land, would have produced basically the same damage as actually occurred.) Assume that apart from City's failure to follow the state statute, there is no other evidence that City behaved negligently in building or maintaining the dam. Farmer has sued City for negligence. Does Farmer win?   Not sure ☐

39. Same basic facts as in the previous question. Now, however, assume that in addition to his crops, Farmer also maintained two pens filled with expensive live mink, which he was breeding for their pelts. The two pens were at different elevations, such that at the time of maximum flooding, one pen had 15 inches of water in it and the other had ten inches of water. The height of a mink is such that it will survive in five inches or less of water but not in any higher water. There were 100 minks in each pen; all were killed. For how many minks may Farmer recover against City?   Not sure ☐

(a) None

(b) 100

(c) 200

40. Abel, while driving his car, hit the brakes as a child ran into the road. Baker, who was tailgating Abel, slammed into Abel. Carr, who was tailgating Baker, slammed into Baker, causing an additional impact on Abel's car. Abel suffered serious whiplash. Abel sued Baker and Carr for his injuries. No party produces evidence as to which crash (Baker into Abel, or Carr into Baker and thence into Abel) caused Abel's whiplash. What is the most likely result?   Not sure ☐

   (a) Both Baker and Carr are liable.

   (b) Neither Baker nor Carr is liable.

41. With Driver at the wheel, Driver and Passenger motored into town. Passenger fell asleep during the trip. Driver parked the car in front of a fire hydrant next to a bank, in violation of a municipal statute and also in violation of what motorists across America know to be prudent practice. Driver went into the bank to make a quick deposit, while Passenger remained asleep. Trucker, who was driving his truck down the street, suddenly swerved to avoid hitting a dog. Trucker's truck smashed into Driver's car, seriously injuring Passenger. Had Driver parked the car anywhere but in front of the hydrant, Trucker's truck would not have hit Driver's car. Passenger has sued Driver for negligence. Will Passenger recover?   Not sure ☐

42. Trucker was driving a truck filled with gasoline cross-country. Trucker realized that he was very sleepy, and that he ought to stop for the night. However, anxious to get to his destination as soon as possible, he drove through the night. He fell asleep at the wheel, crashed through a guardrail and flipped his truck on its side. Driver, who was passing by the accident site in his car, stopped and attempted to pull Trucker out of the wreck. While he was trying to do so, the truck exploded from the leaking gasoline, badly burning both Trucker and Driver. Driver has sued Trucker for negligence. Can Driver recover?   Not sure ☐

43. Tardy, who was late for an appointment, ran down a crowded city street faster than a careful person would under the circumstances. Just as Tardy got to a corner, Bystander walked at an ordinary pace from the other direction. The two collided (though without a very great impact), and Bystander was knocked to the ground. Ordinarily, a person knocked to the ground with that level of force would sustain at most slight cuts or bruises. Bystander suffered a cut on his shin. In an ordinary healthy person, this cut would have healed promptly. However, because Bystander had recently had a kidney transplant, he was taking immunosuppressant drugs that had seriously weakened his immune system. The cut failed to heal and became a raging infection, and Bystander's leg had to be amputated. Bystander has sued Tardy for damages for the loss of his leg. May Bystander recover such damages?   Not sure ☐

44. Dan was driving his car with Patrick as passenger. Dan negligently ran a red light, and an oncoming car driven by Xavier struck his car. Patrick was seriously though not fatally injured. An ambulance was called, which rushed Patrick to the hospital. The ambulance driver drove at an excessive rate of speed (even considering the need to get Patrick to the hospital quickly) and crashed. Patrick was killed. His estate has sued Dan. Assuming the estate may recover for the serious but not fatal injuries sustained by Patrick during the initial collision, may it also recover for Patrick's death?   Not sure ☐

45. Same facts as in the previous question. This time, however, assume that Patrick made it safely to the hospital. While being treated in the hospital, Patrick spoke crossly to Nurse, who was taking care of Patrick. Nurse, who was (unbeknownst to the hospital) psychotic, responded by stabbing Patrick to death. Patrick's estate has sued Dan for his death. Can the estate recover?   Not sure ☐

46. Carmaker, a manufacturer of automobiles, sold a 2007 Sprint to Dealer. Dealer, in turn, sold the car to Abel. In 2008, Carmaker learned of an existing defect in the safety catch, such that the hood could fly open while the car was being driven and block the driver's view. Carmaker notified Dealer of this defect, and Dealer notified Abel of it. Dealer also notified Abel that if Abel would bring in the car for one hour, Dealer would fix the problem for free. Abel declined to bring the car in. Abel then sold the car in 2009 to Babcock, who was unaware of the problem. In 2010, while Babcock was driving the car on the highway, the defective latch released the hood; Babcock was unable to see, so the car crashed, and Babcock suffered serious injuries. Babcock has sued Carmaker in strict product liability for his injuries. May Babcock recover?   Not sure ☐

47. Aggressive, while riding his bicycle on the sidewalk (instead of on the street where he should have been), and riding too fast, nearly hit Bystander. To avoid being hit, Bystander threw himself into the street. Bystander was not seriously injured by the impact with the street. However, before he could get up, Careless, who was driving his car too fast and not paying attention, ran over Bystander, causing Bystander's leg to be amputated. Bystander has chosen to sue only Aggressive for his injuries. May Bystander recover the full value of his lost leg from Aggressive?   Not sure ☐

48. Same facts as in the previous question. Now, however, assume that when Bystander threw himself into the street, he suffered a fractured skull. Then (as in the above question) Careless ran over Bystander, causing Bystander to lose his leg. May Bystander recover for all of his injuries from Careless?   Not sure ☐

49. Factory and Manufacturer each discharged mercury into the Tort River as a byproduct of their manufacturing operations. Farmer, whose land lay downstream from Factory and Manufacturer, was unable to irrigate his crops and suffered $100,000 of economic damage. Evidence showed that 60 percent of the total mercury was released by Factory and 40 percent by Manufacturer. Manufacturer has gone out of business. Farmer now sues Factory for his damages. How much may Farmer recover from Factory?   Not sure ☐

50. One night, as Milquetoast was walking down a dark street, Bully and Dastardly decided, just for fun, to beat him up. Bully held Milquetoast down while Dastardly hit him in the jaw, breaking it. (Bully anticipated that Dastardly would hit Milquetoast somewhere in the face, though he did not anticipate precisely the broken jaw.) Milquetoast brought suit against Bully alone, and recovered the full value of his injuries from Bully, $50,000. Bully then sued Dastardly for a $25,000 contribution. Will Bully succeed in recovering this contribution from Dastardly?   Not sure ☐

51. Darwin and Dexter both drove their cars at an unreasonably high speed. The two cars collided, and Perry, a bystander, was injured as a result. Perry, believing that his case was stronger against Dexter than against Darwin, settled with Darwin for $10,000. Perry then sued Dexter. In that suit, the jury found (in response to a special interrogatory) that Perry's total damages were $100,000. What may Perry recover from Dexter, and what contribution may Dexter receive from Darwin?

Not sure ☐

52. Manufacturer produced a power saw, which it wholesaled to Retailer. Retailer sold the saw to Consumer. Unbeknownst to either Manufacturer or Retailer, the saw was dangerously defective. When Consumer tried to use the saw, it cut off his hand. Consumer sued Retailer and recovered the full amount of his injuries under the doctrine of strict product liability. There is no evidence that Retailer was negligent in failing to inspect the saw. May Retailer obtain indemnity from Manufacturer for the full judgment paid to Consumer?

Not sure ☐

53. Dan was a sociopath who hated many different types of people, including those with physical disabilities. While walking down the street, he spotted Paul, a blind man, who was about to cross the street. Paul thought it was safe to cross because he did not hear any vehicular sounds. As Dan realized, Xerxes, who was riding quite silently on a bicycle, would strike Paul if Paul crossed the street. Dan could have, at no risk and virtually no bother, called out a warning to Paul or physically stopped him from crossing. But because of his hatred of blind people, Dan said nothing. Paul walked into the street and was knocked down and severely injured. Paul has sued Dan for negligence. May Paul recover?

Not sure ☐

54. Same basic facts as in the previous question. Now, however, assume that Xerxes, after colliding with Paul, got up and bicycled away without summoning aid for Paul. Xerxes was not in any way negligent in colliding with Paul in the first place. If Paul had received prompt medical assistance following the collision, he would not have suffered any lasting injuries. But because no help was summoned for half an hour, Paul suffered serious internal bleeding, which in turn caused his death. Paul's estate has sued Xerxes for the death. Can the estate recover?

Not sure ☐

55. Same facts as in the previous two questions. Now, however, assume that Terry, a bystander, realized that Paul had been seriously injured. Terry picked Paul up, put him in Terry's car, and drove off to the hospital. Terry drove at an excessive speed and crashed, killing Paul. Evidence shows that if Terry had left Paul where he was, a doctor who happened to be passing by five minutes later would have successfully treated Paul's initial injuries from the bicycle collision. Paul's estate has sued Terry for Paul's death. Can the estate recover?

Not sure ☐

56. Same facts as in the previous question. Now, however, assume that Terry did not in fact lift Paul into Terry's car. Instead, Terry told Steve, the only other person in the vicinity, "Don't worry about getting medical help—I'll take care of that." Terry then continued walking, intending to go to a pay phone; however, he got distracted and never made the call. Paul's injuries, which could have been treated if help had been summoned promptly by either Terry or Steve, caused his death on the roadway. Paul's estate has sued Terry. Can Paul's estate recover?

Not sure ☐

57. Patricia was walking with her five-year-old son, Colin, across the street. Doug, driving dangerously fast, was unable to come to a full stop and lightly hit Patricia. Patricia was knocked to the ground and suffered minor bruises. She suffered many

sleepless nights mentally replaying the accident, and is now afraid to cross any of the busy streets in her neighborhood. She has sued Doug not only for the bruises but also for her emotional distress arising out of the accident. May she recover for this distress?

Not sure ☐

58. Same basic facts as in the previous question. However, assume that Doug was able to stop his car just before it made contact with Patricia's body. However, during the five seconds before the crash, Patricia thought she was going to be run over (a reasonable fear in the circumstances). Patricia has relived the accident over and over again. The mental consequences of the near-accident have led Patricia to develop an ulcer, for which she is still receiving medical treatment. (The doctor has testified that Patricia probably would not have developed that ulcer except for the near-accident.) May Patricia recover for the ulcer against Doug?

Not sure ☐

59. Same facts as in the previous question. Now, however, assume that Patricia suffered no substantial physical harm requiring a doctor's attention. However, she was dizzy for five minutes shortly after the episode, and then had two sleepless nights. May Patricia recover for her mental anguish (i.e., her fear at thinking she was going to be killed and her after-the-fact anxiety about how close she was to getting killed)?

Not sure ☐

60. Same basic facts as in the previous three questions. Now, however, assume that Patricia remained on the sidewalk while her son Colin ran into the street. Patricia watched, horrified, while Colin was hit by Doug, who was unable to stop in time. Patricia herself was never in any physical danger since she was on the sidewalk, and she realized that she was not in danger. Patricia not only suffered great mental anguish as the result of Colin's severe injuries, but also suffered a miscarriage as a result of her distress. May Patricia recover against Doug for her miscarriage?

Not sure ☐

61. Colin, who was five years old, went out for a walk, crossed the street, and was hit by a car negligently driven by Doug. Patricia, Colin's mother, remained home. She heard the sounds of a collision, rushed outside, and discovered that Colin had been severely injured. Patricia suffered severe emotional distress, leading to a miscarriage. May Patricia recover against Doug for this miscarriage?

Not sure ☐

62. Colin, a five-year-old, crossed the street at the same time that Zena, a complete stranger to him, was walking nearby on the sidewalk. Doug, driving too fast down the street, was unable to stop, and hit Colin. Zena watched the accident up close but was never in physical danger. Zena was so shaken by seeing Colin badly hurt that she suffered a miscarriage. May Zena recover against Doug for this miscarriage?

Not sure ☐

63. Homeowner constructed a swimming pool in her backyard. Homeowner was aware that while she was at work each day, children from the neighborhood frequently swam in the pool, yet Homeowner did not fence in the pool, a step she could have taken relatively cheaply. Peter, who was ten, could not swim very well and understood the dangers of being in deep water. Responding to a dare from his friend Ted (who could not swim either), Peter dove into the deep end of the pool, panicked, and drowned. Peter's parents have sued Homeowner for his death. May they recover?

Not sure ☐

64. Same basic facts as above question. Now, however, assume that what existed on Homeowner's land was a natural pond rather than a man-made swimming pool. Again, assume that Homeowner could have fenced in the pond at relatively little expense. Homeowner knew that children as young as two frequently played on her property and sometimes ended up in the pond. Patty, who was three, entered Homeowner's land, was intrigued by ducks she saw in the pond, went into the water to get closer to them, and drowned. Can Patty's parents recover against Homeowner?

Not sure ☐

65. Farmer owned a relatively small (20-acre) farm. If Farmer had inspected his property even casually after buying it, he would have known that there was an abandoned mine shaft in one corner of it, leading hundreds of feet down with no easy way back to the surface. But because Farmer was a "weekend farmer" who bought the property for its appreciation potential, Farmer never conducted such an inspection, and thus did not know of the shaft's existence. Had such an inspection been made and the mine shaft discovered, it would have cost very little to fence in the shaft. Farmer knew that children from neighboring farms frequently trespassed on his property to play in his barn. Paul, who was six, came onto Farmer's property to play in the barn, happened to walk into the mine shaft after dark, and was killed. His estate has sued Farmer. Can the estate recover?

Not sure ☐

66. Same basic facts as in the previous question. Now, however, assume that Farmer invited Frank, his neighbor in the city, up to the farm for the weekend. As the two of them were walking around the property seeing the sights, Frank fell into the mine shaft and was paralyzed. Frank has sued Farmer for his injuries. Can Frank recover?

Not sure ☐

67. Same facts as in the previous question. Now, however, assume that Farmer knew that there was an open mine shaft on his property (and where it was located), but forgot to warn Frank just before Frank stepped into the shaft. If Farmer had been paying reasonable attention, he would have remembered the shaft's existence and location in time to warn Frank. Frank fell in, was paralyzed, and sued Farmer. Can he recover?

Not sure ☐

68. As the result of snow and rain a day earlier, a platform owned by Railway Co. was covered with ice. Railway had prominently posted a sign saying, "Mind your step—platform is icy," but did not remove the ice (which could have been done at reasonable cost). Harried, who was running late for his commuter train, slipped on the ice and cracked his skull. He has sued Railway for damages. Can Harried recover?

Not sure ☐

69. The City of Einstein maintained a public library open to all residents of Einstein. Peter entered the library for the purpose of borrowing a book. Paul, who was Peter's friend, hated books, and just came along to keep Peter company. While the two of them were riding an elevator in the building, the elevator broke a cable; the two were thrown to the ground, and both were badly injured. Had city personnel conducted reasonable periodic inspections of the elevator, they would have spotted the frayed cable and been able to repair it. However, no such inspections took place, and no one who worked for the city knew of the fraying. Both Peter and Paul have sued the city. Which of them can recover?

Not sure ☐

(a) Peter only

(b) Paul only

(c) Neither

(d) Both

70. Vick, a door-to-door vacuum cleaner salesman, walked up to the front path of Homemaker's house. He noticed a sign that said, "No door-to-door salesmen," but disregarded it. Before he even got to the door, Vick tripped over a pothole in the front walk and injured himself. Homemaker knew about this pothole. A reasonable person in Homemaker's position, knowing that people often came up the walk, would have filled the hole or at least posted a warning sign, but Homemaker had done neither. Vick has sued Homemaker for his injuries; can he recover?

Not sure ☐

71. Same basic facts as in the previous question. Now, however, assume that Vick made it to Homemaker's front porch, rang the bell, and was in the middle of explaining to Homemaker why Homemaker should give Vick ten minutes for a vacuum demonstration when Vick fell through a rotted floorboard on the porch. Homemaker, who because of loneliness had been drinking a bit too much over the past few months, didn't know that the floorboard was rotting. However, a reasonable person in Homemaker's position would have noticed this rot and would have fixed it. Vick has sued Homemaker for his injuries; can he recover?

Not sure ☐

72. Same facts as in the previous question. Now, however, assume that before any catastrophe had befallen Vick, Homemaker said, "Okay, I'd be willing to sit through your ten-minute demonstration of superior vacuuming power." Vick entered the house, plugged his vacuum into what turned out to be a defective wall outlet, and was electrocuted. Homemaker did not know of the defect. However, a reasonably careful owner would have been put on notice by burn marks near the outlet that something was amiss and would have made reasonable investigations, which would have brought the danger to light. Can Vick recover for his electrical injuries?

Not sure ☐

73. Same facts as in the previous question. Now, however, assume that Vick finished his demonstration without mishap. He then said to Homemaker, "May I use your bathroom? I try not to drink very many liquids while I'm on the job, but even so, my bladder has limits and a lot of people slam the door on my face." Homemaker said, "Why, of course. The bathroom is down the hall and to your right." While Vick was on his way to the bathroom, he stumbled over a child's toy that had been left in a poorly lit part of the corridor, and fell. Homemaker was not aware that her two-year-old child had left the toy there. Can Vick recover for his injuries from the fall?

Not sure ☐

74. Landlord rented an apartment to Tenant. The lease provided that Landlord would make all needed repairs. On July 1, Tenant noticed a large crack in the ceiling, but was too busy to notify Landlord about it during the next six weeks. On August 15, Tenant invited Guest, a friend from the office, to dinner at Tenant's apartment. While they were dining, a chunk of plaster fell off near the crack and hit Guest in the head, seriously injuring him. Guest did not want to sue his friend, Tenant, so

he instead sued Landlord for failing to keep the apartment in adequate repair. Can Guest recover?

Not sure ☐

75. A car negligently driven by Daewoo injured Pindar. Pindar was so badly injured that he has been classified as "disabled" under the federal Social Security Act and receives payments of $400 per month indefinitely. If Daewoo is required to pay damages for Pindar's loss of earnings due to the disability, may the amount Daewoo is required to pay be reduced by the net present value of the monthly disability payments?

Not sure ☐

76. Same facts as in the previous question. Now, assume that Pindar was not wearing his seat belt at the time of the collision between his car and Daewoo's car. The evidence shows that if Pindar had been wearing his seat belt (as required by local law), Pindar would have suffered only minor injuries and would soon have been back at work. Instead, Pindar was permanently disabled and will lose earnings over the rest of his life having a net present value of $1,000,000. May Pindar recover the $1,000,000?

Not sure ☐

77. Jogger had heard that a particular stretch of Middle Park in the City of Ames was notoriously dangerous at night, and that a pack of youths frequently robbed and/ or raped women who went there. Normally, Jogger was careful not to go into this section of the park, but one night she carelessly missed a turnoff and found herself right in the dangerous section. She was accosted and struck by Doug, who then stole her purse. Jogger fell, hit her head on a stone, and suffered serious injuries. She brought a battery action against Doug (who was caught by the police shortly after the episode). Doug now asserts that Jogger should be barred by the doctrine of contributory negligence (still applicable in the state). Is Doug right?

Not sure ☐

78. Perry, an avid hiker, negligently wore very thin-soled shoes that were inadequate protection for the sharp stones on the mountain trail that he planned to navigate. About halfway up the trail, Perry badly gashed his foot and passed out in the middle of the trail from lack of blood. Don, riding a mountain bike, arrived at the same point in the trail, saw Perry, negligently believed that he (Don) had enough room on the trail to get by Perry without hitting him, and because of his miscalculation ran over Perry's foot, crushing it. Perry has sued Don for the crushed foot. Don has raised the defense that Perry's contributory negligence was the proximate cause of Perry's injury, since if Perry had worn proper shoes, he would never have gashed his foot, would therefore not have been lying unconscious in the middle of the trail, and would not have been run over by Don. The jurisdiction follows the common law approach to contributory negligence.

(a) What doctrine should Perry assert to rebut Don's defense?

Not sure ☐

(b) May Perry recover?

Not sure ☐

79. Same facts as in the previous question. Now, however, assume that Don was day-dreaming, rather than watching the trail closely. If Don had watched the trail closely, he would have seen Perry's body in time to avoid hitting it. Instead, he ran into the body without ever realizing it was there. Again, Don now asserts that Perry's contributory negligence should bar his recovery against Don. Is Don correct?

Not sure ☐

80. Same facts as in the previous two questions. Now, however, assume that Don was paying close attention, saw Perry's body early, and slammed on the brakes. If Don had carefully maintained his mountain bike, there would have been enough distance that Don's bike would have stopped before hitting Perry's unconscious body. However, due to Don's negligence in the weeks prior to this episode, the brakes had not been properly maintained, and they did not bring the mountain bike to a stop in time, so that Don hit Perry's body. Once again, Don asserts that Perry should be barred from recovery by Perry's contributory negligence. Is Don correct?

Not sure ☐

81. Jay Walker, a pedestrian who was in a hurry, crossed a busy street from between two parked cars in the middle of the street, rather than at a crosswalk. Although this was an act of negligence, it was widely (and properly) perceived as only slightly negligent on this particular street, since crosswalks were few and far between and drivers knew to be on the lookout for pedestrians doing this. Hard Driver, a hard-driving executive, was driving down the street at 70 mph in a 40 mph zone. He never even saw Jay and just slammed into him. Jay never even knew that he was in danger, because Hard's car simply came on too suddenly. Jay was killed in the collision His estate has sued Hard. There are no applicable statutes, and all relevant common law doctrines are in force. May Jay's estate recover?

Not sure ☐

82. Same facts as in the previous question. This time, however, assume that Jay was merely knocked down, not killed, by the collision with Hard. Hard drove away and was never found again. Shortly thereafter, a car driven by Speedy came along. If Speedy had been paying proper attention, he would have noticed Jay's body, and would have been able to avoid hitting it. But because of Speedy's inattentiveness, he hit Jay's body, killing Jay. The jurisdiction has enacted a "pure" comparative negligence statute. In a suit by Jay's estate against Speedy, the jury finds that 30 percent of the fault was Jay's and 70 percent was Speedy's (the jury ignores any fault by Hard, who is not before the court). Jay's estate argues that by the doctrine of last clear chance, Speedy should be liable for 100 percent of the damages. Is the estate correct?

Not sure ☐

83. Theater Buff had a $60 orchestra ticket for a Broadway show that was scheduled to start at 8:30 P.M. He arrived in the neighborhood of the theater at 7:45 P.M. and began looking for a parking garage. All parking garages within a safe walking distance of the theater were filled, except for a garage operated by Dennis. Buff gave his car to Dennis, who gave Buff a receipt. On the back of the receipt was a clause stating that Dennis would have no liability for damage or loss of Buff's car even due to negligence by Dennis. Buff read the ticket, was unhappy about the terms, but stuffed it in his pocket without saying anything, and left the car. Such terms are found on the receipts given by virtually all parking garages in the area. Due to Dennis's negligence, Buff's car was stolen from the garage. May Buff recover from Dennis for the value of the car?

Not sure ☐

84. Same facts as in the previous question. Now, however, assume that there were a number of parking garages in the neighborhood of the theater that had open spaces, and at least some of these did not have a blanket waiver of liability on their receipts. Buff chose to park at Dennis's garage, received the receipt, and stuffed it in his pocket without noticing the fine-print waiver on the reverse. If Buff's car is stolen due to the negligence of Dennis, may Buff recover against Dennis?

Not sure ☐

85. The courts of New York have held that, as a common law matter, any operator of a baseball stadium must furnish each patron with a screened seat so that batted balls will not hit the patron. Fan, who was knowledgeable about baseball and the risks associated with it, attended a New York Yokels baseball game at Yokels Stadium. A particular seat sold to Fan by the Yokels was an unscreened seat, and Fan was aware of this fact. The ticket said nothing about the risk of foul balls. Fan sat in the seat and was hit in the face by a foul ball. The jurisdiction still applies common law contributory negligence. May Fan recover in a negligence suit against the Yokels?

Not sure ☐

86. Same facts as in the previous question. Now, assume that Swede, a tourist from Sweden, attended the game. Swede knew nothing about baseball, did not speak English, and attended the game merely because he guessed that it was some sort of sporting spectacle that he might enjoy. Swede was hit in the face by a foul ball while sitting in an unscreened seat and has sued the Yokels for damages. May he recover?

Not sure ☐

87. Pedestrian was struck and slightly injured by a car driven by Doug. There was no other traffic around, and there were no pay phones nearby. Doug said to Pedestrian, "I'd be happy to drive you to the hospital, but you must understand that my brakes are not working very well—that's the very reason I couldn't stop before I hit you." Pedestrian responded, "Alright, alright, just get me to the hospital as best you can." While Doug was driving to the hospital, he tried to brake to avoid an oncoming car, failed, and smashed into that car, killing Pedestrian. Pedestrian's estate has sued Doug. May the estate recover from Doug for Pedestrian's death (as opposed to the minor injuries he sustained in the first collision)?

Not sure ☐

88. Same facts as in the previous question. Now, however, assume that Doug abandoned Pedestrian in a hit-and-run scenario. Shortly thereafter, Samaritan drove up, offered Pedestrian a ride to the hospital, and said, "But I want you to know I have bad brakes." Pedestrian accepted the ride (there were no other cars around, and no nearby pay phones), and a crash due to Samaritan's bad brakes ensued. The state maintains common law contributory negligence. In a suit against Samaritan, may Pedestrian recover for his injuries from the second collision?

Not sure ☐

89. Same facts as in the previous question. Now, however, assume that the state has enacted comparative negligence. Is Pedestrian barred from recovering against Samaritan under the doctrine of assumption of risk?

Not sure ☐

90. Child, who was three years old, was walking down the sidewalk with Tina, his mother. Tina stopped to talk to a friend and carelessly lost sight of Child, who Tina knew was a very adventurous and active toddler. Child ran into the street and was hit and seriously injured by Driver, who was speeding. Child has sued Driver for his injuries. Driver has impleaded Tina, arguing that Tina, through her negligent failure to supervise Child, was partly responsible for the accident and that Tina should therefore have to pay contribution equal to part of any damage award that Driver may have to pay to Child. The jury has found that Driver is liable for Child's injuries, and that Tina was careless in not supervising Child better. May Driver collect contribution from Tina?

Not sure ☐

91. The U.S. Department of Energy adopted regulations, prepared by senior scientists within the Department, specifying the design and safety features that any nuclear reactor must have. A private company built a nuclear reactor according to these specifications. The specifications turned out to be faulty and negligently prepared. The reactor exploded, injuring Percy, a nearby resident. Percy has sued the United States for negligence. May he recover?

Not sure ☐

92. Joseph, a state court judge, convicted David of conspiracy to sell cocaine, after a bench trial. Joseph's wife, who divorced Joseph after this trial, then told David, "My husband told me that he was quite confident you were innocent of these charges, but he was determined to convict you because your father once stole $10 from his father back in 1953." David, who was by now out of prison, sued Joseph for false imprisonment and intentional infliction of emotional distress. May David recover?

Not sure ☐

93. Cosa Nostra Collectors, Inc. runs a debt collection service. All employees of Cosa are instructed that they should never use violence, or even threats of violence, in attempting to collect a debt. Vincent ("Big Vinny") Testarosa, one of Cosa's collectors, attempted to collect a $10,000 debt that Potter owed to a Cosa client, Carla. Potter refused to pay even though (as Vincent knew) Potter had the money. To soften Potter's resistance, Vincent disregarded his employer's instructions, and with an unlicensed pistol fired a slug through Potter's left kneecap, crippling him for life. Potter then paid the money. Potter (after assuming a new identity and state of residence) has brought suit against Cosa for battery, under the doctrine of *respondeat superior*. Can Potter recover?

Not sure ☐

94. Messenger Service was in the business of hand-delivering packages within New York City. Law Firm engaged Messenger Service to deliver a large box of documents from Law Firm's principal office on the East Side to its branch office on the West Side. Law Firm knew that Messenger Service would use a van, and Law Firm insisted that the van go directly from one office to the other without making any intervening stops. Law Firm directed Messenger Service to perform this task "as quickly as possible." The driver for Messenger Service traveled 50 mph down a 30 mph street and while doing so struck and seriously injured Pedestrian. Because Messenger Service had no substantial assets, Pedestrian sued Law Firm. May Pedestrian recover against Law Firm?

Not sure ☐

95. The City of New Ames desired to repave its principal street, Main Street. After competitive bidding, it awarded the contract to Contractor. Anyone reasonably knowledgeable in roadway construction knows that repaving requires the use of large quantities of sand and gravel, and that contractors often find it useful to dump large piles of sand and gravel on the roadway until it is needed. It is customary in the roadway construction industry to place red warning lights around such piles, especially at night (so that drivers will not run into the piles). The contract between New Ames and Contractor required placement of such warning lights. Contractor dumped several large sand and gravel piles in the street, and (unknown to New Ames or its Director of Public Works) failed to install any warning lights. Driver was unaware of the piles and drove his car into one of them at night, injuring himself. Driver has sued New Ames. May he recover?

Not sure ☐

96. Owen and Fred drove in Owen's car to the neighborhood bar. Owen then had a number of drinks, and Fred just had soda. Fred suggested that he drive home, rather than Owen, because he (Fred) was completely sober and Owen was not. Owen agreed. Fred (who so far as Owen knew was a careful and responsible driver) went through an intersection without carefully checking for oncoming traffic. David, who was traveling down the cross street at a speed 20 mph faster than the speed limit, smashed into Owen's car. Owen was seriously injured. The jurisdiction maintains common law contributory negligence. The jurisdiction also has an "automobile consent" statute, whereby the owner of a vehicle is liable as a defendant for any harm done to third persons by the negligence of anyone driving the car with the owner's consent. May Owen recover against David for his injuries?   Not sure ☐

97. Same basic facts as in the previous question. Now, however, assume that Fred was acting as Owen's chauffeur, for pay, at the time Fred went through the intersection. May Owen recover for his own injuries against David?   Not sure ☐

98. Owner wanted to acquire a watchdog that would protect his property. He acquired Rex, a pit bull, after friends told him that pit bulls generally have a nasty disposition that causes them to attack any stranger. Two days after Owner acquired Rex, Rex escaped through a very narrow hole in Owner's fence (which Owner did not know about and probably would not have found even had he inspected his property) and attacked Penny, a child living next door. Penny has sued Owner. May she recover?   Not sure ☐

99. Utility Co. constructed a nuclear power plant in the town of Langdell. Utility used all possible care in constructing the state-of-the-art plant. Langdell is in a region that suffers occasional earthquakes, so the plant design was earthquake-resistant, though not earthquake-proof. A relatively severe earthquake occurred and caused a rupture in one of the cooling tanks in the plant. A nuclear meltdown occurred, releasing gamma rays into the atmosphere. A large number of these gamma rays struck Peg, a neighboring landowner, as she was standing outside surveying the earthquake damage. Peg suffered severe radiation burns and sued Utility for her injuries. She has been unable to show any respect in which Utility behaved with less than due care. In the Langdell vicinity, nuclear power is an accepted low-cost method of generating power, but is certainly not the only method of doing so. May Peg recover?   Not sure ☐

100. Same facts as in the previous question. Now, however, assume that Utility Co. realized that a meltdown was occurring and posted large signs on all roads leading to within half a mile of the plant, warning "Danger of Gamma Ray Radiation Due to Meltdown. Enter Only at Your Own Risk." Truck Driver, who was inattentive due to his fatigue from the long trip he was engaged on, failed to read the sign; had he done so, he could easily have taken a detour that would have cost him only five minutes. Instead, he drove near the plant and was injured by radiation. He has sued Utility Co. The jurisdiction recognizes common law contributory negligence as a defense. Can Truck Driver recover?   Not sure ☐

101. Same facts as in the previous question. Now, however, assume that Hero, a member of the Langdell Volunteer Ambulance Corps, read the sign, said to himself, "But there may be injured people in there," and drove his ambulance to the plant site, where he was injured by radiation. Can Hero recover against Utility?   Not sure ☐

102. Campfire Soup Company is in the business of making canned soups. It uses only the latest state-of-the-art machinery to blend, cook, and can the soups; it maintains high safety standards; and it conducts rigorous inspections constantly. A particular can of the company's Cream of Snail soup was sold to Wholesaler, who is a distributor for Campfire's products. Wholesaler resold the can to Retailer. In Retailer's store, Charles, a consumer, bought the can. Charles prepared the soup and served it to Gaia, a houseguest and friend of his. As Gaia was eating the soup, she bit down and suffered a terrible gash in her gum. The gash turned out to have been caused by a small fragment of glass in the soup. All available evidence suggests that the glass was in the soup at the time Charles opened the can. The glass is a type used in Campfire's canning equipment, and the most likely (though still somewhat speculative) explanation is that there was a one-in-a-million breakage of the machinery during the making of the batch that included this can. Gaia has sued all people concerned (Campfire, Wholesaler, Retailer, and Charles). Against which of them can she recover, assuming that she produces no evidence other than that already described in this question?

Not sure ☐

103. Slip and Slide Floor Polish, which is poisonous, looks like Flopsy Cola, a popular soft drink and comes in a soda-like bottle with an easily removable lid. The bottle has a warning reading: "This product is poisonous. Keep out of reach of children." Little Bobo, three years old, finds a bottle of polish under the kitchen sink, pops the lid off, and drinks the contents of the bottle, making himself seriously ill in the process. Could Slip and Slide be strictly liable for Bobo's injuries?

Not sure ☐

104. Count Dracula enters the hospital for an operation to correct internal hemorrhaging. During the operation, he receives a transfusion of blood infected with the HIV virus, and as a result he contracts AIDS. Can he successfully sue the hospital in strict product liability?

Not sure ☐

105. Campfire Soup Co. sells a variety of canned soups, including Cream of Avocado. It sold a case of Cream of Avocado to Retailer. Retailer stacked the cans in a pyramid structure as a special display. A stock boy employed by Retailer knocked over the cans, and one of them was, unnoticed by Retailer's employees, slightly dented. Consumer bought that dented can, cooked and ate its contents, and got severe food poisoning. The soup in that can turned out to be infected by botulism, which often results from spoilage in canned goods that are not tightly sealed. Tests of numerous other cans from the same batch (including two cans from the same pyramid pile in Retailer's store) show no spoilage. Consumer has sued Campfire on a strict liability theory. Will Consumer recover?

Not sure ☐

106. Drill Press Corp. (DPC) manufactures drill presses and other machine tools. Drill presses are used to drill a hole in metal or other hard substances, where the object to be drilled is held in position on the drill press. All of DPC's drill presses require (or at least assume) that the operator will hold the object to be drilled in place with the left hand, and will signal the press to drill by using the right hand. All of DPC's drill presses contain a large red bold legend affixed to the front of the press: "WARNING. WHEN YOU HOLD THE OBJECT TO BE DRILLED, MAKE SURE THAT YOUR HAND IS NOT IN THE AREA TO BE PUNCHED." The area to be punched is also drawn in red on the top of the surface where objects to be drilled are placed. Patrick had been operating a DPC drill press for 15 years and had grown somewhat casual about safety. One day, he inattentively held a small piece of metal in such a way that when it was drilled, Patrick's left thumb was in the path of the drill and was severed. Patrick has brought a strict product liability suit against DPC. There is evidence that an alternative design could have been used, at slightly greater cost, whereby all objects to be drilled would have to be clamped down with a vice, and both rather than one hand would have to be on a switch located away from the drilling area to operate the machine. Patrick argues that a press made without these design changes is "defective." The jurisdiction maintains common law contributory negligence. Will Patrick recover against DPC?

Not sure ☐

107. Same facts as in the previous question. Now, however, assume that DPC presents evidence at trial that no drill presses made by any other manufacturer contain the hands-free design that Patrick claims should have been used.

(a) Is this evidence admissible?

Not sure ☐

(b) For this part only, assume that the evidence is admitted. Does the evidence prevent a jury from finding in favor of Patrick?

Not sure ☐

108. Frieda was driving her 1999 Newmobile when she was struck from the side by a speeding driver who drove away and was never found. The impact on Frieda's car was great enough that it caused the car to go through a barrier at the side of the road, where it tumbled over and fell into a seven-foot-deep ravine. The car finally landed on its roof, and Frieda was seriously injured. Medical evidence shows that the only serious injuries to Frieda occurred when the car landed on its roof, the pieces of steel supporting the roof buckled, and the roof therefore collapsed onto Frieda's head and neck. The evidence also shows that had a roll bar been installed in the car to maintain the structural integrity of the passenger compartment in a rollover accident, Frieda would not have sustained her injuries. There is evidence that other manufacturers of similar cars have installed roll bars for this reason.

Frieda sued Newmobile in strict product liability. Newmobile defends on the grounds that a manufacturer of a defective product only has liability when the product is put to its intended use, and that collisions and rollovers are not the intended use for cars. Will Newmobile prevail with this defense?

Not sure ☐

109. After 15 years of testing (the last 10 on a group of 5,000 humans), Drugco Inc. released its long-awaited AIDS vaccine in 1990. At the time the product was released, no person given it in the human tests had ever developed AIDS. Perry, who had a deep-seated fear of contracting AIDS, took one of the early post-release dosages, in 2000. (Perry's fear of AIDS was quite irrational, since he was not a member of any high-risk group and practiced safe monogamous sex.) At the time Perry took the drug, the warning given with the drug (both in printed material given to each patient, and in greater detail given to each doctor) described certain mild side effects, but no serious ones. Unknown to Drugco or anyone else in 1990—and in fact unknowable given the state of medical science at that time— one in every 10,000 patients given the Drugco vaccine will, over the course of the following 15 years, develop AIDS caused by the vaccine itself (which is made from whole killed AIDS viruses). Perry was the unlucky one in 10,000, and contracted the disease in 2009. He has sued Drugco in strict liability. Perry concedes that the product was, in 2000, "unavoidably unsafe." However, he contends that Drugco's failure to warn of actually existing perils (even though Drugco didn't know of those perils) violated Drugco's duty to warn, and thus subjected it to strict product liability. Is Perry correct in his contention?

Not sure ☐

110. The Peach Aircraft Co. constructs its single-propeller Peachcraft Model 202 airplane using parts from hundreds of different suppliers. One of these parts is an altimeter from Altos Corp. Terry bought a Peachcraft 202, and was flying it one night in dark but good weather over mountainous terrain. Based on altimeter readings, Terry believed that he was flying at a safe altitude. In fact, he was flying at only 2,500 feet above sea level, and he collided with a 3,000-foot mountain peak. Terry was killed, and his estate sued Altos on a strict liability theory. (Peachcraft was unavailable for suit because it had gone bankrupt in the interim.) There is no evidence of any negligence in design or assembly by either Altos, Peachcraft, or Terry, but there is clear evidence that (for some unknown reason) the altimeter did not function as it was supposed to. There is also evidence that altimeters are a sealed component whose functioning is generally not affected by the manner in which they are installed into the completed aircraft or the manner in which they are maintained. Will Terry's estate be successful in its strict liability suit against Altos?

Not sure ☐

111. Doctor Lookgood, a plastic surgeon, specializes in breast enlargement operations. To perform such an operation, he inserts a sac of silicon gel, manufactured by Gelco, into each breast. Due to an unforeseeable problem with one of Gelco's sac-manufacturing machines (unpreventable through reasonable inspection methods), a particular gel sac, after being implanted by Lookgood in Pamela, developed a leak. The leaky silicon gel caused an infection, and Pamela lost her entire left breast. Because Gelco had by then gone out of business, Pamela sued Lookgood. She concedes that Lookgood was not negligent (since he could not have known of the defect, and Gelco had a good reputation), but she asserts that he is liable under a strict product liability theory. Is she correct?

Not sure ☐

112. United Automobile Corp. manufactured a 1998 Weep four-wheel-drive vehicle and sold it to Dealer, who resold it to Tim. Tim, after using it for a year, sold it to Peggy. One day, due to a defect in the design of the Weep's radiator, the radiator became clogged, the engine temperature heated up to an unbearable extent, and the engine caught fire. (There is no evidence that United was negligent in the way it designed the radiator—the flaw in design only became apparent long after Peggy's Weep was made, after a couple of fires like the one in Peggy's car.) Peggy escaped the car without injuries, but the car was completely destroyed by the fire. Can Peggy recover for the value of the car against United? If so, on what theory?

Not sure ☐

113. Same facts as above question. Now, however, assume that Peggy was able to put out the fire quite quickly with a fire extinguisher that she happened to keep in the car. The car suffered no significant damage. However, because of the time taken by the fire and

by Peggy's attempts to put it out, Peggy was made late for the closing on a house that she was buying, the contract for which contained a "time is of the essence" clause. The house seller canceled the contract because of Peggy's tardiness (and because he had gotten a higher offer in the meantime), a court upheld the seller's right to do this, and Peggy therefore lost the "benefit of her bargain" on the house, equal to $40,000. May Peggy recover the $40,000 from United? If so, on what theory?

Not sure ☐

114. Same facts as in the previous question. Now, however, assume that as Peggy was attempting to put out the fire with the extinguisher, she suffered a slight burn on her left hand.

    (a) May Peggy recover against United for the burn, and if so, on what theory?

Not sure ☐

    (b) May Peggy recover for her lost house profits?

Not sure ☐

115. Davis Soup Co. is in the business of manufacturing canned soups. Retailer sold a particular can of cream of asparagus soup manufactured by Davis to Parker. Parker cooked the soup, poured a serving into his bowl, and started to eat. A person of normal attentiveness would have noticed that there was a small mouse (dead) in the soup at the time the can was opened. Parker, however, had been smoking a marijuana cigarette just before eating the soup, and was therefore too spaced out to notice the mouse. However, once he took a bite, felt and heard a crunch far too loud to be that of a piece of asparagus, and looked down, he saw the rear half of the mouse's body still in the soup. Parker developed recurring nightmares, had to consult a psychiatrist weekly for the next three months, developed an ulcer, and has ever since been afraid to eat anything that comes from a can. He has sued Davis on a strict liability theory. Davis defends on the grounds that Parker was contributorily negligent. The jurisdiction maintains common law contributory negligence. May Parker recover?

Not sure ☐

116. Pamela's eight-year-old son, Steven, suddenly suffered excruciating abdominal pain, nausea, and fever. Pamela suspected (correctly, as it turned out) that Steven had appendicitis. Pamela owned no car, and the local 911 emergency number was repeatedly busy. Therefore, Pamela asked her neighbor, Nathan, to lend Pamela his car so she could take Steven to the hospital. Nathan replied, "I'm happy to do that, but you should know that the brakes are intermittently defective, according to a recall notice I just got from Carco, the manufacturer." Pamela replied, "Well, I've really got no choice, so I'll take it." She put Steven in the car and drove off at 40 mph (well below the speed limit). En route, a car driven by Jerry, going at right angles to the car Pamela was driving, jumped a stop sign. Pamela saw the danger and immediately slammed on the brakes. With correctly working brakes, Pamela would have been able to avoid the accident, but the brakes of Nathan's car failed due to the defect Nathan had warned Pamela about, and the car slammed into Jerry's car. Pamela was injured, but managed to get a friend to take Steven to the hospital, where he was operated on and cured. Pamela has sued Carco in strict liability for her injuries. Carco defends on the grounds that Pamela assumed the risk. Will this defense prevail?

Not sure ☐

117. Same facts as in the previous question, except that this time, assume that the reason Pamela needed the car was to go to the drugstore to replenish her supply of Passion

No. 6 Perfume. All other facts (including the way the accident developed) remain the same. Will Carco prevail if it defends against Pamela's strict product liability action by claiming that Pamela assumed the risk?

Not sure ☐

118. Eyyon, a large oil refiner, owned a large tanker, the SS *Eyyon*. As the SS *Eyyon*, filled with oil, was approaching the port of Zedlav, its captain failed to notice a large iceberg in the ship's path. The SS *Eyyon* slammed into the iceberg and discharged tens of thousands of gallons of oil into the bay surrounding Zedlav. Evidence later showed that the captain was seriously intoxicated at the time of the accident. The oil killed nearly all fish in the bay. The economy of Zedlav is a diversified one, but commercial fishermen make up a significant (though minority) chunk of its local industry. The fishermen have brought a class action against Eyyon Corp. for their losses.

(a) On what tort theory should the fishermen sue?

Not sure ☐

(b) Will they recover?

Not sure ☐

119. Same facts as in the previous question. Now, however, assume that the plaintiff class consists of all owners of hotels in the Zedlav area, who claim that (1) Zedlav is a much less pleasant place to live since the oil spill, (2) tourism has therefore decreased dramatically, and (3) their own profits have therefore diminished to almost nothing. If the hotel operators bring suit on the same theory as that used by the fishermen in the previous question, will they be able to recover damages against Eyyon?

Not sure ☐

120. Printer maintains certain photosensitive chemicals that he uses to develop photo-offset negatives and plates. These chemicals are not highly toxic. Once a year, Printer changes these chemicals, dumping the old chemicals into a depression on his property. On one occasion, the chemicals so dumped percolated down into an underground stream, where they were carried onto Farmer's property, adjacent to Printer's. When Farmer drew water from a well on his property to irrigate his soybean crop, a large part of the crop (a part worth $5,000) was killed by the presence of the chemicals in this well water. Printer, at the time he dumped the chemicals, did not know of the underground stream or of the fact that the chemicals would be brought onto Farmer's land. Farmer has brought a suit in private nuisance against Printer. Will he recover?

Not sure ☐

121. Same facts as above question. Now, however, assume that after the first dumping, Farmer notified Printer that Farmer's crops had been damaged by the seepage of the chemicals onto Farmer's land. Several months later, Printer dumped more of the same chemical in the same place, causing $5,000 of new damages to Farmer's crop. Printer did not desire to harm Farmer; indeed, he considered Farmer a friend. Nonetheless, Printer concluded that it would cost $1,000 to have the chemicals carted away, and Printer did not want to spend the money. Farmer has brought suit for private nuisance for the second dumping. Will he recover?

Not sure ☐

122. For many years, Utility Co. operated a coal-fired generating plant on Whiteacre. The plant produced smoke, gas, fumes, and particles, some of which settled on

Blackacre, the vacant parcel adjoining Whiteacre. However, since Blackacre was unsettled, the pollution from the plant did not harm Blackacre. After several years of this pollution, Phyllis purchased Blackacre at a somewhat lower price because of the adjoining plant. Phyllis was a landscape gardener, and she attempted to grow small trees and shrubs on Blackacre. The shrubs and trees died because of the pollution. Phyllis has brought a suit for damages against Utility Co., under a theory of private nuisance.

(a) What defense should Utility Co. raise? — Not sure ☐

(b) Will that defense succeed, if it is raised in a summary judgment motion before trial? — Not sure ☐

123. Donald was a professional collector of violins, and was highly knowledgeable about how much various types of violins are worth. As he was traveling in a distant city on business, he happened upon a violin shop run by Pierre. In Pierre's display case, Donald noticed a violin listed for sale at $200. Donald, by virtue of his superior knowledge and training, immediately recognized the violin as a rare Guarnerius, worth at least $100,000. Donald did not tell Pierre his identity, and did not say anything about the nature of the violin. He immediately paid Pierre the $200 list price, and two days later resold the violin for $100,000. Pierre read an account of Donald's "coup" in the newspapers, and sued Donald in tort for fraudulently concealing from him the fact that the violin was worth 500 times Pierre's asking price. May Pierre recover? — Not sure ☐

124. Octavio offered for sale the house in which he lived. Barnaby, who lived in the same town, heard about the house through Sidney, a mutual friend. Sidney told Barnaby, "Go look at Octavio's house, and tell him you're a good friend of mine. He won't steer you wrong." Barnaby went to look at the house, and told Octavio, "Our mutual friend Sidney sent me to look at your house; he told me that you wouldn't steer me wrong." At that time, Octavio knew full well that the house was constructed on a former toxic waste site, that toxic wastes had occasionally found their way into the well that served the property (though the water was not contaminated at present), and that Barnaby would not buy the house if he were aware of these facts. Octavio declined to disclose these facts, even though he realized that Barnaby had no ready way of discovering them for himself, through inspection or otherwise. Barnaby bought the house. After the sale, Barnaby discovered the toxic waste problem and sued Octavio for fraud. Will Barnaby recover? — Not sure ☐

125. Same facts as in the previous question. Now, however, assume that the buyer was Bertram, who did not know Octavio even by reputation, and who came to the house by reading an ad for it placed by Octavio in the newspaper. All other facts (including Octavio's failure to disclose the toxic waste problem) are as in the previous question. Can Bertram recover against Octavio for fraudulent nondisclosure? — Not sure ☐

126. Darlene owned a five-story apartment building in Pound City. Darlene offered the building for sale to Percy. She gave Percy a sheet she had prepared, which stated, "The current rent roll is $5,000 per month, consisting of ten apartments at $500 each." She did not disclose to Percy a fact well known to her, namely, that under the Rent Stabilization ordinance in force in Pound, the highest rent properly chargeable for any of the apartments was $400, and that any tenant who became aware of his rights could sue to have the rent reduced to that amount. Percy was aware that the Rent Stabilization ordinance existed, and was also aware that there were records at the Pound City Hall showing, for each apartment building, the highest rent that could be charged per apartment. Percy decided that Darlene looked honest, so he neglected to check the town records, even though he could have easily done this. He bought the building at a price that appeared economically sensible to him based on a $5,000 per month rent roll, but that he would not have paid had he known the legal rent roll was only $4,000.

Shortly after the closing, the tenants discovered their rights, banded together, and successfully sued to have each person's rental reduced to $400. Percy has sued Darlene for fraudulent misrepresentation and/or nondisclosure. Darlene defends on the grounds that (1) she has no liability for what was essentially nondisclosure; and (2) in any event, Percy was not justified in relying, because he could have easily performed his own investigation which would have disclosed the true facts. Which, if either, of these defenses has merit?

Not sure ☐

127. Developer owned 20 country lots that he wanted to sell. He took out a newspaper ad, in which he stated, "I will build a 20-acre lake, which each of my 20 lots will abut. Any purchaser of one of my lots (as well as a purchaser of any other lot that happens to abut the lake) will have full boating and fishing rights." Developer in fact had no intention of ever building the lake; he simply wanted to make a quick buck and hoped he wouldn't get sued. Clarence Credulous decided that he could not afford any of Developer's lots. He was able, however, to locate a lot owned by Xavier, offered at a lesser price, which would abut the proposed lake to be built by Developer. Clarence bought Xavier's lot, relying heavily on the fact that he would be able to look at, and boat and fish on, the lake. Developer failed to build the lake, and Clarence has sued him for fraudulent misrepresentation. May Clarence recover?

Not sure ☐

128. Pia was contemplating the purchase of a painting that the seller represented to be by the great master Rubens. Pia brought the painting to her friend Dimitrius, whom Pia knew to be one of the world's great experts in Old Masters paintings. Pia asked Dimitrius to give his opinion on whether the painting was really by Rubens. Dimitrius looked at the painting, and said, "Yes, my dear, I'm nearly certain that it really was painted by Rubens himself." In fact, Dimitrius was very unsure whether the painting was by Rubens or rather by one of his students, but he was too embarrassed to tell Pia (whom he longed for romantically) of his uncertainty. Pia bought the painting and suffered financial loss when it was later conclusively shown to have been by one of Rubens's students. Pia has sued Dimitrius for fraudulent misrepresentation. Dimitrius defends on the grounds that he was only stating, as Pia knew, his own opinion. May Pia recover?

Not sure ☐

129. Same facts as the above question. Now, however, assume that the seller of the painting, Darren, said to Pia, "I, too, believe that this painting was by Rubens." Pia knew that Darren was an amateur collector, not a scholar. Darren in fact knew nothing about the painting's provenance, and has no real belief about who painted it. May Pia recover from Darren?

Not sure ☐

130. In 1975, before the danger of asbestos was widely understood, Owner asked Contractor, who was in the commercial renovation business, to look at the insulation around the boiler in an apartment building owned by Owner, and to tell Owner whether that insulation contained asbestos. (Owner was an epidemiologist specializing in asbestos-related diseases, so he appreciated the danger that the world was not yet aware of.) Contractor was not being paid to give his opinion, but he wanted to help Owner because he was hoping to be hired to renovate the building. He told Owner, "The insulation on your boiler was manufactured by Insul Co., and I happen to know that they never used asbestos." In fact, Insul Co. had made a few asbestos-based products, and a reasonable person in Contractor's position would have either known this fact or called to find out; Contractor did not in fact know, and honestly believed he was stating the true facts to Owner.

Owner could and would have sold the building in 1975 had he known of the asbestos covering, and would have gotten full value for the building. Instead, Owner did not discover the asbestos until 1989, when a prospective purchaser conducted an inspection that turned up the true facts. No physical injury resulted, but Owner was required to sell for $40,000 less than had the building not contained asbestos (since this was the amount that the buyer estimated would have to be spent to remove the asbestos). Owner has sued Contractor for negligent misrepresentation. May he recover?

Not sure ☐

131. Same facts as in the previous question. Now, however, assume that Owner repeated Contractor's statement to Owner's friend Investor, who, like Owner, bought and sold commercial real estate. A building that Investor was considering buying happened to have the very same insulation in it as was contained in Owner's building. Investor, reassured by hearing that this insulation was asbestos-free, bought the building, and later suffered financial loss when the insulation turned out to contain asbestos and needed to be removed at great expense. Investor has sued Contractor. May he recover for negligent misrepresentation?

Not sure ☐

132. Same facts as in question 130. Now, however, assume that the boiler in Owner's building was not yet insulated at all. Owner contacted Insul Co. and asked it to propose insulation for the boiler. The Insul Co. representative proposed the company's Apex 332 insulation. Owner asked, "Is this insulation asbestos-free?" The Insul Co. representative replied, "Yes, it is." A third-party supplier in Taiwan made the insulation for Insul Co. Unbeknownst to any Insul Co. employee, including the representative (and in fact not knowable through the exercise of reasonable care), the Taiwanese supplier had just changed the raw materials used in Apex 322 to asbestos, without notifying Insul Co. Owner agreed to take the insulation and signed Insul Co.'s standard form contract, which said nothing about the product's being asbestos-free and contained the statement, "This document shall be the sole agreement between the parties, and no oral representations made prior to or simultaneously herewith shall be deemed to have any effect." The insulation was put in. Owner later discovered the asbestos content and was required to remove it at great expense. No one was injured by the asbestos. Owner has sued Insul Co. for misrepresentation. Insul Co. defends on the grounds that it was not even negligent. Will Owner recover?

Not sure ☐

133. Same facts as in the previous question. Now, however, assume that Owner never discovered the asbestos problem and sold the building to Speculator. To induce Speculator to buy, Owner repeated Insul Co.'s oral representation about the insulation's being asbestos-free (a representation that Owner believed). Speculator bought, later discovered the truth, and has sued Insul Co. for misrepresentation. May Speculator recover?

Not sure ☐

134. Newspaper asserted, in an article about a recent trial of an organized crime figure that ended in a mistrial, "There was strong evidence that a majority of the 12-person jury were bribed by the defendant." The article did not describe the nature of the evidence, nor did it say which jurors were probably bribed. Portia, a member of the jury, bought a libel suit against Newspaper. Putting aside all issues of Newspaper's mental state (e.g., whether it had "actual malice"), will Portia's action satisfy the requirement that Newspaper be shown to have defamed Portia?

Not sure ☐

135. Same basic fact pattern as in the previous question. Now, however, assume that Newspaper published a second article, in which it stated, "One of the jurors, Ted Townsend, told a reporter for this newspaper that he personally witnessed fellow juror Portia Potter receive a bundle of cash during the trial from a man whom Townsend had witnessed conversing with the defendant on prior occasions." Portia has sued Newspaper for libel. Newspaper has raised the defense of truth, and has proved that Townsend did indeed make exactly the accusation that Newspaper reported. Portia, however, has shown that Townsend lied to Newspaper to settle an old score with Portia. May Portia recover (assuming that Newspaper is shown to have whatever degree of fault is required)?

Not sure ☐

136. Shopkeeper, the owner of a small dress shop, fired Cashier, saying to other people in the store, "I just saw Cashier steal $100 by taking $200 in payment for a dress and ringing up the dress as if it were a $100 item." Cashier has sued Shopkeeper for slander. Evidence at trial shows that the dress in question cost $178, that Cashier rang up a $98 tab on the register, and that Cashier thus stole only $80. Assuming that Shopkeeper is shown to have had the required mental state, may Cashier recover?

Not sure ☐

137. Newspaper, in a story on the general subject of how organized crime figures have infiltrated legitimate business, stated, "And Joe's Casino, the big Atlantic City casino, is probably mob controlled, because Joe Picolo, owner of record, has been linked by law enforcement authorities to the mob." Joe has brought a libel suit against Newspaper. At the trial, Newspaper has not come up with any evidence to show that Joe has links to the mob, but Joe has not come up with evidence to show that he does not. Assuming that the truth of Newspaper's allegations is the only issue in the case, who will win the suit?

Not sure ☐

138. Parker sold his business, Little Corp, to Big Corp, in return for Big Corp stock. Shortly thereafter, some irregularities in Big Corp's published financial information came to light, and Big Corp's stock dropped sharply (making the payment effectively received by Parker for Little Corp less than he expected). At a meeting of Big Corp's board of directors (to which Parker had been elected), Parker said, "If you don't sell Little Corp back to me in return for the Big Corp stock I received,

I will bring a suit against Big Corp and all of you directors charging securities law violations." Denise, one of the board members, responded, "Parker, you're a blackmailer, and I vote that we tell this blackmailer to shove it." The board refused Parker's request. Parker then brought a slander action against Denise for calling him a blackmailer. Assuming that Denise knew that Parker had in fact not committed acts that would be punishable by the criminal law as blackmail, may Parker recover?

Not sure ☐

139. Same facts as in the previous question. Now, however, assume that after Denise's statement calling Parker a blackmailer, another director, Dan, stood up and said, "I agree with Denise. Anyway, I've watched Parker's behavior for a number of years, and I think he's a thief, so let's expel him from the board." Assuming that Parker is able to demonstrate that he has not engaged in any conduct that would be punishable as theft, embezzlement, larceny, etc., by the criminal law, may Parker recover for slander against Dan? (Assume that Dan's mental state is not at issue in the case.)

Not sure ☐

140. At a birthday party to celebrate the second birthday of Tommy, Deborah said to Anna, "Did you know that Polly [Tommy's mother] did not marry Tommy's father until a year and a half ago?" Only Anna and Polly heard the remark. The remark happened not to be true, and anyway, Anna did not believe it. Polly was terribly upset by the false accusation, and suffered feelings of rage and several sleepless nights. However, she suffered no other loss, and no financial loss. Polly has sued Deborah for defamation. Assuming that Deborah knew the remark was false when she made it, may Polly recover?

Not sure ☐

141. Same facts as in the previous question. Now, however, assume that Anna, although she did not believe Deborah's statement, said to Barbara, "According to Deborah, Polly gave birth to Tommy before she married Tommy's father." Polly overheard this statement and became even more upset. If Polly brings a defamation action against Anna, may she recover?

Not sure ☐

142. *American Inquisition* magazine published a news article about Paul Prude, a famous TV talk show host. The article said that Prude was a vengeful man who once kept actor Xavier Tiger off his program for ten years because Prude thought (falsely) that Tiger had leered at Prude's wife. The *Inquisition*'s source for this news item was Stan, a servant of Prude. Ed, the editor of the *Inquisition*, knew that Stan was a crack addict and that the money the *Inquisition* was paying him was important to Stan so that he could maintain his drug habit. A journalist of average professionalism would not have believed Stan's report. Ed, however, was an unusually credulous sort, who in fact believed Stan implicitly. Prude has brought a libel action against the *Inquisition*, in which he has proved decisively that he never tried to keep Tiger off his show. May Prude recover?

Not sure ☐

143. Newspaper, a local paper in the town of Chippewa, publishes an column called "Police Blotter" in every day's paper. The "Blotter" purports to be a reprinting of crimes handled by the local police (and listed on the police department's blotter) the previous day. In one edition, the "Blotter" column said, "John Smith was charged by the police with a burglary at 123 Main Street, at the home of John Brown." In fact, this item was not taken from the blotter, but was the result of a conversation between the cub reporter on the police beat and Officer Flatfoot of the Chippewa Police Department. Because the reporter was inexperienced and tired, the article as printed reversed the names—it was really John Brown who was charged with a burglary at the home of John Smith at 123 Main. A reporter of average professional standards would have read his notes back to Flatfoot before leaving the police department, but the cub reporter did not know to do this. Neither the reporter nor Newspaper or any of its other employees knew that the item printed was false. John Smith, a local resident of no special prominence, has brought a libel action against Newspaper. May he recover?

144. Same facts as in the previous question. Now, however, assume that the source for the newspaper story was not the words of Officer Flatfoot, but an official entry in the police blotter stating (correctly) that Brown was arrested for the burglary at Smith's premises. Once again, Newspaper blew the story by getting Brown's and Smith's names switched, so that Smith was reported to have been arrested for a burglary at Brown's place. May Smith recover for libel against Newspaper?

145. Cashier had worked for Anvil Bank for ten years. He was then fired due to the bank's desire to reduce expenses and return to profitability. Cashier next landed a job with Bigelow Bank. Denise, who was a fellow employee of Cashier's at Anvil, believed that the banking world should be run more efficiently. She therefore wrote an anonymous letter to the president of Bigelow, stating, "You really should think twice about keeping Cashier on your payroll. He was fired from Anvil for consistently taking a one-hour lunch period instead of the allowed half-hour." Denise believed that her statement was a correct one; however, if she had used reasonable care she would have discovered that even though Cashier did take longer lunches, this had nothing to do with his firing (which was purely for financial reasons and was based on relative seniority). The president disregarded Denise's letter. Cashier discovered that Denise sent the letter and has sued Denise for libel. Denise defends on the grounds that she was privileged to make the statement she made. Is Denise's assertion correct?

146. Same basic fact pattern as in the previous question. Now, however, assume that the president of Bigelow Bank, after hearing some disquieting rumors about Cashier's efficiency and honesty, telephoned Dorothy, whom he knew to be the personnel director of Anvil Bank, and asked her why Cashier was fired. Dorothy responded, "As I recall, there were rumors that Cashier was a cocaine addict. We were never able to prove anything, but we decided to be safe rather than sorry." Dorothy fully believed the statement she made to the president of Bigelow, but her memory had played tricks on her—she was actually thinking of a similar incident involving Teller, not Cashier (who was really fired for plain old reasons of efficiency and seniority). A reasonably careful person in Dorothy's position would have checked the personnel records before making the statement she made. Cashier has sued Dorothy for slander. Dorothy defends on the grounds that she was privileged. Is Dorothy's assertion correct?

147. Dogged, a notorious paparazzo, makes his living photographing celebrities (usually against their will) and selling the photographs to magazines. Peggy Pulchritudinous, a famous movie star, hated publicity, and especially hated to be photographed. Rumors had spread that Peggy, while still married, was carrying on an affair with one of her costars, Siegfried Sensitive. Each night for a week, Peggy and Siegfried went for an evening stroll, sat on their favorite park bench, and had a cup of coffee at a sidewalk cafe. Each of those nights, Dogged snapped at least one picture of the couple doing this, although they asked him to stop. Dogged then caused two of the pictures showing the couple holding hands (one while they were walking down the street, the other while they were sitting at the cafe) to be published in a national magazine. Peggy wishes to bring a tort action against Dogged. Is there any claim she can make successfully, and if so, what?

Not sure ☐

148. Same basic facts as in the previous question. Now, however, assume that Dogged paid $1,000 to Butler, Siegfried's ex-servant. In return, Siegfried told Dogged that Peggy and Siegfried had indeed been having an adulterous affair, and that the couple was insatiable, often having sex three or four times a day. Dogged caused these assertions (which were true) to be published in a magazine. Peggy has sued Dogged for invasion of privacy. May she recover? If so, for what form of invasion?

Not sure ☐

149. Merchant sold goods to Customer in return for a check written by Customer. The check was returned to Merchant due to insufficient funds. Merchant called Customer's bank to find out what the explanation was, and was told by a bank employee, "Yeah, that's the third check this month that we had to return on Customer's account due to insufficient funds." Merchant asked Customer to pay him cash representing the amount of the check. Customer refused. Merchant then said, "If you don't pay up immediately, I'm going to go to the district attorney." Customer still did not pay. Merchant went to the district attorney, showed him the check, and requested that the DA institute bad-check charges. Merchant did this not because he wanted to see Customer brought to justice, but because he figured that with a criminal charge pending, Customer would be more inclined to reimburse Merchant. The DA brought charges but later dropped them because of the small amount involved and the heavy caseload of his office.

Customer has sued Merchant for malicious prosecution. Customer shows at the trial that at the time he wrote the check to Merchant, he honestly believed he had enough money in his account. (State law defines the crime of bad-check writing to include only those checks written with knowledge that there are insufficient funds.) Will Customer recover against Merchant?

Not sure ☐

150. Slimy, who was poor but shrewd, realized that there was money to be made by being a tort plaintiff. He rode his bicycle next to a car driven by Tycoon, and then fell, pretending to have been hit by Tycoon's car. Claiming whiplash plus other neurological injuries, Slimy sued Tycoon for $1 million. After the case had been pending for six months, Tycoon learned that due to the prevalence of drug cases and the lack of enough judges, the case would not be tried for at least another four years. Tycoon then sued Slimy for wrongful civil proceedings. At this trial (which happened quickly, because it was not a jury case), Tycoon showed by clear evidence that Slimy knew the accident was phony, and was just bringing a "strike suit" that he was willing to settle for $20,000 (less than the cost to Tycoon of defending the suit). Will Tycoon win his wrongful civil proceedings suit?

Not sure ☐

151. Employee, who worked for Employer, injured his back while on the job. Doctor, who worked for Employer, examined Employee. Employer had previously instructed Doctor to keep Employer's workers compensation premiums low by certifying as often as possible that a worker who claimed an on-the-job injury was not in fact injured. Doctor wrote up a report stating that Employee had not been injured. Doctor did so knowing that the report was false, and knowing that it would probably result in a denial of workers compensation benefits to Employee. The insurance company indeed denied such benefits to Employee. Employee has sued Doctor for the lost benefits. May he recover, and if so, on what theory?

Not sure ☐

152. The management of Target Co., a medium-sized oil company, signed a contract with Suitor Co., another oil company, for Suitor to acquire Target for $100 per share. Shortly before the closing, Monster Co., an even bigger oil company, knowing of the Target-Suitor agreement, offered $115 per share for Target. Target's management decided that it was required by its duty to its shareholders to accept the higher offer, and did so. Assuming that Target was really "worth" $115 per share, can Suitor Co. recover $15 per Target share from Monster Co. (Suitor's "benefit of its bargain"), and if so, on what theory?

Not sure ☐

153. Abel Computer Corp. and Baker Computer Corp. were competitors. Baker learned that Abel was about to sign a large contract with Customer, a deal that Abel had been working on for two years. Because Customer was an unusually prestigious account and would provide a good reference, Baker offered Customer a contract for equipment similar to that being proposed by Abel, but at a price that was 20 percent lower; in fact, Baker's price was so low that Baker knew it would lose money on the deal. Customer accepted Baker's offer. Can Abel recover anything from Baker, and if so, on what theory?

Not sure ☐

154. Same facts as in the previous question. Now, however, assume that the reason that Baker offered the below-cost deal to Customer was that Baker's president hated Abel's president because Abel's president had married Baker's girlfriend. Therefore, Baker's president would do anything he could to ruin Abel's president, even if it caused Baker great loss. Does this change the result in a suit brought by Abel against Baker?

Not sure ☐

155. Tina, who was 13 years old, was unhappy living with her father, Pascal (her mother was dead). She felt that although Pascal did not in any way abuse her, he spent very little time with her and was emotionally distant. Therefore, she ran away. While away, she met several members of the Sunnies, a cult devoted to the teachings of the Reverend Sun. The Sunnies convinced Tina that she would be happier with them, and that her father was not worthy of being with her. Pascal located Tina after a year, and requested that she return home. She refused. Does Pascal have any action against the Sunnies, and if so, for what?

Not sure ☐

156. Same basic facts as in the previous question. Now, however, assume that Tina's mother, Doris, is not dead but is divorced from Pascal. Doris induced Tina to leave Pascal, move to Paris (where Doris now lives), and live with Doris. There is no custody decree outstanding. Can Pascal recover against Doris?

Not sure ☐

Torts Answers to Short-Answer Questions

1. Battery. **Battery is the intentional infliction of a harmful or offensive bodily contact. Here, the contact by the piece of bullet casing against Frank's cheek was certainly a "harmful contact," even though it was not a very serious one. The nub of the question relates to** *intent*. **The intent to cause the harmful or offensive contact will of course qualify. Alternatively, the intent to commit an** *assault* **will meet the intent requirement for battery if a harmful or offensive contact actually results.** Jerry intended to commit an assault, since he intended to put Frank in apprehension of an immediate bodily contact (clearly he intended that when Frank heard the blank go off, Frank would believe that a bullet was simultaneously hitting him). This intent to commit assault will also supply the intent required for battery.

2. Assault. **Jerry has intentionally put Frank in apprehension of a harmful or offensive contact.** That is, he has intentionally created in Frank the belief (however short-lived it was) that a bullet would or might hit him. The fact that Jerry intended no harm, and regarded Frank as a close friend, is irrelevant—since he intended to make Frank fear a harmful or offensive bodily contact, that's all that is required for the intent in assault.

3. Battery. **Battery is the intentional causing of either a harmful or** *offensive* **contact.** Here, the splashing of dirty water would definitely be offensive to a reasonable person in Pedestrian's position, so Driver has committed battery even though no bodily harm resulted.

4. None. **For battery or assault, the defendant must either intend to bring about the harmful/offensive contact, or at least know with substantial certainty that the contact will occur.** The mere expectation that the contact will occur, so long as it is not a substantial certainty, is not enough to constitute the requisite intent.

5. Battery. **The fondling was an offensive touching, even though Patient was not aware of it at the time. See Rest. 2d, §18.**

6. None. **In particular, there is no assault. Assault requires that the plaintiff be put in imminent apprehension of a harmful or offensive contact. See Rest. 2d, §22.** Even though Dexter desired to create such apprehension in Paul (so that Dexter had the requisite intent for assault), Paul was not in fact put in such apprehension. The fact that Paul became scared or angry after the fact is irrelevant.

7. No. **A person may recover for assault only if he or she is put in apprehension of a harmful or offensive contact** *with his or her own body*, **not the body of another, even a close relative. See Rest. 2d, §26.**

8. False imprisonment. **A private citizen who merely makes a complaint to the police will not be liable for false imprisonment. But a citizen who goes further, and urges that the arrest be made (rather than merely giving the police the information and letting them decide what to do with it), will be liable for false imprisonment if the arrest itself is unlawful.** Here, the arrest itself by the police officer was unlawful (because the police officer did not have enough information to constitute probable cause to believe that Paula had committed a felony); therefore, Detective is liable for false imprisonment for actively helping to bring about that arrest. (A merchant's privilege of detention to make reasonable investigation applies only where the merchant's suspicion of shoplifting is a *reasonable* one.)

9. Intentional infliction of emotional distress, against both Timid and Tina. **Hulk's conduct was "extreme and outrageous," and he intentionally caused severe emotional distress to Timid (indeed, that was the purpose of his visit). Since Hulk knew that Tina was present, he is also liable for Tina's distress, since she is a member of Timid's immediate family.** At least under the Restatement view, Hulk is liable even if Timid and Tina did not suffer bodily harm, so long as they suffered severe mental distress. See Rest. 2d, §46(1) and §46(2)(a). (Interestingly, Hulk's conduct does *not* constitute assault. The reason is that Hulk did not put Timid or Tina in apprehension of an *imminent* harmful or offensive contact—the threatened contact was not to take place until next week.)

10. No. **Trespass exists only where the entry on land is intentional, negligent, or abnormally dangerous.** Here, although an instrument under Pilot's control (the plane) entered owner's property, this did not happen as the result of any intent or negligence by Pilot. Also, flying (at least of the routine, rather than test-piloting, variety) is sufficiently common today that it is very unlikely to be considered "abnormally dangerous." Therefore, the entry of the plane onto Owner's land would be found to be "accidental," and thus does not constitute trespass.

11. Yes. **An owner's ownership rights include the right to exclusive possession of the space immediately above his or her land.** (Airplane flights above federally prescribed minimum altitudes are usually not considered trespass, but this is because they are beyond the "immediate reaches" of the plaintiff's land.) Therefore, Cable Co. has trespassed on Peter's property even though it has not touched his land. Also, the fact that no physical harm or loss of economic value has been caused to Peter is irrelevant: A trespass can occur even in the absence of actual harm, and Peter would be entitled to collect nominal damages.

12. Trespass to chattels. **When Maven took the car on the joyride, he actually deprived Owner of possession for a brief time. This loss of possession is deemed to be "actual harm," and thus constitutes the tort of trespass to chattels, even if the physical condition of the car is not damaged.** Had Maven merely touched or leaned on the car, this would not have constituted trespass to chattels, unless there was some harm done to the physical condition of the car. Maven would have to pay damages representing the value of use of the car for the brief time (probably a nominal amount).

13. Conversion. **The tort of conversion occurs when the defendant so substantially interferes with the plaintiff's possession or ownership of the property that it is fair to require the defendant to pay the property's full value.** APS intentionally gave dominion over the watch to Neighbor rather than to Owner. The fact that this was due to APS's mistake about who should receive the package is irrelevant.

14. Probably trespass to chattels, but not conversion. **Conversion exists only where the owner's rights are so seriously interfered with that it is fair to make the defendant pay the chattel's full value. Here, the one-day interference with Owner's right to use or possess the watch is not sufficiently great. See Rest. 2d, §222A, Illustr. 9 & 10. On the other hand, the deprivation of use is probably great enough that the tort of trespass to chattels has been committed.** If so, APS would have to pay Owner the value of one day's use of the watch (compared with having to pay the entire value of the watch, as it would on the facts of the prior question).

15. No. **A patient will be deemed as a matter of law to have consented if all the following conditions are met: (1) the patient was unable to give consent (as where he or she was under anesthesia), (2) the action was necessary to save his or her life or safeguard his or her health, (3) the defendant did not know that the patient would refuse to consent if conscious, and (4) a reasonable person**

would have consented in the circumstances. Here, these conditions were all satisfied, so Patient is deemed to have consented. The fact that in reality Patient was idiosyncratic—and would not have consented if given the choice—is irrelevant, since Surgeon had no way of knowing this. (But if Surgeon *knew* of this strong desire on the part of Patient not to have cancerous growths removed, and Surgeon went ahead anyway, this would be battery.)

16. Yes. **Since there was no serious threat to Patient's life or health, Surgeon's extension of the operation to include tonsil removal amounted to a battery—that is, an unauthorized offensive touching.**

17. No. **A person may use deadly force in self-defense if he or she believes that he or she is in danger of death or serious bodily harm. See Rest. 2d, §65.** In the circumstances, Drug Lord reasonably believed that Scarecrow was about to kill or seriously wound him. Therefore, Drug Lord had a privilege to use self-defense if it seemed under the circumstances that he could not obtain his safety in any other way (e.g., by retreating). On the facts as known to Drug Lord, retreat would not have reasonably seemed to be a successful strategy. The fact that Scarecrow was actually a police officer who did not intend serious bodily harm is irrelevant—what matters is the reasonableness and genuineness of Drug Lord's belief that he was in imminent peril. Therefore, Drug Lord has a privilege of self-defense.

18. Yes, at least according to the Restatement and modern views. **These authorities say that rather than using deadly force, a person must retreat if he or she is attacked outside of his or her dwelling and could retreat safely. See Rest. 2d, §65(2).**

19. No. **Even under the Restatement and in those courts generally requiring retreat instead of use of deadly force, a person has no obligation to retreat within his or her own dwelling.** (There is an exception to this exception if the attacker is also a resident of the dwelling. If Peter and Dan had been roommates, Dan would have had the obligation to retreat rather than use his knife, if he could have done so safely.)

20. No, according to the Restatement and most courts. **A property owner is privileged to use deadly force to prevent certain felonies, namely those involving death, serious bodily harm, or the burglary of a dwelling place, if lesser force will not suffice. Rest. 2d, §143(2). Since a homeowner may prevent a burglary directly by the use of deadly force (if lesser force will not suffice), he or she may do the same thing by indirect mechanical means such as a spring gun. Rest. 2d, §85.** (The court that decided the landmark case of *Katko v. Briney*, 183 N.W.2d 657 (Iowa 1971), would presumably answer yes to this question, since that court, like a minority of other courts, allowed the use of deadly force only to prevent violent felonies, and did not recognize burglary as a violent felony. Also, observe that the question posed is different from the fact pattern in *Katko*, in that here the structure was a "dwelling," whereas the farmhouse in *Katko* was boarded up and therefore not a dwelling—so under the Restatement test, the use of deadly force is allowable on the facts of our question even though not allowable on the facts of *Katko*.)

21. Yes. **A property owner (here, Master) has a privilege to use reasonable force to recapture a chattel that has been wrongfully taken from him or her, provided that the owner (1) acts in a timely manner, (2) first makes a request for the return (unless this would be dangerous or clearly futile), and (3) uses no force greater than seems reasonably necessary to effect the recapture.** However, unlike the privilege of self-defense or the right to defend possession of one's land or chattels, the privilege to regain possession of a chattel *never* entitles the owner to use *deadly force*. Here, Master's use of the knife clearly constituted deadly force. Therefore, Master exceeded the scope of the privilege, and since he initiated the scuffle he is liable for battery.

22. Yes. **Unlike the privilege of self-defense or the privilege of defending one's possession of one's land or chattels, a privilege to regain possession of a chattel does *not* exist where the owner makes a reasonable *mistake* about whether the goods really belong to him or her.** Therefore, even though on these facts Master avoided the use of deadly force, he still had no privilege and is therefore liable for battery.

23. No. **Most courts (and the Restatement) recognize a privilege on the part of a merchant who *reasonably* suspects shoplifting to detain the suspect for the length of time reasonably needed to conduct an investigation.** Since Clerk's suspicions were reasonable here, and since the length and scope of the investigation were also reasonable in the circumstances, the privilege applies, so there is no false imprisonment even though Clerk was in fact mistaken.

24. No. **Under the doctrine of *"private necessity,"* a person has a privilege to enter another's property if this is necessary to protect himself or herself (or another) from serious harm. See Rest. 2d, §197, Illustr. 3.** This privilege constitutes a complete defense to Farmer's trespass action.

25. Yes. **Although a person has a privilege to enter another's land to protect himself or herself from serious harm, the person must pay for any damage caused.**

26. Yes, probably. **Pilot had a "private necessity" privilege to be on the land, and Farmer could not directly cause physical harm to Pilot for exercising that privilege.** So long as Farmer's act is found to have been the proximate cause of Pilot's collision, Farmer will be liable.

27. Yes. **As the result of *Tennessee v. Garner*, 471 U.S. 1 (1985), the Fourth Amendment prevents police from using deadly force to apprehend even a fleeing felon, unless the officer has probable cause to believe that the suspect poses a significant threat of death or serious physical injury to the officer or to others.** Here, there was no such probable cause. Also, the fact that Officer aimed at the leg did not stop his shooting from constituting deadly force—deadly force is force that is either intended to, or reasonably likely to, result in death or serious bodily harm, and shooting a running person almost certainly qualifies even when the bullet is aimed at a nonvital area.

28. No, probably. **Officer had the right to use deadly force so long as he believed that the fleeing felony suspect posed a significant threat of death or serious physical injury to others.** There is a sufficiently great chance that a rapist will commit the same crime again, that this probably qualifies for deadly force. The fact that Officer was mistaken as to Suspect's identity will not deprive Officer of the defense that he used force in making an arrest, so long as Officer had probable cause to believe that there really had been a violent felony and that Suspect was the one who did it (and probable cause seems to exist on these facts).

29. Yes, probably. **Where a defendant has a physical disability, the standard for negligence is what a reasonable person with that physical disability would have done. See Rest. 2d, §283C; Rest. 3d (Liab. For Phys. Harm) (Prop. Fin. Dr. #1) §11(a).** A person who has a sudden, first-ever epileptic seizure will clearly not be deemed negligent for, say, losing control of his or her car during the seizure. But Driver knew that he was subject to such seizures. Even if his dropping the medication was not itself negligence (let us assume that this is the case), it was still probably a lack of reasonable care for Driver to drive to the drugstore unmedicated, rather than have someone else get the drug for him.

30. Yes. **Normally, a minor is held merely to the standard of care that would be manifested by a reasonable child of similar "age, intelligence, and experience." But if the child engages in an activity that is normally undertaken only by adults, and for which adult qualifications are required, then the child is held to an adult standard of care. See Rest. 3d (Liab. For Phys. Harm) (Prop. Fin. Dr.**

#1) §10(c). Piloting a large motorboat is almost certainly such an adult activity, so Teen will be held to adult standards, and by those standards is negligent.

31. **(a)** Yes. **The question is always what a reasonable person in Trucker's position would have done.** Evidence that a new safety device was available would certainly be admissible as evidence on whether Trucker was behaving reasonably in choosing not to install the device.

    (b) Yes. **Conversely, the "custom" in an industry is always admissible as tending to show that a person who followed that custom was acting reasonably.**

    (c) Yes. **Neither the availability of a new safety device not used by the defendant, nor the fact that the defendant was following industry customs, will be dispositive on the issue of negligence.** On these facts, a reasonable jury could go either way—by finding that it was not reasonable for Trucker to decline to use an available safety device, or by finding that the lack of widespread adoption of the device meant that a reasonable trucker could decline to use it.

32. Yes. **Generally, a defendant may be required to anticipate the negligence of others if the likelihood of injury is great. See Rest. 2d, §290.** Here, a reasonable person in Owner's position would have declined to lend his car to one who not only was without a license but also had lost the license for recklessness.

33. No. **Violation of a statute will only constitute negligence per se when (among other requirements) the *type of harm* that actually occurs is the type of harm that the statute is intended to protect against.** Here, the statute was intended to protect against people or animals being hit by trains, not their eating poisonous plants near the tracks. Therefore, Child will have to rely on other evidence, apart from the statutory violation, to show that Railroad violated its duty of care.

34. No. **The court is always free to find that, for purposes of a negligence suit, the defendant's failure to comply with the statute was *excused*. See Rest. 3d (Liab. for Phys. Harm) (Prop. Fin. Dr. #1) §15.** Courts do so for a variety of reasons, including the defendant's inability after reasonable diligence to comply. (The sole exception is where the court interprets the statute itself as not permitting such an excuse, but there is no evidence of this here.) Since Owner made reasonable attempts to comply, his violation will be excused, and that violation therefore will not constitute negligence per se.

35. No, probably. **A state or federal safety statute will generally be construed to establish merely a *minimum* standard. If in the particular circumstances a reasonable person would adopt additional precautions, then failure to so adopt can be negligence.** (Occasionally, a federal enactment will be found to have been intended to "preempt" state law as to what constitutes reasonable safety or warnings—as is the case with cigarette labeling—but a general statute saying that all poisons must be marked as such would probably not be held to have been intended as preemptive.) Since a jury could properly find that a reasonably careful manufacturer of an exceptionally dangerous poison would adopt additional safeguards (e.g., a childproof cap), Child's case will be permitted to go to the jury.

36. **(c). The doctrine of *res ipsa loquitur* allows the plaintiff to point to the fact of the accident, and to create an inference that, even without a precise showing of how the defendant behaved, the defendant was probably negligent. See Rest. 2d, §328D, Illustr. 3.** This situation is an appropriate one for application of *res ipsa loquitur*: A plane does not normally crash in clear weather except through the negligence of someone, the airplane was in the exclusive control of Airline at the time it crashed, and Passenger himself was almost certainly not at fault. However, in most courts, even if *res ipsa* applies, it does not *require* an inference of negligence. Rather, the doctrine merely *permits* an inference of negligence; that is, the doctrine allows the plaintiff to be deemed to have met his burden

of production, thus entitling him to get to the jury. Therefore, the judge should send the case to the jury and let the jury decide whether it is more probable than not that the crash was caused by Airline's negligence.

37. (c). **Even though the defendant comes up with evidence tending to show his or her own due care, this will not be enough to entitle him or her to a directed verdict. Once P shows that the requirements for *res ipsa* are satisfied, he is entitled to get to the jury no matter what evidence of due care D comes up with** (provided that D's evidence does not conclusively show that the requirements for *res ipsa* are not satisfied, as would be the case if Airline were able to show that an armed hijacker had boarded the airplane and wrested control from the pilot).

38. No. **For Farmer to recover against City, he must show not only that City was negligent but also that City was the cause in fact, or "but-for" cause, of the damage to him.** On these facts, even if City had constructed a properly high dam (one that could withstand 30 inches of rainfall during a season), there still would have been 10 inches of extra rainfall that would have flowed over the top of the dam. Since these 10 inches would have produced substantially the same damage to Farmer as the 15 inches did, City's negligent construction of too low a dam was not the cause of Farmer's damage, so he cannot recover.

39. (b) 100. **If the plaintiff suffers two distinct harms (here, two different pens, the inhabitants of which are killed) and two different causes (here, the City's negligence plus the unprecedentedly heavy rainfall), the court will attempt to apportion damages between the distinct harm and the distinct causes.** If City had not behaved negligently (i.e., had constructed a dam that would handle up to a 30-inch rainy season), the actual heavy rainfall would have led to 5 inches less of rain in each pen than there really was (i.e., there would have been 5 inches in one pen and 10 inches in the other pen). In that event, the mink in the first pen would have been spared, but the second would not have been. Therefore, Farmer may recover only for the mink in the first pen, since it is only that pen that City's negligence was the "but for" cause of the deaths.

40. (a) Both liable. **When the conduct of two or more defendants is tortious, and plaintiff proves that the harm to him or her has been caused by only one of them, but he or she cannot prove which one, the burden is on each of the defendants to prove that he or she did not cause the harm. See Rest. 2d, §433B, Illustr. 11.** The fact that Baker and Carr were each tailgating the car in front of him establishes that they were each negligent. Abel has certainly proved that the damage resulted from the negligence of either Baker or Carr. Therefore, the burden was placed on Baker and Carr each to show that his negligence was not the cause in fact of Abel's injury—since neither carried this burden, each is liable for the full amount of Abel's injuries (though of course he may not have a double recovery, so that if he recovers the full amount of his injuries from Baker, he may not recover from Carr, and vice versa).

41. No. **Even though Driver was negligent in parking in front of the hydrant, he will only be liable for those consequences that were of a *type* the *risk of which* made Driver's conduct negligent.** What makes parking in front of a hydrant negligent is that fire engines may not be able to get water to put out fires; parking in front of a hydrant does not increase the risk that some other driver will collide with one's own car (since such collisions are equally likely to occur whether there is a hydrant on the sidewalk or not). Because the presence of the hydrant did not increase the risk of such a collision, a court would hold that Driver's negligence was not the proximate cause (or "legal cause") of Passenger's injuries.

42. Yes. ***"Danger invites rescue"*—a person who behaves negligently is liable for injuries to one who attempts a rescue, unless the rescue takes place in a grossly negligent or totally bizarre manner.**

See Rest. 2d, §445, Illustr. 4. It was quite foreseeable that someone might attempt to rescue Trucker from this type of accident, so Trucker's negligence in causing the accident is the proximate cause of injury to the rescuer.

43. Yes. **As a general rule, a tortfeasor *"takes his victim as he finds him."* That is, if the defendant negligently causes an injury to the plaintiff, the defendant is liable for the *full consequences* of that injury even though an unknown and/or rare medical condition of the plaintiff makes the injury much worse than it would ordinarily have been. See Rest. 2d, §461, and Illustr. 2 thereto.**

44. Yes. **A defendant who behaves negligently will be liable for additional damage caused by foreseeable rescue efforts, even if these rescue efforts were themselves conducted with negligence.** It is foreseeable that ambulance drivers will sometimes travel too fast and get in accidents, so Dan's negligence was the proximate or "legal" cause of Patrick's death. (But the result would be different if the ambulance driver behaved in a totally bizarre, unforeseeable, and dangerous manner. For instance, if the driver knew that Patrick had sustained only mild non-life-threatening injuries that could wait half an hour for medical attention, and the driver travelled at 80 mph in a 25 mph zone to shorten the trip from ten minutes to three minutes, Dan would not have been liable for Patrick's death in the resulting ambulance crash.)

45. No. **The original tortfeasor (Dan) is liable for any additional injuries that arise out of third persons' (including doctors' and nurses') efforts to help the victim. But the original tortfeasor is not liable for injuries that are unconnected with assistance efforts, even if these other injuries would not have come about except for the initial tort. See Rest. 2d, §457, Illustr. 5.** The stabbing by Nurse was not part of an effort (negligent or otherwise) to render medical assistance to Patrick, so Dan is not the proximate or legal cause of that stabbing, and is not liable for it. (The estate could try to recover against the hospital instead, on a theory of *respondeat superior*. But the estate would probably lose here, too, since an employer is generally not liable for intentional torts by employees motivated solely by personal concerns.)

46. No, probably. **A court would probably hold that Abel's refusal to cooperate in having the defect repaired for free was a *superseding cause*, making Carmaker's initial sale of the defective car no longer the proximate cause of Babcock's accident. See Rest. 2d, §452, Illustr. 10.** The fact that both Carmaker and Dealer made every reasonable effort to cure the problem, and the lapse of time between their efforts and the accident, would probably lead a court to conclude that the risk and responsibility for the defective latch had *shifted* to Abel. (In fact, Babcock would probably be able to recover against Abel for negligence.)

47. Yes. **Both Aggressive and Careless were proximate and "but for" causes of the injury to Bystander. Therefore, they are jointly and severally liable for the damage to Bystander. (The joint-and-several rule applies only where the harm is not capable of apportionment, and a single injury or death is never apportioned.) Because of the joint-and-several liability, Bystander may get a judgment (and collect it) against either Aggressive alone, Careless alone, or both. (However, Bystander may only collect a single time.) See Rest. 2d, §879, and Illustr. 2 thereto. If Bystander collects the full judgment against Aggressive, Aggressive will be entitled to contribution from Careless.**

48. No. **Careless is not the (or even a) cause in fact of the fractured skull—even if Careless had never come on the scene, Bystander would still have suffered that fractured skull. Therefore, Bystander may recover for all of his injuries (skull plus leg) from Aggressive, since Aggressive**

was both a "but for" and proximate cause of these injuries, but he may recover only for the lost leg from Careless. See Rest. 2d, §433A, Illustr. 2.

49. **$60,000. Where two tortfeasors (acting independently) cause similar damage to a single plaintiff, the court will attempt to *apportion* the harm if there is a reasonable basis for doing so. See Rest. 2d, §433A, Illustr. 5.** Here, the court can plausibly say that each of the tortfeasors has damaged Farmer's land in proportion to the amount of mercury that that tortfeasor has released. Therefore, Factory will not have to pay for the full damage. (Contrast this situation with that of a personal injury or death—a single personal injury or a death is never apportioned, so each tortfeasor is jointly and severally liable for the entire injury or the death.)

50. **No. A tortfeasor who intentionally caused the harm has no right, in most states, to recover contribution from his or her fellow tortfeasor (even if the latter also intentionally caused the harm). See Rest. 2d, §886A(3).**

51. **Split of authority. Some courts would apply the traditional rule—they would allow Perry to collect $90,000 from Dexter, and would allow Dexter to recover $40,000 from Darwin (so that Dexter and Darwin each end up paying half of the total damages). The modern trend is that the nonsettling defendants who are found liable are not permitted to get contribution against the previously settling defendant, but the plaintiff's recovery against the nonsettling defendants is reduced to account for the prior settlement. See Rest. 3d (Apport.) §23.**

52. **Yes. A retailer who is held strictly liable for selling a defective injury-causing product will get indemnity from others further up the distribution chain, including the manufacturer. See Rest. 3d (Apport.) §22(a)(2)(ii).**

53. **No. As a general rule, a person simply has *no general duty to act*—even if the defendant could prevent serious injury to another at little or no effort or risk, he or she will nonetheless not be liable for failing to act.** (But there are a number of exceptions, such as where there is a special relationship between plaintiff and defendant, or where defendant has begun to act.)

54. **Yes. It is true that as a general rule, a person has no duty to act. However, if the defendant endangers or harms the plaintiff, even if he or she does so completely innocently, he or she must render assistance or warning when he or she discovers the problem. See Rest. 3d (Liab. for Phys. Harm) (Prop. Fin. Dr. #1) §39.** Even though Xerxes was entirely blameless in the original collision, once the collision occurred, Xerxes then had a duty to take reasonable affirmative steps to minimize additional harm to Paul. Therefore, Xerxes is liable for the worsening in Paul's condition to the extent that this could have been prevented by prompt medical attention; thus Paul's estate will be able to recover the difference between his injured-but-not-dead condition and his death.

55. **Yes. Even though Terry had no duty to stop and render assistance to Paul, once he did begin to render assistance, he had an obligation to render that aid with reasonable care.** Since Terry's negligence in rendering that assistance increased the risk to Paul, Terry is liable for the resulting harm.

56. **Yes. Once Terry made his promise to render assistance, he was required to fulfill the promise with reasonable care. See Cf. Rest. 3d (Liab. for Phys. Harm) (Prop. Fin. Dr. #1) §42, Illustr. 3.**

57. **Yes. If the defendant's negligence has caused a physical impact with the plaintiff's person, the defendant is liable not only for the physical consequences of that impact but also all the emotional or mental suffering that flows naturally from it.** Thus Patricia, like any physically injured negligence plaintiff, may recover for "mental suffering"—these mental damages are said to be "parasitic" ones (i.e., ones that attach to the physical injury).

58. Yes. A plaintiff can generally recover when he or she suffers fear for his or her own safety, if this fear leads to physical consequences. Here, Patricia can point to her ulcer.

59. No. **Nearly all courts hold that unless the emotional distress produces "physical illness," there can be no recovery for that emotional harm in the absence of impact. See Rest. 2d, §436A.** The occasional sleepless night and the dizziness would not qualify as physical illness.

60. Split of authority. **The Restatement would not allow Patricia to recover since Patricia was never in the "zone of danger" (i.e., she was never subject to a risk of physical harm through nonemotional means). See Rest. 2d, §436. But a substantial number of states, including California, have abandoned the "zone of danger" requirement, and would allow Patricia to recover, since she suffered physical illness as the result of Doug's negligence.**

61. No. **Where the plaintiff has not even witnessed the accident (let alone been in the zone of danger), probably few if any states would allow a recovery for physical harm (such as a miscarriage) that comes via emotional distress.**

62. Probably not, in most states. **The fact that she was a complete stranger who merely happened to be standing by would probably lead most courts to deny recovery, perhaps on the grounds that even the presence of physical illness does not give enough guarantees of genuineness (e.g., Zena might have suffered the miscarriage anyway, so that it wasn't really caused by her distress).** Zena was not within the zone of danger. If she had been closely related to Colin (e.g., his mother), she might nonetheless have been able to recover.

63. No. **A landowner has a duty to use due care to protect trespassing children under certain circumstances. However, one of the requirements for the imposition of such a duty is that the child, because of his or her youth, has not recognized the risk involved. See Rest. 2d, §339.** Peter understood or should have understood the risk to a nonswimmer of diving into a pool with no swimmer nearby for protection. Therefore, the special conditions for the duty to trespassing children do not apply, and Homeowner is not liable.

64. Unclear. **If the pond had been man-made, all the requirements for imposing on Homeowner a duty of reasonable care to trespassing children would be satisfied. (Homeowner knew or should have known of the likely trespass, Homeowner knew or should have known of the great danger, the child did not understand the risk because of her youth, the burden of fencing the pond was not great relative to the danger, and Homeowner failed to use reasonable care to eliminate the danger.) This is the doctrine of *"attractive nuisance."* However, courts are less quick to apply the doctrine where the condition is a naturally occurring one (as here) than where it is man-made. Probably most courts would not find liability on these facts. See Rest. 2d, §339.**

65. No. **Even where all of the conditions are satisfied for imposing on the landowner a duty to use reasonable care to protect trespassing children, the landowner has no affirmative duty to *inspect* his or her land to discover whether hazardous conditions exist; he or she merely has the duty to protect against such conditions if he or she knows or should know that they exist, and knows or should know of the danger to trespassing children. See Rest. 2d, §339, Comment h.**

66. No, in most courts. **Frank, as a social guest, was a *licensee*. As such, Farmer owed him the duty to warn him of dangers known to Farmer, but not the duty to inspect for previously unknown dangers. See Rest. 2d, §342, Comment d.** Since Farmer did not know of the mine shaft, his failure to guard against it or warn Frank about it did not violate any duty that Farmer owed Frank.

67. **Yes. Since Frank was a licensee, Farmer owed him the duty to warn him of dangers known to Farmer (even though he did not owe Frank any duty of inspection).**

68. **Yes. Harried was an invitee, since he was on the premises for business purposes. Therefore, Railway had the obligation to make the premises reasonably safe for him. See Rest. 2d, §343A, Illustr. 8.** While a warning may in many situations be enough to make the premises safe, here this was not the case—it was quite foreseeable that a patron might be running late, and would either not see or disregard the sign, especially where no safe alternative way was made available by Railway.

69. **(a) Peter only. Peter was an invitee, because he came to a public place for the purpose that the public place was held open. Paul, on the other hand, was merely a licensee, not an invitee, because although he came to a public place, he was not there for the purpose (reading or borrowing books) that the place was held open. Therefore, the city owed a duty of inspection only to Peter, not Paul, and it is therefore liable only for Peter's injuries. See Rest. 2d, §332, Illustr. 2.**

70. **No. The general rule is that the landowner owes no duty to a trespasser to make his or her land safe.** Vick was clearly a trespasser. Nor does Vick fall into any of the exceptions under which the owner may have a duty of care even to a trespasser (e.g., constant trespass on limited area, discovered trespasser, trespassing child, etc.). Therefore, the general rule applies here: Homemaker owed no duty to Vick, as trespasser, to make Homemaker's land safe for him or to warn him of dangers.

71. **No. A licensee is a person who has the owner's consent to be on the property, but is not there for a business purpose. For licensees, a landowner has no duty to inspect to find any hidden dangers.** At this point, Vick was a *licensee*. (By Homemaker's willingness to hear his introductory pitch, she upgraded Vick's status from trespasser to licensee—he had her permission to be there but was not yet really conducting business with her.) Therefore, Homemaker had a duty to warn Vick of dangers that Homemaker was aware of but not an affirmative duty to inspect her property.

72. **Yes. Once Vick was permitted in the house to make his demonstration, he became an *invitee*— that is, he was on the premises for a business purpose.** At that point, Homemaker had the obligation to use reasonable care to make the premises safe for Vick, including the obligation to make reasonable inspections and consequent repairs.

73. **No. Here, Vick was once again merely a licensee, not an invitee—he was no longer on the premises for business purposes, but was instead merely being accommodated in his need to use the bathroom. As a licensee, Homemaker owed Vick no duty of inspection and danger removal, merely the duty to warn him of dangers known to Homemaker (which this was not).**

74. **No. Most courts today hold that if a landlord agrees in a lease to perform repairs, he or she will be liable for personal injuries caused by his or her failure to perform the repairs in a reasonable manner. See Rest. 2d, §357.** However, such a clause is almost never held to impose on the Landlord the affirmative duty of inspecting the premises; the landlord must merely make those repairs the need for which he or she is put on notice. Since Landlord was not put on notice of the need to fix the crack in Tenant's ceiling, he has no liability.

75. **No. According to the "*collateral source rule*," no payment received by the plaintiff on account of his or her injuries (except for payments made by or on behalf of the defendant or by some other defendant) will reduce the amount of damages payable by the defendant.** Therefore, in a sense Pindar will end up being "ahead" by the $400 per month.

76. Split of authority. **At least a respectable minority of courts, if not a majority, would recognize a "*seat belt defense*" for Daewoo here. That is, they would hold that Pindar may not recover for the**

loss of earnings, since he could have avoided this loss by the use of reasonable care. Such a result is most likely in a contributory negligence jurisdiction, but might also be reached even in a comparative negligence jurisdiction, and even if the jury found that Pindar's negligence was much smaller than Daewoo's negligence.

77. No. **Contributory negligence is never recognized as a defense to an intentional tort.**

78. (a) Last clear chance. **By the doctrine of *"last clear chance,"* if the plaintiff is helpless to avoid his or her peril, and the defendant discovers that peril and negligently fails to avoid it, the defendant's subsequent negligence (his or her squandering of his or her last clear chance to avoid the accident) wipes out the effect of the plaintiff's contributory negligence.**

    (b) Yes. **Perry was helpless to avoid the peril (since he was unconscious), and Don knew of the peril and negligently failed to avoid it. So the last clear chance doctrine applies and wipes out the effect of Perry's negligence.**

79. No, in most courts. **In this "helpless plaintiff, inattentive defendant" situation, most courts apply the last clear chance doctrine, just as they do in the "helpless plaintiff, defendant discovers danger" situation covered by the prior question.**

80. Yes, most states. **The doctrine of last clear chance only applies where the defendant could, by the exercise of reasonable care at the time of the accident, have avoided it.** Here, however, nothing Don could reasonably have been expected to do *at or just before the time of the accident* would have avoided the collision. Don's "antecedent negligence" (i.e., his negligence in not maintaining the brakes during the weeks before) is irrelevant for this purpose—most courts would treat Don as not having had a last clear chance, so Perry's contributory negligence would bar him from recovery (since the jurisdiction follows the common law contributory negligence principle).

81. No. **This is a classic situation in which Jay's contributory negligence would completely bar him from recovery, even though his degree of fault is much less than that of Hard. Also, last clear chance does not apply, because virtually no courts apply the doctrine in this "inattentive plaintiff, inattentive defendant" situation.**

82. Split of authority. **Some states that have enacted comparative negligence statutes hold that this doctrine abolishes the need for the last clear chance doctrine, and that to retain it would merely give the plaintiff a windfall. (California falls into this group.) In these states, Speedy would be 70 percent liable. Other states maintain the last clear chance doctrine even after enacting comparative negligence, on the theory that the defendant's failure to use his last clear chance means that the plaintiff's comparative fault is not really the proximate cause of the accident. (In these states, Speedy would be 100 percent liable.) Probably states abolishing last clear chance as a consequence of comparative negligence are in the majority.**

83. Yes. **There is an exception to the general enforceability of express agreements to assume risk where the court concludes that there is some overriding public interest that demands that the court refuse to enforce the exculpatory clause.** Even if Dennis raises the defense of *express assumption of risk*, he will probably lose. This is because Dennis had greatly superior bargaining power—he was virtually the only available parking garage in the area at a time when Buff had essentially no choice but to use a parking garage, and in any event all neighborhood parking garages imposed the same limit. Therefore, the court would probably hold that the agreement on the receipt, whereby Buff expressly assumed the risk of negligence, should be treated as void as against public policy.

84. Yes. **Again, most courts would not enforce the limitation of liability on the back of the receipt.** This time, it would be because Buff did not, and a reasonable person in Buff's position would not realize that the receipt was in fact intended to be an express waiver of liability. That is, the waiver will only be effective if Dennis shows that Buff actually agreed to it, and the facts here indicate that he was not even aware of it.

85. No. **The defendants would be successful in asserting that Fan *assumed the risk*, and was thus barred from recovery. A plaintiff will be barred by the doctrine of implied assumption of risk if he or she understands a risk of harm to himself or herself, and nonetheless voluntarily chooses to accept that risk, assuming that no strong public policy forbids application of the doctrine. See Rest. 2d, §496C, Illustr. 4.** Fan understood the risk of foul balls, and voluntarily chose to expose himself to that danger (rather than either requesting a different seat or simply declining to attend the game). Also, probably no strong public policy prevents the application of the implied assumption of risk doctrine to foul ball dangers. Therefore, Fan would be barred from recovery.

86. Yes. **Swede will not be barred by the doctrine of implied assumption of risk because he did not truly understand the risk and therefore cannot be said to have voluntarily assumed it. See Rest. 2d, §496C, Illustr. 5.**

87. Yes. **Pedestrian will not be held to have assumed the risk of Doug's bad brakes, because it was Doug's own tortious conduct that left Pedestrian no reasonable alternative course but to accept Doug's offer of a ride. See Rest. 2d, §496E.**

88. No. **Here, Pedestrian has voluntarily assumed the risk of the bad brakes. Even though Pedestrian behaved quite reasonably, and in fact had no other reasonable alternative to accepting Samaritan's offer of a ride, Pedestrian will be deemed to have voluntarily accepted the risk, because the lack of alternatives was not due to Samaritan's tortious conduct. See Rest. 2d, §496E.**

89. Split of authority. **Some states would apply assumption of risk here just as they would if common law contributory negligence still applied. But other states, representing a growing trend (although not necessarily a majority), would hold that assumption of risk no longer exists as a separate doctrine, and that all that counts is whether the plaintiff was negligent.** Since Pedestrian was not negligent at all, these latter courts would presumably not only not bar him from recovery but also not even reduce his recovery at all.

90. Probably not. **First, if the state has maintained common law parent-child immunity, then there can clearly be no contribution. (A person can only be required to pay contribution if he or she could have been primarily liable to the original defendant; since Tina would be immune from a direct suit by Child, she cannot be required to give contribution to defray part of Driver's liability to Child.) If the state has abolished parent-child immunity, the question is more difficult. Probably most courts would hold, as New York has, that even after abolition of parent-child immunity, a child may not sue his or her parent for negligent failure to supervise. If so, the court would deny contribution for the same reason it would deny it if parent-child immunity were still in force (since there would be no possibility of primary liability of Tina to Child, and thus no scope for contribution). See *Holodook v. Spencer*, 324 N.E.2d 338 (N.Y. 1974), a New York case denying contribution to one in Driver's situation.** If the court did allow a suit by a child against a parent for negligent failure to supervise, then in theory the court should allow Driver to recover contribution from Tina on these facts.

91. No. **The United States has only partially waived its sovereign immunity. Under the Federal Tort Claims Act (FTCA), the United States is not liable for its exercise of a "discretionary function."**

The adoption of design and safety standards for nuclear reactors would almost certainly be held to be a discretionary function, since it involves a leadership or planning function, rather than the carrying out of policy.

92. No. **Judges receive complete immunity at common law for any act that is even arguably "judicial" in nature. This is true even if the act was motivated by corrupt or improper motives. See Rest. 2d, §895D, Comment c.** Since Joseph's decision to convict David was clearly "judicial" even though improper, Joseph gets the full immunity.

93. Yes. **Even if the tort committed by servant is an intentional one, the master will be held liable for it under the doctrine of *respondeat superior*, provided that the tort was committed in some sense *in furtherance of the employer's business.*** According to most courts, it does not matter that the employer expressly forbade the method or action used, as long as it was done in furtherance of the employment. Since Vincent, when he fired the slug into Potter's kneecap, was attempting to collect the debt (and indeed the slug helped him succeed), a court would almost certainly find that Vincent was acting in furtherance of his employment with Cosa, so that Cosa would be liable under *respondeat superior*.

94. No. **Law Firm has itself not been negligent, so the only way it can be liable is under the doctrine of *respondeat superior*. However, Messenger Service was clearly an *independent contractor*, not an employee. Therefore, the master (Law Firm) will only be liable for the torts of the servant/ independent contractor (Messenger Service) if Law Firm should have recognized that the work to be done would pose a *peculiar risk* of physical harm to others unless special precautions were taken. See Rest. 2d, §416, and Comment d.** There was no "peculiar risk" associated with the job of driving the package across town; the risk that Messenger Service would speed and strike someone was no different from the risk that any other vehicle would do so. Therefore, Law Firm is not liable under the doctrine of *respondeat superior*. (But if Law Firm actually had hired an individual messenger as an *employee*, and he sped and struck a pedestrian, Law Firm would be liable under the doctrine of *respondeat superior* even though there was no "peculiar risk" and no direct negligence by Law Firm.)

95. Yes. **If the master should have known that the independent contractor's work creates a peculiar risk, the master will be liable. See Rest. 2d, §416.** Even though Contractor was an independent contractor, not an employee, of New Ames, this situation presents one of the exceptions to the general rule that one who hires an independent contractor will not be liable under *respondeat superior* for the latter's torts. Here, New Ames should have known that failure to put warning lights around piles of sand and gravel in the roadway would pose a *peculiar risk* of harm to motorists. Therefore, New Ames will be liable under *respondeat superior* for Contractor's failure to do so.

96. Yes. **Formerly, the doctrine of *"imputed contributory negligence"* might have been applied, so as to impute Fred's negligence to Owen, and thereby bar Owen from recovery on the grounds that he was effectively contributorily negligent. But today, the doctrine of imputed contributory negligence is applied only sparingly, and only in a few special situations (e.g., a servant's negligence during the scope of his employment is imputed to bar the master's right to recover against a third party).** Virtually no courts today would apply the imputed doctrine here, even though Owen as owner would be liable *as a defendant* in a suit brought by Fred (if Fred had not been contributorily negligent) under the automobile consent statute.

97. No. **This is one of the few situations in which the doctrine of imputed contributory negligence will still be applied by most courts: A servant's negligence during the performance of his or her employment will be imputed to the master in a suit brought by the master against a third party.**

Since Fred would be barred by common law contributory negligence if *he* were to sue David, Owen as employer is similarly barred. (But Owen could sue Fred without being barred.)

98. Yes. **An owner will be *strictly liable* for injuries caused by his or her animal if the animal is either "wild" or is a domestic animal that has dangerous characteristics that the owner knows of or should know of.** Here, even though Rex was a "domesticated" animal, Owner knew or should have known that Rex would be dangerous if he escaped, so Owner is strictly liable for damages done by Rex—that is, Owner is liable even if he used due care in attempting to fence Rex in.

99. Yes. **Even though Utility Co. was not negligent, it will be strictly liable for carrying out an *abnormally dangerous activity*. An abnormally dangerous activity is one that cannot be carried out safely, even with reasonable care. This seems to be true of nuclear power plants, at least under present technology. See Rest. 2d, §520, Comment h.** The fact that Utility Co. might have been "reasonable" in choosing to build a nuclear plant rather than, say, a coal-fired plant, is irrelevant—a nuclear plant is not so enormously valuable to Langdell that this should outweigh the plant's dangers (as might be the case, for instance, for a reservoir used for irrigation in an arid farming state). (There is some chance that the court might view the earthquake as an "act of God" that relieved Utility of liability. But since the risk of damage in an earthquake is one of the very things that makes a nuclear power plant abnormally dangerous, probably the court would not so reason.)

100. Yes. **Ordinary contributory negligence by the plaintiff generally does not bar him or her from strict liability recovery.** This is certainly true whenever (as here) the plaintiff's contributory negligence consists of inattentiveness (i.e., P was not aware of the risk, even though he should have been).

101. Probably not. **Probably Utility would be successful in raising the "assumption of risk" defense.** Hero knew of and voluntarily subjected himself to the risk of radiation. Assumption of risk will probably be applied whether Hero was reasonable or unreasonable in subjecting himself to this risk.

102. Campfire, Wholesaler, and Retailer, but not Charles. **Campfire, Wholesaler, and Retailer will all have *strict product liability* each sold a product that was both defective and unreasonably dangerous. Since they did so, it does not matter that they may all have behaved with more than reasonable care. See Rest. 2d, §402A, and Illustr. 1 thereto.** It does not even matter that Wholesaler and Retailer had absolutely no chance to discover the defect no matter how diligent they were—since they were in the business of selling products of this type, they became liable for dangerous defects in the product without reference to their level of care. But the same is not true of Charles—since he was not in the business of selling soups, he can be liable only for his negligence, and the facts do not suggest that he was negligent here. (But if he should have noticed the glass and through inattention did not, then he would be liable to Gaia for negligence).

103. Yes. **Strict liability applies to products in a defective condition unreasonably dangerous to consumers.** It is foreseeable that children will find the bottle, and Slip and Slide designed theirs to look like soda pop. As such, Slip and Slide will likely be strictly liable. The warning won't exculpate Slip and Slide—a reasonable warning is an additional requirement, added to the requirement that a product not be sold in a defective/unreasonably dangerous condition.

104. No. **Strict liability can only be imposed for the sale of defective products, not services.** Blood transfusions are generally considered a service, not a product, and as a result strict liability cannot be imposed for infusion with infected blood.

105. No. **The plaintiff in a product liability suit bears the burden of showing that the defect existed** *at the time the product left the defendant's hands.* Normally, the plaintiff who is suing a manufacturer of defective canned goods will benefit from an inference of defective manufacture similar to *res ipsa loquitur*. But here, there is evidence that the botulism was caused by the denting, and this will be enough to undo the inference of defective manufacture, unless Consumer comes up with separate evidence of defective manufacture (which on the above facts he has not done).

106. Yes, probably. **The Third Restatement defines a product as being "defective in design" "when the foreseeable risks of harm posed by the product could have been reduced or avoided by the adoption of a reasonable alternative design by the seller . . . and the omission of the alternative design renders the product not reasonably safe." Rest. 3d (Prod. Liab.) §2(b).** Here, the slight increase in cost is probably outweighed by the gain in safety.

107. (a) Yes. **The evidence is admissible as bearing on whether Patrick's proposed alternative design was a feasible one. (The fact that no other manufacturer adopted that design suggests, but does not prove, that the design was not feasible or at least not cost-effective.)**

   (b) No. **The jury is still free to conclude that despite the universal lack of acceptance of Patrick's proposed hands-free design, this design was sufficiently feasible and cost-effective that a product without the feature was defectively dangerous and thus gives rise to strict liability.**

108. No. **Strict product liability will be found whenever the product is dangerously defective if used in a "*foreseeable*" way, not merely when used in an "intended" way.** Since it is quite foreseeable that a car may be involved in an accident, including a rollover accident, Newmobile is unlikely to prevail with this defense. (Newmobile might prevail by showing that installation of a roll bar would be prohibitively expensive in light of the infrequency with which it would prove beneficial, but this is another matter.)

109. No. **A manufacturer has no duty to warn of dangers that it neither knew of nor, in the exercise of reasonable care, should have known of at the time of sale.** Especially in the case of prescription drugs and other items of great social utility, a contrary holding would make the manufacturer a virtual insurer of the product, something courts do not want to do for fear of keeping valuable products off the market.

110. Yes. **If a component is defective, and is then incorporated in a larger product, the component's manufacturer will be liable if the defect leads to a failure of the larger product and that failure in turn leads to injury. See Rest. 3d (Prod. Liab.) §5(a).** Terry's estate will get the benefit of a *res ipsa*–like inference to enable it to establish that the altimeter was probably defective when it left Altos's plant.

111. No, according to most courts. **Most courts treat strict products liability as being inapplicable to one who furnishes the defective good as part of the provision of professional services (e.g., use of medical or dental devices by doctors and dentists).**

112. Yes, probably, but only on a warranty theory. **Most courts (and the Third Restatement) would say that since the damage here consists solely of damage to the defective product itself, strict products liability does not apply.** That is, most courts would treat this as a form of intangible economic loss, not "property damage," and strict product liability generally doesn't apply to intangible economic loss. In such a court, Peggy will have to proceed on a warranty theory (since by hypothesis there is no negligence). The problem is that United didn't sell directly to Peggy, but rather to Tim, who then resold to Peggy. States vary in whether they find that the implied warranty of merchantability (which would probably cover this fact pattern) applies to the subsequent purchaser.

113. No. **There is virtually no chance that Peggy can recover on a strict liability theory, since she has suffered only intangible economic harm, and virtually all courts deny recovery for intangible economic harm by itself** (unaccompanied by personal injury or property damage).

114. (a) Yes, certainly on a strict liability theory and perhaps on a warranty theory as well. **Peggy has suffered personal injury as a result of a defective product, so assuming that the product was "unreasonably dangerous" (a likely assumption, given that it caused a fire to break out in the car), Peggy can clearly recover in strict liability for her personal injuries.** (Also, she will probably be able to recover for breach of the UCC implied warranty of merchantability, even though she was a remote purchaser; assuming that United's warranty did not expressly extend to purchasers other than the original purchaser Tim Peggy would be able to recover if the state has enacted either alternative B or C to §2-318, but not if it has enacted alternative A.)

(b) Yes, probably. **Peggy will now probably be able to recover for her lost house profits, which are intangible economic losses. Clearly in a negligence action, once the plaintiff shows physical injury, he or she may "tack on" his or her intangible economic losses as an additional element of damages.** But Peggy probably cannot succeed with her basic negligence action, since there is nothing in the facts to suggest that United was negligent. If Peggy sues in strict liability or for breach of warranty, it is not so clear whether she can tack on these additional intangible economic losses, but there is a good chance that she will be allowed to do so.

115. Yes. **Even though a consumer of ordinary attentiveness might well have looked at his or her food before eating it and would have discovered the risk, most courts would not apply comparative negligence to reduce a plaintiff's recovery, on the theory that a consumer is entitled to expect that a product will not contain a manufacturing defect.** See Rest. 3d (Prod. Liab) §17, Comment d.

116. No. **Assumption of risk, in the sense of a voluntary and *unreasonable* encountering of a known risk, is a defense in strict liability cases just as it is in negligence cases.** But Pamela's acceptance of the risk of defective brakes was not unreasonable—under the circumstances, she really had no choice. Therefore, she will not be deemed to have assumed the risk.

117. Yes. **Where the plaintiff voluntarily and unreasonably encounters a known risk from a defective product, this will give rise to the defense of assumption of risk just as it would in a negligence action.** Pamela has undertaken the known risk both voluntarily and *unreasonably*. (She has behaved unreasonably because the danger from defective brakes far outweighs the benefits of having perfume one day sooner.)

118. (a) They should sue on a "public nuisance" theory. **That is, they should sue Eyyon for having "unreasonably interfered with a right common to the general public" (see Rest. 2d, §821B(1)).** In this case, the right common to the general public would be the right to an unpolluted waterway.

(b) Yes, probably. **The fishermen must show, in addition to the fact that Eyyon unreasonably interfered with a right common to the general public, that Eyyon's conduct fell within one of the three usual classes of tortious behavior (intention, negligent, or abnormally dangerous activity).** Here, the fishermen's best hope is to show that Eyyon was negligent—the captain was clearly negligent in failing to see the iceberg, and his negligence will be imputed to Eyyon by the doctrine of **respondeat superior**. The most significant issue is whether the fishermen suffered a "harm of a kind different from that suffered by other members of the public," as is required for public nuisance suits. (See Rest. 2d, §821C(1).) Probably the fishermen will meet this test, since the subject matter of their livelihood—the fish—were directly killed by Eyyon's creation of the nuisance.

119. Probably not. **A key requirement for a public nuisance action for damages is that the plaintiff must have suffered "harm of a kind different from that suffered by other members of the public." Rest. 2d, §821C(1).** A court would probably hold that every member of the Zedlav community suffered from the fact that the region was no longer as attractive in light of the oil spill. While the hotel operators may have suffered greater pecuniary loss than other residents, the court would probably hold that their loss was merely greater in degree, not different in kind.

120. No. **True, Farmer's interest in the private use and enjoyment of his land has been invaded and substantially injured. But Farmer still has to prove that Printer's interference with Farmer's use and enjoyment was either intentional, negligent, or arising from an abnormally dangerous activity or condition. See Rest. 2d, §822.** There is nothing in the facts to suggest that Printer's conduct was negligent or involved an abnormally dangerous activity. If Printer had known that it was substantially certain that the chemicals would come onto Farmer's land and interfere with his use and enjoyment of that land, Printer would be liable for "intentional" nuisance (even if he did not desire to harm Farmer). But this was not the case here. Therefore, given that there is no "strict liability" for private nuisance, Farmer cannot recover.

121. Yes, probably. **Farmer has to prove that Printer's interference with Farmer's use and enjoyment was either intentional, negligent, or arising from an abnormally dangerous activity or condition. See Rest. 2d, §822.** Now, Printer's conduct will be treated as having been intentional, in the sense that Printer knew that the chemicals were substantially certain to come on Farmer's land and cause harm there. Farmer will therefore be able to recover as long as Printer's conduct is found to be "unreasonable." Since Farmer's loss was substantially greater than the money saved by Printer in avoiding cartage fees, the unreasonableness requirement will probably be deemed met.

122. (a) That Phyllis "came to the nuisance." **Courts consider the fact that a plaintiff has "come to the nuisance" as a factor to be considered when assessing liability.** Utility should point out that Phyllis bought the land after the nearby nuisance already existed.

   (b) No, at least under modern case law. **Traditionally, if the plaintiff "came to the nuisance," he or she automatically lost. But the modern approach (represented by Rest. 2d, §840D) is that coming to the nuisance is merely one factor among several in determining whether defendant's conduct is unreasonable, so it does not automatically bar the plaintiff.** Therefore, Phyllis will be entitled to a trial at which she can show that, under all the circumstances, she should not be required to bear the full burden of Utility Co.'s knowing pollution of her land. (If "coming to the nuisance" were an automatic bar to Phyllis, then the prior owner of Blackacre would be treated unfairly, since he would never be compensated for the fact that Utility Co. was in effect eliminating certain types of purchasers of Blackacre, such as landscape gardeners like Phyllis.)

123. No. **These facts illustrate the general rule that one party to a business transaction normally has no obligation to disclose even highly relevant facts to the other. This basic rule is especially likely to be applied where it is the buyer, not the seller, who has the superior knowledge. See Rest. 2d, §551, Illustr. 6.**

124. Yes, probably. **Courts are quicker today than formerly to conclude that notwithstanding the general rule that silence will not constitute fraud, special facts may impose upon a party with superior knowledge (especially a seller) a duty to disclose basic facts to the other party. As Rest.**

2d, §551(2)(e) puts it, one party must disclose "facts basic to the transaction, if he or she knows that the other is about to enter into it under a mistake as to them, and that the other, because of the *relationship between them*, the customs of the trade or other objective circumstances, would reasonably expect a disclosure of those facts." Octavio knew that Barnaby expected Octavio to be honest and forthcoming, if only because of their mutual friendship with Sidney. Since the toxic waste problem was certainly a "basic fact," this situation would probably fall within the Restatement's special "relationship between the parties" rule, and Octavio would therefore be liable.

125. Unclear. **There is no special relationship between the parties, so Bertram's case is clearly weaker than Barnaby's. However, a court might hold that in residential real estate transactions, the "customs of the trade" now require the disclosure of essential defects if these cannot be found by reasonable inspection.** For instance, a number of courts have held that an arm's-length seller has the obligation to tell the buyer about termite damage to the house; a court so holding would presumably find Octavio liable here.

126. Neither. **First, Darlene has not merely failed to disclose; she has made a material (and fraudulent) misrepresentation in the form of a "half-truth." That is, she has told Percy that the current rent roll is $5,000, but has not given him the additional facts (that the current rents being charged are illegal) necessary to make the statement that she did make not misleading. See Rest. 2d, §529, Illustr. 2. Second, it is not a defense to a fraudulent misrepresentation action that the other party failed to perform an investigation that he could reasonably have performed a party to a transaction has no duty to investigate, even if his failure to do so is unreasonable and thus amounts to contributory negligence. See Rest. 2d, §540. So Percy will recover for fraud.**

127. No, probably. **The fact that Developer only stated his intention is not a defense—if a person states that he or she intends to do X when he or she knows full well that he or she will not do X, that's misrepresentation, just as if the statement had been made about a matter of present fact. (Of course, if a person says that he or she intends to do X, and later changes his or her mind or is prevented by developments beyond his or her control from doing X, there is no fraud and thus no liability.)**

    However, Developer will probably escape liability, because he was not intending to influence those who brought "lakefront" lots from sellers other than Developer. Developer would be liable to anyone who actually bought a lot *from him*, since these people fall within the *"class of persons who he intends or has reason to expect to act . . . in reliance upon the misrepresentation."* Rest. 2d, §531. This may include people whose specific identity Developer did not know, and even people who learned of the misrepresentation only when it was repeated by some third person. But Developer is only liable to those who acted in the *"type of transaction"* that Developer had in mind. Here, the purchase by Clarence of a lot not from Developer but from a third party is probably not the "type of transaction" that Developer had in mind, so he probably will not be liable.

128. Yes. **A statement of opinion will not usually give rise to liability for intentional misrepresentation. However, courts are quicker to find liability for an opinion when the opinion is expressed by one who is not an "adverse party" to the listener (i.e., where the two parties are not on opposite sides of a business transaction). See Rest. 2d, §539, Illustr. 3.** Here, Dimitrius and Pia were not on opposite sides, as they would have been had Dimitrius been trying to sell the painting to Pia; therefore, a court will be quicker to find Dimitrius liable than if he were the seller. Also, the courts are quicker to find liability even for an opinion where the other party believes that the speaker has reason to know special facts that the listener does not. Here, Pia reasonably understood Dimitrius to be implying

that he knew facts sufficient to lead him to his opinion of the genuineness of the painting. Therefore, Dimitrius will be liable since he knew that he did not have such facts.

129. **No, probably. Courts are very reluctant to hold a person liable for an opinion when suit is brought by an** *"adverse party"* **(i.e., the other party to a business transaction). See Rest. 2d, §542.** Even if the parties are on opposite sides of the transaction, an opinion will sometimes be actionable (e.g., where the speaker stands in a fiduciary relationship with the listener, or purports to have special knowledge of the matter that the listener does not have, etc.). But none of these special facts is present here (especially since Pia knew that Ted was an amateur who had no special skill in ascertaining authorship).

130. Yes. **Contractor made a false statement in the course of his business or profession and supplied it to guide another (Owner) in the course of a business-related transaction by that other Owner (possible replacement of a furnace in an investment property).** Neither the fact that Contractor was only negligent rather than deceitful, nor the fact that Owner suffered no physical injury or direct property damage, will save Contractor from liability for negligent misrepresentation. Nor will the fact that Contractor was not paid for his opinion save him; he gave the opinion in the course of his business, and he had a business motive for doing so (the hope of getting construction work from Owner by being helpful to him).

131. **No. The suit is for negligent (not intentional) misrepresentation. Therefore, Contractor can at most be liable to members of a** *"limited group of persons"* **for whose benefit and guidance he intended to supply the information, or a limited class to whom, as Contractor knew, the recipient (Owner) intended to supply the information. See Rest. 2d, §552(2).** Since Contractor did not intend for Owner to communicate his representation to Investor, and did not know that Owner intended to pass on the communication to Investor, Contractor is off the hook (whereas he might still be on the hook had he made his misrepresentation knowingly). Also, the transaction that Contractor intended to influence (Owner's decision whether to sell *his* building) was not the same as, or very similar to, the transaction that ended up being influenced (Investor's decision to buy the other building), so Contractor would escape liability for that reason as well.

132. **Yes. At least in cases involving a sale, rental, or exchange transaction, a material representation by the seller will make him or her liable even if the misrepresentation is** *"innocent"* **(i.e., not even negligent).** Observe that a tort suit for misrepresentation is probably the only way that Owner could recover against Insul Co., since a breach of warranty suit would probably be foreclosed by application of the parol evidence rule (by which the written document wiped out the effect of prior oral statements by the Insul Co. representative).

133. **No. Even in a sale or exchange transaction, a speaker will be liable for** *innocent* **misrepresentation only to the person to whom the representation is directly made, not to some third party who learns of it. See Rest. 2d, §552C, Comment d.** Even if Insul Co. knew that Owner would be repeating the representation to any prospective purchaser of the building, this fact would not change Insul Co.'s nonliability. (Thus the scope of liability for innocent misrepresentation is much narrower than for negligent misrepresentation, and the scope of liability for negligent misstatement is in turn narrower than where the misstatement is intentional.)

134. Yes, probably. **Even though Newspaper was effectively saying only that seven or more of the 12 jurors were dishonest, a court would probably hold that a reasonable jury could find that suspicion attached to the plaintiff, as one of the 12 jurors, a majority of whom were bribed. See Rest. 2d, §564A, Comment c.**

135. **Yes. If a person repeats a defamatory statement that he or she attributes to some other person, it is not enough for the repeater to show that the statement was made by the other instead, the repeater (the defendant) must show the truth of the defamatory charges, not the truth of the fact that the charges were made. See Rest. 2d, §581A, Comment e.** Therefore, the fact that Newspaper proves that Townsend made exactly the charges that Newspaper said he did is irrelevant.

136. **No. To recover for slander (or libel), plaintiff must show that the statement was "false." It is not enough for the plaintiff to show that there was some small inaccuracy in defendant's statement. Instead, defendant will be relieved of liability so long as the *basic substance* of his or her statement was correct.** Since the basic substance of Shopkeeper's statement was that Cashier had stolen money by ringing up a lesser amount and pocketing the difference, Cashier has not proved "falsity," and she will lose.

137. **Newspaper. If the statement involves a matter of public interest and the defendant is a media organization, the First Amendment requires that the plaintiff bear the burden of proving that the statement was false. This is true even if the plaintiff is a private figure. See *Philadelphia Newspapers v. Hepps*, 475 U.S. 767 (1986).** Therefore, even though it may seem unfair to Joe to make him prove a negative fact (very difficult to do), this is what Joe must do, and he loses since he did not do it.

138. **No. Statements of pure opinion (i.e., statements that do not imply the assertion of undisclosed defamatory facts that form the basis for the speaker's opinion) are protected by the First Amendment, and thus may not be made the subject of a defamation action. See Rest. 2d, §566, Comment c.** Denise's statement was fairly understood as being merely an expression of pure opinion, not a statement of fact. That is, a reasonable person in the position of the other board members would not have understood Denise as saying that Parker was punishable at criminal law as a blackmailer, but rather, as asserting that Parker was trying to coerce the board and behaving in a reprehensible manner.

139. **Yes. Although Dan's statement is on its face merely an expression of opinion, it could also reasonably be understood by one or more other board members as being based upon unstated facts known to Dan that would justify his belief that Parker is really a thief. See Rest. 2d, §566, Illustr. 3.** Dan's statement is quite different from Denise's. Denise's epithet of "blackmailer" was spoken in connection with factual allegations known to the entire board (demand for undoing of the original stock transaction), so it should have been clear to all of the other board members that Denise was merely expressing her distaste for Parker's conduct, not stating that he was punishable at criminal law as a blackmailer. But Dan has not stated the factual background for his assertion that Parker is a thief. The judge should therefore send the case to the jury, and the jury could properly find Dan defamed Parker.

140. **Yes. Normally, a person may not recover for slander except by showing "special harm" (i.e., some economic or pecuniary loss). However, there are four well-known exceptions to this rule (i.e., situations in which a person may recover for *"slander per se"*) without a showing of special harm. One of these is where the slanderous statement accuses the plaintiff of serious sexual misconduct. See Rest. 2d, §574, Illustr. 2.** Deborah's accusation that Polly not only had sex before marriage but also bore Tommy out of wedlock would presumably qualify, even in this more liberal modern age.

141. **Yes. One who repeats a slanderous statement originally made by another person is liable as if he or she were the originator of the statement, even if the repeater gives the source, or says that the statement is only a rumor. See Rest. 2d, §578, Comment c.**

142. **No. Prude, because he is a famous TV personality, is unquestionably a "public figure." Therefore, he can only recover for defamation if he shows that the defendant acted with "actual malice" (i.e., with either knowledge that his statement was false or with reckless disregard of whether it was true or false).** *New York Times v. Sullivan*, 376 U.S. 254 (1964). Here, the facts indicate that Ed was negligent, but that he honestly believed the truth of the material he was about to print. Therefore, the *Inquisition*'s actions do not satisfy the *New York Times* "actual malice" standard, and Prude cannot recover.

143. **Yes. John Smith is clearly a "private figure." As such, the** *New York Times* **"actual malice" requirement does not apply to his libel suit. Therefore, to recover he only has to prove that Newspaper and its reporter were negligent, not intentionally false or reckless. Also, because the item originated with the unofficial words of Officer Flatfoot, the conditional privilege to report on public proceedings does not apply.**

144. **Yes, probably. There is a common law privilege to report on official proceedings, and an entry on the police blotter would probably be held to be an official proceeding. However, this common law privilege is merely the privilege to report** *accurately* **on official proceedings (even if what is said at the proceeding, and later reported, is itself defamatory). See Rest. 2d, §611, including Comments b and h.** Since Newspaper negligently failed to report correctly what happened at the proceeding, its privilege to report on official proceedings would probably be lost. Also, since Smith is a private figure, he would only have to show negligence.

145. **No. A person indeed has a qualified privilege to supply information to a third person if the third person's important interest would be affected by the information. However, the supplying of the information must be within "generally accepted standards of decent conduct." Rest. 2d, §595(1) (b).** The mailing of an anonymous letter to the plaintiff's new employer, where the allegation concerns a relatively trivial matter, would almost certainly not be found to be within generally accepted standards of decent conduct. Therefore, since this statement was also false (and Denise was negligent in making it), she will be liable for libel.

It is important to note that Cashier is able to recover against Denise only because he is a private figure. If Cashier were a public figure (e.g., a major movie star defamed by a statement by a coworker made anonymously to a studio contemplating hiring the star to do a picture), it would not be enough for him to show negligence. In that situation, the plaintiff would lose, not because the defendant was privileged, but because *New York Times v. Sullivan* would require him to show "actual malice" (knowledge of falsity or reckless disregard of the facts) rather than negligence. To put it another way, a privilege will only exist and matter where the plaintiff is a private figure and the defendant has behaved negligently but not recklessly (because if the defendant was reckless, the qualified privilege is deemed "abused").

146. **Yes, probably. A person indeed has a qualified privilege to supply information to a third person if the third person's important interest would be affected by the information. However, the supplying of the information must be within "generally accepted standards of decent conduct." Rest. 2d, §595.** This situation differs from that in the previous question in two respects: (1) the information being reported is much more serious and bears much more directly on the recipient's (Bigelow's) interests, so the case for qualified privilege is much stronger; and (2) Dorothy, unlike

Denise, was responding to a request for information from the third person, rather than volunteering. These two factors make it quite likely that what Dorothy did would be found to be within generally accepted standards of "decent conduct," so that her statement was privileged (even though negligent and incorrect).

147. Probably not. **Obviously, Peggy would like to allege invasion of privacy. "Invasion of privacy" is not a single tort, but is rather four different torts, three of which might conceivably (but probably would not) apply here.** Peggy might claim that her solitude was intruded upon. However, this tort is generally committed only when the defendant has intruded into a private place—here, everything Dogged captured in his photographs was visible to a member of the public, so Peggy will probably not win on this claim. Alternatively, Peggy could claim that her likeness and name had been appropriated. But the problem with this theory is that the tort is usually found to exist only when the defendant makes use of the plaintiff's name or likeness to publicize a product. A newspaper's publication of a photograph of a public figure, even where the item's news value is weak, is unlikely to be held to be the sort of "appropriation" that is protected against.

   Finally, Peggy could claim that the details of her private life have been unreasonably publicized. However, the tort does not exist when the material that is publicized is of "legitimate concern to the public." Here, since Peggy is a "voluntary public figure" (she has sought her stardom), probably even the somewhat personal details of her romantic life would be held to be of legitimate public concern. Also, the First Amendment might prevent states from making Dogged liable on these facts. So in summary, Peggy probably loses on all three of her invasion of privacy claims.

148. Yes, for "unreasonable publicity given to private life." **Here, Dogged has stepped over the line, and would almost certainly be liable for the "publicity given to private life" branch of invasion of privacy. The matter disclosed must be "highly offensive to a reasonable person" and "not of legitimate concern to the public." Rest. 2d, §652B.** Both these requirements seem satisfied: Surely the disclosure of intimate details like the frequency of sexual intercourse would be highly offensive to a reasonable person (even if disclosure of the basic fact that two people have a sexual relationship would not be). Also, despite Peggy's celebrity status, it is doubtful that the public has a legitimate entitlement to know such details.

149. No. **Customer can satisfy three of the four requirements for the tort of malicious prosecution: (1) that Merchant took an active part in instigating and encouraging the prosecution; (2) that the criminal proceedings were terminated in Customer's favor (since dismissal by the prosecutor, when not part of a plea bargain, is deemed to be in the accused's favor); and (3) that Merchant had an improper purpose (coercing Customer to pay the bill, rather than seeing that Customer is brought to justice). However, Customer cannot meet the fourth requirement: that Merchant be shown to have lacked probable cause to institute the proceedings.** The facts known to Merchant (especially the fact that there had been two prior checks returned by the bank during the prior month) gave Merchant probable cause to believe that the crime of bad-check writing had been committed. Even though Customer later showed in the malicious prosecution action that he had not really known he lacked funds (thus establishing his substantive innocence of the charge), the facts known to Merchant still gave Merchant probable cause. Therefore, Merchant wins.

150. No. **The plaintiff in a suit for wrongful use of civil proceedings must show three things: (1) that the original plaintiff (defendant in the wrongful-civil-proceedings action) acted without probable cause; (2) that the original plaintiff acted primarily for an improper purpose (i.e., a purpose other than securing proper adjudication of his or her claim); and (3) that the proceedings have terminated in favor of the person against whom they were brought.** Tycoon can easily meet

requirements (1) and (2), but he cannot satisfy (3), since the accident suit has not yet been terminated in his favor. It is not enough that the judge in the wrongful civil proceedings suit is convinced that Tycoon *will* win the accident suit—Tycoon must wait until he has in fact won.

151. Yes, on a theory of "injurious falsehood." **To recover, Employee will have to show that (1) Doctor made to a third person a false statement harmful to Employee's interest, which caused Employee pecuniary harm; (2) Doctor recognized or should have recognized that Employee would suffer pecuniary harm by virtue of the statement; and (3) Doctor knew the statement was false or acted in reckless disregard of its truth or falsity. See Rest. 2d, §623A.** Employee can make all three of these showings. (The tort of "injurious falsehood" usually occurs in cases of so-called trade libel— that is, cases where the defendant falsely disparages the plaintiff's goods or business. But the tort is broader than that, to include any injurious falsehood that causes the plaintiff economic damage, as in the present fact situation.)

152. Yes, on a theory of interference with contract. **The defendant will be liable for interference with contract if he or she intentionally and improperly interfered with the performance of a contract between another and a third person.** Since Monster knew of the contract between Target and Suitor, and by its own higher offer induced Suitor to break that contract, Monster will be liable for the amount by which the price in the Suitor-Target contract was less than the true value of Target.

153. No. **Abel could assert the tort of interference with prospective contractual relations, or as it is sometimes called, "*interference with prospective advantage.*"** But Abel would lose. The reason is that where the plaintiff has not yet made a contract with the third person, the defendant has a *privilege* to interfere by making his or her own contract with that third person, so long as he or she does so for proper business purposes. If plaintiff and defendant are competitors, and defendant wants to get the business for himself or herself, this is a proper purpose, so long as defendant does not employ wrongful means (e.g., bribery, restraint of trade, etc.). Even though Baker is taking a loss on the contract, a court is very unlikely to regard this as an improper means, because of the long-term competitive benefit to Baker of having Customer as a reference account.

154. Yes. **A defendant in an interference-with-prospective-advantage case can successfully raise the defense that he or she was privileged to induce a third party to do business with the defendant rather than with another only if the defendant's purpose was to protect his or her own *valid economic objectives*. Where the interference with the prospective contract was motivated solely by malice, not business interests, the privilege does not exist. See Rest. 2d, §769, Comment e.**

155. Yes, for interference with custody of a minor. **"One who, with knowledge that the parent does not consent . . . induces a minor child to leave a parent legally entitled to its custody, or not to return to the parent after it has left him, is subject to liability to the parent." Rest. 2d, §700.** The fact that the defendant is inspired by motives of kindness or affection rather than malice to the parent is irrelevant. (But the Sunnies might have a privilege if they reasonably believed that Tina was being physically abused by her father.)

156. No. **In the absence of a custody decree, each parent is equally entitled to custody. Therefore, a parent cannot be liable for inducing the child to leave the other parent and come live with him or her. Rest. 2d, §700, Comment c.** It is irrelevant that the defendant parent lives outside the United States.

Torts Essay Questions

QUESTION 1:   Before attending law school in Bristol, Texas, Robert owned a petting zoo back in his hometown of Cut-and-Shoot, Texas. He left the zoo in the care of his brother-in-law, Ian. Three months into the semester, Ian called Robert and said he could no longer take care of the animals because he had a new and lucrative job working as a test subject at STU Labs in Austin, Texas. He'd been able to sell or give away most of the animals, but those he couldn't sell or find a home for he had decided to send to Robert. He told Robert the animals from the zoo would be arriving in Bristol the next day. Soon thereafter, a truck pulled up to Robert's house with a horse, a dog, a lion, and a cat.

Robert convinced his friend Susie to let him keep the horse on her large farm. The horse had a tendency to bite anyone who put their hands near its face. One day, after warning Susie about the horse's tendency to bite, Robert let Susie take the horse for a ride. When Susie and the horse passed a schoolyard, several schoolchildren begged to pet the horse. Before Susie could stop them, one of the children reached to pet the horse, and the horse promptly bit her.

Robert lived in a house in downtown Bristol with a large, fenced-in backyard. He decided to keep the dog in the backyard. One night, Robert forgot to close the back gate, and the dog wandered onto Steve's yard. Steve, who was taking a late-night stroll on his property, did not see the dog and stumbled over it. He suffered an injury to his hand.

Since Robert's house had been robbed twice, he decided to keep the lion in his side yard fastened to a post by a chain. Because of a defect in the chain that Robert could not be expected to detect, the lion broke free and attacked Gillian as she was walking on the sidewalk, injuring her.

Robert decided to keep the cat inside his house. While the cat was at the petting zoo, Robert had had to keep it away from customers because it was always jumping on their faces and biting them. Several times, the cat had sent a customer to the hospital. Since he was keeping the cat inside, he decided to take it to Thom, a groomer. Robert warned Thom of the cat's dangerous tendencies, and Thom said he could handle the cat. As soon as Robert handed the cat over to Thom, it jumped up and bit Thom's face, sending him to the hospital.

Please discuss Robert's potential liability. Do not discuss issues concerning comparative negligence.

QUESTION 2:   Alan decides to build a pool on his property. He knows all the neighborhood kids trespass across his yard to get to the public playground on the other side. Even so, after he uses a backhoe to dig a 20-foot-deep hole to put the pool in, he fails to mark it or block it off with a fence, figuring that even kids will notice the giant hole in the ground and avoid it. One particularly dark night, Neil, age eight, is running across Alan's property when he falls into the hole and severely injures himself. At the same time, as Neil's dad is walking around the neighborhood looking for Neil, a large potted plant falls out of Grace's window and hits Neil's dad in the head, knocking him to the ground and giving him a concussion. As he lies there, Stella, in the neighboring house, yells, "Look out below!" and throws out a television set (she is having a fight with her husband at the time). Neil's dad is hit in the leg with the television, which causes injuries. He comes to you for advice.

QUESTION 3:   WPRV, "the Rock of Rhode Island," was a modern-rock radio station that was listened to by more than 55 percent of Rhode Island and southern Massachusetts teenagers. The station's nearest rival was WBOR, a classic-rock station that had an audience of 8 percent of the area's teenagers. To attract an even larger portion of the available audience and thus increase advertising revenue, WPRV launched a promotion in July 2011 entitled "the Super Wonderful Plastic Fantastic Lobster Summer Spectacular." The Spectacular, with a budget of approximately $40,000 for the month, was specifically designed to make the radio station "more exciting." Among the programs included in the Spectacular was a contest broadcast on July 27, 2011. On that day, Dave "Quahog" Jones, a WPRV disc jockey and television personality, traveled in a bright red Hummer to a number of areas in the Providence metropolitan area (which includes Fall River and New Bedford, Massachusetts). Periodically, he told WPRV his whereabouts and his intended destination, and the station broadcast this information to its listeners. The first person to physically locate Quahog and fulfill a specified condition received a cash prize. In addition, the winning contestant participated in a brief interview on the air with Quahog. The July 27 broadcast included the following announcements: "Holy smoke! 9:30 and Quahog is back on his feet again and is headed for the Braga Bridge! Thought I would give you a warning so you can get your kids off the street." "Quahog is in Bristol near those crazy kids at Big University. I'm at the main entrance! You know where that is! You were drunk there last week! I'm standing here, waiting to give out some money. Be the first person there to tell me what type of car we gave away yesterday—that's the make and model. If you know, you should be making like a tree! I mean leave!"

In Providence, 17-year-old Harold Lovecraft was listening to WPRV in his car while searching for Quahog. Upon hearing that Quahog was headed toward Warren, he immediately drove to that vicinity. Meanwhile, in New Bedford, 19-year-old Harriet Melville heard and responded to the same information. Both arrived in Warren to find that someone had already claimed the prize. Without knowledge of the other, each decided to follow Quahog's vehicle to its next stop and thus be first to arrive when the contest question or condition was announced. For the next few miles, the Lovecraft and Melville cars jockeyed for position closest to Quahog's vehicle, reaching speeds up to 80 miles an hour. However, Quahog never exceeded the legal speed limit. About a mile and a half from Exit 2, the teenagers heard, "11:15—Quahog is heading for Exit 2 to give away some of that sweet green chorizo at the Double D across from Manny's Furniture— looks like a great place to stop and give out some cash!" Quahog's vehicle left I-95 at Exit 2. Lovecraft and Melville, in attempting to follow, forced another car, driven by Hunting, onto the center divider, where it overturned. Hunting was severely injured. Lovecraft stopped to report the accident. Melville, after pausing momentarily to relate the accident to a passing police officer, continued to pursue Quahog, successfully located him, and collected a cash prize. Hunting brings an action against all relevant parties. Please discuss each party's potential liability.

QUESTION 4:   Alvin is walking down the street to his weekly football game when Bertie and her girl-friends walk up to him. Bertie doesn't like how Alvin looks, so as Alvin walks by, Bertie sprays her perfume in his face. Bertie and her friends laugh and run away. Alvin coughs and blinks his eyes hard but continues on to the game. At the game (which is touch football, meaning a person is "down" when he is tagged by another player—no one is supposed to tackle anyone), Calvin, who is dating Bertie, smells her distinctive perfume on Alvin. Believing Alvin and Bertie are having an affair, on the next play, Calvin shoves Alvin hard into a tree, breaking his nose. Alvin gets up and stumbles into a nearby bathroom to look at his nose in the mirror. Calvin sneaks up to the door of the bathroom and yells, "If you come out of that bathroom, I'm going to beat you up!" Alvin, who is now justifiably frightened and confused by Calvin's anger, cowers in the bathroom. Bertie then passes by the bathroom, and Calvin tells her he has Alvin trapped inside. Bertie yells to Alvin, "Calvin is going to kill your dog! Dead dog! Woof, woof!" Alvin is so upset he has a mild heart attack. Alvin later comes to your office says he wants to sue Bertie and Calvin for his injuries. What torts have been committed?

QUESTION 5:   During a huge storm, Captain Pete moors his ship on Del's dock to avoid being ship-wrecked by the heavy seas. Del, seeing Captain Pete's ship and objecting to what he thinks is a trespass, unmoors the ship, causing the ship to sink and Captain Pete to be injured. The next day, Mark, Captain Pete's first mate, is walking along the beach looking for stuff tossed up by the storm. He sees something up in the trees and walks over to take a look (unbeknownst to him, crossing onto Del's land from the public beach). Next to the tree, he sees a handbag. On top of it is a plate of still-warm porridge and a cold beer. Mark moves the food, and then carries the handbag down to the beach to look inside. As he walks away, Del, who had set the handbag next to the tree, realizes it is gone. He spends ten minutes looking for it and then sees Mark at the far end of the beach. He runs after Mark shouting, "Hey! That's my bag!" Mark hands it over immediately without taking anything. Del says, "I'm going to sue you, boy-o! Along with that no-good friend of yours, Captain Pete!" Del comes to you for advice regarding his potential lawsuits.

Sample Answers to Torts Essay Questions

ANSWER TO QUESTION 1:

Horse

Robert is likely strictly liable for the horse's bites. **An owner or possessor of a domestic animal that the owner or possessor knows or has reason to know has dangerous tendencies abnormal for the animal's category is subject to strict liability for physical harm caused by the animal if the harm ensues from that dangerous activity. A domestic animal is one commonly kept for work or as a pet. Under strict liability, the defendant is liable for any harms simply because the defendant engaged in that activity. All that needs to be established for liability is causation and damages.** As a riding horse from a petting zoo, the horse is likely a domestic animal. Robert knew of its tendency to bite when people got near its face, and the horse did in fact bite when the children reached to pet it. Since Robert knew, and the harm arose from the horse's abnormally dangerous tendency of biting people, Robert is strictly liable, and it is irrelevant that Robert warned Susie before giving her permission to ride.

Dog

For the same reasons as above, the dog is likely a domestic animal. **If harm arises from the keeping of domestic animals, a person's liability is analyzed based on standard negligence. Negligence occurs when the defendant's conduct imposes an unreasonable risk upon another, resulting in an injury to that other. To show negligence, a plaintiff has to show that there was a duty, a breach, causation, and damages.** Robert likely had a duty to keep his gate closed and his animal from straying from his yard due to the duty to act with reasonable care when creating a risk. Keeping a dog in downtown Bristol creates a risk. He breached that duty by leaving the gate open and allowing the dog to get loose and injure Steve.

Lion

Robert is likely strictly liable for Gillian's injuries. **An owner or possessor of a wild animal is subject to strict liability for physical harm caused by the wild animal. A wild animal is an animal that belongs to a category of animals that have not been generally domesticated and that are likely, unless restrained, to cause personal injury. As stated above, under strict liability, all that needs to be established for liability is causation and damages.** Robert's lion is likely a wild animal, because lions have not been generally domesticated and it is likely to cause personal injury unless restrained. The lion got loose, attacked Gillian, and injured her. Despite his exercise of reasonable care in his attempt to confine the lion, Robert is liable to Gillian for her injuries.

Cat

Robert is likely not liable for Thom's injuries. **Strict liability for abnormally dangerous animals does not apply if the person suffers physical or emotional harm as a result of making contact with or coming into proximity to the defendant's animal with the purpose of securing some benefit from that contact or proximity.** As a groomer who accepted the cat from Robert, Thom was deriving financial benefits from the acceptance of the animal, so strict liability does not apply. Also, there was no indication that Robert was negligent in handing the cat over to Thom, as he clearly warned him of the cat's dangerous tendency, and Thom told him he could handle it. Consequently, Robert is not liable to Thom for his injuries.

ANSWER TO QUESTION 2:

Neil v. Alan

The issue is whether Alan owed any duty to Neil, a trespasser. **A landowner owes a duty of reasonable care to a trespassing child if (1) the owner knows that the area is one where children are likely to trespass; (2) the owner has reason to know that the condition poses an unreasonable risk of serious injury or death to trespassing children; (3) the injured child either does not discover the condition or does not realize the danger, due to his or her youth; (4) the benefit to the owner of maintaining the condition in its dangerous form is slight weighed against the risk to the children; and (5) the owner fails to use reasonable care to eliminate the danger.** Since Alan knew children often trespassed across his property, he should have used reasonable care to eliminate the danger caused by the 20-foot-deep hole. Neil had no way of knowing the hole was out there in the dark until he fell into it. Importantly, Alan did absolutely nothing, and it would have been relatively cheap and easy for him to mark the hole or otherwise fence it off. Since a 20-foot-deep hole posed a significant danger, Alan is likely liable to Neil. However, Alan may argue that Neil's comparative negligence in running across his land during a very dark night contributed to his injuries. If so, Neil's recovery may be reduced by the amount of his negligence.

Neil's Dad v. Grace

Neil's dad is likely to recover against Grace under the doctrine of *res ipsa loquitur.* **Under *res ipsa loquitur*, a plaintiff can point to the fact of the accident and create an inference that, even without a precise showing of how the defendant behaved, the defendant was probably negligent.** At trial, as long as Neil's dad can show that the plant fell out of Grace's window, and that plants do not fall out of windows without some negligence, Neil's dad has presented enough evidence to justify a verdict for him. Consequently, unless Grace comes up with some rebuttal evidence that the plant did not come from her window or did not fall out from negligence, Grace is liable for Neil's dad's injuries to his head.

Neil's Dad v. Stella

The issue is whether Stella is liable for Neil's dad's injuries even though she shouted out a warning. **Even if a person gives a warning, this does not immunize the person from negligence liability—if the person's activity is unreasonably dangerous (evaluated by its benefits against its risks) despite the warning, the person will still be liable.** It is so dangerous to throw heavy objects out of a window, and so easy to discard the object by safer means, that giving the warning did not make the total benefits of Stella's conduct outweigh its dangers. Importantly, she was in the middle of having a fight with her husband, and was likely launching the television simply out of spite rather than any real desire to discard it. Consequently, she will be liable for the injuries to Neil's dad's leg.

Joint and Several Liability of Grace and Stella

The issue is whether Grace and Stella are jointly and severally liable for Neil's dad's injuries. **Even where the traditional rule of joint and several liability is in force, it applies only where a person's harm is "indivisible," or not capable of being divided.** From the facts, it is clear that Grace's plant caused Neil's dad's head injuries and that Stella's television caused his leg injuries. Consequently, each will be responsible only for the directly attributable harm.

ANSWER TO QUESTION 3:

Hunting v. Quahog

The issue here is whether Quahog can be held liable for Hunting's injuries. **The tort of negligence occurs when a person's conduct imposes an unreasonable risk upon another, resulting in injury to** that other. **The five components of a prima facie case for negligence are duty, failure to conform to that duty, causation in fact, proximate cause, and actual damage.** Quahog had the duty to behave with the care that would be shown by a reasonable person. Although Quahog never drove over the speed limit, he likely breached that duty by driving all over Rhode Island and encouraging teenagers to chase him for money. Quahog was likely the cause in fact of Hunting's injuries, because had Quahog not acted negligently by holding this particular contest, Hunting would not have been injured. Finally, Hunting suffered damages when he was injured in the car wreck. However, Quahog could claim that he was not the proximate cause of Hunting's injuries. The proximate cause requirement is a policy determination that a defendant, even one who has behaved negligently, should not be automatically liable for all the consequences, no matter how improbable or far-reaching, of his or her act. Today, this requirement usually means that the defendant will not be liable for the consequences that are very unforeseeable. While Quahog could claim that Lovecraft and Melville are the real causes of Hunting's injuries, it was likely foreseeable that holding this contest and speeding around the highway would cause other drivers to speed and chase him and potentially get into accidents. Consequently, a court will likely hold Quahog liable in negligence.

Hunting v. WPRV

For the same reasons as Quahog, WPRV is likely liable in negligence for holding the contest. However, it may also be liable under respondeat superior. **Under respondeat superior, an employer is normally vicariously liable for torts committed by its employees. However, the employer is only liable for torts committed by the employee during the scope of employment. Normally, this means that there will be liability only when the employee is acting in furtherance of the employer's business interests.** Quahog appears to be a full-time employee of the station rather than an independent contractor (since the facts state he is one of the station's popular on-air personalities). Additionally, he is holding and participating in the contest to promote and benefit the station. Consequently, WPRV is likely responsible for Quahog's actions under respondeat superior.

Hunting v. Lovecraft

The issue is whether Lovecraft is liable for Hunting's injuries, either because of her own negligence or because of her failure to render aid. **The rule for negligence is stated above. Additionally, if a defendant endangers or harms the plaintiff, even if he or she does so completely innocently, he or she must render assistance or warning when he or she discovers the problem. A number of "hit and run" driving statutes in various states require a driver to render assistance to one whom he or she has hit; these have sometimes been held to result in negligence per se, and civil liability, where the driver does not comply with the statute.** Although Lovecraft is only 17, he was engaged in the adult activity of driving, so he owed the same duty of driving as a reasonable adult would. He likely breached that duty by speeding and chasing after Quahog. He was both the cause in fact and proximate cause of Hunting's injuries, since his driving (at least partly) forced Hunting off the road. He did stop to render aid, as he was required to do under common law and probably state statute. However, stopping to render aid will not relieve him of liability for his initial negligence.

Hunting v. Melville

The issue is whether Melville will be liable for Hunting's injuries. **The rules for negligence and rendering assistance are stated above.** Melville is likely liable for the same reasons as Lovecraft. Additionally, even if she was not engaged in the adult activity of driving, as a 19-year-old, she likely cannot claim that she should be judged on the same standard as a minor. Also, while she stopped only to tell a police officer and did not stay at the scene of the accident, whether she would be liable for her failure to render aid as well likely depends on what is required under the state's "hit-and-run" statute, if the state has one.

ANSWER TO QUESTION 4:

Battery by Bertie

The issue is whether Bertie committed a battery on Alvin. **A battery is the intentional infliction of a harmful or offensive bodily contact. An offensive contact is a contact that damages a person's reasonable sense of dignity.** Bertie, because she didn't like how Alvin looked, intentionally sprayed him in the face with her perfume. It seemed to harm him (in that he coughed and rubbed his eyes), but even if it did not do so, spraying perfume into the face of another person is likely damaging to a reasonable sense of dignity. Consequently, Bertie has committed a battery.

Battery by Calvin

The issue here is whether Alvin consented to being shoved by Calvin. **The plaintiff's consent to a touching is a complete defense to battery. However, a battery can occur where a plaintiff consents to a certain level of bodily contact, but the defendant goes beyond the consented-to level of contact. At that point, any consent to touching becomes invalid, and a battery results.** In joining the football game, Alvin probably consented to tagging, maybe some pushing, and other touching involved in a touch football game. However, he did not consent to being intentionally shoved into a tree. While an accidental shove might have been protected by the consent rule, an intentional shove, such as the one here, is unlikely to fall under the scope of Alvin's consent.

False Imprisonment by Calvin

The issue here is whether Calvin falsely imprisoned Alvin. **False imprisonment is the intentional infliction of a confinement. The idea of a confinement is that the plaintiff is held within certain limits. Importantly, the imprisonment can be accomplished by threats.** Alvin was confined inside the bathroom by Calvin's threats that he would "beat him" if he came out. Consequently, even though Alvin wasn't physically confined by anything, Calvin falsely imprisoned Alvin with his threats of violence.

Intentional Infliction of Emotional Distress by Bertie

The issue is whether Bertie committed the tort of intentional infliction of emotional distress. **An intentional infliction of emotional distress occurs when a defendant's extreme and outrageous conduct cause severe emotional or mental distress in the plaintiff.** By yelling that Calvin was going to kill Alvin's dog, it was clear Bertie was intentionally trying to cause Alvin distress. Yelling that one is going to kill another's pet is likely extreme and outrageous, and Bertie's taunts did in fact give Alvin a heart attack. Consequently, it's likely that Bertie is liable for intentional infliction of emotional distress.

ANSWER TO QUESTION 5:

Del v. Captain Pete

The issue is whether Del can sue Captain Pete for trespass. **Under the defense of necessity, a person has a privilege to harm the property of another where this is necessary to prevent greater harm to third persons or the person himself or herself.** Captain Pete moored his ship at Del's dock because he was in danger of wrecking his entire ship (which did indeed happen). The harm of having Captain Pete's ship temporarily moored at Del's dock was so much less than the harm of the ship going down or Captain Pete being injured that Del is likely liable to Captain Pete for the damages.

Del v. Mark for Trespass

The issue is whether Mark committed a trespass when he unknowingly crossed onto Del's property. **A trespass occurs when a person intentionally enters another's land without permission. If the person has the intent to commit a physical contact with the other person's land, the person will have the requisite intent for trespass even if his or her decision to make the contact was the result of a mistake.** Even though Mark did not know he had crossed into Del's land, he intended to walk up to the trees to take a closer look at the handbag. Consequently, he committed the tort of trespass.

Del v. Mark for Trespass to Chattels

The issue is whether Mark could be liable for moving the handbag from Del's land. **Trespass to chattels is defined as any intentional interference with a person's use or possession of a chattel. If a person loses possession of the chattel for any time, recovery is allowed even if the chattel is returned unharmed.** Here, Mark interfered with Del's possession of the handbag for at least ten minutes. While he might argue that he thought the bag was abandoned or lost, the freshness of the food sitting on top likely made such a belief unreasonable. Consequently, even though he gave it back to Del as soon as Del asked for it, he could still be held liable for trespass to chattels. However, since his interference with Del's use was so slight, any damages awarded as a result are likely to be minimal.